Alexander Roberts, James Sir Donaldson

The Clementine Homilies and the Apostolic Constitutions

Ante-Nicene Christian library Volume 17

Alexander Roberts, James Sir Donaldson

The Clementine Homilies and the Apostolic Constitutions
Ante-Nicene Christian library Volume 17

ISBN/EAN: 9783742854711

Manufactured in Europe, USA, Canada, Australia, Japa

Cover: Foto ©Lupo / pixelio.de

Manufactured and distributed by brebook publishing software (www.brebook.com)

Alexander Roberts, James Sir Donaldson

The Clementine Homilies and the Apostolic Constitutions

ANTE-NICENE CHRISTIAN LIBRARY:

TRANSLATIONS OF
THE WRITINGS OF THE FATHERS
DOWN TO A.D. 325.

EDITED BY THE
REV. ALEXANDER ROBERTS, D.D.,
AND
JAMES DONALDSON, LL.D.

VOL. XVII.

THE CLEMENTINE HOMILIES.
THE APOSTOLICAL CONSTITUTIONS.

EDINBURGH:
T. & T. CLARK, 38, GEORGE STREET.
MDCCCLXX.

PRINTED BY MURRAY AND GIBB,

FOR

T. & T. CLARK, EDINBURGH.

LONDON, ... HAMILTON, ADAMS, AND CO.
DUBLIN, ... JOHN ROBERTSON AND CO.
NEW YORK, . . . C. SCRIBNER AND CO.

THE CLEMENTINE

HOMILIES.

EDINBURGH:
T. & T. CLARK, 38, GEORGE STREET.
MDCCCLXX.

BOOKS I. TO V. HAVE BEEN TRANSLATED BY REV. THOMAS SMITH, D.D.; BOOKS VI.–XII. BY PETER PETERSON, M.A.; AND BOOKS XIII.–XX. BY DR. DONALDSON.

CONTENTS.

	PAGE
EPISTLE OF PETER TO JAMES,	1
EPISTLE OF CLEMENT TO JAMES,	6
THE CLEMENTINE HOMILIES—	
Homily I.,	17
Homily II.,	32
Homily III.,	57
Homily IV.,	90
Homily V.,	101
Homily VI.,	115
Homily VII.,	130
Homily VIII.,	137
Homily IX.,	149
Homily X.,	161
Homily XI.,	173
Homily XII.,	192
Homily XIII.,	211
Homily XIV.,	225
Homily XV.,	234
Homily XVI.,	242
Homily XVII.,	257
Homily XVIII.,	274
Homily XIX.,	290
Homily XX.,	312

INTRODUCTORY NOTICE.

E have already given an account of the *Clementines* in the Introductory Notice to the *Recognitions*. All that remains for us to do here, is to notice the principal editions of the *Homilies*. The first edition was published by Cotelerius in his collection of the *Apostolic Fathers*, from a manuscript in the Royal Library at Paris, the only manuscript of the work then known to exist. He derived assistance from an epitome of the work which he found in the same library. The text of Cotelerius was revised by Clericus in his edition of Cotelerius, but more carefully by Schwegler, Stuttgart 1847. The Paris MS. breaks off in the middle of the fourteenth chapter of the nineteenth book.

In 1853 (Göttingen) Dressel published a new recension of the *Homilies*, having found a complete manuscript of the twenty Homilies in the Ottobonian Library in Rome. In 1859 (Leipzig) he published an edition of two Epitomes of the Homilies,—the one previously edited by Turnebus and Cotelerius being given more fully, and the other appearing for the first time. To these Epitomes were appended notes by Frederic Wieseler on the Homilies. The last edition of the *Clementines* is by Paul de Lagarde (Leipzig, 1865), which has no new sources, is pretentious, but far from accurate.

EPISTLE OF PETER TO JAMES.

ETER to James, the lord and bishop of the holy church, under the Father of all, through Jesus Christ, wishes peace always.

CHAP. I.—*Doctrine of reserve.*

Knowing, my brother, your eager desire after that which is for the advantage of us all, I beg and beseech you not to communicate to any one of the Gentiles the books of my preachings which I sent to you, nor to any one of our own tribe before trial; but if any one has been proved and found worthy, then to commit them to him, after the manner in which Moses delivered [his books] to the Seventy who succeeded to his chair. Wherefore also the fruit of that caution appears even till now. For his countrymen keep the same rule of monarchy and polity everywhere, being unable in any way to think otherwise, or to be led out of the way of the much-indicating Scriptures. For, according to the rule delivered to them, they endeavour to correct the discordances of the Scriptures, if any one, haply not knowing the traditions, is confounded at the various utterances of the prophets. Wherefore they charge no one to teach, unless he has first learned how the Scriptures must be used. And thus they have amongst them one God, one law, one hope.

CHAP. II.—*Misrepresentation of Peter's doctrine.*

In order, therefore, that the like may also happen to those among us as to these Seventy, give the books of my preachings to our brethren, with the like mystery of initiation, that they may indoctrinate those who wish to take part in teaching; for if it be not so done, our word of truth will be rent into many opinions. And this I know, not as being a prophet, but as already seeing the beginning of this very evil. For some from among the Gentiles have rejected my legal preaching, attaching themselves to certain lawless and trifling preaching of the man who is my enemy. And these things some have attempted while I am still alive, to transform my words by certain various interpretations, in order to the dissolution of the law; as though I also myself were of such a mind, but did not freely proclaim it, which God forbid! For such a thing were to act in opposition to the law of God which was spoken by Moses, and was borne witness to by our Lord in respect of its eternal continuance; for thus He spoke: "The heavens and the earth shall pass away, but one jot or one tittle shall in no wise pass from the law."[1] And this He has said, that all things might come to pass. But these men, professing, I know not how, to know my mind, undertake to explain my words, which they have heard of me, more intelligently than I who spoke them, telling their catechumens that this is my meaning, which indeed I never thought of. But if, while I am still alive, they dare thus to misrepresent me, how much more will those who shall come after me dare to do so!

Chap. III.—*Initiation.*

Therefore, that no such thing may happen, for this end I have prayed and besought you not to communicate the books of my preaching which I have sent you to any one, whether of our own nation or of another nation, before trial; but if any one, having been tested, has been found worthy, then to hand them over to him, according to the initiation of Moses, by which he delivered [his books] to the Seventy who succeeded to his chair; in order that thus they may keep the faith, and everywhere deliver the rule of truth, explaining all things after our tradition; lest being themselves dragged down by ignorance, being drawn into error by conjectures after their mind, they bring others into

---

[1] Mark xiii. 31; Matt. v. 18.

the like pit of destruction. Now the things that seemed good to me, I have fairly pointed out to you; and what seems good to you, do you, my lord, becomingly perform. Farewell.

CHAP. IV.—*An adjuration concerning the receivers of the book.*

1. Therefore James, having read the epistle, sent for the elders; and having read it to them, said: "Our Peter has strictly and becomingly charged us concerning the establishing of the truth, that we should not communicate the books of his preachings, which have been sent to us, to any one at random, but to one who is good and religious, and who wishes to teach, and who is circumcised, and faithful. And these are not all to be committed to him at once; that, if he be found injudicious in the first, the others may not be entrusted to him. Wherefore let him be proved not less than six years. And then according to the initiation of Moses, he [that is to deliver the books] should bring him to a river or a fountain, which is living water, where the regeneration of the righteous takes place, and should make him, not swear —for that is not lawful—but to stand by the water and adjure, as we ourselves, when we were regenerated, were made to do for the sake of not sinning.

2. "And let him say: 'I take to witness heaven, earth, water, in which all things are comprehended, and in addition to all these, that air also which pervades all things, and without which I cannot breathe, that I shall always be obedient to him who gives me the books of the preachings; and those same books which he may give me, I shall not communicate to any one in any way, either by writing them, or giving them in writing, or giving them to a writer, either myself or by another, or through any other initiation, or trick, or method, or by keeping them carelessly, or placing them before [any one], or granting him permission [to see them], or in any way or manner whatsoever communicating them to another; unless I shall ascertain one to be worthy, as I myself have been judged, or even more so, and that after a probation of

not less than six years; but to one who is religious and good, chosen to teach, as I have received them, so I will commit them, doing these things also according to the will of my bishop.

3. "'But otherwise, though he were my son or my brother, or my friend, or otherwise in any way pertaining to me by kindred, if he be unworthy, that I will not vouchsafe the favour to him, as is not meet; and I shall neither be terrified by plot nor mollified by gifts. But if even it should ever seem to me that the books of the preachings given to me are not true, I shall not so communicate them, but shall give them back. And when I go abroad, I shall carry them with me, whatever of them I happen to possess. But if I be not minded to carry them about with me, I shall not suffer them to be in my house, but shall deposit them with my bishop, having the same faith, and setting out from the same persons [as myself].[1] But if it befall me to be sick, and in expectation of death, and if I be childless, I shall act in the same manner. But if I die having a son who is not worthy, or not yet capable, I shall act in the same manner. For I shall deposit them with my bishop, in order that if my son, when he grows up, be worthy of the trust, he may give them to him as his father's bequest, according to the terms of this engagement.

4. "'And that I shall thus do, I again call to witness heaven, earth, water, in which all things are enveloped, and in addition to all these, the all-pervading air, without which I cannot breathe, that I shall always be obedient to him who giveth me these books of the preachings, and shall observe in all things as I have engaged, or even something more. To me, therefore, keeping this covenant, there shall be a part with the holy ones; but to me doing anything contrary to what I have covenanted, may the universe be hostile to me, and the all-pervading ether, and the God who is over all, to whom none is superior, than whom none is greater. But if even I should come to the acknowledgment of another God, I now swear

[1] Unless the reading be corrupt here, I suppose the reference must be to episcopal succession.

by him also, be he or be he not, that I shall not do otherwise. And in addition to all these things, if I shall lie, I shall be accursed living and dying, and shall be punished with everlasting punishment.'

"And after this, let him partake of bread and salt with him who commits them to him."

Chap. v.—*The adjuration accepted.*

James having thus spoken, the elders were in an agony of terror. Therefore James, perceiving that they were greatly afraid, said: "Hear me, brethren and fellow-servants. If we should give the books to all indiscriminately, and they should be corrupted by any daring men, or be perverted by interpretations, as you have heard that some have already done, it will remain even for those who really seek the truth, always to wander in error. Wherefore it is better that they should be with us, and that we should communicate them with all the fore-mentioned care to those who wish to live piously, and to save others. But if any one, after taking this adjuration, shall act otherwise, he shall with good reason incur eternal punishment. For why should not he who is the cause of the destruction of others not be destroyed himself?" The elders, therefore, being pleased with the sentiments of James, exclaimed, "Blessed be He who, as foreseeing all things, has graciously appointed thee as our bishop;" and when they had said this, we all rose up, and prayed to the Father and God of all, to whom be glory for ever. Amen.

EPISTLE OF CLEMENT TO JAMES.

LEMENT to James, the lord,[1] and the bishop of bishops, who rules Jerusalem, the holy church of the Hebrews, and the churches everywhere excellently founded by the providence of God, with the elders and deacons, and the rest of the brethren, peace be always.

CHAP. I.—*Peter's martyrdom.*

Be it known to you, my lord, that Simon, who, for the sake of the true faith, and the most sure foundation of his doctrine, was set apart to be the foundation of the church, and for this end was by Jesus Himself, with His truthful mouth, named Peter, the first-fruits of our Lord, the first of the apostles; to whom first the Father revealed the Son; whom the Christ, with good reason, blessed; the called, and elect, and associate at table and in the journeyings [of Christ]; the excellent and approved disciple, who, as being fittest of all, was commanded to enlighten the darker part of the world, namely the West, and was enabled to accomplish it,—and to what extent do I lengthen my discourse, not wishing to indicate what is sad, which yet of necessity, though reluctantly, I must tell you,—he himself, by reason of his immense love towards men, having come as far as Rome, clearly and publicly testifying, in opposition to the wicked one who withstood him, that there is to be a good King over all the world, while saving men by his God-inspired doctrine,

[1] More probably "the Lord's brother." So it must have been in the text from which Rufinus translated.

himself, by violence, exchanged this present existence for life.

CHAP. II.—*Ordination of Clement.*

But about that time, when he was about to die, the brethren being assembled together, he suddenly seized my hand, and rose up, and said in presence of the church: "Hear me, brethren and fellow-servants. Since, as I have been taught by the Lord and Teacher Jesus Christ, whose apostle I am, the day of my death is approaching, I lay hands upon this Clement as your bishop; and to him I entrust my chair of discourse, even to him who has journeyed with me from the beginning to the end, and thus has heard all my homilies—who, in a word, having had a share in all my trials, has been found stedfast in the faith; whom I have found, above all others, pious, philanthropic, pure, learned, chaste, good, upright, large-hearted, and striving generously to bear the ingratitude of some of the catechumens. Wherefore I communicate to him the power of binding and loosing, so that with respect to everything which he shall ordain in the earth, it shall be decreed in the heavens. For he shall bind what ought to be bound, and loose what ought to be loosed, as knowing the rule of the church. Therefore hear him, as knowing that he who grieves the president of the truth, sins against Christ, and offends the Father of all. Wherefore he shall not live; and therefore it becomes him who presides to hold the place of a physician, and not to cherish the rage of an irrational beast."

CHAP. III.—*Nolo episcopari.*

While he thus spoke, I knelt to him, and entreated him, declining the honour and the authority of the chair. But he answered: "Concerning this matter do not ask me; for it has seemed to me to be good that thus it be, and all the more if you decline it. For this chair has not need of a presumptuous man, ambitious of occupying it, but of one pious in conduct and deeply skilled in the word [of God]. But show me a better [than yourself], who has travelled more with me, and has heard more of my discourses, and has learned better the regulations of the church, and I shall not force you to do well against your will. But it will not be in your power to show me your superior; for you are the choice first-fruits of the multitudes saved through me. However, consider this further, that if you do not undertake the administration of the church, through fear of the danger of sin, you may be sure that you sin more, when you have it in your power to help the godly, who are, as it were, at sea and in danger, and will not do so, providing only for your own interest, and not for the common advantage of all. But that it behoves you altogether to undertake the danger, while I do not cease to ask it of you for the help of all, you well understand. The sooner, therefore, you consent, so much the sooner will you relieve me from anxiety.

CHAP. IV.—*The recompense of the reward.*

" But I myself also, O Clement, know the griefs and anxieties, and dangers and reproaches, that are appointed you from the uninstructed multitudes; and these you will be able to bear nobly, looking to the great reward of patience bestowed on you by God. But also consider this fairly with me: When has Christ need of your aid? Now, when the wicked one has sworn war against His bride; or in the time to come, when He shall reign victorious, having no need of further help? Is it not evident to any one who has even the least understanding, that it is now? Therefore with all good-will hasten in the time of the present necessity to do battle on the side of this good King, whose character it is to give great rewards after victory. Therefore take the oversight gladly; and all the more in good time, because you have learned from me the administration of the church, for the safety of the brethren who have taken refuge with us.

CHAP. V.—*A charge.*

" However, I wish, in the presence of all, to remind you, for the sake of all, of the things belonging to the administration. It becomes you, living without reproach, with the greatest earnestness to shake off all the cares of life, being neither a surety, nor an advocate, nor involved in any other secular business. For Christ does not wish to appoint you either a judge or an arbitrator in business, or negotiator of the secular affairs of the present life, lest, being confined to the present cares of men, you should not have leisure by the word of truth to separate the good among men from the bad. But let the disciples perform these offices to one another, and not withdraw [you] from the discourses which are able to save. For as it is wicked for you to undertake secular cares, and to omit the doing of what you have been commanded to do, so it is sin for every layman, if they do not stand by one another even in secular necessities. And if all do not understand to take order that you be without care in respect of the things in which you ought to be, let them learn it from the deacons; that you may have the care of the church always, in order both to your administering it well, and to your holding forth the words of truth.

Chap. VI.—*The duty of a bishop.*

"Now, if you were occupied with secular cares, you should deceive both yourself and your hearers. For not being able, on account of occupation, to point out the things that are advantageous, both you should be punished, as not having taught what was profitable, and they, not having learned, should perish by reason of ignorance. Wherefore do you indeed preside over them without occupation, so as to send forth seasonably the words that are able to save them; and so let them listen to you, knowing that whatever the ambassador of the truth shall bind upon earth is bound also in heaven, and what he shall loose is loosed. But you shall bind what ought to be bound, and loose what ought to be loosed. And these, and such like, are the things that relate to you as president.

Chap. VII.—*Duties of presbyters.*

"And with respect to the presbyters, take these [instructions]. Above all things, let them join the young betimes in marriage, anticipating the entanglements of youthful lusts. But neither let them neglect the marriage of those who are already old; for lust is vigorous even in some old men. Lest, therefore, fornication find a place among you, and bring upon you a very pestilence, take precaution, and search, lest at any time the fire of adultery be secretly kindled among you. For adultery is a very terrible thing, even such that it holds the second place in respect of punishment, the first being assigned to those who are in error, even although they be chaste. Wherefore do you, as elders of the church, exercise the spouse of Christ to chastity (by the spouse I mean the body of the church); for if she be apprehended to be chaste by her royal Bridegroom, she shall obtain the greatest honour; and you, as wedding guests, shall receive great commendation. But if she be caught having sinned, she herself indeed shall be cast out; and you shall suffer punishment, if at any time her sin has been through your negligence.

CHAP. VIII.—" *Do good unto all.*"

"Wherefore above all things be careful about chastity; for fornication has been marked out as a bitter thing in the estimation of God. But there are many forms of fornication, as also Clement himself will explain to you. The first is adultery, that a man should not enjoy his own wife alone, or a woman not enjoy her own husband alone. If any one be chaste, he is able also to be philanthropic, on account of which he shall obtain eternal mercy. For as adultery is a great evil, so philanthropy is the greatest good. Wherefore love all your brethren with grave and compassionate eyes, performing to orphans the part of parents, to widows that of husbands, affording them sustenance with all kindliness, arranging marriages for those who are in their prime, and for those who are without a profession the means of necessary support through employment; giving work to the artificer, and alms to the incapable.

CHAP. IX.—" *Let brotherly love continue.*"

"But I know that ye will do these things if you fix love into your minds; and for its entrance there is one only fit means, viz. the common partaking of food.¹ Wherefore see to it that ye be frequently one another's guests, as ye are able, that you may not fail of it. For it is the cause of well-doing, and well-doing of salvation. Therefore all of you present your provisions in common to all your brethren in God, knowing that, giving temporal things, you shall receive eternal things. Much more feed the hungry, and give drink to the thirsty, and clothing to the naked; visit the sick; showing yourselves to those who are in prison, help them as ye are able, and receive strangers into your houses with all alacrity. However, not to speak in detail, philanthropy will teach you to do everything that is good, as misanthropy suggests ill-doing to those who will not be saved.

CHAP. X.—" *Whatsoever things are honest.*"

"Let the brethren who have causes to be settled not be judged by the secular authorities; but let them by all means be reconciled by the elders of the church, yielding ready obedience to them. Moreover, also, flee avarice, inasmuch as it is able, under pretext of temporal gain, to deprive you of eternal blessings. Carefully keep your balances, your measures, your weights, and the things belonging to your traffic, just. Be faithful with respect to your trusts. Moreover, you will persevere in doing these things, and things similar to these, until the end, if you have in your hearts an ineradicable remembrance of the judgment that is from God. For who would sin, being persuaded that at the end of life there is a judgment appointed of the righteous God, who only now is long-suffering and good,² that the good may in future enjoy for ever unspeakable blessings; but the sinners being found as evil, shall obtain an eternity of unspeakable punishment. And, indeed, that these things are so, it would be reasonable to doubt, were it not that the Prophet of the truth has said and sworn that it shall be.

¹ Literally, "of salt."
² The common reading would give "who alone is now long-suffering;" but the change of a letter gives the reading which we have adopted.

Chap. XI.—*Doubts to be satisfied.*

"Wherefore, being disciples of the true Prophet, laying aside double-mindedness, from which comes ill-doing, eagerly undertake well-doing. But if any of you doubt concerning the things which I have said are to be, let him confess it without shame, if he cares for his own soul, and he shall be satisfied by the president. But if he has believed rightly, let his conversation be with confidence, as fleeing from the great fire of condemnation, and entering into the eternal good kingdom of God.

Chap. XII.—*Duties of deacons.*

"Moreover let the deacons of the church, going about with intelligence, be as eyes to the bishop, carefully inquiring into the doings of each member of the church, [ascertaining] who is about to sin, in order that, being arrested with admonition by the president, he may haply not accomplish the sin. Let them check the disorderly, that they may not desist from assembling to hear the discourses, so that they may be able to counteract by the word of truth those anxieties that fall upon the heart from every side, by means of worldly casualties and evil communications; for if they long remain fallow, they become fuel for the fire. And let them learn who are suffering under bodily disease, and let them bring them to the notice of the multitude who do not know of them, that they may visit them, and supply their wants according to the judgment of the president. Yea, though they do this without his knowledge, they do nothing amiss. These things, then, and things like to these, let the deacons attend to.

Chap. XIII.—*Duties of catechists.*

"Let the catechists instruct, being first instructed; for it is a work relating to the souls of men. For the teacher of the word must accommodate himself to the various judgments of the learners. The catechists must therefore be learned, and unblameable, of much experience, and approved, as you will know that Clement is, who is to be your instructor after me.

For it were too much for me now to go into details. However, if ye be of one mind, you shall be able to reach the haven of rest, where is the peaceful city of the great King.

CHAP. XIV.—*The vessel of the church.*

"For the whole business of the church is like unto a great ship, bearing through a violent storm men who are of many places, and who desire to inhabit the city of the good kingdom. Let, therefore, God be your shipmaster; and let the pilot be likened to Christ, the mate[1] to the bishop, the sailors to the deacons, the midshipmen to the catechists, the multitude of the brethren to the passengers, the world to the sea; the foul winds to temptations, persecutions, and dangers; and all manner of afflictions to the waves; the land winds and their squalls to the discourses of deceivers and false prophets; the promontories and rugged rocks to the judges in high places threatening terrible things; the meetings of two seas, and the wild places, to unreasonable men and those who doubt of the promises of truth. Let hypocrites be regarded as like to pirates. Moreover, account the strong whirlpool, and the Tartarean Charybdis, and murderous wrecks, and deadly founderings, to be nought but sins. In order, therefore, that, sailing with a fair wind, you may safely reach the haven of the hoped-for city, pray so as to be heard. But prayers become audible by good deeds.

CHAP. XV.—*Incidents of the voyage.*

"Let therefore the passengers remain quiet, sitting in their own places, lest by disorder they occasion rolling or careening. Let the midshipmen give heed to the fare. Let the deacons neglect nothing with which they are entrusted; let the presbyters, like sailors, studiously arrange what is needful for each one. Let the bishop, as the mate, wakefully ponder the words of the pilot alone. Let Christ, even the Saviour, be loved as the pilot, and alone believed in the matters of which He speaks; and let all pray to God for a prosperous voyage.

---

[1] It is impossible to translate these terms very accurately. I suppose the πρωρεύς was rather the "bow-oarsman" in the galley.

Let those sailing expect every tribulation, as travelling over a great and troubled sea, the world: sometimes, indeed, disheartened, persecuted, dispersed, hungry, thirsty, naked, hemmed in; and, again, sometimes united, congregated, at rest; but also sea-sick, giddy, vomiting, that is, confessing sins, like disease-producing bile,—I mean the sins proceeding from bitterness, and the evils accumulated from disorderly lusts, by the confession of which, as by vomiting, you are relieved of your disease, attaining healthful safety by means of carefulness.

CHAP. XVI.—*The bishop's labours and reward.*

"But know all of you that the bishop labours more than you all; because each of you suffers his own affliction, but he his own and that of every one. Wherefore, O Clement, preside as a helper to every one according to your ability, being careful of the cares of all. Whence I know that in your undertaking the administration, I do not confer, but receive, a favour. But take courage and bear it generously, as knowing that God will recompense you when you enter the haven of rest, the greatest of blessings, a reward that cannot be taken from you, in proportion as you have undertaken more labour for the safety of all. So that, if many of the brethren should hate you on account of your lofty righteousness, their hatred shall nothing hurt you, but the love of the righteous God shall greatly benefit you. Therefore endeavour to shake off the praise that arises from injustice, and to attain the profitable praise that is from Christ on account of righteous administration."

CHAP. XVII.—*The people's duties.*

Having said this, and more than this, he looked again upon the multitude, and said: "And you also, my beloved brethren and fellow-servants, be subject to the president of the truth in all things, knowing this, that he who grieves him has not received Christ, with whose chair he has been entrusted; and he who has not received Christ shall be regarded as having despised the Father; wherefore he shall be cast out of the good kingdom. On this account, endeavour to come to all the assemblies, lest as deserters you incur the charge of sin through the disheartening of your captain. Wherefore all of you think before all else of the things that relate to him, knowing this, that the wicked one, being the more hostile on account of every one of you, wars against him alone. Do you therefore strive to live in affection towards him, and in kindliness towards one another, and to obey him, in order that both he may be comforted and you may be saved.

CHAP. XVIII.—"*As a heathen man and a publican.*"

"But some things also you ought of yourselves to consider, on account of his not being able to speak openly by reason of the plots. Such as: if he be hostile to any one, do not wait for his speaking; and do not take part with that man, but prudently follow the bishop's will, being enemies to those to whom he is an enemy, and not conversing with those with whom he does not converse, in order that every one, desiring to have you all as his friends, may be reconciled to him and be saved, listening to his discourse. But if any one remain a friend of those to whom he is an enemy, and speak to those with whom he does not converse, he also himself is one of those who would waste the church. For, being with you in body, but not with you in judgment, he is against you; and is much worse than the open enemies from without, since with seeming friendship he disperses those who are within."

CHAP. XIX.—*Installation of Clement.*

Having thus spoken, he laid his hands upon me in the presence of all, and compelled me to sit in his own chair. And when I was seated, he immediately said to me: "I entreat you, in the presence of all the brethren here, that whensoever I depart from this life, as depart I must, you send to James the brother of the Lord a brief account of your reasonings from your boyhood, and how from the beginning until now you have journeyed with me, hearing the discourses preached by me in every city, and [seeing] my deeds. And then at the end you will not fail to inform him of the manner of my death, as I said before. For that event will not grieve him very much, when he knows that I piously went through what it behoved me to suffer. And he will get the greatest comfort when he learns, that not an unlearned man, or one ignorant of life-giving words, or not knowing the rule of the church, shall be entrusted with the chair of the teacher after me. For the discourse of a deceiver destroys the souls of the multitudes who hear."

CHAP. XX.—*Clement's obedience.*

Whence I, my lord James, having promised as I was ordered, have not failed to write in books by chapters the greater part of his discourses in every city, which have been already written to you, and sent by himself, as for a token; and thus I despatched them to you, inscribing them *Clement's Epitome of the Popular Sermons of Peter.* However, I shall begin to set them forth, as I was ordered.

THE CLEMENTINE HOMILIES.

HOMILY I.

CHAP. I.—*Boyish questionings.*

CLEMENT, being a Roman citizen, even from my earliest youth was able to live chastely, my mind from my boyhood drawing away the lust that was in me to dejection and distress. For I had a habit of reasoning—how originating I know not—making frequent cogitations concerning death: When I die, shall I neither exist, nor shall any one ever have any remembrance of me, while boundless time bears all things of all men into forgetfulness? and shall I then be without being, or acquaintance with those who are; neither knowing nor being known, neither having been nor being? And has the world ever been made? and was there anything before it was made? For if it has been always, it shall also continue to be; but if it has been made, it shall also be dissolved. And after its dissolution, shall there ever be anything again, unless, perhaps, silence and forgetfulness? Or perhaps something shall be which it is not possible now to conceive.

CHAP. II.—*Good out of evil.*

As I pondered without ceasing these and such like questions—I know not whence arising—I had such bitter grief, that, becoming pale, I wasted away; and, what was most terrible, if at any time I wished to drive away this meditation as unprofitable, my suffering became all the more severe; and I grieved over this, not knowing that I had a fair inmate, even my thought, which was to be to me the cause of a blessed immortality, as I afterwards knew by experience, and gave thanks to God, the Lord of all. For it was by this thought, which at first afflicted me, that I was compelled to come to the search and the finding of things; and then I pitied those whom at first, through ignorance, I ventured to call blessed.

CHAP. III.—*Perplexity.*

From my boyhood, then, being [involved] in such reasonings, in order to learn something definite, I used to resort to the schools of the philosophers. But nought else did I see than the setting up and knocking down of doctrines, and strifes, and seeking for victory, and the arts of syllogisms, and the skill of assumptions; and sometimes one [opinion] prevailed, —as, for example, that the soul is immortal, and sometimes that it is mortal. If, therefore, at any time the doctrine prevailed that it is immortal, I was glad; and when the doctrine prevailed that it is mortal, I was grieved. And again, I was the more disheartened because I could not establish either doctrine to my satisfaction. However, I perceived that the opinions on subjects under discussion are taken as true or false, according to their defenders, and do not appear as they really are. Perceiving, therefore, now that the acceptance does not depend on the real nature of the subjects discussed, but that opinions are proved to be true or false according to ability of those who defend them, I was still more than ever at a loss in regard of things. Wherefore I groaned from the depth of my soul. For neither was I able to establish anything, nor could I shake off the consideration of such things, though, as I said before, I wished it. For although I frequently charged myself to be at peace, in some way or other thoughts on these subjects, accompanied with a feeling of pleasure, would come into my mind.

CHAP. IV.—*More perplexity.*

And again, living in doubt, I said to myself, Why do I labour in vain, when the matter is clear, that if I lose existence when I die, it is not fitting that I should distress myself now while I do exist? Wherefore I shall reserve my grief till that [day], when, ceasing to exist, I shall not be affected with grief. But if I am to exist, what does it profit me now to distress myself gratuitously? And immediately after this another reasoning assailed me; for I said, Shall I not have something worse to suffer then than that which distresses me now, if I have not lived piously; and shall I not be delivered over, according to the doctrines of some philosophers, to Pyriphlegethon and Tartarus, like Sisyphus, or Tityus, or Ixion, or Tantalus, and be punished for ever in Hades? But again I replied, saying: But there are no such things as these. Yet again I said: But if there be? Therefore, said I, since the matter is uncertain, the safer plan is for me rather to live piously. But how shall I be able, for the sake of righteousness, to subdue bodily pleasures, looking, as I do, to an uncertain hope? But I am neither fully persuaded what is that righteous thing that is pleasing to God, nor do I know whether the soul is immortal or mortal. Neither can I find any well-established doctrine, nor can I abstain from such debatings.

CHAP. V.—*A resolution.*

What, then, am I to do, unless this? I shall go into Egypt, and I shall become friendly with the hierophants of the shrines, and with the prophets; and I shall seek and find a magician, and persuade him with large bribes to effect the calling up of a soul, which is called necromancy, as if I were going to inquire of it concerning some business. And the inquiry shall be for the purpose of learning whether the soul is immortal. But the answer of the soul that it is immortal shall not give me the knowledge from its speaking or my hearing, but only from its being seen; so that, seeing it with my very eyes, I may have a self-sufficient and fit assurance, from the very fact of its appearing, that it exists; and never again shall the uncertain words of hearing be able to overturn the things which the eyes have made their own. However, I submitted this very plan to a certain companion who was a philosopher; and he counselled me not to venture upon it, and that on many accounts. "For if," said he, "the soul shall not listen to the magician, you will live with an evil conscience, as having acted against the laws which forbid the doing of these things. But if it shall listen to him, then, besides your living with an evil conscience, I think that matters of piety will not be promoted to you on account of your making this attempt. For they say that the Deity is angry with those who disturb souls after their release from the body."[1] And I, when I heard this, became indeed more backward to undertake such a thing, but I did not abandon my original plan; but I was distressed, as being hindered in the execution of it.

CHAP. VI.—*Tidings from Judea.*

And, not to discuss such matters to you in a long speech, while I was occupied with such reasonings and doings, a certain report, taking its rise in the spring-time, in the reign of Tiberius Cæsar, gradually grew everywhere, and ran through the world as truly the good tidings of God, being unable to stifle the counsel of God in silence. Therefore it everywhere became greater and louder, saying that a certain One in Judea, beginning in the spring season, was preaching to the Jews the kingdom of the invisible God, and saying that whoever of them would reform his manner of living should enjoy it. And in order that He might be believed that He uttered these things full of the Godhead, He wrought many wonderful miracles and signs by His mere command, as having received power from God. For He made the deaf to hear, the blind to see, the lame to walk, raised up the bowed down, drove away every disease, put to flight every demon; and even scabbed lepers, by only looking on Him from a distance, were sent away cured by Him; and the dead, being brought to Him, were raised; and there was nothing which He could not do. And as time advanced, so much the greater, through the arrival of more persons, and the stronger grew—I say not now the report, but—the truth of the thing; for now at length there were

[1] This rendering is from the text in the corresponding passage of the *Epitome de gestis S. Petri.*

meetings in various places for consultation and inquiry as to who He might be that had appeared, and what was His purpose.

Chap. VII.—*The gospel in Rome.*

And then in the same year, in the autumn season, a certain one, standing in a public place, cried and said, "Men of Rome, hearken. The Son of God is come in Judea, proclaiming eternal life to all who will, if they shall live according to the counsel of the Father, who hath sent Him. Wherefore change your manner of life from the worse to the better, from things temporal to things eternal; for know ye that there is one God, who is in heaven, whose world ye unrighteously dwell in before His righteous eyes. But if ye be changed, and live according to His counsel, then, being born into the other world, and becoming eternal, ye shall enjoy His unspeakable good things. But if ye be unbelieving, your souls, after the dissolution of the body, shall be thrown into the place of fire, where, being punished eternally, they shall repent of their unprofitable deeds. For every one, the term of repentance is the present life." I therefore, when I heard these things, was grieved, because no one among so great multitudes, hearing such an announcement, said: I shall go into Judea, that I may know if this man who tells us these things speaks the truth, that the Son of God has come into Judea, for the sake of a good and eternal hope, revealing the will of the Father who sent Him. For it is no small matter which they say that He preaches: for He asserts that the souls of some, being [themselves] immortal, shall enjoy eternal good things; and that those of others, being thrown into unquenchable fire, shall be punished for ever.

Chap. VIII.—*Departure from Rome.*

While I spoke thus concerning others, I also lectured myself, saying, Why do I blame others, being myself guilty of the very same crime of heedlessness? But I shall hasten into Judea, having first arranged my affairs. And when I had thus made up my mind, there occurred a long time of delay, my worldly affairs being difficult to arrange. Therefore, meditating further on the nature of life, that by involving[1] men in hope it lays snares for those who are making haste, yea, and how much time I had been robbed of while tossed by hopes, and that we men die while thus occupied, I left all my affairs as they were, and sped to Portus;[2] and coming to the harbour, and being taken on board a ship, I was borne by adverse winds to Alexandria instead of Judea; and being detained there by stress of weather, I consorted with the philosophers, and told them about the rumour and the sayings of him who had appeared in Rome. And they answered that indeed they knew nothing of him who had appeared in Rome; but concerning Him who was born in Judea, and who was said by the report to be the Son of God, they had heard from many who had come from thence, and had learned respecting all the wonderful things that He did with a word.

CHAP. IX.—*Preaching of Barnabas.*

And when I said that I wished I could meet with some one of those who had seen Him, they immediately brought me to one, saying, "There is one here who not only is acquainted with Him, but is also of that country, a Hebrew, by name Barnabas, who says that he himself is one of His disciples; and hereabouts he resides, and readily announces to those who will the terms of His promise." Then I went with them; and when I came, I stood listening to his words with the crowd that stood round him; and I perceived that he was speaking truth not with dialectic art, but was setting forth simply and without preparation what he had heard and seen the manifested Son of God do and say. And even from the crowd who stood around him he produced many witnesses of the miracles and discourses which he narrated.

CHAP. X.—*Cavils of the philosophers.*

But while the multitudes were favourably disposed towards the things that he so artlessly spoke, the philosophers, impelled

---

[1] For ἐκπλοκῶν Wieseler proposes ἐκκλίπτων, "that deceiving by hopes it lays snares," etc.

[2] Portus, the port of Rome. One MS. reads πόντον, "the sea."

by their worldly learning, set upon laughing at him and
making sport of him, upbraiding and reproaching him with
excessive presumption, making use of the great armoury of
syllogisms. But he set aside their babbling, and did not
enter into their subtle questioning, but without embarrassment
went on with what he was saying. And then one of them
asked, Wherefore it was that a gnat, although it be so small,
and has six feet, has wings also; while an elephant, the largest
of beasts, is wingless, and has but four feet? But he, after
the question had been put, resuming his discourse, which had
been interrupted, as though he had answered the question,
resumed his original discourse, only making use of this pre-
face after each interruption: "We have a commission only
to tell you the words and the wondrous doings of Him who
sent us; and instead of logical demonstration, we present to
you many witnesses from amongst yourselves who stand by,
whose faces I remember, as living images. These sufficient
testimonies it is left to your choice to submit to, or to disbelieve.[1] But I shall not cease to declare unto you what
is for your profit; for to be silent were to me a loss, and to
disbelieve is ruin to you. But indeed I could give answers
to your frivolous questions, if you asked them through love
of truth. But the reason of the different structure of the
gnat and the elephant it is not fitting to tell to those who are
ignorant of the God of all."

CHAP. XI.—*Clement's zeal.*

When he said this, they all, as in concert, set up a shout
of laughter, trying to silence him and put him out, as a barbarous madman. But I, seeing this, and seized, I know not
how, with enthusiasm, could no longer keep silence with
righteous indignation, but boldly cried out, saying, "Well
has God ordained that His counsel should be incapable of
being received by you, foreseeing you to be unworthy, as
appears manifestly to such of those who are now present as

[1] We have here adopted a conjectural reading of Davis. The common
text is thus translated: "whose faces I remember, and who as being
living images are satisfactory testimonies. These it is left," etc.

have minds capable of judging. For whereas now heralds of His counsel have been sent forth, not making a show of grammatical art, but setting forth His will in simple and inartificial words, so that whosoever hear can understand what is spoken, and not with any invidious feeling, as though unwilling to offer it to all; you come here, and besides your not understanding what is for your advantage, to your own injury you laugh at the truth, which, to your condemnation, consorts with the barbarians, and which you will not entertain when it visits you, by reason of your wickedness and the plainness of its words, lest you be convicted of being merely lovers of words, and not lovers of truth and lovers of wisdom. How long will you be learning to speak, who have not the power of speech?[1] For many sayings of yours are not worth one word. What, then, will your Grecian multitude say, being of one mind, if, as he says, there shall be a judgment? "Why, O God, didst Thou not proclaim to us Thy counsel?" Shall you not, if you be thought worthy of an answer at all, be told this? "I, knowing before the foundation of the world all characters that were to be, acted towards each one by anticipation according to his deserts without making it known;[2] but wishing to give full assurance to those who have fled to me that this is so, and to explain why from the beginning, and in the first ages, I did not suffer my counsel to be publicly proclaimed; I now, in the end of the world,[3] have sent heralds to proclaim my will, and they are insulted and flouted by those who will not be benefited, and who wilfully reject my friendship. Oh, great wrong! The preachers are exposed to danger even to the loss of life,[4] and that by the men who are called to salvation.

CHAP. XII.—*Clement's rebuke of the people.*

"And this wrongful treatment of my heralds would have

---

[1] The Vatican MS. and Epit. have "the power of speaking well."
[2] Lit., "I met each one beforehand secretly." The Latin has, "unicuique prævius occurri."
[3] The Greek is βίου, "life."
[4] The Paris MS. reads φθόνου, "envy," instead of φόνου, "murder."

been against all from the beginning, if from the beginning the unworthy had been called to salvation. For that which is now done wrongfully by these men serves to the vindication of my righteous foreknowledge, that it was well that I did not choose from the beginning to expose uselessly to public contempt the word which is worthy of honour; but determined to suppress it, as being honourable, not indeed from those who were worthy from the beginning—for to them also I imparted it—but from those, and such as those, unworthy, as you see them to be,—those who hate me, and who will not love themselves. And now, give over laughing at this man, and hear me with respect to his announcement, or let any one of the hearers who pleases answer. And do not bark like vicious dogs, deafening with disorderly clamour the ears of those who would be saved, ye unrighteous and God-haters, and perverting the saving method to unbelief. How shall you be able to obtain pardon, who scorn him who is sent to speak to you of the Godhead of God? And this you do towards a man whom you ought to have received on account of his good-will towards you, even if he did not speak truth."

CHAP. XIII.—*Clement instructed by Barnabas.*

While I spake these words, and others to the same effect, there arose a great excitement among the crowd; and some, as pitying Barnabas, sympathized with me; but others, being senseless, terribly gnashed their teeth against me. But, as the evening had already come, I took Barnabas by the hand, and by force conducted him, against his will, to my lodging, and constrained him to remain there, lest some one might lay hands on him. And having spent several days, and instructed me briefly in the true doctrine, as well as he could in a few days, he said that he should hasten into Judea for the observance of the festival, and also because he wished for the future to consort with those of his own nation.

CHAP. XIV.—*Departure of Barnabas.*

But it plainly appeared to me that he was disconcerted.

For when I said to him, "Only set forth to me the words which you have heard of the Man who has appeared, and I will adorn them with my speech, and preach the counsel of God; and if you do so, within a few days I will sail with you, for I greatly desire to go to the land of Judea, and perhaps I shall dwell with you all my life;"—when he heard this, he answered: "If you wish to inquire into our affairs, and to learn what is for your advantage, sail with me at once. But if you will not, I shall now give you directions to my house, and that of those whom you wish [to meet], that when you choose to come you may find us. For I shall set out to-morrow for my home." And when I saw that he could not be prevailed upon, I went with him as far as the harbour; and having learned of him the directions which he had promised to give me for finding the dwellings, I said to him, "Were it not that to-morrow I am to recover a debt that is due to me, I should straightway set sail with you. But I shall soon overtake you." And having said this, and having given him in charge to those who commanded the ship, I returned grieving, remembering him as an excellent and dear friend.

CHAP. XV.—*Introduction to Peter.*

But having spent [some] days, and not having been able to recover the whole debt, for the sake of speed I neglected the balance, as being a hindrance, and myself also set sail for Judea, and in fifteen days arrived at Cæsarea Stratonis. And when I had landed, and was seeking for a lodging, I learned that one named Peter, who was the most esteemed disciple of the Man who had appeared in Judea, and had done signs and wonders, was going to have a verbal controversy next day with Simon, a Samaritan of Gitthi. When I heard this, I begged to be shown his lodging; and as soon as I learned it, I stood before the door. And those who were in the house, seeing me, discussed the question who I was, and whence I had come. And, behold, Barnabas came out; and as soon as he saw me he embraced me, rejoicing greatly, and weeping. And he took me by the hand, and conducted me to where Peter was, saying to me, "This is Peter, of whom I told you as being the greatest in the wisdom of God, and I have spoken to him of you continually. Therefore enter freely,[1] for I have told him your excellent qualities, without falsehood; and, at the same time, have disclosed to him your intention, so that he himself also is desirous to see you. Therefore I offer him a great gift when by my hands I present you to him." Thus saying, he presented me, and said, "This, O Peter, is Clement."

CHAP. XVI.—*Peter's salutation.*

Then the blessed man, springing forward as soon as he heard my name, kissed me; and making me sit down, straightway said, "You acted nobly in entertaining Barnabas, a herald of the truth, to the honour of the living God, being magnanimously not ashamed, nor fearing the resentment of the rude multitude. Blessed shall you be. For as you thus with all honour entertained the ambassador of the truth, so also truth herself shall constitute you, who are a stranger, a citizen of her own city. And thus you shall greatly rejoice, because you have now lent a small favour; I mean the kindness of good words. You shall be heir of blessings which are both eternal and cannot possibly be taken from you. And do not trouble yourself to detail to me your manner of life; for the veracious Barnabas has detailed to us everything relating to you, making favourable mention of you almost every day. And in order that I may tell to you briefly, as to a genuine friend, what is in hand, travel with us, unless anything hinders you, partaking of the words of truth which I am going to speak from city to city, as far as Rome itself. And if you wish [to say] anything, speak on."

CHAP. XVII.—*Questions propounded.*

Then I set forth my purpose from the beginning, and how I had spent myself upon difficult questions, and all the things

---

[1] The text is corrupt. Dressel's reading is adopted in the text, being based on Rufinus's translation. Some conjecture, "as you will know of your own accord."

that I disclosed to you at the outset, so that I need not write the same things again. Then I said, "I hold myself in readiness to journey with you; for this, I know not how, I gladly wish. However, I wish first to be convinced concerning the truth, that I may know whether the soul is mortal or immortal; and whether, if it is eternal, it is to be judged concerning the things which it hath done here. Also, whether there is anything that is righteous and well-pleasing to God; and whether the world was made, and for what end it was made; and whether it shall be dissolved; and if it shall be dissolved, whether it shall be made better, or shall not be at all." And not to mention them in detail, I said that I wished to learn these things, and things consequent upon these. And to this he answered: "I shall shortly convey to you, O Clement, the knowledge of the things that are; and even now listen.

CHAP. XVIII.—*Causes of ignorance.*

"The will of God has been [kept] in obscurity in many ways. In the first place, there is evil instruction, wicked association, terrible society, unseemly discourses, wrongful prejudice. Thereby is error, then fearlessness, unbelief, fornication, covetousness, vainglory; and ten thousand other such evils, filling the world as a quantity of smoke fills a house, have obscured the sight of the men inhabiting the world, and have not suffered them to look up and become acquainted with God the Creator from the delineation [of Himself which He has given], and to know what is pleasing to Him. Wherefore it behoves the lovers of truth, crying out inwardly from their breasts, to call for aid, with truth-loving reason, that some one living within the house[1] which is filled with smoke may approach and open the door, so that the light of the sun which is without may be admitted into the house, and the smoke of the fire which is within may be driven out.

CHAP. XIX.—*The true Prophet.*

"Now the Man who is the helper I call the true Prophet;

[1] A conjectural reading, "being without the house," seems preferable.

and He alone is able to enlighten the souls of men, so that with our own eyes we may be able to see the way of eternal salvation. But otherwise it is impossible, as you also know, since you said a little while ago that every doctrine is set up and pulled down, and the same is thought true or false, according to the power of him who advocates it; so that doctrines do not appear as they are, but take the appearance of being or not being truth or falsehood from those who advocate them. On this account the whole business of religion needed a true prophet, that he might tell us things that are, as they are, and how we must believe concerning all things. So that it is first necessary to test the prophet by every prophetic sign, and having ascertained that he is true, thereafter to believe him in everything, and not to sit in judgment upon his several sayings, but to receive them as certain, being accepted indeed by seeming faith, yet by sure judgment. For by our initial proof, and by strict inquiry on every side, all things are received with right reason. Wherefore before all things it is necessary to seek after the true Prophet, because without Him it is impossible that any certainty can come to men."

CHAP. XX.—*Peter's satisfaction with Clement.*

And, at the same time, he satisfied me by expounding to me who He is, and how He is found, and holding Him forth to me as truly to be found, showing that the truth is more manifest to the ear by the discourse of the prophet than things that are seen with the eye; so that I was astonished, and wondered that no one sees those things which are sought after by all, though they lie before him. However, having written this discourse concerning the Prophet by his order, he caused the volume to be despatched to you from Cæsarea Stratonis, saying that he had a charge from you to send you his discourses and his acts year by year.[1] Thus, on the very first

---

[1] The text is probably corrupt or defective. As it stands, grammatically Peter writes the discourse and sends it, and yet "by his order" must also apply to Peter. The Recognitions make Clement write the book and send it. The passage is deemed important, and is accordingly discussed in Schliemann, p. 83; Hilgenfeld, p. 37; and Uhlhorn, p. 101.

day, beginning only concerning the prophet of the truth, he confirmed me in every respect; and then he spoke thus: "Henceforth give heed to the discussions that take place between me and those on the other side; and even if I come off at a disadvantage, I am not afraid of your ever doubting of the truth that has been delivered to you, knowing well that I seem to be beaten, but not the doctrine that has been delivered to us by the Prophet. However, I hope not to come off in our inquiries at a disadvantage with men who have understanding—I mean lovers of truth, who are able to know what discourses are specious, artificial, and pleasant, and what are unartificial and simple, trusting only to the truth [that is conveyed] through them."

CHAP. XXI.—*Unalterable conviction.*

When he had thus spoken, I answered: "Now do I thank God; for as I wished to be convinced, so He has vouchsafed to me. However, so far as concerns me, be you so far without anxiety that I shall never doubt; so much so, that if you yourself should ever wish to remove me from the prophetic doctrine, you should not be able, so well do I know what I have received. And do not think that it is a great thing that I promise you that I shall never doubt; for neither I myself, nor any man who has heard your discourse concerning the Prophet, can ever doubt of the true doctrine, having first heard and understood what is the truth of the prophetic announcement. Wherefore have confidence in the God-willed dogma; for every art of wickedness has been conquered. For against prophecy, neither arts of discourses, nor tricks of sophisms, nor syllogisms, nor any other contrivance, can prevail anything; that is, if he who has heard the true Prophet really is desirous of truth, and does not give heed to aught else under pretext of truth. So that, my lord Peter, be not disconcerted, as though you had presented the greatest good to a senseless person; for you have presented it to one sensible of the favour, and who cannot be seduced from the truth that has been committed to him. For I know that it is one of those things which one wishes to receive quickly, and not to attain slowly. Therefore I know that I should not despise, on account of the quickness [with which I have got it], what has been committed to me, what is incomparable, and what alone is safe."

CHAP. XXII.—*Thanksgiving.*

When I had thus spoken, Peter said: "I give thanks to God, both for your salvation and for my satisfaction. For I am truly pleased to know that you apprehend what is the greatness of prophecy. Since, then, as you say, if I myself should ever wish—which God forbid—to transfer you to another doctrine, I shall not be able to persuade you, begin from to-morrow to attend upon me in the discussions with the adversaries. And to-morrow I have one with Simon Magus." And having spoken thus, and he himself having partaken of food in private, he ordered me also to partake; and having blessed the food, and having given thanks after being satisfied, and having given me an account of this matter, he went on to say: "May God grant you in all things to be made like unto me, and having been baptized, to partake of the same table with me." And having thus spoken, he enjoined me to go to rest; for now indeed my bodily nature demanded sleep.

HOMILY II.

CHAP. I.—*Peter's attendants.*

THEREFORE the next day, I Clement, awaking from sleep before dawn, and learning that Peter was astir, and was conversing with his attendants concerning the worship of God (there were sixteen of them, and I have thought good to set forth their names, as I subsequently learned them, that you may also know who they were. The first of them was Zaccheus, who was once a publican, and Sophonias his brother; Joseph and his foster-brother Michaias; also Thomas and Eliezer the twins; also Æneas and Lazarus the priests; besides also Elisaeus, and Benjamin the son of Saphrus; as also Rubilus and Zacharias the builders; and Ananias and Haggæus the Jamminians; and Nicetas and Aquila the friends),—accordingly I went in and saluted him, and at his request sat down.

CHAP. II.—*A sound mind in a sound body.*

And he, breaking off the discourse in which he was engaged, assured me, by way of apology, why he had not awakened me that I might hear his discourses, assigning as the reason the discomfort of my voyage. As he wished this to be dispelled,[1] he had suffered me to sleep. "For," said he, "whenever the soul is distracted concerning some bodily want, it does not properly approach the instructions that are presented to it. On this account I am not willing to converse, either with those who are greatly grieving through some calamity, or are immoderately angry, or are turned to the frenzy of love, or are suffering under bodily exhaustion, or are

[1] Literally, "to be boiled out of me."

distressed with the cares of life, or are harassed with any other sufferings, whose soul, as I said, being downcast, and sympathizing with the suffering body, occupies also its own intelligence therewith.

CHAP. III.—*Forewarned is forearmed.*

"And let it not be said, Is it not, then, proper to present comforts and admonitions to those who are in any bad case? To this I answer, that if, indeed, any one is able, let him present them; but if not, let him bide his time. For I know[1] that all things have their proper season. Wherefore it is proper to ply men with words which strengthen the soul in anticipation of evil; so that, if at any time any evil comes upon them, the mind, being forearmed with the right argument, may be able to bear up under that which befalls it: for then the mind knows in the crisis of the struggle to have recourse to him who succoured it by good counsel.

CHAP. IV.—*A request.*

"However, I have learned, O Clement, how that in Alexandria Barnabas perfectly expounded to you the word respecting prophecy. Was it not so?" I answered, "Yes, and exceeding well." Then Peter: "Therefore it is not necessary now to occupy with the instructions which you know, the time which may serve us for other instructions which you do not know." Then said I: "You have rightly said, O Peter. But vouchsafe this to me, who purpose always to attend upon you, continuously to expound to me, a delighted hearer, the doctrine of the Prophet. For, apart from Him, as I learned from Barnabas, it is impossible to learn the truth."

CHAP. V.—*Excellence of the knowledge of the true Prophet.*

And Peter, being greatly pleased with this, answered: "Already hath the rectifying process taken its end, as regards you, knowing as you do the greatness of the infallible prophecy, without which it is impossible for any one to receive that which is supremely profitable. For of many

[1] Eccles. iii. 1.

and diverse blessings which are in the things which are or which may be, the most blessed of all—whether it be eternal life, or perpetual health, or a perfect understanding, or light, or joy, or immortality, or whatever else there is or that can be supremely good in the nature of things—cannot be possessed without first knowing things as they are; and this knowledge cannot be otherwise obtained than by first becoming acquainted with the Prophet of the truth.

CHAP. VI.—*The true Prophet.*

"Now the Prophet of the truth is He who always knows all things—things past as they were, things present as they are, things future as they shall be; sinless, merciful, alone entrusted with the declaration of the truth. Read, and you shall find that those [were deceived][1] who thought that they had found the truth of themselves. For this is peculiar to the Prophet, to declare the truth, even as it is peculiar to the sun to bring the day. Wherefore, as many as have even desired to know the truth, but have not had the good fortune to learn it from Him, have not found it, but have died seeking it. For how can he find the truth who seeks it from his own ignorance? And even if he find it, he does not know it, and passes it by as if it were not. Nor yet shall he be able to obtain possession of the truth from another, who, in like manner, promises to him knowledge from ignorance; excepting only the knowledge of morality and things of that sort, which can be known through reason, which affords to every one the knowledge that he ought not to wrong another, through his not wishing [himself] to be wronged.

CHAP. VII.—*Unaided quest of truth profitless.*

"All therefore who ever sought the truth, trusting to themselves to be able to find it, fell into a snare. This is what both the philosophers of the Greeks, and the more intelligent of the barbarians, have suffered. For, applying themselves to things visible, they have given decisions by conjecture on

---

[1] "Were deceived" is not in the text, but the sense demands that some such expression should be supplied.

things not apparent, thinking that that was truth which at any time presented itself to them [as such]. For, like persons who know the truth, they, still seeking the truth, reject some of the suppositions that are presented to them, and lay hold of others, as if they knew, while they do not know, what things are true and what are false. And they dogmatize concerning truth, even those who are seeking after truth, not knowing that he who seeks truth cannot learn it from his own wandering. For not even, as I said, can he recognise her when she stands by him, since he is unacquainted with her.

CHAP. VIII.—*Test of truth.*

"And it is by no means that which is true, but that which is pleasing, which persuades every one who seeks to learn from himself. Since, therefore, one thing is pleasing to one, and another to another, one thing prevails over one as truth, and another thing over another. But the truth is that which is approved by the Prophet, not that which is pleasant to each individual. For that which is one would be many, if the pleasing were the true; which is impossible. Wherefore also the Grecian philologers—rather than philosophers[1]—going about matters by conjectures, have dogmatized much and diversely, thinking that the apt sequence of hypotheses is truth, not knowing that when they have assigned to themselves false beginnings, their conclusion has corresponded with the beginning.

CHAP. IX.—"*The weak things of the world.*"

"Whence a man ought to pass by all else, and commit himself to the Prophet of the truth alone. And we are all able to judge of Him, whether he is a prophet, even although we be wholly unlearned, and novices in sophisms, and unskilled in geometry, and uninitiated in music. For God, as caring for all, has made the discovery concerning Himself easier to all, in order that neither the barbarians might be powerless, nor the Greeks unable to find Him. Therefore the discovery concerning Him is easy; and thus it is:

---

[1] φιλόλογοι, οὐ φιλόσοφοι, "lovers of words, not lovers of wisdom."

CHAP. X.—*Test of the prophet.*

"If he is a Prophet, and is able to know how the world was made, and the things that are in it, and the things that shall be to the end, if He has foretold us anything, and we have ascertained that it has been perfectly accomplished, we easily believe that the things shall be which [He says] are to be, from the things that have been already; we believe Him, I say, as not only knowing, but foreknowing. To whom then, however limited an understanding he may have, does it not appear, that it behoves us, with respect to the things that are pleasing to God, to believe beyond all others Him who beyond all men knows, even though He has not learned? Wherefore, if any one should be unwilling to concede the power of knowing the truth to such an one—I mean to Him who has foreknowledge through the divinity of the Spirit that is in Him—conceding the power of knowing to any one else, is he not void of understanding, in conceding to him who is no prophet, that power of knowing which he would not concede to the Prophet?

CHAP. XI.—*Ignorance, knowledge, foreknowledge.*

"Wherefore, before all things, we must test the Prophet with all judgment by means of the prophetic promise; and having ascertained Him to be the Prophet, we must undoubtingly follow the other words of His teaching; and having confidence concerning things hoped for, we must conduct ourselves according to the first judgment, knowing that He who tells us these things has not a nature to lie. Wherefore, if any of the things that are afterwards spoken by Him do not appear to us to be well spoken, we must know that it is not that it has been spoken amiss, but that it is that we have not conceived it aright. For ignorance does not rightly judge knowledge, and so neither is knowledge competent truly to judge foreknowledge; but foreknowledge affords knowledge to the ignorant.

CHAP. XII.—*Doctrine of the true Prophet.*

"Hence, O beloved Clement, if you would know the things pertaining to God, you have to learn them from Him alone, because He alone knows the truth. For if any one else knows anything, he has received it from Him or from His disciples. And this is His doctrine and true proclamation, that there is one God, whose work the world is; who being altogether righteous, shall certainly at some time render to every one according to his deeds.

CHAP. XIII.—*Future rewards and punishments.*

"For there is every necessity, that he who says that God is by His nature righteous, should believe also that the souls of men are immortal: for where would be His justice, when some, having lived piously, have been evil-treated, and sometimes violently cut off, while others who have been wholly impious, and have indulged in luxurious living, have died the common death of men? Since therefore, without all contradiction, God who is good is also just, He shall not otherwise be known to be just, unless the soul after its separation from the body be immortal, so that the wicked man, being in hell,[1] as having here received his good things, may there be punished for his sins; and the good man, who has been punished here for his sins, may then, as in the bosom of the righteous, be constituted an heir of good things. Since therefore God is righteous, it is fully evident to us that there is a judgment, and that souls are immortal.

CHAP. XIV.—*Righteousness and unrighteousness.*

"But if any one, according to the opinion of this Simon the Samaritan, will not admit that God is just, to whom then can any one ascribe justice, or the possibility of it? For if the Root of all have it not, there is every necessity to think that it must be impossible to find it in human nature, which is, as it were, the fruit. And if it is to be found in man, how much more in God! But if righteousness can be found no-

---

[1] Lit. Hades.

where, neither in God nor in man, then neither can unrighteousness. But there is such a thing as righteousness, for unrighteousness takes its name from the existence of righteousness; for it is called unrighteousness, when righteousness is compared with it, and it is found to be opposite to it.

CHAP. XV.—*Pairs.*

"Hence therefore God, teaching men with respect to the truth of existing things, being Himself one, has distinguished all principles into pairs and opposites,[1] Himself being one and sole God from the beginning, having made heaven and earth, day and night, light and fire, sun and moon, life and death. But man alone amongst these He made self-controlling, having a fitness to be either righteous or unrighteous. To him also he hath varied the figures of combinations, placing before him small things first, and great ones afterwards, such as the world and eternity. But the world that now is, is temporary; that which shall be, is eternal. First is ignorance, then knowledge. So also has He arranged the leaders of prophecy. For, since the present world is female, as a mother bringing forth the souls of her children, but the world to come is male, as a father receiving his children [from their mother], therefore in this world there come a succession of prophets, as being sons of the world to come, and having knowledge of men. And if pious men had understood this mystery, they would never have gone astray, but even now they should have known that Simon, who now enthralls all men, is a fellow-worker of error and deceit. Now, the doctrine of the prophetic rule is as follows.

CHAP. XVI.—*Man's ways opposite to God's.*

"As in the beginning God, who is one, like a right hand and a left, made the heavens first and then the earth, so also He constituted all the combinations in order; but upon men He no more does this, but varies all the combinations. For whereas from Him the greater things come first, and the inferior second, we find the opposite in men—the first worse,

[1] Literally, "twofoldly and oppositely."

and the second superior. Therefore from Adam, who was made after the image of God, there sprang first the unrighteous Cain, and then the righteous Abel. Again, from him who amongst you is called Deucalion,[1] two forms of spirits were sent forth, the impure namely, and the pure, first the black raven, and then the white dove. From Abraham also, the patriarchs of our nation, two firsts[2] sprang—Ishmael first, then Isaac, who was blessed of God. And from Isaac himself, in like manner, there were again two—Esau the profane, and Jacob the pious. So, first in birth, as the first born in the world, was the high priest [Aaron], then the lawgiver [Moses].

CHAP. XVII.—*First the worse, then the better.*

"In like manner, the combination with respect to Elias, which behoved to have come, has been willingly put off to another time, having determined to enjoy it conveniently hereafter.[3] Wherefore, also, he who was among those born of woman came first; then he who was among the sons of men came second. It were possible, following this order, to perceive to what series Simon belongs, who came before me to the Gentiles, and to which I belong who have come after him, and have come in upon him as light upon darkness, as knowledge upon ignorance, as healing upon disease. And thus, as the true Prophet has told us, a false prophet must first come from some deceiver; and then, in like manner, after the removal of the holy place, the true gospel must be secretly sent abroad for the rectification of the heresies that shall be. After this, also, towards the end, Antichrist must first come, and then our Jesus must be revealed to be indeed the Christ; and after this, the eternal light having sprung up, all the things of darkness must disappear.

---

[1] Noah.

[2] For "first" Wieseler conjectures "different,"—two different persons.

[3] In this sentence the text is probably corrupted. The general meaning seems to be, that he does not enter fully at present into the subject of Elias, or John the Baptist, the greatest of those born of woman, coming first, and Christ, the greatest among the sons of men, coming after, but that he will return to the subject on a fitting occasion.

CHAP. XVIII.—*Mistake about Simon Magus.*

"Since, then, as I said, some men do not know the rule of combination, thence they do not know who is my precursor Simon. For if he were known, he would not be believed; but now, not being known, he is improperly believed; and though his deeds are those of a hater, he is loved; and though an enemy, he is received as a friend; and though he be death, he is desired as a saviour; and though fire, he is esteemed as light; and though a deceiver, he is believed as a speaker of truth."

Then I Clement, when I heard this, said, "Who then, I pray you, is this who is such a deceiver? I should like to be informed." Then said Peter: "If you wish to learn, it is in your power to know it from those from whom I also got accurate information on all points respecting him.

CHAP. XIX.—*Justa, a proselyte.*

"There is amongst us one Justa, a Syro-Phœnician, by race a Canaanite, whose daughter was oppressed with a grievous disease. And she came to our Lord, crying out, and entreating that He would heal her daughter. But He, being asked also by us, said, 'It is not lawful to heal the Gentiles, who are like to dogs on account of their using various[1] meats and practices, while the table in the kingdom has been given to the sons of Israel.' But she, hearing this, and begging to partake like a dog of the crumbs that fall from this table, having changed what she was,[2] by living like the sons of the kingdom, she obtained healing for her daughter, as she asked. For she being a Gentile, and remaining in the same course of life, He would not have healed had she remained a Gentile, on account of its not being lawful to heal her as a Gentile.[3]

---

[1] For διαφόροις Duncker proposes ἀδιαφόροις, "meats without distinction."

[2] That is, having ceased to be a Gentile, by abstaining from forbidden foods.

[3] There are several various readings in this sentence, and none of them can be strictly construed; but the general sense is obvious.

Chap. XX.—*Divorced for the faith.*

"She, therefore, having taken up a manner of life according to the law, was, with the daughter who had been healed, driven out from her home by her husband, whose sentiments were opposed to ours. But she, being faithful to her engagements, and being in affluent circumstances, remained a widow herself, but gave her daughter in marriage to a certain man who was attached to the true faith, and who was poor. And, abstaining from marriage for the sake of her daughter, she bought two boys and educated them, and had them in place of sons. And they being educated from their boyhood with Simon Magus, have learned all things concerning him. For such was their friendship, that they were associated with him in all things in which he wished to unite with them.

Chap. XXI.—*Justa's adopted sons, associates with Simon.*

"These men having fallen in with Zaccheus, who sojourned here, and having received the word of truth from him, and having repented of their former innovations, and immediately denouncing Simon as being privy with him in all things, as soon as I came to sojourn here, they came to me with their foster-mother, being presented to me by him [Zaccheus], and ever since they continue with me, enjoying instructions in the truth." When Peter had said this, he sent for them, and charged them that they should accurately relate to me all things concerning Simon. And they, having called God to witness that in nothing they would falsify, proceeded with the relation.

Chap. XXII.—*Doctrines of Simon.*

First Aquila began to speak in this wise: "Listen, O dearest brother, that you may know accurately everything about this man, whose he is, and what, and whence; and what the things are which he does, and how and why he does them. This Simon is the son of Antonius and Rachel, a Samaritan by race, of the village of Gitthæ, which is six schoeni distant from the city. He having disciplined himself greatly in Alexandria,¹ and being very powerful in magic, and being ambitious, wishes to be accounted a certain supreme power, greater even than the God who created the world. And sometimes intimating that he is Christ, he styles himself the Standing One. And this epithet he employs, as intimating that he shall always stand, and as not having any cause of corruption so that his body should fall. And he neither says that the God who created the world is the Supreme, nor does he believe that the dead will be raised. He rejects Jerusalem, and substitutes Mount Gerizzim for it. Instead of our Christ, he proclaims himself. The things of the law he explains by his own presumption; and he says, indeed, that there is to be a judgment, but he does not expect it. For if he were persuaded that he shall be judged by God, he would not dare be impious towards God Himself. Whence some not knowing that, using religion as a cloak, he spoils the things of the truth, and faithfully believing the hope and the judgment which in some way he says are to be, are ruined.

CHAP. XXIII.—*Simon a disciple of the Baptist.*

"But that he came to deal with the doctrines of religion happened on this wise. There was one John, a day-baptist,² who was also, according to the method of combination, the forerunner of our Lord Jesus; and as the Lord had twelve apostles, bearing the number of the twelve months of the sun, so also he [John] had thirty chief men, fulfilling the monthly reckoning of the moon, in which number was a certain woman called Helena, that not even this might be without a dispensational significance. For a woman, being half a man, made up the imperfect number of the triacontad; as also in the case of the moon, whose revolution does not make the complete course of the month. But of these thirty, the first and the most esteemed by John was Simon; and the reason of his not being chief after the death of John was as follows:—

¹ The Vatican MS. adds, "which is in Egypt [or, on the Nile], in Greek culture."

² A day-baptist is taken to mean "one who baptizes every day."

Chap. XXIV.—*Electioneering stratagems.*

"He being absent in Egypt for the practice of magic, and John being killed, Dositheus desiring the leadership, falsely gave out that Simon was dead, and succeeded to the seat. But Simon, returning not long after, and strenuously holding by the place as his own, when he met with Dositheus did not demand the place, knowing that a man who has attained power beyond his expectations cannot be removed from it. Wherefore with pretended friendship he gives himself for a while to the second place, under Dositheus. But taking his place after a few days among the thirty fellow-disciples, he began to malign Dositheus as not delivering the instructions correctly. And this he said that he did, not through unwillingness to deliver them correctly, but through ignorance. And on one occasion, Dositheus, perceiving that this artful accusation of Simon was dissipating the opinion of him with respect to many, so that they did not think that he was the standing one, came in a rage to the usual place of meeting, and finding Simon, struck him with a staff. But it seemed to pass through the body of Simon as if he had been smoke. Thereupon Dositheus, being confounded, said to him, 'If you are the standing one, I also will worship you.' Then Simon said that he was; and Dositheus, knowing that he himself was not the standing one, fell down and worshipped; and associating himself with the twenty-nine chiefs, he raised Simon to his own place of repute; and thus, not many days after, Dositheus himself, while he (Simon) stood, fell down and died.

Chap. XXV.—*Simon's deceit.*

"But Simon is going about in company with Helena, and even till now, as you see, is stirring up the people. And he says that he has brought down this Helena from the highest heavens to the world; being queen, as the all-bearing being, and wisdom, for whose sake, says he, the Greeks and barbarians fought, having before their eyes but an image of truth;[1] for she, who really is the truth, was then with the chiefest god. Moreover, by cunningly explaining certain things of this sort, made up from Grecian myths, he deceives many; especially as he performs many signal marvels, so that if we did not know that he does these things by magic, we ourselves should also have been deceived. But whereas we were his fellow-labourers at the first, so long as he did such things without doing wrong to the interests of religion; now that he has madly begun to attempt to deceive those who are religious, we have withdrawn from him.

CHAP. XXVI.—*His wickedness.*

"For he even began to commit murder, as himself disclosed to us, as a friend to friends, that, having separated the soul of a child from its own body by horrid incantations, as his assistant for the exhibition of anything that he pleased, and having drawn the likeness of the boy, he has it set up in the inner room where he sleeps, saying that he once formed the boy of air, by divine arts, and having painted his likeness, he gave him back again to the air. And he explains that he did the deed thus. He says that the first soul of man, being turned into the nature of heat, drew to itself, and sucked in the surrounding air, after the fashion of a gourd;[2] and then that he changed it into water, when it was within the form of the spirit; and he said that he changed into the nature of blood the air that was in it, which could not be poured out on account of the consistency of the spirit, and that he made the blood solidified into flesh; then, the flesh being thus consolidated, that he exhibited a man not [made] from earth, but from air. And thus, having persuaded himself that he was able to make a new [sort of] man, he said that he reversed the changes, and again restored him to the air. And when he told this to others, he was believed; but by us who were present at his ceremonies he was religiously disbelieved.

[1] We have here an allusion to the tradition that it was only an image of Helen that was taken to Troy, and not the real Helen herself.
[2] Which was used by the ancients as cupping-glasses are now used.

Wherefore we denounced his impieties, and withdrew from him."

CHAP. XXVII.—*His promises.*

When Aquila had thus spoken, his brother Nicetas said: "It is necessary, O Clement our brother, for me to mention what has been left out by Aquila. For, in the first place, God is witness that we assisted him in no impious work, but that we looked on while he wrought; and as long as he did harmless things, and exhibited them, we were also pleased. But when, in order to deceive the godly, he said that he did, by means of godhead, the things that were done by magic, we no longer endured him, though he made us many promises, especially that our statues should be thought worthy of [a place in] the temple,[1] and that we should be thought to be gods, and should be worshipped by the multitude, and should be honoured by kings, and should be thought worthy of public honours, and enriched with boundless wealth.

CHAP. XXVIII.—*Fruitless counsel.*

"These things, and things reckoned greater than these, he promised us, on condition only that we should associate with him, and keep silence as to the wickedness of his undertaking, so that the scheme of his deceit might succeed. But still we would not consent, but even counselled him to desist from such madness, saying to him: 'We, O Simon, remembering our friendship towards you from our childhood, and out of affection for you, give you good counsel. Desist from this attempt. You cannot be a God. Fear Him who is really God. Know that you are a man, and that the time of your life is short; and though you should get great riches, or even become a king, few things accrue to the short time of your life for enjoyment, and things wickedly gotten soon flee away, and procure everlasting punishment for the adventurer. Wherefore we counsel you to fear God, by whom

---

[1] The Vatican MS. and Epitome read, "that a shrine and statues should be erected in honour of us."

the soul of every one must be judged for the deeds that he hath done here.'

CHAP. XXIX.—*Immortality of the soul.*

"When he heard this he laughed; and when we asked him why he laughed at us for giving him good counsel, he answered: 'I laugh at your foolish supposition, because you believe that the soul of man is immortal.' Then I said: 'We do not wonder, O Simon, at your attempting to deceive us, but we are confounded at the way in which you deceive even yourself. Tell me, O Simon, even if no one else has been fully convinced that the soul is immortal, at all events you and we [ought to be so]: you as having separated one from a human body, and conversed with it, and laid your commands upon it; and we as having been present, and heard your commands, and clearly witnessed [the performance of] what was ordered.' Then said Simon: 'I know what you mean; but you know nothing of the matters concerning which you reason.' Then said Nicetas: 'If you know, speak; but if you do not know, do not suppose that we can be deceived by your saying that you know, and that we do not. For we are not so childish, that you can sow in us a shrewd suspicion that we should think that you know some unutterable things, and so that you should take and hold us in subjection, by holding us in restraint through means of desire.'

CHAP. XXX.—*An argument.*

"Then Simon said: 'I am aware that you know that I separated a soul from a human body; but I know that you are ignorant that it is not the soul of the dead person that ministers to me, for it does not exist; but a certain demon works, pretending to be the soul.' Then said Nicetas: 'Many incredible things we have heard in our lifetime, but aught more senseless than this speech we do not expect ever to hear. For if a demon pretends to be the soul of the dead person, what is the use of the soul at all, that it should be separated from the body? Were not we ourselves present, and heard you conjuring the soul from the body? And how comes it that, when one is conjured, another who is not conjured obeys, as if it were frightened? And you yourself, when at any time we have asked you why the conferences sometimes cease, did not you say that the soul, having fulfilled the time upon earth which it was to have passed in the body, goes to Hades? And you added, that the souls of those who commit suicide are not easily permitted to come, because, having gone home into Hades, they are guarded.'"

CHAP. XXXI.—*A dilemma.*

Nicetas having thus spoken, Aquila himself in turn said: "This only should I wish to learn of you, Simon, whether it is the soul or whether it is a demon that is conjured: what is it afraid of, that it does not despise the conjuration?" Then Simon said: "It knows that it should suffer punishment if it were disobedient." Then said Aquila: "Therefore, if the soul comes when conjured, there is also a judgment. If, therefore, souls are immortal, assuredly there is also a judgment. As you say, then, that those which are conjured on wicked business are punished if they disobey, how are you not afraid to compel them, when those that are compelled are punished for disobedience? For it is not wonderful that you do not already suffer for your doings, seeing the judgment has not yet come, when you are to suffer the penalty of those deeds which you have compelled others to do, and when that which has been done under compulsion shall be pardoned, as having been out of respect for the oath which led to the evil action."[1] And he hearing this was enraged, and threatened death to us if we did not keep silence as to his doings.

CHAP. XXXII.—*Simon's prodigies.*

Aquila having thus spoken, I Clement inquired: "What, then, are the prodigies that he works?" And they told me that he makes statues walk, and that he rolls himself on the fire, and is not burnt; and sometimes he flies; and he makes

[1] The Latin translates: "as having preferred the oath to the evil action."

loaves of stones; he becomes a serpent; he transforms himself into a goat; he becomes two-faced; he changes himself into gold; he opens lockfast gates; he melts iron; at banquets he produces images of all manner of forms. In his house he makes dishes be seen as borne of themselves to wait upon him, no bearers being seen. I wondered when I heard them speak thus; but many bore witness that they had been present, and had seen such things.

CHAP. XXXIII.—*Doctrine of pairs.*

These things having been thus spoken, the excellent Peter himself also proceeded to speak: "You must perceive, brethren, the truth of the rule of conjunction, from which he who departs not cannot be misled. For since, as we have said, we see all things in pairs and contraries, and as the night is first, and then the day; and first ignorance, then knowledge; first disease, then healing, so the things of error come first into our life, then truth supervenes, as the physician upon the disease. Therefore straightway, when our God-loved nation was about to be ransomed from the oppression of the Egyptians, first diseases were produced by means of the rod turned into a serpent, which was given to Aaron, and then remedies were superinduced by the prayers of Moses. And now also, when the Gentiles are about to be ransomed from the superstition with respect to idols, wickedness, which reigns over them, has by anticipation sent forth her ally like another serpent, even this Simon whom you see, who works wonders to astonish and deceive, not signs of healing to convert and save. Wherefore it behoves you also from the miracles that are done to judge the doers, what is the character of the performer, and what that of the deed. If he do unprofitable miracles, he is the agent of wickedness; but if he do profitable things, he is a leader of goodness.

CHAP. XXXIV.—*Useless and philanthropic miracles.*

"Those, then, are useless signs, which you say that Simon did. But I say that the making statues walk, and rolling himself on burning coals, and becoming a dragon, and being changed into a goat, and flying in the air, and all such things, not being for the healing of man, are of a nature to deceive many. But the miracles of compassionate truth are philanthropic, such as you have heard that the Lord did, and that I after Him accomplish by my prayers; at which most of you have been present, some being freed from all kinds of diseases, and some from demons, some having their hands restored, and some their feet, some recovering their eyesight, and some their hearing, and whatever else a man can do, being of a philanthropic spirit."

CHAP. XXXV.—*Discussion postponed.*

When Peter had thus spoken, towards dawn Zaccheus entered and saluted us, and said to Peter: "Simon puts off the inquiry till to-morrow; for to-day is his Sabbath, which occurs at intervals of eleven days." To him Peter answered: "Say to Simon, Whenever thou wishest; and know thou that we are always in readiness to meet thee, by divine providence, when thou desirest." And Zaccheus hearing this, went out to return the answer.

CHAP. XXXVI.—*All for the best.*

But he (Peter) saw me disheartened, and asked the reason; and being told that it proceeded from no cause but the postponement of the inquiry, he said: "He who has apprehended that the world is regulated by the good providence of God, O beloved Clement, is not vexed by things howsoever occurring, considering that things take their course advantageously under the providence of the Ruler. Whence, knowing that He is just, and living with a good conscience, he knows how by right reason to shake off from his soul any annoyance that befalls him, because, when complete, it must come to some unknown good. Now then, let not Simon the magician's postponement of the inquiry grieve you; for perhaps it has happened from the providence of God for your profit. Wherefore I shall not scruple to speak to you as being my special friend.

CHAP. XXXVII.—*Spies in the enemy's camp.*

"Some of our people attend feignedly upon Simon as companions, as if they were persuaded by his most atheistic error, in order that they may learn his purpose and disclose it to us, so that we may be able to encounter this terrible man on favourable terms. And now I have learned from them what arguments he is going to employ in the discussion. And knowing this, I give thanks to God on the one hand, and I congratulate you on the other, on the postponement of the discussion; for you, being instructed by me before the discussion, of the arguments that are to be used by him for the destruction of the ignorant, will be able to listen without danger of falling.

CHAP. XXXVIII.—*Corruption of the law.*

"For the Scriptures have had joined to them many falsehoods against God on this account. The prophet Moses having by the order of God delivered the law, with the explanations, to certain chosen men, some seventy in number, in order that they also might instruct such of the people as chose, after a little the written law had added to it certain falsehoods contrary to the law of God,[1] who made the heaven and the earth, and all things in them; the wicked one having dared to work this for some righteous purpose. And this took place in reason and judgment, that those might be convicted who should dare to listen to the things written against God, and those who, through love towards Him, should not only disbelieve the things spoken against Him, but should not even endure to hear them at all, even if they should happen to be true, judging it much safer to incur danger with respect to religious faith, than to live with an evil conscience on account of blasphemous words.

CHAP. XXXIX.—*Tactics.*

" Simon, therefore, as I learn, intends to come into public, and to speak of those chapters against God that are added to

[1] The Vatican MS. reads: " against the only God."

the Scriptures, for the sake of temptation, that he may seduce
as many wretched ones as he can from the love of God. For
we do not wish to say in public that these chapters are added
to the Bible, since we should thereby perplex the unlearned
multitudes, and so accomplish the purpose of this wicked
Simon. For they not having yet the power of discerning,
would flee from us as impious; or, as if not only the blasphemous chapters were false, they would even withdraw from
the word. Wherefore we are under a necessity of assent-
ing to the false chapters, and putting questions in return to
him concerning them, to draw him into a strait, and to give
in private an explanation of the chapters that are spoken
against God to the well-disposed after a trial of their faith;
and of this there is but one way, and that a brief one. It is
this.

CHAP. XL.—*Preliminary instruction.*

"Everything that is spoken or written against God is
false. But that we say this truly, not only for the sake of
reputation, but for the sake of truth, I shall convince you
when my discourse has proceeded a little further. Whence
you, my most beloved Clement, ought not to be sorry at
Simon's having interposed a day between this and the discussion. For to-day, before the discussion, you shall be
instructed concerning the chapters added to the Scriptures;
and then in the discussion concerning the only one and good
God, the Maker also of the world, you ought not to be distracted. But in the discussion you will even wonder how
impious men, overlooking the multitudes of things that are
spoken in the Scriptures for God, and looking at those that
are spoken against Him, gladly bring these forward; and
thus the hearers, by reason of ignorance, believing the things
against God, become outcasts from His kingdom. Wherefore
you, by advantage of the postponement, learning the mystery
of the Scriptures, and gaining the [means of] not sinning
against God, will incomparably rejoice."

CHAP. XLI.—*Asking for information, not contradiction.*

Then I Clement, hearing this, said: "Truly I rejoice, and I give thanks to God, who in all things doeth well. However, he knows that I shall be able to think nothing other than that all things are for God. Wherefore do not suppose that I ask questions, as doubting the words concerning God,[1] or those that are to be spoken, but rather that I may learn, and so be able myself to instruct another who is ingenuously willing to learn. Wherefore tell me what are the falsehoods added to the Scriptures, and how it comes that they are really false." Then Peter answered: "Even although you had not asked me, I should have gone on in order, and afforded you the exposition of these matters, as I promised. Learn, then, how the Scriptures misrepresent Him in many respects, that you may know when you happen upon them.

CHAP. XLII.—*Right notions of God essential to holiness.*

"But what I am going to tell you will be sufficient by way of example. But I do not think, my dear Clement, that any one who possesses ever so little love to God and ingenuousness, will be able to take in, or even to hear, the things that are spoken against Him. For how is it that he can have a monarchic[2] soul, and be holy, who supposes that there are many gods, and not one only? But even if there be but one, who will cherish zeal to be holy, that finds Him in many defects, since he will hope that the Beginning of all things, by reason of the defects of his own nature, will not visit the crimes of others?

CHAP. XLIII.—A priori *argument on the divine attributes.*

"Wherefore, far be it from us to believe that the Lord of all, who made the heaven and the earth, and all things that

[1] The text has ὑπό, "by," which has been altered into ὑπέρ. Davis would read σου, "by you."

[2] Cotelerius doubts whether this expression means a soul ruling over his body, or a soul disposed to favour monarchical rule. The former explanation seems to us the more probable.

are in them, shares His government with others, or that He lies. For if He lies, then who speaks truth? Or that He makes experiments as in ignorance; for then who foreknows? And if He deliberates, and changes His purpose, who is perfect in understanding and permanent in design? If He envies, who is above rivalry? If He hardens hearts, who makes wise? If He makes blind and deaf, who has given sight and hearing? If He commits pilfering, who administers justice? If He mocks, who is sincere? If He is weak, who is omnipotent? If He is unjust, who is just? If He makes evil things, who shall make good things? If He does evil, who shall do good?

CHAP. XLIV.—*The same continued.*

"But if He desires the fruitful hill,[1] whose then are all things? If He is false, who then is true? If He dwells in a tabernacle, who is without bounds? If He is fond of fat, and sacrifices, and offerings, and drink-offerings, who then is without need, and who is holy, and pure, and perfect? If He is pleased with candles and candlesticks, who then placed the luminaries in heaven? If He dwells in shadow, and darkness, and storm, and smoke, who is the light that lightens the universe? If He comes with trumpets, and shoutings, and darts, and arrows, who is the looked-for tranquillity of all? If He loves war, who then wishes peace? If He makes evil things, who makes good things? If He is without affection, who is a lover of men? If He is not faithful to His promises, who shall be trusted? If He loves the wicked, and adulterers, and murderers, who shall be a just judge? If He changes His mind, who is stedfast? If He chooses evil men, who then takes the part of the good?

CHAP. XLV.—*How God is to be thought of.*

"Wherefore, Clement, my son, beware of thinking otherwise of God, than that He is the only God, and Lord, and Father, good and righteous, the Creator, long-suffering, merciful, the sustainer, the benefactor, ordaining love of men, counselling

[1] Wieseler considers this corrupt, and amends: "if He desires more."

purity, immortal and making immortal, incomparable, dwelling in the souls of the good, that cannot be contained and yet is contained,[1] who has fixed the great world as a centre in space, who has spread out the heavens and solidified the earth, who has stored up the water, who has disposed the stars in the sky, who has made the fountains flow in the earth, has produced fruits, has raised up mountains, hath set bounds to the sea, has ordered winds and blasts, who by the spirit of counsel has kept safely the body comprehended in a boundless sea.

CHAP. XLVI.—*Judgment to come.*

"This is our Judge, to whom it behoves us to look, and to regulate our own souls, thinking all things in His favour, speaking well of Him, persuaded that by His long-suffering He brings to light the obstinacy of all, and is alone good. And He, at the end of all, shall sit as a just Judge upon every one of those who have attempted what they ought not."

CHAP. XLVII.—*A pertinent question.*

When I Clement heard this, I said, "Truly this is godliness; truly this is piety." And again I said: "I would learn, therefore, why the Bible has written anything of this sort? For I remember that you said that it was for the conviction of those who should dare to believe anything that was spoken against God. But since you permit us, we venture to ask, at your command: If any one, most beloved Peter, should choose to say to us, 'The Scriptures are true, although to you the things spoken against God seem to be false,' how should we answer him?"

CHAP. XLVIII.—*A particular case.*

Then Peter answered: "You speak well in your inquiry; for it will be for your safety. Therefore listen: Since there are many things that are spoken by the Scriptures against

---

[1] The Latin has here, "imperceptus et perceptus;" but Wieseler points out that χωρούμενος has reference to God's dwelling in the souls of the good, and thus He is contained by them.

God, as time presses on account of the evening, ask with respect to any one matter that you please, and I will explain it, showing that it is false, not only because it is spoken against God, but because it is really false." Then I answered: "I wish to learn how, when the Scriptures say that God is ignorant, you can show that He knows?"

CHAP. XLIX.—*Reductio ad absurdum.*

Then Peter answered: "You have presented us with a matter that can easily be answered. However, listen, how God is ignorant of nothing, but even foreknows. But first answer me what I ask of you. He who wrote the Bible, and told how the world was made, and said that God does not foreknow, was he a man or not?" Then I said: "He was a man." Then Peter answered: "How, then, was it possible for him, being a man, to know assuredly how the world was made, and that God does not foreknow?"

CHAP. L.—*A satisfactory answer.*

Then I, already perceiving the explanation, smiled, and said that he was a prophet. And Peter said: "If, then, he was a prophet, being a man, he was ignorant of nothing, by reason of his having received foreknowledge from God; how then, should He, who gave to man the gift of foreknowledge, being God, Himself be ignorant?" And I said: "You have spoken rightly." Then Peter said: "Come with me one step further. It being acknowledged by us that God foreknows all things, there is every necessity that the scriptures are false which say that He is ignorant, and those are true which say that He knows." Then said I: "It must needs be so."

CHAP. LI.—*Weigh in the balance.*

Then Peter said: "If, therefore, some of the Scriptures are true and some false, with good reason said our Master, 'Be ye good money-changers,'[1] inasmuch as in the Scriptures there

---

[1] This is quoted three times in the *Homilies* as a saying of our Lord, viz. here and in Homily iii. chap. l., and Homily xviii. chap. xx. It is probably taken from one of the apocryphal Gospels. In Homily xviii.

are some true sayings and some spurious. And to those who err by reason of the false scriptures He fitly showed the cause of their error, saying, 'Ye do therefore err, not knowing the true things of the Scriptures;[1] for this reason ye are ignorant also of the power of God.'" Then said I: "[You have spoken] very excellently."

CHAP. LII.—*Sins of the saints denied.*

Then Peter answered: "Assuredly, with good reason, I neither believe anything against God, nor against the just men recorded in the law, taking for granted that they are impious imaginations. For, as I am persuaded, neither was Adam a transgressor, who was fashioned by the hands of God; nor was Noah drunken, who was found righteous above all the world;[2] nor did Abraham live with three wives at once, who, on account of his sobriety, was thought worthy of a numerous posterity; nor did Jacob associate with four —of whom two were sisters—who was the father of the twelve tribes, and who intimated the coming of the presence of our Master; nor was Moses a murderer, nor did he learn to judge from an idolatrous priest—he who set forth the law of God to all the world, and for his right judgment has been testified to as a faithful steward.

CHAP. LIII.—*Close of the conference.*

"But of these and such like things I shall afford you an explanation in due time. But for the rest, since, as you see, the evening has come upon us, let what has been said be enough for to-day. But whenever you wish, and about whatever you wish, ask boldly of us, and we shall gladly explain it at once." Thus having spoken, he rose up. And then, having partaken of food, we turned to sleep, for the night had come upon us.

---

chap. xx. the meaning is shown to be, that as it is the part of a money-changer to distinguish spurious coins from genuine, so it is the part of a Christian to distinguish false statements from true.

[1] A corruption of the texts, Matt. xxii. 29, Mark xii. 24.
[2] Gen. vii. 1.

HOMILY III.

CHAP. I.—*The morning of the discussion.*

TWO days, therefore, having elapsed, and while the third was dawning, I Clement, and the rest of our companions, being roused about the second cock-crowing, in order to the discussion with Simon, found the lamp still alight, and Peter kneeling in prayer. Therefore, having finished his supplication, and turning round, and seeing us in readiness to hear, he said :

CHAP. II.—*Simon's design.*

"I wish you to know that those who, according to our arrangement, associate with Simon that they may learn his intentions, and submit them to us, so that we may be able to cope with his variety of wickedness, these men have sent to me, and informed me that Simon to-day is, as he arranged, prepared to come before all, and show from the Scriptures that He who made the heaven and the earth, and all things in them, is not the Supreme God, but that there is another, unknown and supreme, as being in an unspeakable manner God of gods; and that He sent two gods, one of whom is he who made the world, and the other he who gave the law. And these things he contrives to say, that he may dissipate the right faith of those who would worship the one and only God who made heaven and earth.

CHAP. III.—*His object.*

"When I heard this, how was I not disheartened! Wherefore I wished you also, my brethren, who associate with me, to know that I am beyond measure grieved in my soul, seeing the wicked one awake for the temptation of men, and men wholly indifferent about their own salvation. For to those from amongst the Gentiles who were about being persuaded respecting the earthly images that they are no gods, he has contrived to bring in opinions of many other gods, in order that, if they cease from the polytheo-mania, they may be deceived to speak otherwise, and even worse [than they now do], against the sole government of God, so that they may not yet value the truths connected with that monarchy, and may never be able to obtain mercy. And for the sake of this attempt Simon comes to do battle with us, armed with the false chapters of the Scriptures. And what is more dreadful, he is not afraid to dogmatize thus against the true God from the prophets whom he does not [in fact] believe.

CHAP. IV.—*Snares laid for the Gentiles.*

"And with us, indeed, who have had handed down from our forefathers the worship of the God who made all things, and also the mystery of the books which are able to deceive, he will not prevail; but with those from amongst the Gentiles who have the polytheistic fancy bred in them, and who know not the falsehoods of the Scriptures, he will prevail much. And not only he; but if any other shall recount to those from among the Gentiles any vain, dreamlike, richly set out story against God, he will be believed, because from their childhood their minds are accustomed to take in things spoken against God. And few there shall be of them, as a few out of a multitude, who through ingenuousness shall not be willing so much as to hear an evil word against the God who made all things. And to these alone from amongst the Gentiles it shall be vouchsafed to be saved. Let not any one of you, therefore, altogether complain of Simon, or of any one else; for nothing happens unjustly, since even the falsehoods of Scripture are with good reason presented for a test."

CHAP. V.—*Use of errors.*

Then I Clement, hearing this, said: "How say you, my lord, that even the falsehoods of the Scriptures are set forth happily for the proof of men?" And he answered: "The falsehoods of the Scriptures have been permitted to be written for a certain righteous reason, at the demand of evil. And when I say happily, I mean this: In the account of God, the wicked one, not loving God less than the good one, is exceeded by the good in this one thing only, that he, not pardoning those who are impious on account of ignorance, through love towards that which is profound, desires the destruction of the impious; but the good one desires to present them with a remedy. For the good one desires all to be healed by repentance, but saves those only who know God. But those who know Him not He does not heal: not that He does not wish to do so, but because it is not lawful to afford to those who, through want of judgment, are like to irrational animals, the good things which have been prepared for the children of the kingdom.

Chap. VI.—*Purgatory and hell.*

"Such is the nature of the one and only God, who made the world, and who created us, and who has given us all things, that as long as any one is within the limit of piety, and does not blaspheme His Holy Spirit, through His love towards him He brings the soul to Himself by reason of His love towards it. And although it be sinful, it is His nature to save it, after it has been suitably punished for the deeds it hath done. But if any one shall deny Him, or in any other way be guilty of impiety against Him, and then shall repent, he shall be punished indeed for the sins he hath committed against Him, but he shall be saved, because he turned and lived. And perhaps excessive piety and supplication shall even be delivered from punishment, ignorance being admitted as a reason for the pardon of sin after repentance.[1] But those who do not repent shall be destroyed by the punishment of fire, even though in all other things they are most holy. But, as I said, at an appointed time a fifth[2] part, being punished with eternal fire, shall be consumed. For they cannot endure for ever who have been impious against the one God.

---

[1] The text manifestly corrupt.
[2] Perhaps, rather, "the greater part."

Chap. VII.—*What is impiety?*

"But impiety against Him is, in the matter of religion, to die saying there is another God, whether superior or inferior, or in any way saying that there is one besides Him who really is. For He who truly is, is He whose form the body of man bears; for whose sake the heaven and all the stars, though in their essence superior, submit to serve him who is in essence inferior, on account of the form of the Ruler. So much has God blessed man above all, in order that, loving the Benefactor in proportion to the multitude of His benefits, by means of this love he may be saved for the world to come.

Chap. VIII.—*Wiles of the devil.*

"Therefore the love of men towards God is sufficient for salvation. And this the wicked one knows; and while we are hastening to sow the love towards Him which makes immortal in the souls of those who from among the Gentiles are ready to believe in the one and only God, this wicked one, having sufficient armour against the ignorant for their destruction, hastens to sow the supposition of many gods, or at least of one greater, in order that men, conceiving and being persuaded of what is not wisdom, may die, as in the crime of adultery, and be cast out from His kingdom.

Chap. IX.—*Uncertainty of the Scriptures.*

"Worthy, therefore, of rejection is every one who is willing so much as to hear anything against the monarchy of God; but if any one dares to hear anything against God, as trusting in the Scriptures, let him first of all consider with me that if any one, as he pleases, form a dogma agreeable to himself, and then carefully search the Scriptures, he will be able to produce many testimonies from them in favour of the dogma that he has formed. How, then, can confidence be placed in them against God, when what every man wishes is found in them?

CHAP. X.—*Simon's intention.*

"Therefore Simon, who is going to discuss in public with us to-morrow, is bold against the monarchy of God, wishing to produce many statements from these Scriptures, to the effect that there are many gods, and a certain one who is not He who made this world, but who is superior to Him; and, at the same time, he is going to offer many scriptural proofs. But we also can easily show many passages from them that He who made the world alone is God, and that there is none other besides Him. But if any one shall wish to speak otherwise, he also shall be able to produce proofs from them at his pleasure. For the Scriptures say all manner of things, that no one of those who inquire ungratefully may find the truth, but [simply] what he wishes to find, the truth being reserved for the grateful; now gratitude is to preserve our love to Him who is the cause of our being.

CHAP. XI.—*Distinction between prediction and prophecy.*

"Whence it must before all things be known, that nowhere can truth be found unless from a prophet of truth. But He is a true Prophet, who always knows all things, and even the thoughts of all men, who is without sin, as being convinced respecting the judgment of God. Wherefore we ought not simply to consider respecting His foreknowledge, but whether His foreknowledge can stand, apart from other cause. For physicians predict certain things, having the pulse of the patient as matter submitted to them; and some predict by means of having fowls, and some by having sacrifices, and others by having many various matters submitted to them; yet these are not prophets.

CHAP. XII.—*The same.*

"But if any one should say that the foreknowledge [shown] by these predictions is like to that foreknowledge which is really implanted, he were much deceived. For he only declares such things as being present, and that if he speaks truth. However, even these things are serviceable to me, for they establish that there is such a thing as foreknowledge. But the foreknowledge of the one true Prophet does not only know things present, but stretches out prophecy without limit as far as the world to come, and needs nothing for its interpretation, not prophesying darkly and ambiguously, so that the things spoken would need another prophet for the interpretation of them; but clearly and simply, as our Master and Prophet, by the inborn and ever-flowing Spirit, always knew all things.

CHAP. XIII.—*Prophetic knowledge constant.*

"Wherefore He confidently made statements respecting things that are to be—I mean sufferings, places, limits. For, being a faultless Prophet, and looking upon all things with the boundless eye of His soul, He knows hidden things. But if we should hold, as many do, that even the true Prophet, not always, but sometimes, when He has the Spirit, and through it, foreknows, but when He has it not is ignorant,—if we should suppose thus, we should deceive ourselves and mislead others. For such a matter belongs to those who are madly inspired by the spirit of disorder—to those who are drunken beside the altars, and are gorged with fat.

CHAP. XIV.—*Prophetic spirit constant.*

"For if it were permitted to any one who will profess prophecy to have it believed in the cases in which he was found false, that then he had not the Holy Spirit of foreknowledge, it will be difficult to convict him of being a false prophet; for among the many things that he speaks, a few come to pass, and then he is believed to have the Spirit, although he speaks the first things last, and the last first; speaks of past events as future, and future as already past; and also without sequence; or things borrowed from others and altered, and some that are lessened, unformed, foolish, ambiguous, unseemly, obscure, proclaiming all unconscientiousness.

Chap. XV.—*Christ's prophecies.*

"But our Master did not prophesy after this fashion; but, as I have already said, being a prophet by an inborn and ever-flowing Spirit, and knowing all things at all times, He confidently set forth, plainly as I said before, sufferings, places, appointed times, manners, limits. Accordingly, therefore, prophesying concerning the temple, He said: 'See ye these buildings? Verily I say to you, There shall not be left here one stone upon another which shall not be taken away; and this generation shall not pass until the destruction begin. For they shall come, and shall sit here, and shall besiege it, and shall slay your children here.'[1] And in like manner He spoke in plain words the things that were straightway to happen, which we can now see with our eyes, in order that the accomplishment might be among those to whom the word was spoken. For the Prophet of truth utters the word of proof in order to the faith of His hearers.

Chap. XVI.—*Doctrine of conjunction.*

"However, there are many proclaimers of error, having one chief, even the chief of wickedness, just as the Prophet of truth, being one, and being also the chief of piety, shall in His own times have as His prophets all who are found pure. But the chief cause of men being deceived is this, their not understanding beforehand the doctrine of conjunction, which I shall not fail to expound to you in private every day, summarily; for it were too long to speak in detail. Be you therefore to me truth-loving judges of the things that are spoken.

Chap. XVII.—*Whether Adam had the Spirit.*

"But I shall begin the statement now. God having made all things, if any one will not allow to a man, fashioned by His hands, to have possessed His great and Holy Spirit of foreknowledge, how does not he greatly err who attributes it to another born of a spurious stock! And I do not think that

[1] Matt. xxiv. 2, 34; Luke xix. 43.

he will obtain pardon, though he be misled by spurious scripture to think dreadful things against the Father of all. For he who insults the image and the things belonging to the eternal King, has the sin reckoned as committed against Him in whose likeness the image was made. But then, says he, the Divine Spirit left him when he sinned. In that case [the Spirit] sinned along with him; and how can he escape peril who says this? But perhaps he received the Spirit after he sinned. Then it is given to the unrighteous; and where is justice? But it was afforded to the just and the unjust. This were most unrighteous of all. Thus every falsehood, though it be aided by ten thousand reasonings, must receive its refutation, though after a long time.

CHAP. XVIII.—*Adam not ignorant.*

"Be not deceived. Our father was ignorant of nothing; since, indeed, even the law publicly current, though charging him with the crime of ignorance for the sake of the unworthy, sends to him those desirous of knowledge, saying, 'Ask your father, and he will tell you; your elders, and they will declare to you.'[1] This father, these elders ought to be inquired of. But you have not inquired whose is the time of the kingdom, and whose is the seat of prophecy, though He Himself points out Himself, saying, 'The scribes and the Pharisees sit in Moses' seat; all things whatsoever they say to you, hear them.'[2] Hear *them,* He said, as entrusted with the key of the kingdom, which is knowledge, which alone can open the gate of life, through which alone is the entrance to eternal life. But truly, He says, they possess the key, but those wishing to enter they do not suffer to do so.

CHAP. XIX.—*Reign of Christ.*

"On this account, I say, He Himself, rising from His seat as a father for his children, proclaiming the things which from the beginning were delivered in secret to the worthy, extending mercy even to the Gentiles, and compassionating the souls of all, neglected His own kindred. For He, being

[1] Deut. xxxii. 7.   [2] Matt. xxii. 2.

thought worthy to be King of the world to come, [fights against¹] him who, by predestination, has usurped the kingdom that now is. And the thing which exceedingly grieved Him is this, that by those very persons for whom, as for sons, he did battle, He was assailed, on account of their ignorance. And yet He loved even those who hated Him, and wept over the unbelieving, and blessed those who slandered Him, and prayed for those who were in enmity against Him.² And not only did He do this as a father, but also taught His disciples to do the like, bearing themselves as towards brethren.³ This did our Father, this did our Prophet. This is reasonable, that He should be King over His children; that by the affection of a father towards his children, and the engrafted respect of children towards their father, eternal peace might be produced. For when the good man reigneth, there is true joy among those who are ruled over, on account of him who rules.

CHAP. XX.—*Christ the only Prophet has appeared in different ages.*

"But give heed to my first discourse of the truth. If any one do not allow the man fashioned by the hands of God to have had the Holy Spirit of Christ, how is he not guilty of the greatest impiety in allowing another born of an impure stock to have it? But he would act most piously, if he should not allow to another to have it, but should say that he alone has it, who has changed his forms and his names from the beginning of the world, and so reappeared again and again in the world, until coming upon his own times, and being anointed with mercy for the works of God, he shall enjoy rest for ever. His honour it is to bear rule and lordship over all things, in air, earth, and waters. But in addition to these, himself having made man, he had breath, the indescribable garment of the soul, that he might be able to be immortal.

CHAP. XXI.—*The eating of the forbidden fruit denied.*

"He himself being the only true prophet, fittingly gave

¹ From a conjectural reading by Neander.
² Matt. xxiii. 37; Luke xiii. 34; Luke xxiii. 34.   ³ Matt. v. 44.

names to each animal, according to the merits of its nature, as having made it. For if he gave a name to any one, that was also the name of that which was made, being given by him who made it.[1] How, then, had he still need to partake of a tree, that he might know what is good and what is evil, if he was commanded not to eat of it? But this senseless men believe, who think that a reasonless beast was more powerful than the God who made these things.

CHAP. XXII.—*Male and female.*

"But a companion was created along with him, a female nature, much differing from him, as quality from substance, as the moon from the sun, as fire from light. She, as a female ruling the present world as her like,[2] was entrusted to be the first prophetess, announcing prophecy with all amongst those born of woman.[3] But the other, as the son of man, being a male, prophesies better things to the world to come as a male.

CHAP. XXIII.—*Two kinds of prophecy.*

"Let us then understand that there are two kinds of prophecy:[4] the one male; and let it be defined that the first, being the male, has been ranked after the other in the order of advent; but the second, being female, has been appointed to come first in the advent of the pairs. This second, therefore, being amongst those born of woman, as the female superintendent of this present world, wishes to be thought masculine. Wherefore, stealing the seeds of the male, and sowing them with her own seeds of the flesh, she brings forth the fruits—that is, words—as wholly her own. And she promises that she will give the present earthly riches as

---

[1] Gen. ii. 20.
[2] That is, the present world is female, and is under the rule of the female; the world to come is male, and is under the rule of the male.
[3] The allusion is to the fact that John the Baptist is called the greatest of those born of woman, while Christ is called the Son of man.
[4] Literally, "Let there be to us two genuine prophecies."

a dowry, wishing to change the slow for the swift, the small for the greater.

CHAP. XXIV.—*The prophetess a misleader.*

"However, she, not only presuming to say and to hear that there are many gods, but also believing herself to be one, and in hope of being that which she had not a nature to be, and throwing away what she had, and as a female being in her courses at the offering of sacrifices, is stained with blood; and then she pollutes those who touch her. But when she conceives and brings forth temporary kings, she stirs up wars, shedding much blood; and those who desire to learn truth from her, by telling them all things contrary, and presenting many and various services, she keeps them always seeking and finding nothing, even until death. For from the beginning a cause of death lies upon blind men; for she, prophesying deceit, and ambiguities, and obliquities, deceives those who believe her.

CHAP. XXV.—*Cain's name and nature.*

"Hence the ambiguous name which she gave to her first-born son, calling him *Cain*, which has a capability of interpretation in two ways; for it is interpreted both *possession* and *envy*, as signifying that in the future he was to envy either a woman, or possessions, or the love of the parents towards her.[1] But if it be none of these, then it will befall him to be called the *possession*. For she possessed him first, which also was advantageous to him. For he was a murderer and a liar, and with his sins was not willing to be at peace with respect to the government. Moreover, those who came forth by succession from him were the first adulterers. And there were psalteries, and harps, and forgers of instruments of war. Wherefore also the prophecy of his descendants being full of adulterers and of psalteries, secretly by means of pleasures excites to wars.

[1] Qu. "towards Abel"?

CHAP. XXVI.—*Abel's name and nature.*

"But he who amongst the sons of men had prophecy innate to his soul as belonging to it, expressly, as being a male, indicating the hopes of the world to come, called his own son Abel, which without any ambiguity is translated *grief.* For he assigns to his sons to grieve over their deceived brethren. He does not deceive them when he promises them comfort in the world to come. When he says that we must pray to one only God, he neither himself speaks of gods, nor does he believe another who speaks of them. He keeps the good which he has, and increases more and more. He hates sacrifices, bloodshed, and libations; he loves the chaste, the pure, the holy. He quenches the fire of altars, represses wars, teaches pious preachers wisdom, purges sins, sanctions marriage, approves temperance, leads all to chastity, makes men liberal, prescribes justice, seals those of them who are perfect, publishes the word of peace, prophesies explicitly, speaks decidedly, frequently makes mention of the eternal fire of punishment, constantly announces the kingdom of God, indicates heavenly riches, promises unfading glory, shows the remission of sins by works.

CHAP. XXVII.—*The prophet and the prophetess.*

"And what need is there to say more? The male is wholly truth, the female wholly falsehood. But he who is born of the male and the female, in some things speaks truth, in some falsehood. For the female, surrounding the white seed of the male with her own blood, as with red fire, sustains her own weakness with the extraneous supports of bones, and, pleased with the temporary flower of flesh, and spoiling the strength of the judgment by short pleasures, leads the greater part into fornication, and thus deprives them of the coming excellent Bridegroom. For every person is a bride, whenever, being sown with the true Prophet's whole word of truth, he is enlightened in his understanding.

Chap. XXVIII.—*Spiritual adultery.*

" Wherefore, it is fitting to hear the one only Prophet of the truth, knowing that the word that is sown by another bearing the charge of fornication, is, as it were, cast out by the Bridegroom from His kingdom. But to those who know the mystery, death is also produced by spiritual adultery. For whenever the soul is sown by others, then it is forsaken by the Spirit, as guilty of fornication or adultery; and so the living body, the life-giving Spirit being withdrawn, is dissolved into dust, and the rightful punishment of sin is suffered at the time of the judgment by the soul, after the dissolution of the body; even as, among men, she who is caught in adultery is first cast out from the house, and then afterwards is condemned to punishment."

Chap. XXIX.—*The signal given.*

While Peter was about to explain fully to us this mystic word, Zaccheus came, saying: "Now indeed, O Peter, is the time for you to go out and engage in the discussion; for a great crowd awaits you, packed together in the court; and in the midst of them stands Simon, like a war-chieftain attended by his spearmen." And Peter, hearing this, ordered me to withdraw for prayer, as not yet having received baptism for salvation, and then said to those who were already perfected: "Let us rise and pray that God, by His unfailing mercies, may help me striving for the salvation of the men whom He has made." And having thus said, and having prayed, he went out into the uncovered portion of the court, which was a large space; and there were many come together for the purpose of seeing him, his pre-eminence having made them more eagerly hasten to hear.

Chap. XXX.—*Apostolic salutation.*

Therefore, standing and seeing all the people gazing upon him in profound silence, and Simon the magician standing in the midst, he began to speak thus: "Peace be to all you who are in readiness to give your right hands to the truth of God, which, being His great and incomparable gift in the present world, He who sent us, being an infallible Prophet of that which is supremely profitable, gave us in charge, by way of salutation before our words of instruction, to announce to you, in order that if there be any son of peace among you, peace may take hold of him through our teaching; but if any of you will not receive it, then we, shaking off for a testimony the road-dust of our feet, which we have borne through our toils, and brought to you that you may be saved, will go to the abodes and the cities of others.[1]

CHAP. XXXI.—*Faith in God.*

"And we tell you truly, it shall be more tolerable in the day of judgment to dwell in the land of Sodom and Gomorrha, than in the place of unbelief. In the first place, because you have not preserved of yourselves what is reasonable; in the second place, because, hearing the things concerning us, you have not come to us; and in the third place, because you have disbelieved us when we have come to you. Wherefore, being concerned for you, we pray of our own accord that our peace may come upon you. If therefore ye will have it, you must readily promise not to do injustice, and generously to bear wrong; which the nature of man would not sustain, unless it first received the knowledge of that which is supremely profitable, which is to know the righteous nature of Him who is over all, that He defends and avenges those who are wronged, and does good for ever to the pious.

CHAP. XXXII.—*Invitation.*

"Do you, therefore, as thankful servants of God, perceiving of yourselves what is reasonable, take upon you the manner of life that is pleasing to Him, that so, loving Him, and being loved of Him, you may enjoy good for ever. For to Him alone is it most possible to bestow it, who gave being to things that were not, who created the heavens, settled the earth, set bounds to the sea, stored up the things that are in Hades, and filled all places with air.

[1] Matt. x. 12; Mark vi. 11; Luke x. 5.

CHAP. XXXIII.—*Works of creation.*

"He alone turned into the four contrary elements[1] the one, first, simple substance. Thus combining them, He made of them myriads of compounds, that, being turned into opposite natures, and mingled, they might effect the pleasure of life from the combination of contraries. In like manner, He alone, having created races of angels and spirits by the *fiat* of His will, peopled the heavens; as also He decked the visible firmament with stars, to which also He assigned their paths and arranged their courses. He compacted the earth for the production of fruits. He set bounds to the sea, marking out a dwelling-place on the dry land.[2] He stores up the things in Hades, designating it as the place of souls; and He filled all places with air, that all living creatures might be able to breathe safely in order that they might live.

CHAP. XXXIV.—*Extent of creation.*

"O the great hand of the wise God, which doeth all in all! For a countless multitude of birds have been made by Him, and those various, differing in all respects from one another; I mean in respect of their colours, beaks, talons, looks, senses, voices, and all else. And how many different species of plants, distinguished by boundless variety of colours, qualities, and scents! And how many animals on the land and in the water, of which it were impossible to tell the figures, forms, habitats, colour, food, senses, natures, multitude! Then also the multitude and height of mountains, the varieties of stones, awful caverns, fountains, rivers, marshes, seas, harbours, islands, forests, and all the inhabited world, and places uninhabited!

CHAP. XXXV.—"*These are a part of His ways.*"

"And how many things besides are unknown, having eluded the sagacity of men! And of those that are within our

[1] This is rather a paraphrase than a strict translation.
[2] Various reading, "assigning it [the sea] as a habitation for aquatic animals."

comprehension, who of mankind knows the limit? I mean, how the heaven rolls, how the stars are borne in their courses, and what forms they have, and the subsistence of their being,[1] and what are their ethereal paths. And whence the blasts of winds are borne around, and have different energies; whence the fountains ceaselessly spring, and the rivers, being ever flowing, run down into the sea, and neither is that [fountain] emptied whence they come, nor do they fill that [sea] whither they come! How far reaches the unfathomable depth of the boundless Tartarus! Upon what the heaven is upborne which encircles all! How the clouds spring from air, and are absorbed into air! What is the nature of thunder and lightning, snow, hail, mist, ice, storms, showers, hanging clouds! And how He makes plants and animals! And these things, with all accuracy, continually perfected in their countless varieties!

CHAP. XXXVI.—*Dominion over the creatures.*

"Therefore, if any one shall accurately scan the whole with reason, he shall find that God has made them for the sake of man. For showers fall for the sake of fruits, that man may partake of them, and that animals may be fed, that they may be useful to men. And the sun shines, that he may turn the air into four seasons, and that each time may afford its peculiar service to man. And the fountains spring, that drink may be given to men. And, moreover, who is lord over the creatures, so far as is possible? Is it not man, who has received wisdom to till the earth, to sail the sea; to make fishes, birds, and beasts his prey; to investigate the course of the stars, to mine the earth, to sail the sea, to build cities, to define kingdoms, to ordain laws, to execute justice, to know the invisible God, to be cognizant of the names of angels, to drive away demons, to endeavour to cure diseases by medicines, to find charms against poison-darting serpents, to understand antipathies?

[1] Literally, "of their life," according to the idea prevalent of old, that the heavenly bodies were living creatures.

CHAP. XXXVII.—" *Whom to know is life eternal.*"

But if thou art thankful, O man, understanding that God is thy benefactor in all things, thou mayest even be immortal, the things that are made for thee having continuance through thy gratitude. And now thou art able to become incorruptible, if thou acknowledge Him whom thou didst not know, if thou love Him whom thou didst forsake, if thou pray to Him alone who is able to punish or to save thy body and soul. Wherefore, before all things, consider that no one shares His rule, no one has a name in common with Him—that is, is called God. For He alone is both called and is God. Nor is it lawful to think that there is any other, or to call any other by that name. And if any one should dare do so, eternal punishment of soul is his."

CHAP. XXXVIII.—*Simon's challenge.*

When Peter had thus spoken, Simon, at the outside of the crowd, cried aloud: " Why would you lie, and deceive the unlearned multitude standing around you, persuading them that it is unlawful to think that there are gods, and to call them so, when the books that are current among the Jews say that there are many gods? And now I wish, in the presence of all, to discuss with you from these books on the necessity of thinking that there are gods; first showing respecting him whom you call God, that he is not the supreme and omnipotent [Being], inasmuch as he is without foreknowledge, imperfect, needy, not good, and underlying many and innumerable grievous passions. Wherefore, when this has been shown from the Scriptures, as I say, it follows that there is another, not written of, foreknowing, perfect, without want, good, removed from all grievous passions. But he whom you call the Creator is subject to the opposite [evils].

CHAP. XXXIX.—*Defects ascribed to God.*

" Therefore also Adam, being made at first after his likeness, is created blind, and is said not to have knowledge of good or evil, and is found a transgressor, and is driven out of paradise, and is punished with death. In like manner also, he who made him, because he sees not in all places, says with reference to the overthrow of Sodom, 'Come, and let us go down, and see whether they do according to their cry which comes to me; or if not, that I may know.'[1] Thus he shows himself ignorant. And in his saying respecting Adam, 'Let us drive him out, lest he put forth his hand and touch the tree of life, and eat, and live for ever;'[2] in saying *lest* he is ignorant; and in driving him out lest he should eat and live for ever, he is also envious. And whereas it is written that "God[3] repented that he had made man," this implies both repentance and ignorance. For this reflection is a view by which one, through ignorance, wishes to inquire into the result of the things which he wills, or it is the act of one repenting on account of the event not being according to his expectation. And whereas it is written, 'And the Lord smelled a scent of sweetness,'[4] it is the part of one in need; and his being pleased with the fat of flesh is the part of one who is not good. But his tempting, as it is written, 'And God did tempt Abraham,'[5] is the part of one who is wicked, and who is ignorant of the issue of the experiment."

CHAP. XL.—*Peter's answer.*

In like manner Simon, by taking many passages from the Scriptures, seemed to show that God is subject to every infirmity. And to this Peter said: "Does he who is evil, and wholly wicked, love to accuse himself in the things in which he sins? Answer me this." Then said Simon: "He does not." Then said Peter: "How, then, can God be evil and wicked, seeing that those evil things which have been commonly written regarding Him, have been added by His own will!" Then said Simon: "It may be that the charge against Him is written by another power, and not according to His choice." Then said Peter: "Let us then, in the first place, inquire into this. If, indeed, He has of His own will accused

---

[1] Gen. xviii. 21.   [2] Gen. iii. 22.   [3] Gen. vi. 6.
[4] Gen. viii. 21.   [5] Gen. xxii. 1.

Himself, as you formerly acknowledged, then He is not wicked; but if it is done by another power, it must be inquired and investigated with all energy who hath subjected to all evils Him who alone is good."

Chap. XLI.—"*Status quæstionis.*"

Then said Simon: "You are manifestly avoiding the hearing of the charge from the Scriptures against your God." Then Peter: "You yourself appear to me to be doing this; for he who avoids the order of inquiry, does not wish a true investigation to be made. Hence I, who proceed in an orderly manner, and wish that the writer should first be considered, am manifestly desirous to walk in a straight path." Then Simon: "First confess that if the things written against the Creator are true, he is not above all, since, according to the Scriptures, he is subject to all evil; then afterwards we shall inquire as to the writer." Then said Peter: "That I may not seem to speak against your want of order through unwillingness to enter upon the investigation,[1] I answer you. I say that if the things written against God are true, they do not show that God is wicked." Then said Simon: "How can you maintain that?"

Chap. XLII.—*Was Adam blind?*

Then said Peter: "Because things are written opposite to those sayings which speak evil of him; wherefore neither the one nor the other can be confirmed." Then Simon: "How, then, is the truth to be ascertained, of those Scriptures that say he is evil, or of those that say he is good?" Then Peter: "Whatever sayings of the Scriptures are in harmony with the creation that was made by Him are true, but whatever are contrary to it are false." Then Simon said: "How can you show that the Scriptures contradict themselves?" And Peter said: "You say that Adam was created blind, which was not so; for He would not have pointed out the tree of the knowledge of good and evil to a blind man, and com-

---

[1] The text of this passage in all the editions is meaningless. It becomes clear by a change of punctuation.

manded him not to taste of it." Then said Simon: "He meant that his mind was blind." Then Peter: "How could he be blind in respect of his mind, who, before tasting of the tree, in harmony with Him who made him, imposed appropriate names on all the animals?" Then Simon: "If Adam had foreknowledge, how did he not foreknow that the serpent would deceive his wife?" Then Peter: "If Adam had not foreknowledge, how did he give names to the sons of men as they were born with reference to their future doings, calling the first Cain (which is interpreted 'envy'), who through envy killed his brother Abel (which is interpreted 'grief'); for his parents grieved over him, the first slain?

CHAP. XLIII.—*God's foreknowledge.*

"But if Adam, being the work of God, had foreknowledge, much more the God who created him. And that is false which is written that God reflected, as if using reasoning on account of ignorance; and that the Lord tempted Abraham, that He might know if he would endure it; and that which is written, 'Let us go down, and see if they are doing according to the cry of them which cometh to me; and if not, that I may know.' And, not to extend my discourse too far, whatever sayings ascribe ignorance to Him, or anything else that is evil, being upset by other sayings which affirm the contrary, are proved to be false. But because He does indeed foreknow, He says to Abraham, 'Thou shalt assuredly know that thy seed shall be sojourners in a land that is not their own; and they shall enslave them, and shall evil entreat them, and humble them four hundred years. But the nation to which they shall be in bondage will I judge, and after that they shall come out hither with much property; but thou shalt depart to thy fathers with peace, being nourished in a good old age; and in the fourth generation they shall return hither, for the sins of the Amorites are hitherto not filled up.'[1]

CHAP. XLIV.—*God's decrees.*

"But what? Does not Moses pre-intimate the sins of the

[1] Gen. xv. 13-16.

people, and predict their dispersion among the nations? But if He gave foreknowledge to Moses, how can it be that He had it not Himself? But He has it. And if He has it, as we have also shown, it is an extravagant saying that He reflected, and that He repented, and that He went down to see, and whatever else of this sort. Whatsoever things being foreknown before they come to pass as about to befall, take issue by a wise economy, without repentance.

CHAP. XLV.—*Sacrifices.*

"But that He is not pleased with sacrifices, is shown by this, that those who lusted after flesh were slain as soon as they tasted it, and were consigned to a tomb, so that it was called the grave of lusts.[1] He then who at the first was displeased with the slaughtering of animals, not wishing them to be slain, did not ordain sacrifices as desiring them; nor from the beginning did He require them. For neither are sacrifices accomplished without the slaughter of animals, nor can the first-fruits be presented. But how is it possible for Him to abide in darkness, and smoke, and storm (for this also is written), who created a pure heaven, and created the sun to give light to all, and assigned the invariable order of their revolutions to innumerable stars? Thus, O Simon, the handwriting of God—I mean the heaven—shows the counsels of Him who made it to be pure and stable.

CHAP. XLVI.—*Disparagements of God.*

"Thus the sayings accusatory of the God who made the heaven are both rendered void by the opposite sayings which are alongside of them, and are refuted by the creation. For they were not written by a prophetic hand. Wherefore also they appear opposite to the hand of God, who made all things." Then said Simon: "How can you show this?"

CHAP. XLVII.—*Foreknowledge of Moses.*

Then said Peter: "The law of God was given by Moses, without writing, to seventy wise men, to be handed down,

---
[1] That is, Kibroth-Hattaavah; Num. xi. 34.

that the government might be carried on by succession. But after that Moses was taken up, it was written by some one, but not by Moses. For in the law itself it is written, 'And Moses died; and they buried him near the house of Phogor,[1] and no one knows his sepulchre till this day.' But how could Moses write that Moses died? And whereas in the time after Moses, about 500 years or thereabouts, it is found lying in the temple which was built, and after about 500 years more it is carried away, and being burnt in the time of Nebuchadnezzar it is destroyed; and thus being written after Moses, and often lost, even this shows the foreknowledge of Moses, because he, foreseeing its disappearance, did not write it; but those who wrote it, being convicted of ignorance through their not foreseeing its disappearance, were not prophets."

CHAP. XLVIII.—*Test of truth.*

Then said Simon: "Since, as you say, we must understand the things concerning God by comparing them with the creation, how is it possible to recognise the other things in the law which are from the tradition of Moses, and are true, and are mixed up with these falsehoods?" Then Peter said: "A certain verse has been recorded without controversy in the written law, according to the providence of God, so as to show clearly which of the things written are true and which are false." Then said Simon: "Which is that? Show it us."

CHAP. XLIX.—*The true Prophet.*

Then Peter said: "I shall tell you forthwith. It is written in the first book of the law, towards the end: 'A ruler shall not fail from Judah, nor a leader from his thighs, until He come whose it is; and He is the expectation of the nations.'[2] If, therefore, any one can apprehend Him who came after the failure of ruler and leader from Judah, and who was to be expected by the nations, he will be able by this verse to recognise Him as truly having come;[3] and believing His

---

[1] Septuagint version of Deut. xxxiv. 8.
[2] Gen. xlix. 10.   [3] From the amended reading of Davis.

teaching, he will know what of the Scriptures are true and what are false." Then said Simon: "I understand that you speak of your Jesus as Him who was prophesied of by the scripture. Therefore let it be granted that it is so. Tell us, then, how he taught you to discriminate the Scriptures."

CHAP. L.—*His teaching concerning the Scriptures.*

Then Peter: "As to the mixture of truth with falsehood, I remember that on one occasion He, finding fault with the Sadducees, said, 'Wherefore ye do err, not knowing the true things of the Scriptures; and on this account ye are ignorant of the power of God.'[1] But if He cast up to them that they knew not the true things of the Scriptures, it is manifest that there are false things in them. And also, inasmuch as He said, 'Be ye prudent money-changers,'[2] it is because there are genuine and spurious words. And whereas He said, 'Wherefore do ye not perceive that which is reasonable in the Scriptures?' He makes the understanding of him stronger who voluntarily judges soundly.

CHAP. LI.—*His teaching concerning the law.*

"And His sending to the scribes and teachers of the existing Scriptures, as to those who knew the true things of the law that then was, is well known. And also that He said, 'I am not come to destroy the law,'[3] and yet that He appeared to be destroying it, is the part of one intimating that the things which He destroyed did not belong to the law. And His saying, 'The heaven and the earth shall pass away, but one jot or one tittle shall not pass from the law,'[4] intimated that the things which pass away before the heaven and the earth do not belong to the law in reality.

CHAP. LII.—*Other sayings of Christ.*

"Since, then, while the heaven and the earth still stand,

---

[1] Matt. xxii. 29.

[2] This is frequently quoted as a saying of Christ. It is probably from one of the apocryphal gospels.

[3] Matt. v. 17. [4] Matt. v. 18.

sacrifices have passed away, and kingdoms, and prophecies among those who are born of woman, and such like, as not being ordinances of God; hence therefore He says, 'Every plant which the heavenly Father has not planted shall be rooted up.'[1] Wherefore He, being the true Prophet, said, 'I am the gate of life;'[2] he who entereth through me entereth into life,' there being no other teaching able to save. Wherefore also He cried, and said, 'Come unto me, all who labour,'[3] that is, who are seeking the truth, and not finding it; and again, 'My sheep hear my voice;'[4] and elsewhere, 'Seek and find,'[5] since the truth does not lie on the surface.

CHAP. LIII.—*Other sayings of Christ.*

"But also a witnessing voice was heard from heaven, saying, 'This is my beloved Son, in whom I am well pleased; hear Him.'[6] And in addition to this, willing to convict more fully of error the prophets from whom they asserted that they had learned, He proclaimed that they died desiring the truth, but not having learned it, saying, 'Many prophets and kings desired to see what ye see, and to hear what you hear; and verily I say to you, they neither saw nor heard.'[7] Still further He said, 'I am he concerning whom Moses prophesied, saying, A Prophet shall the Lord our God raise unto you of your brethren, like unto me: Him hear in all things; and whosoever will not hear that Prophet shall die.'[8]

CHAP. LIV.—*Other sayings.*

"Whence it is impossible without His teaching to attain to saving truth, though one seek it for ever where the thing that is sought is not. But it was, and is, in the word of our Jesus. Accordingly, He, knowing the true things of the law, said to the Sadducees, asking on what account Moses permitted to marry seven, 'Moses gave you commandments according to your hard-heartedness; for from the beginning

---

[1] Matt. xv. 13. [2] John x. 9. [3] Matt. xi. 28.
[4] John x. 3. [5] Matt. vii. 7. [6] Matt. xvii. 5.
[7] Matt. xiii. 17; Luke x. 24.
[8] Deut. xviii. 15-19; Acts iii. 22, vii. 37.

it was not so: for He who created man at first, made him male and female.'[1]

CHAP. LV.—*Teaching of Christ.*

"But to those who think, as the Scriptures teach, that God swears, He said, 'Let your yea be yea, and nay, nay; for what is more than these is of the evil one.'[2] And to those who say that Abraham and Isaac and Jacob are dead, He said, 'God is not of the dead, but of the living.'[3] And to those who suppose that God tempts, as the Scriptures say, He said, 'The tempter is the wicked one,'[4] who also tempted Himself. To those who suppose that God does not foreknow, He said, 'For your heavenly Father knoweth that ye need all these things before ye ask Him.'[5] And to those who believe, as the Scriptures say, that He does not see all things, He said, 'Pray in secret, and your Father, who seeth secret things, will reward you.'[6]

CHAP. LVI.—*Teaching of Christ.*

"And to those who think that He is not good, as the Scriptures say, He said, 'From which of you shall his son ask bread, and he will give him a stone; or shall ask a fish, and he will give him a serpent? If ye then, being evil, know to give good gifts to your children, how much more shall your heavenly Father give good things to those who ask Him, and to those who do His will!'[7] But to those who affirmed that He was in the temple, He said, 'Swear not by heaven, for it is God's throne; nor by the earth, for it is the footstool of His feet.'[8] And to those who supposed that God is pleased with sacrifices, He said, 'God wishes mercy, and not sacrifices'[9]—the knowledge of Himself, and not holocausts.

[1] Matt. xix. 8; Mark x. 5. [2] Matt. v. 37.
[3] Matt. xxii. 32; Mark xii. 27; Luke xx. 38.
[4] Perhaps Matt. xiii. 39. [5] Matt. vi. 8, 32. [6] Matt. vi. 6.
[7] Matt. vii. 9–11. [8] Matt. v. 34, 35.
[9] Matt ix. 13, xii. 7.

Chap. LVII.—*Teaching of Christ.*

"But to those who are persuaded that He is evil, as the Scriptures say, He said, 'Call not me good, for One [only] is good.'[1] And again, 'Be ye good and merciful, as your Father in the heavens, who makes the sun rise on good and evil men, and brings rain upon just and unjust.'[2] But to those who were misled to imagine many gods, as the Scriptures say, He said, 'Hear, O Israel; the Lord your God is one Lord.'"[3]

Chap. LVIII.—*Flight of Simon.*

Therefore Simon, perceiving that Peter was driving him to use the Scriptures as Jesus taught, was unwilling that the discussion should go into the doctrine concerning God, even although Peter had changed the discussion into question and answer, as Simon himself asked. However, the discussion occupied three days. And while the fourth was dawning, he set off darkling as far as Tyre of Phœnicia. And not many days after, some of the precursors came and said to Peter: "Simon is doing great miracles in Tyre, and disturbing many of the people there; and by many slanders he has made you to be hated."

Chap. LIX.—*Peter's resolution to follow.*

Peter, hearing this, on the following night assembled the multitude of hearers; and as soon as they were come together, he said: "While I am going forth to the nations which say that there are many gods, to teach and to preach that God is one, who made heaven and earth, and all things that are in them, in order that they may love Him and be saved, evil has anticipated me, and by the very law of conjunction has sent Simon before me, in order that these men, if they shall cease to say that there are many gods, disowning those upon earth that are called gods, may think that there are many gods in heaven; so that, not feeling the excellency

[1] Matt. xix. 17; Mark x. 18; Luke xviii. 19.
[2] Matt. v. 44, 45.   [3] Mark xii. 29.

of the monarchy, they may perish with eternal punishment. And what is most dreadful, since true doctrine has incomparable power, he forestalls me with slanders, and persuades them to this, not even at first to receive me; lest he who is the slanderer be convicted of being himself in reality a devil, and the true doctrine be received and believed. Therefore I must quickly catch him up, lest the false accusation, through gaining time, wholly get hold of all men.

CHAP. LX.—*Successor to be appointed.*

"Since, therefore, it is necessary to set apart some one instead of me to fill my place, let us all with one consent pray to God, that He would make manifest who amongst us is the best, that, sitting in the chair of Christ, he may piously rule His church. Who, then, shall be set apart? For by the counsel of God that man is set forth as blessed, 'whom his Lord shall appoint over the ministry of his fellow-servants, to give them their meat in their season, not thinking and saying in his heart, My Lord delayeth His coming, and who shall not begin to beat his fellow-servants, eating and drinking with harlots and drunkards. And the Lord of that servant shall come in an hour when he doth not look for Him, and in a day when he is not aware, and shall cut him in sunder, and shall assign his unfaithful part with the hypocrites.'[1]

CHAP. LXI.—*Monarchy.*

"But if any one of those present, being able to instruct the ignorance of men, shrink from it, thinking only of his own ease, let him expect to hear this sentence: 'O wicked and slothful servant, thou oughtest to have given my money to the exchangers, and I at my coming should have got my own. Cast out the unprofitable servant into the outer darkness.'[2] And with good reason; 'for,' says He, 'it is thine, O man, to prove my words, as silver and money are proved among the exchangers.'[3] Therefore the multitude of the

---

[1] Matt. xxiv. 45–50.   [2] Matt. xxv. 27–30.
[3] Probably from an apocryphal gospel.

faithful ought to obey some one, that they may live in harmony. For that which tends to the government of one person, in the form of monarchy, enables the subjects to enjoy peace by means of good order; but in case of all, through desire of ruling, being unwilling to submit to one only, they must altogether fall by reason of division.

Chap. LXII.—*Obedience leads to peace.*

"But, further, let the things that are happening before your eyes persuade you; how wars are constantly arising through there being now many kings all over the earth. For each one holds the government of another as a pretext for war. But if one were universal superior, he, having no reason why he should make war, would have perpetual peace. In short, therefore, to those who are thought worthy of eternal life, God appoints one universal King in the world that shall then be, that by means of monarchy there may be unfailing peace. It behoves all, therefore, to follow some one as a leader, honouring him as the image of God; and it behoves the leader to be acquainted with the road that entereth into the holy city.

Chap. LXIII.—*Zacchæus appointed.*

"But of those who are present, whom shall I choose but Zacchæus, to whom also the Lord went in[1] and rested, judging him worthy to be saved?" And having said this, he laid his hand upon Zacchæus, who stood by, and forced him to sit down in his own chair. But Zacchæus, falling at his feet, begged that he would permit him to decline the rulership; promising, at the same time, and saying, "Whatever it behoves the ruler to do, I will do; only grant me not to have this name: for I am afraid of assuming the name of the rulership, for it teems with bitter envy and danger."

Chap. LXIV.—*The bishopric.*

Then Peter said: "If you are afraid of this, do not be called *ruler*, but *the appointed one*, the Lord having permitted

[1] Luke xix. 5.

you to be so called, when He said, 'Blessed is that man whom his Lord shall *appoint* to the ministry of his fellow-servants.'[1] But if you wish it to be altogether unknown that you have authority of administration, you seem to me to be ignorant that the acknowledged authority of the president has great influence as regards the respect of the multitude. For every one obeys him who has received authority, having conscience as a great constraint. And are you not well aware that you are not to rule as the rulers of the nations, but as a servant ministering to them, as a father to the oppressed, visiting them as a physician, guarding them as a shepherd,—in short, taking all care for their salvation? And do you think that I am not aware what labours I compel you to undertake, desiring you to be judged by multitudes whom it is impossible for any one to please. But it is most possible for him who does well to please God. Wherefore I entreat you to undertake it heartily, by God, by Christ, for the salvation of the brethren, for their ordering, and your own profit.

Chap. LXV.—*Nolo episcopari.*

"And consider this other thing, that in proportion as there is labour and danger in ruling the church of Christ, so much greater is the reward. And yet again the greater is also the punishment to him who can, and refuses. I wish, therefore, knowing that you are the best instructed of my attendants, to turn to account those noble powers of judging with which you have been entrusted by the Lord, in order that you may be saluted with the *Well done, good and faithful servant,* and not be found fault with, and declared liable to punishment, like him who hid the one talent. But if you will not be appointed a good guardian of the church, point out another in your stead, more learned and more faithful than yourself. But you cannot do this; for you associated with the Lord, and witnessed His marvellous doings, and learned the administration of the church.

[1] Luke xii. 42.

Chap. LXVI.—*Danger of disobedience.*

"And your work is to order what things are proper; and that of the brethren is to submit, and not to disobey. Therefore submitting they shall be saved, but disobeying they shall be punished by the Lord, because the president is entrusted with the place of Christ. Wherefore, indeed, honour or contempt shown to the president is handed on to Christ, and from Christ to God. And this I have said, that these brethren may not be ignorant of the danger they incur by disobedience to you, because whosoever disobeys your orders, disobeys Christ; and he who disobeys Christ offends God.

Chap. LXVII.—*Duties of church office-bearers.*

"It is necessary, therefore, that the church, as a city built upon a hill, have an order approved of God, and good government. In particular, let the bishop, as chief, be heard in the things which he speaks; and let the elders give heed that the things ordered be done. Let the deacons, going about, look after the bodies and the souls of the brethren, and report to the bishop. Let all the rest of the brethren bear wrong patiently; but if they wish judgment to be given concerning wrongs done to them, let them be reconciled in presence of the elders; and let the elders report the reconciliation to the bishop.

Chap. LXVIII.—"*Marriage always honourable.*"

"And let them inculcate marriage not only upon the young, but also upon those advanced in years, lest burning lust bring a plague upon the church by reason of whoredom or adultery. For, above every other sin, the wickedness of adultery is hated by God, because it not only destroys the person himself who sins, but those also who eat and associate with him. For it is like the madness of a dog, because it has the nature of communicating its own madness. For the sake of chastity, therefore, let not only the elders, but even all, hasten to accomplish marriage. For the sin of him who commits adultery necessarily comes upon all. Therefore, to urge the brethren to be chaste, this is the first charity. For it is the healing of the soul. For the nourishment of the body is rest.

CHAP. LXIX.—"*Not forsaking the assembling of yourselves together.*"

"But if you love your brethren, take nothing from them, but share with them such things as ye have. Feed the hungry; give drink to the thirsty; clothe the naked; visit the sick; so far as you can, help those in prison; receive strangers gladly into your own abodes; hate no one. And how you must be pious, your own mind will teach you, judging rightly. But before all else, if indeed I need say it to you, come together frequently, if it were every hour, especially on the appointed days of meeting. For if you do this, you are within a wall of safety. For disorderliness is the beginning of perdition. Let no one therefore forsake the assembly on the ground of envy towards a brother. For if any one of you forsake the assembly, he shall be regarded as of those who scatter the church of Christ, and shall be cast out with adulterers. For as an adulterer, under the influence of the spirit that is in him, he separates himself on some pretext, and gives place to the wicked one against himself,—a sheep for the stealing, as one found outside the fold.[1]

CHAP. LXX.—"*Hear the bishop.*"

"However, hear your bishop, and do not weary of giving all honour to him; knowing that, by showing it to him, it is borne to Christ, and from Christ it is borne to God; and to him who offers it, is requited manifold.[2] Honour, therefore, the throne of Christ. For you are commanded even to honour the chair of Moses, and that although they who

[1] There seems to be a corruption of the text here, but the general meaning is evident enough.

[2] There are several conjectural readings of this sentence. We have not exactly followed any one of them, but have ventured on a conjecture of our own.

occupy it are accounted sinners.[1] And now I have said enough to you; and I deem it superfluous to say to him how he is to live unblameably, since he is an approved disciple of Him who taught me also.

CHAP. LXXI.—*Various duties of Christians.*

"But, brethren, there are some things that you must not wait to hear, but must consider of yourselves what is reasonable. Zaccheus alone having given himself up wholly to labour for you, and needing sustenance, and not being able to attend to his own affairs, how can he procure necessary support? Is it not reasonable that you are to take forethought for his living? not waiting for his asking you, for this is the part of a beggar. But he will rather die of hunger than submit to do this. And shall not you incur punishment, not considering that the workman is worthy of his hire? And let no one say: Is, then, the word sold which was freely given? Far be it. For if any one has the means of living, and takes anything, he sells the word; but if he who has not takes support in order to live—as the Lord also took at supper and among His friends, having nothing, though He alone is the owner of all things—he sins not. Therefore suitably honour elders, catechists, useful deacons, widows who have lived well, orphans as children of the church. But wherever there is need of any provision for an emergency, contribute all together. Be kind one to another, not shrinking from the endurance of anything whatever for your own salvation."

CHAP. LXXII.—*Ordination.*

And having thus spoken, he placed his hand upon Zaccheus, saying, "O Thou Ruler and Lord of all, Father and God, do Thou guard the shepherd with the flock. Thou art the cause, Thou the power. We are that which is helped; Thou the helper, the physician, the saviour, the wall, the life, the hope, the refuge, the joy, the expectation, the rest. In a word, Thou art all things to us. In order to the eternal

[1] Matt. xxiii. 2.

attainment of salvation, do Thou co-operate, preserve, protect. Thou canst do all things. For Thou art the Ruler of rulers, the Lord of lords, the Governor of kings. Do Thou give power to the president to loose what ought to be loosed, to bind what ought to be bound. Do Thou make him wise. Do Thou, as by His name, protect the church of Thy Christ as a fair bride. For Thine is eternal glory. Praise to the Father and the Son and the Holy Ghost to all ages. Amen."

CHAP. LXXIII.—*Baptisms.*

And having thus spoken, he afterwards said: "Whoever of you wish to be baptized, begin from to-morrow to fast, and have hands laid upon you day by day, and inquire about what matters you please. For I mean still to remain with you ten days." And after three days, having begun to baptize, he called me, and Aquila, and Nicetas, and said to us: "As I am going to set out for Tyre after seven days, I wish you to go away this very day, and to lodge secretly with Bernice the Canaanite, the daughter of Justa, and to learn from her, and write accurately to me what Simon is about. For this is of great consequence to me, that I may prepare myself accordingly. Therefore depart straightway in peace." And leaving him baptizing, as he commanded, we preceded him to Tyre of Phœnicia.

HOMILY IV.

Chap. I.—*Bernice's hospitality.*

THUS I Clement, departing from Cæsarea Stratonis, together with Nicetas and Aquila, entered into Tyre of Phœnicia; and according to the injunction of Peter, who sent us, we lodged with Bernice, the daughter of Justa the Canaanitess. She received us most joyfully; and striving with much honour towards me, and with affection towards Aquila and Nicetas, and speaking freely as a friend, through joy she treated us courteously, and hospitably urged us to take bodily refreshment. Perceiving, therefore, that she was endeavouring to impose a short delay upon us, I said: "You do well, indeed, to busy yourself in fulfilling the part of love; but the fear of our God must take the precedence of this. For, having a combat on hand on behalf of many souls, we are afraid of preferring our own ease before their salvation.

Chap. II.—*Simon's practices.*

"For we hear that Simon the magician, being worsted at Cæsarea in the discussion with our lord Peter, immediately hastened hither, and is doing much mischief. For he is slandering Peter, in opposition to truth, to all the adversaries, and stealing away the souls of the multitude. For he being a magician, calls him a magician; and he being a deceiver, proclaims him as a deceiver. And although in the discussions he was beaten in all points, and fled, yet he says that he was victorious; and he constantly charges them that they ought not to listen to Peter,—as if, forsooth, he were anxious that they may not be fascinated by a terrible magician.

CHAP. III.—*Object of the mission.*

"Therefore our lord Peter, having learned these things, has sent us to be investigators of the things that have been told him; that if they be so, we may write to him and let him know, so that he may come and convict him face to face of the accusations that he has uttered against him. Since, therefore, danger on the part of many souls lies before us, on this account we must neglect bodily rest for a short time; and we would learn truly from you who live here, whether the things which we have heard be true. Now tell us particularly."

CHAP. IV.—*Simon's doings.*

But Bernice, being asked, said: "These things are indeed as you have heard; and I will tell you other things respecting this same Simon, which perhaps you do not know. For he astonishes the whole city every day, by making spectres and ghosts appear in the midst of the market-place; and when he walks abroad, statues move, and many shadows go before him, which, he says, are souls of the dead. And many who attempted to prove him an impostor he speedily reconciled to him; and afterwards, under pretence of a banquet, having slain an ox, and given them to eat of it, he infected them with various diseases, and subjected them to demons. And in a word, having injured many, and being supposed to be a god, he is both feared and honoured.

CHAP. V.—*Discretion the better part of valour.*

"Wherefore I do not think that any one will be able to quench such a fire as has been kindled. For no one doubts his promises; but every one affirms that this is so. Wherefore, lest you should expose yourselves to danger, I advise you not to attempt anything against him until Peter come, who alone shall be able to resist such a power, being the most esteemed disciple of our Lord Jesus Christ. For so much do I fear this man, that if he had not elsewhere been vanquished in disputing with my lord Peter, I should counsel you to persuade even Peter himself not to attempt to oppose Simon."

CHAP. VI.—*Simon's departure.*

Then I said: "If our lord Peter did not know that he himself alone can prevail against this power, he would not have sent us before him with orders to get information secretly concerning Simon, and to write to him." Then, as evening had come on, we took supper,[1] and went to sleep. But in the morning, one of Bernice's friends came and said that Simon had set sail for Sidon, and that he had left behind him Appion Pleistonices,[2]—a man of Alexandria, a grammarian by profession, whom I knew as being a friend of my father; and a certain astrologer, Annubion the Diospolitan, and Athenodorus the Athenian, attached to the doctrine of Epicurus. And we, having learned these things concerning Simon, in the morning wrote and despatched a letter to Peter, and went to take a walk.

CHAP. VII.—*Appion's salutation.*

And Appion met us, not only with the two companions just named, but with about thirty other men. And as soon as he saw me, he saluted and kissed me, and said, "This is Clement, of whose noble birth and liberal education I have often told you; for he, being related to the family of Tiberius Cæsar, and equipped with all Grecian learning, has been seduced by a certain barbarian called Peter to speak and act after the manner of the Jews. Wherefore I beg of you to strive together with me for the setting of him right. And in your presence I now ask him. Let him tell me, since he thinks that he has devoted himself to piety, whether he is not acting most impiously, in forsaking the customs of his country, and falling away to those of the barbarians."

[1] Literally, "partook of salt."
[2] This epithet means, "the conqueror of very many." Suidas makes Appion the son of Pleistonices.

Chap. VIII.—*A challenge.*

I answered: "I accept, indeed, your kindly affection towards me, but I take exception to your ignorance. For your affection is kindly, because you wish me to continue in those [customs] which you consider to be good. But your inaccurate knowledge strives to lay a snare for me, under the guise of friendship." Then said Appion: "Does it seem to you to be ignorance, that one should observe the customs of his fathers, and judge after the manner of the Greeks?" Then I answered: "It behoves one who desires to be pious not altogether to observe the customs of his fathers; but to observe them if they be pious, and to shake them off if they be impious. For it is possible that one who is the son of an impious father, if he wishes to be pious, should not desire to follow the religion of his father."[1] Then answered Appion: "What then? Do you say that your father was a man of an evil life?" Then said I: "He was not of an evil life, but of an evil opinion." Then Appion: "I should like to know what was his evil apprehension." Then said I: "Because he believed the false and wicked myths of the Greeks." Then Appion asked: "What are these false and evil myths of the Greeks?" Then I said: "The wrong opinion concerning the gods, which, if you will bear with me, you shall hear, with those who are desirous to learn.

Chap. IX.—*Unworthy ends of philosophers.*

"Wherefore, before beginning our conversation, let us now withdraw into some quieter place, and there I shall converse with you. And the reason why I wish to speak privately is this, because neither the multitude, nor even all the philosophers, approach honestly to the judgment of things as they are. For we know many, even of those who pride themselves on their philosophy, who are vainglorious, or who have put on the philosopher's robe for the sake of gain, and not for the sake of virtue itself; and they, if they do not find that

---

[1] We have adopted the emendation of Wieseler, who reads σιβάσματι for σιβάσματα. He also proposes ἴθει (habit) instead of σιβάσματι. The readings in the MSS. vary.

for which they take to philosophy, turn to mockery. Therefore, on account of such as these, let us choose some place fit for private conference."

Chap. X.—*A cool retreat.*

And a certain one amongst them—a rich man, and possessing a garden of evergreen plants[1]—said: "Since it is very hot, let us retire for a little from the city to my gardens." Accordingly they went forth, and sat down in a place where there were pure streams of cool water, and a green shade of all sorts of trees. There I sat pleasantly, and the others round about me; and they being silent, instead of a verbal request made to me, showed by their eager looks to me that they required the proof of my assertion. And therefore I proceeded to speak thus:

Chap. XI.—*Truth and custom.*

"There is a certain great difference, O men of Greece, between truth and custom. For truth is found when it is honestly sought; but custom, whatsoever be the character of the custom received, whether true or false, is strengthened by itself without the exercise of judgment; and he who has received it is neither pleased with it as being true, nor grieved with it as false. For such an one has believed not by judgment, but by prejudice, resting his own hope on the opinion of those who have lived before him on a mere peradventure. And it is not easy to cast off the ancestral garment, though it be shown to himself to be wholly foolish and ridiculous.

Chap. XII.—*Genesis.*

"Therefore I say that the whole learning of the Greeks is a most dreadful fabrication of a wicked demon. For they have introduced many gods of their own, and these wicked, and subject to all kinds of passion; so that he who wishes to do the like things may not be ashamed, which belongs to a

---

[1] The text here is corrupt. If we adopt Lobeck's emendation of ταμμιούσων into ταμπλούσιον, the literal translation is, "possessing a property around him continually rich in leaves."

man, having as an example the wicked and unquiet lives of the mythological gods. And through his not being ashamed, such an one affords no hope of his repenting. And others have introduced fate, which is called genesis, contrary to which no one can suffer or do anything. This, therefore, also is like to the first. For any one who thinks that no one has aught to do or suffer contrary to genesis easily falls into sin; and having sinned, he does not repent of his impiety, holding it as his apology that he was borne on by genesis to do these things. And as he cannot rectify genesis, he has no reason to be ashamed of the sins he commits.

CHAP. XIII.—*Destiny.*

"And others introduce an unforeseeing destiny, as if all things revolved of their own accord, without the superintendence of any master. But thus to think these things is, as we have said, the most grievous of all opinions. For, as if there were no one superintending and fore-judging and distributing to every one according to his deserving, they easily do everything as they can through fearlessness. Therefore those who have such opinions do not easily, or perhaps do not at all, live virtuously; for they do not foresee the danger which might have the effect of converting them. But the doctrine of the barbarous Jews, as you call them, is most pious, introducing One as the Father and Creator of all this world, by nature good and righteous; good, indeed, as pardoning sins to those who repent; but righteous, as visiting to every one after repentance according to the worthiness of his doings.

CHAP. XIV.—"*Doctrine according to godliness.*"

"This doctrine, even if it also be mythical, being pious, would not be without advantage for this life. For every one, in expectation of being judged by the all-seeing God, receives the greater impulse towards virtue. But if the doctrine be also true, it withdraws him who has lived virtuously from eternal punishment, and endows him with eternal and unspeakable blessings from God.

CHAP. XV.—*Wickedness of the gods.*

" But I return to the foremost doctrine of the Greeks, that which states in stories[1] that there are gods many, and subject to all kinds of passions. And not to spend much time upon things that are clear, referring to the impious deeds of every one of those who are called gods, I could not tell all their amours; those of Zeus and Poseidon, of Pluto and Apollo, of Dionysus and Hercules, and of them all singly. And of these you are yourselves not ignorant, and have been taught their manners of life, being instructed in the Grecian learning, that, as competitors with the gods, you might do like things.

CHAP. XVI.—*Wickedness of Jupiter.*

" But I shall begin with the most royal Zeus, whose father Kronos, having, as you say, devoured his own children, and having shorn off the members of his father Uranus with a sickle of adamant, showed to those who are zealous for the mysteries of the gods an example of piety towards parents and of love towards children. And Jupiter himself bound his own father, and imprisoned him in Tartarus; and he also punishes the other gods.[2] And for those who wish to do things not to be spoken of, he begat Metis, and devoured her. But Metis was seed; for it is impossible to devour a child. And for an excuse to abusers of themselves with mankind, he carries away Ganymedes. And as a helper of adulterers in their adultery, he is often found an adulterer. And to those who wish to commit incest with sisters, he sets the example in his intercourse with his sisters Hera and Demeter, and the heavenly Aphrodite, whom some call Dodona.[3] And to those who wish to commit incest with their daughters, there is a wicked example from his story, in his committing incest with Persephone. But in myriads of instances he acted impiously, that by reason of his excessive

---

[1] μυθολογοῦσαν.

[2] Wieseler proposes θείους instead of θεούς; and he punishes his uncles also, as in vi. 2, 21.

[3] This is properly regarded as a mistake for Dione, or Didone, which is another form of the name Dione.

wickedness the fable of his being a god might be received by impious men.

CHAP. XVII.—"*Their makers are like unto them.*"

"You would hold it reasonable for ignorant men to be moderately indignant at these fancies. But what must we say to the learned, some of whom, professing themselves to be grammarians and sophists, affirm that these acts are worthy of gods ? For, being themselves incontinent, they lay hold of this mythical pretext; and as imitators of the gods,[1] they practise unseemly things with freedom.

CHAP. XVIII.—*Second nature.*

"On this account, they who live in the country sin much less than they do, not having been indoctrinated in those things in which they have been indoctrinated who dare do these things, having learned from evil instruction to be impious. For they who from their childhood learn letters by means of such fables, while their soul is yet pliant, engraft the impious deeds of those who are called gods into their own minds; whence, when they are grown up, they ripen fruit, like evil seeds cast into the soul. And what is worst of all, the rooted impurities cannot be easily cut down, when they are perceived to be bitter by them when they have attained to manhood. For every one is pleased to remain in those habits which he forms in childhood ; and thus, since custom is not much less powerful than nature, they become difficult to be converted to those good things which were not sown in their souls from the beginning.

CHAP. XIX.—"*Where ignorance is bliss.*"

"Wherefore it behoves the young not to be satisfied with those corrupting lessons, and those who are in their prime should carefully avoid listening to the mythologies of the Greeks. For lessons about their gods are much worse than ignorance, as we have shown from the case of those dwelling in the country, who sin less through their not having been

---

[1] Lit. " of those who are superior or better."

instructed by Greeks. Truly, such fables of theirs, and spectacles, and books, ought to be shunned, and if it were possible, even their cities. For those who are full of evil learning, even with their breath infect as with madness those who associate with them, with their own passions. And what is worst, whoever is most instructed among them, is so much the more turned from the judgment which is according to nature.

CHAP. XX.—*False theories of philosophers.*

"And some of those amongst them who even profess to be philosophers, assert that such sins are indifferent, and say that those who are indignant at such practices are senseless. For they say that such things are not sins by nature, but have been proscribed by laws made by wise men in early times, through their knowing that men, through the instability of their minds, being greatly agitated on these accounts, wage war with one another; for which reason, wise men have made laws to proscribe such things as sins. But this is a ridiculous supposition. For how can they be other than sins, which are the cause of tumults, and murders, and every confusion? For do not shortenings of life[1] and many more evils proceed from adultery?

CHAP. XXI.—*Evils of adultery.*

"But why, it is said, if a man is ignorant of his wife's being an adulteress, is he not indignant, enraged, distracted? why does he not make war? Thus these things are not evil by nature, but the unreasonable opinion of men make them terrible. But I say, that even if these dreadful things do not occur, it is usual for a woman, through association with an adulterer, either to forsake her husband, or if she continue to live with him, to plot against him, or to bestow upon the adulterer the goods procured by the labour of her husband; and having conceived by the adulterer while her husband is absent, to attempt the destruction of that which is in her womb, through shame of conviction, and so to become a child-

[1] The Vatican MS. inserts here, "upturning of houses, magic practices, deceptions, perplexities."

murderer; or even, while destroying it, to be destroyed along with it. But if while her husband is at home she conceives by the adulterer and bears a child, the child when he grows up does not know his father, and thinks that he is his father who is not; and thus he who is not the father, at his death leaves his substance to the child of another. And how many other evils naturally spring from adultery! And the secret evils we do not know. For as the mad dog destroys all that he touches, infecting them with the unseen madness, so also the hidden evil of adultery, though it be not known, effects the cutting off of posterity.

CHAP. XXII.—*A more excellent way.*

"But let us pass over this now. But this we all know, that universally men are beyond measure enraged on account of it, that wars have been waged, that there have been overthrows of houses, and captures of cities, and myriads of other evils. On this account I betook myself to the holy God and law of the Jews, putting my faith in the well-assured conclusion that the law has been assigned by the righteous judgment of God, and that the soul must at some time receive according to the desert of its deeds."

CHAP. XXIII.—"*Whither shall I go from Thy presence?*"

When I had thus spoken, Appion broke in upon my discourse. "What!" said he; "do not the laws of the Greeks also forbid wickedness, and punish adulterers?" Then said I: "Then the gods of the Greeks, who acted contrary to the laws, deserve punishment. But how shall I be able to restrain myself, if I suppose that the gods themselves first practised all wickednesses as well as adultery, and did not suffer punishment; whereas they ought the rather to have suffered, as not being slaves to lust? But if they were subject to it, how were they gods?" Then Appion said: "Let us have in our eye not the gods, but the judges; and looking to them, we shall be afraid to sin." Then I said: "This is not fitting, O Appion: for he who has his eye upon men will dare to sin, in hope of escaping detection; but he who sets before his soul the all-seeing God, knowing that he cannot escape His notice, will refrain from sinning even in secret."

CHAP. XXIV.—*Allegory.*

When Appion heard this, he said: "I knew, ever since I heard that you were consorting with Jews, that you had alienated your judgment. For it has been well said by some one, 'Evil communications corrupt good manners.'" Then said I: "Therefore good communications correct evil manners." And Appion said: "To-day I am fully satisfied to have learned your position; therefore I permitted you to speak first. But to-morrow, in this place, if it is agreeable to you, I will show, in the presence of these friends when they meet, that our gods are neither adulterers, nor murderers, nor corrupters of children, nor guilty of incest with sisters or daughters. But the ancients, wishing that only lovers of learning should know the mysteries, veiled them with those fables of which you have spoken. For they speak physiologically of boiling substance under the name of Zen, and of time under that of Kronos, and of the ever-flowing nature of water under that of Rhea. However, as I have promised, I shall to-morrow exhibit the truth of things, explaining them one by one to you when you come together in the morning." In reply to this I said: "To-morrow, as you have promised, so do. But now hear something in opposition to what you are going to say.

CHAP. XXV.—*An engagement for to-morrow.*

"If the doings of the gods, being good, have been veiled with evil fables, the wickedness of him who wove the veil is shown to have been great, because he concealed noble things with evil narratives, that no one imitate them. But if they really did things impious, they ought, on the contrary, to have veiled them with good narratives, lest men, regarding them as their superiors, should set about sinning in like manner." As I spoke thus, those present were evidently beginning to be well-disposed towards the words spoken by me; for they repeatedly and earnestly asked me to come on the following day, and departed.

HOMILY V.

Chap. I.—*Appion does not appear.*

THE next day, therefore, in Tyre, as we had agreed, I came to the quiet place, and there I found the rest, with some others also. Then I saluted them. But as I did not see Appion, I asked the reason of his not being present; and some one said that he had been unwell ever since last evening. Then, when I said that it was reasonable that we should immediately set out to visit him, almost all begged me first to discourse to them, and that then we could go to see him. Therefore, as all were of one opinion, I proceeded to say:

Chap. II.—*Clement's previous knowledge of Appion.*

"Yesterday, when I left this, O friends, I confess that, through much anxiety about the discussion that was to take place with Appion, I was not able to get any sleep. And while I was unable to sleep, I remembered a trick that I played upon him in Rome. It was this. From my boyhood I Clement was a lover of truth, and a seeker of the things that are profitable for the soul, and spending my time in raising and refuting theories; but being unable to find anything perfect, through distress of mind I fell sick. And while I was confined to bed Appion came to Rome, and being my father's friend, he lodged with me; and hearing that I was in bed, he came to me, as being not unacquainted with medicine, and inquired the cause of my being in bed. But I, being aware that the man exceedingly hated the Jews, as also that he had written many books against them, and that he had formed a friendship with this

Simon, not through desire of learning, but because he knew that he was a Samaritan and a hater of the Jews, and that he had come forth in opposition to the Jews, therefore he had formed an alliance with him, that he might learn something from him against the Jews;—

CHAP. III.—*Clement's trick.*

"I, knowing this before concerning Appion, as soon as he asked me the cause of my sickness, answered feignedly, that I was suffering and distressed in my mind after the manner of young men. And to this he said, 'My son, speak freely as to a father: what is your soul's ailment?' And when I again groaned feignedly, as being ashamed to speak of love, by means of silence and down-looking I conveyed the impression of what I wished to intimate. But he, being persuaded that I was in love with a woman, said: 'There is nothing in life which does not admit of help. For indeed I myself, when I was young, being in love with a most accomplished woman, not only thought it impossible to obtain her, but did not even hope ever to address her. And yet, having fallen in with a certain Egyptian who was exceedingly well versed in magic, and having become his friend, I disclosed to him my love, and not only did he assist me in all that I wished, but, honouring me more bountifully, he hesitated not to teach me an incantation by means of which I obtained her; and as soon as I had obtained her, by means of his secret instruction, being persuaded by the liberality of my teacher, I was cured of love.

CHAP. IV.—*Appion's undertaking.*

"'Whence, if you also suffer any such thing after the manner of men, use freedom with me with all security; for within seven days I shall put you fully in possession of her.' When I heard this, looking at the object I had in view, I said: 'Pardon me that I do not altogether believe in the existence of magic; for I have already tried many who have made many promises, and have deceived me. However, your undertaking influences me, and leads me to hope. But when I think of the matter, I am afraid that the demons are sometimes not subject to the magicians with respect to the things that are commanded them.'

Chap. V.—*Theory of magic.*

"Then Appion said: 'Admit that I know more of these things than you do. However, that you may not think that there is nothing in what you have heard from me in reference to what you have said, I will tell you how the demons are under necessity to obey the magicians in the matters about which they are commanded. For as it is impossible for a soldier to contradict his general, and impossible for the generals themselves to disobey the king— for if any one oppose those set over him, he is altogether deserving of punishment—so it is impossible for the demons not to serve the angels who are their generals; and when they are adjured by them, they yield trembling, well knowing that if they disobey they shall be fully punished. But the angels also themselves, being adjured by the magicians in the name of their ruler, obey, lest, being found guilty of disobedience, they be destroyed. For unless all things that are living and rational foresaw vengeance from the ruler, confusion would ensue, all revolting against one another.'

Chap. VI.—*Scruples.*

"Then said I: 'Are those things correct, then, which are spoken by poets and philosophers, that in Hades the souls of the wicked are judged and punished for their attempts; such as those of Ixion, and Tantalus, and Tityus, and Sisyphus, and the daughters of Danaus, and as many others as have been impious here? And how, if these things are not so, is it possible that magic can subsist?' Then he having told me that these things are so in Hades, I asked him: 'Why are not we ourselves afraid of magic, being persuaded of the punishment in Hades for adultery? For I do not admit that it is a righteous thing to compel to adultery a woman who is unwilling; but if any one will engage to persuade her, I am ready for that, besides confessing my thanks.'

CHAP. VII.—*A distinction with a difference.*

"Then Appion said: 'Do you not think it is the same thing, whether you obtain her by magic, or by deceiving her with words?' Then said I: 'Not altogether the same; for these differ widely from one another. For he who constrains an unwilling woman by the force of magic, subjects himself to the most terrible punishment, as having plotted against a chaste woman; but he who persuades her with words, and puts the choice in her own power and will, does not force her. And I am of opinion, that he who has persuaded [a woman] will not suffer so great punishment as he who has forced her. Therefore, if you can persuade her, I shall be thankful to you when I have obtained her; but otherwise, I had rather die than force her against her will.'

CHAP. VIII.—*Flattery or magic.*

"Then Appion, being really puzzled, said: 'What am I to say to you? For at one time, as one perturbed with love, you pray to obtain her; and anon, as if you loved her not, you make more account of your fear than your desire: and you think that if you can persuade her you shall be blameless, as without sin; but obtaining her by the power of magic, you will incur punishment. But do you not know that it is the end of every action that is judged, the fact that it has been committed, and that no account is made of the means by which it has been effected? And if you commit adultery, being enabled by magic, shall you be judged as having done wickedly; and if by persuasion, shall you be absolved from sin in respect of the adultery?' Then I said: 'On account of my love, there is a necessity for me to choose one or other of the means that are available to procure the object of my love; and I shall choose, as far as possible, to cajole her rather than to use magic. But neither is it easy to persuade her by flattery, for the woman is very much of a philosopher.'

CHAP. IX.—*A love-letter.*

"Then Appion said: 'I am all the more hopeful to be able

to persuade her, as you wish, provided only we be able to converse with her.' 'That,' said I, 'is impossible.' Then Appion asked if it were possible to send a letter to her. Then I said: 'That indeed may be done.' Then Appion said: 'This very night I shall write a paper on encomiums of adultery, which you shall get from me and despatch to her; and I hope that she shall be persuaded, and consent.' Appion accordingly wrote the paper, and gave it to me; and I thought of it this very night, and I remembered that fortunately I have it by me, along with other papers which I carry about with me." Having thus spoken, I showed the paper to those who were present, and read it to them as they wished to hear it; and having read it, I said: "This, O men, is the instruction of the Greeks, affording a bountiful licence to sin without fear. The paper was as follows:

CHAP. X.—*The lover to the beloved one.*

"'Anonymously, on account of the laws of foolish men. At the bidding of Love, the first-born of all, salutation: I know that you are devoted to philosophy, and for the sake of virtue you affect the life of the noble. But who are nobler then the gods among all, and philosophers among men? For these alone know what works are good or evil by nature, and what, not being so, are accounted so by the imposition of laws. Now, then, some have supposed that the action which is called adultery is evil, although it is in every respect good. For it is by the appointment of Eros for the increase of life. And Eros is the eldest of all the gods. For without Eros there can be no mingling or generation either of elements, or gods, or men, or irrational animals, or aught else. For we are all instruments of Eros. He, by means of us, is the fabricator of all that is begotten, the mind inhabiting our souls. Hence it is not when we ourselves wish it, but when we are ordered by him, that we desire to do his will. But if, while we desire according to his will, we attempt to restrain the desire for the sake of what is called chastity, what do we do but the greatest impiety, when we oppose the oldest of all gods and men?

CHAP. XI.—"*All uncleanness with greediness.*"

"'But let all doors be opened to him, and let all baneful and arbitrary laws be set aside, which have been ordained by fanatical men, who, under the power of senselessness, and not willing to understand what is reasonable, and, moreover, suspecting those who are called adulterers, are with good reason mocked with arbitrary laws by Zeus himself, through Minos and Rhadamanthus. For there is no restraining of Eros dwelling in our souls; for the passion of lovers is not voluntary. Therefore Zeus himself, the giver of these laws, approached myriads of women; and, according to some wise men, he sometimes had intercourse with human beings, as a benefactor for the production of children. But in the case of those to whom he knew that his being unknown would be a favour,[1] he changed his form, in order that he might neither grieve them, nor seem to act in opposition to the laws given by himself. It becomes you, therefore, who are debaters of philosophy, for the sake of a good life, to imitate those who are acknowledged to be the nobler, who have had sexual intercourse ten thousand times.

CHAP. XII.—*Jupiter's amours.*

"'And not to spend the time to no purpose in giving more examples, I shall begin with mentioning some embraces of Zeus himself, the father of gods and men. For it is impossible to mention all, on account of their multitude. Hear, therefore, the amours of this great Jupiter, which he concealed by changing his form, on account of the fanaticism of senseless men. For, in the first place, wishing to show to wise men that adultery is no sin, when he was going to marry, being, according to the multitude, knowingly an adulterer, in his first marriage, but not being so in reality, by means, as I said, of a seeming sin he accomplished a sinless marriage.[2] For he married his own sister Hera, assum-

---

[1] We have adopted the punctuation of Wieseler.
[2] I have no doubt that this is the general meaning; but the text is hopelessly corrupt.

ing the likeness of a cuckoo's wing; and of her were born Hebe and Ilithyia. For he gave birth to Metis without copulation with any one, as did also Hera to Vulcan.

CHAP. XIII.—*Jupiter's amours continued.*

"'Then he committed incest with his sister, who was born of Kronos and Thalasse, after the dismemberment of Kronos, and of whom were born Eros and Cypris, whom they call also Dodone. Then, in the likeness of a satyr, he had intercourse with Antiope the daughter of Nycteus, of whom were born Amphion and Zethus. And he embraced Alcmene, the wife of Amphitryon, in the form of her husband Amphitryon, of whom was born Hercules. And, changed into an eagle, he approached Ægina, the daughter of Asclepius, of whom Æacus was born. And in the form of a bear he lay with Amalthea the daughter of Phocus; and in a golden shower he fell upon Danae, the daughter of Acrisius, of whom sprang Perseus. He became wild as a lion to Callisto the daughter of Lycaon, and begat Arcus the second. And with Europa the daughter of Phœnix he had intercourse by means of a bull, of whom sprang Minos, and Rhadamanthus, and Sarpedon; and with Eurymedusa the daughter of Achelous, changing himself into an ant, of whom was born Myrmidon. With a nymph of Hersæus, in the form of a vulture, from whom sprang the wise men of old in Sicily. He came to Juno the earth-born in Rhodes, and of her were born Pargæus, Kronius, Kytis. And he deflowered Ossia, taking the likeness of her husband Phœnix, of whom Anchinous was born to him. Of Nemesis the daughter of Thestius, who is also thought to be Leda, he begot Helena, in the form of a swan or goose; and again, in the form of a star, he produced Castor and Polydeuces. With Lamia he was transformed into a hoopoo.

CHAP. XIV.—*Jupiter's undisguised amours.*

"'In the likeness of a shepherd he made Mnemosyne mother of the Muses. Setting himself on fire, he married Semele, the daughter of Cadmus, of whom he begat Dionysus. In the likeness of a dragon he deflowered his daughter Persephone, thought to be the wife of his brother Pluto. He had intercourse with many other women without undergoing any change in his form; for the husbands had no ill-will to him as if it were a sin, but knew well that in associating with their wives he bountifully produced children for them, bestowing upon them the Hermeses, the Apollos, the Dionysi, the Endymions, and others whom we have spoken of, most excellent in beauty through his fatherhood.

CHAP. XV.—*Unnatural lusts.*

"'And not to spend the time in an endless exposition, you will find numerous unions with Jupiter of all the gods. But senseless men call these doings of the gods adulteries; even of those gods who did not refrain from the abuse of males as disgraceful, but who practised even this as seemly. For instance, Jupiter himself was in love with Ganymede; Poseidon with Pelops; Apollo with Cinyras, Zacynthus, Hyacinthus, Phorbas, Hylas, Admetus, Cyparissus, Amyclas, Troilus, Branchus the Tymnæan, Parus the Potnian, Orpheus; Dionysus with Laonis, Ampelus, Hymenæus, Hermaphrodites, Achilles; Asclepius with Hippolytus, and Hephæstus with Peleus; Pan with Daphnis; Hermes with Perseus, Chrysas, Theseus, Odrysus; Hercules with Abderus, Dryops, Jocastus, Philoctetes, Hylas, Polyphemus, Hæmon, Chonus, Eurystheus.

CHAP. XVI.—*Praise of unchastity.*

"'Thus have I in part set before you the amours of all the more noted gods, beloved, that you may know that fanaticism respecting this thing is confined to senseless men. Therefore they are mortal, and spend their lives sadly, because through their zeal they proclaim those things to be evil which the gods esteem as excellent. Therefore for the future you will be blessed, imitating the gods, and not men. For men, seeing you preserving that which is thought to be chastity, on account of what they themselves feel, praise you indeed, but do not help you. But the gods, seeing you like unto themselves, will both praise and help.

CHAP. XVII.—*The constellations.*

"'For reckon to me how many mistresses they have rewarded, some of whom they have placed among the stars; and of some they have blessed both the children and the associates. Thus Zeus made Callisto a constellation, called the Little Bear, which some also call the Dog's Tail. Poseidon also placed the dolphin in the sky for the sake of Amphitrite; and he gave a place among the stars to Orion the son of Euryale, the daughter of Minos, for the sake of his mother Euryale. And Dionysus made a constellation of the crown of Ariadne, and Zeus invested the eagle which assisted him in the rape of Ganymede, and Ganymede himself with the honour of the Water-pourer. Also he honoured the bull for the sake of Europa; and also having bestowed Castor, and Polydeuces, and Helena upon Leda, he made them stars. Also Perseus for the sake of Danae; and Arcus for the sake of Callisto. The virgin who also is Dice, for the sake of Themis; and Heracles for the sake of Alcmene. But I do not enlarge further; for it were long to tell particularly how many others the gods have blessed for the sake of their many mistresses, in their intercourse with human beings, which senseless men repudiate as evil deeds, not knowing that pleasure is the great advantage among men.

CHAP. XVIII.—*The philosophers advocates of adultery.*

"'But why? Do not the celebrated philosophers extol pleasure, and have they not had intercourse with what women they would? Of these the first was that teacher of Greece, of whom Phœbus himself said, "Of all men, Socrates is the wisest." Does not he teach that in a well-regulated state women should be common?[1] and did he not conceal the fair Alcibiades under his philosopher's gown? And the Socratic Antisthenes writes of the necessity of not abandoning what is called adultery. And even his disciple Diogenes, did not

[1] This from a marginal reading.

he freely associate with Lais, for the hire of carrying her on his shoulders in public? Does not Epicurus extol pleasure? Did not Aristippus anoint himself with perfumes, and devote himself wholly to Aphrodite? Does not Zeno, intimating indifference, say that the deity pervades all things, that it may be known to the intelligent, that with whomsoever a man has intercourse, it is as with himself; and that it is superfluous to forbid what are called adulteries, or intercourse with mother, or daughter, or sister, or children. And Chrysippus, in his erotic epistles, makes mention of the statue in Argos, representing Hera and Zeus in an obscene position.

CHAP. XIX.—*Close of the love-letter.*

"'I know that to those uninitiated in the truth these things seem dreadful and most base; but not so to the gods and the philosophers of the Greeks, nor to those initiated in the mysteries of Dionysus and Demeter. But above all these, not to waste time in speaking of the lives of all the gods, and all the philosophers, let the two chief be your marks—Zeus the greatest of the gods, and Socrates of philosophic men. And the other things which I have mentioned in this letter, understand and attend to, that you may not grieve your lover; since, if you act contrarily to gods and heroes, you will be judged wicked, and will subject yourself to fitting punishment. But if you offer yourself to every lover, then, as an imitator of the gods, you shall receive benefits from them. For the rest, dearest one, remember what mysteries I have disclosed to you, and inform me by letter of your choice. Fare thee well.'

CHAP. XX.—*The use made of it.*

"I therefore, having received this billet from Appion, as though I were really going to send it to a beloved one, pretended as if she had written in answer to it; and the next day, when Appion came, I gave him the reply, as if from her, as follows:

CHAP. XXI.—*Answer to Appion's letter.*

" 'I wonder how, when you commend me for wisdom, you write to me as to a fool. For, wishing to persuade me to your passion, you make use of examples from the mythologies of the gods, that Eros is the eldest of all, as you say, and above all gods and men, not being afraid to blaspheme, that you might corrupt my soul and insult my body. For Eros is not the leader of the gods,—he, I mean, who has to do with lusts. For if he lusts willingly, he is himself his own suffering and punishment; and he who should suffer willingly could not be a god. But if against his will he lust for copulation, and, pervading our souls as through the members of our bodies, is borne into intermeddling with our minds, then he that impels him to love is greater than he. And again, he who impels him, being himself impelled by another desire, another greater than he is found impelling him. And thus we come to an endless succession of lovers,[1] which is impossible. Thus, neither is there an impeller nor an impelled; but it is the lustful passion of the lover himself, which is increased by hope and diminished by despair.

CHAP. XXII.—*Lying fables.*

" 'But those who will not subdue base lusts belie the gods, that, by representing the gods as first doing the things which they do, they may be set free from blame. For if those who are called gods committed adulteries for the sake of begetting children, and not through lasciviousness, why did they also debauch males? But it is said they complimented their mistresses by making them stars. Therefore before this were there no stars, until such time as, by reason of wantonness, the heaven was adorned with stars by adulterers? And how is it that the children of those who have been made stars are punished in Hades,—Atlas loaded, Tantalus tortured with thirst, Sisyphus pushing a stone, Tityus thrust through the bowels, Ixion continually rolled round a wheel? How is it that these divine lovers made stars of the women whom they defiled, but gave no such grace to these?

---

[1] I suspect it should rather be *impellers*, reading φερόντων for ἐρώντων.

Chap. XXIII.—*The gods no gods.*

"'They were not gods, then, but representations of tyrants. For a certain tomb is shown among the Caucasian mountains, not in heaven, but in earth, as that of Kronus, a barbarous man and a devourer of children. Further, the tomb of the lascivious Zeus, so famed in story, who in like manner devoured his own daughter Metis, is to be seen in Crete, and those of Pluto and Poseidon in the Acherusian lake; and that of Helius in Astra, and of Selene in Carræ, of Hermes in Hermopolis, of Ares in Thrace, of Aphrodite in Cyprus, of Dionysus in Thebes, and of the rest in other places. At all events, the tombs are shown of those that I have named; for they were men, and in respect of these things, wicked men and magicians. For else they should not have become despots —I mean Zeus, renowned in story, and Dionysus—but that by changing their forms they prevailed over whom they pleased, for whatever purpose they designed.

Chap. XXIV.—*If a principle be good, carry it out.*

"'But if we must emulate their lives, let us imitate not only their adulteries, but also their banquets. For Kronus devoured his own children, and Zeus in like manner his own daughter. And what must I say? Pelops served as a supper for all the gods. Wherefore let us also, before unhallowed marriages, perpetrate a supper like that of the gods; for thus the supper would be worthy of the marriages. But this you would never consent to; no more will I to adultery. Besides this, you threaten me with the anger of Eros as of a powerful god. Eros is not a god, as I conceive him, but a desire occurring from the temperament of the living creature in order to the perpetuation of life, according to the foresight of Him who worketh all things, that the whole race may not fail, but by reason of pleasure another may be produced out of the substance of one who shall die, springing forth by lawful marriage, that he may know to sustain his own father in old age. And this those born from adultery cannot do, not having the nature of affection towards those who have begotten them.

CHAP. XXV.—*Better to marry than to burn.*

"'Since, therefore, the erotic desire occurs for the sake of continuation and legitimate increasing, as I have said, it behoves parents providing for the chastity of their children to anticipate the desire, by imbuing them with instruction by means of chaste books, and to accustom them beforehand by excellent discourses; for custom is a second nature. And in addition to this, frequently to remind them of the punishments appointed by the laws, that, using fear as a bridle, they may not run on in wicked pleasures. And it behoves them also, before the springing of the desire, to satisfy the natural passion of puberty by marriage, first persuading them not to look upon the beauty of another woman.

CHAP. XXVI.—*Close of the answer.*

"'For our mind, whenever it is impressed delightfully with the image of a beloved one, always seeing the form as in a mirror, is tormented by the recollection; and if it do not obtain its desire, it contrives ways of obtaining it; but if it do obtain it, it is rather increased, like fire having a supply of wood, and especially when there is no fear impressed upon the soul of the lover before the rise of passion. For as water extinguishes fire, so fear is the extinguisher of unreasonable desire. Whence I, having learned from a certain Jew both to understand and to do the things that are pleasing to God, am not to be entrapped into adultery by your lying fables. But may God help you in your wish and efforts to be chaste, and afford a remedy to your soul burning with love.'

CHAP. XXVII.—*A reason for hatred.*

"When Appion heard the pretended answer, he said: 'Is it without reason that I hate the Jews? Here now some Jew has fallen in with her, and has converted her to his religion, and persuaded her to chastity, and it is henceforth impossible that she ever have intercourse with another man; for these fellows, setting God before them as the universal inspector of actions, are extremely persistent in chastity, as being unable to be concealed from Him.'

CHAP. XXVIII.—*The hoax confessed.*

"When I heard this, I said to Appion: 'Now I shall confess the truth to you. I was not enamoured of the woman, or of any one else, my soul being exceedingly spent upon other desires, and upon the investigation of true doctrines. And till now, although I have examined many doctrines of philosophers, I have inclined to none of them, excepting only that of the Jews,—a certain merchant of theirs having sojourned here in Rome, selling linen clothes, and a fortunate meeting having set simply before me the doctrine of the unity of God.'

CHAP. XXIX.—*Appion's resentment.*

"Then Appion, having heard from me the truth, with his unreasonable hatred of the Jews, and neither knowing nor wishing to know what their faith is, being senselessly angry, forthwith quitted Rome in silence. And as this is my first meeting with him since then, I naturally expect his anger in consequence. However, I shall ask him in your presence what he has to say concerning those who are called gods, whose lives, fabled to be filled with all passions, are constantly celebrated to the people, in order to their imitation; while, besides their human passions, as I have said, their graves are also shown in different places."

CHAP. XXX.—*A discussion promised.*

The others having heard these things from me, and desiring to learn what would ensue, accompanied me to visit Appion. And we found him bathed, and sitting at a table furnished. Wherefore we inquired but little into the matter concerning the gods. But he, understanding, I suppose, our wish, promised that next day he would have something to say about the gods, and appointed to us the same place where he would converse with us. And we, as soon as he had promised, thanked him, and departed, each one to his home.

HOMILY VI.

Chap. I.—*Clement meets Appion.*

AND on the third day, when I came with my friends to the appointed place in Tyre, I found Appion sitting between Anubion and Athenodorus, and waiting for us, along with many other learned men. But in no wise dismayed, I greeted them, and sat down opposite Appion. And in a little he began to speak:

"I wish to start from the following point, and to come with all speed at once to the question. Before you, my son Clement, joined us, my friend Anubion here, and Athenodorus, who yesterday were among those who heard you discourse, were reporting to me what you said of the numerous false accusations I brought against the gods when I was visiting you in Rome, at the time you were shamming love, how I charged them with pæderasty, lasciviousness, and numerous incests of all kinds. But, my son, you ought to have known that I was not in earnest when I wrote such things about the gods, but was concealing the truth, from my love to you. That truth, however, if it so please you, you may hear from me now.

Chap. II.—*The myths are not to be taken literally.*

"The wisest of the ancients, men who had by hard labour learned all truth, kept the path of knowledge hid from those who were unworthy and had no taste for lessons in divine things. For it is not really true that from Ouranos and his mother Ge were born twelve children, as the myth counts them: six sons, Okeanos, Koios, Krios, Hyperion, Japetos, Kronos; and six daughters, Thea, Themis, Mnemosyne, Demeter, Tethys, and Rhea. Nor that Kronos, with the knife of adamant, mutilated his father Ouranos, as you say, and threw the part into the sea; nor that Aphrodite sprang from the drops of blood which flowed from it; nor that Kronos associated with Rhea, and devoured his first-begotten son Pluto, because a certain saying of Prometheus led him to fear that a child born from him would wax stronger than himself, and spoil him of his kingdom; nor that he devoured in the same way Poseidon, his second child; nor that, when Zeus was born next, his mother Rhea concealed him, and when Kronos asked for him that he might devour him, gave him a stone instead; nor that this, when it was devoured, pressed those who had been previously devoured, and forced them out, so that Pluto, who was devoured first, came out first, and after him Poseidon, and then Zeus;[1] nor that Zeus, as the story goes, preserved by the wit of his mother, ascended into heaven, and spoiled his father of the kingdom; nor that he punished his father's brothers; nor that he came down to lust after mortal women; nor that he associated with his sisters, and daughters, and sisters-in-law, and was guilty of shameful pæderasty; nor that he devoured his daughter Metis, in order that from her he might make Athene be born out of his own brain (and from his thigh might bear Dionysos,[2] who is said to have been rent in pieces by the Titans); nor that he held a feast at the marriage of Peleus and Thetis; nor that he excluded Eris (discord) from the marriage; nor that Eris on her part, thus dishonoured, contrived an occasion of quarrelling and discord among the feasters; nor that she took a golden apple from the gardens of the Hesperides, and wrote on it 'For the fair.' And then they fable how Hera, and Athena, and Aphrodite, found the apple, and quarrelling about it, came to Zeus; and he did not decide it for them, but sent them by Hermes to the shepherd Paris, to

[1] The passage seems to be corrupt.
[2] The common story about Dionysus is, that he was the unborn son, not of Metis, but of Semele. Wieseler supposes that some words have fallen out, or that the latter part of the sentence is a careless interpolation.

be judged of their beauty. But there was no such judging of the goddesses; nor did Paris give the apple to Aphrodite; nor did Aphrodite, being thus honoured, honour him in return, by giving him Helen to wife. For the honour bestowed by the goddess could never have furnished a pretext for a universal war, and that to the ruin of him who was honoured, himself nearly related to the race of Aphrodite. But, my son, as I said, such stories have a peculiar and philosophical meaning, which can be allegorically set forth in such a way that you yourself would listen with wonder." And I said, "I beseech you not to torment me with delay." And he said, "Do not be afraid; for I shall lose no time, but commence at once.

Chap. III.—*Appion proceeds to interpret the myths.*

"There was once a time when nothing existed but chaos and a confused mixture of orderless elements, which were as yet simply heaped together. This nature testifies, and great men have been of opinion that it was so. Of these great men I shall bring forward to you him who excelled them all in wisdom, Homer, where he says, with a reference to the original confused mass, 'But may you all become water and earth;'[1] implying that from these all things had their origin, and that all things return to their first state, which is chaos, when the watery and earthy subtances are separated. And Hesiod in the *Theogony* says, 'Assuredly chaos was the very first to come into being.'[2] Now, by 'come into being,' he evidently means that chaos came into being, as having a beginning, and did not always exist, without beginning. And Orpheus likens chaos to an egg, in which was the confused mixture of the primordial elements. This chaos, which Orpheus calls an egg, is taken for granted by Hesiod, having a beginning, produced from infinite matter, and originated in the following way.

Chap. IV.—*Origin of chaos.*

"This matter, of four kinds, and endowed with life, was

[1] *Iliad*, vii. 99.   [2] L. 116.

an entire infinite abyss, so to speak, in eternal stream, borne about without order, and forming every now and then countless but ineffectual combinations (which therefore it dissolved again from want of order); ripe indeed, but not able to be bound so as to generate a living creature. And once it chanced that this infinite sea, which was thus by its own nature driven about with a natural motion, flowed in an orderly manner from the same to the same (back on itself), like a whirlpool, mixing the substances in such a way that from each[1] there flowed down the middle of the universe (as in the funnel of a mould) precisely that which was most useful and suitable for the generation of a living creature. This was carried down by the all-carrying whirlpool, drew to itself the surrounding spirit, and having been so conceived that it was very fertile, formed a separate substance. For just as a bubble is usually formed in water, so everything round about contributed to the conception of this ball-like globe. Then there came forth to the light, after it had been conceived in itself, and was borne upwards by the divine spirit which surrounded it,[2] perhaps the greatest thing ever born; a piece of workmanship, so to speak, having life in it which had been conceived from that entire infinite abyss, in shape like an egg, and as swift as a bird.

CHAP. V.—*Kronos and Rhea explained.*

"Now you must think of Kronos as time (*chronos*), and Rhea as the flowing (*rheon*) of the watery substance. For the whole body of matter was borne about for some *time*, before it brought forth, like an egg, the sphere-like, all-embracing heaven (*ouranos*), which at first was full of productive marrow, so that it was able to produce out of itself elements and colours of all sorts, while from the one substance and the one colour it produced all kinds of forms. For as a peacock's egg seems to have only one colour, while potentially it has in it all the colours of the animal that is to be,

---

[1] This is the emendation of Davisius. The Greek has ἐξ ἀκουστοῦ; the Latin, "mirum in modum." Wieseler suggests ἐξακοντιστός.

[2] This is Wieseler's emendation for "received."

so this living egg, conceived out of infinite matter, when set in motion by the underlying and ever-flowing matter, produces many different forms. For within the circumference a certain living creature, which is both male and female, is formed by the skill of the indwelling divine spirit. This Orpheus calls Phanes, because when it appeared (*phaneis*) the universe shone forth from it, with the lustre of that most glorious of the elements, fire, perfected in moisture. Nor is this incredible, since in glowworms nature gives us to see a moist light.

CHAP. VI.—*Phanes and Pluto.*

"This egg, then, which was the first substance, growing somewhat hot, was broken by the living creature within, and then there took shape and came forth something;[1] such as Orpheus also speaks of, where he says, 'when the capacious egg was broken,'[2] etc. And so by the mighty power of that which appeared (*phaneis*) and came forth, the globe attained coherency, and maintained order, while it itself took its seat, as it were, on the summit of heaven, there in ineffable mystery diffusing light through endless ages. But the productive matter left inside the globe, separated the substances of all things. For first its lower part, just like dregs, sank downwards of its own weight; and this they called Pluto from its gravity, and weight, and great quantity (*polu*) of underlying matter, styling it the king of Hades and the dead.

CHAP. VII.—*Poseidon, Zeus, and Metis.*

"When, then, they say that this primordial substance, although most filthy and rough, was devoured by Kronos, that is, time, this is to be understood in a physical sense, as meaning that it sank downwards. And the water which flowed together after this first sediment, and floated on the

---

[1] Wieseler corrects to "some such being," etc.; and below, "of him who appeared," etc.; and "he took his seat."

[2] The first word of this quotation gives no sense, and has been omitted in the translation. Lobeck suggests "at its prime;" Hermann, "Heracapeian;" Duentzer, "ancient;" and Wieseler, "white."

surface of the first substance, they called Poseidon. And then what remained, the purest and noblest of all, for it was translucent fire, they called Zeus, from its glowing (*zeousa*) nature. Now since fire ascends, this was not swallowed, and made to descend by time or Kronos; but, as I said, the fiery substance, since it has life in it, and naturally ascends, flew right up into the air, which from its purity is very intelligent. By his own proper heat, then, Zeus—that is, the glowing substance—draws up what is left in the underlying moisture, to wit, that very strong[1] and divine spirit which they called Metis.

CHAP. VIII.—*Pallas and Hera.*

"And this, when it had reached the summit of the æther, was devoured by it (moisture being mixed with heat, so to say); and causing in it that ceaseless palpitation, it begat intelligence, which they call Pallas from this palpitating (*pallesthai*). And this is artistic wisdom, by which the ætherial artificer wrought out the whole world. And from all-pervading Zeus, that is, from this very hot æther, air (*aer*) extends all the way to our earth; and this they call Hera. Wherefore, because it has come below the æther, which is the purest substance (just as a woman, as regards purity, is inferior), when the two were compared to see which was the better, she was rightly regarded as the sister of Zeus, in respect of her origin from the same substance, but as his spouse, as being inferior like a wife.

CHAP. IX.—*Artemis.*

"And Hera we understand to be a happy tempering of the atmosphere, and therefore she is very fruitful; but Athena, as they call Pallas, was reckoned a virgin, because on account of the intense heat she could produce nothing. And in a similar fashion Artemis is explained: for her they take as the lowest depth of air, and so they called her a virgin, because she could not bear anything on account of the extreme cold. And that troubled and drunken composition which arises from the upper and lower vapours

---
[1] The Paris MS. has "very fine."

they called Dionysus, as troubling the intellect. And the water under the earth, which is in nature indeed one, but which flows through all the paths of earth, and is divided into many parts, they called Osiris, as being cut in pieces. And they understand Adonis as favourable seasons, Aphrodite as coition and generation, Demeter as the earth, the Girl (Proserpine) as seeds; and Dionysus some understand as the vine.

CHAP. X.—*All such stories are allegorical.*

"And I must ask you to think of all such stories as embodying some such allegory. Look on Apollo as the wandering Sun (*peri-polôn*), a son of Zeus, who was also called Mithras, as completing the period of a year. And these said transformations of the all-pervading Zeus must be regarded as the numerous changes of the seasons, while his numberless wives you must understand to be years, or generations. For the power which proceeds from the æther and passes through the air unites with all the years and generations in turn, and continually varies them, and so produces or destroys the crops. And ripe fruits are called his children, the barrenness of some seasons being referred to unlawful unions."

CHAP. XI.—*Clement has heard all this before.*

While Appion was allegorizing in this way, I became plunged in thought, and seemed not to be following what he was saying. So he interrupted his discourse, and said to me, "If you do not follow what I am saying, why should I speak at all?" And I answered, "Do not suppose that I do not understand what you say. I understand it thoroughly; and that the more that this is not the first time I have heard it. And that you may know that I am not ignorant of these things, I shall epitomize what you have said, and supply in their order, as I have heard them from others, the allegorical interpretations of those stories you have omitted." And Appion said: "Do so."

Chap. XII.—*Epitome of Appion's explanation.*

And I answered: "I shall not at present speak particularly of that living egg, which was conceived by a happy combination out of infinite matter, and from which, when it was broken, the masculo-feminine Phanes leaped forth, as some say. I say little about all that, up to the point when this broken globe attained coherency, there being left in it some of its marrow-like matter; and I shall briefly run over the description of what took place in it by the agency of this matter, with all that followed. For from Kronos and Rhea were born, as you say—that is, by time and matter—first Pluto, who represents the sediment which settled down; and then Poseidon, the liquid substance in the middle,[1] which floated over the heavier body below; and the third child—that is, Zeus—is the æther, and is highest of all. It was not devoured; but as it is a fiery power, and naturally ascends, it flew up as with a bound to the very highest æther.

Chap. XIII.—*Kronos and Aphrodite.*

"And the bonds of Kronos are the binding together of heaven and earth, as I have heard others allegorizing; and his mutilation is the separation and parting of the elements; for they all were severed and separated, according to their respective natures, that each kind might be arranged by itself. And time no longer begets anything; but the things which have been begotten of it, by a law of nature, produce their successors. And the Aphrodite who emerged from the sea is the fruitful substance which arises out of moisture, with which the warm spirit mixing, causes that sexual desire, and perfects the beauty of the world.

Chap. XIV.—*Peleus and Thetis, Prometheus, Achilles, and Polyxena.*

"And the marriage banquet, at which Zeus held the feast on the occasion of the marriage of the Nereid Thetis and the beautiful Peleus, has in it this allegory,—that you may

[1] This is Wieseler's conjecture.

know, Appion, that you are not the only one from whom I
have heard this sort of thing. The banquet, then, is the
world, and the twelve are these heavenly props of the Fates,[1]
called the Zodiac. Prometheus is foresight (*prometheia*), by
which all things arose; Peleus is clay (*pelos*), namely, that
which was *collected*[2] from the earth and mixed with Nereis,
or water, to produce man; and from the mixing of the two,
i.e. water and earth, the first offspring was not begotten, but
fashioned complete, and called Achilles, because he never
put his lips (*cheile*) to the breast.[3] Still in the bloom of life,
he is slain by an arrow while desiring to have Polyxena,
that is, something other than the truth, and foreign (*xene*) to
it, death stealing on him through a wound in his foot.

Chap. XV.—*The judgment of Paris.*

"Then Hera, and Athena, and Aphrodite, and Eris, and
the apple, and Hermes, and the judgment, and the shepherd,
have some such hidden meaning as the following:—Hera is
dignity; Athena, manliness; Aphrodite, pleasure; Hermes,
language, which interprets (*hermeneutikos*) thought; the
shepherd Paris, unreasoned and brutish passion. Now if,
in the prime of life, reason, that shepherd of the soul, is
brutish, does not regard its own advantage, will have nothing
to do with manliness and temperance, chooses only pleasure,
and gives the prize to lust alone, bargaining that it is to
receive in return from lust what may delight it,—he who
thus judges incorrectly will choose pleasure to his own destruction and that of his friends. And Eris is jealous spite;
and the golden apples of the Hesperides are perhaps riches,
by which occasionally even temperate persons like Hera are
seduced, and manly ones like Athena are made jealous, so
that they do things which do not become them, and the

---

[1] The Latin takes "moira" in the sense of "district," and translates,
"these props of the districts of the sky."

[2] This is Wieseler's conjecture for the reading of the MSS., "contrived."

[3] This is Schwegler's restoration of the passage. Davisius proposes,
"He is in the bloom of life, at which time if any one desires," etc.

soul's beauty like Aphrodite is destroyed under the guise of refinement. To speak briefly, in all men riches provoke evil discord.

CHAP. XVI.—*Hercules.*

"And Hercules, who slew the serpent which led and guarded riches, is the true philosophical reason which, free from all wickedness, wanders all over the world, visiting the souls of men, and chastising all it meets,—namely, men like fierce lions, or timid stags, or savage boars, or multiform hydras; and so with all the other fabled labours of Hercules, they all have a hidden reference to moral valour. But these instances must suffice, for all our time would be insufficient if we were to go over each one.

CHAP. XVII.—*They are blameworthy who invented such stories.*

"Now, since these things can be clearly, profitably, and without prejudice to piety, set forth in an open and straightforward manner, I wonder you call those men sensible and wise who concealed them under crooked riddles, and overlaid them with filthy stories, and thus, as if impelled by an evil spirit, deceived almost all men. For either these things are not riddles, but real crimes of the gods, in which case they should not have been exposed to contempt, nor should these their deeds have been set before men at all as models; or things falsely attributed to the gods were set forth in an allegory, and then, Appion, they whom you call wise erred, in that, by concealing under unworthy stories things in themselves worthy, they led men to sin, and that not without dishonouring those whom they believed to be gods.

CHAP. XVIII.—*The same.*

"Wherefore do not suppose that they were wise men, but rather evil spirits, who could cover honourable actions with wicked stories, in order that they who wish to imitate their betters may emulate these deeds of so-called gods, which yesterday in my discourse I spoke so freely of,—namely, their parricides, their murders of their children, their incests of all kinds, their shameless adulteries and countless impurities. The most impious of them are those who wish these stories to be believed, in order that they may not be ashamed when they do the like. If they had been disposed to act reverently, they ought, as I said a little ago, even if the gods really did the things which are sung of them, to have veiled their indecencies under more seemly stories, and not, on the contrary, as you say they did, when the deeds of the gods were honourable, clothed them in wicked and indecent forms, which, even when interpreted, can only be understood by much labour; and when they were understood by some, they indeed got for their much toil the privilege of not being deceived, which they might have had without the toil, while they who were deceived were utterly ruined. (Those, however, who trace the allegories to a more honourable source I do not object to; as, for instance, those who explain one allegory by saying that it was wisdom which sprang from the head of Zeus.) On the whole, it seems to me more probable that wicked men, robbing the gods of their honour, ventured to promulgate these insulting stories.

CHAP. XIX.—*None of these allegories are consistent.*

"Nor do we find the poetical allegory about any of the gods consistent with itself. To go no further than the fashioning of the universe, the poets now say that nature was the first cause of the whole creation, now that it was mind. For, say they, the first moving and mixing of the elements came from nature, but it was the foresight of mind which arranged them in order. Even when they assert that it was nature which fashioned the universe, being unable absolutely to demonstrate this on account of the traces of design in the work, they inweave the foresight of mind in such a way that they are able to entrap even the wisest. But we say to them: If the world arose from self-moved nature, how did it ever take proportion and shape, which cannot come but from a superintending wisdom, and can be comprehended only by knowledge, which alone can trace such things? If, on the other hand, it is by wisdom that all things subsist and maintain order, how can it be that those things arose from self-moved chance?

CHAP. XX.—*These gods were really wicked magicians.*

"Then those who chose to make dishonourable allegories of divine things—as, for instance, that Metis was devoured by Zeus—have fallen into a dilemma, because they did not see that they who in these stories about the gods indirectly taught physics, denied the very existence of the gods, resolving all kinds of gods into mere allegorical representations of the various substances of the universe. And so it is more likely that the gods these persons celebrate were some sort of wicked magicians, who were in reality wicked men, but by magic assumed different shapes, committed adulteries, and took away life, and thus to the men of old who did not understand magic seemed to be gods by the things they did; and the bodies and tombs of these men are to be seen in many towns.

CHAP. XXI.—*Their graves are still to be seen.*

"For instance, as I have mentioned already, in the Caucasian mountains there is shown the tomb of a certain Kronos, a man, and a fierce monarch who slew his children. And the son of this man, called Zeus, became worse [than his father]; and having by the power of magic been declared ruler of the universe, he committed many adulteries, and inflicted punishment on his father and uncles, and so died; and the Cretans show his tomb. And in Mesopotamia there lie buried a certain Helios at Atir, and a certain Selene at Carrhæ. A certain Hermes, a man, lies buried in Egypt; Ares in Thrace; Aphrodite in Cyprus; Æsculapius in Epidaurus; and the tombs of many other such persons are to be seen.

CHAP. XXII.—*Their contemporaries, therefore, did not look on them as gods.*

"Thus, to right thinking men, it is clear that they were admitted to be mortals. And their contemporaries, knowing that they were mortal, when they died paid them no more heed; and it was length of time which clothed them with the glory of gods. Nor need you wonder that they who lived in the times of Æsculapius and Hercules were deceived, or the contemporaries of Dionysus or any other of the men of that time, when even Hector in Ilium, and Achilles in the island of Leuce, are worshipped by the inhabitants of those places; and the Opuntines worship Patroclus, and the Rhodians Alexander of Macedon.

CHAP. XXIII.—*The Egyptians pay divine honours to a man.*

"Moreover, among the Egyptians even to the present day, a man is worshipped as a god before his death. And this truly is a small impiety, that the Egyptians give divine honours to a man in his lifetime; but what is of all things most absurd is, that they worship birds and creeping things, and all kinds of beasts. For the mass of men neither think nor do anything with discretion. But look, I pray you, at what is most disgraceful of all: he who is with them the father of gods and men is said by them to have had intercourse with Leda; and many of them set up in public a painting of this, writing above it the name Zeus. To punish this insult, I could wish that they would paint their own present king in such base embraces as they have dared to do with Zeus, and set it up in public, that from the anger of a temporary monarch, and him a mortal, they might learn to render honour where it is due. This I say to you, not as myself already knowing the true God; but I am happy to say that even if I do not know who is God, I think I at least know clearly what God is.

CHAP. XXIV.—*What is not God.*

"And first, then, the four original elements cannot be God, because they have a cause. Nor can that mixing be God, nor that compounding, nor that generating, nor that globe which surrounds the visible universe; nor the dregs which flow together in Hades, nor the water which floats over them; nor the fiery substance, nor the air which extends from it to our earth. For the four elements, if they lay outside one another, could not have been mixed together so as to generate animal life without some great artificer. If they have always been united, even in this case they are fitted together by an artistic mind to what is requisite for the limbs and parts of animals, that they may be able to preserve their respective proportions, may have a clearly defined shape, and that all the inward parts may attain the fitting coherency. In the same way also the positions suitable for each are determined, and that very beautifully, by the artificer mind. To be brief, in all other things which a living creature must have, this great being of the world is in no respect wanting.

CHAP. XXV.—*The universe is the product of mind.*

"Thus we are shut up to the supposition that there is an unbegotten artificer, who brought the elements together, if they were separate; or, if they were together, artistically blended them so as to generate life, and perfected from all one work. For it cannot be that a work which is completely wise can be made without a mind which is greater than it. Nor will it do to say that love is the artificer of all things, or desire, or power, or any such thing. All these are liable to change, and transient in their very nature. Nor can that be God which is moved by another, much less what is altered by time and nature, and can be annihilated."

CHAP. XXVI.—*Peter arrives from Cæsarea.*

While I was saying these things to Appion, Peter drew near from Cæsarea, and in Tyre the people were flocking together, hurrying to meet him and unite in an expression of gratification at his visit. And Appion withdrew, accompanied by Anubion and Athenodorus only; but the rest of us hurried to meet Peter, and I was the first to greet him at the gate, and I led him towards the inn. When we arrived, we dismissed the people; and when he deigned to ask what had taken place, I concealed nothing, but told him of Simon's slanders, and the monstrous shapes he had taken, and all the diseases he had sent after the sacrificial feast, and that some of the sick persons were still there in Tyre, while others had gone on with Simon to Sidon just as I arrived, hoping to be cured by him, but that I had heard that none of them had been cured by him. I also told Peter of the controversy I had had with Appion; and he, from his love to me, and desiring to encourage me, praised and blessed me. Then, having supped, he betook himself to the rest the fatigues of his journey rendered so necessary.

HOMILY VII.

Chap. I.—*Peter addresses the people.*

AND on the fourth day of our stay in Tyre, Peter went out about daybreak, and there met him not a few of the dwellers round about, with very many of the inhabitants of Tyre itself, who cried out, and said, "God through you have mercy upon us, God through you heal us!" And Peter stood on a high stone, that all might see him; and having greeted them in a godly manner, thus began:

Chap. II.—*Reason of Simon's power.*

"God, who created the heavens and the whole universe, does not want occasion for the salvation of those who would be saved. Wherefore let no one, in seeming evils, rashly charge Him with unkindness to man. For men do not know the issue of those things which happen to them, nay, suspect that the result will be evil; but God knows that they will turn out well. So is it in the case of Simon. He is a power of the left hand of God, and has authority to do harm to those who know not God, so that he has been able to involve you in diseases; but by these very diseases, which have been permitted to come upon you by the good providence of God, you, seeking and finding him who is able to cure, have been compelled to submit to the will of God on the occasion of the cure of the body, and to think of believing, in order that in this way you may have your souls as well as your bodies in a healthy state.

Chap. III.—*The remedy.*

"Now I have been told, that after he had sacrificed an ox he feasted you in the middle of the forum, and that you, being carried away with much wine, made friends with not only the evil demons, but their prince also, and that in this way the most of you were seized by these sicknesses, unwittingly drawing upon yourselves with your own hands the sword of destruction. For the demons would never have had power over you, had not you first supped with their prince. For thus from the beginning was a law laid by God, the Creator of all things, on each of the two princes, him of the right hand and him of the left, that neither should have power over any one whom they might wish to benefit or to hurt, unless first he had sat down at the same table with them. As, then, when you partook of meat offered to idols, you became servants to the prince of evil, in like manner, if you cease from these things, and flee for refuge to God through the good Prince of His right hand, honouring Him without sacrifices, by doing whatsoever He wills, know of a truth that not only will your bodies be healed, but your souls also will become healthy. For He only, destroying with His left hand, can quicken with His right; He only can both smite and raise the fallen.

Chap. IV.—*The golden rule.*

"Wherefore, as then ye were deceived by the forerunner Simon, and so became dead in your souls to God, and were smitten in your bodies; so now, if you repent, as I said, and submit to those things which are well-pleasing to God, you may get new strength to your bodies, and recover your soul's health. And the things which are well-pleasing to God are these: to pray to Him, to ask from Him, recognising that He is the giver of all things, and gives with discriminating law; to abstain from the table of devils, not to taste dead flesh, not to touch blood; to be washed from all pollution; and the rest in one word,—as the God-fearing Jews have heard, do you also hear, and be of one mind in many bodies; let each man be minded to do to his neighbour those good things he wishes for himself. And you may all find out what *is* good, by holding some such conversation as the following with yourselves: You would not like to be murdered; do not murder another man: you would not like your wife to be seduced by another; do not you commit adultery: you would not like any of your things to be stolen from you; steal nothing from another. And so understanding by yourselves what is reasonable, and doing it, you will become dear to God, and will obtain healing; otherwise in the life which now is your bodies will be tormented, and in that which is to come your souls will be punished."

CHAP. V.—*Peter departs for Sidon.*

After Peter had spent a few days in teaching them in this way, and in healing them, they were baptized. And after that,[1] all sat down together in the market-places in sackcloth and ashes, grieving because of his other wondrous works, and repenting their former sins. And when they of Sidon heard it, they did likewise, and sent to beseech Peter, since they could not come themselves for their diseases. And Peter did not spend many days in Tyre; but when he had instructed all its inhabitants, and freed them from all manners of diseases, and had founded a church, and set over it as bishop one of the elders who were with him, he departed for Sidon. But when Simon heard that Peter was coming, he straightway fled to Beyrout with Appion and his friends.

CHAP. VI.—*Peter in Sidon.*

And as Peter entered Sidon, they brought many in couches, and laid them before him. And he said to them: "Think not, I pray you, that I can do anything to heal you, who

[1] We have adopted Wieseler's emendation. The text may be translated thus: "And after that, among his other wondrous deeds, all the rest (who had not been baptized) sat down," etc.

am a mortal man, myself subject to many evils. But I shall not refuse to show you the way in which you must be saved. For I have learned from the Prophet of truth the conditions fore-ordained of God before the foundation of the world; that is to say, the evil deeds which if men do He has ordained that they shall be injured by the prince of evil, and in like manner the good deeds for which He has decreed that they who have believed in Him as their Physician shall have their bodies made whole, and their souls established in safety.

CHAP. VII.—*The two paths.*

"Knowing, then, these good and evil deeds, I make known unto you as it were two paths, and I shall show you by which travellers are lost and by which they are saved, being guided of God. The path of the lost, then, is broad and very smooth—it ruins them without troubling them; but the path of the saved is narrow, rugged, and in the end it saves, not without much toil, those who have journeyed through it. And these two paths are presided over by unbelief and faith; and these journey through the path of unbelief, those who have preferred pleasure, on account of which they have forgotten the day of judgment, doing that which is not pleasing to God, and not caring to save their souls by the word, and have not anxiously sought their own good. Truly they know not that the counsels of God are not like men's counsels; for, in the first place, He knows the thoughts of all men, and all must give an account not only of their actions, but also of their thoughts. And their sin is much less who strive to understand well and fail, than that of those who do not at all strive after good things. Because it has pleased God that he who errs in his knowledge of good, as men count errors, should be saved after being slightly punished. But they who have taken no care at all to know the better way, even though they may have done countless other good deeds, if they have not stood in the service He has Himself appointed, come under the charge of indifference, and are severely punished, and utterly destroyed.

CHAP. VIII.—*The service of God's appointment.*

"And this is the service He has appointed: To worship Him only, and trust only in the Prophet of truth, and to be baptized for the remission of sins, and thus by this pure baptism to be born again unto God by saving water; to abstain from the table of devils, that is, from food offered to idols, from dead carcases, from animals which have been suffocated or caught by wild beasts, and from blood; not to live any longer impurely; to wash after intercourse; that the women on their part should keep the law of purification; that all should be sober-minded, given to good works, refraining from wrong-doing, looking for eternal life from the all-powerful God, and asking with prayer and continual supplication that they may win it." Such was Peter's counsel to the men of Sidon also. And in few days many repented and believed, and were healed. And Peter having founded a church, and set over it as bishop one of the elders who were with him, left Sidon.

CHAP. IX.—*Simon attacks Peter.*

No sooner had he reached Beyrout than an earthquake took place; and the multitude, running to Peter, said, "Help us, for we are afraid we shall all utterly perish." Then Simon ventured, along with Appion and Anubion and Athenodorus, and the rest of his companions, to cry out to the people against Peter in public: "Flee, friends, from this man! he is a magician; trust us, he it was who caused this earthquake: he sent us these diseases to terrify us, as if he were God Himself." And many such false charges did Simon and his friends bring against Peter, as one who could do things above human power. But as soon as the people gave him a moment's quiet, Peter with surprising boldness gave a little laugh, and said, "Friends, I admit that I can do, God willing, what these men say; and more than that, I am ready, if you do not believe what I say, to overturn your city from top to bottom."

CHAP. X.—*Simon is driven away.*

And the people were afraid, and promised to do whatever he should command. "Let none of you, then," said Peter, "either hold conversation with these sorcerers, or have anything to do with them." And as soon as the people heard this concise command, they took up sticks, and pursued them till they had driven them wholly out of the town. And they who were sick and possessed with devils came and cast themselves at Peter's feet. And he seeing all this, and anxious to free them from their terror, said to them :

CHAP. XI.—*The way of salvation.*

"Were I able to cause earthquakes, and do all that I wish, I assure you I would not destroy Simon and his friends (for not to destroy men am I sent), but would make him my friend, that he might no longer, by his slanders against my preaching the truth, hinder the salvation of many. But if you believe me, he himself is a magician; he is a slanderer; he is a minister of evil to them who know not the truth. Therefore he has power to bring diseases on sinners, having the sinners themselves to help him in his power over them. But I am a servant of God the Creator of all things, and a disciple of His Prophet who is at His right hand. Wherefore I, being His apostle, preach the truth: to serve a good man I drive away diseases, for I am His second messenger, since first the disease comes, but after that the healing. By that evil-working magician, then, you were stricken with disease because you revolted from God. By me, if you believe on Him ye shall be cured; and so having had experience that He is able, you may turn to good works, and have your souls saved."

CHAP. XII.—*Peter goes to Byblus and Tripolis.*

As he said these things, all fell on their knees before his feet. And he, lifting up his hands to heaven, prayed to God, and healed them all by his simple prayer alone. And he remained not many days in Beyrout; but after he had accustomed many to the service of the one God, and had baptized them, and had set over them a bishop from the elders who were with him, he went to Byblus. And when he came there, and learned that Simon had not waited for them for a day, but had gone straightway to Tripolis, he remained there only a few days; and after that he had healed not a few, and exercised them in the Scriptures, he followed in Simon's track to Tripolis, preferring to pursue him rather than flee from him.

HOMILY VIII.

Chap. I.—*Peter's arrival at Tripolis.*

NOW, as Peter was entering Tripolis, the people from Tyre and Sidon, Berytus and Byblus, who were eager[1] to get instruction, and many from the neighbourhood, entered along with him; and not least were there gatherings of the multitudes from the city itself wishing to see him. Therefore there met with us in the suburbs the brethren who had been sent forth by him to ascertain as well other particulars respecting the city, as the proceedings of Simon, and to come and explain them. They received him, and conducted him to the house of Maroones.

Chap. II.—*Peter's thoughtfulness.*

But he, when he was at the very gate of his lodging, turned round, and promised to the multitudes that after the next day he would converse with them on the subject of religion. And when he had gone in, the forerunners assigned lodgings to those who had come with him. And the hosts and the entertainers did not fall short of the desire of those who sought hospitality. But Peter, knowing nothing of this, being asked by us to partake of food, said that he would not himself partake until those who had come with him were settled. And on our assuring him that this was already done, all having received them eagerly by reason of their affection towards him, so that those were grieved beyond measure who had no guests to entertain,—Peter hearing this, and being pleased with their eager philanthropy, blessed them and went out, and having bathed in the sea, partook of

---

[1] Lit.: more willing to learn [than the others].

food with the forerunners; and then, the evening having come, he slept.

CHAP. III.—*A conversation interrupted.*

But awaking about the second cock-crowing, he found us astir. We were in all sixteen, viz. Peter himself, and I Clement, Nicetas and Aquila, and the twelve who had preceded us. Having therefore saluted us, he said, "To-day, not being occupied with those without, we are free to be occupied with one another. Wherefore I shall tell you the things that happened after your departure from Tyre; and do you minutely relate to me what have been the doings of Simon here." While, therefore, we were answering one another by narratives on either side, one of our friends entered, and announced to Peter that Simon, learning of his arrival, had set off for Syria, and that the multitudes, thinking this one night to be like a year's time, and not able to wait for the appointment which he had made, were standing before the doors conversing with one another in knots and circles about the accusation brought by Simon, and how that, having raised their expectations, and promised that he would charge Peter when he came with many evils, he had fled by night when he knew of his arrival. "However," said he, "they are eager to hear you; and I know not whence some rumour has reached them to the effect that you are going to address them to-day. In order, therefore, that they may not when they are very tired be dismissed without reason, you yourself know what it is proper for you to do."

CHAP. IV.—*Many called.*

Then Peter, wondering at the eagerness of the multitudes, answered, "You see, brethren, how the words of our Lord are manifestly fulfilled. For I remember His saying, 'Many shall come from the east and from the west, the north and the south, and shall recline on the bosoms of Abraham, and Isaac, and Jacob.'[1] 'But many,' said He also, 'are called, but few chosen.'[2] The coming, therefore, of these called

---
[1] Matt. viii. 11; Luke xiii. 29.   [2] Matt. xx. 16.

ones is fulfilled. But inasmuch as it is not of themselves, but of God who has called them and caused them to come, on this account alone they have no reward, since it is not of themselves, but of Him who has wrought in them. But if, after being called, they do things that are excellent, for this is of themselves, then for this they shall have a reward.

Chap. v.—*Faith the gift of God.*

"For even the Hebrews who believe Moses, and do not observe the things spoken by him, are not saved, unless they observe the things that were spoken to them. For their believing Moses was not of their own will, but of God, who said to Moses, 'Behold, I come to thee in a pillar of cloud, that the people may hear me speaking to thee, and may believe thee for ever.'[1] Since, therefore, both to the Hebrews and to those who are called from the Gentiles, believing in the teachers of truth is of God, while excellent actions are left to every one to do by his own judgment, the reward is righteously bestowed upon those who do well. For there would have been no need of Moses, or of the coming of Jesus, if of themselves they would have understood what is reasonable. Neither is there salvation in believing in teachers and calling them lords.

Chap. vi.—*Concealment and revelation.*

"For on this account Jesus is concealed from the Jews, who have taken Moses as their teacher, and Moses is hidden from those who have believed Jesus. For, there being one teaching by both, God accepts him who has believed either of these. But believing a teacher is for the sake of doing the things spoken by God. And that this is so our Lord Himself says, 'I thank thee, Father of heaven and earth, because Thou hast concealed these things from the wise and elder, and hast revealed them to sucking babes.'[2] Thus God Himself has concealed a teacher from some, as foreknowing what they ought to do, and has revealed him to others, who are ignorant what they ought to do.

[1] Ex. xix. 9.   [2] Matt. xi. 25.

CHAP. VII.—*Moses and Christ.*

"Neither, therefore, are the Hebrews condemned on account of their ignorance of Jesus, by reason of Him who has concealed Him, if, doing the things [commanded] by Moses, they do not hate Him whom they do not know. Neither are those from among the Gentiles condemned, who know not Moses on account of Him who hath concealed him, provided that these also, doing the things spoken by Jesus, do not hate Him whom they do not know. And some will not be profited by calling the teachers lords, but not doing the works of servants. For on this account our Jesus Himself said to one who often called Him Lord, but did none of the things which He prescribed, 'Why call ye me Lord, Lord, and do not the things which I say?'[1] For it is not saying that will profit any one, but doing. By all means, therefore, is there need of good works. Moreover, if any one has been thought worthy to recognise both as preaching one doctrine, that man has been counted rich in God, understanding both the old things as new in time, and the new things as old."

CHAP. VIII.—*A large congregation.*

While Peter was thus speaking, the multitudes, as if they had been called by some one, entered into the place where Peter was. Then he, seeing a great multitude, like the smooth current of a river gently flowing towards him, said to Maroones, "Have you any place here that is better able to contain the crowd?" Then Maroones conducted him to a garden-plot in the open air, and the multitudes followed. But Peter, standing upon a base of a statue which was not very high, as soon as he had saluted the multitude in pious fashion, knowing that many of the crowd that stood by were tormented with demons and many sufferings of long standing, and [hearing them] shrieking with lamentation, and falling down [before him] in supplication, rebuked them, and commanded them to hold their peace; and promising healing to them after the discourse, began to speak on this wise:—

[1] Matt. vii. 21.

CHAP. IX.—" *Vindicate the ways of God to men.*"

" While beginning to discourse on the worship of God to those who are altogether ignorant of everything, and whose minds have been corrupted by the accusations of our adversary Simon, I have thought it necessary first of all to speak of the blamelessness of the God who hath made all things, starting from the occasion seasonably afforded by Him according to His providence, that it may be known how with good reason many are held by many demons, and subjected to strange sufferings, that in this the justice of God may appear; and that those who through ignorance blame Him, now may learn by good speaking and well-doing what sentiments they ought to hold, and recall themselves from their previous accusation, assigning ignorance as the cause of their evil presumption, in order that they may be pardoned.

CHAP. X.—*The original law.*

" But thus the matter stands. The only good God having made all things well, and having handed them over to man, who was made after His image, he who had been made breathing of the divinity of Him who made him, being a true prophet and knowing all things, for the honour of the Father who had given all things to him, and for the salvation of the sons born of him, as a genuine father preserving his affection towards the children born of him, and wishing them, for their advantage, to love God and be loved of Him, showed them the way which leads to His friendship, teaching them by what deeds of men the one God and Lord of all is pleased; and having exhibited to them the things that are pleasing to Him, appointed a perpetual law to all, which neither can be abrogated by enemies, nor is vitiated by any impious one, nor is concealed in any place, but which can be read by all. To them, therefore, by obedience to the law, all things were in abundance,—the fairest of fruits, fulness of years, freedom from grief and from disease, bestowed upon them without fear, with all salubrity of the air.

CHAP. XI.—*Cause of the fall of man.*

"But they, because they had at first no experience of evils, being insensible to the gift of good things, were turned to ingratitude by abundance of food and luxuries, so that they even thought that there is no Providence, since they had not by previous labour got good things as the reward of righteousness, inasmuch as no one of them had fallen into any suffering or disease, or any other necessity; so that, as is usual for men afflicted on account of wicked transgression, they should look about for the God who is able to heal them.[1] But immediately after their despite, which proceeded from fearlessness and secure luxury, a certain just punishment met them, as following from a certain arranged harmony, removing from them good things as having hurt them, and introducing evil things instead, as advantageous.

CHAP. XII.—*Metamorphoses of the angels.*

"For of the spirits who inhabit the heaven, the angels who dwell in the lowest region, being grieved at the ingratitude of men to God, asked that they might come into the life of men, that, really becoming men, by more intercourse they might convict those who had acted ungratefully towards Him, and might subject every one to adequate punishment. When, therefore, their petition was granted, they metamorphosed themselves into every nature; for, being of a more godlike substance, they are able easily to assume any form. So they became precious stones, and goodly pearl, and the most beauteous purple, and choice gold, and all matter that is held in most esteem. And they fell into the hands of some, and into the bosoms of others, and suffered themselves to be stolen by them. They also changed themselves into beasts and reptiles, and fishes and birds, and into whatsoever they pleased. These things also the poets among yourselves, by reason of fearlessness, sing, as they befell, attributing to one the many and diverse doings of all.

---

[1] The general meaning seems to be as given; but the text is undoubtedly corrupt, and scarcely intelligible.

Chap. XIII.—*The fall of the angels.*

"But when, having assumed these forms, they convicted as covetous those who stole them, and changed themselves into the nature of men, in order that, living holily, and showing the possibility of so living, they might subject the ungrateful to punishment, yet having become in all respects men, they also partook of human lust, and being brought under its subjection they fell into cohabitation with women; and being involved with them, and sunk in defilement and altogether emptied of their first power, were unable to turn back to the first purity of their proper nature, their members turned away from their fiery substance:[1] for the fire itself, being extinguished by the weight of lust, [and changed] into flesh, they trode the impious path downward. For they themselves, being fettered with the bonds of flesh, were constrained and strongly bound; wherefore they have no more been able to ascend into the heavens.

Chap. XIV.—*Their discoveries.*

"For after the intercourse, being asked to show what they were before, and being no longer able to do so, on account of their being unable to do aught else after their defilement, yet wishing to please their mistresses, instead of themselves, they showed the bowels[2] of the earth; I mean, the choice metals,[3] gold, brass, silver, iron, and the like, with all the most precious stones. And along with these charmed stones, they delivered the arts of the things pertaining to each, and imparted the discovery of magic, and taught astronomy, and the powers of roots, and whatever was impossible to be found out by the human mind; also the melting of gold and silver, and the like, and the various dyeing of garments. And all things, in short, which are for the adornment and delight of women, are the discoveries of these demons bound in flesh.

---

[1] The text is somewhat obscure; but the following sentence shows this to be the meaning of it.

[2] Literally, "the marrow."

[3] Literally, "the flowers of metals."

Chap. xv.—*The giants.*

"But from their unhallowed intercourse spurious men sprang, much greater in stature than [ordinary] men, whom they afterwards called giants; not those dragon-footed giants who waged war against God, as those blasphemous myths of the Greeks do sing, but wild in manners, and greater than men in size, inasmuch as they were sprung of angels; yet less than angels, as they were born of women. Therefore God, knowing that they were barbarized to brutality, and that the world was not sufficient to satisfy them (for it was created according to the proportion of men and human use), that they might not through want of food turn, contrary to nature, to the eating of animals, and yet seem to be blameless, as having ventured upon this through necessity, the Almighty God rained manna upon them, suited to their various tastes; and they enjoyed all that they would. But they, on account of their bastard nature, not being pleased with purity of food, longed only after the taste of blood. Wherefore they first tasted flesh.

Chap. xvi.—*Cannibalism.*

"And the men who were with them there for the first time were eager to do the like. Thus, although we are born neither good nor bad, we become [one or the other]; and having formed habits, we are with difficulty drawn from them. But when irrational animals fell short, these bastard men tasted also human flesh. For it was not a long step to the consumption of flesh like their own, having first tasted it in other forms.

Chap. xvii.—*The flood.*

"But by the shedding of much blood, the pure air being defiled with impure vapour, and sickening those who breathed it, rendered them liable to diseases, so that thenceforth men died prematurely. But the earth being by these means greatly defiled, these first teemed with poison-darting and deadly creatures. All things, therefore, going from bad to worse, on account of these brutal demons, God wished to cast them away like an evil leaven, lest each generation from a wicked seed, being like to that before it, and equally impious, should empty the world to come of saved men. And for this purpose, having warned a certain righteous man, with his three sons, together with their wives and their children, to save themselves in an ark, He sent a deluge of water, that all being destroyed, the purified world might be handed over to him who was saved in the ark, in order to a second beginning of life. And thus it came to pass.

CHAP. XVIII.—*The law to the survivors.*

" Since, therefore, the souls of the deceased giants were greater than human souls, inasmuch as they also excelled their bodies, they, as being a new race, were called also by a new name. And to those who survived in the world a law was prescribed of God through an angel, how they should live. For being bastards in race, of the fire of angels and the blood of women, and therefore liable to desire a certain race of their own, they were anticipated by a certain righteous law. For a certain angel was sent to them by God, declaring to them His will, and saying :

CHAP. XIX.—*The law to the giants or demons.*

" ' These things seem good to the all-seeing God, that you lord it over no man ; that you trouble no one, unless any one of his own accord subject himself to you, worshipping you, and sacrificing and pouring libations, and partaking of your table, or accomplishing aught else that they ought not, or shedding blood, or tasting dead flesh, or filling themselves with that which is torn of beasts, or that which is cut, or that which is strangled, or aught else that is unclean. But those who betake themselves to my law, you not only shall not touch, but shall also do honour to, and shall flee from, their presence. For whatsoever shall please them, being just, respecting you, that you shall be constrained to suffer. But if any of those who worship me go astray, either committing adultery, or practising magic, or living impurely, or

K

doing any other of the things which are not well-pleasing to me, then they will have to suffer something at your hands or those of others, according to my order. But upon them, when they repent, I, judging of their repentance, whether it be worthy of pardon or not, shall give sentence. These things, therefore, ye ought to remember and to do, well knowing that not even your thoughts shall be able to be concealed from Him.'

CHAP. XX.—*Willing captives.*

"Having charged them to this effect, the angel departed. But you are still ignorant of this law, that every one who worships demons, or sacrifices to them, or partakes with them of their table, shall become subject to them and receive all punishment from them, as being under wicked lords. And you who, on account of ignorance of this [law], have been corrupted beside their altars,[1] and have been satiated with [food offered to] them, have come under their power, and do not know how you have been in every way injured in respect of your bodies. But you ought to know that the demons have no power over any one, unless first he be their table-companion; since not even their chief can do anything contrary to the law imposed upon them by God, wherefore he has no power over any one who does not worship him; but neither can any one receive from them any of the things that he wishes, nor in anything be hurt by them, as you may learn from the following statement.

CHAP. XXI.—*Temptation of Christ.*

"For once the king of the present time came to our King of righteousness, using no violence, for this was not in his power, but inducing and persuading, because the being persuaded lies in the power of every one. Approaching him, therefore, as being king of things present, he said to the King of things future, 'All the kingdoms of the present world are subject to me; also the gold and the silver and all the luxury of this world are under my power. Wherefore fall down

[1] τοῖς αὐτῶν βωμοῖς προσφθαρέντις καὶ αὐτῶν ἐκπληρωθέντις.

and worship me, and I will give you all these things.' And this he said, knowing that after He worshipped him he would have power also over Him, and thus would rob Him of the future glory and kingdom. But He, knowing all things, not only did not worship him, but would not receive aught of the things that were offered by him. For He pledged Himself with those that are His, to the effect that it is not lawful henceforth even to touch the things that are given over to him. Therefore He answered and said, 'Thou shalt fear the Lord thy God, and Him only shalt thou serve.'[1]

Chap. XXII.—*The marriage supper.*

"However, the king of the impious, striving to bring over to his own counsel the King of the pious, and not being able, ceased his efforts, undertaking to persecute Him for the remainder of His life. But you, being ignorant of the fore-ordained law, are under his power through evil deeds. Wherefore you are polluted in body and soul, and in the present life you are tyrannized over by sufferings and demons, but in that which is to come you shall have your souls to be punished. And this not you alone suffer through ignorance, but also some of our nation, who by evil deeds having been brought under the power of the prince of wickedness, like persons invited to a supper by a father celebrating the marriage of his son, have not obeyed.[2] But instead of those who through preoccupation disobeyed, the Father celebrating the marriage of his Son, has ordered us, through the Prophet of the truth, to come into the partings of the ways, that is, to you, and to invest you with the clean wedding-garment, which is baptism, which is for the remission of the sins done by you, and to bring the good to the supper of God by repentance, although at the first they were left out of the banquet.

Chap. XXIII.—*The assembly dismissed.*

"If, therefore, ye wish to be the vesture of the Divine Spirit, hasten first to put off your base presumption, which is

[1] Matt. iv.; Luke iv.   [2] Matt. xxii.

an unclean spirit and a foul garment. And this you cannot otherwise put off, than by being first baptized in good works. And thus being pure in body and in soul, you shall enjoy the future eternal kingdom. Therefore neither believe in idols, nor partake with them of the impure table, nor commit murder, nor adultery, nor hate those whom it is not right to hate, nor steal, nor set upon any evil deeds; since, being deprived of the hope of future blessings in the present life, you shall be subjected to evil demons and terrible sufferings, and in the world to come you shall be punished with eternal fire. Now, then, what has been said is enough for to-day. For the rest, those of you who are afflicted with ailments remain for healing; and of the others, you who please go in peace."

CHAP. XXIV.—*The sick healed.*

When he had thus spoken, all of them remained, some in order to be healed, and others to see those who obtained cures. But Peter, only laying his hands upon them, and praying, healed them; so that those who were straightway cured were exceeding glad, and those who looked on exceedingly wondered, and blessed God, and believed with a firm hope, and with those who had been healed departed to their own homes, having received a charge to meet early on the following day. And when they had gone, Peter remained there with his associates, and partook of food, and refreshed himself with sleep.

HOMILY IX.

Chap. I.—*Peter's discourse resumed.*

THEREFORE on the next day, Peter going out with his companions, and coming to the former place, and taking his stand, proceeded to say: "God having cut off by water all the impious men of old, having found one alone amongst them all that was pious, caused him to be saved in an ark, with his three sons and their wives. Whence may be perceived that it is His nature not to care for a multitude of wicked, nor to be indifferent to the salvation of one pious. Therefore the greatest impiety of all is forsaking the sole Lord of all, and worshipping many, who are no gods, as if they were gods.

Chap. II.—*Monarchy and polyarchy.*

"If, therefore, while I expound and show you that this is the greatest sin, which is able to destroy you all, it occur to your mind that you are not destroyed, being great multitudes, you are deceived. For you have the example of the old world deluged. And yet their sin was much less than that which is chargeable against you. For they were wicked with respect to their equals, murdering or committing adultery. But you are wicked against the God of all, worshipping lifeless images instead of Him or along with Him, and attributing His divine name to every kind of senseless matter. In the first place, therefore, you are unfortunate in not knowing the difference between monarchy and polyarchy—that monarchy, on the one hand, is productive of concord, but polyarchy is effective of wars. For unity does not fight with itself, but multitude has occasion of undertaking battle one against another.

Chap. III.—*Family of Noe.*

"Therefore, straightway after the flood, Noe continued to live three hundred and fifty years with the multitude of his descendants in concord, being a king according to the image of the one God. But after his death many of his descendants were ambitious of the kingdom, and being eager to reign, each one considered how it might be effected; and one attempted it by war, another by deceit, another by persuasion, and one in one way and another in another; one of whom was of the family of Ham, whose descendant was Mestren, from whom the tribes of the Egyptians and Babylonians and Persians were multiplied.

Chap. IV.—*Zoroaster.*

"Of this family there was born in due time a certain one, who took up with magical practices, by name Nebrod, who chose, giant-like, to devise things in opposition to God. Him the Greeks have called Zoroaster. He, after the deluge, being ambitious of sovereignty, and being a great magician, by magical arts compelled the world-guiding star of the wicked one who now rules, to the bestowal of the sovereignty [as a gift] from him. But he,[1] being a prince, and having authority over him who compelled him,[2] wrathfully poured out the fire of the kingdom, that he might both bring to allegiance, and might punish him who at first constrained him.

Chap. V.—*Hero-worship.*

"Therefore the magician Nebrod, being destroyed by this lightning falling on earth from heaven, for this circumstance had his name changed to Zoroaster, on account of the living (ζῶσαν) stream of the star (ἀστέρος) being poured upon him. But the unintelligent amongst the men who then were, thinking that through the love of God his soul had been sent for

---
[1] That is, I suppose, the wicked one.
[2] I suppose Nimrod, or Zoroaster.

by lightning, buried the remains of his body, and honoured his burial-place with a temple among the Persians, where the descent of the fire occurred, and worshipped him as a god. By this example also, others there bury those who die by lightning as beloved of God, and honour them with temples, and erect statues of the dead in their own forms. Thence, in like manner, the rulers in different places were emulous [of like honour], and very many of them honoured the tombs of those who were beloved of them, though not dying by lightning, with temples and statues, and lighted up altars, and ordered them to be adored as gods. And long after, by the lapse of time, they were thought by posterity to be really gods.

CHAP. VI.—*Fire-worship.*

"Thus, in this fashion, there ensued many partitions of the one original kingdom. The Persians, first taking coals from the lightning which fell from heaven, preserved them by ordinary fuel, and honouring the heavenly fire as a god, were honoured by the fire itself with the first kingdom, as its first worshippers. After them the Babylonians, stealing coals from the fire that was there, and conveying it safely to their own home, and worshipping it, they themselves also reigned in order. And the Egyptians, acting in like manner, and calling the fire in their own dialect *Phthaë*, which is translated *Hephaistus* or *Osiris*, he who first reigned amongst them is called by its name. Those also who reigned in different places, acting in this fashion, and making an image, and kindling altars in honour of fire, most of them were excluded from the kingdom.

CHAP. VII.—*Sacrificial orgies.*

"But they did not cease to worship images, by reason of the evil intelligence of the magicians, who found excuses for them, which had power to constrain them to the foolish worship. For, establishing these things by magical ceremonies, they assigned them feasts from sacrifices, libations, flutes, and shoutings, by means of which senseless men, being deceived, and their kingdom being taken from them, yet did not desist from the worship that they had taken up with. To such an extent did they prefer error, on account of its pleasantness, before truth. They also howl after their sacrificial surfeit, their soul from the depth, as it were by dreams, forewarning them of the punishment that is to befall such deeds of theirs.

CHAP. VIII.—*The best merchandise.*

"Many forms of worship, then, having passed away in the world, we come, bringing to you, as good merchantmen, the worship that has been handed down to us from our fathers, and preserved; showing you, as it were, the seeds of plants, and placing them under your judgment and in your power. Choose that which seems good unto you. If, therefore, ye choose our wares, not only shall ye be able to escape demons, and the sufferings which are inflicted by demons, but yourselves also putting them to flight, and having them reduced to make supplication to you, shall for ever enjoy future blessings.

CHAP. IX.—*How demons get power over men.*

"Since, on the other hand, you are oppressed by strange sufferings inflicted by demons, on your removal from the body you shall have your souls also punished for ever; not indeed by God's inflicting vengeance, but because such is the judgment of evil deeds. For the demons, having power by means of the food given to them, are admitted into your bodies by your own hands; and lying hid there for a long time, they become blended with your souls. And through the carelessness of those who think not, or even wish not, to help themselves, upon the dissolution of their bodies, their souls being united to the demon, are of necessity borne by it into whatever places it pleases. And what is most terrible of all, when at the end of all things the demon is first consigned to the purifying fire, the soul which is mixed with it is under the necessity of being horribly punished, and the demon of being pleased. For the soul, being made of light, and not capable of bearing the heterogeneous flame of fire, is tortured; but the demon, being in the substance of his own kind, is greatly pleased, becoming the strong chain of the soul that he has swallowed up.

CHAP. X.—*How they are to be expelled.*

"But the reason why the demons delight in entering into men's bodies is this. Being spirits, and having desires after meats and drinks, and sexual pleasures, but not being able to partake of these by reason of their being spirits, and wanting organs fitted for their enjoyment, they enter into the bodies of men, in order that, getting organs to minister to them, they may obtain the things that they wish, whether it be meat, by means of men's teeth, or sexual pleasure, by means of men's members. Hence, in order to the putting of demons to flight, the most useful help is abstinence, and fasting, and suffering of affliction. For if they enter into men's bodies for the sake of sharing [pleasures], it is manifest that they are put to flight by suffering. But inasmuch as some,[1] being of a more malignant kind, remain by the body that is undergoing punishment, though they are punished with it, therefore it is needful to have recourse to God by prayers and petitions, refraining from every occasion of impurity, that the hand of God may touch him for his cure, as being pure and faithful.

CHAP. XI.—*Unbelief the demon's stronghold.*

"But it is necessary in our prayers to acknowledge that we have had recourse to God, and to bear witness, not to the apathy, but to the slowness of the demon. For all things are done to the believer, nothing to the unbeliever. Therefore the demons themselves, knowing the amount of faith of those of whom they take possession, measure their stay proportionately. Wherefore they stay permanently with the unbelieving, tarry for a while with the weak in faith; but

[1] The gender is here changed, but the sense shows that the reference is still to the demons. I suppose the author forgot that in the preceding sentences he had written δαίμονες (*masc.*) and not δαιμόνια (*neut.*).

with those who thoroughly believe, and who do good, they cannot remain even for a moment. For the soul being turned by faith, as it were, into the nature of water, quenches the demon as a spark of fire. The labour, therefore, of every one is to be solicitous about the putting to flight of his own demon. For, being mixed up with men's souls, they suggest to every one's mind desires after what things they please, in order that he may neglect his salvation.

CHAP. XII.—*Theory of disease.*

"Whence many, not knowing how they are influenced, consent to the evil thoughts suggested by the demons, as if they were the reasoning of their own souls. Wherefore they become less active to come to those who are able to save them, and do not know that they themselves are held captive by the deceiving demons. Therefore the demons who lurk in their souls induce them to think that it is not a demon that is distressing them, but a bodily disease, such as some acrid matter, or bile, or phlegm, or excess of blood, or inflammation of a membrane, or something else. But even if this were so, the case would not be altered of its being a kind of demon. For the universal and earthly soul, which enters on account of all kinds of food, being taken to excess by overmuch food, is itself united to the spirit, as being cognate, which is the soul of man; and the material part of the food being united to the body, is left as a dreadful poison to it. Wherefore in all respects moderation is excellent.

CHAP. XIII.—*Deceits of the demons.*

" But some of the maleficent demons deceive in another way. For at first they do not even show their existence, in order that care may not be taken against them; but in due time, by means of anger, love, or some other affection, they suddenly injure the body, by sword, or halter, or precipice, or something else, and at last bring to punishment the deceived souls of those who have been mixed up with them, as we said, withdrawing into the purifying fire. But others, who are deceived in another way, do not approach us, being

seduced by the instigations of maleficent demons, as if they
suffered these things at the hands of the gods themselves,
on account of their neglect of them, and were able to reconcile them by sacrifices, and that it is not needful to come to
us, but rather to flee from and hate us. And at the same
time[1] they hate and flee from those who have greater compassion for them, and who follow after them in order to do
good to them.

CHAP. XIV.—*More tricks.*

"Therefore shunning and hating us they are deceived, not
knowing how it happens that they devise things opposed to
their health. For neither can we compel them against their
will to incline towards health, since now we have no such
power over them, nor are they able of themselves to understand the evil instigation of the demon; for they know not
whence these evil instigations are suggested to them. And
these are they whom the demons affright, appearing in such
forms as they please. And sometimes they prescribe remedies for those who are diseased, and thus they receive divine
honours from those who have previously been deceived. And
they conceal from many that they are demons, but not from
us, who know their mystery, and why they do these things,
changing themselves in dreams against those over whom they
have power; and why they terrify some, and give oracular
responses to others, and demand sacrifices from them, and
command them to eat with them, that they may swallow up
their souls.

CHAP. XV.—*Test of idols.*

"For as dire serpents draw sparrows to them by their
breath, so also these draw to their own will those who partake of their table, being mixed up with their understanding
by means of food and drink, changing themselves in dreams
according to the forms of the images, that they may increase
error. For the image is neither a living creature, nor has
it a divine spirit, but the demon that appeared abused the

[1] Some read οὕτως, thus.

form.[1] How many, in like manner, have been seen by others in dreams; and when they have met one another when awake, and compared them with what they saw in their dream, they have not accorded: so that the dream is not a manifestation, but is either the production of a demon or of the soul, giving forms to present fears and desire. For the soul, being struck with fear, conceives forms in dreams. But if you think that images, as being alive, can accomplish such things, place them on a beam accurately balanced, and place an equipoise in the other scale, then ask them to become either heavier or lighter; and if this be done, then they are alive. But it does not so happen. But if it were so, this would not prove them to be gods. For this might be accomplished by the finger of the demon. Even maggots move, yet they are not called gods.

CHAP. XVI.—*Powers of the demons.*

"But that the soul of each man embodies the forms of demons after his own preconceptions, and that those who are called gods do not appear, is manifest from the fact that they do not appear to the Jews. But some one will say, How then do they give oracular responses, forecasting future things? This also is false. But suppose it were true, this does not prove them to be gods; for it does not follow, if anything prophesies, that it is a god. For pythons prophesy, yet they are cast out by us as demons, and put to flight. But some one will say, They work cures for some persons. It is false. But suppose it were true, this is no proof of Godhead; for physicians also heal many, yet are not gods. But, says one, physicians do not completely heal those of whom they take charge, but these heal oracularly. But the demons know the remedies that are suited to each disease. Wherefore, being skilful physicians, and able to cure those diseases which can be cured by men, and also being prophets, and knowing when each disease is healed of itself, they so arrange their

---

[1] The meaning is: "the idols or images of the heathen deities are not living, but the demons adopt the forms of these images when they appear to men in dreams."

remedies that they may gain the credit of producing the cure.

CHAP. XVII.—*Reasons why their deceits are not detected.*

"For why do they oracularly foretell cures after a long time? And why, if they are almighty, do they not effect cures without administering any medicine? And for what reason do they prescribe remedies to some of those who pray to them, while to some, and it may be more suitable cases, they give no response? Thus, whenever a cure is going to take place spontaneously, they promise, in order that they may get the credit of the cure; and others, having been sick, and having prayed, and having recovered spontaneously, attributed the cure to those whom they had invoked, and make offerings to them. Those, however, who, after praying, have failed, are not able to offer their sacrifices. But if the relatives of the dead, or any of their children, inquired into the losses, you would find the failures to be more than the successes. But no one who has been taken in by them is willing to exhibit an accusation against them, through shame or fear; but, on the other hand, they conceal the crimes which they believe them to be guilty of.

CHAP. XVIII.—*Props of the system.*

"And how many also falsify the responses given and the cures effected by them, and confirm them with an oath! And how many give themselves up to them for hire, undertaking falsely to suffer certain things, and thus proclaiming their suffering, and being restored by remedial means, they say that they oracularly promised them healing, in order that they may assign as the cause the senseless worship! And how many of these things were formerly done by magical art, in the way of interpreting dreams, and divining! Yet in course of time these things have disappeared. And how many are there now, who, wishing to obtain such things, make use of charms! However, though a thing be prophetical or healing, it is not divine.

Chap. XIX.—*Privileges of the baptized.*

"For God is almighty. For He is good and righteous, now long-suffering to all, that those who will, repenting of the evils which they have done, and living well, may receive a worthy reward in the day in which all things are judged. Wherefore now begin to obey God by reason of good knowledge, and to oppose your evil lusts and thoughts, that you may be able to recover the original saving worship which was committed to humanity. For thus shall blessings straightway spring up to you, which, when you receive, you will thenceforth quit the trial of evils. But give thanks to the Giver; being kings for ever of unspeakable good things, with the King of peace. But in the present life, washing in a flowing river, or fountain, or even in the sea, with the thrice-blessed invocation, you shall not only be able to drive away the spirits which lurk in you; but yourselves no longer sinning, and undoubtingly believing God, you shall drive out evil spirits and dire demons, with terrible diseases, from others. And sometimes they shall flee when you but look on them. For they know those who have given themselves up to God. Wherefore, honouring them, they flee affrighted, as you saw yesterday, how, when after the address I delayed praying for those who were suffering these maladies, through respect towards the worship they cried out, not being able to endure it for a short hour.

Chap. XX.—*"Not almost, but altogether such as I am."*

"Do not then suppose that we do not fear demons on this account, that we are of a different nature [from you]. For we are of the same nature, but not of the same worship. Wherefore, being not only much but altogether superior to you, we do not grudge you becoming such [as we are]; but, on the other hand, counsel you, knowing that all these [demons] beyond measure honour and fear those who are reconciled to God.

CHAP. XXI.—*The demons subject to the believer.*

"For, in like manner as the soldiers who are put under one of Cæsar's captains know to honour him who has received authority on account of him who gave it, so that the commanders say to this one, Come, and he comes, and to another, Go, and he goes; so also he who has given himself to God, being faithful, is heard when he only speaks to demons and diseases; and the demons give place, though they be much stronger than they who command them. For with unspeakable power God subjects the mind of every one to whom He pleases. For as many captains, with whole camps and cities, fear Cæsar, who is but a man, every one's heart being eager to honour the image of all;[1] for by the will of God, all things being enslaved by fear, do not know the cause; so also all disease-producing spirits, being awed in some natural way, honour and flee from him who has had recourse to God, and who carries right faith as His image in his heart.

CHAP. XXII.—*"Rather rejoice."*

"But still, though all demons, with all diseases, flee before you, you are not to rejoice in this only, but in that, through grace, your names, as of the ever-living, are written in heaven. Thus also the Divine Holy Spirit rejoices, because man hath overcome death; for the putting of the demons to flight makes for the safety of another. But this we say, not as denying that we ought to help others, but that we ought not to be inflated by this and neglect ourselves. It happens, also, that the demons flee before some wicked men by reason of the honoured name, and both he who expels the demon and he who witnesses it are deceived: he who expels him, as if he were honoured on account of righteousness, not knowing the wickedness of the demon. For he has at once honoured the name, and by his flight has brought the wicked man into a thought of his righteousness, and so deceived him

---

[1] I prefer here the common text to any of the proposed emendations, and suppose that the author represents Cæsar, though but one man, as the image or personification of the whole empire.

away from repentance. But the looker-on, associating with the expeller as a pious man, hastens to a like manner of life, and is ruined. Sometimes also they pretend to flee before adjurations not made in the name of God, that they may deceive men, and destroy them whom they will.

CHAP. XXIII.—*The sick healed.*

"This then we would have you know, that unless any one of his own accord give himself over as a slave to demons, as I said before, the demon has no power against him. Choosing, therefore, to worship one God, and refraining from the table of demons, and undertaking chastity with philanthropy and righteousness, and being baptized with the thrice-blessed invocation for the remission of sins, and devoting yourselves as much as you can to the perfection of purity, you can escape everlasting punishment, and be constituted heirs of eternal blessings."

Having thus spoken, he ordered those to approach who were distressed with diseases; and thus many approached, having come together through the experience of those who had been healed yesterday. And he having laid his hands upon them and prayed, and immediately healed them, and having charged them and the others to come earlier, he bathed and partook of food, and went to sleep.

HOMILY X.

CHAP. I.—*The third day in Tripolis.*

THEREFORE on the third day in Tripolis, Peter rose early and went into the garden, where there was a great water-reservoir, into which a full stream of water constantly flowed. There having bathed, and then having prayed, he sat down; and perceiving us sitting around and eagerly observing him, as wishing to hear something from him, he said:

CHAP. II.—*Ignorance and error.*

"There seems to me to be a great difference between the ignorant and the erring. For the ignorant man seems to me to be like a man who does not wish to set out for a richly stored city, through his not knowing the excellent things that are there; but the erring man to be like one who has learned indeed the good things that are in the city, but who has forsaken the highway in proceeding towards it, and so has wandered. Thus, therefore, it seems to me that there is a great difference between those who worship idols and those who are faulty in the worship of God. For they who worship idols are ignorant of eternal life, and therefore they do not desire it; for what they do not know, they cannot love. But those who have chosen to worship one God, and who have learned of the eternal life given to the good, if they either believe or do anything different from what is pleasing to God, are like to those who have gone out from the city of punishment, and are desirous to come to the well-stored city, and on the road have strayed from the right path."

CHAP. III.—*Man the lord of all.*

While he was thus discoursing to us, there entered one of our people, who had been appointed to make the following announcement to him, and said: "My lord Peter, there are great multitudes standing before the doors." With his consent, therefore, a great multitude entered. Then he rose up, and stood on the basis, as he had done the day before; and having saluted them in religious fashion, he said: "God having formed the heaven and the earth, and having made all things in them, as the true Prophet has said to us, man, being made after the image and likeness of God, was appointed to be ruler and lord of things, I say, in air and earth and water, as may be known from the very fact that by his intelligence he brings down the creatures that are in the air, and brings up those that are in the deep, hunts those that are on the earth, and that although they are much greater in strength than he; I mean elephants, and lions, and such like.

CHAP. IV.—*Faith and duty.*

"While, therefore, he was righteous, he was also superior to all sufferings, as being unable by his immortal body to have any experience of pain; but when he sinned, as I showed you yesterday and the day before, becoming as it were the servant of sin, he became subject to all sufferings, being by a righteous judgment deprived of all excellent things. For it was not reasonable, the Giver having been forsaken, that the gifts should remain with the ungrateful. Whence, of His abundant mercy, in order to our receiving, with the first, also future blessings, He sent His Prophet. And the Prophet has given in charge to us to tell you what you ought to think, and what to do. Choose, therefore; and this is in your power. What, therefore, you ought to think is this, to worship the God who made all things; whom if you receive in your minds, you shall receive from Him, along with the first excellent things, also the future eternal blessings.

Chap. v.—*The fear of God.*

"Therefore you shall be able to persuade yourselves with respect to the things that are profitable, if, like charmers, you say to the horrible serpent which lurks in your heart, 'The Lord God thou shalt fear, and Him alone thou shalt serve.'[1] On every account it is advantageous to fear Him alone, not as an unjust, but as a righteous God. For one fears an unjust being, lest he be wrongfully destroyed, but a righteous one, lest he be caught in sin and punished. You can therefore, by fear towards Him, be freed from many hurtful fears. For if you do not fear the one Lord and Maker of all, you shall be the slaves of all evils to your own hurt, I mean of demons and diseases, and of everything that can in any way hurt you.

Chap. vi.—*Restoration of the divine image.*

"Therefore approach with confidence to God, you who at first were made to be rulers and lords of all things: ye who have His image in your bodies, have in like manner the likeness of His judgment in your minds. Since, then, by acting like irrational animals, you have lost the soul of man from your soul, becoming like swine, you are the prey of demons. If, therefore, you receive the law of God, you become men. For it cannot be said to irrational animals, 'Thou shalt not kill, thou shalt not commit adultery, thou shalt not steal,' and so forth. Therefore do not refuse, when invited, to return to your first nobility; for it is possible, if ye be conformed to God by good works. And being accounted to be sons by reason of your likeness to Him, you shall be reinstated as lords of all.

Chap. vii.—*Unprofitableness of idols.*

"Begin, then, to divest yourselves of the injurious fear of vain idols, that you may escape unrighteous bondage. For they have become your masters, who even as servants are unprofitable to you. I speak of the material of the lifeless

[1] Matt. iv. 10.

images, which are of no use to you as far as service is concerned. For they neither hear nor see nor feel, nor can they be moved. For is there any one of you who would like to see as they see, and to hear as they hear, and to feel as they feel, and to be moved as they are? God forbid that such a wrong should be done to any man bearing the image of God, though he have lost His likeness.

CHAP. VIII.—*No gods which are made with hands.*

"Therefore reduce your gods of gold and silver, or any other material, to their original nature; I mean into cups and basins and all other utensils, such as may be useful to you for service; and those good things which were given you at first shall be able to be restored. But perhaps you will say, The laws of the emperors do not permit us to do this. You say well that it is the law, and not the power of the vain idols themselves, which is nothing. How, then, have ye regarded them as gods, who are avenged by human laws, guarded by dogs, kept by multitudes?—and that if they are of gold, or silver, or brass. For those of wood or earthenware are preserved by their worthlessness, because no man desires to steal a wooden or earthenware god! So that your gods are exposed to danger in proportion to the value of the material of which they are made. How, then, can they be gods, which are stolen, molten, weighed, guarded?

CHAP. IX.—"*Eyes have they, but they see not,*" etc.

"Oh the minds of wretched men, who fear things deader than dead men! For I cannot call them even dead, which have never lived, unless they are the tombs of ancient men. For sometimes a person, visiting unknown places, does not know whether the temples which he sees are monuments of dead men, or whether they belong to the so-called gods; but on inquiring and hearing that they belong to the gods, he worships, without being ashamed that if he had not learned on inquiring, he would have passed them by as the monument of a dead man, on account of the strictness of the resemblance. However, it is not necessary that I should adduce much proof in regard to such superstition. For it is easy for any one who pleases to understand that it [an idol] is nothing, unless there be any one who does not see. However, now at least hear that it does not hear, and understand that it does not understand. For the hands of a man who is dead made it. If, then, the maker is dead, how can it be that that which was made by him shall not be dissolved? Why, then, do you worship the work of a mortal which is altogether senseless? whereas those who have reason do not worship animals, nor do they seek to propitiate the elements which have been made by God,—I mean the heaven, the sun, the moon, lightning, the sea, and all things in them,—rightly judging not to worship the things that He has made, but to reverence the Maker and Sustainer of them. For in this they themselves also rejoice, that no one ascribes to them the honour that belongs to their Maker.

CHAP. X.—*Idolatry a delusion of the serpent.*

"For His alone is the excellent glory of being alone uncreated, while all else is created. As, therefore, it is the prerogative of the uncreated to be God, so whatever is created is not God indeed. Before all things, therefore, you ought to consider the evil-working suggestion of the deceiving serpent that is in you, which seduces you by the promise of better reason, creeping from your brain to your spinal marrow, and setting great value upon deceiving you.

CHAP. XI.—*Why the serpent tempts to sin.*

"For he knows the original law, that if he bring you to the persuasion of the so-called gods, so that you sin against the one good of monarchy, your overthrow becomes a gain to him. And that for this reason, because he being condemned eats earth, he has power to eat him who through sin being dissolved into earth, has become earth, your souls going into his belly of fire. In order, therefore, that you may suffer these things, he suggests every thought to your hurt.

Chap. XII.—*Ignorantia neminem excusat.*

"For all the deceitful conceptions against the monarchy are sown in your mind by him to your hurt. First, that you may not hear the discourses of piety, and so drive away ignorance, which is the occasion of evils, he ensnares you by a pretence of knowledge, giving in the first instance, and using throughout this presumption, which is to think and to be unhappily advised, that if any one do not hear the word of piety, he is not subject to judgments. Wherefore also some, being thus deceived, are not willing to hear, that they may be ignorant, not knowing that ignorance is of itself a sufficient deadly drug. For if any one should take a deadly drug in ignorance, does he not die? So naturally sins destroy the sinner, though he commit them in ignorance of what is right.

Chap. XIII.—*Condemnation of the ignorant.*

"But if judgment follows upon disobedience to instruction, much more shall God destroy those who will not undertake His worship. For he who will not learn, lest that should make him subject to judgment, is already judged as knowing, for he knew what he will not hear; so that that imagination avails nothing as an apology in presence of the heart-knowing God. Wherefore avoid that cunning thought suggested by the serpent to your minds. But if any one end this life in real ignorance, this charge will lie against him, that, having lived so long, he did not know who was the bestower of the food supplied to him; and as a senseless, and ungrateful, and very unworthy servant, he is rejected from the kingdom of God.

Chap. XIV.—*Polytheistic illustration.*

"Again, the terrible serpent suggests this supposition to you, to think and to say that very thing which most of you do say; viz., We know that there is one Lord of all, but there also are gods. For in like manner as there is one Cæsar, but he has under him procurators, proconsuls, prefects, commanders of thousands, and of hundreds, and of tens; in the same way, there being one great God, as there is one Cæsar, there also, after the manner of inferior powers, are gods, inferior indeed to Him, but ruling over us. Hear, therefore, ye who have been led away by this conception as by a terrible poison—I mean the evil conception of this illustration—that you may know what is good and what is evil. For you do not yet see it, nor do you look into the things that you utter.

CHAP. XV.—*Its inconclusiveness.*

"For if you say that, after the manner of Cæsar, God has subordinate powers—those, namely, which are called gods— you do not thus go by your illustration. For if you went by it, you must of necessity know that it is not lawful to give the name of Cæsar to another, whether he be consul, or prefect, or captain, or any one else, and that he who gives such a name shall not live, and he who takes it shall be cut off. Thus, according to your own illustration, the name of God must not be given to another; and he who is tempted either to take or give it is destroyed. Now, if this insult of a man induces punishment, much more they who call others gods shall be subject to eternal punishment, as insulting God. And with good reason; because you subject to all the insult that you can the name which it was committed to you to honour, in order to His monarchy. For GOD is not properly His name; but you having in the meantime received it, insult what has been given you, that it may be accounted as done against the real name, according as you use that. But you subject it to every kind of insult.

CHAP. XVI.—*Gods of the Egyptians.*

"Therefore you ringleaders among the Egyptians, boasting of meteorology, and promising to judge the natures of the stars, by reason of the evil opinion lurking in them, subjected that name to all manner of dishonour as far as in them lay. For some of them taught the worship of an ox called Apis, some that of a he-goat, some of a cat, some of a serpent; yea, even of a fish, and of onions, and rumblings in the stomach,[1]

[1] γαστρῶν πνεύματα.

and common sewers, and members of irrational animals, and to myriads of other base abominations [they gave the name of god]."

CHAP. XVII.—*The Egyptians' defence of their system.*

On Peter's saying this, the surrounding multitude laughed. Then Peter said to the laughing multitude: "You laugh at their proceedings, not knowing that you are yourselves much more objects of ridicule to them. But you laugh at one another's proceedings; for, being led by evil custom into deceit, you do not see your own. But I admit that you have reason to laugh at the idols of the Egyptians, since they, being rational, worship irrational animals, and these altogether dying. But listen to what they say when they deride you. We, they say, though we worship dying creatures, yet still such as have once had life; but you reverence things that never lived. And in addition to this, they say, We wish to honour the form of the one God, but we cannot find out what it is, and so we choose to give honour to every form. And so, making some such statements as these, they think that they judge more rightly than you do.

CHAP. XVIII.—*Answer to the Egyptians.*

"Wherefore answer them thus: You lie, for you do not worship these things in honour of the true God, for then all of you would worship every form; not as ye do. For those of you who suppose the onion to be the divinity, and those who worship rumblings in the stomach, contend with one another; and thus all in like manner preferring some one thing, revile those that are preferred by others. And with diverse judgments, one reverences one and another another of the limbs of the same animal. Moreover, those of them who still have a breath of right reason, being ashamed of the manifest baseness, attempt to drive these things into allegories, wishing by another vagary to establish their deadly error. But we should confute the allegories, if we were there, the foolish passion for which has prevailed to such an extent as to constitute a great disease of the understanding. For it is not necessary to apply a plaster to a whole part of the body, but to a diseased part. Since then, you, by your laughing at the Egyptians, show that you are not affected with their disease, with respect to your own disease it were reasonable I should afford to you a present cure of your own malady.

CHAP. XIX.—*God's peculiar attribute.*

"He who would worship God ought before all things to know what alone is peculiar to the nature of God, which cannot pertain to another, that, looking at His peculiarity, and not finding it in any other, he may not be seduced into ascribing godhead to another. But this is peculiar to God, that He alone is, as the Maker of all, so also the best of all. That which makes is indeed superior in power to that which is made; that which is boundless is superior in magnitude to that which is bounded: in respect of beauty, that which is comeliest; in respect of happiness, that which is most blessed; in respect of understanding, that which is most perfect. And in like manner, in other respects, He has incomparably the pre-eminence. Since then, as I said, this very thing, viz. to be the best of all, is peculiar to God, and the all-comprehending world was made by Him, none of the things made by Him can come into equal comparison with Him.

CHAP. XX.—*Neither the world nor any of its parts can be God.*

"But the world, not being incomparable and unsurpassable, and altogether in all respects without defect, cannot be God. But if the whole world cannot be God, in respect of its having been made, how much more should not its parts be reasonably called God; I mean the parts that are by you called gods, being made of gold and silver, brass and stone, or of any other material whatsoever; and they constructed by mortal hand. However, let us further see how the terrible serpent through man's mouth poisons those who are seduced by his solicitations.

CHAP. XXI.—*Idols not animated by the Divine Spirit.*

"For many say, We do not worship the gold or the silver,

the wood or the stone, of the objects of our worship. For we also know that these are nothing but lifeless matter, and the art of mortal man. But the spirit that dwells in them, that we call God. Behold the immorality of those who speak thus! For when that which appears is easily proved to be nothing, they have recourse to the invisible, as not being able to be convicted in respect of what is non-apparent. However, they agree with us in part, that one half of their images is not God, but senseless matter. It remains for them to show how we are to believe that these images have a divine spirit. But they cannot prove to us that it is so, for it is not so; and we do not believe them [when they say that they] have seen it. We shall afford them proofs that they have not a divine spirit, that lovers of truth, hearing the refutation of the thought that they are animated, may turn away from the hurtful delusion.

CHAP. XXII.—*Confutation of idol-worship.*

"In the first place, indeed, if you worship them as being animated, why do you also worship the sepulchres of memorable men of old, who confessedly had no divine spirit? Thus you do not at all speak truth respecting this. But if your objects of worship were really animated, they would move of themselves; they would have a voice; they would shake off the spiders that are on them; they would thrust forth those that wish to surprise and to steal them; they would easily capture those who pilfer the offerings. But now they do none of these things, but are guarded, like culprits, and especially the more costly of them, as we have already said. But what? Is it not so, that the rulers demand of you imposts and taxes on their account, as if you were greatly benefited by them? But what? Have they not often been taken as plunder by enemies, and been broken and scattered? And do not the priests, more than the outside worshippers, carry off many of the offerings, thus acknowledging the uselessness of their worship?

Chap. XXIII.—*Folly of idolatry.*

"Nay, it will be said; but they are detected by their foresight. It is false; for how many of them have not been detected? And if on account of the capture of some it be said that they have power, it is a mistake. For of those who rob tombs, some are found out and some escape; but it is not by the power of the dead that those who are apprehended are detected. And such ought to be our conclusion with respect to those who steal and pilfer the gods. But it will be said, The gods that are in them take no care of their images. Why, then, do you tend them, wiping them, and washing them, and scouring them, crowning them, and sacrificing to them? Wherefore agree with me that you act altogether without right reason. For as you lament over the dead, so you sacrifice and make libations to your gods.

Chap. XXIV.—*Impotence of idols.*

" Nor yet is that in harmony with the illustration of Cæsar, and of the powers under him, to call them administrators; whereas you take all care of them, as I said, tending your images in every respect. For they, having no power, do nothing. Wherefore tell us what do they administer? what do they of that sort which rulers in different places do? and what influence do they exert, as the stars of God? Do they show anything like the sun, or do you light lamps before them? Are they able to bring showers, as the clouds bring rain,—they which cannot even move themselves, unless men carry them? Do they make the earth fruitful to your labours, these to whom you supply sacrifices? Thus they can do nothing.

Chap. XXV.—*Servants become masters.*

"But if they were able to do something, you should not be right in calling them gods : for it is not right to call the elements gods, by which good things are supplied; but only Him who ordereth them, to accomplish all things for our use, and who commandeth them to be serviceable to man,—

Him alone we call God in propriety of speech, whose beneficence you do not perceive, but permit those elements to rule over you which have been assigned to you as your servants. And why should I speak of the elements, when you not only have made and do worship lifeless images, but deign to be subject to them in all respects as servants? Wherefore, by reason of your erroneous judgments, you have become subject to demons. However, by acknowledgment of God Himself, by good deeds you can again become masters, and command the demons as slaves, and as sons of God be constituted heirs of the eternal kingdom."

CHAP. XXVI.—*The sick healed.*

Having said this, he ordered the demoniacs, and those taken with diseases, to be brought to him; and when they were brought, he laid his hands on them, and prayed, and dismissed them healed, reminding them and the rest of the multitude to attend upon him there every day that he should discourse. Then, when the others had withdrawn, Peter bathed in the reservoir that was there, with those who pleased; and then ordering a table to be spread on the ground under the thick foliage of the trees, for the sake of shade, he ordered us each to recline, according to our worth; and thus we partook of food. Therefore having blessed and having given thanks to God for the enjoyment, according to the accustomed faith of the Hebrews; and there being still a long time before us, he permitted us to ask him questions about whatever we pleased; and thus, though there were twenty of us putting questions to him all round, he satisfied every one. And now evening having descended, we all went with him into the largest apartment of the lodging, and there we all slept.

HOMILY XI.

Chap. I.—*Morning exercises.*

THEREFORE on the fourth day at Tripolis, Peter rising and finding us awake, saluted us and went out to the reservoir, that he might bathe and pray; and we also did so after him. To us, therefore, when we had prayed together, and were set down before him, he gave a discourse touching the necessity of purity. And when thereafter it was day, he permitted the multitudes to enter. Then, when a great crowd had entered, he saluted them according to custom, and began to speak.

Chap. II.—*" Giving all diligence."*

"Inasmuch as, by long-continued neglect on your part, to your own injury, your mind has caused to sprout many hurtful conceptions about religion, and ye have become like land fallow by the carelessness of the husbandman, you need a long time for your purification, that your mind, receiving like good seed the true word that is imparted to you, may not choke it with evil cares, and render it unfruitful with respect to works that are able to save you. Wherefore it behoves those who are careful of their own salvation to hear more constantly, that their sins which have been long multiplying may, in the short time that remains, be matched with constant care for their purification. Since, therefore, no one knows the time of his end, hasten to pluck out the many thorns of your hearts; but not by little and little, for then you cannot be purified, for you have been long fallow.

Chap. III.—*" Behold what indignation."*

"But not otherwise will you endure to undertake much

care for your purification unless you be angry with yourselves, and chastise yourselves for those things with which, as unprofitable servants, you have been ensnared, consenting to your evil lusts, that you may be able to let in your righteous indignation upon your mind, as fire upon a fallow field. If, therefore, ye have not righteous fire, I mean indignation, against evil lusts, learn from what good things ye have been seduced, and by whom ye have been deceived, and for what punishment ye are prepared; and thus, your mind being sober, and kindled into indignation like fire by the teaching of Him who sent us, may be able to consume the evil things of lust. Believe me, that if you will, you can rectify all things.

CHAP. IV.—*The golden rule.*

"Ye are the image of the invisible God. Whence let not those who would be pious say that idols are images of God, and therefore that it is right to worship them. For the image of God is man. He who wishes to be pious towards God does good to man, because the body of man bears the image of God. But all do not as yet bear His likeness, but the pure mind of the good soul does. However, as we know that man was made after the image and after the likeness of God, we tell you to be pious towards him, that the favour may be accounted as done to God, whose image he is. Therefore it behoves you to give honour to the image of God, which is man—in this wise: food to the hungry, drink to the thirsty, clothing to the naked, care to the sick, shelter to the stranger, and visiting him who is in prison, to help him as you can. And not to speak at length, whatever good things any one wishes for himself, so let him afford to another in need, and then a good reward can be reckoned to him as being pious towards the image of God. And by like reason, if he will not undertake to do these things, he shall be punished as neglecting the image.

CHAP. V.—*Forasmuch as ye did it unto one of these.*

"Can it therefore be said that, for the sake of piety towards God, ye worship every form, while in all things ye injure man who is really the image of God, committing murder, adultery, stealing, and dishonouring him in many other respects? But you ought not to do even one evil thing on account of which man is grieved. But now you do all things on account of which man is disheartened, for wrong is also distress. Wherefore you murder and spoil his goods, and whatever else you know which you would not receive from another. But you, being seduced by some malignant reptile to malice, by the suggestion of polytheistic doctrine, are impious towards the real image, which is man, and think that ye are pious towards senseless things.

CHAP. VI.—*Why God suffers objects of idolatry to subsist.*

"But some say, Unless He wished these things to be, they should not be, but He would take them away. But I say this shall assuredly be the case, when all shall show their preference for Him, and thus there shall be a change of the present world. However, if you wished him to act thus, so that none of the things that are worshipped should subsist, tell me what of existing things you have not worshipped. Do not some of you worship the sun, and some the moon, and some water, and some the earth, and some the mountains, and some plants, and some seeds, and some also man, as in Egypt? Therefore God must have suffered nothing, not even you, so that there should have been neither worshipped nor worshipper. Truly this is what the terrible serpent which lurks in you would have, and spares you not. But so it shall not be. For it is not the thing that is worshipped that sins; for it suffers violence at the hands of him who will worship it. For though unjust judgment is passed by all men, yet not by God. For it is not just that the sufferer and the disposer receive the same punishment, unless he willingly receive the honour which belongs only to the Most Honourable.

CHAP. VII.—"*Let both grow together till the harvest.*"

"But it will be said that the worshippers themselves ought to be taken away by the true God, that others may not do it.

But you are not wiser than God, that you should give Him counsel as one more prudent than He. He knows what He does; for He is long-suffering to all who are in impiety, as a merciful and philanthropic father, knowing that impious men become pious. And of those very worshippers of base and senseless things, many becoming sober have ceased to worship these things and to sin, and many Greeks have been saved so as to pray to the true God.

CHAP. VIII.—*Liberty and necessity.*

"But, you say, God ought to have made us at first so that we should not have thought at all of such things. You who say this do not know what is free-will, and how it is possible to be really good; that he who is good by his own choice is really good; but he who is made good by another under necessity is not really good, because he is not what he is by his own choice. Since therefore every one's freedom constitutes the true good, and shows the true evil, God has contrived that friendship or hostility should be in each man by occasions. But no, it is said: everything that we think He makes us to think. Stop! Why do you blaspheme more and more, in saying this? For if we are under His influence in all that we think, you say that He is the cause of fornications, lusts, avarice, and all blasphemy. Cease your evil-speaking, ye who ought to speak well of Him, and to bestow all honour upon Him. And do not say that God does not claim any honour; for if He Himself claims nothing, you ought to look to what is right, and to answer with thankful voice Him who does you good in all things.

CHAP. IX.—*God a jealous God.*

"But, you say, we do better when we are thankful at once to Him and to all others. Now, when you say this, you do not know the plot that is formed against you. For as, when many physicians of no power promise to cure one patient, one who is really able to cure him does not apply his remedy, considering that, if he should cure him, the others would get the credit; so also God does not do you good, when He is asked along with many who can do nothing. What! it will be said, is God enraged at this, if, when He cures, another gets the credit? I answer: Although He be not indignant, at all events He will not be an accomplice in deceit; for when He has conferred a benefit, the idol, which has done nothing, is credited with the power. But also I say to you, if he who crouches in adoration before senseless idols had not been injured naturally, perhaps He (God) would have endured even this. Wherefore watch ye that you may attain to a reasonable understanding on the matter of salvation.[1] For God being without want, neither Himself needs anything, nor receives hurt; for it belongs to us to be profited or injured. For in like manner as Cæsar is neither hurt when he is evil spoken of, nor profited when he is thanked, but safety accrues to the renderer of thanks, and ruin to the evil-speaker, so they who speak well of God indeed profit Him nothing, but save themselves; and in like manner, those who blaspheme Him do not indeed injure Him, but themselves perish.

CHAP. X.—*The creatures avenge God's cause.*

"But it will be said that the cases are not parallel between God and man; and I admit that they are not parallel: for the punishment is greater to him who is guilty of impiety against the greater, and less to him who sins against the less. As, therefore, God is greatest of all, so he who is impious against Him shall endure greater punishment, as sinning against the greater; not through His defending Himself with His own hand, but the whole creation being indignant at him, and naturally taking vengeance on him. For to the blasphemer the sun will not give his light, nor the earth her fruits, nor the fountain its water, nor in Hades shall he who is there constituted prince give rest to the soul; since even now, while the constitution of the world subsists, the whole creation is indignant at him. Wherefore neither do [the clouds] afford sufficient rains, nor the earth fruits, whereby many perish; yea, even the air itself, inflamed with anger,

[1] We have adopted the reading of Codex O. The reading in the others is corrupt.

is turned to pestilential courses. However, whatsoever good things we enjoy, He of His mercy compels the creature to our benefits. Still, against you who dishonour the Maker of all, the whole creation is hostile.

CHAP. XI.—*Immortality of the soul.*

"And though by the dissolution of the body you should escape punishment, how shall you be able by corruption to flee from your soul, which is incorruptible? For the soul even of the wicked is immortal, for whom it were better not to have it incorruptible. For, being punished with endless torture under unquenchable fire, and never dying, it can receive no end of its misery. But perhaps some one of you will say, 'You terrify us, O Peter.' Teach us then how we can be silent [about these things, and yet] tell you things as they are, for not otherwise can we tell you them. But if we should be silent, you should be ensnared by evils through ignorance. But if we speak, we are suspected of terrifying you with a false theory. How then shall we charm that wicked [serpent] that lurks in your [soul], and subtilely insinuates suspicions hostile to God, under the guise of love to God? Be reconciled with yourselves; for in order to your salvation recourse is to Him with well-doing. Unreasonable lust in you is hostile to God, for by conceit of wisdom it strengthens ignorance.

CHAP. XII.—*Idols unprofitable.*

"But others say, God does not care for us. This also is false. For if really He did not care, He would neither cause His sun to rise on the good and the evil, nor send His rain on the just and the unjust. But others say, We are more pious [than you], since we worship both him and images. I do not think, if one were to say to a king, 'I give you an equal share of honour with that which I give to corpses and to worthless dung'—I do not think that he would profit by it. But some one will say, Do you call our objects of worship dung? I say Yes, for you have made them useless to yourselves by setting them aside for worship, whereas their substance might perhaps have been serviceable for some other purpose, or for the purpose of manure. But now it is not useful even for this purpose, since you have changed its shape and worship it. And how do you say that you are more pious, you who are the most wicked of all, who deserve destruction of your souls by this very one incomparable sin, at the hands of Him who is true, if you abide in it? For as if any son having received many benefits from his father, give to another, who is not his father, the honour that is due to his father, he is certainly disinherited; but if he live according to the judgment of his father, and so thanks him for his kindnesses, he is with good reason made the heir.

CHAP. XIII.—*Arguments in favour of idolatry answered.*

"But others say, We shall act impiously if we forsake the objects of worship handed down to us by our fathers; for it is like the guarding of a deposit. But on this principle the son of a robber or a debauchee ought not to be sober and to choose the better part, lest he should act impiously, and sin by doing differently from his parents! How foolish, then, are they who say, We worship these things that we may not be troublesome to Him; as if God were troubled by those who bless Him, and not troubled by those who ungratefully blaspheme Him. Why is it, then, that when there is a withholding of rain, you look only to heaven and pour out prayers and supplications; and when you obtain it, you quickly forget? For when you have reaped your harvest or gathered your vintage, you distribute your firstfruits among those idols which are nothing, quickly forgetting God your benefactor; and thus you go into groves and temples, and offer sacrifices and feasts. Wherefore some of you say, These things have been excellently devised for the sake of good cheer and feasting.

CHAP. XIV.—*Heathen orgies.*

"Oh men without understanding! Judge ye rightly of what is said. For if it were necessary to give one's self to some pleasure for the refreshment of the body, whether were it better to do so among the rivers and woods and groves, where there are entertainments and convivialities and shady places, or where there is the madness of demons, and cuttings of hands, and emasculations, and fury and mania, and dishevelling of hair, and shoutings and enthusiasms and howlings, and all those things which are done with hypocrisy for the confounding of the unthinking, when you offer your prescribed prayers and thanksgivings even to those who are deader than the dead?

CHAP. XV.—*Heathen worshippers under the power of the demon.*

"And why do ye take pleasure in these doings? Since the serpent which lurks in you, which has sown in you fruitless lust, will not tell you, I shall speak and put it on record. Thus the case stands. According to the worship of God, the proclamation is made to be sober, to be chaste, to restrain passion, not to pilfer other men's goods, to live uprightly, moderately, fearlessly, gently; rather to restrain one's self in necessities, than to supply his wants by wrongfully taking away the property of another. But with the so-called gods the reverse is done. And ye renounce some things [as done by you], in order to the admiration of [your] righteousness; whereas, although you did all that you are commanded, ignorance with respect to God is alone sufficient for your condemnation. But meeting together in the places which you have dedicated to them, you delight in making yourselves drunk, and you kindle your altars, of which the diffused odour through its influence attracts the blind and deaf spirits to the place of their fumigation. And thus, of those who are present, some are filled with inspirations, and some with strange fiends, and some betake themselves to lasciviousness, and some to theft and murder. For the exhalation of blood, and the libation of wine, satisfies even these unclean spirits, which lurk within you and cause you to take pleasure in the things that are transacted there, and in dreams surround you with false phantasies, and punish you with myriads of diseases. For under the show of the so-called sacred victims you are filled with dire demons, which, cunningly concealing themselves, destroy you, so that you should not understand the plot that is laid for you. For, under the guise of some injury, or love, or anger, or grief, or strangling you with a rope, or drowning you, or throwing you from a precipice, or by suicide, or apoplexy, or some other disease, they deprive you of life.

CHAP. XVI.—*All things work for good to them that love God.*

"But no one of us can suffer such a thing; but they themselves are punished by us, when, having entered into any one, they entreat us that they may go out slowly. But some one will say perhaps, Even some of the worshippers of God fall under such sufferings. I say that that is impossible. For he is a worshipper of God, of whom I speak, who is truly pious, not one who is such only in name, but who really performs the deeds of the law that has been given him. If any one acts impiously, he is not pious; in like manner as, if he who is of another tribe keeps the law, he is a Jew; but he who does not keep it is a Greek. For the Jew believes God and keeps the law, by which faith he removes also other sufferings, though like mountains and heavy.[1] But he who keeps not the law is manifestly a deserter through not believing God; and thus as no Jew, but a sinner, he is on account of his sin brought into subjection to those sufferings which are ordained for the punishment of sinners. For, by the will of God prescribed at the beginning, punishment righteously follows those who worship Him on account of transgressions; and this is so, in order that, having reckoned with them by punishment for sin as for a debt, he may set forth those who have turned to Him pure in the universal judgment. For as the wicked here enjoy luxury to the loss of eternal blessings, so punishments are sent upon the Jews who transgress for a settlement of accounts, that, expiating their transgression here, they may there be set free from eternal punishments.

[1] Matt. xvii. 19.

Chap. XVII.—*Speaking the truth in love.*

"But you cannot speak thus; for you do not believe that things are then as we say; I mean, when there is a recompense for all. And on this account, you being ignorant of what *is* advantageous, are seduced by temporal pleasures from taking hold of eternal things. Wherefore we attempt to make to you exhibitions of what is profitable, that, being convinced of the promises that belong to piety, you may by good deeds inherit with us the griefless world. Until then you know us, do not be angry with us, as if we spoke falsely of the good things which we desire for you. For the things which are regarded by us as true and good, these we have not scrupled to bring to you, but, on the contrary, have hastened to make you fellow-heirs of good things, which we have considered to be such. For thus it is necessary to speak to the unbelievers. But that we really speak the truth in what we say, you cannot know otherwise than by first listening with love of the truth.

Chap. XVIII.—*Charming of the serpent.*

"Wherefore, as to the matter in hand, although in ten thousand ways the serpent that lurks in you suggesting evil reasonings and hindrances, wishes to ensnare you, therefore so much the more ought ye to resist him, and to listen to us assiduously. For it behoves you, consulting, as having been grievously deceived, to know how he must be charmed. But in no other way is it possible. But by charming I mean the setting yourselves by reason in opposition to their evil counsels, remembering that by promise of knowledge he brought death into the world at the first.

Chap. XIX.—*Not peace, but a sword.*

"Whence the Prophet of the truth, knowing that the world was much in error, and seeing it ranged on the side of evil, did not choose that there should be peace to it while it stood in error. So that till the end he sets himself against all those who are in concord with wickedness, setting [truth] over against error, sending as it were fire upon those who are sober, namely wrath against the seducer, which is likened to a sword,[1] and by holding forth the word he destroys ignorance by knowledge, cutting, as it were, and separating the living from the dead. Therefore, while wickedness is being conquered by lawful knowledge, war has taken hold of all. For the submissive son is, for the sake of salvation, separated from the unbelieving father, or the father from the son, or the mother from the daughter, or the daughter from the mother, and relatives from relatives, and friends from associates.

CHAP. XX.—*What if it be already kindled?*

" And let not any one say, How is this just, that parents should be separated from their children, and children from their parents? It is just, even entirely. For if they remained with them, and, after profiting them nothing, were also destroyed along with them, how is it not just that he who wishes to be saved should be separated from him who will not, but who wishes to destroy him along with himself. Moreover, it is not those who judge better that wish to be separated, but they wish to stay with them, and to profit them by the exposition of better things; and therefore the unbelievers, not wishing to hearken to them, make war against them, banishing, persecuting, hating them. But those who suffer these things, pitying those who are ensnared by ignorance, by the teaching of wisdom pray for those who contrive evil against them, having learned that ignorance is the cause of their sin. For the Teacher Himself, being nailed to [the cross], prayed to the Father that the sin of those who slew Him might be forgiven, saying, ' Father, forgive them their sins, for they know not what they do.'[2] They also therefore, being imitators of the Teacher in their sufferings, pray for those who contrive them, as they have been taught. Therefore they are not separated as hating their parents, since they make constant prayers even for those who are neither parents nor relatives, but enemies, and strive to love them, as they have been commanded.

[1] Matt. x. 34.   [2] Luke xxiii. 34.

CHAP. XXI.—"*If I be a father, where is my fear?*"

"But tell me, how do you love your parents? If, indeed, you do it as always regarding what is right, I congratulate you; but if you love them as it happens, then not so, for then you may on a small occasion become their enemies. But if you love them intelligently, tell me, what are parents? You will say they are the sources of our being. Why, then, do ye not love the [source of the] being of all things, if indeed you have with right understanding elected to do this? But you will now say again, we have not seen Him. Why, then, do ye not seek for Him, but worship senseless things? But what? If it were even difficult for you to know what God is, you cannot fail to know what is not God, so as to reason that God is not wood, nor stone, nor brass, nor anything else made of corruptible matter.

CHAP. XXII.—"*The gods that have not made the heavens.*"

"For are not they graven with iron? And has not the graving iron been softened by fire? And is not the fire itself extinguished with water? And has not the water its motion from the spirit? And has not the spirit the beginning of its course from the God who hath made all things? For thus said the prophet Moses: 'In the beginning God made the heaven and the earth. And the earth was unsightly, and unadorned; and darkness was over the deep: and the Spirit of God was borne above the waters.' Which Spirit, at the bidding of God, as it were His hand, makes all things, dividing light from darkness, and after the invisible heaven spreading out the visible, that the places above might be inhabited by the angels of light, and those below by man, and all the creatures that were made for his use.

CHAP. XXIII.—"*To whom much is given.*"

"For on thy account, O man, God commanded the water to retire upon the face of the earth, that the earth might be able to bring forth fruits for thee. And He made water-courses, that He might provide for thee fountains, and that river-beds might be disclosed, that animals might teem forth; in a word, that He might furnish thee with all things. For is it not for thee that the winds blow, and the rains fall, and the seasons change for the production of fruits? Moreover, it is for thee that the sun and moon, with the other heavenly bodies, accomplish their risings and settings; and rivers and pools, with all fountains, serve thee. Whence to thee, O senseless one, as the greater honour has been given, so for thee, ungrateful, the greater punishment by fire has been prepared, because thou wouldest not know Him whom it behoved thee before all things to know.

CHAP. XXIV.—"*Born of water.*"

"And now from inferior things learn the cause of all, reasoning that water makes all things, and water receives the production of its movement from spirit, and the spirit has its beginning from the God of all. And thus you ought to have reasoned, in order that by reason you might attain to God, that, knowing your origin, and being born again by the first-born water, you may be constituted heir of the parents who have begotten you to incorruption.

CHAP. XXV.—*Good works to be well done.*

"Wherefore come readily, as a son to a father, that God may assign ignorance as the cause of your sins. But if after being called you will not, or delay, you shall be destroyed by the just judgment of God, not being willed, through your not willing. And do not think, though you were more pious than all the pious that ever were, but if you be unbaptized, that you shall ever obtain hope. For all the more, on this account, you shall endure the greater punishment, because you have done excellent works not excellently. For well-doing is excellent when it is done as God has commanded. But if you will not be baptized according to His pleasure, you serve your own will and oppose His counsel.

CHAP. XXVI.—*Baptism.*

"But perhaps some one will say, What does it contribute to

piety to be baptized with water? In the first place, because you do that which is pleasing to God; and in the second place, being born again to God of water, by reason of fear you change your first generation, which is of lust, and thus you are able to obtain salvation. But otherwise it is impossible. For thus the prophet has sworn to us, saying, "Verily I say to you, Unless ye be regenerated by living water into the name of Father, Son, and Holy Spirit, you shall not enter the kingdom of heaven.[1] Wherefore approach. For there is there something that is merciful from the beginning, borne upon the water, and rescues from the future punishment those who are baptized with the thrice-blessed invocation, offering as gifts to God the good deeds of the baptized whenever they are done after their baptism. Wherefore flee to the waters, for this alone can quench the violence of fires. He who will not now come to it still bears the spirit of strife, on account of which he will not approach the living water for his own salvation.

Chap. XXVII.—*All need baptism.*

"Therefore approach, be ye righteous or unrighteous. For if you are righteous, baptism alone is lacking in order to salvation. But if you are unrighteous, come to be baptized for the remission of the sins formerly committed in ignorance. And to the unrighteous man it remains that his well-doing after baptism be according to the proportion of his [previous] impiety. Wherefore, be ye righteous or unrighteous, hasten to be born to God, because delay brings danger, on account of the fore-appointment of death being unrevealed; and show by well-doing your likeness to the Father, who begetteth you of water. As a lover of truth, honour the true God as your Father. But His honour is that you live as He, being righteous, would have you live. And the will of the righteous One is that you do no wrong. But wrong is murder, hatred, envy, and such like; and of these there are many forms.

[1] Altered from John iii. 5.

Chap. XXVIII.—*Purification.*

"However, it is necessary to add something to these things which has not community with man, but is peculiar to the worship of God. I mean purification, not approaching to a man's own wife when she is in separation, for so the law of God commands. But what? If purity be not added to the service of God, you would roll pleasantly like the dung-flies. Wherefore as man, having something more than the irrational animals, namely, rationality, purify your hearts from evil by heavenly reasoning, and wash your bodies in the bath. For purification according to the truth is not that the purity of the body precedes purification after the heart, but that purity follows goodness. For our Teacher also, [dealing with] certain of the Pharisees and Scribes among us, who are separated, and as Scribes know the matters of the law more than others, still He reproved them as hypocrites, because they cleansed only the things that appear to men, but omitted purity of heart and the things seen by God alone.

Chap. XXIX.—*Outward and inward purity.*

"Therefore He made use of this memorable expression, speaking the truth with respect to the hypocrites of them, not with respect to all. For to some He said that obedience was to be rendered, because they were entrusted with the chair of Moses. However, to the hypocrites he said, 'Woe to you, Scribes and Pharisees, hypocrites, for ye make clean the outside of the cup and the platter, but the inside is full of filth. Thou blind Pharisee, cleanse first the inside of the cup and the platter, that their outsides may be clean also.' And truly: for when the mind is enlightened by knowledge, the disciple is able to be good, and thereupon purity follows; for from the understanding within a good care of the body without is produced. As from negligence with respect to the body, care of the understanding cannot be produced, so the pure man can purify both that which is without and that which is within. And he who, purifying the things without, does it looking to the praise of men, and by the praise of those who look on, he has nothing from God.

CHAP. XXX.—" *Whatsoever things are pure.*"

"But who is there to whom it is not manifest that it is better not to have intercourse with a woman in her separation, but purified and washed. And also after copulation it is proper to wash. But if you grudge to do this, recall to mind how you followed after the parts of purity when you served senseless idols; and be ashamed that now, when it is necessary to attain, I say not more, but to attain the one and whole of purity, you are more slothful. Consider, therefore, Him who made you, and you will understand who He is that casts upon you this sluggishness with respect to purity.

CHAP. XXXI.—" *What do ye more than others?*"

"But some one of you will say, Must we then do whatsoever things we did while we were idolaters? I say to you, Not all things; but whatsoever you did well, you must do now, and more: for whatsoever is well done in error hangs upon truth, as if anything be ill done in the truth it is from error. Receive, therefore, from all quarters the things that are your own, and not those that are another's, and do not say, If those who are in error do anything well we are not bound to do it. For, on this principle, if any one who worships idols do not commit murder, we ought to commit murder, because he who is in error does not commit it.

CHAP. XXXII.—" *To whom much is given.*"

"No; but rather, if those who are in error do not kill, let us not be angry; if he who is in error do not commit adultery, let us not lust even in the smallest degree; if he who is in error loves him who loves him, let us love even those who hate us; if he who is in error lends to those who have, let us [give] to those who have not. Unquestionably we ought—we who hope to inherit eternal life—to do better things than the good things that are done by those who know only the present life, knowing that if their works, being judged with ours in the day of judgment, be found equal in goodness, we shall have shame, and they perdition, having acted against themselves through error. And I say that we shall be put to shame on this account, because we have not done more than they, though we have known more than they. And if we shall be put to shame if we show well-doing equal to theirs, and no more, how much more if we show less than their well-doing?

CHAP. XXXIII.—*The queen of the south and the men of Nineveh.*

"But that indeed in the day of judgment the doings of those who have known the truth are compared with the good deeds of those who have been in error, the unlying One Himself has taught us, saying to those who neglected to come and listen to Him, 'The queen of the south shall rise up with this generation, and shall condemn it; because she came from the extremities of the earth to hear the wisdom of Solomon: and behold, a greater than Solomon is here,'[1] and ye do not believe Him. And to those amongst the people who would not repent at His preaching He said, 'The men of Nineveh shall rise up with this generation and shall condemn it, for they heard and repented on the preaching of Jonas: and behold, a greater is here, and no one believes.'[2] And thus, setting over against all their impiety those from among the Gentiles who have done [well], in order to condemn those who, possessing the true religion, had not acted so well as those who were in error, he exhorted those having reason not only to do equally with the Gentiles whatsoever things are excellent, but more than they. And this speech has been suggested to me, taking occasion from the necessity of respecting the separation, and of washing after copulation, and of not denying such purity, though those who are in error do the same, since those who in error do well, without being saved, are for the condemnation of those who are in the worship of God, [and do ill]; because their

[1] Matt. xii. 42.   [2] Luke xi. 32.

respect for purity is through error, and not through the worship of the true Father and God of all."

CHAP. XXXIV.—*Peter's daily work.*

Having said this, he dismissed the multitudes; and according to his custom, having partaken of food with those dearest to him, he went to rest. And thus doing and discoursing day by day, he strongly buttressed the law of God, challenging the reputed gods with the reputed *genesis*, and arguing that there is no automatism, but that the world is governed according to providence.

CHAP. XXXV.—*"Beware of false prophets."*

Then after three months were fulfilled, he ordered me to fast for several days, and then brought me to the fountains that are near to the sea, and baptized me as in ever-flowing water. Thus, therefore, when our brethren rejoiced at my God-gifted regeneration, not many days after he turned to the elders in presence of all the church, and charged them, saying: " Our Lord and Prophet, who hath sent us, declared to us that the wicked one, having disputed with Him forty days, and having prevailed nothing against Him, promised that he would send apostles from amongst his subjects, to deceive. Wherefore, above all, remember to shun apostle or teacher or prophet who does not first accurately compare his preaching with [that of] James, who was called the brother of my Lord, and to whom was entrusted to administer the church of the Hebrews in Jerusalem,—and that even though he come to you with witnesses;[1] lest the wickedness which disputed forty days with the Lord, and prevailed nothing, should afterwards, like lightning falling from heaven upon the earth, send a preacher to your injury, as now he has sent Simon upon us, preaching, under pretence of the truth, in the name of the Lord, and sowing error. Wherefore He who hath sent us, said, 'Many shall come to me in sheep's cloth-

---

[1] A conjectural reading, which seems probable, is, Unless he come to you with credentials, viz. from James.

ing, but inwardly they are ravening wolves. By their fruits ye shall know them.'"

CHAP. XXXVI.—*Farewell to Tripolis.*

Having spoken thus, he sent the harbingers into Antioch of Syria, bidding them expect him there forthwith. Then when they had gone, Peter having driven away diseases, sufferings, and demons from great multitudes who were persuaded, and having baptized them in the fountains which are near to the sea, and having celebrated[1] the eucharist, and having appointed Maroones, who had received him into his house, and was now perfected, as their bishop, and having set apart twelve elders, and having designated deacons, and arranged matters relating to widows, and having discoursed on the common good what was profitable for the ordering of the church, and having counselled them to obey the bishop Maroones, three months being now fulfilled, he bade those in Tripolis of Phœnicia farewell, and took his journey to Antioch of Syria, all the people accompanying us with due honour.

[1] Literally, "having broken."

HOMILY XII.

Chap. I.—*Two bands.*

THEREFORE starting from Tripolis of Phœnicia to go to Antioch of Syria, on the same day we came to Orthasia, and there stayed. And on account of its being near the city which we had left, almost all having heard the preaching before, we stopped there only one day, and set out to Antaradus. And as there were many who journeyed with us, Peter, addressing Nicetus and Aquila, said, "Inasmuch as the great crowd of those who journey with us draws upon us no little envy as we enter city after city, I have thought that we must of necessity arrange, so that neither, on the one hand, these may be grieved at being prevented from accompanying us, nor, on the other hand, we, by being so conspicuous, may fall under the envy of the wicked.[1] Wherefore I wish you, Nicetus and Aquila, to go before me in two separate bodies, and enter secretly into the Gentile cities.

Chap. II.—*Love of preachers and their converts.*

"I know, indeed, that you are distressed at being told to do this, being separated from me by a space of two days. I would have you know, therefore, that we the persuaders love you the persuaded much more than you love us who have persuaded you. Therefore loving one another as we do by not unreasonably doing what we wish, let us provide, as much as in us lies, for safety. For I prefer, as you also know, [to go] into the more notable cities of the provinces, and to remain some days, and discourse. And for the pre-

---

[1] Literally, " of wickedness."

sent lead the way into the neighbouring Laodicea, and, after two or three days, so far as it depends upon my choice, I shall overtake you. And do you alone receive me at the gates, on account of the confusion, that thus we may enter along with you without tumult. And thence, in like manner, after some days' stay, others in your stead will go forward by turns to the places beyond, preparing lodgings for us."

Chap. III.—*Submission.*

When Peter had thus spoken they were compelled to acquiesce, saying, "It does not altogether grieve us, my lord, to do this on account of its being your command; in the first place, indeed, because you have been chosen by the providence of God, as being worthy to think and counsel well in all things; and in addition to this, for the most part we shall be separated from you only for two days by the necessity of preceding you. And that were indeed a long time to be without sight of thee, O Peter, did we not consider that they will be more grieved who are sent much farther forward, being ordered to wait for thee longer in every city, distressed that they are longer deprived of the sight of thy longed-for countenance. And we, though not less distressed than they, make no opposition, because you order us to do it for profit." Thus, having spoken, they went forward, having it in charge that at the first stage they should address the accompanying multitude that they should enter the cities apart from one another.

Chap. IV.—*Clement's joy.*

When, therefore, they had gone, I, Clement, rejoiced greatly that he had ordered me to remain with himself. Then I answered and said, "I thank God that you have not sent me away as you have done the others, as I should have died of grief." But he said, "But what? If there shall ever be any necessity that you be sent away for the sake of teaching, would you, on account of being separated for a little while from me, and that for an advantageous purpose, would you die for that? Would you not rather impress upon yourself the duty of bearing the things that are arranged for you through necessity, and cheerfully submit? And do you not know that friends are present with one another in their memories, although they are separated bodily; whereas some, being bodily present, wander from their friends in their souls, by reason of want of memory?"

Chap. V.—*Clement's office of service.*

Then I answered, "Do not think, my lord, that I should endure that grief foolishly, but with some good reason. For since I hold you, my lord, in place of all, father, mother, brothers, relatives, you who are the means through God of my having the saving truth, holding you in place of all, I have the greatest consolation. And in addition to this, being afraid of my natural youthful lust, I was concerned lest, being left by you (being but a young man, and having now such a resolution that it would be impossible to desert you without incurring the anger of God,)[1] I should be overcome by lust. But since it is much better and safer for me to remain with you, when my mind is with good reason set upon venerating, therefore I pray that I may always remain with you. Moreover, I remember you saying in Cæsarea, 'If any one wishes to journey with me, let him piously journey.' And by *piously* you meant, that those who are devoted to the worship of God should grieve no one in respect of God, such as by leaving parents, an attached wife, or any others.[2] Whence I am in all respects a fitting fellow-traveller for you, to whom, if you would confer the greatest favour, you would allow to perform the functions of a servant."

Chap. VI.—*Peter's frugality.*

Then Peter, hearing, smiled and said, "What think you, then, O Clement? Do you not think that you are placed by very necessity in the position of my servant? For who else

---

[1] Here the text is hopelessly corrupt, and the meaning can only be guessed at.

[2] I have ventured to make a very slight change on the reading here, so as to bring out what I suppose to be the sense.

shall take care of those many splendid tunics, with all my changes of rings and sandals? And who shall make ready those pleasant and artistic dainties, which, being so various, need many skilful cooks, and all those things which are procured with great eagerness, and are prepared for the appetite of effeminate men as for some great wild beast? However, such a choice has occurred to you, perhaps, without you understanding or knowing my manner of life, that I use only bread and olives, and rarely pot-herbs; and that this is my only coat and cloak which I wear; and I have no need of any of them, nor of aught else: for even in these I abound. For my mind, seeing all the eternal good things that are there, regards none of the things that are here. However, I accept of your good will; and I admire and commend you, for that you, a man of refined habits, have so easily submitted your manner of living to your necessities. For we, from our childhood, both I and Andrew, my brother, who is also my brother as respects God, not only being brought up in the condition of orphans, but also accustomed to labour through poverty and misfortune, easily bear the discomforts of our present journeys. Whence, if you would obey me, you would allow me, a working man, to fulfil the part of a servant to you."

CHAP. VII.—"*Not to be ministered unto, but to minister.*"

But I, when I heard this, fell a-trembling and weeping, that such a word should be spoken by a man to whom all the men of this generation are inferior in point of knowledge and piety. But he, seeing me weeping, asked the cause of my tears. Then I said, "In what have I sinned so that you have spoken to me such a word?" Then Peter answered, "If it were wrong of me to speak of being your servant, you were first in fault in asking to be mine." Then I said, "The cases are not parallel; for to do this indeed becomes me well; but it is terrible for you, the herald of God, and who savest our souls, to do this to me." Then Peter answered, "I should agree with you, but that[1] our Lord, who came for the salvation of

[1] A negative particle seems to be dropped from the text.

all the world, being alone noble above all, submitted to the condition of a servant, that He might persuade us not to be ashamed to perform the ministrations of servants to our brethren, however well-born we may be." Then I said, "If I think to overcome you in argument, I am foolish. However, I thank the providence of God, that I have been thought worthy to have you instead of parents."

Chap. VIII.—*Family history.*

Then Peter inquired, "Are you really, then, alone in your family?" Then I answered, "There are indeed many and great men, being of the kindred of Cæsar. Wherefore Cæsar himself gave a wife of his own family to my father, who was his foster-brother; and of her three sons of us were born, two before me, who were twins and very like each other, as my father told me. But I scarcely know either them or our mother, but bear about with me an obscure image of them, as through dreams. My mother's name was Mattidia, and my father's, Faustin; and of my brothers one was called Faustinus, and the other Faustinianus. Then after I, their third son, was born, my mother saw a vision—so my father told me—[which told her,] that unless she immediately took away her twin sons, and left the city of Rome for exile for twelve years, she and they must die by an all-destructive fate.

Chap. IX.—*The lost ones.*

"Therefore my father, being fond of his children, supplying them suitably for the journey with male and female servants, put them on board ship, and sent them to Athens with her to be educated, and kept me alone of his sons with him for his comfort; and for this I am very thankful, that the vision had not ordered me also to depart with my mother from the city of Rome. Then, after the lapse of a year, my father sent money to them to Athens, and at the same time to learn how they did. But those who went on this errand did not return. And in the third year, my father being distressed, sent others in like manner with supplies, and they returned in the fourth year with the tidings that they had seen neither my mother nor my brothers, nor had they ever arrived at Athens, nor had they found any trace of any one of those who set out with them.

CHAP. X.—*The seeker lost.*

"Then my father, hearing this, and being stupefied with excessive grief, and not knowing where to go in quest of them, used to take me with him and go down to the harbour, and inquire of many where any one of them had seen or heard of a shipwreck four years ago. And one turned one place, and another another. Then he inquired whether they had seen the body of a woman with [two] children cast ashore. And when they told him that they had seen many corpses in many places, my father groaned at the information. But, with his bowels yearning, he asked unreasonable questions, that he might try to search so great an extent of sea. However, he was pardonable, because, through affection towards those whom he was seeking for, he fed on vain hopes. And at last, placing me under guardians, and leaving me at Rome when I was twelve years old, he himself, weeping, went down to the harbour, and went on board ship, and set out upon the search. And from that day till this I have neither received a letter from him, nor do I know whether he be alive or dead. But I rather suspect that he is dead somewhere, either overcome by grief, or perished by shipwreck. And the proof of that is that it is now the twentieth year that I have heard no true intelligence concerning him."

CHAP. XI.—*The afflictions of the righteous.*

But Peter, hearing this, wept through sympathy, and immediately said to the gentlemen who were present: "If any worshipper of God had suffered these things, such as this man's father hath suffered, he would immediately have assigned the cause of it to be his worship of God, ascribing it to the wicked one. Thus also it is the lot of the wretched Gentiles to suffer; and we worshippers of God know it not. But with good reason I call them wretched, because here they are ensnared, and the hope that is thine they obtain not. For those who in the worship of God suffer afflictions, suffer them for the expiation of their transgressions."

CHAP. XII.—*A pleasure trip.*

When Peter had spoken thus, a certain one amongst us ventured to invite him, in the name of all, that next day, early in the morning, he should sail to Aradus, an island opposite, distant, I suppose, not quite thirty stadia, for the purpose of seeing two pillars of vine-wood that were there, and that were of very great girth. Therefore the indulgent Peter consented, saying, "When you leave the boat, do not go many of you together to see the things that you desire to see; for I do not wish that the attention of the inhabitants should be turned to you." And so we sailed, and in short time arrived at the island. Then landing from the boat, we went to the place where the vine-wood pillars were, and along with them we looked at several of the works of Phidias.

CHAP. XIII.—*A woman of a sorrowful spirit.*

But Peter alone did not think it worth while to look at the sights that were there; but noticing a certain woman sitting outside before the doors, begging constantly for her support, he said to her, "O woman, is any of your limbs defective, that you submit to such disgrace—I mean that of begging,—and do not rather work with the hands which God has given you, and procure your daily food?" But she, groaning, answered, "Would that I had hands able to work! But now they retain only the form of hands, being dead and rendered useless by my gnawing of them." Then Peter asked her, "What is the cause of your suffering so terribly?" And she answered, "Weakness of soul; and nought else. For if I had the mind of a man, there was a precipice or a pool whence I should have thrown myself, and have been able to rest from my tormenting misfortunes."

CHAP. XIV.—*Balm in Gilead.*

Then said Peter, "What then? Do you suppose, O

woman, that those who destroy themselves are freed from punishment? Are not the souls of those who thus die punished with a worse punishment in Hades for their suicide?" But she said, "Would that I were persuaded that souls are really found alive in Hades; then I should love death, making light of the punishment, that I might see, were it but for an hour, my longed-for sons!" Then said Peter, "What is it that grieves you? I should like to know, O woman. For if you inform me, in return for this favour, I shall satisfy you that souls live in Hades; and instead of precipice or pool, I shall give you a drug, that you may live and die without torment."

CHAP. XV.—*The woman's story.*

Then the woman, not understanding what was spoken ambiguously, being pleased with the promise, began to speak thus:—"Were I to speak of my family and my country, I do not suppose that I should be able to persuade any one. But of what consequence is it to you to learn this, excepting only the reason why in my anguish I have deadened my hands by gnawing them? Yet I shall give you an account of myself, so far as it is in your power to hear it. I, being very nobly born, by the arrangement of a certain man in authority, became the wife of a man who was related to him. And first I had twin sons, and afterwards another son. But my husband's brother, being thoroughly mad, was enamoured of wretched me, who exceedingly affected chastity. And I, wishing neither to consent to my lover nor to expose to my husband his brother's love of me, reasoned thus: that I may neither defile myself by the commission of adultery nor disgrace my husband's bed, nor set brother at war with brother, nor subject the whole family, which is a great one, to the reproach of all, as I said. I reasoned that it was best for me to leave the city for some time with my twin children, until the impure love should cease of him who flattered me to my disgrace. The other son, however, I left with his father, to remain for a comfort to him.

CHAP. XVI.—*The shipwreck.*

"However, that matters might be thus arranged, I resolved to fabricate a dream, to the effect that some one stood by me by night, and thus spoke: 'O woman, straightway leave the city with your twin children for some time, until I shall charge you to return hither again; otherwise you forthwith shall die miserably, with your husband and all your children.' And so I did. For as soon as I told the false dream to my husband, he being alarmed, sent me off by ship to Athens with my two sons, and with slaves, maids, and abundance of money, to educate the boys, until, said he, it shall please the giver of the oracle that you return to me. But, wretch that I am, while sailing with my children, I was driven by the fury of the winds into these regions, and the ship having gone to pieces in the night, I was wrecked. And all the rest having died, my unfortunate self alone was tossed by a great wave and cast upon a rock; and while I sat upon it in my misery, I was prevented, by the hope of finding my children alive, from throwing myself into the deep then, when I could easily have done it, having my soul made drunk by the waves.

CHAP. XVII.—*The fruitless search.*

"But when the day dawned, I shouted aloud, and howled miserably, and looked around, seeking for the dead bodies of my hapless children. Therefore the inhabitants took pity on me, and seeing me naked, they first clothed me and then sounded the deep, seeking for my children. And when they found nothing of what they sought, some of the hospitable women came to me to comfort me, and every one told her own misfortunes, that I might obtain comfort from the occurrences of similar misfortunes. But this only grieved me the more; for I said that I was not so wicked that I could take comfort from the misfortunes of others. And so, when many of them asked me to accept their hospitality, a certain poor woman with much urgency constrained me to come into her cottage, saying to me, 'Take courage, woman, for my husband, who was a sailor, also died at sea, while he was still in the bloom of his youth; and ever since, though many have asked me in marriage, I have preferred living as a widow, regretting the loss of my husband. But we shall have in common whatever we can both earn with our hands.'

CHAP. XVIII.—*Trouble upon trouble.*

" And not to lengthen out unnecessary details, I went to live with her, on account of her love to her husband. And not long after, my hands were debilitated by my gnawing of them; and the woman who had taken me in, being wholly seized by some malady, is confined in the house. Since then the former compassion of the woman has declined, and I and the woman of the house are both of us helpless. For a long time I have sat here, as you see, begging; and whatever I get I convey to my fellow-sufferer for our support. Let this suffice about my affairs. For the rest, what hinders your fulfilling of your promise to give me the drug, that I may give it to her also, who desires to die; and thus I also, as you said, shall be able to escape from life?"

CHAP. XIX.—*Evasions.*

While the woman thus spoke, Peter seemed to be in suspense on account of many reasonings. But I came up and said, "I have been going about seeking you for a long time. And now, what is in hand?" But Peter ordered me to lead the way, and wait for him at the boat; and because there was no gainsaying when he commanded, I did as I was ordered. But Peter, as he afterwards related the whole matter to me, being struck in his heart with some slight suspicion, inquired of the woman, saying, "Tell me, O woman, your family, and your city, and the names of your children, and presently I shall give you the drug." But she, being put under constraint, and not wishing to speak, yet being eager to obtain the drug, cunningly said one thing for another. And so she said that she was an Ephesian, and her husband a Sicilian; and in like manner she changed the names of the three children. Then Peter, supposing that she spoke the truth, said, "Alas! O woman, I thought that this day was to bring you great joy, suspecting that you are a certain person of whom I was thinking, and whose affairs I have heard and accurately know." But she adjured him, saying, "Tell me, I entreat of you, that I may know if there is among women any one more wretched than myself."

CHAP. XX.—*Peter's account of the matter.*

Then Peter, not knowing that she had spoken falsely, through pity towards her, began to tell her the truth: "There is a certain young man in attendance upon me, thirsting after the discourses on religion, a Roman citizen, who told me how that, having a father and two twin brothers, he has lost sight of them all. For," says he, "my mother, as my father related to me, having seen a vision, left the city Rome for a time with her twin children, lest she should perish by an evil fate, and having gone away with them, she cannot be found; and her husband, the young man's father, having gone in search of her, he also cannot be found."

CHAP. XXI.—*A disclosure.*

While Peter thus spoke, the woman, who had listened attentively, swooned away as if in stupor. But Peter approached her, and caught hold of her, and exhorted her to restrain herself, persuading her to confess what was the matter with her. But she, being powerless in the rest of her body, as through intoxication, turned her [head] round, being able to sustain the greatness of the hoped-for joy, and rubbing her face: "Where," said she, "is this youth?" And he, now seeing through the whole affair, said, "Tell me first; for otherwise you cannot see him." Then she earnestly said, "I am that youth's mother." Then said Peter, "What is his name?" And she said, "Clement." Then Peter said, "It is the same, and he it was that spoke to me a little while ago, whom I ordered to wait for me in the boat. And she, falling at Peter's feet, entreated him to make haste to come to the boat." Then Peter, "If you will keep terms with me, I shall do so." Then she said, "I will do anything; only show me my only child. For I shall seem to see in him my two children who died here." Then Peter said, "When ye see him, be quiet, until we depart from the island." And she said, "I will."

CHAP. XXII.—*The lost found.*

Peter, therefore, took her by the hand, and led her to the boat. But I, when I saw him leading the woman by the hand, laughed, and approaching, offered to lead her instead of him, to his honour. But as soon as I touched her hand, she gave a motherly shout, and embraced me violently, and eagerly kissed me as her son. But I, being ignorant of the whole affair, shook her off as a madwoman. But, through my respect for Peter, I checked myself.

CHAP. XXIII.—*Reward of hospitality.*

But Peter said, "Alas! What are you doing, my son Clement, shaking off your real mother?" But I, when I heard this, wept, and falling down by my mother, who had fallen, I kissed her. For as soon as this was told me, I in some way recalled her appearance indistinctly. Then great crowds ran together to see the beggar woman, telling one another that her son had recognised her, and that he was a man of consideration. Then, when we would have straightway left the island with my mother, she said to us, "My much longed-for son, it is right that I should bid farewell to the woman who entertained me, who, being poor and wholly debilitated, lies in the house." And Peter hearing this, and all the multitude who stood by, admired the good disposition of the woman. And immediately Peter ordered some persons to go and bring the woman on her couch. And as soon as the couch was brought and set down, Peter said, in the hearing of the whole multitude, "If I be a herald of the truth, in order to the faith of the bystanders, that they may know that there is one God, who made the world, let her straightway rise whole." And while Peter was still speaking, the woman arose healed, and fell down before Peter, and kissed her dear associate, and asked her what it all meant. Then she briefly detailed to her the whole business of the recognition, to the astonishment of the hearers. Then also my mother, seeing her hostess cured, entreated that she herself also might obtain healing. And his placing his hand upon her, cured her also.

CHAP. XXIV.—*All well arranged.*

And then Peter having discoursed concerning God and the service accorded to Him, he concluded as follows: "If any one wishes to learn these things accurately, let him come to Antioch, where I have resolved to remain some length of time, and learn the things that pertain to his salvation. For if you are familiar with leaving your country for the sake of trading or of warfare, and coming to far-off places, you should not be unwilling to go three days' journey for the sake of eternal salvation." Then, after the address of Peter, I presented the woman who had been healed, in the presence of all the multitude, with a thousand drachmas, for her support, giving her in charge to a certain good man, who was the chief man of the city, and who of his own accord joyfully undertook the charge. Further, having distributed money amongst many other women, and thanked those who at any time had comforted my mother, I sailed away to Antaradus, along with my mother, and Peter, and the rest of our companions; and thus we proceeded to our lodging.

CHAP. XXV.—*Philanthropy and friendship.*

And when we were arrived and had partaken of food, and given thanks according to our custom, there being still time, I said to Peter: "My lord Peter, my mother has done a work of philanthropy in remembering the woman her hostess." And Peter answered, "Have you indeed, O Clement, thought truly that your mother did a work of philanthropy in respect of her treatment of the woman who took her in after her shipwreck, or have you spoken this word by way of greatly complimenting your mother? But if you spoke truly, and not by way of compliment, you seem to me not to know what the greatness of philanthropy is, which is affection towards any one whatever in respect of his being a man, apart from physical persuasion. But not even do I venture to call the hostess who received your mother after her shipwreck, philanthropic; for she was impelled by pity, and persuaded to become the benefactress of a woman who had been shipwrecked, who was grieving for her children,—a stranger, naked, destitute, and greatly deploring her misfortunes. When, therefore, she was in such circumstances, who that saw her, though he were impious, could but pity her? So that it does not seem to me that even the stranger-receiving woman did a work of philanthropy, but to have been moved to assist her by pity for her innumerable misfortunes. And how much more is it true of your mother, that when she was in prosperous circumstances and requited her hostess, she did a deed, not of philanthropy, but of friendship! for there is much difference between friendship and philanthropy, because friendship springs from requital. But philanthropy, apart from physical persuasion, loves and benefits every man as he is a man. If, therefore, while she pitied her hostess, she also pitied and did good to her enemies who have wronged her, she would be philanthropic; but if, on one account she is friendly or hostile, and on another account is hostile or friendly, such an one is the friend or enemy of some quality, not of man as man."

CHAP. XXVI.—*What is philanthropy?*

Then I answered, "Do you not think, then, that even the stranger-receiver was philanthropic, who did good to a stranger whom she did not know?" Then Peter said, "Compassionate, indeed, I can call her, but I dare not call her philanthropic, just as I cannot call a mother philoteknic, for she is prevailed on to have an affection for them by her pangs, and by her rearing of them. As the lover also is gratified by the company and enjoyment of his mistress, and the friend by return of friendship, so also the compassionate man by misfortune. However the compassionate man is near to the philanthropic, in that he is impelled, apart from hunting after the receipt of anything, to do the kindness. But he is not yet philanthropic." Then I said, " By what deeds, then, can any one be philanthropic?" And Peter answered, "Since I see that you are eager to hear what is the work of philanthropy, I shall not object to telling you. He is the philanthropic man who does good even to his enemies. And that it is so, listen : Philanthropy is masculo-feminine; and the feminine part of it is called *compassion*, and the male part is named love to our neighbour. But every man is neighbour to every man, and not merely this man or that; for the good and the bad, the friend and the enemy, are alike men. It behoves, therefore, him who practises philanthropy to be an imitator of God, doing good to the righteous and the unrighteous, as God Himself vouchsafes His sun and His heavens to all in the present world. But if you will do good to the good, but not to the evil, or even will punish them, you undertake to do the work of a judge, you do not strive to hold by philanthropy."

CHAP. XXVII.—*Who can judge?*

Then I said, "Then even God, who, as you teach us, is at some time to judge, is not philanthropic." Then said Peter, "You assert a contradiction; for because He shall judge, on that very account He is philanthropic. For he who loves and compassionates those who have been wronged, avenges those who have wronged them." Then I said, "If, then, I also do good to the good, and punish the wrong-doers in respect of their injuring men, am I not philanthropic?" And Peter answered, "If along with knowledge[1] you had also authority to judge, you would do this rightly on account of your having received authority to judge those whom God made, and on account of your knowledge infallibly justifying some as the righteous, and condemning some as unrighteous." Then I said, "You have spoken rightly and truly; for it is impossible for any one who has not knowledge to judge rightly. For sometimes some persons seem good, though they perpetrate wickedness in secret, and some good persons are conceived to be bad through the accusation of their enemies. But even

---

[1] The word repeatedly rendered *knowledge* and once *omniscience* in this passage, properly signifies *foreknowledge*. The argument shows clearly that it means omniscience, of which foreknowledge is the most signal manifestation.

if one judges, having the power of torturing and examining, not even so should he altogether judge righteously. For some persons, being murderers, have sustained the tortures, and have come off as innocent; while others, being innocent, have not been able to sustain the tortures, but have confessed falsely against themselves, and have been punished as guilty."

CHAP. XXVIII.—*Difficulty of judging.*

Then said Peter, "These things are ordinary: now hear what is greater. There are some men whose sins or good deeds are partly their own, and partly those of others; but it is right that each one be punished for his own sins, and rewarded for his own merits. But it is impossible for any one except a prophet, who alone has omniscience, to know with respect to the things that are done by any one, which are his own, and which are not; for all are seen as done by him." Then I said, "I would learn how some of men's wrong-doings or right-doings are their own, and some belong to others."

CHAP. XXIX.—*Sufferings of the good.*

Then Peter answered, "The prophet of the truth has said, 'Good things must needs come, and blessed, said he, is he by whom they come; in like manner evil things must needs come, but woe to him through whom they come.'[1] But if evil things come by means of evil men, and good things are brought by good men, it must needs be in each man as his own to be either good or bad, and proceeding from what he has proposed, in order to the coming of the subsequent good or evil,[2] which, being of his own choice, are not arranged by the providence of God to come from him. This being so, this is the judgment of God, that he who, as by a combat, comes through all misfortune and is found blameless, he is deemed worthy of eternal life; for those who by their own will continue in goodness, are tempted by those who continue in evil by their own will, being persecuted, hated, slandered, plotted

---

[1] An incorrect quotation from Matt. xviii., Luke xvii.
[2] This from a various reading.

against, struck, cheated, accused, tortured, disgraced,—suffering all these things by which it seems reasonable that they should be enraged and stirred up to vengeance.

CHAP. XXX.—*Offences must come.*

"But the Master knowing that those who wrongfully do these things are guilty by means of their former sins, and that the spirit of wickedness works these things by means of the guilty, has counselled to compassionate men, as they are men, and as being the instruments of wickedness through sin; [and this counsel] He has given to His disciples as claiming philanthropy, and, as much as in us lies, to absolve the wrong-doers from condemnation, that, as it were, the temperate may help the drunken, by prayers, fastings, and benedictions, not resisting, not avenging, lest they should compel them to sin more. For when a person is condemned by any one to suffer, it is not reasonable for him to be angry with him by whose means the suffering comes; for he ought to reason, that if he had not ill-used him, yet because he was to be ill-used, he must have suffered it by means of another. Why, then, should I be angry with the dispenser, when I was condemned at all events to suffer? But yet, further: if we do these same things to the evil on pretence of revenge, we who are good do the very things which the evil do, excepting that they do them first, and we second; and, as I said, we ought not to be angry, as knowing that in the providence of God, the evil punish the good. Those, therefore, who are bitter against their punishers, sin, as disdaining the messengers of God; but those who honour them, and set themselves in opposition to those who think to injure them,[1] are pious towards God who has thus decreed."

CHAP. XXXI.—"*Howbeit, they meant it not.*"

To this I answered, "Those, therefore, who do wrong are not guilty, because they wrong the just by the judgment of God." Then Peter said, "They indeed sin greatly, for they have given themselves to sin. Wherefore knowing this,

[1] That is, I suppose, who render good for evil.

[God] chooses from among them [some] to punish those who righteously repented of their former sins, that the evil things done by the just before their repentance may be remitted through this punishment. But to the wicked who punish and desire to ill-use them, and will not repent, it is permitted to ill-use the righteous for the filling up of their own punishment. For without the will of God, not even a sparrow can fall into a girn.[1] Thus even the hairs of the righteous are numbered by God.

Chap. XXXII.—*The golden rule.*

"But he is righteous who for the sake of what is reasonable fights with nature. For example, it is natural to all to love those who love them. But the righteous man tries also to love his enemies and to bless those who slander him, and even to pray for his enemies, and to compassionate those who do him wrong. Wherefore also he refrains from doing wrong, and blesses those who curse him, pardons those who strike him, and submits to those who persecute him, and salutes those who do not salute him, shares such things as he has with those who have not, persuades him that is angry with him, conciliates his enemy, exhorts the disobedient, instructs the unbelieving, comforts the mourner; being distressed, he endures; being ungratefully treated, he is not angry. But having devoted himself to love his neighbour as himself, he is not afraid of poverty, but becomes poor by sharing his possessions with those who have none. But neither does he punish the sinner. For he who loves his neighbour as himself, as he knows that when he has sinned he does not wish to be punished, so neither does he punish those who sin. And as he wishes to be praised, and blessed, and honoured, and to have all his sins forgiven, thus he does to his neighbour, loving him as himself.[2] In one word, what he wishes for himself, he wishes also for his neighbour. For this is the law of God and of the prophets;[3] this is the doctrine of truth. And this perfect love towards every man is the male part of philanthropy, but the female part of it is compassion; that

[1] See Luke xii. 6, 7.   [2] Matt. xxii. 39.   [3] Matt. vii. 12.

is, to feed the hungry,[1] to give drink to the thirsty, to clothe the naked, to visit the sick, to take in the stranger, to show herself to, and help to the utmost of her power, him who is in prison, and, in short, to have compassion on him who is in misfortune."

CHAP. XXXIII.—*Fear and love.*

But I, hearing this, said: "These things, indeed, it is impossible to do; but to do good to enemies, bearing all their insolences, I do not think can possibly be in human nature." Then Peter answered: "You have said truly; for philanthropy, being the cause of immortality, is given for much." Then I said, "How then is it possible to get it in the mind?" Then Peter answered: "O beloved Clement, the way to get it is this: if any one be persuaded that enemies, ill-using for a time those whom they hate, become the cause to them of deliverances from eternal punishment; and forthwith he will ardently love them as benefactors. But the way to get it, O dear Clement, is but one, which is the fear of God. For he who fears God cannot indeed from the first love his neighbour as himself; for such an order does not occur to the soul. But by the fear of God he is able to do the things of those who love; and thus, while he does the deeds of love, the bride *Love* is, as it were, brought to the bridegroom *Fear*. And thus this bride, bringing forth philanthropic thoughts, makes her possessor immortal, as an accurate image of God, which cannot be subject in its nature to corruption." Thus while he expounded to us the doctrine of philanthropy, the evening having set in, we turned to sleep.

[1] Matt. xxv. 35, 36.

HOMILY XIII.

CHAP. I.—*Journey to Laodicea.*

NOW at break of day Peter entered, and said: "Clement, and his mother Mattidia, and my wife, must take their seats immediately on the waggon." And so they did straightway. And as we were hastening along the road to Balanææ, my mother asked me how my father was; and I said: "My father went in search of you, and of my twin brothers Faustinus and Faustinianus, and is now nowhere to be found. But I fancy he must have died long ago, either perishing by shipwreck, or losing his way,[1] or wasted away by grief." When she heard this, she burst into tears, and groaned through grief; but the joy which she felt at finding me, mitigated in some degree the painfulness of her recollections. And so we all went down together to Balanææ. And on the following day we went to Paltus, and from that to Gabala; and on the next day we reached Laodicea. And, lo! before the gates of the city Nicetas and Aquila met us, and embracing us, brought us to our lodging. Now Peter, seeing that the city was beautiful and great, said: "It is worth our while to stay here for some days; for, generally speaking, a populous place is most capable of yielding us those whom we seek."[2] Nicetas and Aquila asked me who that strange woman was; and I said: "My mother, whom God, through my lord Peter, has granted me to recognise."

---

[1] Cotelerius conjectured σφαγέντα for σφαλέντα—"being slain on our journey."

[2] The first Epitome explains "those whom we seek" as those who are worthy to share in Christ or in Christ's gospel.

CHAP. II.—*Peter relates to Nicetas and Aquila the history of Clement and his family.*

On my saying this, Peter gave them a summary account of all the incidents,—how, when they had gone on before, I Clement had explained to him my descent, the journey undertaken by my mother with her twin children on the false pretext of the dream; and furthermore, the journey undertaken by my father in search of her; and then how Peter himself, after hearing this, went into the island, met with the woman, saw her begging, and asked the reason of her so doing; and then ascertained who she was, and her mode of life, and the feigned dream, and the names of her children —that is, the name borne by me, who was left with my father, and the names of the twin children who travelled along with her, and who, she supposed, had perished in the deep.

CHAP. III.—*Recognition of Nicetas and Aquila.*

Now when this summary narrative had been given by Peter, Nicetas and Aquila in amazement said: "Is this indeed true, O Ruler and Lord of the universe, or is it a dream?" And Peter said: "Unless we are asleep, it certainly is true." On this they waited for a little in deep meditation, and then said: "We are Faustinus and Faustinianus. From the commencement of your conversation we looked at each other, and conjectured much with regard to ourselves, whether what was said had reference to us or not; for we reflected that many coincidences take place in life. Wherefore we remained silent while our hearts beat fast. But when you came to the end of your narrative, we saw clearly[1] that your statements referred to us, and then we avowed who we were." And on saying this, bathed in tears, they rushed in to see their mother; and although they found her asleep, they were yet anxious to embrace her. But Peter forbade them, saying: "Let me bring you and present you to your mother, lest she should, in consequence

[1] The text is somewhat doubtful. We have given the meaning contained in the first Epitome.

of her great and sudden joy, lose her reason, as she is slumbering, and her spirit is held fast by sleep."

CHAP. IV.—*The mother must not take food with her son. The reason stated.*

As soon as my mother had enough of sleep, she awoke, and Peter at once began first to talk to her of [true] piety, saying: "I wish you to know, O woman, the course of life involved in our religion.[1] We worship one God, who made the world which you see; and we keep His law, which has for its chief injunctions to worship Him alone, and to hallow His name, and to honour our parents, and to be chaste, and to live piously. In addition to this, we do not live with all indiscriminately; nor do we take our food from the same table as Gentiles, inasmuch as we cannot eat along with them, because they live impurely. But when we have persuaded them to have true thoughts, and to follow a right course of action, and have baptized them with a thrice blessed invocation, then we dwell with them. For not even if it were our father, or mother, or wife, or child, or brother, or any other one having a claim by nature on our affection, can we venture to take our meals with him; for our religion compels us to make a distinction. Do not, therefore, regard it as an insult if your son does not take his food along with you, until you come to have the same opinions and adopt the same course of conduct as he follows."

CHAP. V.—*Mattidia wishes to be baptized.*

When she heard this, she said: "What, then, prevents me from being baptized this day? for before I saw you I turned away from the so-called gods, induced by the thought that, though I sacrificed much to them almost every day, they did not aid me in my necessities. And with regard to adultery, what need I say? for not even when I was rich was I betrayed into this sin by luxury, and the poverty which succeeded has been unable to force me into it, since I cling to

[1] Θρησκεία.

my chastity as constituting the greatest beauty,[1] on account of which I fell into so great distress. But I do not at all imagine that you, my lord Peter, are ignorant that the greatest temptation[2] arises when everything looks bright. And therefore, if I was chaste in my prosperity, I do not in my despondency give myself up to pleasures. Yea, indeed, you are not to suppose that my soul has now been freed from distress, although it has received some measure of consolation by the recognition of Clement. For the gloom which I feel in consequence of the loss of my two children rushes in upon me, and throws its shadow to some extent over my joy; for I am grieved, not so much because they perished in the sea, but because they were destroyed, both soul and body, without possessing true[3] piety towards God. Moreover, my husband, their father, as I have learned from Clement, went away in search of me and his sons, and for so many years has not been heard of; and, without doubt, he must have died. For the miserable man, loving me as he did in chastity, was fond of his children; and therefore the old man, deprived of all of us who were dear to him above everything else, died utterly broken-hearted."

CHAP. VI.—*The sons reveal themselves to the mother.*

The sons, on hearing their mother thus speak, could no longer, in obedience to the exhortation of Peter, restrain themselves, but rising up, they clasped her in their arms, showering down upon her tears and kisses. But she said: "What is the meaning of this?" And Peter answered: "Courageously summon up your spirits, O woman, that you may enjoy your children; for these are Faustinus and Faustinianus, your sons, who, you said, had perished in the deep. For how they are alive, after they had in your opinion died

---

[1] One MS. and the first Epitome read, "as being the greatest blessing."

[2] Lit., "desire."

[3] The Greek has, "apart from divine piety towards God." As Wieseler remarks, the epithet "divine" is corrupt. The meaning may be, "without having known the proper mode of worshipping God."

on that most disastrous night, and how one of them now bears the name of Nicetas, and the other that of Aquila, they will themselves be able to tell you; for we, as well as you, have yet to learn this." When Peter thus spoke, my mother fainted away through her excessive joy, and was like to die. But when we had revived her she sat up, and coming to herself, she said: "Be so good, my darling children, as tell us what happened to you after that disastrous night."

CHAP. VII.—*Nicetas tells what befell him.*

And Nicetas, who in future is to be called Faustinus, began to speak. "On that very night when, as you know, the ship went to pieces, we were taken up by some men, who did not fear to follow the profession of robbers on the deep. They placed us in a boat, and brought us along the coast, sometimes rowing and sometimes sending for provisions, and at length took us to Cæsarea Stratonis,[1] and there tormented us by hunger, fear, and blows, that we might not recklessly disclose anything which they did not wish us to tell; and, moreover, changing our names, they succeeded in selling us. Now the woman who bought us was a proselyte of the Jews, an altogether worthy person, of the name of Justa. She adopted us as her own children, and zealously brought us up in all the learning of the Greeks. But we, becoming discreet with our years, were strongly attached to her religion, and we paid good heed to our culture, in order that, disputing with the other nations, we might be able to convince them of their error. We also made an accurate study of the doctrines of the philosophers, especially the most atheistic,—I

---

[1] This clause, literally translated, is, "and sometimes impelling it with oars, they brought us along the land; and sometimes sending for provisions, they conveyed us to Cæsarea Stratonis." The Latin translator renders "to land," not "along the land." The passage assumes a different form in the Recognitions, the first Epitome, and the second Epitome; and there is, no doubt, some corruption in the text. The text has λακρύοντας, which makes no sense. We have adopted the rendering given in the Recognitions. Various attempts have been made to amend the word.

mean those of Epicurus and Pyrrho,—in order that we might be the better able to refute them.

CHAP. VIII.—*Nicetas like to be deceived by Simon Magus.*

"We were brought up along with one Simon, a magician; and in consequence of our friendly intercourse with him, we were in danger of being led astray. Now there is a report in regard to some man, that, when he appears, the mass of those who have been pious are to live free from death and pain in his kingdom. This matter, however, mother, will be explained more fully at the proper time. But when we were going to be led astray by Simon, a friend of our lord Peter, by name Zacchæus, came to us and warned us not to be led astray by the magician; and when Peter came, he brought us to him that he might give us full information, and convince us in regard to those matters that related to piety. Wherefore we beseech you, mother, to partake of those blessings which have been vouchsafed to us, that we may unite around the same table!¹ This, then, is the reason, mother, why you thought we were dead. On that disastrous night we had been taken up in the sea by pirates, but you supposed that we had perished."

CHAP. IX.—*The mother begs baptism for herself and her hostess.*

When Faustinus had said this, our mother fell down at Peter's feet, begging and entreating him to send for her and her hostess, and baptize them immediately, in order that, says she, not a single day may pass after the recovery of my children, without my taking food with them. When we united with our mother in making the same request, Peter said: "What can you imagine? Am I alone heartless, so as not to wish that you should take your meals with your mother, baptizing her this very day? But yet it is incumbent on her to fast one day before she be baptized. And it is only one day, because, in her simplicity, she said something in her own behalf, which I looked on as a sufficient

---
¹ Lit., "that we may be able to partake of common salt and table."

indication of her faith; otherwise, her purification must have lasted many days."

CHAP. X.—*Mattidia values baptism aright.*

And I said: "Tell us what it was that she said which made her faith manifest." And Peter said: "Her request that her hostess and benefactress should be baptized along with her. For she would not have besought this to be granted to her whom she loves, had she not herself first felt that baptism was a great gift. And for this reason I condemn many that, after being baptized, and asserting that they have faith, they yet do nothing worthy of faith; nor do they urge those whom they love—I mean their wives, or sons, or friends—to be baptized.[1] For if they had believed that God grants eternal life with good works on the acceptance of baptism,[2] they without delay would urge those whom they loved to be baptized. But some one of you will say, 'They do love them, and care for them.' That is nonsense. For do they not, most assuredly, when they see them sick, or led away along the road that ends in death, or enduring any other trial, lament over them and pity them? So, if they believed that eternal fire awaits those who worship not God, they would not cease admonishing them, or being in deep distress for them as unbelievers, if they saw them disobedient, being fully assured that punishment awaits them. But now I shall send for the hostess, and question her as to whether she deliberately accepts the law which is proclaimed through us;[3] and so, according to her state of mind, shall we do what ought to be done.

CHAP. XI.—*Mattidia has unintentionally fasted one day.*

"But since your mother has real confidence in the efficacy of baptism,[4] let her fast at least one day before her baptism."

---

[1] Lit., "to this."

[2] ἐπὶ τῷ βαπτίσματι; lit., "on the condition of baptism."

[3] Lit., "the law which is by means of us." But the Epitomes, and a various reading in Cotelerius, give "our law."

[4] Lit., "since your mother is faithfully disposed in regard to baptism."

But she swore: "During the two past days, while I related to the woman[1] all the events connected with the recognition, I could not, in consequence of my excessive joy, partake of food; only yesterday I took a little water." Peter's wife bore testimony to her statement with an oath, saying: "In truth she did not taste anything." And Aquila, who must rather be called Faustinianus[2] in future, said: "There is nothing, therefore, to prevent her being baptized." And Peter, smiling, replied: "But that is not a baptismal fast which has not taken place on account of the baptism itself." And Faustinus answered: "Perhaps God, not wishing to separate our mother a single day after our recognition from our table, has arranged beforehand the fast. For as she was chaste in the times of her ignorance, doing what the true religion inculcated,[3] so even now perhaps God has arranged that she should fast one day before for the sake of the true baptism, that, from the first day of her recognising us, she might take her meals along with us."

CHAP. XII.—*The difficulty solved.*

And Peter said: "Let not wickedness have dominion over us, finding a pretext in Providence and your affection for your mother; but rather abide this day in your fast, and I shall join you in it, and to-morrow she will be baptized. And, besides, this hour of the day is not suitable for baptism." Then we all agreed that it should be so.

CHAP. XIII.—*Peter on chastity.*

That same evening we all enjoyed the benefit of Peter's instruction. Taking occasion by what had happened to our mother, he showed us how the results of chastity are good, while those of adultery are disastrous, and naturally bring destruction on the whole race, if not speedily, at all events slowly. "And to such an extent," he says, "do deeds of

---

[1] The second Epitome makes her the wife of Peter: a various reading mentions also her hostess.
[2] Dressel strangely prefers the reading "Faustinus."
[3] Lit., "doing what was becoming to the truth."

chastity please God, that in this life He bestows some small favour on account of it, even on those who are in error; for salvation in the other world is granted only to those who have been baptized on account of their trust[1] in Him, and who act chastely and righteously. This ye yourselves have seen in the case of your mother, that the results of chastity are in the end good. For perhaps she would have been cut off if she had committed adultery; but God took pity on her for having behaved chastely, rescued her from the death that threatened her, and restored to her her lost children.

Chap. XIV.—*Peter's speech continued.*

"But some one will say, 'How many have perished on account of chastity?' Yes; but it was because they did not perceive the danger. For the woman who perceives that she is in love with any one, or is beloved by any one, should immediately shun all association with him as she would shun a blazing fire or a mad dog. And this is exactly what your mother did, for she really loved chastity as a blessing: wherefore she was preserved, and, along with you, obtained the full knowledge of the everlasting kingdom. The woman who wishes to be chaste, ought to know that she is envied by wickedness, and that because of love many lie in wait for her. If, then, she remain holy through a stedfast persistence in chastity, she will gain the victory over all temptations, and be saved; whereas, even if she were to do all that is right, and yet should once commit the sin of adultery, she must be punished, as said the prophet.

Chap. XV.—*Peter's speech continued.*

"The chaste wife, doing the will of God, is a good reminiscence of His first creation; for God, being one, created one woman for one man. She is also still more chaste if she does not forget her own creation, and has future punishment before her eyes, and is not ignorant of the loss of eternal blessings. The chaste woman takes pleasure in those who wish to be saved, and is a pious example to the pious, for she

[1] Lit., "hope."

is the model of a good life. She who wishes to be chaste, cuts off all occasions for slander; but if she be slandered as by an enemy, though affording him no pretext, she is blessed and avenged by God. The chaste woman longs for God, loves God, pleases God, glorifies God; and to men she affords no occasion for slander. The chaste woman perfumes the church with her good reputation, and glorifies it by her piety. She is, moreover, the praise of her teachers, and a helper to them in their chastity.[1]

CHAP. XVI.—*Peter's speech continued.*

"The chaste woman is adorned with the Son of God as with a bridegroom. She is clothed with holy light. Her beauty lies in a well-regulated soul; and she is fragrant with ointment, even with a good reputation. She is arrayed in beautiful vesture, even in modesty. She wears about her precious pearls, even chaste words. And she is radiant, for[2] her mind has been brilliantly lighted up. Into a beautiful mirror does she look, for she looks into God. Beautiful cosmetics[3] does she use, namely, the fear of God, with which she admonishes her soul. Beautiful is the woman, not because she has chains of gold on her,[4] but because she has been set free from transient lusts. The chaste woman is greatly desired by the great King;[5] she has been wooed, watched, and loved by Him. The chaste woman does not furnish occasions for being desired, except by her own husband. The chaste woman is grieved when she is desired by another. The chaste woman loves her husband from the heart, embraces, soothes, and pleases him, acts the slave to him, and is obedient to him in all things, except when she would be disobedient to God. For she who obeys God is

---

[1] The Greek is αὐτοῖς σωφρονοῦσι. The Latin translator and Lehmann (*Die Clementinischen Schriften*, Gotha 1869) render, "to those who are chaste, *i.e.* love or practise chastity," as if the reading were τοῖς σωφρονοῦσι.

[2] Lit., "when."

[3] κόσμῳ—properly ornaments; but here a peculiar meaning is evidently required.

[4] Lit., "as being chained with gold."   [5] Ps. xlv. 11.

without the aid of watchmen chaste in soul and pure in body.

CHAP. XVII.—*Peter's speech continued.*

"Foolish, therefore, is every husband who separates his wife from the fear of God; for she who does not fear God is not afraid of her husband. If she fear not God, who sees what is invisible, how will she be chaste in her unseen choice?[1] And how will she be chaste, who does not come to the assembly to hear chaste-making words? And how could she obtain admonition? And how will she be chaste without watchmen, if she be not informed in regard to the coming judgment of God, and if she be not fully assured that eternal punishment is the penalty for the slight pleasure? Wherefore, on the other hand, compel her even against her will always to come to hear the chaste-making word, yea, coax her to do so.

CHAP. XVIII.—*Peter's speech continued.*

"Much better is it if you will take her by the hand and come, in order that you yourself may become chaste; for you will desire to become chaste, that you may experience the full fruition of a holy marriage, and you will not scruple, if you desire it, to become a father,[2] to love your own children, and to be loved by your own children. He who wishes to have a chaste wife is also himself chaste, gives her what is due to a wife, takes his meals with her, keeps company with her, goes with her to the word that makes chaste, does not grieve her, does not rashly quarrel with her, does not make himself hateful to her, furnishes her with all the good things he can, and when he has them not, he makes up the deficiency

---

[1] "In her unseen choice" means, in what course of conduct she really prefers in her heart. This reading occurs in one MS.; in the other MS. it is corrupt. Schwegler amended it into, "How shall she be chaste towards him who does not see [what is invisible]?" and the emendation is adopted by Dressel.

[2] There seems to be some corruption in this clause. Literally it is, "and you will not scruple, if you love, I mean, to become a father."

by caresses. The chaste wife does not expect to be caressed, recognises her husband as her lord, bears his poverty when he is poor, is hungry with him when he is hungry, travels with him when he travels, consoles him when he is grieved, and if she have a large[1] dowry, is subject to him as if she had nothing at all. But if the husband have a poor wife, let him reckon her chastity a great dowry. The chaste wife is temperate in her eating and drinking, in order that the weariness of the body, thus pampered, may not drag the soul down to unlawful desires. Moreover, she never assuredly remains alone with young men, and she suspects[2] the old; she turns away from disorderly laughter, gives herself up to God alone; she is not led astray; she delights in listening to holy words, but turns away from those which are not spoken to produce chastity.

CHAP. XIX.—*Peter's speech ended.*

"God is my witness: one adultery is as bad as many murders; and what is terrible in it is this, that the fearfulness and impiety of its murders are not seen. For, when blood is shed, the dead body remains lying, and all are struck by the terrible nature of the occurrence. But the murders of the soul caused by adultery, though they are more frightful, yet, since they are not seen by men, do not make the daring a whit less eager in their impulse. Know, O man, whose breath it is that thou hast to keep thee in life, and thou shalt not wish that it be polluted. By adultery alone is the breath of God polluted. And therefore it drags him who has polluted it into the fire; for it hastens to deliver up its insulter to everlasting punishment."

CHAP. XX.—*Peter addresses Mattidia.*

While Peter was saying this, he saw the good and chaste Mattidia weeping for joy; but thinking that she was grieved at having suffered so much in past times, he said: "Take

[1] Lit., "larger" [than usual].
[2] ὑποπτεύει. The Latin translator and Lehmann render "respects" or "reveres."

courage, O woman; for while many have suffered many evils on account of adultery, you have suffered on account of chastity, and therefore you did not die. But if you had died, your soul would have been saved. You left your native city of Rome on account of chastity, but through it you found the truth, the diadem of the eternal kingdom. You underwent danger in the deep, but you did not die; and even if you had died, the deep itself would have proved to you, dying on account of chastity, a baptism for the salvation of your soul. You were deprived of your children for a little; but these, the true offspring of your husband, have been found in better circumstances. When starving, you begged for food, but you did not defile your body by fornication. You exposed your body to torture, but you saved your soul; you fled from the adulterer, that you might not defile the couch of your husband: but, on account of your chastity, God, who knows your flight, will fill up the place of your husband. Grieved and left desolate, you were for a short time deprived of husband and children, but all these you must have been deprived of, some time or other, by death, the preordained lot of man. But better is it that you were willingly deprived of them on account of chastity, than that you should have perished unwillingly after a time, simply on account of sins.

CHAP. XXI.—*The same subject continued.*

"Much better is it, then, that your first circumstances should be distressing. For when this is the case, they do not so deeply grieve you, because you hope that they will pass away, and they yield joy through the expectation of better circumstances. But, above all, I wish you to know how much chastity is pleasing to God. The chaste woman is God's choice, God's good pleasure, God's glory, God's child. So great a blessing is chastity,[1] that if there had not been a law that not even a righteous person should enter into the kingdom of God unbaptized, perhaps even the erring

[1] We have adopted an emendation of Wieseler's. The emendation is questionable; but the sense is the best that can be got out of the words.

Gentiles might have been saved solely on account of chastity. Wherefore I am exceedingly sorry for those erring ones who are chaste because they shrink from baptism—thus choosing to be chaste without good hope. Wherefore they are not saved; for the decree of God is clearly set down, that an unbaptized person cannot enter into His kingdom." When he said this, and much more, we turned to sleep.

HOMILY XIV.

CHAP. I.—*Mattidia is baptized in the sea.*

MUCH earlier than usual Peter awoke, and came to us, and awaking us, said: "Let Faustinus and Faustinianus, along with Clement and the household, accompany me, that we may go to some sheltered spot by the sea, and there be able to baptize her without attracting observation." Accordingly, when we had come to the sea-shore, he baptized her between some rocks, which supplied a place at once free from wind and dust.[1] But we brothers, along with our brother and some others, retired because of the women and bathed, and coming again to the women, we took them along with us, and thus we went to a secret place and prayed. Then Peter, on account of the multitude, sent the women on before, ordering them to go to their lodging by another way, and he permitted us alone of the men to accompany our mother and the rest of the women.[2] We went then to our lodging, and while waiting for Peter's arrival, we conversed with each other. Peter came several hours after, and breaking the bread for the eucharist,[3] and putting salt upon it, he gave it first to our mother, and, after her, to us her sons. And thus we took food along with her, and blessed God.

[1] Lit., "tranquil and clean."
[2] We have adopted an emendation of Schwegler's. The MSS. read either "these" or "the same" for "the rest of."
[3] The words "for the eucharist" might be translated "after thanksgiving." But it is much the same which, for the eucharist is plainly meant. The Epitomes have it: "taking the bread, giving thanks, blessing, and consecrating it, he gave it;" but no mention is made of salt.

CHAP. II.—*The reason of Peter's lateness.*

Then, at length, Peter seeing that the multitude had entered, sat down, and bidding us sit down beside him, he related first of all why he had sent us on before him after the baptism, and why he himself had been late in returning. He said that the following was the reason: "At the time that you came up,"[1] he says, "an old man, a workman, entered along with you, concealing himself out of curiosity. He had watched us before, as he himself afterwards confessed, in order to see what we were doing when we entered into the sheltered place, and then he came out secretly and followed us. And coming up to me at a convenient place, and addressing me, he said, 'For a long time I have been following you and wishing to talk with you, but I was afraid that you might be angry with me, as if I were instigated by curiosity; but now I shall tell you, if you please, what I think is the truth.' And I replied, 'Tell us what you think is good, and we shall approve your conduct, even should what you say not be really good, since with a good purpose you have been anxious to state what you deem to be good.'

CHAP. III.—*The old man does not believe in God or Providence.*

"The old man began to speak as follows: 'When I saw you after you had bathed in the sea retire into the secret place, I went up and secretly watched what might be your object in entering into a secret place, and when I saw you pray, I retired;[2] but taking pity on you, I waited that I might speak with you when you came out, and prevail on you not to be led astray. For there is neither God nor providence; but all things are subject to Genesis.[3] Of this I am fully assured in consequence of what I have myself

---

[1] We have adopted an emendation of Wieseler's. The text has, "at the time that you went away."

[2] Wieseler thinks that the reading should be: "I did not retire."

[3] Genesis is destiny determined by the stars which rule at each man's birth.

endured, having for a long time made a careful study of the science.[1] Do not therefore be deceived, my child. For whether you pray or not, you must endure what is assigned to you by Genesis. For if prayers could have done anything or any good, I myself should now be in better circumstances. And now, unless my needy garments mislead you, you will not refuse to believe what I say. I was once in affluent circumstances; I sacrificed much to the gods, I gave liberally to the needy; and yet, though I prayed and acted piously, I was not able to escape my destiny.' And I said: 'What are the calamities you have endured?' And he answered: 'I need not tell you now; perhaps at the end you shall learn who I am, and who are my parents, and into what straitened circumstances I have fallen. But at present I wish you to become fully assured that everything is subject to Genesis.'

CHAP. IV.—*Peter's arguments against Genesis.*

"And I said: 'If all things are subject to Genesis, and you are fully convinced that this is the case, your thoughts and advice are contrary to your own opinion.[2] For if it is impossible even to think in opposition to Genesis, why do you toil in vain, advising me to do what cannot be done? Yea, moreover, even if Genesis subsists, do not make haste to prevail on me not to worship Him who is also Lord of the stars, by whose wish that a thing should not take place, that thing becomes an impossibility. For always that which is subject must obey that which rules. As far, however, as the worship of the common gods is concerned, that is superfluous, if Genesis has sway. For neither does anything happen contrary to what seems good to fate, nor are they themselves able to do anything, since they are subject to their own universal Genesis. If Genesis exists, there is this objection to it, that that which is not first has the rule; or [in other

[1] μάθημα, mathematical science specially, which was closely connected with astrology.

[2] Lit., "thinking you counsel what is contrary to yourself."

words] the uncreated cannot be subject, for the uncreated, as being uncreated, has nothing that is older than itself.'[1]

CHAP. V.—*Practical refutation of Genesis.*

"While we were thus talking, a great multitude gathered round us. And then I looked to the multitude, and said: 'I and my tribe have had handed down to us from our ancestors the worship of God, and we have a commandment to give no heed to Genesis, I mean to the science of astrology; and therefore I gave no attention to it. For this reason I have no skill in astrology, but I shall state that in which I have skill. Since I am unable to refute Genesis by an appeal to the science which relates to Genesis, I wish to prove in another way that the affairs [of this world] are managed by a providence, and that each one will receive reward or punishment according to his actions. Whether he shall do so now or hereafter, is a matter of no consequence to me; all I affirm is, that each one without doubt will reap the fruit of his deeds. The proof that there is no Genesis is this. If any one of you present has been deprived of eyes, or has his hand maimed, or his foot lame, or some other part of the body wrong, and if it is utterly incurable, and entirely beyond the range of the medical profession,—a case, indeed, which not even the astrologers profess to cure, for no such cure has taken place within the lapse of a vast period,—yet I praying to God will cure it,[2] although[3] it could never have been set right by Genesis. Since this is so, do not they sin who blaspheme the God that fashioned all things?' And the old man answered: 'Is it then blasphemy to say that all things are subject to Genesis?' And I replied: 'Most certainly it is. For if all the sins of men, and all their

---

[1] The argument here is obscure. Probably what is intended is as follows: Genesis means origination, coming into being. Origination cannot be the ruling power, for there must be something unoriginated which has given rise to the origination. The origination, therefore, as not being first, cannot have sway, and it must itself be subject to that which is unoriginated.

[2] We have adopted the reading given in the two Epitomes.

[3] Lit., "when."

acts of impiety and licentiousness, owe their origin to the stars, and if the stars have been appointed by God to do this work, so as to be the efficient causes of all evils, then the sins of all are traced up to Him who placed Genesis[1] in the stars.'

CHAP. VI.—*The old man opposes his personal experience to the argument of Peter.*

"And the old man answered: 'You have spoken truly,[2] and yet, notwithstanding all your incomparable demonstration, I am prevented from yielding assent by my own personal knowledge. For I was an astrologer, and dwelt first at Rome; and then forming a friendship with one who was of the family of Cæsar, I ascertained accurately the genesis of himself and his wife. And tracing their history, I find all the deeds actually accomplished in exact accordance with their genesis, and therefore I cannot yield to your argument. For the arrangement[3] of her genesis was that which makes women commit adultery, fall in love with their own slaves, and perish abroad in the water. And this actually took place; for she fell in love with her own slave, and not being able to bear the reproach, she fled with him, hurried to a foreign land, shared his bed, and perished in the sea.'

CHAP. VII.—*The old man tells his story.*

"And I answered: 'How then do you know that she who fled and took up her residence in a foreign land married the slave, and marrying him died?' And the old man said: 'I am quite sure that this is true, not indeed that she married him, for I did not know even that she fell in love with him; but after her departure, a brother of her husband's told me the whole story of her passion, and how he acted as an honourable man, and did not, as being his brother, wish to pollute his couch, and how she the wretched woman (for she is not blameable, inasmuch as she was compelled to do and suffer all this in consequence of Genesis) longed for him, and

---

[1] That is, the power of origination.
[2] One ms. adds "greatly," and an Epitome "great things."
[3] That is, the position of the stars at her birth.

yet stood in awe of him and his reproaches, and how she devised a dream, whether true or false I cannot tell; for he stated that she said, "Some one in a vision stood by me, and ordered me to leave the city of the Romans immediately with my children." But her husband being anxious that she should be saved with his sons, sent them immediately to Athens for their education, accompanied by their mother and slaves, while he kept the third and youngest son with himself, for he who gave the warning in the dream permitted this son to remain with his father. And when a long time had elapsed, during which[1] he received no letters from her, he himself sent frequently to Athens, and at length took me, as the truest of all his friends, and went in search of her. And much did I exert myself along with him in the course of our travels with all eagerness; for I remembered that, in the old times of his prosperity, he had given me a share of all he had, and loved me above all his friends. At length we set sail from Rome itself, and so we arrived in these parts of Syria, and we landed at Seleucia, and not many days after we had landed he died of a broken heart. But I came here, and have procured my livelihood from that day till this by the work of my hands.'

CHAP. VIII.—*The old man gives information in regard to Faustus the father of Clement.*

"When the old man had thus spoken, I knew from what he said that the old man who he stated had died, was no other than your father. I did not wish, however, to communicate your circumstances to him until I should confer with you. But I ascertained where his lodging was, and I pointed out mine to him; and to make sure [that my conjecture was right], I put this one question to him: 'What was the name of the old man?' And he said, 'Faustus.' 'And what were the names of his twin sons?' And he answered, 'Faustinus and Faustinianus.' 'What was the name of the third son?' He said, 'Clement.' 'What was their mother's name?' He said, 'Mattidia.' Accordingly, from

[1] We have inserted ὡς from the Epitomes.

compassion, I shed tears along with him, and, dismissing the multitudes, I came to you, in order that I might take counsel with you after we had partaken of food[1] together. But I did not wish to disclose the matter to you before we had partaken of food, lest perchance you should be overcome by sorrow, and continue sad on the day of baptism, when even angels rejoice." At these statements of Peter we all fell a weeping along with our mother. But he beholding us in tears, said: "Now let each one of you, through fear of God, bear bravely what has been said; for certainly it was not to-day that your father died, but long ago, as you conjecturing said."

CHAP. IX.—*Faustus himself appears.*

When Peter said this, our mother could no longer endure it, but cried out, "Alas! my husband! loving us, you died by your own decision,[2] while we are still alive, see the light, and have just partaken of food." This one scream had not yet ceased, when, lo! the old man came in, and at the same time wishing to inquire into the cause of the cry, he looked on the woman and said, "What does this mean? Whom do I see?" And going up to her, and looking at her, and being looked at more carefully, he embraced her. But they were like to die through the sudden joy, and wishing to speak to each other, they could not get the power in consequence of their unsatisfied joy, for they were seized with speechlessness. But not long after, our mother said to him: "I now have you, Faustus, in every way the dearest being to me. How then are you alive, when we heard a short time ago that you were dead? But these are our sons, Faustinus, Faustinianus, and Clement." And when she said this, we all three fell on him, and kissed him, and in rather an indistinct way we recalled his form to our memory.

CHAP. X.—*Faustus explains his narrative to Peter.*

Peter seeing this, said: "Are you Faustus, the husband of

[1] Lit., "of salt."
[2] Lit., "you died by a judgment;" but it is thought that κρίσει is corrupt.

this woman, and the father of her children?" And he said: "I am." And Peter said: "How, then, did you relate to me your own history as if it were another's; telling me of your toils, and sorrow, and burial?" And our father answered: "Being of the family of Cæsar, and not wishing to be discovered, I devised the narrative in another's name, in order that it might not be perceived who I was. For I knew that, if I were recognised, the governors in the place would learn this, and recall me to gratify Cæsar, and would bestow upon me that former prosperity to which I had formerly bidden adieu with all the resolution I could summon. For I could not give myself up to a luxurious life when I had pronounced the strongest condemnation on myself, because I believed that I had been the cause of death to those who were loved by me."[1]

CHAP. XI.—*Discussion on Genesis.*

And Peter said: "You did this according to your resolution. But in regard to Genesis, were you merely playing a part when you affirmed it, or were you in earnest in asserting that it existed?" Our father said: "I will not speak falsely to you. I was in earnest when I maintained that Genesis existed. For I am not uninitiated in the science; on the contrary, I associated with one who is the best of the astrologers, an Egyptian of the name of Annubion, who became my friend in the commencement of my travels, and disclosed to me the death of my wife and children." And Peter said: "Are you not now convinced by facts, that the doctrine of Genesis has no firm foundation?" And my father answered: "I must lay before you all the ideas that occur to my mind, that listening to them I may understand your refutation of them.[2] I know, indeed, that astrologers both make many mistakes, and frequently speak the truth.

---

[1] Lit., "Having judged the greatest things in regard to those who were loved by me, as having died." The text is doubtful; for the first Epitome has something quite different.

[2] Here MSS. and Epitomes differ in their readings. The text adopted seems a combination of two ideas: "that you may listen and refute them, and that I may thus learn the truth."

I suspect, therefore, that they speak the truth so far as they are accurately acquainted with the science, and that their mistakes are the result of ignorance; so that I conjecture that the science has a firm foundation, but that the astrologers themselves speak what is false solely on account of ignorance, because they cannot know all things with absolute[1] accuracy." And Peter answered: "Consider[2] whether their speaking of the truth is not accidental, and whether they do not make their declarations without knowing the matters accurately. For it must by all means happen that, when many prophecies are uttered, some of them should come true." And the old man said: "How, then, is it possible to be fully convinced of this, whether the science of Genesis has a sure foundation or not?"

CHAP. XII.—*Clement undertakes the discussion.*

When both were silent, I said: "Since I know accurately the science, but our lord and our father are not in this condition, I should like if Annubion himself were here, to have a discussion with him in the presence of my father. For thus would the matter be able to become public, when one practically acquainted with the subject has held the discussion with one equally informed."[3] And our father answered: "Where, then, is it possible to fall in with Annubion?" And Peter said: "In Antioch, for I learn that Simon Magus is there, whose inseparable companion Annubion is. When, then, we go there, if we come upon them, the discussion can take place." And so, when we had discussed many subjects, and rejoiced at the recognition and given thanks to God, evening came down upon us, and we turned to sleep.

[1] We have adopted the reading of Codex O, πάντως. The other MS. reads, " that all cannot know all things accurately."

[2] The MSS. read ἄτεχε, "hold back." The reading of the text is in an Epitome.

[3] Lit., "when artist has had discussion with fellow-artist."

HOMILY XV.

CHAP. I.—*Peter wishes to convert Faustus.*

T break of day our father, with our mother and his three sons, entered the place where Peter was, and accosting him, sat down. Then we also did the same at his request; and Peter looking at our father, said: "I am anxious that you should become of the same mind as your wife and children, in order that here you may live along with them, and in the other world,[1] after the separation of the soul from the body, you will continue to be with them free from sorrow. For does it not grieve you exceedingly that you should not associate with each other?" And my father said: "Most assuredly." And Peter said: "If, then, separation from each other here gives you pain, and if without doubt the penalty awaits you that after death you should not be with each other, how much greater will your grief be that you, a wise man, should be separated from your own family on account of your opinions? They, too, must[2] feel the more distressed from the consciousness that eternal punishment awaits you because you entertain different opinions from theirs, and deny the established truth."[3]

CHAP. II.—*Reason for listening to Peter's arguments.*

Our father said: "But it is not the case, my very dear

[1] Lit., "there."

[2] We have inserted a δεῖ, probably omitted on account of the previous δέ.

[3] The words are peculiar. Lit., "eternal punishment awaits you thinking other things, through denial of the fixed dogma" (ἡττοῦ δόγματος). The Latin translator gives: "ob veri dogmatis negationem."

friend, that souls are punished in Hades, for the soul is dissolved into air as soon as it leaves the body." And Peter said: "Until we convince you in regard to this point, answer me, does it not appear to you that you are not grieved as having no faith in a [future] punishment, but they who have full faith in it must be vexed in regard to you?" And our father said: "You speak sense." And Peter said: "Why, then, will you not free them from the greatest grief they can have in regard to you by agreeing to their religion, not, I mean, through dread, but through kindly feeling, listening and judging about what is said by me, whether it be so or not? and if the truth is as we state it, then here you will enjoy life with those who are dearest to you, and in the other world you will have rest with them; but if, in examining the arguments, you show that what is stated by us is a fictitious story,[1] you will thus be doing good service, for you will have your friends on your side, and you will put an end to their leaning upon false hopes, and you will free them from false fears."

CHAP. III.—*Obstacles to faith.*

And our father said: "There is evidently much reason in what you say." And Peter said: "What is it, then, that prevents you from coming to our faith? Tell me, that we may begin our discussion with it. For many are the hindrances. The faithful are hindered by occupation with merchandise, or public business, or the cultivation of the soil, or cares, and such like; the unbelievers, of whom you also are one, are hindered by ideas such as that the gods, which do not exist, really exist, or that all things are subject to Genesis, or chance,[2] or that souls are mortal, or that our doctrines are false because there is no providence.

CHAP. IV.—*Providence seen in the events of the life of Faustus and his family.*

"But I maintain, from what has happened to you, that all things are managed by the providence of God, and that your separation from your family for so many years was providen-

[1] μῦθός τινα ψευδῆ.   [2] Properly, self-action.

tial;[1] for since, if they had been with you, they perhaps would not have listened to the doctrines of the true religion, it was arranged that your children should travel with their mother, should be shipwrecked, should be supposed to have perished, and should be sold;[2] moreover, that they should be educated in the learning of the Greeks, especially in the atheistic doctrines, in order that, as being acquainted with them, they might be the better able to refute them; and in addition to this, that they should become attached to the true religion, and be enabled to be united with me, so as to help me in my preaching; furthermore, that their brother Clement should meet in the same place, and that thus his mother should be recognised, and through her cure[3] should be fully convinced of the right worship of God;[4] that after no long interval the twins should recognise and be recognised, and the other day should fall in with you, and that you should receive back your own. I do not think, then, that such a speedy filling in of circumstances, coming as it were from all quarters, so as to accomplish one design, could have happened without the direction of Providence."

CHAP. V.—*Difference between the true religion and philosophy.*

And our father began to say: "Do not suppose, my dearest Peter, that I am not thinking of the doctrines preached by you. I was thinking of them. But during the past night, when Clement urged me earnestly to give in my adhesion to the truth preached by you, I at last answered, 'Why should I? for what new commandment can any one give more than what the ancients urged us to obey?' And he, with a gentle smile, said, 'There is a great difference, father, between the doctrines of the true religion and those of philosophy; for the true religion receives its proof from prophecy, while

---

[1] We have adopted a reading suggested by the second Epitome.

[2] The word ἀπρασίαι is corrupt. We have adopted the emendation πρᾶσις. The word is not given in the MS. O, nor in the Epitomes.

[3] ὑπὸ θεραπείας, which Cotelerius translates *recuperata sanitate.*

[4] Lit., "convinced of the Godhead." "Godhead" is omitted in the Epitomes.

philosophy, furnishing us with beautiful sentences, seems to present its proofs from conjecture.' On saying this, he took an instance, and set before us the doctrine of philanthropy,[1] which you had explained to him,[2] which rather appeared to me to be very unjust. And I shall tell you how. He alleged that it was right to present to him who strikes you on the one cheek the other[3] also, and to give to him who takes away your cloak your tunic also, and to go two miles with him who compels you to go one, and such like."

CHAP. VI.—*The love of man.*

And Peter answered: "You have deemed unjust what is most just. If you are inclined, will you listen to me?" And my father said: "With all my heart." And Peter said: "What is your opinion? Suppose that there were two kings, enemies to each other, and having their countries cut off from each other; and suppose that some one of the subjects of one of them were to be caught in the country of the other, and to incur the penalty of death on this account: now if he were let off from the punishment by receiving a blow instead of death, is it not plain that he who let him off is a lover of man?" And our father said: "Most certainly." And Peter said: "Now suppose that this same person were to steal from some one something belonging to him or to another; and if when caught he were to pay double, instead of suffering the punishment that was due to him, namely, paying four times the amount, and being also put to death, as having been caught in the territories of the enemy; is it

---

[1] Or "love of man" in all its phases—kindliness, gentleness, humanity, etc.

[2] Hom. xii. 25 ff.

[3] Matt. v. 39–41; Luke vi. 29. The writer of the Homilies changes the word χιτῶνα, "tunic," of the New Testament into μαφόριον, which Suicer describes "a covering for the head, neck, and shoulders, used by women." Wieseler is in doubt whether the writer of the Homilies uses μαφόριον as equivalent to χιτῶνα, or whether he intentionally changed the word, for the person who lost both cloak and tunic would be naked altogether; and this, the writer may have imagined, Christ would not have commanded.

not your opinion that he who accepts double, and lets him off from the penalty of death, is a lover of man?" And our father said: "He certainly seems so." And Peter said: "Why then? Is it not the duty of him who is in the kingdom of another, and that, too, a hostile and wicked monarch, to be pleasing to all[1] for the sake of life, and when force is applied to him, to yield still more, to accost those who do not accost him, to reconcile enemies, not to quarrel with those who are angry, to give his own property freely to all who ask, and such like?" And our father said: "He should with reason endure all things rather, if he prefers life to them."

CHAP. VII.—*The explanation of a parable; the present and the future life.*

And Peter[2] said: "Are not those, then, who you said received injustice, themselves transgressors, inasmuch as they are in the kingdom of the other, and is it not by overreaching that they have obtained all they possess? while those who are thought to act unjustly are conferring a favour on each subject of the hostile kingdom, so far as they permit him to have property. For these possessions belong to those who have chosen the present.[3] And they are so far kind as to permit the others to live. This, then, is the parable; now listen to the actual truth. The prophet of the truth who appeared [on earth] taught us that the Maker and God of all gave two kingdoms to two,[4] good and evil; granting to the evil the sovereignty over the present world along with law, so that he [it] should have the right to punish those who act

---

[1] Lit., "to flatter."

[2] The following words would be more appropriately put in the mouth of the father, as is done in fact by the Epitomes. Peter's address would commence, "And the parable is." The Epitomes differ much from each other and the text, and there seems to be confusion in the text.

[3] This sentence would be more appropriate in the explanation of the parable.

[4] The Greek leaves it uncertain whether it is two persons or two things,—whether it is a good being and an evil being, or good and evil. Afterwards, a good being and an evil are distinctly introduced.

unjustly; but to the good He gave the eternal[1] age to come. But He made each man free with the power to give himself up to whatsoever he prefers, either to the present evil or the future good. Those men who choose the present have power to be rich, to revel in luxury, to indulge in pleasures, and to do whatever they can. For they will possess none of the future goods. But those who have determined to accept the blessings of the future reign have no right to regard as their own the things that are here, since they belong to a foreign king, with the exception only of water and bread, and those things procured with sweat to maintain life (for it is not lawful for them to commit suicide),[2] and also one garment, for they are not permitted to go naked on account of the all-seeing[3] Heaven.

CHAP. VIII.—*The present and the future.*

"If, then, you wish to have an accurate account of the matter, listen. Those of whom you said a little before that they receive injustice, rather act unjustly themselves; for they who have chosen the future blessings, live along with the bad in the present world, having many enjoyments the same as the bad,—such as life itself, light, bread, water, clothing, and others of a like nature. But they who are thought by you to act unjustly, shall not live with the good men in[4] the coming age." And our father replied to this: "Now when you have convinced me that those who act unjustly suffer injustice themselves, while those who suffer injustice have by far the advantage, the whole affair seems to me still more the most unjust of transactions; for those who seem to act unjustly grant many things to those who have chosen the future blessings, but those who seem to receive injustice do themselves commit injustice, because they do not give in the other world, to those who have given them blessings here, the same advantages which these gave to them." And Peter

---

[1] The word αἴδιος, properly and strictly "eternal," is used.
[2] Lit., "to die willingly."
[3] We have adopted an obvious emendation, πάντα for παντός.
[4] We have translated Schwegler's emendation. He inserted ἐν.

said: "This is not unjust at all, because each one has the power to choose the present or the future goods, whether they be small or great. He who chooses by his own individual judgment and wish, receives no injustice,—I mean, not even should his choice rest on what is small, since the great lay within his choice, as in fact did also the small." And our father said: "You are right; for it has been said by one of the wise men of the Greeks, 'The blame rests with those who chose—God is blameless.'[1]

CHAP. IX.—*Possessions are transgressions.*

"Will you be so good as to explain this matter also? I remember Clement saying to me, that we suffer injuries and afflictions for the forgiveness of our sins." Peter said: "This is quite correct. For we, who have chosen the future things, in so far as we possess more goods than these, whether they be clothing, or food or drink, or any other thing, possess sins, because we ought not to have anything, as I explained to you a little ago. To all of us possessions are sins.[2] The deprivation of these, in whatever way it may take place, is the removal of sins." And our father said: "That seems reasonable, as you explained that these were the two boundary lines of the two kings, and[3] that it was in the power of each to choose whatever he wished of what was under their authority. But why are the afflictions sent, or[4] do we suffer them justly?" And Peter said: "Most justly; for since the boundary line of the saved is, as I said, that no one should possess anything, but since many have many possessions, or in other words sins, for this reason the exceeding love of God sends afflictions on those who do not act in purity of heart, that on account of their having some measure of the love of God, they might, by temporary inflictions, be saved from eternal punishments."

[1] Plato, *Rep.* x. 617 E.
[2] One MS. inserts before this sentence: "For if in all of us possessions are wont to occasion sins in those who have them."
[3] We have adopted Wieseler's emendation of τά into καί.
[4] We have changed εἰ into ἤ.

CHAP. X.—*Poverty not necessarily righteous.*

And our father said: "How then is this? Do we not see many impious men poor? Then do these belong to the saved on this account?" And Peter said: "Not at all; for that poverty is not acceptable which longs for what it ought not. So that some are rich as far as their choice goes, though poor in actual wealth, and they are punished because they desire to have more. But one is not unquestionably righteous because he happens to be poor. For he can be a beggar as far as actual wealth is concerned, but he may desire and even do what above everything he ought not to do. Thus he may worship idols, or be a blasphemer or fornicator, or he may live indiscriminately, or perjure himself, or lie, or live the life of an unbeliever. But our teacher pronounced the faithful poor blessed;[1] and he did so, not because they had given anything, for they had nothing, but because they were not to be condemned, as having done no sin, simply because they gave no alms, because they had nothing to give." And our father said: "In good truth all seems to go right as far as the subject of discussion is concerned; wherefore I have resolved to listen to the whole of your argument in regular order."

CHAP. XI.—*Exposition of the true religion promised.*

And Peter said: "Since, then, you are eager henceforth to learn what relates to our religion, I ought to explain it in order, beginning with God Himself, and showing that we ought to call Him alone God, and that we ought neither to speak of the others as gods nor deem them such, and that he who acts contrary to this will be punished eternally, as having shown the greatest impiety to Him who is the Lord of all." And saying this, he laid his hands on those who were vexed by afflictions, and were diseased, and possessed by demons; and, praying, he healed them, and dismissed the multitudes. And then entering in this way, he partook of his usual food, and went to sleep.

[1] Matt. v. 3. The Epitomes run thus: "Our Lord Jesus Christ, the Son of the living God, said." And then they quote the words of our Gospel.

HOMILY XVI.

Chap. I.—*Simon wishes to discuss with Peter the unity of God.*

T break of day Peter went out, and reaching the place where he was wont to discourse, he saw a great multitude assembled. At the very time when he was going to discourse, one of his deacons entered, and said: "Simon has come from Antioch, starting as soon as it was evening, having learned that you promised to speak on the unity[1] of God; and he is ready, along with Athenodorus the Epicurean, to come to hear your speech, in order that he may publicly oppose all the arguments ever adduced by you for the unity of God." Just as the deacon said this, lo! Simon himself entered, accompanied by Athenodorus and some other friends. And before Peter spoke at all, he took the first word, and said:

Chap. II.—*The same subject continued.*

"I heard that you promised yesterday to Faustus to prove this day, giving out your arguments in regular order, and beginning with Him who is Lord of the universe, that we ought to say that He alone is God, and that we ought neither to say nor to think that there are other gods, because he that acts contrary to this will be punished eternally. But, above all, I am truly amazed at your madness in hoping to convert a wise man, and one far advanced in years, to your state of mind. But you will not succeed in your designs; and all the more that I am present, and can thoroughly refute

[1] The word properly signifies the "sole government or monarchy of God." It means that God alone is ruler.

your false arguments. For perhaps, if I had not been present, the wise old man might have been led astray, because he has no critical acquaintance[1] with the books publicly believed in amongst the Jews.[2] At present I shall omit much, in order that I may the more speedily refute that which you have promised to prove. Wherefore begin to speak what you promised to say before us, who know the Scriptures. But if, fearing our refutation, you are unwilling to fulfil your promise in our presence, this of itself will be sufficient proof that you are wrong, because you did not venture to speak in the presence of those who know the Scriptures. And now, why should I wait till you tell me, when I have a most satisfactory witness of your promise in the old man who is present?" And, saying this, he looked to my father, and said: "Tell me, most excellent of all men, is not this the man who promised to prove to you to-day that God is one, and that we ought not to say or think that there is any other god, and that he who acts contrary to this will be punished eternally, as committing the most heinous sin? Do you, then, refuse to reply to me?"

CHAP. III.—*The mode of the discussion.*

And our father said: "Well might you have demanded testimony from me, Simon, if Peter had first denied [that he had made the promise]. But now I shall feel no shame in saying what I am bound to say. I think that you wish to enter on the discussion inflamed with anger. Now this is a state of mind in which it is improper for you to speak and for us to listen to you; for we are no longer being helped on to the truth, but we are watching the progress of a contest. And now, having learned from Hellenic culture how those who seek [the truth] ought to act, I shall remind you. Let

---

[1] Ἰδιώτης.

[2] τῶν παρὰ Ἰουδαίοις δημοσίᾳ πεπιστευμένων βίβλων. The literal translation, given in the text, means that the Jews as a community believed in these books as speaking the truth. Cotelerius translates: "the books which were publicly entrusted to the Jews." One MS. reads, πεπιστευμένων, which might mean, "deemed trustworthy among the Jews."

each of you give an exposition of his own opinion,[1] and let the right of speech pass from the one to the other.[2] For if Peter alone should wish to expound his thought, but you should be silent as to yours, it is possible that some argument adduced by you might crush both your and his opinion; and both of you, though defeated by this argument, would not appear defeated, but only the one who expounded his opinion; while he who did not expound his, though equally defeated, would not appear defeated, but would even be thought to have conquered." And Simon answered: "I will do as you say; but I am afraid lest you do not turn out a truth-loving judge, as you have been already prejudiced by his arguments."

CHAP. IV.—*The prejudices of Faustus rather on the side of Simon than on that of Peter.*

Our father answered: "Do not compel me to agree with you without any exercise of my judgment in order that I may seem to be a truth-loving judge; but if you wish me to tell you the truth, my prepossessions are rather on the side of your opinions." And Simon said: "How is this the case, when you do not know what my opinions are?" And our father said: "It is easy to know this, and I will tell you how. You promised that you would convict Peter of error in maintaining the unity of God; but if one undertakes to convict of error him who maintains the unity of God, it is perfectly plain that he, as being in the right,[3] does not hold the same opinion. For if he holds the same opinion as the man who is thoroughly in error, then he himself is in error; but if he gives his proofs holding opposite opinions, then he is in the right. Not well[4] then do you assert that he who main-

---

[1] δόγμα.
[2] One MS. and an Epitome have: "And you must address your arguments to another who acts as judge."
[3] The words translated "error," ψεῦσμα, and "to be in the right," ἀληθεύειν, are, properly rendered, "falsehood," and "to speak the truth."
[4] The MSS. read: "not otherwise." The reading of the text is found in an Epitome.

tains the unity of God is wrong, unless you believe that there are many gods. Now I maintain that there are many gods. Holding, therefore, the same opinion as you before the discussion, I am prepossessed rather in your favour. For this reason you ought to have no anxiety in regard to me, but Peter ought, for I still hold opinions contrary to his. And so after your discussion I hope that, as a truth-loving judge, who has stripped himself of his prepossessions, I shall agree to that doctrine which gains the victory." When my father said this, a murmur of applause burst insensibly from the multitudes because my father had thus spoken.

CHAP. V.—*Peter commences the discussion.*

Peter then said: "I am ready to do as the umpire of our discussion has said; and straightway without any delay I shall set forth my opinion in regard to God. I then assert that there is one God who made the heavens and the earth, and all things that are in them. And it is not right to say or to think that there is any other." And Simon said: "But I maintain that the Scriptures believed in amongst the Jews say that there are many gods, and that God is not angry at this, because He has Himself spoken of many gods in His Scriptures.

CHAP. VI.—*Simon appeals to the Old Testament to prove that there are many gods.*

"For instance, in the very first words of the law, He evidently speaks of them as being like even unto Himself. For thus it is written, that, when the first man received a commandment from God to eat of every tree that was in the garden,[1] but not to eat of the tree of the knowledge of good and evil, the serpent having persuaded them by means of the woman, through the promise that they would become gods, made them look up;[2] and then, when they had thus looked up,

[1] παραδείσῳ, "paradise." Gen. ii. 16, 17.

[2] ἀναβλίψαι. It signifies either to look up, or to recover one's sight. Possibly the second meaning is the one intended here, corresponding to the words of our version: "Then your eyes shall be opened."

God said,[1] 'Behold, Adam is become as one of us.' When, then, the serpent said,[2] 'Ye shall be as gods,' he plainly speaks in the belief that gods exist; all the more as God also added His testimony, saying, 'Behold, Adam is become as one of us.' The serpent, then, who said that there are many gods, did not speak falsely. Again, the scripture,[3] 'Thou shalt not revile the gods, nor curse the rulers of thy people,' points out many gods whom it does not wish even to be cursed. But it is also somewhere else written,[4] 'Did another god dare to enter and take him a nation from the midst of [another] nation, as did I the Lord God?' When He says, 'Did another God dare?' He speaks on the supposition that other gods exist. And elsewhere:[5] 'Let the gods that have not made the heavens and the earth perish;' as if those who had made them were not to perish. And in another place, when it says,[6] 'Take heed to thyself lest thou go and serve other gods whom thy fathers knew not,' it speaks as if other gods existed whom they were not to follow. And again:[7] 'The names of other gods shall not ascend upon thy lips.' Here it mentions many gods whose names it does not wish to be uttered. And again it is written,[8] 'Thy God is the Lord, He is God of gods.' And again:[9] 'Who is like unto Thee, O Lord, among the gods?' And again:[10] 'God is Lord of gods.' And again:[11] 'God stood in the assembly of gods: He judgeth among the gods.' Wherefore I wonder how, when there are so many passages in writing which testify that there are many gods, you have asserted that we ought neither to say nor to think that there are many. Finally, if you have anything to say against what has been spoken so distinctly, say it in the presence of all."

---

[1] Gen. iii. 22.   [2] Gen. iii. 5.   [3] Ex. xxii. 28.
[4] Deut. iv. 34.   [5] Jer. x. 11.   [6] Deut. xiii. 6.
[7] Josh. xxiii. 7, Sept.   [8] Deut. x. 17.
[9] Ps. xxxv. 10, lxxxvi. 8.   [10] Ps. l. 1.   [11] Ps. lxxxii. 1.

CHAP. VII.—*Peter appeals to the Old Testament to prove the unity of God.*

And Peter said: "I shall reply briefly to what you have said. The law, which frequently speaks of gods, itself says to the Jewish multitude,[1] 'Behold, the heaven of heavens is the Lord's thy God, with all that therein is;' implying that, even if there are gods, they are under Him, that is, under the God of the Jews. And again:[2] 'The Lord thy God, He is God in heaven above, and upon the earth beneath, and there is none other except Him.' And somewhere else the Scripture says to the Jewish multitude,[3] 'The Lord your God is God of gods;' so that, even if there are gods, they are under the God of the Jews. And somewhere else the Scripture says in regard to Him,[4] 'God, the great and true, who regardeth not persons, nor taketh reward, He doth execute the judgment of the fatherless and widow.' The Scripture, in calling the God of the Jews great and true, and executing judgment, marked out the others as small, and not true. But also somewhere else the Scripture says,[5] 'As I live, saith the Lord, there is no other God but me. I am the first, I am after this; except me there is no God.' And again:[6] 'Thou shalt fear the Lord thy God, and Him only shalt thou serve.' And again:[7] 'Hear, O Israel, the Lord your God is one Lord.' And many passages besides seal with an oath that God is one, and except Him there is no God. Whence I wonder how, when so many passages testify that there is one God, you say that there are many."

CHAP. VIII.—*Simon and Peter continue the discussion.*

And Simon said: "My original stipulation with you was that I should prove from the Scriptures that you were wrong in maintaining that we ought not to speak of many gods. Accordingly I adduced many written passages to show that the divine Scriptures themselves speak of many gods." And

---

[1] Deut. x. 14.   [2] Deut. iv. 39.   [3] Deut. x. 17.
[4] Deut. x. 17.   [5] Isa. xlix. 18, xlv. 21, xliv. 6.
[6] Deut. vi. 13.   [7] Deut. vi. 4.

Peter said: "Those very Scriptures which speak of many gods, also exhorted us, saying, 'The names of other gods shall not ascend upon thy lips.'[1] Thus, Simon, I did not speak contrary to what was written." And Simon said: "Do you, Peter, listen to what I have to say. You seem to me to sin in speaking against them,[2] when the Scripture says,[3] 'Thou shalt not revile [the gods], nor curse the rulers of thy people.'" And Peter said: "I am not sinning, Simon, in pointing out their destruction according to the Scriptures; for thus it is written:[4] 'Let the gods who did not make the heavens and the earth perish.' And He said thus, not as though *some* had made the heavens and were not to perish, as you interpreted the passage. For it is plainly declared that He who made them is one in the very first part of Scripture:[5] 'In the beginning God created the heaven and the earth.' And it did not say, 'the gods.' And somewhere else it says,[6] 'And the firmament showeth His handiwork.' And in another place it is written,[7] 'The heavens themselves shall perish, but Thou shalt remain for ever.'"

CHAP. IX.—*Simon tries to show that the Scriptures contradict themselves.*

And Simon said: "I adduced clear passages from the Scriptures to prove that there are many gods; and you, in reply, brought forward as many or more from the same Scriptures, showing that God is one, and He the God of the Jews. And when I said that we ought not to revile gods, you proceeded to show that He who created is one, because those who did not create will perish. And in reply to my assertion that we ought to maintain that there are gods, because the Scriptures also say so, you showed that we ought not to utter their names, because the same Scripture tells us not to utter the names of other gods. Since, then, these very

---

[1] Josh. xxiii. 7 in the Septuagint.   [2] Namely, the gods.
[3] Ex. xxii. 28. The MSS. omit θεούς, though they insert it in the passage as quoted a little before this. One MS. reads "the ruler" with our version.
[4] Jer. x. 11.   [5] Gen. i. 1.   [6] Ps. xix. 1.   [7] Ps. cii. 26, 27.

Scriptures say at one time that there are many gods, and at another that there is only one; and sometimes that they ought not to be reviled, and at other times that they ought; what conclusion ought we to come to in consequence of this, but that the Scriptures themselves lead us astray?"

CHAP. X.—*Peter's explanation of the apparent contradictions of Scripture.*

And Peter said: "They do not lead astray, but convict and bring to light the evil disposition against God which lurks like a serpent in each one. For the Scriptures lie before each one like many divers types. Each one, then, has his own disposition like wax, and examining the Scriptures and finding everything in them, he moulds his idea of God according to his wish, laying upon them, as I said, his own disposition, which is like wax. Since, then, each one finds in the Scriptures whatever opinion he wishes to have in regard to God, for this reason he [Simon] moulds from them the forms[1] of many gods, while we moulded the form of Him who truly exists, coming to the knowledge of the true type from our own shape.[2] For assuredly the soul within us is clothed with His image for immortality. If I abandon the parent of this soul, it also will abandon me to just judgment, making known the injustice by the very act of daring;[3] and as coming from one who is just, it will justly abandon me; and so, as far as the soul is concerned, I shall, after punishment, be destroyed, having abandoned the help that comes from it. But if there is another [god], first let him put on another form, another shape, in order that by the new shape of the body I may recognise the new god. But if he should change the shape, does he thereby change the substance of the soul? But if he should change it also, then I am no longer myself, having become another both in shape and in substance. Let him, therefore, create others, if there

---

[1] ἰδίας.   [2] μορφῆς.
[3] Probably τολμήματι should be changed into ὁρμήματι, or some such word: making known that an act of injustice has been committed by taking its departure.

is another. But there is not. For if there had been, he would have created. But since he has not created, then let him, as non-existent, leave him who is really existent.¹ For he is nobody,² except only in the opinion of Simon. I do not accept of any other god but Him alone who created me."

CHAP. XI.—*Gen. i. 26 appealed to by Simon.*

And Simon said: "Since I see that you frequently speak of the God who created you, learn from me how you are impious even to Him. For there are evidently two who created, as the Scripture says:³ 'And God said, Let us make man in our image, after our likeness.' Now 'let us make' implies two or more; certainly not one only."

CHAP. XII.—*Peter's explanation of the passage.*

And Peter answered: "One is He who said to His Wisdom, 'Let us make man.' But His Wisdom⁴ was that with which He Himself always rejoiced⁵ as with His own spirit. It is united as soul to God, but it is extended by Him, as hand, fashioning the universe. On this account, also, one man was made, and from him went forth also the female. And being a unity generically, it is yet a duality, for by expansion and contraction the unity is thought to be a duality. So that I act rightly in offering up all the honour to one God as to parents." And Simon said: "What then? Even if the Scriptures say that there are other gods, will you not accept the opinion?"

CHAP. XIII.—*The contradictions of the Scriptures intended to try those who read them.*

And Peter answered: "If the Scriptures or prophets speak

---

¹ This might possibly be translated, "let him leave him who exists to him who exists;" *i.e.* let him leave the real God to man, who really exists.
² Wieseler proposes, "for he exists to no one." ³ Gen. i. 26.
⁴ This is the only passage in the Homilies relating to the σοφία. The text is in some parts corrupt. It is critically discussed by Uhlhorn, some of whose emendations are adopted by Dressel and translated here.
⁵ Prov. viii. 30.

of gods, they do so to try those who hear. For thus it is written:[1] 'If there arise among you a prophet, giving signs and wonders, and that sign and wonder shall then come to pass, and he say to thee, Let us go after and worship other gods which thy fathers have not known, ye[2] shall not hearken to the words of that prophet; let thy hands be among the first to stone him. For he hath tried to turn thee from the Lord thy God. But if thou say in thy heart, How did he do that sign or wonder? thou shalt surely know that he who tried thee, tried thee to see if thou dost fear the Lord thy God.' The words 'he who tried thee, tried thee,' have reference to the earliest times;[3] but it appears to be otherwise after the removal to Babylon. For God, who knows all things, would not, as can be proved by many arguments, try in order that He Himself might know, for He foreknows all things. But, if you like, let us discuss this point, and I shall show that God foreknows. But it has been proved that the opinion is false that He does not know, and that this was written to try us. Thus we, Simon, can be led astray[4] neither by the Scriptures nor by any one else; nor are we deceived into the admission of many gods, nor do we agree to any statement that is made against God.

CHAP. XIV.—*Other beings called gods.*

"For we ourselves also know that angels are called gods by the Scriptures,—as, for instance, He who spake at the bush, and wrestled with Jacob,—and the name is likewise applied to Him who is born Emmanuel, and who is called the mighty God.[5] Yea, even Moses became a god to Pharaoh, though

---

[1] Deut. xiii. 1 ff.

[2] The change from the singular to the plural is in the Greek.

[3] Lit., "But it had been said that he who tried, tried." The idea seems to be, Before the removal to Babylon true prophets tested the people by urging them to worship these gods; but after that event false prophets arose who really wished to seduce the Jews from the worship of the true God.

[4] Lit., "nor can we be made to stumble from the Scriptures nor by any one else [or anything else]."

[5] Isa. ix. 6.

in reality he was a man. The same is the case also with the idols of the Gentiles. But we have but one God, one who made creation and arranged the universe, whose Son is the Christ. Obeying Christ,[1] we learn to know what is false from the Scriptures. Moreover, being furnished by our ancestors with the truths of the Scriptures, we know that there is only one who has made the heavens and the earth, the God of the Jews, and of all who choose to worship Him. Our fathers, with pious thought, setting down a fixed belief in Him as the true God, handed down this belief to us, that we may know that if anything is said against God, it is a falsehood. I shall add this remark over and above what I need say: If the case be not as I have said, then may I, and all who love the truth, incur danger in regard to the praise of the God who made us."

CHAP. XV.—*Christ not God, but the Son of God.*

When Simon heard this, he said: "Since you say that we ought not to believe even the prophet that gives signs and wonders if he say that there is another god, and that you know that he even incurs the penalty of death, therefore your teacher also was with reason cut off for having given signs and wonders." And Peter answered: "Our Lord neither asserted that there were gods except the Creator of all, nor did He proclaim Himself to be God, but He with reason pronounced blessed him who called Him the Son of that God who has arranged the universe." And Simon answered: "Does it not seem to you, then, that he who comes from God is God?" And Peter said: "Tell us how this is possible; for we cannot affirm this, because we did not hear it from Him.

CHAP. XVI.—*The unbegotten and the begotten necessarily different from each other.*

"In addition to this, it is the peculiarity of the Father not to have been begotten, but of the Son to have been begotten; but what is begotten cannot be compared with that which is

[1] Lit., "whom obeying:" the "whom" might refer to God.

unbegotten or self-begotten." And Simon said: "Is it not the same on account of its origin?"[1] And Peter said: "He who is not the same in all respects as some one, cannot have all the same appellations applied to him as that person." And Simon said: "This is to assert, not to prove." And Peter said: "Why, do you not see that if[2] the one happens to be self-begotten or unbegotten, they cannot be called the same; nor can it be asserted of him who has been begotten that he is of the same substance as he is who has begotten him? Learn this also: The bodies of men have immortal souls, which have been clothed with the breath of God; and having come forth from God, they are of the same substance, but they are not gods. But if they are gods, then in this way the souls of all men, both those who have died, and those who are alive, and those who shall come into being, are gods. But if in a spirit of controversy you maintain that these also are gods, what great matter is it, then, for Christ to be called God? for He has only what all have.

CHAP. XVII.—*The nature of God.*

"We call Him God whose peculiar attributes cannot belong to the nature of any other; for, as He is called the Unbounded because He is boundless on every side, it must of necessity be the case that it is no other one's peculiar attribute to be called unbounded, as another cannot in like manner be boundless. But if any one says that it is possible, he is wrong; for two things boundless on every side cannot coexist, for the one is bounded by the other. Thus it is in the nature[3] of things that the unbegotten is one. But if he possesses a figure, even in this case the figure is one and incomparable.[4] Wherefore He is called the Most High, be-

[1] The word γένεσις, "arising, coming into being," is here used, not γέννησις, "begetting." The idea fully expressed is: "Is not that which is begotten identical in essence with that which begets it?"

[2] We have inserted εἰ. The passage is amended in various ways; this seems to be the simplest.

[3] Lit., "thus it is nature."

[4] We have adopted an emendation here. The text has: "Even thus the incomparable is one."

cause, being higher than all, He has the universe subject to Him."

Chap. XVIII.—*The name of God.*

And Simon said: "Is this word 'God' His ineffable name, which all use, because you maintain so strongly in regard to a name that it cannot be given to another?" And Peter said: "I know that this is not His ineffable name, but one which is given by agreement among men; but if you give it to another, you will also assign to this other that which is not used; and that, too, deliberately.[1] The name which is used is the forerunner of that which is not used. In this way insolence is attributed even to that which has not yet been spoken, just as honour paid to that which is known is handed on to that which has not yet been known."

Chap. XIX.—*The shape of God in man.*

And Simon said: "I should like to know, Peter, if you really believe that the shape of man has been moulded after the shape of God."[2] And Peter said: "I am really quite certain, Simon, that this is the case." And Simon said: "How can death dissolve the body, impressed as it has thus been with the greatest seal?" And Peter said: "It is the shape of the just God. When, then, the body begins to act unjustly, the form which is in it takes to flight, and thus the body is dissolved, by the shape disappearing, in order that an unjust body may not have the shape of the just God. The dissolution, however, does not take place in regard to the seal, but in regard to the sealed body. But that which is sealed is not dissolved without Him who sealed it. And thus it is not permitted to die without judgment." And Simon said: "What necessity was there to give the shape of such a being to man, who was raised from the earth?" And Peter said: "This was done because of the love of God, who made man. For while, as far as substance is concerned,

---

[1] Wieseler proposes to join this clause with the following: "And in point of choice the name which."

[2] Lit., "of that one, of Him."

all things are superior to the flesh of man,—I mean the ether, the sun, the moon, the stars, the air, the water, the fire—in a word, all the other things which have been made for the service of man,—yet, though superior in substance, they willingly endure to serve the inferior in substance, because of the shape of the superior. For as they who honour the clay image of a king have paid honour to the king himself, whose shape the clay happens to have, so the whole creation with joy serves man, who is made from earth, looking to the honour thus paid to God.

CHAP. XX.—*The character of God.*

"Behold, then, the character of that God to whom you, Simon, wish to persuade us to be ungrateful, and the earth continues to bear you, perhaps wishing to see who will venture to entertain similar opinions to yours. For you were the first to dare what no other dared: you were the first to utter what we first heard. We first and alone have seen the boundless long-suffering of God in bearing with such great impiety as yours, and that God no other than the Creator of the world, against whom you have dared to act impiously. And yet openings of the earth took not place, and fire was not sent down from heaven and went not forth to burn up men, and rain was not poured out,[1] and a multitude of beasts was not sent from the thickets, and upon us ourselves the destructive wrath of God did not begin to show itself, on account of one who sinned the sin, as it were, of spiritual adultery, which is worse than the carnal. For it is not God the Creator of heaven and earth that in former times punished sins, since now, when He is blasphemed in the highest degree, He would inflict the severest punishment.[2] But, on the contrary, He is long-suffering, calls to

---

[1] One MS. reads, "was not restrained."

[2] We have inserted *ἄν*, and suppose the sentence to be ironical. The meaning might be the same without *ἄν*. The text of Dressel is as follows: "For is not He who then punished the sins God, Creator of heaven and earth; since even now, being blasphemed in the highest degree, He punished it in the highest degree?"

repentance, having the arrows which end in the destruction of the impious laid up in His treasures, which He will discharge like living animals when He shall sit down to give judgment to those that are His.[1] Wherefore let us fear the just God, whose shape the body of man bears for honour."

CHAP. XXI.—*Simon promises to appeal to the teaching of Christ. Peter dismisses the multitudes.*

When Peter said this, Simon answered: "Since I see you skilfully hinting that what is written in the books[2] against the framer[3] [of the world] does not happen to be true, to-morrow I shall show, from the discourses of your teacher, that he asserted that the framer [of the world] was not the highest God." And when Simon said this, he went out. But Peter said to the assembled multitudes: "If Simon can do no other injury to us in regard to God, he at least prevents you from listening to the words that can purify the soul." On Peter saying this, much whispering arose amongst the crowds, saying, "What necessity is there for permitting him to come in here, and utter his blasphemies against God?" And Peter heard, and said, "Would that the doctrines against God which are intended to try men[4] went no further than Simon! For there will be, as the Lord said, false apostles,[5] false prophets, heresies, desires for supremacy, who, as I conjecture, finding their beginning in Simon, who blasphemes God, will work together in the assertion of the same opinions against God as those of Simon." And saying this with tears, he summoned the multitudes to him by his hand; and when they came, he laid his hands upon them and prayed, and then dismissed them, telling them to come at an earlier hour next day. Saying this, and groaning, he entered and went to sleep, without taking food.

---

[1] Cotelerius translates: "to His enemies."   [2] *i.e.* the Scriptures.

[3] A distinction has to be made between the Creator, or maker out of nothing, and the framer, or fashioner, or Demiurge, who puts the matter into shape.

[4] Lit., "the word against God for the trial of men."

[5] Comp. Matt. xxiv. 24.

HOMILY XVII.

CHAP. I.—*Simon comes to Peter.*

THE next day, therefore, as Peter was to hold a discussion with Simon, he rose earlier than usual and prayed. On ceasing to pray, Zacchæus came in, and said: "Simon is seated without, discoursing with about thirty of his own special followers." And Peter said: "Let him talk until the multitude assemble, and then let us begin the discussion in the following way. We shall hear all that has been said by him, and having fitted our reply to this, we shall go out and discourse." And assuredly so it happened. Zacchæus, therefore, went out, and not long after entered again, and communicated to Peter the discourse delivered by Simon against him.[1]

CHAP. II.—*Simon's speech against Peter.*

Now he said: "He accuses you, Peter, of being the servant of wickedness, of having great power in magic, and as charming the souls of men in a way worse than idolatry. To prove that you are a magician, he seemed to me to adduce the following evidence, saying: 'I am conscious of this, that when I come to hold a discussion with him, I do not remember a single word of what I have been meditating on by myself. For while he is discoursing, and my mind is engaged in recollecting what it is that I thought of saying on coming to a conference with him, I do not hear anything whatsoever of what he is saying. Now, since I do not experience this in the presence of any other than in his alone, is it not plain that I am under the influence of his magic? And as

---
[1] The text has: "against Peter."

to his doctrines being worse than those of idolatry, I can make that quite clear to any one who has understanding. For there is no other benefit than this, that the soul should be freed from images[1] of every kind. For when the soul brings an image before its eye, it is bound by fear, and it pines away through anxiety lest it should suffer some calamity; and being altered, it falls under the influence of a demon; and being under his influence, it seems to the mass to be wise.

CHAP. III.—*Simon's accusation of Peter.*

"'Peter does this to you while promising to make you wise. For, under the pretext of proclaiming one God, he seems to free you from many lifeless images, which do not at all injure those who worship them, because they are seen by the eyes themselves to be made of stone, or brass, or gold, or of some other lifeless material. Wherefore the soul, because it knows that what is seen is nothing, cannot be spell-bound by fear in an equal degree by means of what is visible. But looking to a terrible God through the influence of deceptive teaching, it has all its natural foundations overturned. And I say this, not because I exhort you to worship images, but because Peter, seeming to free your souls from terrible images,[2] drives mad the mind of each one of you by a more terrible image, introducing God in a shape, and that, too, a God extremely just,—an image which is accompanied by what is terrible and awful to the contemplative soul, by that which can entirely destroy the energy of a sound mind. For the mind, when in the midst of such a storm, is like the depth stirred by a violent wind, perturbed and darkened. Wherefore, if he comes to benefit you, let him not, while seeming to dissolve your fears which gently proceed from lifeless shapes, introduce in their stead the terrible shape of God. But has God a shape? If He has, He possesses a figure. And if He has a figure, how is He not limited? And if limited, He is in space. But if He is in space, He is less than the space which encloses Him. And if less than anything, how is He greater than all, or

[1] εἰδώλων, idols.   [2] ἰδεῶν.

superior to all, or the highest of all? This, then, is the state of the case.

CHAP. IV.—*It is asserted that Christ's teaching is different from Peter's.*

"'And that he does not really believe even the doctrines proclaimed by his teacher is evident, for he proclaims doctrines opposite to his. For he said to some one, as I learn,[1] "Call me not good, for the good is one." Now, in speaking of the good one, he no longer speaks of that just one,[2] whom the Scriptures proclaim, who kills and makes alive,—kills those who sin, and makes alive those who live according to His will. But that he did not really call Him who is the framer of the world good, is plain to any one who can reflect. For the framer of the world was known to Adam whom He had made, and to Enoch who pleased Him, and to Noah who was seen to be just by Him; likewise to Abraham, and Isaac, and Jacob; also to Moses, and the people, and the whole world. But Jesus, the teacher of Peter himself, came and said,[3] "No one knew the Father except the Son, as no one knoweth[4] even the Son except the Father, and those to whom the Son may wish to reveal Him." If, then, it was the Son himself who was present, it was from the time of his appearance that he began to reveal to those to whom he wished, Him who was unknown to all. And thus the Father was unknown to all who lived before him, and could not thus be He who was known to all.

CHAP. V.—*Jesus inconsistent in his teaching.*

"'In saying this, Jesus is consistent not even with himself. For sometimes by other utterances, taken from the Scriptures, he presents God as being terrible and just, saying,[5] "Fear not him who killeth the body, but can do nothing to the soul; but fear Him who is able to cast both body and soul into the geenna of fire. Yea, I say unto you, fear Him." But

---

[1] Matt. xix. 17.
[2] The Gnostic distinction between the God who is just and the God who is good, is here insisted on.
[3] Matt. xi. 27.   [4] One MS. reads, " saw."   [5] Matt. x. 28.

that he asserted that He is really to be feared as being a just God, to whom he says those who receive injustice cry, is shown in a parable of which he gives the interpretation, saying:[1] "If, then, the unjust judge did so, because he was continually entreated, how much more will the Father avenge those who cry to Him day and night? Or do you think that, because He bears long with them, He will not do it? Yea, I say to you, He will do it, and that speedily." Now he who speaks of God as an avenging and rewarding God, presents Him as naturally just, and not as good. Moreover he gives thanks to the Lord of heaven and earth.[2] But if He is Lord of heaven and earth, He is acknowledged to be the framer of the world, and if framer, then He is just. When, therefore, he sometimes calls Him good and sometimes just, he is not consistent with himself in this point. But his wise disciple maintained yesterday a third point, that real sight[3] is more satisfactory than vision, not knowing that real sight can be human, but that vision confessedly proceeds from divinity.'

CHAP. VI.—*Peter goes out to answer Simon.*

"These and such like were the statements, Peter, which Simon addressed to the multitudes while he stood outside; and he seems to me to be disturbing the minds of the greater number. Wherefore go forth immediately, and by the power of truth break down his false statements." When Zacchæus said this, Peter prayed after his usual manner and went out, and standing in the place where he spoke the day before, and saluting the multitudes according to the custom enjoined by his religion, he began to speak as follows: "Our Lord Jesus Christ, who is the true prophet (as I shall prove conclusively at the proper time), made concise declarations in regard to those matters that relate to the truth, for these two

---

[1] Luke xviii. 6. [2] Matt. xi. 25.
[3] The MSS. read ἐνέργειαν, "activity." Clericus amended it into ἐνάργειαν, which means, vision or sight in plain open day with one's own eyes, in opposition to the other word ὀπτασία, vision in sleep, or ecstasy, or some similar unusual state.

reasons: first, because He was in the habit of addressing the pious, who had knowledge enough to enable them to believe the opinions uttered by Him by way of declaration; for His statements were not strange to their usual mode of thought; and in the second place, because, having a limited time assigned Him for preaching, He did not employ the method of demonstration in order that He might not spend all His limited time in arguments, for in this way it might happen that He would be fully occupied in giving the solutions of a few problems which might be understood by mental exertion, while He would not have given us to any great extent[1] those statements which relate to the truth. Accordingly He stated any opinions He wished, as to a people who were able to understand Him, to whom we also belong, who, whenever we did not understand anything of what had been said by Him,—a thing which rarely happened,—inquired of Him privately, that nothing said by Him might be unintelligible to us.

CHAP. VII.—*Man in the shape of God.*

"Knowing therefore that we knew all that was spoken by Him, and that we could supply the proofs, He sent us to the ignorant Gentiles to baptize them for remission of sins,[2] and commanded us to teach them first. Of His commandments this is the first and great one, to fear the Lord God, and to serve Him only. But He meant us to fear that God whose angels they are who are the angels of the least of the faithful amongst us,[3] and who stand in heaven continually beholding the face of the Father. For He has shape, and He has every limb primarily and solely for beauty's sake, and not for use. For He has not eyes that He may see with them; for He sees on every side, since He is incomparably more brilliant in His body than the visual spirit which is in us, and He is more splendid than everything, so that in comparison with Him the light of the sun may be reckoned as darkness. Nor has He ears that He may hear; for He hears, perceives, moves, energizes, acts on every side. But He has the most beautiful shape on account of man, that the

[1] Lit., "to a greater extent."   [2] Matt. xxviii. 19.   [3] Matt. xviii. 10.

pure in heart[1] may be able to see Him, that they may rejoice because they suffered. For He moulded man in His own shape as in the grandest seal, in order that he may be the ruler and lord of all, and that all may be subject to him. Wherefore, judging that He is the universe, and that man is His image (for He is Himself invisible, but His image man is visible), the man who wishes to worship Him honours His visible image, which is man. Whatsoever therefore any one does to man, be it good or bad, is regarded as being done to Him. Wherefore the judgment which proceeds from Him shall go before, giving to every one according to his merits. For He avenges His own shape.

CHAP. VIII.—*God's figure: Simon's objection therefrom refuted.*

"But some one will say, If He has shape, then He has figure also, and is in space; but if He is in space, and is, as being less, enclosed by it, how is He great above everything? How can He be everywhere if He has figure? The first remark I have to make to him who urges these objections is this: The Scriptures persuade us to have such sentiments and to believe such statements in regard to Him; and we know that their declarations are true, for witness is borne to them by our Lord Jesus Christ, by whose orders we are bound to afford proofs to you that such is the case. But first I shall speak of space. The space of God is the non-existent, but God is that which exists. But that which is non-existent cannot be compared with that which is existent. For how can space be existent? unless it be a second space, such as heaven, earth, water, air, and if there is any other body that fills up the vacuity, which is called vacuity on this account, that it is nothing. For 'nothing' is its more appropriate name. For what is that which is called vacuity but as it were a vessel which contains nothing, except the vessel itself? But being vacuity, it is not itself space; but space is that in which vacuity itself is, if indeed it is the vessel. For it must be the case that that which exists is in that which does not exist.

[1] Matt. v. 8.

But by this which is non-existent I mean that which is called by some, space, which is nothing. But being nothing, how can it be compared with that which is, except by expressing the contrary, and saying that it is that which does not exist, and that that which does not exist is called space? But even if it were something, there are many examples which I have at hand, but I shall content myself with one only, to show that that which encloses is not unquestionably superior to that which is enclosed. The sun is a circular figure, and is entirely enclosed by air, yet it lightens up the air, it warms it, it divides it; and if the sun be away from it, it is enveloped in darkness; and from whatsoever part of it the sun is removed, it becomes cold as if it were dead; but again it is illuminated by its rising, and when it has been warmed up by it, it is adorned with still greater beauty. And it does this by giving a share of itself, though it has its substance limited. What, then, is there to prevent God, as being the Framer and Lord of this and everything else, from possessing figure and shape and beauty, and having the communication of these qualities proceeding from Himself extended infinitely?

CHAP. IX.—*God the centre or heart of the universe.*

"One, then, is the God who truly exists, who presides in a superior shape, being the heart of that which is above and that which is below twice,[1] which sends forth from Him as from a centre the life-giving and incorporeal power; the whole universe with the stars and regions[2] of the heaven, the air, the fire, and if anything else exists, is proved to be a substance infinite in height, boundless in depth, immeasurable in breadth, extending the life-giving and wise nature from Him over three infinites.[3] It must be, therefore, that this

---

[1] The whole of this chapter is full of corruptions; "twice" occurs in one MS. Various attempts have been made to amend the passage.

[2] An emendation.

[3] The text is corrupt. We have translated ἐπ' ἀπείρους τρεῖς. Some think "three" should be omitted. The three infinites are in respect of height, depth, and breadth.

infinite which proceeds from Him on every side exists,[1] having as its heart Him who is above all, and who thus possesses figure; for wherever He be, He is as it were in the centre of the infinite, being the limit of the universe. And the extensions taking their rise with Him, possess the nature of six infinites; of whom the one taking its rise with Him penetrates[2] into the height above, another into the depth below, another to the right hand, another to the left, another in front, and another behind; to whom He Himself, looking as to a number that is equal on every side,[3] completes the world in six temporal intervals,[4] Himself being the rest,[5] and having the infinite age to come as His image, being the beginning and the end. For in Him the six infinites end, and from Him they receive their extension to infinity.

CHAP. X.—*The nature and shape of God.*

"This is the mystery of the hebdomad. For He Himself is the rest of the whole who grants Himself as a rest to those who imitate His greatness within their little measure. For He is alone, sometimes comprehensible, sometimes incomprehensible, [sometimes limitable,[6]] sometimes illimitable, having extensions which proceed from Him into infinity. For thus He is comprehensible and incomprehensible, near and far, being here and there, as being the only existent one, and as giving a share of that mind which is infinite on every hand, in consequence of which souls breathe and possess life;[7] and if they be separated from the body and be found with a longing for Him, they are borne along into His

---

[1] As punctuated in Dressel, this reads, "that the infinite is the heart."
[2] The emendation of the transcriber of one of the MSS.
[3] This refers to the following mode of exhibiting the number: where each side presents the number three.
[4] The creation of the world in six days.
[5] The seventh day on which God rested, the type of the rest of the future age. See *Epistle of Barnabas*, c. xv.
[6] The words within brackets are inserted by conjecture. "Sometimes incomprehensible, sometimes illimitable," occur only in one MS.
[7] We have adopted Wieseler's suggestions.

bosom, as in the winter time the mists of the mountains, attracted by the rays of the sun, are borne along immortal[1] to it. What affection ought therefore to arise within us if we gaze with our mind on His beautiful shape! But otherwise it is absurd [to speak of beauty]. For beauty cannot exist apart from shape; nor can one be attracted to the love of God, nor even deem that he can see Him, if God has no form.

CHAP. XI.—*The fear of God.*

"But some who are strangers to the truth, and who give their energies to the service of evil, on pretext of glorifying God, say that He has no figure, in order that, being shapeless and formless, He may be visible to no one, so as not to be longed for. For the mind, not seeing the form of God, is empty of Him. But how can any one pray if he has no one to whom he may flee for refuge, on whom he may lean? For if he meets with no resistance, he falls out into vacuity. Yea, says he, we ought not to fear God, but to love Him. I agree; but the consciousness of having done well in each good act will accomplish this. Now well-doing proceeds from fearing. But fear, says he, strikes death into the soul. Nay, but I affirm that it does not strike death, but awakens the soul, and converts it. And perhaps the injunction not to fear God might be right, if we men did not fear many other things; such, for instance, as plots against us by those who are like us, and wild beasts, serpents, diseases, sufferings, demons, and a thousand other ills. Let him, then, who asks us not to fear God, rescue us from these, that we may not fear them; but if he cannot, why should he grudge that we should be delivered from a thousand fears by one fear, the fear of the Just One, and that it should be possible by a slight[2] faith in Him to remove a thousand afflictions from ourselves and others, and receive instead an exchange of

---

[1] This word is justly suspected. The passage is in other respects corrupt.

[2] The word "slight" is not used in reference to the character of the faith, but to indicate that the act of faith is a small act compared with the results that flow from it.

blessings, and that, doing no ill in consequence of fear of the God who sees everything, we should continue in peace even in the present life.

CHAP. XII.—*The fear and love of God.*

"Thus, then, grateful service to Him who is truly Lord, renders us free from service to all other masters.[1] If, then, it is possible for any one to be free from sin without fearing God, let him not fear; for under the influence of love to Him one cannot do what is displeasing to Him. For, on the one hand, it is written that we are to fear Him, and we have been commanded to love Him, in order that each of us may use that prescription which is suitable to his constitution. Fear Him, therefore, because He is just; but whether you fear Him or love Him, sin not. And may it be the case that any one who fears Him shall be able to gain the victory over unlawful desires, shall not lust after what belongs to others, shall practise kindness, shall be sober, and act justly! For I see some who are imperfect in their fear of Him sinning very much. Let us therefore fear God, not only because He is just; for it is through pity for those who have received injustice that He inflicts punishment on those who have done the injustice. As water therefore quenches fire, so does fear extinguish the desire for evil practices. He who teaches fearlessness does not himself fear; but he who does not fear, does not believe that there will be a judgment, strengthens his lusts, acts as a magician, and accuses others of the deeds which he himself does."

CHAP. XIII.—*The evidence of the senses contrasted with that from supernatural vision.*

Simon, on hearing this, interrupted him, and said: "I know against whom you are making these remarks; but in order that I may not spend any time in discussing subjects which I do not wish to discuss, repeating the same statements to refute you, reply to that which is concisely stated by us. You professed that you had well understood the doctrines and

[1] We have adopted an emendation of a passage which is plainly corrupt.

deeds[1] of your teacher because you saw them before you with your own eyes,[2] and heard them with your own ears, and that it is not possible for any other to have anything similar by vision or apparition. But I shall show that this is false. He who hears any one with his own ears, is not altogether fully assured of the truth of what is said; for his mind has to consider whether he is wrong or not, inasmuch as he is a man as far as appearance goes. But apparition not merely presents an object to view, but inspires him who sees it with confidence, for it comes from God. Now reply first to this."

CHAP. XIV.—*The evidence of the senses more trustworthy than that of supernatural vision.*

And Peter said: "You proposed to speak to one point, you replied to another.[3] For your proposition was, that one is better able to know more fully, [and to attain confidence,[4]] when he hears in consequence of an apparition, than when he hears with his own ears; but when you set about the matter, you were for persuading us that he who hears through an apparition is surer than he who hears with his own ears. Finally, you alleged that, on this account, you knew more satisfactorily the doctrines of Jesus than I do, because you heard His words through an apparition. But I shall reply to the proposition you made at the beginning. The prophet, because he is a prophet, having first given certain information with regard to what is objectively[5] said

---

[1] Doctrines and deeds; lit., the things of your teacher.

[2] The MSS. have here ἐνεργείᾳ, "activity." This has been amended into ἐναργείᾳ, "with plainness, with distinctness." Ἐνάργεια is used throughout in opposition to ὀπτασία, ὅραμα, and ἐνύπνιον, and means the act of seeing and hearing by our own senses in plain daylight, when to doubt the fact observed is to doubt the senses; ὀπτασία is apparition or vision in ecstasy, or some extraordinary way but that of sleep; ὅραμα and ἐνύπνιον are restricted to visions in sleep. The last term implies this. The first means simply "a thing seen."

[3] Probably it should be ἀπεκλίνω instead of ἀπεκρίνω, "you turned aside to another."

[4] The words inserted in brackets are inserted conjecturally, to fill up a lacuna in the best MS.

[5] ἐναργῶς, "with reference to things palpable to our senses."

by him, is believed with confidence; and being known beforehand to be a true prophet, and being examined and questioned as the disciple wishes, he replies: But he who trusts to apparition or vision and dream is insecure. For he does not know to whom he is trusting. For it is possible either that he may be an evil demon or a deceptive spirit, pretending in his speeches to be what he is not. But if any one should wish to inquire of him who he is who has appeared, he can say to himself whatever he likes. And thus, gleaming forth like a wicked one, and remaining as long as he likes, he is at length extinguished, not remaining with the questioner so long as he wished him to do for the purpose of consulting him. For any one that sees by means of dreams cannot inquire about whatever he may wish. For reflection is not in the special power of one who is asleep. Hence we, desiring to have information in regard to something in our waking hours, inquire about something else in our dreams; or without inquiring, we hear about matters that do not concern us, and awaking from sleep we are dispirited because we have neither heard nor inquired about those matters which we were eager to know."

CHAP. XV.—*The evidence from dreams discussed.*

And Simon said: "If you maintain that apparitions do not always reveal the truth, yet for all that, visions and dreams, being God-sent, do not speak falsely in regard to those matters which they wish to tell." And Peter said: "You were right in saying that, being God-sent, they do not speak falsely. But it is uncertain if he who sees has seen a God-sent dream." And Simon said: "If he who has had the vision is just, he has seen a true vision." And Peter said: "You were right. But who is just, if he stands in need of a vision that he may learn what he ought to learn, and do what he ought to do?" And Simon said: "Grant me this, that the just man alone can see a true vision, and I shall then reply to that other point. For I have come to the conclusion that an impious man does not see a true dream." And Peter said: "This is false; and I can prove it both apart from Scripture and by Scripture; but I do not undertake to persuade you. For the man who is inclined to fall in love with a bad woman, does not change his mind so as to care for a lawful union with another woman in every respect good; but sometimes they love the worse woman through prepossessions, though they are conscious that there is another who is more excellent. And you are ignorant, in consequence of some such state of mind." And Simon said: "Dismiss this subject, and discuss the matter on which you promised to speak. For it seems to me impossible that impious men should receive dreams from God in any way whatever."

CHAP. XVI.—*None but evil demons appear to the impious.*

And Peter said: "I remember that I promised to prove this point, and to give my proofs in regard to it from Scripture and apart from Scripture. And now listen to what I say. We know that there are many (if you will pardon me the statement; and if you don't, I can appeal to those who are present as judges) who worship idols, commit adultery, and sin in every way, and yet they see true visions and dreams, and some of them have also apparitions of demons. For I maintain that the eyes of mortals cannot see the incorporeal form of the Father or Son, because it is illumined by exceeding great light. Wherefore it is not because God envies, but because He pities, that He cannot be seen by man who has been turned into flesh. For he who sees [God] cannot live. For the excess of light dissolves the flesh of him who sees; unless by the secret power of God the flesh be changed into the nature of light, so that it can see light, or the substance of light be changed into flesh, so that it can be seen by flesh. For the power to see the Father, without undergoing any change, belongs to the Son alone. But the just shall also in like manner behold God;[1] for in the resurrection of the dead, when they have been

---

[1] We have translated a bold conjecture. The text has, "The just not in like manner," without any verb, which Schwegler amended: "To the just this power does not belong in like manner."

changed, as far as their bodies are concerned, into light, and become like the angels, they shall be able to see Him. Finally, then, if any angel be sent that he may be seen by a man, he is changed into flesh, that he may be able to be seen by flesh. For no one can see the incorporeal power not only of the Son, but not even of an angel. But if one sees an apparition, he should know that this is the apparition of an evil demon.

CHAP. XVII.—*The impious see true dreams and visions.*

"But it is manifest that the impious see true visions and dreams, and I can prove it from Scripture. Finally, then, it is written in the law, how Abimelech, who was impious, wished to defile the wife of just Abraham by intercourse, and how he heard the commandment from God in his sleep, as the Scripture saith, not to touch her,[1] because she was dwelling with her husband. Pharaoh, also an impious man, saw a dream in regard to the fulness and thinness of the ears of corn,[2] to whom Joseph said, when he gave the interpretation, that the dream had come from God.[3] Nebuchadnezzar, who worshipped images, and ordered those who worshipped God to be cast into fire, saw a dream[4] extending over the whole age of the world.[5] And let no one say, 'No one who is impious sees a vision when awake.' That is false. Nebuchadnezzar himself, having ordered three men to be cast into fire, saw a fourth when he looked into the furnace, and said, 'I see the fourth as the Son of God.'[6] And nevertheless, though they saw apparitions, visions, and dreams, they were impious. Thus, we cannot infer with absolute certainty that the man who has seen visions, and dreams, and apparitions, is undoubtedly pious. For in the case of the pious man, the truth gushes up natural and pure[7] in his mind, not worked up through dreams, but granted to the good through intelligence.

---

[1] Gen. xx. 3.   [2] Gen. xli. 6.   [3] Gen. xli. 25.   [4] Dan. ii. 31.
[5] Lit., of the whole length of the age.   [6] Dan. iii. 25.
[7] We have amended this passage. The text applies the words "natural [or innate] and pure" to the mind.

Chap. XVIII.—*The nature of revelation.*

"Thus to me also was the Son revealed by the Father. Wherefore I know what is the meaning of revelation, having learned it in my own case. For at the very time when the Lord said, 'Who do they say that I am?'[1] and when I heard one saying one thing of Him, and another another, it came into my heart to say (and I know not, therefore, how I said it), 'Thou art the Son of the living God.'[2] But He, pronouncing me blessed, pointed out to me that it was the Father who had revealed it to me; and from this time I learned that revelation is knowledge gained without instruction, and without apparition and dreams. And this is indeed the case. For in the [soul[3]] which has been placed in us by[4] God, there is all the truth; but it is covered and revealed by the hand of God, who works so far as each one through his knowledge deserves.[5] But the declaration of anything by means of apparitions and dreams from without is a proof, not that it comes from revelation, but from wrath. Finally, then, it is written in the law, that God, being angry, said to Aaron and Miriam,[6] 'If a prophet arise from amongst you, I shall make myself known to him through visions and dreams, but not so as to my servant Moses; because I shall speak to him in an [outward] appearance, and not through dreams, just as one will speak to his own friend.' You see how the statements of wrath are made through visions and dreams, but the statements to a friend are made face to face, in [outward] appearance, and not through riddles and visions and dreams, as to an enemy.

---

[1] Matt. xvi. 13.   [2] Matt. xvi. 16.

[3] This word is not in the text. Schliemann proposed the word "heart." Possibly "breath" or "spirit" may be the lost word. See above.

[4] "By" should properly be "from."

[5] Lit., "who produces according to the merit of each one knowing." Cotelerius translated, "who, knowing the merit of each man, does to him according to it." The idea seems to be, that God uncovers the truth hidden in the soul to each man according to his deserts.

[6] Num. xii. 6; Ex. xxxiii. 11.

CHAP. XIX.—*Opposition to Peter unreasonable.*

"If, then, our Jesus appeared to you in a vision, made Himself known to you, and spoke to you, it was as one who is enraged with an adversary; and this is the reason why it was through visions and dreams, or through revelations that were from without, that He spoke to you. But can any one be rendered fit for instruction through apparitions? And if you will say, 'It is possible,' then I ask, 'Why did our teacher abide and discourse a whole year to those who were awake?' And how are we to believe your word, when you tell us that He appeared to you? And how did He appear to you, when you entertain opinions contrary to His teaching? But if you were seen and taught by Him, and became His apostle for a single hour, proclaim His utterances, interpret His sayings, love His apostles, contend not with me who companied with Him. For in direct opposition to me, who am a firm rock, the foundation of the church,[1] you now stand. If you were not opposed to me, you would not accuse me, and revile the truth proclaimed by me, in order that I may not be believed when I state what I myself have heard with my own ears from the Lord, as if I were evidently a person that was condemned and in bad repute.[2] But if you say that I am condemned, you bring an accusation against God, who revealed the Christ to me, and you inveigh against Him who pronounced me blessed on account of the revelation. But if, indeed, you really wish to work in the cause of truth, learn first of all from us what we have learned from Him, and, becoming a disciple of the truth, become a fellow-worker with us."

CHAP. XX.—*Another subject for discussion proposed.*

When Simon heard this, he said: "Far be it from me to become his or your disciple. For I am not ignorant of what I ought to know; but the inquiries which I made as a learner

[1] Matt. xvi. 18.
[2] We have adopted an emendation of Schwegler's. The text reads, "in good repute."

were made that I may see if you can prove that actual sight is more distinct than apparition.[1] But you spoke according to your own pleasure; you did not prove. And now, to-morrow I shall come to your opinions in regard to God, whom you affirmed to be the framer of the world; and in my discussion with you, I shall show that he is not the highest, nor good, and that your teacher made the same statements as I now do; and I shall prove that you have not understood him." On saying this he went away, not wishing to listen to what might be said to the propositions which he had laid down.

[1] This passage is corrupt in the text. Dressel reads, " that activity is more distinct than apparition." By activity would be meant, " acting while one is awake, and in full possession of his senses; " and thus the meaning would be nearly the same as in our translation.

HOMILY XVIII.

CHAP. I.—*Simon maintains that the framer of the world is not the highest God.*

T break of day, when Peter went forth to discourse, Simon anticipated him, and said : " When I went away yesterday, I promised to you to return to-day, and in a discussion show that he who framed the world is not the highest God, but that the highest God is another who alone is good, and who has remained unknown up to this time. At once, then, state to me whether you maintain that the framer of the world is the same as the lawgiver or not ? If, then, he is the lawgiver, he is just ; but if he is just, he is not good. But if he is not good, then it was another that Jesus proclaimed, when he said,[1] ' Do not call me good ; for one is good, the Father who is in the heavens.' Now a lawgiver cannot be both just and good, for these qualities do not harmonize." And Peter said : " First tell us what are the actions which in your opinion constitute a person good, and what are those which constitute him just, in order that thus we may address our words to the same mark." And Simon said : " Do you state first what in your opinion is goodness, and what justice."

CHAP. II.—*Definition of goodness and justice.*

And Peter said : " That I may not waste my time in contentious discussions, while I make the fair demand that you should give answers to my propositions, I shall myself answer those questions which I put, as is your wish. I then affirm that the man who bestows[2] [goods] is good, just as I see the Framer of the world doing when He gives the sun

---

[1] Matt. xix. 17.
[2] There is a lacuna in one of the MSS. here, which is supplied in various ways. We have inserted the word " goods."

to the good, and the rain to the just and unjust." And Simon said: "It is most unjust that he should give the same things to the just and the unjust." And Peter said: "Do you, then, in your turn state to us what course of conduct would constitute Him good." And Simon said: "It is you that must state this." And Peter said: "I will. He who gives the same things to the good and just, and also to the evil and unjust, is not even just according to you; but you would with reason call Him just if He gave goods to the good and evils to the evil. What course of conduct, then, would He adopt, if He does not adopt the plan of giving things temporal to the evil, if perchance they should be converted, and things eternal to the good, if at least they remain [good]? And thus by giving to all, but by gratifying the more excellent,[1] His justice is good; and all the more long-suffering in this, that to sinners who repent He freely grants forgiveness of their sins, and to those who have acted well He assigns even eternal life. But judging at last, and giving to each one what he deserves, He is just. If, then, this is right, confess it; but if it appears to you not to be right, refute it."

CHAP. III.—*God both good and just.*

And Simon said: "I said once for all, 'Every lawgiver, looking to justice, is just.'" And Peter said: "If it is the part of him who is good not to lay down a law, but of him who is just to lay down a law, in this way the Framer of the world is both good and just. He is good, inasmuch as it is plain that He did not lay down a law in writing from the times of Adam to Moses; but inasmuch as He had a written law from Moses to the present times,[2] He is just also." And Simon said: "Prove to me from the utterances of your teacher that it is within the power of the same man to be good and just; for to me it seems impossible that the law-

---

[1] This translation of Cotelerius is doubtful. More correctly it would be, "by gratifying different people," which does not make sense. Wieseler proposes, "by gratifying in different ways."

[2] The text seems corrupt here. Literally it is, "from Moses to the present times, as has been written, He is just also."

giver who is good should also be just." And Peter said: "I shall explain to you how goodness itself is just. Our teacher Himself first said to the Pharisee who asked Him,[1] 'What shall I do to inherit eternal life?' 'Do not call me good; for one is good, even the Father who is in the heavens;' and straightway He introduced these words, 'But if thou shalt wish to enter into life, keep the commandments.' And when he said, 'What commandments?' He pointed him to those of the law. Now He would not, if He were indicating some other good being, have referred him to the commandments of the Just One. That indeed justice and goodness are different I allow, but you do not know that it is within the power of the same being to be good and just. For He is good, in that He is now long-suffering with the penitent, and welcomes them; but just, when acting as judge He will give to every one according to his deserts."

CHAP. IV.—*The unrevealed God.*

And Simon said: "How, then, if the framer of the world, who also fashioned Adam, was known, and known too by those who were just according to the law, and moreover by the just and unjust, and the whole world, does your teacher, coming after all these, say,[2] 'No one has known the Father but the Son, even as no one knoweth the Son but the Father, and those to whom the Son may wish to reveal Him?' But he would not have made this statement, had he not proclaimed a Father who was still unrevealed, whom the law speaks of as the highest, and who has not given any utterance either good or bad (as Jeremiah testifies in the Lamentations[3]); who also, limiting the nations to seventy languages, according to the number of the sons of Israel who entered Egypt, and according to the boundaries of these nations, gave to his own Son, who is also called Lord, and who brought into order the heaven and the earth, the Hebrews as his portion, and defined him to be God of gods, that is, of the gods who received the other nations as their portions. Laws, therefore,

[1] Luke xviii. 19; Matt. xix. 17.
[2] Matt. xi. 27.   [3] Lam. iii. 38.

proceeded from all the so-called gods to their own divisions, which consist of the other nations. In like manner also from the Son of the Lord of all came forth the law which is established among the Hebrews. And this state of matters was determined on, that if any one should seek refuge in the law of any one, he should belong to the division of him whose law he undertook to obey. No one knew the highest Father, who was unrevealed, just as they did not know that his Son was his Son. Accordingly at this moment you yourself, in assigning the special attributes of the unrevealed Most High to the Son, do not know that he is the Son, being the Father of Jesus, who with you is called the Christ."

CHAP. V.—*Peter doubts Simon's honesty.*

When Simon had made these statements, Peter said to him: "Can you call to witness that these are your beliefs that being Himself,—I do not mean Him whom you speak of now as being unrevealed, but Him in whom you believe, though you do not confess Him? For you are talking nonsense when you define one thing instead of another. Wherefore, if you call Him to witness that you believe what you say, I shall answer you. But if you continue discussing with me what you do not believe, you compel me to strike the empty air." And Simon said: "It is from some of your own disciples that I have heard [that this is the truth[1]]." And Peter said: "Do not bear false witness?" And Simon said: "Do not rebuke me, most insolent man." And Peter said: "So long as you do not tell who it was who said so, [I affirm that] you are a liar." And Simon said: "Suppose that I myself have got up these doctrines, or that I heard them from some other, give me your answer to them. For if they cannot be overturned, then I have learned that this is the truth." And Peter said: "If it is a human invention, I will not reply to it; but if you are held fast by the supposition that it is the truth, acknowledge to me that this is the case, and I can then myself say something in regard to

[1] The words in brackets are inserted to fill up a lacuna which occurs here in the Vatican MS.

the matter." And Simon said: "Once for all, then, these doctrines seem to me to be true. Give me your reply, if you have aught to say against them."

CHAP. VI.—*The nature of revelation.*

And Peter said: "If this is the case, you are acting most impiously. For if it belongs to the Son, who arranged heaven and earth, to reveal His unrevealed Father to whomsoever He wishes, you are, as I said, acting most impiously in revealing Him to those to whom He has not revealed Him." And Simon said: "But he himself wishes me to reveal him." And Peter said: "You do not understand what I mean, Simon. But listen and understand. When it is said that the Son will reveal Him to whom He wishes, it is meant that such an one is to learn of Him not by instruction, but by revelation only. For it is revelation when that which lies secretly veiled in all the hearts of men is revealed [unveiled] by His [God's] own will without any utterance. And thus knowledge comes to one, not because he has been instructed, but because he has understood. And yet the person who understands it cannot demonstrate it to another, since he did not himself receive it by instruction; nor can he reveal it, since he is not himself the Son, unless he maintains that he is himself the Son. But you are not the standing Son. For if you were the Son, assuredly you would know those who are worthy of such a revelation. But you do not know them. For if you knew them, you would do as they do who know."

CHAP. VII.—*Simon confesses his ignorance.*

And Simon said: "I confess I have not understood what you mean by the expression, 'You would do as they do who know.'" And Peter said: "If you have not understood it, then you cannot know the mind of every one; and if you are ignorant of this, then you do not know those who are worthy of the revelation. You are not the Son, for[1] the Son knows. Wherefore He reveals [Him] to whomsoever He wishes, be-

[1] The Greek has "but."

cause they are worthy." And Simon said: "Be not deceived. I know those who are worthy, and I am not the Son. And yet I have not understood what meaning you attach to the words, 'He reveals [Him] to whomsoever He wishes.' But I said that I did not understand it, not because I did not know it, but because I knew that those who were present did not understand it, in order that you may state it more distinctly, so that they may perceive what are the reasons why we are carrying on this discussion." And Peter said: "I cannot state the matter more clearly: explain what meaning you have attached to the words." And Simon said: "There is no necessity why I should state your opinions." And Peter said: "You evidently, Simon, do not understand it, and yet you do not wish to confess, that you may not be detected in your ignorance, and thus be proved not to be the standing Son. For you hint this, though you do not wish to state it plainly; and, indeed, I who am not a prophet, but a disciple of the true Prophet, know well from the hints you have given what your wishes are. For you, though you do not understand even what is distinctly said, wish to call yourself son in opposition to us." And Simon said: "I will remove every pretext from you. I confess I do not understand what can be the meaning of the statement, 'The Son reveals [Him] to whomsoever He wishes.' State therefore what is its meaning more distinctly."

CHAP. VIII.—*The work of revelation belongs to the Son alone.*

And Peter said: "Since, at least in appearance, you have confessed that you do not understand it, reply to the question I put to you, and you will learn the meaning of the statement. Tell me, do you maintain that the Son, whoever he be, is just, or that he is not just?" And Simon said: "I maintain that he is most just." And Peter said: "Seeing He is just, why does He not make the revelation to all, but only to those to whom He wishes?" And Simon said: "Because, being just, he wishes to make the revelation only to the worthy." And Peter said: "Must He not therefore know the mind of each one, in order that He may make the revelation to the worthy?" And Simon said: "Of course he must." And Peter said: "With reason, therefore, has the work of giving the revelation been confined to Him alone, for He alone knows the mind of every one; and it has not been given to you, who are not able to understand even that which is stated by us."

CHAP. IX.—*How Simon bears his exposure.*

When Peter said this, the multitudes applauded. But Simon, being thus exposed,[1] blushed through shame, and rubbing his forehead, said: "Well, then, do they declare that I, a magician, yea, even I who syllogize, am conquered by Peter? It is not so. But if one should syllogize, though carried away and conquered, he still retains the truth that is in him. For the weakness in the defender is not identical with the truth in the conquered man.[2] But I assure you that I have judged all those who are bystanders worthy to know the unrevealed Father. Wherefore, because I publicly reveal him to them, you yourself, through envy, are angry with me who wish to confer a benefit on them."

CHAP. X.—*Peter's reply to Simon.*

And Peter said: "Since you have thus spoken to please the multitudes who are present, I shall speak to them, not to please them, but to tell them the truth. Tell me how you know all those who are present to be worthy, when not even one of them agreed with your exposition of the subject;

[1] Lit., "caught in the act."
[2] This passage is deemed corrupt by commentators. We have made no change in the reading of the MSS., except that of νενικημένης into νενικημένος, and perhaps even this is unnecessary. The last sentence means: "A man may overcome the weakness of his adversary; but he does not therefore strip him of the truth, which he possesses even when he is conquered." The Latin translation of Cotelerius, with some emendations from later editors, yields this: "But they say that I, a magician, am not merely conquered by Peter, but reduced to straits by his reasonings. But not even though one be reduced to straits by reasonings, has he the truth which is in him conquered. For the weakness of the defender is not the truth of the conqueror."

for the giving of applause to me in opposition to you is not the act of those who agree with you, but of those who agree with me, to whom they gave the applause for having spoken the truth. But since God, who is just, judges the mind of each one—a doctrine which you affirm to be true—He would not have wished this to be given through the left hand to those on the right hand, exactly as the man who receives anything from a robber is himself guilty. So that, on this account, He did not wish them to receive what is brought by you; but they are to receive the revelation through the Son, who has been set apart for this work. For to whom is it reasonable that the Father should give a revelation, but to His only Son, because He knows Him to be worthy of such a revelation? And so this is a matter which one cannot teach or be taught, but it must be revealed by the ineffable hand to him who is worthy to know it."

CHAP. XI.—*Simon professes to utter his real sentiments.*

And Simon said: "It contributes much to victory, if the man who wars uses his own weapons; for what one loves he can in real earnest defend, and that which is defended with genuine earnestness has no ordinary power in it. Wherefore in future I shall lay before you my real opinions. I maintain that there is some unrevealed power, unknown to all, even to the Creator himself, as Jesus himself has also declared, though he did not know what he said. For when one talks a great deal he sometimes hits the truth, not knowing what he is saying. I am referring to the statement which he uttered, 'No one knows the Father.'" And Peter said: "Do not any longer profess that you know His doctrines." And Simon said: "I do not profess to believe his doctrines; but I am discussing points in which he was by accident right." And Peter said: "Not to give you any pretext for escape, I shall carry on the discussion with you in the way you wish. At the same time, I call all to witness that you do not yet believe the statement which you just now made. For I know your opinions. And in order that you may not imagine that I am not speaking the truth, I shall expound your opinions, that you may know that you are discussing with one who is well acquainted with them.

CHAP. XII.—*Simon's opinions expounded by Peter.*

"We, Simon, do not assert that from the great power, which is also called the dominant[1] power, two angels were sent forth, the one to create the world, the other to give the law; nor that each one when he came proclaimed himself, on account of what he had done, as the sole creator; nor that there is one who stands, will stand, and is opposed.[2] Learn how you disbelieve even in respect to this subject. If you say that there is an unrevealed power, that power is full of ignorance. For it did not foreknow the ingratitude of the angels who were sent by it." And Simon became exceedingly angry with Peter for saying this, and interrupted his discourse, saying: "What nonsense is this you speak, you daring and most impudent of men, revealing plainly before the multitudes the secret doctrines, so that they can be easily learned?" And Peter said: "Why do you grudge that the present audience should receive benefit?" And Simon said: "Do you then allow that such knowledge is a benefit?" And Peter said: "I allow it: for the knowledge of a false doctrine is beneficial, inasmuch as you do not fall into it because of ignorance." And Simon said: "You are evidently not able to reply to the propositions I laid before you. I maintain that even your teacher affirms that there is some Father unrevealed."

CHAP. XIII.—*Peter's explanation of the passage.*

And Peter said: "I shall reply to that which you wish me to speak of,—namely, the passage, 'No one knows the Father but the Son, nor does any one know the Son but the Father,

---

[1] Κυρία.
[2] The text is corrupt. Various emendations have been proposed, none of which are satisfactory. Uhlhorn proposes, "that there is a standing one, one who will stand. You who are opposed, learn how you disbelieve, and that this subject which you say is the power unrevealed is full of ignorance." P. 283, note.

and they to whom the Son may wish to reveal Him.' First, then, I am astonished that, while this statement admits of countless interpretations, you should have chosen the very dangerous position of maintaining that the statement is made in reference to the ignorance of the Creator (Demiurge), and all who are under him. For, first, the statement can apply to all the Jews who think that David is the father of Christ, and that Christ himself is his son, and do not know that He is the Son of God. Wherefore it is appropriately said, 'No one knows the Father,' since, instead of God, they affirmed David to be His father; and the additional remark, that no one knows even the Son, is quite correct, since they did not know that He was the Son. The statement also, 'to whomsoever the Son may wish to reveal Him,' is also correct; for He, being the Son from the beginning, was alone appointed to give the revelation to those to whom He wishes to give it. And thus the first man (protoplast) Adam must have heard of Him; and Enoch, who pleased [God], must have known Him; and Noah, the righteous one, must have become acquainted with Him; and Abraam His friend must have understood Him; and Isaac must have perceived Him; and Jacob, who wrestled with Him, must have believed in Him; and the revelation must have been given to all among the people who were worthy.

CHAP. XIV.—*Simon refuted.*

"But if, as you say, it will be possible to know Him, because He is now revealed to all through Jesus,[1] are you not stating what is most unjust, when you say that these men did not know Him, who were the seven pillars of the world, and who were able to please the most just God, and that so many now from all nations who were impious know Him in every respect? Were not those who were superior to every one not deemed worthy to know Him?[2] And how can that be good which is not just? unless you wish to give the name

[1] The text is corrupt. We have placed διά τό after εἰδέναι.
[2] Another reading is: "Were not those deemed better worthy than any one else to know Him?"

of 'good,' not to him who does good to those who act justly, but to him who loves the unjust, even though they do not believe, and reveals to them the secrets which he would not reveal to the just. But such conduct is befitting neither in one who is good nor just, but in one who has come to hate the pious. Are not you, Simon, the standing one, who have the boldness to make these statements which never have been so made before?"

CHAP. XV.—*Matthew* xi. 25 *discussed.*

And Simon, being vexed at this, said: "Blame your own teacher, who said, 'I thank Thee, Lord of heaven and earth, that what was concealed from the wise, Thou hast revealed to suckling babes.'"[1] And Peter said: "This is not the way in which the statement was made; but I shall speak of it as if it had been made in the way that has seemed good to you. Our Lord, even if He had made this statement, 'What was concealed from the wise, the Father revealed to babes,' could not even thus be thought to point out another God and Father in addition to Him who created the world. For it is possible that the concealed things of which He spoke may be those of the Creator (Demiurge) himself; because Isaiah[2] says, 'I will open my mouth in parables, and I will belch forth things concealed from the foundation of the world.' Do you allow, then, that the prophet was not ignorant of the things concealed, which Jesus says were concealed from the wise, but revealed to babes? And how was the Creator (Demiurge) ignorant of them, if his prophet Isaiah was not ignorant of them? But our Jesus did not in reality say 'what was concealed,' but He said what seems a harsher statement; for He said, ['Thou hast concealed these things from the wise, and[3]]

---

[1] Matt. xi. 25.

[2] The passage does not occur in Isaiah, but in Ps. lxxviii. 2. The words are quoted not from the Septuagint, but from the Gospel of Matthew (xiii. 35), where in some MSS. they are attributed to Isaiah. See Uhlhorn, p. 119.

[3] The words in brackets are omitted in the MSS.; but the context leaves no doubt that they were once in the text.

hast revealed them to sucking babes.' Now the word 'Thou hast concealed' implies that they had once been known to them; for the key of the kingdom of heaven, that is, the knowledge of the secrets, lay with them.

CHAP. XVI.—*These things hidden justly from the wise.*

"And do not say He acted impiously towards the wise in hiding these things from them. Far be such a supposition from us. For He did not act impiously; but since they hid the knowledge of the kingdom,[1] and neither themselves entered nor allowed those who wished to enter, on this account, and justly, inasmuch as they hid the ways from those who wished, were in like manner the secrets hidden from them, in order that they themselves might experience what they had done to others, and with what measure they had measured, an equal measure might be meted out to them.[2] For to him who is worthy to know, is due that which he does not know; but from him who is not worthy, even should he seem to have anything, it is taken away,[3] even if he be wise in other matters; and it is given to the worthy, even should they be babes as far as the times of their discipleship are concerned.

CHAP. XVII.—*The way to the kingdom not concealed from the Israelites.*

"But if one shall say nothing was concealed from the sons of Israel, because it is written,[4] 'Nothing escaped thy notice, O Israel (for do not say, O Jacob, The way is hid from me),' he ought to understand that the things that belong to the kingdom had been hid from them, but that the way that leads to the kingdom, that is, the mode of life, had not been hid from them. Wherefore it is that He says, 'For say not that the way has been hid from me.' But by the way is meant the mode of life; for Moses says,[5] 'Behold, I have set before thy face the way of life and the way of death.' And the Teacher spoke in harmony with this:[6] 'Enter ye through the

[1] Luke xi. 52.   [2] Matt. vii. 2.   [3] Luke viii. 18.
[4] Isa. xl. 26, 27.   [5] Deut. xxx. 15.   [6] Matt. vii. 13, 14.

strait and narrow way, through which ye shall enter into life.' And somewhere else, when one asked Him,[1] 'What shall I do to inherit eternal life?' He pointed out to him the commandments of the law.

CHAP. XVIII.—*Isaiah i. 3 explained.*

"From the circumstance that Isaiah said, in the person of God,[2] 'But Israel hath not known me, and the people hath not understood me,' it is not to be inferred that Isaiah indicated another God besides Him who is known;[3] but he meant that the known God was in another sense unknown, because the people sinned, being ignorant of the just character of the known God, and imagined that they would not be punished by the good God. Wherefore, after he said, 'But Israel hath not known me, and the people hath not understood me,' he adds, 'Alas! a sinful nation, a people laden with sins.' For, not being afraid, in consequence of their ignorance of His justice, as I said, they became laden with sins, supposing that He was merely good, and would not therefore punish them for their sins.

CHAP. XIX.—*Misconception of God in the Old Testament.*

"And some sinned thus, on account of imagining that there would be no judgment[4] because of His goodness. But others took an opposite course. For, supposing the expressions of the Scriptures which are against God, and are unjust and false, to be true, they did not know His real divinity and power. Therefore, in the belief that He was ignorant and rejoiced in murder, and let off the wicked in consequence of the gifts of sacrifices; yea, moreover, that He deceived and spake falsely, and did everything that is unjust, they

---

[1] Luke xviii. 18; Matt. xix. 17.   [2] Isa. i. 3.
[3] Cotelerius' MS. inserts "the Creator" (Demiurge).
[4] We have adopted the Latin translation here, as giving the meaning which was intended by the writer; but the Greek will scarcely admit of such a translation. Probably the text is corrupt, or something is omitted. The literal translation is, "in consequence of the unjudging supposition on account of the goodness."

themselves did things like to what their God did, and thus sinning, asserted that they were acting piously. Wherefore it was impossible for them to change to the better, and when warned they took no heed. For they were not afraid, since they became like their God through such actions.

CHAP. XX.—*Some parts of the Old Testament written to try us.*

"But one might with good reason maintain that it was with reference to those who thought Him to be such that the statement was made, 'No one knoweth the Father but the Son, as no one knoweth even the Son, but the Father.' And reasonably. For if they had known, they would not have sinned, by trusting to the books written against God, really for the purpose of trying. But somewhere also He says, wishing to exhibit the cause of their error more distinctly to them, 'On this account ye do err, not knowing the true things of the Scriptures, on which account ye are ignorant also of the power of God.'[1] Wherefore every man who wishes to be saved must become, as the Teacher said, a judge of the books written to try us. For thus He spake: 'Become experienced bankers.' Now the need of bankers arises from the circumstance that the spurious is mixed up with the genuine."

CHAP. XXI.—*Simon's astonishment at Peter's treatment of the Scriptures.*

When Peter said this, Simon pretended to be utterly astonished at what was said in regard to the Scriptures; and as if in great agitation, he said: "Far be it from me, and those who love me, to listen to your discourses. And, indeed, as long as I did not know that you held these opinions in regard to the Scriptures, I endured you, and discussed with you; but now I retire. Indeed, I ought at the first to have withdrawn, because I heard you say, 'I, for my part, believe no one who says anything against Him who created the world, neither angels, nor prophets, nor Scrip-

[1] Mark xii. 24.

tures, nor priests, nor teachers, nor any one else, even though one should work signs and miracles, even though he should lighten brilliantly in the air, or should make a revelation through visions or through dreams.' Who, then, can succeed in changing your mind, whether well or ill, so as that you should hold opinions different from what you have determined on, seeing that you abide so persistently and immoveably in your own decision?"

CHAP. XXII.—*Peter worships one God.*

When Simon said this, and was going to depart, Peter said: "Listen to this one other remark, and then go where you like." Whereupon Simon turned back and remained, and Peter said: "I know how you were then astonished when you heard me say, 'Whosoever says anything whatever against God who created the world, I do not believe him.' But listen now to something additional, and greater than this. If God who created the world has in reality such a character as the Scriptures assign Him, and if somehow or other He is incomparably wicked, more wicked[1] than either the Scriptures were able to represent Him, or any other can even conceive Him to be, nevertheless[2] I shall not give up worshipping Him alone, and doing His will. For I wish you to know and to be convinced, that he who has not affection for his own Creator, can never have it towards another. And if he has it towards another, he has it contrary to nature, and he is ignorant that he has this passion for the unjust from the evil one. Nor will he be able to retain even it stedfastly. And, indeed, if there is another above the Creator (Demiurge), he will welcome me, since he is good, all the more that I love my own Father; and he will not welcome you, as he knows that you have abandoned your own natural Creator: for I do not call Him Father, influenced by a greater hope, and not caring for what is

[1] "Incomparably wicked, more wicked than;" literally, "incomparably wicked as."
[2] The Greek has ὁμοίως, "in like manner." We have translated ὅμως.

reasonable. Thus, even if you find one who is superior to Him, he knows that you will one day abandon him; and the more so that he has not been your father, since you have abandoned Him who was really your Father.

Chap. XXIII.—*Simon retires.*

"But you will say, 'He knows that there is no other above him, and on this account he cannot be abandoned.' Thanks, then, to there being no other; but He knows that the state of your mind is one inclined to ingratitude. But if, knowing you to be ungrateful, He welcomes you, and knowing me to be grateful, He does not receive me, He is inconsiderate, according to your own assertion, and does not act reasonably. And thus, Simon, you are not aware that you are the servant of wickedness." And Simon answered: "Whence, then, has evil arisen? tell us." And Peter said: "Since to-day you were the first to go out, and you declared that you would not in future listen to me as being a blasphemer, come to-morrow, if indeed you wish to learn, and I shall explain the matter to you, and I will permit you to ask me any questions you like, without any dispute." And Simon said: "I shall do as shall seem good to me." And saying this, he went away. Now, none of those who entered along with him went out along with him; but, falling at Peter's feet, they begged that they might be pardoned for having been carried away with Simon, and on repenting, to be welcomed. But Peter, admitting those persons who repented, and the rest of the multitudes, laid his hands upon them, praying, and healing those who were sick amongst them; and thus dismissing them, he urged them to return early about dawn. And saying this, and going in with his intimate friends, he made the usual preparations for immediate repose, for it was now evening.

HOMILY XIX.

Chap. I.—*Simon undertakes to prove that the Creator of the world is not blameless.*

HE next day Peter came forth earlier than usual; and seeing Simon with many others waiting for him, he saluted the multitude, and began to discourse. But no sooner did he begin than Simon interrupted him, and said: "Pass by these long introductions of yours, and answer directly the questions I put to you. Since I perceive that you [1] (as I know from what I heard at the beginning, that you have no other purpose, than by every contrivance to show that the Creator himself is alone the blameless God),—since, as I said, I perceive that you have such a decided desire to maintain this, that you venture to declare to be false some portions of the Scriptures that clearly speak against him, for this reason I have determined to-day to prove that it is impossible that he, being the Creator of all, should be blameless. But this proof I can now begin, if you reply to the questions which I put to you.

Chap. II.—*The existence of the devil affirmed.*

"Do you maintain that there is any prince of evil or not? For if you say that there is not, I can prove to you from many statements, and those too of your teacher, that there is; but if you honestly allow that the evil one exists, then I shall speak in accordance with this belief." And Peter said: "It is impossible for me to deny the assertion of my Teacher. Wherefore I allow that the evil one exists, because my Teacher, who spoke the truth in all things, has

[1] This passage is corrupt. Wieseler has proposed to amend it by a bold transposition of the clauses. We make one slight alteration in the text.

frequently asserted that he exists. For instance, then, he acknowledges that he conversed with Him, and tempted Him for forty days.[1] And I know that He has said somewhere else, 'If Satan casts out Satan, he is divided against himself: how then is his kingdom to stand?'[2] And He pointed out that He saw the evil one like lightning falling down from heaven.[3] And elsewhere He said, 'He who sowed the bad seed is the devil.'[4] And again, 'Give no pretext to the evil one.'[5] Moreover, in giving advice, He said, 'Let your yea be yea, and your nay nay; for what is more than these is of the evil one.'[6] Also, in the prayer which He delivered to us, we have it said, 'Deliver us from the evil one.'[7] And in another place, He promised that He would say to those who are impious, 'Go ye into outer darkness, which the Father prepared for the devil and his angels.'[8] And not to prolong this statement further, I know that my Teacher often said that there is an evil one. Wherefore I also agree in thinking that he exists. If, then, in future you have anything to say in accordance with this belief, say it, as you promised."

CHAP. III.—*Peter refuses to discuss certain questions in regard to the devil.*

And Simon said: "Since, then, you have honestly confessed, on the testimony of the Scriptures, that the evil one exists, state to us how he has come into existence, if indeed he has come into existence, and by whom, and why." And Peter said: "Pardon me, Simon, if I do not dare to affirm what has not been written. But if you say that it has been written, prove it. But if, since it has not been written, you cannot prove it, why should we run risk in stating our opinions in regard to what has not been written? For if we discourse too daringly in regard to God, it is either because

---

[1] Mark i. 13. [2] Matt. xii. 26.
[3] Luke x. 18. [4] Matt. xiii. 39.
[5] This passage is not found in the New Testament. It resembles Eph. iv. 27.
[6] Matt. v. 37; Jas. v. 12. [7] Matt. vi. 13. [8] Matt. xxv. 41.

we do not believe that we shall be judged, or that we shall be judged only in respect to that which we do, but not also in regard to what we believe and speak."[1] But Simon, understanding that Peter referred to his own madness, said: "Permit me to run the risk; but do not you make what you assert to be blasphemy a pretext for retiring. For I perceive that you wish to withdraw, in order that you may escape refutation before the masses, sometimes as if you were afraid to listen to blasphemies, and at other times by maintaining that, as nothing has been written as to how, and by whom, and why the evil one came into existence, we ought not to dare to assert more than the Scripture. Wherefore also as a pious man you affirm this only, that he exists. But by these contrivances you deceive yourself, not knowing that, if it is blasphemy to inquire accurately regarding the evil one, the blame rests with me, the accuser, and not with you, the defender of God. And if the subject inquired into is not in Scripture,[2] and on this account you do not wish to inquire into it, there are some satisfactory methods which can prove to you what is sought not less effectively than the Scriptures. For instance, must it not be the case that the evil one, who you assert exists, is either originated or unoriginated?"[3]

CHAP. IV.—*Suppositions in regard to the devil's origin.*

And Peter said: "It must be so." And Simon: "Therefore, if he is originated, he has been made by that very God who made all things, being either born as an animal, or sent forth substantially, and resulting from an external mixture [of elements]. For either[4] the matter, being living or lifeless,

[1] This passage is probably corrupt. We have adopted the readings of Cotelerius—ἤ, ἤ, instead of εἰ and μή.

[2] Lit., "unwritten."

[3] The words γενητός and ἀγένητος are difficult to translate. The first means one who has somehow or other come into being; the second, one who has never *come* into being, but has always been. The MSS. confound γενητός with γεννητός, begotten, and ἀγένητος with ἀγέννητος, unbegotten.

[4] We have changed εἰ into ἤ.

from which he was made was outside of him,[1] or he came into being through God Himself, or through his own self, or he resulted from things non-existent, or he is a mere relative thing, or he always existed. Having thus, as I think, clearly pointed out all the possible ways by which we may find him, in going along some one of these we must find him. We must therefore go along each one of these in search of his origin; and when we find him who is his author, we must perceive that he is to blame. Or how does the matter seem to you?"

CHAP. V.—*God not deserving of blame in permitting the existence of the devil.*

And Peter said: "It is my opinion that, even if it be evident that he was made by God, the Creator who made him should not be blamed; for it might perchance be found that the service he performs[2] was an absolute necessity. But if, on the other hand, it should be proved that he was not created, inasmuch as he existed for ever, not even is the Creator to be blamed in this respect, since He is better than all [others], even if He has not been able to put an end to a being who had no beginning, because his nature did not admit of it; or if, being able, He does not make away with him, deeming it unjust to put an end to that which did not receive a beginning, and pardoning that which was by nature wicked, because he could not have become anything else, even if he were to wish to do so.[3] But if, wishing to do good, He is not able, even in this case He is good in that He has the will, though He has not the power; and while He has not the power, He is yet the most powerful of all, in that the power is not left to another. But if there is some other that is able, and yet does not accomplish it, it must be allowed that, in so far as, being able, he does not accomplish it, he

---

[1] By "Him" is understood God, though it may mean the devil.
[2] Lit., "his usefulness was most necessary of all."
[3] This sentence is obscure in the original. We have, with Wieseler, read ἐπεί, omitting ἀρχή. Instead of supplying μή, we have turned συγγινώσκειν into the participle.

is wicked in not putting an end to him, as if he took pleasure in the deeds done by him. But if not even he is able, then he is better who, though unable, is yet not unwilling to benefit us according to his ability."

CHAP. VI.—*Peter accuses Simon of being worse than the devil.*

And Simon said: "When you have discussed all the subjects which I have laid before you, I shall show you the cause of evil. Then I shall also reply to what you have now said, and prove that that God whom you affirm to be blameless is blameable." And Peter said: "Since I perceive from what you say at the commencement that you are striving after nothing else than to subject God, as being the author of evil, to blame, I have resolved to go along with you all the ways you like, and to prove that God is entirely free from blame." And Simon said: "You say this as loving God, whom you suppose you know; but you are not right." And Peter said: "But you, as being wicked, and hating God whom you have not known, utter blasphemous words." And Simon said: "Remember that you have likened me to the author of evil." And Peter said: "I confess it, I was wrong in comparing you to the evil one; for I was compelled to do so, because I have not found one who is your equal, or worse than you. For this reason I likened you to the evil one; for you happen to be much more wicked than the author of evil. For no one can prove that the evil one spoke against God; but all of us who are present see you speaking daringly against Him." And Simon said: "He who seeks the truth ought not to gratify any one in any respect contrary to what is really true. For why does he make the inquiry at all? Why, I ask? for I am not also able, laying aside the accurate investigation of things, to spend all my time in the praise of that God whom I do not know."[1]

[1] We have adopted the pointing of Wieseler.

CHAP. VII.—*Peter suspects Simon of not believing even in a God.*

And Peter said: "You are not so blessed as to praise Him, nor indeed can you do such a good deed as this; for then you would be full of Him. For thus said our Teacher, who always spoke the truth: 'Out of the abundance of the heart the mouth speaketh.'[1] Whence you, abounding in evil purposes, through ignorance speak against the only good God. And not yet suffering what you deserve to suffer for the words which you have dared to utter,[2] you either imagine that there will be no judgment, or perchance you think that there is not even a God. Whence, not comprehending such long-suffering as His, you are moving on to still greater madness." And Simon said: "Do not imagine that you will frighten me into not investigating the truth of your examples. For I am so eager for the truth, that for its sake I will not shrink from undergoing danger. If, then, you have anything to say in regard to the propositions made by me at the commencement, say it now."

CHAP. VIII.—*Peter undertakes to discuss the devil's origin.*

And Peter said: "Since you compel us, after we have made accurate investigations into the contrivances of God, to venture to state them, and that, too, to men who are not able to comprehend thoroughly the contrivances of their fellow-men, for the sake at least of those who are present, I, instead of remaining silent—a course which would be most pious—shall discuss the subjects of which you wish me to speak. I agree with you in believing that there is a prince of evil, of whose origin the Scripture has ventured to say nothing either true or false. But let us follow out the inquiry in many ways, as to how he has come into existence, if it is the fact that he has come into existence; and of the opinions which present themselves, let us select that which is most reverential, since,

[1] Matt. xii. 34.
[2] We have altered the punctuation. Editors connect this clause with the previous sentence, and change ᾗ of the MSS. into εἰ.

in the case of probable opinions, that one is assumed with confidence which [is based on the principle] that we ought to attribute to God that which is more reverential; and all the more so, if, when all other suppositions are removed, there still remains one which is adequate and involves less danger.[1] But I promise you, before I proceed with the investigation, that every method in the investigation can show that God alone is blameless.

CHAP. IX.—*Theories in regard to the origin of the devil.*

"But, as you said, if the evil one is created, either he has been begotten as an animal, or he has been sent forth substantially by Him,[2] or he has been compounded externally, or his will has arisen through composition; or it happened that he came into existence from things non-existent, without composition and the will of God; or he has been made by God from that which in no manner and nowhere exists; or the matter, being lifeless or living, from which he has arisen was outside of God; or he fashioned himself, or he was made by God, or he is a relative thing, or he ever existed: for we cannot say that he does not exist, since we have agreed in thinking that he does exist." And Simon said: "Well have you distinguished all the methods of accounting for his existence in a summary manner. Now it is my part to examine these various ideas, and to show that the Creator is blameable. But it is your business to prove, as you promised, that he is free from all blame. But I wonder if you will be able. For, first, if the devil has been begotten from God as an animal, the vice

---

[1] This sentence is regarded as corrupt by Wieseler. We have retained the reading of the Paris MS., ὁ, and understand λαμβάνεται after it. Δἱ would naturally be inserted after ταύτη, but it is not necessary. Καθαρθεισῶν is translated in the Latin *purgatis*, which may mean the same as in our translation if we take it in the sense of "washed away;" but καθαιρεθεισῶν would be a better reading. The translation of Cotelerius gives, "Since this is reasonably assumed with firmness,—namely, that it is right to give to God," etc.

[2] The text here is evidently corrupt in many places. If the reading "by him" is to be retained, we must suppose, with Wieseler, that "by God" is omitted in the previous clause. Probably it should be, "by himself."

which is his is accordingly the same as that of him who sends him forth." And Peter said: "Not at all. For we see many men who are good the fathers of wicked children, and others who are wicked the fathers of good children, and others again who are wicked producing both good [and wicked[1]] children, and others who are good having both wicked and good children. For instance, the first man who was created produced the unrighteous Cain and the righteous Abel." To this Simon said: "You are acting foolishly, in using human examples when discoursing about God." And Peter said: "Speak you, then, to us about God without using human examples, and yet so that what you say can be understood; but you are not able to do so.

CHAP. X.—*The absolute God entirely incomprehensible by man.*

"For instance, then, what did you say in the beginning? If the wicked one has been begotten of God, being of the same substance as He, then God is wicked. But when I showed you, from the example which you yourself adduced, that wicked beings come from good, and good from wicked, you did not admit the argument, for you said that the example was a human one. Wherefore I now do not admit that the term 'being begotten'[2] can be used with reference to God; for it is characteristic of man, and not of God, to beget. Not only so; but God cannot be good or evil, just or unjust. Nor indeed can He have intelligence, or life, or any of the other attributes which can exist in man; for all these are peculiar to man. And if we must not, in our investigations in regard to God, give Him the good attributes which belong to man, it is not possible for us to have any thought or make any statement in regard to God; but all we can do is to investigate one point alone,—namely, what is His will which He has Himself allowed us to apprehend, in order that, being judged, we might be without excuse in regard to those laws which we have not observed, though we knew them."

[1] "And bad" is not in the MSS., but is required by the context.
[2] The text is corrupt here. Literally it is, "I do not admit that God has been begotten."

CHAP. XI.—*The application of the attributes of man to God.*

And Simon, hearing this, said: "You will not force me through shame to remain silent in regard to His substance, and to inquire into His will alone. For it is possible both to think and to speak of His substance. I mean from the good attributes that belong to man. For instance, life and death are attributes of man; but death is not an attribute of God, but life, and eternal life. Furthermore, men may be both evil and good; but God can be only incomparably good. And, not to prolong the subject too much, the better attributes of man are eternal attributes of God." And Peter said: "Tell me, Simon, is it an attribute of man to beget evil and good, and to do evil and good?" And Simon said: "It is." And Peter said: "Since you made this assertion, we must assign the better attributes of man to God; and so, while men beget evil and good, God can beget good only; and while men do evil and good, God rejoices only in doing good. Thus, with regard [to God], we must either not predicate any of the attributes of man and be silent, or it is reasonable that we should assign the best of the good attributes to Him. And thus He alone is the cause of all good things."

CHAP. XII.—*God produced the wicked one, but not evil.*

And Simon said: "If, then, God is the cause only of what is good, what else can we think than that some other principle begot the evil one;[1] or is evil unbegotten?" And Peter said: "No other power begot the wicked one, nor is evil unbegotten, as I shall show in the conclusion; for now my object is to prove, as I promised in the commencement, that God is blameless in every[2] respect. We have granted, then, that God possesses in an incomparable way the better attributes that belong to men. Wherefore also it is possible for Him to have been the producer of the four substances,— heat, I mean, and cold, moist and dry. These, as being at first simple and unmixed, were naturally indifferent in their

---

[1] "Evil" is not in the MSS. It is inserted from the next sentence.
[2] "Every" is inserted by a conjecture of Schwegler's.

desire;[1] but being produced by God, and mixed externally, they would naturally become a living being, possessing the free choice to destroy those who are evil. And thus, since all things have been begotten from Him, the wicked one is from no other source. Nor has he derived his evil from the God who has created all things (with whom it is impossible that evil should exist), because the substances were produced by Him in a state of indifference, and carefully separated from each other; and when they were externally blended through his art, there arose through volition the desire for the destruction of the evil ones. But the good cannot be destroyed by the evil that arose, even though it should wish to do so: for it exercises its power only[2] against those who sin. Ignorant, then, of the character of each, he[3] makes his attempt against him, and convicting him, he punishes him." And Simon said: "God being able to mingle the elements, and to make His mixtures so as to produce any dispositions that He may wish, why did He not make the composition of each such as that it would prefer what is good?"

CHAP. XIII.—*God the maker of the devil.*

And Peter said: "Now indeed our object is to show how and by whom the evil one came into being, since he did come into being; but we shall show if he came into being blamelessly, when we have finished the subject now in hand. Then I shall show how and on account of what he came into being, and I shall fully convince you that his Creator is blameless.[4] We said, then, that the four substances were produced by God. And thus, through the volition of Him who mingled them, arose, as He wished, the choice of evils. For if it had arisen contrary to His determination, or from some other substance or cause, then God would not have had firmness of will: for perchance, even though He should not wish it, leaders of evil might continually arise, who would war against His wishes.

---

[1] Lit., "naturally had their desire towards neither."
[2] The MSS. have "by law." We have changed νόμῳ into μόνον.
[3] The devil is plainly meant by the "he."
[4] This passage is evidently corrupt. But it is not easy to amend it.

But it is impossible that this should be the case. For no living being, and especially one capable of giving guidance, can arise from accident: for everything that is produced must be produced by some one."

CHAP. XIV.—*Is matter eternal?*

And Simon said: "But what if matter, being coeval with Him, and possessing equal power, produces as His foe leaders who hinder His wishes?" And Peter said: "If matter is eternal, then it is the foe of no one: for that which exists for ever is impassible, and what is impassible is blessed; but what is blessed cannot be receptive of hatred, since, on account of its eternal creation,[1] it does not fear that it will be deprived of anything. But how does not matter rather love the Creator, when [2] it evidently sends forth its fruits to nourish all who are made by Him? And how does it not fear Him as superior, as trembling through earthquakes it confesses, and as, though its billows ran high, yet, when the Teacher was sailing on it and commanded a calm, it immediately obeyed and became still?[3] What! did not the demons go out through fear and respect for Him, and others of them desired to enter into swine; but they first entreated Him before going, plainly because they had no power to enter even into swine without His permission?"[4]

CHAP. XV.—*Sin the cause of evil.*

And Simon said: "But what if, being lifeless, it possesses a nature capable of producing what is evil and what is good?" And Peter said: "According to this statement, it is neither good nor evil, because it does not act by free choice, being lifeless and insensible. Wherefore it is possible to perceive distinctly in this matter, how, being lifeless, it produces as if it were living;[5] and being insensible, it yet

---

[1] Probably "eternity" should be read, instead of "eternal creation."
[2] At this word the MS. of Cotelerius breaks off; and we have the rest only in the Ottobonian MS., first edited by Dressel.
[3] Matt. xxvii. 51, viii. 24.   [4] Matt. viii. 31.
[5] Possibly the right reading is ἐμψύχους, "it produces living beings."

plainly fashions artistic shapes both in animals and plants."
And Simon said: "What! if God Himself gave it life, is not
He, then, the cause of the evils which it produces?" And
Peter said: "If God gave it life according to His own will,
then it is His Spirit that produces it, and no longer is it anything hostile to God, or of equal power with Him; or it is
impossible that everything made by Him is made according
as He wishes. But you will say, He Himself is the cause
of evil, since He Himself produces the evils through it.
What sort, then, are the evils of which you speak? Poisonous serpents and deadly plants, or demons, or any other of
those things that can disturb men?—which things would not
have been injurious had not man sinned, for which reason [1]
death came in. For if man were sinless, the poison of serpents would have no effect, nor the activities of injurious
plants, nor would there be the disturbances of demons, nor
would man naturally have any other suffering; but losing his
immortality on account of his sin, he has become, as I said,
capable of every suffering. But if you say, Why, then, was
the nature of man made at the beginning capable of death?
I tell you, because of free-will; for if we were not capable
of death, we could not, as being immortal, be punished on
account of our voluntary sin. And thus, on account of our
freedom from suffering, righteousness would be still more
weakened if we were wicked by choice; for those who should
have evil purposes could not be punished, on account of their
being incapable of suffering.[2]

CHAP. XVI.—*Why the wicked one is entrusted with power.*

And Simon said to this: "I have one thing more to say in
regard to the wicked one. Assuredly, since God made him
out of nothing, he is in this respect wicked,[3] especially since
he was able to make him good, by giving him at his creation
a nature in no way capable of selecting wickedness." And
Peter said: "The statement that He created him out of

---

[1] Or, "on whose account." [2] The text is corrupt.
[3] The MS. reads: "In this respect he who made him is wicked, who gave existence to what was non-existent."

nothing, with a power of choice, is like the statement we have made above, that, having made such a constitution as can rejoice in evils, He Himself appears to be the cause of what took place. But since there is one explanation of both statements, we shall show afterwards why it was that He made him rejoice in the destruction of the wicked." And Simon said: "If he made the angels also voluntary agents, and the wicked one departed from a state of righteousness, why has he been honoured with a post of command? Is it not plain that he who thus honoured him takes pleasure in the wicked, in that he has thus honoured him?"[1] And Peter said: "If God set him by law, when he rebelled, to rule over those who were like him, ordering him to inflict punishment on those who sin, He is not unjust. But if it be the case that He has honoured him even after his revolt, He who honoured him saw beforehand his usefulness; for the honour is temporary, and it is right that the wicked should be ruled by the wicked one, and that sinners should be punished by him."

CHAP. XVII.—*The devil has not equal power with God.*

And Simon said: "If, then, he exists for ever, is not the fact of the sole government [of God] thus destroyed, since there is another power, namely, that concerned with matter, which rules along with Him?" And Peter said: "If they are different in their substances, they are different also in their powers, and the superior rules the inferior. But if they are of the same substance, then they are equal in power, and they are in like manner good or bad. But it is plain that they are not equal in power; for the Creator put matter into that shape of a world into which He willed to put it. Is it then at all possible to maintain that it always existed, being a substance; and is not matter, as it were, the storehouse of God? For it is not possible to maintain that there was a time[2] when God possessed nothing, but He always

---

[1] The Greek is either ungrammatical or corrupt, but the sense is evident.

[2] This passage is supposed by most to be defective, and various words have been suggested to supply the lacuna.

was the only ruler of it. Wherefore also He is an eternal sole ruler;[1] and on this account it would justly be said to belong to Him who exists, and rules, and is [eternal[2]]." And Simon said: "What then? Did the wicked one make himself? And was God good in such a way, that, knowing he would be the cause of evil, he yet did not destroy him at his origination, when he could have been destroyed, as not yet being perfectly made? For if he came into being suddenly and complete, then on that account[3] he is at war with the Creator, as having come suddenly into being, possessed of equal power with him."

CHAP. XVIII.—*Is the devil a relation?*

And Peter said: "What you state is impossible; for if he came into existence by degrees, He could have cut him off as a foe by His own free choice. And knowing beforehand that he was coming into existence, He would not have allowed him as a good, had He not known that by reason of him what was useful was being brought into existence.[4] And he could not have come into existence suddenly, complete, of his own power. For he who did not exist could not fashion himself; and he neither could become complete out of nothing, nor could any one justly say that he had substance,[5] so as always to be equal in power if he were begotten." And Simon said: "Is he then a mere relation, and in this way wicked?[6]—being injurious, as water is injurious to fire, but good for the seasonably thirsty land; as iron is

[1] Or, "monarch." But only two letters of the word are in the MS.; the rest is filled in by conjecture.
[2] Supplied by conjecture.
[3] Three words are struck out of the text of the MS. by all editors, as being a repetition.
[4] The editors punctuate differently, thus: "And knowing beforehand that he was becoming not good, He would not have allowed him, unless He knew that he would be useful to Himself." We suppose the reference in the text to be to Gen. i. 31.
[5] Or, "self-subsistence." We have supposed a transposition of the words in the text. The text is without doubt corrupt.
[6] We have adopted an emendation of Lagarde's.

good for the cultivation of the land, but bad for murders; and lust is not evil in respect of marriage, but bad in respect of adultery; as murder is an evil, but good for the murderer so far as his purpose is concerned; and cheating is an evil, but pleasant to the man who cheats; and other things of a like character are good and bad in like manner. In this way, neither is evil evil, nor good good; for the one produces the other. For does not that which seems to be done injuriously rejoice the doer, but punish the sufferer? And though it seems unjust that a man should, out of self-love, gratify himself by every means in his power, to whom, on the other hand, does it not seem unjust that a man should suffer severe punishments at the hand of a just judge for having loved himself?"

CHAP. XIX.—*Some actions really wicked.*

And Peter said: "A man ought to punish himself through self-restraint,[1] when his lust wishes to hurry on to the injury of another, knowing [that[2]] the wicked one can destroy the wicked, for he has received power over them from the beginning. And not yet is this an evil to those who have done evil; but that their souls should remain punished after the destruction, you are right in thinking to be really harsh, though the man who has been fore-ordained for evil should say that it is right.[3] Wherefore, as I said, we ought to avoid doing injury[4] to another for the sake of a shortlived pleasure, that we may not involve ourselves in eternal punishment for the sake of a little pleasure." And Simon said: "Is it the case, then, that there is nothing either bad or good by nature, but the difference arises through law and custom? [For is it not[5]] the habit of the Persians to marry their own mothers, sisters, and daughters, while marriage with other women is

---

[1] Dressel translates *viriliter*, "manfully."
[2] This word is supplied by conjecture.
[3] This passage is hopelessly corrupt. We have changed δικαίως into δικαίοις, the verb, and τὸν προδιωρισμένον into τοῦ προδιωρισμένου.
[4] We have adopted Wieseler's emendation of ἄδικον into ἀδικεῖν.
[5] This is a conjectural filling up of a blank.

prohibited[1] as most barbarous? Wherefore, if it is not settled what things are evil, it is not possible for all to look forward to the judgment of God." And Peter said: "This cannot hold; for it is plain to all that cohabitation with mothers is abominable, even though the Persians, who are a mere fraction of the whole, should under the effects of a bad custom fail to see the iniquity of their abominable conduct. Thus also the Britons publicly cohabit in the sight of all, and are not ashamed; and some men eat the flesh of others, and feel no disgust; and others eat the flesh of dogs; and others practise other unmentionable deeds. Thus, then, we ought not to form our judgments with a perception which through habit has been perverted from its natural action. For to be murdered is an evil, even if all were to deny it; for no one wishes to suffer it himself, and in the case of theft[2] no one rejoices at his own punishment. If, then, no one[3] were at all ever to confess that these are sins, it is right even then to look forward of necessity to a judgment in regard to sins." When Peter said this, Simon answered: "Does this, then, seem to you to be the truth in regard to the wicked one? Tell me."

CHAP. XX.—*Pain and death the result of sin.*

And Peter said: "We remember that our Lord and Teacher, commanding us, said, 'Keep the mysteries for me and the sons of my house.' Wherefore also He explained to His disciples privately the mysteries of the kingdom of heaven.[4] But to you who do battle with us, and examine into nothing else but our statements, whether they be true or false, it would be impious to state the hidden [truths]. But that none of the bystanders may imagine that I am contriving excuses,[5] because I am unable to reply to the assertions

---

[1] This is partly conjecture, to fill up a blank.
[2] The text is likely corrupt.
[3] Uhlhorn changed οὖν ἑνός into οὐδενός. We have changed καὶ τρίτην into καὶ τότε τῆν. Various emendations have been proposed.
[4] Mark iv. 34.
[5] We have adopted an emendation of Wieseler's.

made by you, I shall answer you by first putting the question, If there had been a state of painlessness, what is the meaning of the statement, 'The evil one was?'" And Simon said: "The words have no meaning." And Peter: "Is then evil the same as pain and death?" And Simon: "It seems so." And Peter said: "Evil, then, does not exist always, yea, it cannot even exist at all substantially; for pain and death belong to the class of accidents, neither of which can co-exist with abiding strength. For what is pain but the interruption of harmony? And what is death but the separation of soul from body? There is therefore no pain when there is harmony. For death does not even at all belong to those things which substantially exist: for death is nothing, as I said, but the separation of soul from body; and when this takes place, the body, which is by nature incapable of sensation, is dissolved; but the soul, being capable of sensation, remains in life and exists substantially. Hence, when there is harmony there is no pain, no death, no, not even deadly plants nor poisonous reptiles, nor anything of such a nature that its end is death. And hence, where immortality reigns, all things will appear to have been made with reason. And this will be the case when, on account of righteousness, man becomes immortal through the prevalence of the peaceful reign of Christ, when his composition will be so well arranged as not [to give rise[1]] to sharp impulses; and his knowledge, moreover, will be unerring, so as that he shall not [mistake[1]] evil for good; and he will suffer no pain, so that he will not be mortal."[2]

CHAP. XXI.—*The uses of lust, anger, grief.*

And Simon said: "You were right in saying this; but in the present world does not man seem to you to be capable of every kind of affection,—as, for instance, of lust, anger, grief, and the like?" And Peter said: "Yes, these belong to the things that are accidental, not to those that always

[1] The words in brackets supplied by conjecture.
[2] This last sentence has two blanks, which are filled up by conjecture; and one emendation has been adopted.

exist, and it will be found that they now occur with advantage to the soul. For lust has, by the will of Him who created all things well, been made to arise within the living being, that, led by it to intercourse, he may increase humanity, from a selection of which a multitude of superior beings arise who are fit for eternal life. But if it were not for lust, no one would trouble himself with intercourse with his wife; but now, for the sake of pleasure, and, as it were, gratifying himself, man carries out His will. Now, if a man uses lust for lawful marriage, he does not act impiously; but if he rushes to adultery, he acts impiously, and he is punished because he makes a bad use of a good ordinance. And in the same way, anger has been made by God to be lighted up naturally within us, in order that we may be induced by it to ward off injuries. Yet if any one indulges it without restraint, he acts unjustly; but if he uses it within due bounds, he does what is right. Moreover, we are capable of grief, that we may be moved with sympathy at the death of relatives, of a wife, or children, or brothers, or parents, or friends, or some others, since, if we were not capable of sympathy, we should be inhuman. In like manner, all the other affections will be found to be adapted for us, if at least the reason for their existence[1] be considered."

CHAP. XXII.—*Sins of ignorance.*

And Simon: "Why is it, then, that some die prematurely, and periodical diseases arise; and that there are, moreover, attacks of demons, and of madness, and all other kinds of afflictions which can greatly punish?" And Peter said: "Because men, following their own pleasure in all things, cohabit without observing the proper times; and thus the deposition of seed, taking place unseasonably, naturally produces a multitude of evils. For they ought to reflect, that as a season has been fixed suitable for planting and sowing,[2] so days have been appointed as appropriate for cohabitation, which are carefully to be observed. Accordingly some one

---

[1] We have adopted an emendation of Lagarde's.
[2] Eccles. iii. 2.

well instructed in the doctrines taught by Moses, finding fault with the people for their sins, called them sons of the new moons and the sabbaths.[1] Yet in the beginning of the world men lived long, and had no diseases. But when through carelessness they neglected the observation of the proper times, then the sons in succession cohabiting through ignorance at times when[2] they ought not, place their children under innumerable afflictions. Whence our Teacher, when we inquired of Him[3] in regard to the man who was blind from his birth, and recovered his sight, if this man sinned, or his parents, that he should be born blind, answered, 'Neither did he sin at all, nor his parents, but that the power of God might be made manifest through him in healing the sins of ignorance.'[4] And, in truth, such afflictions arise because of ignorance; as, for instance, by not knowing when one ought to cohabit with his wife, as if she be pure from her discharge. Now the afflictions which you mentioned before are the result of ignorance, and not, assuredly, of any wickedness that has been perpetrated. Moreover, give me the man who sins not, and I will show you the man who suffers not; and you will find that he not only does not suffer himself, but that he is able[5] to heal others. For instance, Moses, on account of his piety, continued free from suffering all his life, and by his prayers he healed the Egyptians when they suffered on account of their sins."

CHAP. XXIII.—*The inequalities of lot in human life.*

And Simon said: "Let me grant that this is the case: does not the inequality of lot amongst men seem to you most unjust? For one is in penury, another is rich; one is sick, another is in good health: and there are innumerable differences of a like character in human life." And Peter said: "Do you not perceive, Simon, that you are again shooting

---

[1] Lit., "new moons that are according to the moon." Gal. iv. 10.
[2] "At times when" is supplied by conjecture.
[3] We have followed an emendation of Wieseler's.
[4] John ix. 2, 3.
[5] We have adopted an obvious emendation of Wieseler's.

your observations beyond the mark? For while we were discussing evil, you have made a digression, and introduced the question of the anomalies that appear in this world. But I shall speak even to this point. The world is an instrument artistically contrived, that for the male who is to exist eternally, the female may bear eternal righteous sons. Now they could not have been rendered perfectly pious here, had there been no needy ones for them to help. In like manner there are the sick, that they may have objects for their care. And the other afflictions admit of a like explanation." And Simon said: "Are not those in humble circumstances unfortunate? for they are subjected to distress, that others may be made righteous." And Peter said: "If their humiliation were eternal, their misfortune would be very great. But the humiliations and exaltations of men take place according to lot; and he who is not pleased with his lot can appeal,[1] and by trying his case according to law, he can exchange his mode of life for another." And Simon said: "What do you mean by this lot and this appeal?" And Peter said: "You are now demanding the exposition of another topic; but if you permit me, we can show you how, being born again, and changing your origin, and living according to law, you will obtain eternal salvation."

CHAP. XXIV.—*Simon rebuked by Faustus.*

And Simon hearing this, said: "Do not imagine that, when I, while questioning you, agreed with you in each topic, I went to the next, as being fully assured of the truth of the previous; but I appeared to yield to your ignorance, that you might go on to the next topic, in order that, becoming acquainted with the whole range of your ignorance, I might condemn you, not through mere conjecture, but from full knowledge.[2] Allow me now to retire for three days, and I shall come back and show that you know nothing." When Simon said this, and was on the point of going out, my

---

[1] An emendation of Wieseler's.
[2] The whole of this sentence is corrupt. We have adopted the conjectures of Wieseler, though they are not entirely satisfactory.

father said: "Listen to me, Simon, for a moment, and then go wherever you like. I remember that in the beginning, before the discussion, you accused me of being prejudiced, though as yet you had had no experience of me. But now, having heard you discuss in turn, and judging that Peter has the advantage, and now assigning to him the merit of speaking the truth, do I appear to you to judge correctly, and with knowledge;[1] or is it not so? For if you should say that I have judged correctly, but do not agree, then you are plainly prejudiced, inasmuch as you do not wish to agree, after confessing your defeat. But if I was not correct in maintaining that Peter has the advantage in the discussion, do you convince us how we have not judged correctly, or you will cease[2] to discuss with him before all, since you will always be defeated and agree, and in consequence your own soul will suffer pain, condemned as you will be, and in disgrace, through your own conscience, even if you do not feel shame before all the listeners as the greatest torture; for we have seen you conquered, in fact, and we have heard your own lips confess it. Finally, therefore, I am of opinion that you will not return to the discussion, as you promised; but that you may seem not to have been defeated,[3] you have promised, when going away, that you will return."

CHAP. XXV.—*Simon retires. Sophonias asks Peter to state his real opinions in regard to evil.*

And Simon hearing this, gnashed his teeth for rage, and went away in silence. But Peter (for a considerable portion of the day still remained) laid his hands on the large multitude to heal them; and having dismissed them, went into the house with his more intimate friends, and sat down. And one of his attendants, of the name of Sophonias, said:

[1] Possibly something is corrupt here. The words may be translated: "Is it not plain that I know how to judge correctly?"
[2] The MS. has, "do not cease." We have omitted μὴ, and changed παύσῃ into παύσει. We have inserted the μὴ after ᾗ, changed into εἰ before αἰδεῖσθαι.
[3] We have adopted an emendation of Wieseler's.

"Blessed is God, O Peter, who selected you and instructed[1] you for the comfort of the good. For, in truth, you discussed with Simon with dignity and great patience. But we beg of you to discourse to us of evil; for we expect that you will state to us your own genuine belief in regard to it,— not, however, at the present moment, but to-morrow, if it seems good to you: for we spare you, because of the fatigue you feel on account of your discussion." And Peter said: "I wish you to know, that he who does anything with pleasure, finds rest in the very toils themselves; but he who does not do what he wishes, is rendered exceedingly weary by the very rest he takes. Wherefore you confer on me a great rest when you make me discourse on topics which please me." Content, then, with his disposition, and sparing him on account of his fatigue, we requested him to put the discussion off till the night, when it was his custom to discourse to his genuine friends. And partaking of salt, we turned to sleep.

[1] An emendation of Wieseler's.

HOMILY XX.

Chap. I.—*Peter is willing to gratify Sophonias.*

In the night-time Peter rose up and wakened us, and then sat down in his usual way, and said: " Ask me questions about anything you like."
And Sophonias was the first to begin to speak to him: " Will you explain to us who are eager to learn what is the real truth in regard to evil ?" And Peter said: "I have already explained it in the course of my discussion with Simon; but because I stated the truth in regard to it in combination with other topics, it was not altogether clearly put; for many topics that seem to be of equal weight with the truth afford some kind of knowledge of the truth to the masses. So that, if now I state what I formerly stated to Simon along with many topics, do not imagine that you are [not[1]] honoured with honour equal to his." And Sophonias said: " You are right; for if you now separate it for us from many of the topics that were then discussed, you will make the truth more evident."

Chap. II.—*The two ages.*

And Peter said: " Listen, therefore, to the truth of the harmony in regard to the evil one. God appointed two kingdoms, and established two ages, determining that the present world should be given to the evil one, because it is small, and passes quickly away; but He promised to preserve for the good one the age to come, as it will be great and eternal. Man, therefore, He created with free-will, and possessing the capability of inclining to whatever actions he wishes. And his body consists of three parts, deriving its origin from

[1] " Not " is supplied by conjecture.

the female; for it has lust, anger, and grief, and what is consequent on these. But the spirit not being uniform,[1] but consisting of three parts, derives its origin from the male; and it is capable of reasoning, knowledge, and fear, and what is consequent on these. And each of these triads has one root, so that man is a compound of two mixtures, the female and the male. Wherefore also two ways have been laid before him—those of obedience and disobedience to law; and two kingdoms have been established,—the one called[2] the kingdom of heaven, and the other the kingdom of those who are now kings upon earth. Also two kings have been appointed, of whom the one is selected to rule by law over the present and transitory world, and his composition is such that he rejoices in the destruction of the wicked. But the other and good[3] one, who is the King of the age to come, loves the whole nature of man; but not being able to have boldness in the present world, he counsels what is advantageous, like one who tries to conceal who he really is.

CHAP. III.—*The work of the good one and of the evil one.*

"But of these two, [the one[4]] acts violently towards the other by the command of God. Moreover, each man has power to obey whichever of them he pleases for the doing of good or evil. But if any one chooses to do what is good, he becomes the possession of the future good king; but if any one should do evil, he becomes the servant of the present evil one, who, having received power over him by just judgment on account of his sins, and wishing [to use it[5]] before the coming age, rejoices in punishing him in the present life, and thus by gratifying, as it were, his own private passion, he accomplishes the will of God. But the other, being made to rejoice in power over the righteous, when he finds a right-

---

[1] A doubtful emendation of Wieseler's for the senseless τρισογενής. Possibly it may be for τρισογενής, original, and is underived.
[2] An obvious correction of the MS. is adopted.
[3] We have changed αὐτός into ἀγαθός.
[4] "One" is supplied by Dressel's conjecture.
[5] The words in brackets are supplied by Dressel's conjecture.

eous man, is exceedingly glad, and saves him with eternal life; and he also, as if gratifying himself, traces the gratification which he feels on account of these to God. Now it is within the power of every unrighteous man to repent and be saved; and every righteous man may have to undergo punishment for sins committed at the end of his career. Moreover, these two leaders are the swift hands of God, eager to anticipate Him so as to accomplish His will. But that this is so, has been said even by the law in the person of God: 'I will kill, and I will make alive; I will strike, and I will heal.'[1] For, in truth, He kills and makes alive. He kills through the left hand, that is, through the evil one, who has been so composed as to rejoice in afflicting the impious. And he saves and benefits through the right hand, that is, through the good one, who has been made to rejoice in the good deeds and salvation of the righteous. Now these have not their substances outside of God: for there is no other primal source. Nor, indeed, have they been sent forth as animals from God, for they were of the same mind with Him; nor are they accidental,[2] arising spontaneously in opposition to His will, since thus the greatest exercise of His power would have been destroyed. But from God have been sent forth the four first elements—heat and cold, moist and dry. In consequence of this, He is the father of every substance, but not of the disposition[3] which may arise from the combination of the elements; for when these were combined from without, disposition was begotten in them as a child. The wicked one, then, having served God blamelessly to the end of the present world, can become good by a change in his composition,[4] since he assuredly is not of one uniform substance whose sole bent is towards sin. For not even more does he do evil, although he is evil, since he has received power to afflict lawfully."

[1] Deut. xxxii. 39.
[2] We have adopted an obvious emendation of Wieseler's.
[3] We have changed οὔσης into οὐ τῆς.
[4] We have given a meaning to μετασυγκριθείς not found in dictionaries, but warranted by etymology, and demanded by the sense.

CHAP. IV.—*Men sin through ignorance.*

When Peter said this, Micah, who was himself one of his followers, asked: "What, then, is the reason why men sin?" And Peter said: "It is because they are ignorant that they will without doubt be punished for their evil deeds when judgment takes place.[1] For this reason they, having lust, as I elsewhere said, for the continuance of life, gratify it in any accidental way, it may be by the vitiation of boys,[2] or by some other flattering sin. For in consequence of their ignorance, as I said before, they are urged on through fearlessness to satisfy their lust in an unlawful manner. Wherefore God is not evil, who has rightly placed lust within man, that there may be a continuance of life, but they are most impious who have used the good of lust badly. The same considerations apply to anger also, that if one uses it righteously, as is within his power, he is pious; but going beyond measure, and taking judgment to himself,[3] he is impious."

CHAP. V.—*Sophonias maintains that God cannot produce what is unlike Himself.*

And Sophonias said again: "Your great patience, my lord Peter, gives us boldness to ask you many questions for the sake of accuracy. Wherefore we make our inquiries with confidence in every direction. I remember, then, that Simon said yesterday, in his discussion with you, that the evil one, if he was born of God, possesses in consequence the same substance as He does who sent him forth, and he ought to have been good, and not wicked. But you answered that this was not always the case, since many wicked sons are born of good parents, as from Adam two unlike[4] sons

---

[1] Part of this is supplied by Dressel's conjecture.
[2] There is a lacuna, which has been filled up in various ways. We have supposed ἐμ to be for ἢ μ., possibly μητέρων ἢ. Wieseler supposes "immature boys."
[3] Dressel translates, "drawing judgment on himself."
[4] An emendation of Wieseler's.

were begotten, one of whom was bad and the other good. And when Simon found fault with you for having used human examples, you answered that in this way we ought not to admit that God begets at all; for this also is a human example. And I, Sophonias, admit that God begets; but I do not allow that He begets what is bad, even though the good among men beget bad children. And do not imagine[1] that I am without reason attributing to God some of the qualities that distinguish men, and refusing to attribute others, when I grant that He begets, but do not allow that He begets what is unlike Himself. For men, as you might expect, beget sons who are unlike them in their dispositions for the following reason. Being composed of four parts, they change their bodies variously, according to the various changes of the year; and thus, the appropriate change either of increase or decrease taking place in the human body, each season destroys the harmonious combination. Now, when the combinations do not always remain exactly in the same position, the seeds, having sometimes one combination, sometimes another, are sent off; and these are followed, according to the combination belonging to the season, by dispositions either good or bad. But in the case of God we cannot suppose any such thing; for, being unchangeable and always existing, whenever He wishes to send forth, there is an absolute necessity that what is sent forth should be in all respects in the same position as that which has begotten, I mean in regard to substance and disposition. But if any one should wish to maintain that He is changeable, I do not know how it is possible for him to maintain that He is immortal."

CHAP. VI.—*God's power of changing Himself.*

When Peter heard this, he thought for a little, and said: "I do not think that any one can converse about evil without doing the will of the evil one. Therefore knowing this, I do not know what I shall do, whether I shall be silent or speak. For if I be silent, I should incur the laughter of the

[1] An emendation of Wieseler's.

multitude, because, professing to proclaim the truth, I am ignorant of the explanation of vice. But if I should state my opinion, I am afraid lest it be not at all pleasing to God that we should seek after evil, for only seeking after good is pleasing to Him. However, in my reply to the statements of Sophonias, I shall make my ideas more plain. I then agree with him in thinking that we ought not to attribute to God all the qualities of men. For instance, men not having bodies that are convertible are not converted; but they have a nature that admits of alteration by the lapse of time through the seasons of the year. But this is not the case with God; for through His inborn[1] Spirit He becomes, by a power which cannot be described, whatever body He likes. And one can the more easily believe this, as the air, which has received such a nature from Him, is converted into dew by the incorporeal mind permeating it, and being thickened becomes water, and water being compacted becomes stone and earth, and stones through collision light up fire. According to such[2] a change and conversion, air becomes first water, and ends in being fire through conversions, and the moist is converted into its natural opposite. Why? Did not God convert the rod of Moses into an animal, making it a serpent,[3] which He reconverted into a rod? And by means of this very converted rod he converted the water of the Nile[4] into blood, which again he reconverted into water. Yea, even man, who is dust, He changed by the inbreathing of His breath[5] into flesh, and changed him back again into dust.[6] And was not Moses,[7] who himself was flesh, converted into the grandest light, so that the sons of Israel could not look him in the face? Much more, then, is God completely able to convert Himself into whatsoever He wishes.

[1] ἐμφύτου.
[2] We have changed τοιοῦτον into τοιαύτην.
[3] Ex. iv. 3, 4.
[4] Ex. vii. 19, 20.
[5] Gen. ii. 7.
[6] Eccles. iii. 20.
[7] Ex. xxxiv. 29.

CHAP. VII.—*The objection answered, that one cannot change himself.*

" But perhaps some one of you thinks that one may become something under the influence of one, and another under the influence of another, but no one can change himself into whatever he wishes, and that it is the characteristic of one who grows old, and who must die according to his nature,[1] to change, but we ought not to entertain such thoughts of immortal beings. For were not angels, who are free from old age, and of a fiery substance,[2] changed into flesh,—those, for instance, who received the hospitality of Abraham,[3] whose feet men washed, as if they were the feet of men of like substance?[4] Yea, moreover, with Jacob,[5] who was a man, there wrestled an angel, converted into flesh that he might be able to come to close quarters with him. And, in like manner, after he had wrestled by his own will, he was converted into his own natural form; and now, when he was changed into fire, he did not burn up the broad sinew of Jacob, but he inflamed it, and made him lame. Now, that which cannot become anything else, whatever it may wish, is mortal, inasmuch as it is subject to its own nature; but he who can become whatever he wishes, whenever he wishes, is immortal, returning to a new condition, inasmuch as he has control over his own nature. Wherefore much more does the power of God change the substance of the body into whatever He wishes, and whenever He wishes; and by the change that takes place[6] He sends forth what, on the one hand, is of similar substance, but, on the other, is not of equal power. Whatever, then, he who sends forth turns into a different substance, that he can again turn back into his own;[7] but he who is sent forth, arising in consequence

---

[1] One word of this is supplied conjecturally by Dressel.
[2] Gen. vi. 2.   [3] Part of this is conjectural.
[4] Gen. xviii. 4.   [5] Gen. xxxii. 24.
[6] We have adopted Wieseler's emendation of μὴ into μὲν.
[7] This passage is corrupt. We have changed ὅτι into ὅ,τι, and supplied τρίτει.

of the change which proceeds from him, and being his child, cannot become anything else without the will of him who sent him forth, unless he wills it."

CHAP. VIII.—*The origin of the good one different from that of the evil one.*

When Peter said this, Micah,[1] who was himself also one of the companions that attended on him, said: "I also should like to learn from you if the good one has been produced in the same way that the evil one came into being. But if they came into being in a similar manner, then they are brothers in my opinion." And Peter said: "They have not come into being in a similar way: for no doubt you remember what I said in the beginning, that the substance of the body of the wicked one, being fourfold in origin, was carefully selected and sent forth by God; but when it was combined externally, according to the will of Him who sent it forth, there arose, in consequence of the combination, the disposition which rejoices in evils:[2] so that you may see that the substance, fourfold in origin, which was sent forth by Him, and which also always exists, is the child of God; but that the accidentally arising disposition which rejoices in evils has supervened when the substance[3] was combined externally by him. And thus this disposition has not been begotten by God, nor by any one else, nor indeed has it been sent forth by Him, nor has it come forth spontaneously,[4] nor did it always exist, like the substance before the combination; but it has come on as an accident by external combination, according to the will of God. And we have often said that it must be so. But the good one having been begotten from the most beautiful change of God, and not having arisen accidentally through an external combination, is really His Son. Yet,

---

[1] Dressel remarks that this cannot be the true reading. Some other name mentioned in Hom. ii. c. 1 must be substituted here or in c. 4.

[2] This passage is corrupt. We have adopted Wieseler's emendations for the most part.

[3] We have read τῆς with Wieseler for τις.

[4] Wieseler translates "accidentally."

since these doctrines are unwritten, and are confirmed to us only by conjecture, let us by no means deem it as absolutely certain that this is the true state of the case. For if we act otherwise, our mind will cease from investigating the truth, in the belief that it has already fully comprehended it. Remember these things, therefore; for I must not state such things to all, but only to those who are found after trial most trustworthy. Nor ought we rashly to maintain such assertions towards each other, nor ought ye to dare to speak as if you were accurately acquainted with the discovery of secret truths, but you ought simply to reflect over them in silence; for in stating, perchance, that a matter is so,[1] he who says it will err, and he will suffer punishment for having dared to speak even to himself what has been honoured with silence."

Chap. IX.—*Why the wicked one is appointed over the wicked by the righteous God.*

When Peter said this, Lazarus, who also was one of his followers, said: "Explain to us the harmony, how it can be reasonable that the wicked one should be appointed by the righteous God to be the punisher of the impious, and yet should himself afterwards be sent into lower darkness along with his angels and with sinners: for I remember that the Teacher Himself said this."[2] And Peter said: "I indeed allow that the evil one does no evil, inasmuch as he is accomplishing the law given to him. And although he has an evil disposition, yet through fear of God he does nothing unjustly; but, accusing the teachers of truth so as to entrap the unwary, he is himself named the accuser (the devil). But the statement of our unerring Teacher, that he and his angels, along with the deluded sinners, shall go into lower darkness, admits of the following explanation. The evil one, having obtained the lot[3] of rejoicing in darkness according to his composition, delights to go down to the darkness of Tartarus along with angels who are his fellow-slaves; for

[1] We have changed οὐχ ὡς ἔχον into οὕτως ἔχειν.   [2] Matt. xxv. 41.
[3] We have adopted an emendation of Wieseler's.

darkness is dear to fire. But the souls of men, being drops of pure light, are absorbed by the substance fire, which is of a different class; and not possessing a nature capable of dying, they are punished according to their deserts. But if he who is the leader of men [1] into vice is not sent into darkness, as not rejoicing in it, then his composition, which rejoices in evils, cannot be changed by another combination into the disposition for good. And thus he will be adjudged to be with the good,[2] all the more because, having obtained a composition which rejoices in evils, through fear of God he has done nothing contrary to the decrees of the law of God. And did not the Scripture by a mysterious hint [3] point out by the statement [4] that the rod of the high priest Aaron became a serpent, and was again converted into a rod, that a change in the composition of the wicked one would afterwards take place?"

CHAP. X.—*Why some believe, and others do not.*

And after Lazarus, Joseph, who also was one of his followers, said: "You have spoken all things rightly. Teach me also this, as I am eager to know it, why, when you give the same discourses to all, some believe and others disbelieve?" And Peter said: "It is because my discourses are not charms, so that every one that hears them must without hesitation believe them. The fact that some believe, and others do not, points out to the intelligent the freedom of the will." And when he said this, we all blessed him.

CHAP. XI.—*Arrival of Appion and Annubion.*

And as we were going to take our meals, some one ran in and said: "Appion Pleistonices has just come with Annubion from Antioch, and he is lodging with Simon." And my father hearing this, and rejoicing, said to Peter: "If you permit me, I shall go to salute Appion and Annubion, who

---

[1] Wieseler's emendation.
[2] We have changed ἀγαθός into ἀγαθοῖς.
[3] An emendation of Wieseler's.
[4] Ex. vii. 9.

have been my friends from childhood. For perchance I shall persuade Annubion to discuss genesis with Clement." And Peter said: "I permit you, and I praise you for fulfilling the duties of a friend. But now consider how in the providence of God there come together from all quarters considerations which contribute to your full assurance, rendering the harmony complete. But I say this because the arrival of Annubion happens advantageously for you." And my father: "In truth, I see that this is the case." And saying this, he went to Simon.

CHAP. XII.—*Faustus appears to his friends with the face of Simon.*

Now all of us who were with Peter asked each other questions the whole of the night, and continued awake, because of the pleasure and joy we derived from what was said. But when at length the dawn began to break, Peter, looking at me and my brothers, said: "I am puzzled to think what your father has been about." And just as he was saying this, our father came in and caught Peter talking to us of him; and seeing him displeased, he accosted him, and rendered an apology for having slept outside. But we were amazed when we looked at him: for we saw the form of Simon, but heard the voice of our father Faustus. And when we were fleeing from him, and abhorring him, our father was astonished at receiving such harsh and hostile treatment from us. But Peter alone saw his natural shape, and said to us: "Why do you in horror turn away from your own father?" But we and our mother said: "It is Simon that we see before us, with the voice of our father." And Peter said: "You recognise only his voice, which is unaffected by magic; but as my eyes also are unaffected by magic, I can see his form as it really is, that he is not Simon, but your father Faustus." Then, looking to my father, he said: "It is not your own true form that is seen by them, but that of Simon, our deadliest foe, and a most impious man."[1]

[1] There are some blanks here, supplied from the Epitome.

Chap. XIII.—*The flight of Simon.*

While Peter was thus talking, there entered one of those who had gone before to Antioch, and who, coming back from Antioch, said to Peter: "I wish you to know, my lord, that Simon, by doing many miracles publicly in Antioch, and calling you a magician and a juggler [and a murderer[1]], has worked them up to such hatred against you, that every man is eager to taste your very flesh if you should sojourn there.[2] Wherefore we who went before, along with our brethren who were in pretence attached by you to Simon, seeing the city raging wildly against you, met secretly and considered what we ought to do. And assuredly, while we were in great perplexity, Cornelius the centurion arrived, who had been sent by the emperor to the governor of the province. He was the person whom our Lord cured when he was possessed of a demon in Cæsarea. This man we sent for secretly; and informing him of the cause of our despondency, we begged his help. He promised most readily that he would alarm Simon, and make him take to flight, if we should assist him in his effort. And when we all promised that we should readily do everything, he said, 'I shall spread abroad the news[3] through many friends that I have secretly come to apprehend him; and I shall pretend that I am in search of him, because the emperor, having put to death many magicians, and having received information in regard to him, has sent me to search him out, that he may punish him as he punished the magicians before him; while those of your party who are with him must report to him, as if they had heard it from a secret source, that I have been sent to apprehend him. And perchance when he hears it from

---

[1] Supplied from Epitome. The passage in Epitome Second renders it likely that the sentence ran: "But Simon, while doing many miracles publicly in Antioch, did nothing else by his discourses than excite hatred amongst them against you, and by calling you," etc.

[2] This passage is amended principally according to Wieseler and the *Recognitions*.

[3] An emendation of Wieseler's.

them, he will be alarmed and take to flight.' When, therefore, we had intended to do something else, nevertheless the affair turned out in the following way. For when he heard the news from many strangers who gratified him greatly by secretly informing him, and also from our brethren who pretended to be attached to him, and took it as the opinion of his own followers, he resolved on retiring. And hastening away from Antioch, he has come here with Athenodorus, as we have heard. Wherefore we advise you not yet to enter that city, until we ascertain whether they can forget in his absence the accusations which he brought against you."

CHAP. XIV.—*The change in the form of Faustus caused by Simon.*

When the person who had gone before gave this report, Peter looked to my father, and said: "You hear, Faustus; the change in your form has been caused by Simon the magician, as is now evident. For, thinking that [a servant[1]] of the emperor was seeking him to punish him, he became afraid and fled, putting you into his own shape, that if you were put to death, your children might have sorrow." When my father heard this, he wept and lamented, and said: "You have conjectured rightly, Peter. For Annubion, who is my dear friend,[2] hinted his design to me; but I did not believe him, [miserable man that I am,[3]] since I deserved to suffer."

CHAP. XV.—*The repentance of Faustus.*

When my father said this, after no long time [Annubion came[4]] to us to announce to us the flight of Simon, and how that very night he had hurried to Judea. And he found our father wailing, and with lamentations saying: "Alas, alas! unhappy man! I did not believe when I was told that he was a magician. Miserable man that I am! I have been

---

[1] Inserted by conjecture.
[2] Part of this is supplied from the *Recognitions*.
[3] Inserted from the *Recognitions*.
[4] These words are taken from the *Recognitions*.

recognised for one day by my wife and children, and have speedily gone back to my previous sad condition when I was still ignorant." And my mother lamenting, plucked her hair; and we groaned in distress on account of the transformation of our father, and could not comprehend what in the world it could be. But Annubion stood speechless, seeing and hearing these things; while Peter said to us, his children, in the presence of all: "Believe me, this is Faustus your father. Wherefore I urge you to attend to him as being your father. For God will vouchsafe some occasion for his putting off the shape of Simon, and exhibiting again distinctly that of your father." And saying this, and looking to my father, he said: "I permitted you to salute Appion and Annubion, since you asserted that they were your friends from childhood, but I did not permit you to associate with the magician Simon."

CHAP. XVI.—*Why Simon gave to Faustus his own shape.*

And my father said: "I have sinned; I confess it." And Annubion said: "I also along with him beg you to forgive the noble and good old man who has been deceived: for the unfortunate man has been the sport of that notorious fellow. But I shall tell you how it took place.[1] The good old man came to salute us. But at that very hour we who were there happened to be listening to Simon, who wished to run away that night, for he had heard that some people had come to Laodicea in search of him by the command of the emperor. But as Faustus was entering, he [turned[2]] his own rage on him, and thus addressed us: 'Make him, when he comes, share your meals; and I will prepare an ointment, so that, when he has supped, he may take some of it, and anoint his face with it, and then he will appear to all to have my shape. But I will anoint you with the juice[3] of some plant,

---

[1] An emendation of Dressel's.
[2] Supplied by Dressel from the *Recognitions.*
[3] An emendation of Wieseler's.

and then you will not be deceived by his new[1] shape; but to all others Faustus will seem to be Simon.'

CHAP. XVII.—*Annubion's services to Faustus.*

"And while he stated this beforehand, I said, 'What, then, is the advantage you now expect to get from such a contrivance?' And Simon said, 'First, those who seek me, when they apprehend him, will give up the search after me. But if he be executed by the hand of the emperor, very great sorrow will fall upon his children, who left me, and fleeing [to Peter], now aid him in his work.' And now, Peter, I confess the truth to you: I was prevented by fear [of Simon] from informing [Fau]stus of this. But Simon did not even give us an opportunity for private conversation, [lest] some one of us might reveal[2] to him the wicked design of Simon. Simon then rose up in the middle of the night and fled to Judea, convoyed by Appion and Athenodorus. Then I pretended that I was sick, in order that, remaining after they had gone, I might make Faustus go back immediately to his own people, if by any chance he might be able, by being concealed with you, to escape observation, lest, being caught as Simon by those who were in search of Simon, he might be put to death through the wrath of the emperor. At the dead of night, therefore, I sent him away to you; and in my anxiety for him I came by night to see him, with the intention of returning before those who convoyed Simon should return." And looking to us, he said: "I, Annubion, see the true shape of your father; for I was anointed, as I related to you before, by Simon himself, that the true shape of Faustus might be seen by my eyes. Astonished, therefore, I exceedingly wonder at the magic power of Simon, in that standing[3] you do not recognise your own father." And

---

[1] MS. reads "empty." Wieseler proposed "new" or "assumed."

[2] An emendation of Wieseler's. The parts within brackets are supplied by conjecture.

[3] We should have expected "standing near" or something similar, as Wieseler remarks; but the Latin of the *Recognitions* agrees with the Greek in having the simple "standing."

while our father and our mother and we ourselves wept on account of the calamity common to all of us, Annubion also through sympathy wept with us.

CHAP. XVIII.—*Peter promises to restore to Faustus his own shape.*

Then Peter promised to us to restore the shape of our father, and he said to him: " Faustus, you heard how matters stand with us. When, therefore, the deceptive shape which invests you has been useful to us, and you have assisted us in doing what I shall tell you to do, then I shall restore to you your true form, when you have first performed my commands." And when my father said, " I shall do everything that is in my power most willingly; only restore to my own people my own form;" Peter answered, " You yourself heard with your own ears how those who went before me came back from Antioch, and said that Simon had been there, and had strongly excited the multitudes against me by calling me a magician and a murderer, a deceiver and a juggler, to such an extent that all the people there were eager to taste my flesh. You will do, then, as I tell you. You will leave Clement with me, and you will go before us into Antioch with your wife, and your sons Faustinus and Faustinianus. And some others will accompany you whom I deem capable of helping forward my design.

CHAP. XIX.—*Peter's instructions to Faustus.*

" When [you are] with these in Antioch, while you look like Simon, proclaim publicly your [repentance], saying, ' I Simon proclaim this to you: I confess[1] that all my statements in regard to Peter are [utterly false;[2] for he is not] a deceiver, nor a murderer, nor a juggler; nor are any of the evil things true which I, urged on by wrath, said previously in regard to him. I myself therefore beg of you, I who have been the cause of your hatred to him, cease from hating him; for he is the true apostle of the true Prophet that was sent

[1] Amended according to Epitome.
[2] Partly filled up from Epitome and *Recognitions*.

by God for the salvation of the world. Wherefore also I counsel you to believe what he preaches;[1] for if you do not, your whole city will be utterly destroyed. Now I wish you to know for what reason I have made this confession to you. This night angels of God scourged me, the impious one, terribly, as being an enemy to the herald of the truth. I beseech you, therefore, do not listen to me, even if I myself should come at another time and attempt to say anything against Peter. For I confess to you I am a magician, I am a deceiver, I am a juggler. Yet perhaps it is possible for me by repentance to wipe out the sins which were formerly committed by me.'"

CHAP. XX.—*Faustus, his wife, and sons, prepare to go to Antioch.*

When Peter suggested this, my father said: "I know what you want; wherefore take no trouble. For assuredly I shall take good care, when I reach that place, to make such statements in regard to you as I ought to make." And Peter again suggested: "When, then, you perceive the city changing from its hatred of me, and longing to see me, send information to me of this, and I shall come to you immediately. And when I arrive there, that same day I shall remove the strange shape which now invests you, and I shall make your own unmistakeably visible to your own people and to all others." Saying this, he made his sons, my brothers, and our mother Mattidia to go along with him; and he also commanded some of his more intimate acquaintances to accompany him. But my mother was[2] unwilling to go with him, and said: "I seem to be an adulteress if I associate with the shape of Simon; but if I shall be compelled to go along with him, it is impossible for me to recline on the same couch with him.[3] But I do not know if I

---

[1] MS. reads, "I preach."
[2] We have changed εἶδε into εἶχε, and added καὶ εἶπε, according to the *Recognitions*.
[3] One word, τύχης, is superfluous.

shall be persuaded to go along with him." And while she was very unwilling to go, Annubion urged her, saying: "Believe me and Peter, and the very voice itself, that this is [Faustus] your husband, whom I love not less than you. And I myself [will go[1]] along with him." When Annubion said this, our mother promised to go with him.

CHAP. XXI.—*Appion and Athenodorus return in quest of Faustus.*

But Peter said: "God arranges our affairs in a most satisfactory manner;[2] for we have with us Annubion the [astro]loger.[3] For when we arrive at Antioch, he will in future discourse regarding genesis, giving us his genuine opinions as a friend." Now when, after midnight, our father hurried with those whom Peter had ordered to go along with him and with Annubion to Antioch, which was near, early next day, before Peter went forth to discourse, Appion and Athenodorus, who had convoyed Simon, returned to Laodicea in search of our father. But Peter, ascertaining the fact, urged them to enter. And when they came in and sat down, and said, "Where is Faustus?" Peter answered: "We know not; for since the evening, when he went to you, he has not been seen by his kinsmen. But yesterday morning Simon came in search of him; and when we made no reply to him, something seemed to come over him,[4] for he called himself Faustus; but not being believed, he wept and lamented, and threatened to kill himself, and then rushed out in the direction of the sea."

CHAP. XXII.—*Appion and Athenodorus return to Simon.*

When Appion and those who were with him heard this, they howled and lamented, saying: "Why did you not

[1] Supplied from the *Recognitions*.
[2] We read ἐπιτηδειότατα, in harmony with the *Recognitions*.
[3] Part within brackets supplied from *Recognitions*.
[4] The Greek is probably corrupt here; but there can scarcely be a doubt about the meaning.

receive him?" And when at the same time Athenodorus wished to say to me, "It was Faustus, your father;" Appion anticipated him, and said, "We learned from some one that Simon, finding him, urged him [to go along with him¹]. Faustus himself entreating him, since he did not wish to see his sons after they had become Jews. And hearing this, we came, for his own sake, in search of him. But since he is not here, it is plain that he spake the truth who gave us the information which we, hearing it from him, have given to you." And I Clement, perceiving the design of Peter, that he wished to beget a suspicion in them that he intended to look out among them for the old man, that they might be afraid and take to flight, assisted in his design, and said to Appion: "Listen to me, my dearest Appion. We were eager to give to him, as being our father, what we ourselves deemed to be good. But if he himself did not wish to receive it, but, on the contrary, fled from us in horror, I shall make a somewhat harsh remark, 'Nor do we care for him.'" And when I said this, they went away, as if irritated by my savageness; and, as we learned next day, they went to Judea in the track of Simon.

CHAP. XXIII.—*Peter goes to Antioch.*

Now, when ten days had passed away, [there came one of our people²] from our father to announce to us how our father [stood forward] publicly [in the] shape [of Simon], accusing him;³ and how by praising Peter he had made the whole city of Antioch long for him: and in consequence of this, all said that they were eager to see him, and that there were some who were angry with him as being Simon, on account of their surpassing affection for Peter, and wished to lay hands on Faustus, believing he was Simon. Wherefore he, fearing that he might be put to death, had sent to request Peter to come immediately if he wished to meet him alive,

---

¹ This is supplied purely by conjecture.
² Supplied from the *Recognitions*.
³ This part is restored by means of the *Recognitions*.

and to appear at the proper time to the city, when it was at the height of its longing for him. Peter, hearing this, called the multitude together to deliberate, and appointed one of his attendants bishop; and having remained three days in Laodicea baptizing and healing, he hastened to the neighbouring city of Antioch. Amen.

INDEXES.

I.—TEXTS OF SCRIPTURE QUOTED.

GENESIS.
i. 1,	.	248
i. 26,	.	250
ii. 7,	.	317
ii. 16, 17,	.	245
ii. 20,	.	66
iii. 5,	.	246
iii. 22,	74,	246
vi. 2,	.	318
vi. 6,	.	74
vii. 1,	.	56
viii. 21,	.	74
xv. 13-16,	.	76
xviii. 4,	.	318
xviii. 21,	.	74
xx. 3,	.	270
xxii. 1,	.	74
xxxii. 24,	.	318
xli. 6,	.	270
xli. 25,	.	270
xlix. 10,	.	78

EXODUS.
iv. 3, 4,	.	317
vii. 9,	.	321
vii. 19, 20,	.	317
xix. 9,	.	139
xxii. 28,	246,	248
xxxiii. 11,	.	271
xxxiv. 29,	.	317

NUMBERS.
xi. 34,	.	77
xii. 6,	.	271

DEUTERONOMY.
iv. 34,	.	246
iv. 39,	.	247
vi. 4,	.	247
vi. 13,	.	247
x. 14,	.	247
x. 17,	246,	247 bis

xiii. 1, etc.,	.	251
xiii. 6,	.	246
xviii. 15-19,	.	80
xxx. 15,	.	285
xxxii. 7,	.	64
xxxii. 39,	.	314
xxxiv. 8,	.	78

JOSHUA.
xxiii. 7,	247,	248

PSALMS.
xix. 1,	.	248
xxxv. 10,	.	246
xlv. 11,	.	220
l. 1,	.	246
lxxii. 1,	.	246
lxxviii. 2,	.	284
lxxxvi. 8,	.	246
cii. 26, 27,	.	248

PROVERBS.
viii. 30,	.	250

ECCLESIASTES.
iii. 1,	.	33
iii. 2,	.	307
iii. 20,	.	317

ISAIAH.
i. 3,	.	286
iv.,	.	147
ix. 6,	.	251
xl. 26, 27,	.	285
xliv. 6,	.	247
xlv. 21,	.	247
xlix. 18,	.	247

JEREMIAH.
x. 11,	246,	248

LAMENTATIONS.
iii. 38,	.	276

DANIEL.
ii. 31,	.	270
iii. 25,	.	270

MATTHEW.
iv.,	.	147
iv. 10,	.	163
v. 3,	.	241
v. 8,	.	262
v. 17,	.	79
v. 18,	.	2, 19
v. 34, 35,	.	81
v. 37,	81,	291
v. 39-41,	.	237
v. 44,	.	65
v. 44, 45,	.	82
vi. 6,	.	81
vi. 8, 32,	.	81
vi. 13,	.	291
vii. 2,	.	285
vii. 7,	.	80
vii. 9-11,	.	81
vii. 12,	.	209
vii. 13, 14,	.	215
vii. 21,	.	140
viii. 11,	.	138
viii. 24,	.	300
viii. 31,	.	300
ix. 13,	.	81
x. 12,	.	70
x. 28,	.	259
x. 34,	.	183
xi. 25,	139, 260,	284
xi. 27,	.	259, 276
xi. 28,	.	80
xii. 7,	.	81
xii. 26,	.	291
xii. 34,	.	295
xii. 42,	.	189
xiii. 17,	.	80
xiii. 39,	.	81, 291
xv. 13,	.	80

xvi. 13,	.	. 271	xxviii. 19,	.	. 261	xviii. 19,	.	82, 276
xvi. 16,	.	. 271				xix. 5,	.	. 84
xvi. 18,	.	. 272	MARK.			xix. 43,	.	. 63
xvii. 5,	.	. 80	i. 13,	.	. 291	xx. 38,	.	. 81
xvii. 19,	.	. 181	iii. 31,	.	. 2	xxiii. 34,	.	65, 183
xviii. 7,	.	. 207	iv. 34,	.	. 305			
xviii. 10,	.	. 261	vi. 11,	.	. 70	JOHN.		
xix. 8,	.	. 81	x. 5,	.	. 81	iii. 5,	.	. 186
xix. 17,	82, 259, 274,		x. 18,	.	. 82	ix. 2, 3,	.	. 308
	276, 286		xii. 24,	.	56, 287	x. 3,	.	. 80
xx. 16,	.	. 138	xii. 27,	.	. 81	x. 9,	.	. 80
xxii.,	.	. 147	xii. 29,	.	. 82			
xxii. 2,	.	. 64				ACTS.		
xxii. 29,	.	56, 79	LUKE.			iii. 22,	.	. 80
xxii. 32,	.	. 81	viii. 18,	.	. 285	vii. 37,	.	. 80
xxii. 39,	.	. 209	x. 5,	.	. 70			
xxiii. 2,	.	. 88	x. 18,	.	. 291	GALATIANS.		
xxiii. 37,	.	. 65	xi. 32,	.	. 189	iv. 10,	.	. 309
xxiv. 2, 34,	.	. 63	xi. 52,	.	. 285			
xxiv. 24,	.	. 256	xii. 42,	.	. 85	EPHESIANS.		
xxiv. 45-50,	.	. 82	xiii. 29,	.	. 138			
xxv. 27-30,	.	. 82	xiii. 34,	.	. 65	iv. 27,	.	. 291
xxv. 35, 36,	.	. 210	xvii.,	.	. 207			
xxv. 41,	.	291, 320	xviii. 6,	.	. 260	JAMES.		
xxvii. 51,	.	. 300	xviii. 18,	.	. 286	v. 12,	.	. 29

II.—PRINCIPAL SUBJECTS.

ABEL, his name and nature, 68.
Actions, wicked, to be avoided, 304.
Adam, had he the Spirit? 63; was not ignorant, 64.
Adultery, the evils of, 98, 99; advocated by some philosophers, 109, 110.
Adultery, spiritual, 69.
Afflictions, the, of the righteous, suffered for the remission of sins, 240.
Ages, the two, 312.
Allegory, the bad actions ascribed to the gods attempted to be explained by, 100, 121; the inventors of these stories of the gods blameworthy, 124.
Amours, the, of Jupiter, 106, 107.
Angels, the metamorphoses of, 142; the fall of, and its cause, 143; discoveries made by, 143; the giant offspring of, 144; demons sprung from the fallen, 145.
Antaradus, 192.
Annubion, 92, 321, 326.

Appion, meets and salutes Clement, 92; discussion with Clement, 93, etc.; previous acquaintance of Clement with, and trick played on, 101, 102, etc.; second discussion with Clement, 115, etc.; and Annubion, 321, 326; in quest of Faustus, and return to Peter, 229.
Aquila, declares the doctrine of Simon Magus to Clement, 41, etc.; and Nicetas deceived by Simon Magus, but finding out his true character, forsake him, 41, 44; sent with Nicetas and Clement to observe and report concerning Simon, 89, 90; and Nicetas, recognise each other as brothers, 212.
Artemis, 120.
Assembling together, the duty of, 87.
Athenodorus, 329.
Attendants of Peter, names of the, 32.
Attribute, the peculiar, of God, 169.

BAPTISM, 89; for the remission of sins, 134; the wedding garment, 147; in good works, 148; the use of, 185, 186; all have need of, 186.
Baptized, the privileges of the, 158.
Barnabas, preaches at Alexandria, 22; interrupted by the crowd, 22, 23; defended by Clement, 23-25; instructs Clement, 25; leaves Alexandria, 25, 26.
Bernice, the daughter of the Canaanitess, 89; receives Clement at Tyre, 90; reports the doings of Simon Magus, 90, 91.
Bishop, the duty of a, 9; labours and reward of a, 14; to be heard and obeyed, 86, 87.
Books, Christian, to be imparted to the initiated only, 1-4.
Born of water, 185.
Boyish questionings, the, of Clement, 17.

CAIN, his name and nature, 67.
Cannibals, the first, 144.
Catechists, the duties of, 12.
Chaos, the origin of, 117, 118.
Chaste woman, the, 220.
Chastity, 218-224.
Christ, the true prophet, 34, 61, 78; hidden from the Jews, 139; and Moses, 140; not God, but the Son of God, 252.
Christ, His prophecies, 63.
Christ, the reign of, 64.
Christ, His teaching respecting the interpretation of Scripture, 79-81.
Church, the, a ship, 13.
Church, duties of the members of the, 88.
Church office-bearers, the duties of, 86.
Clement, epistle of, to James, 6, etc.; ordained by Peter his successor, 7-16; installation of, 15; his boyish questioning — an autobiographic sketch of, 17; his perplexities arising from the teaching of philosophers, 18, 19; his resolution, 19; hears good tidings out of Judea, 20; the gospel reaches him in Rome, 21; sets out for Judea, but is driven by contrary winds to Alexandria, 21, 22; meets with Barnabas at Alexandria, 22; his zeal in defence of Barnabas, 23-25; is instructed in Christianity by Barnabas, 25; introduced to Peter, 26; Peter's salutation of, 27; questions proposed by, to Peter, 27, 28; instructed by Peter, 28; Peter's satisfaction with, 29; convinced of the truth of Christianity, 30; Peter's thanksgiving on account of, 31; sent by Peter to Tyre, to learn and report concerning Simon Magus, 89, 90; meets his friend Appion, and holds a discussion with him, 92; relates his previous acquaintance with Appion, 101; and the successful trick he played on him, 101, 102, etc.; result of the trick he played on Appion, 114; meets Appion again for discussion, 115, etc.; the joy of, for being permitted by Peter to remain with him, 193; his office of service, 194; grief because Peter speaks of being his servant, 195; the family history of, 196, 197; the mother of, her story of herself and family, 198, etc.; introduced by Peter to his mother, 203, etc.; Peter relates the history of, to Nicetas and Aquila, 212; the father of, discovered, 226, 229, 230, 231; undertakes to discuss the subject of genesis, 233.
Concealment and revelation, 139.
Conjunction, the doctrine of, 63.
Constellations, the, 109.
Contradictions of Scripture, 61, 74-77, 249, 250. See Scripture.
Converts and preachers, their mutual love, 192.
Creation, the works of, 71; the extent of, 71; boundless, 71, 72; man's dominion over, 72.
Creatures, avengers of God's cause, 177.
Custom, a second nature, 97.
Custom and truth, 94.
Customs of one's country and fathers, are they to be observed? 93.

DEACONS, the duties of, 12.
Demons, the subjection of, to angel generals, 103; origin of, 143, 144, 145; the law given to, 145, 146; how they enter men, 146; how they get power over men, 152; how they are expelled, 153; unbelief the stronghold of, 153, 154; deceits of, 154; tricks of, 155; power of, 156; reasons why the deceits of, are not detected, 157; props of the system of, 159; the

baptized have power to drive away, 158; subject to believers, 159; none but evil, appear to the impious, 269.
Destiny, 95.
Devil, the, the existence of, asserted, 290; Peter refuses to discuss certain questions relating to, 291; suppositions as to the origin of, 292; God is not blameable for permitting the existence of, 293; Peter accuses Simon Magus of being worse than, 294; theories in regard to the origin of, 296; the creation of, 299; why entrusted with power, 301; has not equal power with God, 302; is he a mere relation? 303, 304.
Devil, the wiles of the, 60.
Discussion between Clement and Appion, 103, etc., 115, etc.; of Peter with Simon Magus, 242, etc.
Disease, a theory of, 154.
Disobedience, the danger of, 86.
Doctrine according to godliness, the, 95.
Dositheus and Simon Magus, the contest between, for pre-eminence, 43.
Dreams, evidence furnished by, discussed, 268; the impious see true visions and, 270.

EGYPTIANS, gods of the, 167; their defence of their system exposed, 168.
Eros, 105, 111, 112.
Errors, the use of, 58, 59.
Evil, sin the cause of, 300, 301.
Evil one, the. See Devil.

FAITH, the gift of God, 139; obstacles to, 235.
Faith and duty, 162.
Fall, the, of man, the cause of, 142; of angels, 143.
Father, love to God as our, 184.
Father, no one knows the, how to be understood, 282, 284.
Faustus, 226, 229, 230.
Fear and love, 210.
Fear of God, 163, 265; and love of, 266.
Female prophetess, the, 66; a deceiver, 67.
Few shall be saved, 58.
Fire-worship, the origin of, 150, 151.
Flattery or magic, which the more potent, 104.

Flesh, the, persons who first ate, 144.
Flood, the cause of the, 144.
Foreknowledge, 61.
Forewarned, forearmed, 33.
Fornication, 10.
Freedom, the, of man, 176.

GENESIS, 94, 95; Peter's argument against, 227; a practical refutation of, 228; discussion concerning, 232, etc.
Giants, the, who? 144.
God, what is not, 127.
God, good and just, 37; the ways of, 38, 39; attributes of, 52, 53; how to be thought of, 53, 54; His works of creation, 70-72; the excellency of the knowledge of, 73; the, of the Jews, 95; vindicated as blameless, 141; peculiar attributes of, 169; neither the world nor any part of it to be considered as being, 169; jealous, 176; creatures avenge the cause of, 177; the nature of, 253; the name of, 254; the shape of, in man, 254; the character of, 255; man in the shape of, 261; the figure of, 262; the centre and heart of the universe, 263; the nature and shape of, further noticed, 264; the fear of, 265; the fear and love of, 266; both good and just, 275; misconceptions respecting, in the Old Testament, 286, 287; not blameable for permitting the existence of the devil, 293; incomprehensible, 297; produced the evil one, but not evil, 298; the maker of the devil, 299; His power of changing Himself, 316; not the author of the evil one, so as He is of the good one, 319; why He appoints the evil one over the wicked, 320.
God, the Son of, 252.
God, the unrevealed, of Simon, 277.
Gods of the heathen, the, the wickedness of, 96; evil influence of the example of, 97; attempted explanation of the bad actions ascribed to, 100; not really gods, 112; imitation of, 112; really wicked magicians, 126; graves of, 126; the contemporaries of, did not look on them as being gods, 127; those which are made by hands are not, 164; of the Egyp-

tians, 167; the, which have not made the heavens, 185.
Golden rule, the, 132, 174, 209.
Good, out of evil, 17.
Good, the sufferings of the, 207.
Good one, the, and the evil one, the different origins of, 319.
Goodness and justice defined, 274, 275.

HAM, the family of, 150.
Helena and Simon Magus, 42; what Simon says of, 43, 44.
Hell and purgatory, 59.
Hercules, 124.
Hero-worship, 150.
Honesty, 11.
Hospitality, 201.
Human life, the inequalities of lot in, 308.

IDOLATRY, a delusion of the serpent, 165; the folly of, 171; why God suffers, 175.
Idols, the test of, 155, 156; the unprofitableness of, 163, 178; not animated by the Divine Spirit, 169; confutation of the worship of, 170; folly of the worship of, 171; heathen worshippers of, under the power of the demon, 180.
Ignorance and error, no excuse for the sinner, 166.
Ignorant, the, the condemnation of, 166.
Image of God, man made after the, 174.
Image of God, the, restoration to, 163.
Imitation of the gods, 97.
Immoral teaching of the Greeks, the, illustrated, 101-105.
Immortality of the soul, Clement's perplexities about, 18, 19; the belief of, necessary to a knowledge of God, 37; asserted by Peter, 178.
Impiety, what it is, 60.
Inequalities of lot in human life, 308.
Initiation, necessary before possessing the privilege of reading Christian books, 2; mode of, 3; vow and adjuration connected with, 3, 4.
Israel, the way of knowledge revealed to, 285; how ignorant of God, 286.

JAMES, the epistle of Peter to, 1, 2,
etc.; epistle of Clement to, 6, etc.
Jealous God, a, God is, 176.
John the Baptist, Simon Magus formerly a disciple of, 42.
Judging, who qualified for, 206, 207.
Justa, the Syrophœnician woman, the daughter of, 40, 41.
Jupiter, the wickedness of, 96; the amours of, 106, 107.

KING of the present time, the, and the King of righteousness, 146, 147.
Kingdom, the way to, not concealed from the Israelites, 285, 286.
Kronos, 96; and Rea, 118.

LAODICEA, a journey to, 211.
Law, the original, 141.
Law, the, of the Old Testament, the corruption of—not written by Moses, 50.
Liberty and necessity, 176.
Life, human, inequalities of lot in the, 308.
Love and fear, 210.
Love of God, 266.
Love of man, 237.
Love-letter, a, written by Appion for Clement, 105, etc.; a reply to, 111, etc.
Lust, anger, and grief, the uses of, 306.

MAGIC, the power of, 102, 103.
Male and female, 66.
Man, the original state of, 141; the fall of, 142; the lord of all, 162; in the shape of God, 203; as created by God, 313; his power to choose good or evil, 313, 314; sins through ignorance, 315.
Marriage, urged on presbyters, 9, 10; always honourable, 86.
Marriage supper, the, 147.
Matter, is it eternal? 300.
Mattidia, 196; the story of, 198, etc., 211; wishes to be baptized, 213; values baptism aright, 217; unintentionally fasted one day, 217, 218; baptized in the sea, 225.
Meeting together, the duty of, urged on Christians, 87.
Merchants, the best, 152.
Micah, question addressed by, to Peter, 319.
Ministry, the support of the, 319.

Miracles, useless and philanthropic, the, of Simon Magus, 48, 49.
Monarchy and polyarchy, 149.
Moses, how he delivered his writings, 70-72; the law not written by, 77, 78.
Moses and Christ, 140.
Myths, the heathen, not to be taken literally, according to Appion, 115, etc., 117, etc., 120, 121; the inventors of such vile, blameworthy, 124, 125.

NAMES, the giving of, to animals, 65, 66.
Nebrod, or Zoroaster, 150.
Nicetas, statement of, concerning Simon Magus, 45-47; and Aquila, recognise each other as brothers, 212; and relate what befell each other, 215; near being deceived by Simon Magus, 216.
Nineveh, the men of, 189.
Noah, 148; the family of, 150.
"*Nolo episcopari*," 85.

OBEDIENCE leads to peace, 84; danger of the contrary, 86.
Offences must come, 208.
Office-bearers in the church, the duties of, 86.
Old Testament, misconceptions of God in the, 286; some parts of, written to try us, 287.
Order, God's, 38, 39.
Ordination, the, of Zacharias by Peter, 88, 89.
Orgies, 151, 179, 180.
Orthasia, 192.

PAIN and death, the result of sin, 305.
Pairs, the doctrine of, 38, 48, 66.
Paris, the judgment of, 123.
Paths, the two, 138.
Pallas and Hera, 120.
Peculiar attributes of God, the, 169.
Persians, the, fire-worshippers, 151.
Peter, the martyrdom of, 6; ordains Clement his successor, 7, 8; his charge to Clement, 9; Clement tells of his introduction to, and instruction by, 26-31; names of the attendants of, 32; tactics of, in regard to Simon Magus, 50, 51; meets Simon, 69; his discussion with Simon, 73, etc.; after the flight of Simon, sends Clement to Tyre to inquire and report concerning him, 89, 90; arrival of, at Cæsarea, 128; addresses the people at Tyre, 130; departs to Sidon, 132; founds a church in Sidon, 134; attacked by Simon, 134; goes to Byblus and Tripolis, 135; arrives at Tripolis, 137; thoughtfulness of, 137, 138; his third day in Tripolis, 161; at Antaradus, 192; frugality of, 194; journeys to Laodicea, 211; baptizes Mattidia, 225; his discussion with an old man, 226; wishes to convert Faustus, 234; his discussion with Simon respecting the unity of God, 242; mode of the discussion, 243; his reply to Simon's appeal to the Old Testament, and other objections, 247, etc.; close of first day's discussion with Simon, 256; second day's discussion with Simon, 257, etc.; third day's discussion with Simon, 274; fourth day's discussion with Simon, 290; Simon is confounded by, and retires, 310; reply to the questions of Sophonios, 312, etc.; promises to restore Faustus to his own proper shape, 327; goes to Antioch, 330.
Peter, epistle of, to James, 1, etc.
Phanes and Pluto, 119.
Philanthropy and friendship, 204; what is philanthropy? 205.
Philosophers, the unworthy ends of, 93; false and impious theories of, 98; advocates of adultery, 109, 110.
Philosophy and religion, the difference between, 236.
Polyarchy and monarchy, 149.
Polytheism, a sophistical illustration in favour of, exposed, 167, etc.
Poseidon, Zeus, and Metis, 119.
Possessions, sins, 240.
Poverty, not necessarily righteous, 241.
Prediction and prophecy, the distinction between, 61.
Presbyters, the duties of the, 9.
Present, the, and the future, 239.
Prince, the, of the left hand, and the, of the right hand of God, 130, 131.
Prophecies of Christ, 63.
Prophecy, two kinds of, 66.
Prophet, the true, 34, 61, 78; all may judge of the, 35; the test

of, 30; doctrines of, 37; has appeared in different ages, 65.
Prophet and prophetess, the, 66, 68.
Prophetic knowledge, constant, 62.
Prophetic spirit, the, constant, 62.
Prophets, false, to be avoided, 190.
Punishment, reformatory, 181.
Purgatory and hell, 59.
Purification, 187.
Purity, outward and inward, 187, 188.

QUEEN of the South, the, 189.

RELIGION and philosophy, the difference between, 236.
Reserve, the doctrine of, 1.
Responsibility, 188, 189.
Revelation, the nature of, 271, 278; the work of, belongs to the Son, 279.
Righteous, the, afflictions of, 197.
Rule, the golden, 209.

SACRIFICES, 77.
Sacrificial orgies, 151.
Saved, the number of the, 58, 59.
Scripture, the, false and blasphemous chapters added to, 50, 51, 52; misrepresentations of God in, 54, 55; some things in, false, and some true, 55, 56; Simon makes use of the alleged falsehoods of, in argument with Peter, 58; use of the falsehoods of, 58, 59; the uncertainty of, 66; contradictions of, 61, 74-77; how to discriminate the true from the false in, 79-81; Peter's explanation of contradictions in, 249; the contradictions in, intended to try the readers of, 250, etc.
Senses, the testimony of the, more trustworthy than that of supernatural vision, 267.
Service, the, which God requires, 134.
Serpent, the, idolatry, a delusion of, 165; why he tempts to sin, 165; charming the, 182.
Sidon, Peter comes to, 132; Peter preaches to the people of, 132, 133; Peter attacked there by Simon, 134; Simon driven from, 135.
Simon Magus, mistakes about, 40; the doctrines of, 41; once a disciple of the Baptist, 42; and Dositheus, the contest between, for precedence, 43; the wickedness and knavish tricks of, 44; statement of Nicetas respecting, and counsel to, 45-47; proceedings of, 47, etc.; the design and object of, exposed by Peter, 57; comes to dispute with Peter, 69; his discussion with Peter, 73, etc.; driven into a corner by Peter's arguments, he quits the field, 82; Clement sent to watch, and report concerning, 89; tricks of, at Tyre, 91; reason of the power of, 138, 139; attacks Peter, 134; is driven away, 135; departs from Tripolis to Syria, 138; comes from Antioch to discuss with Peter the unity of God, 242; appeals to the Old Testament to prove that there are many gods, 245; tries to show that the Scriptures contradict themselves, 248; accuses Peter of using magic, and of teaching doctrines different from those taught by Christ, 257, 258; asserts that Jesus is not consistent with Himself, 259, 260; asserts that the Framer of the world is not the highest God, 274; asserts an unrevealed God, 277; the opinions of, expounded and refuted by Peter, 282, 283; retires from the discussion, 289; is rebuked by Faustus, 309; changes the face of Faustus into the exact resemblance of his own, 322, 324, 325; flight of, 323.
Sin, the cause of evil, 300, 301; the cause of pain and death, 305.
Sins of ignorance, 307.
Son of God, the, 252.
Sophonias, his questions, and Peter's replies to, 311, 312.
Soul, Clement's former perplexities about the immortality of, 32, 33; the belief of the immortality of, necessary to correct views of God. 37; the immortality of, asserted by Peter, 178.
Sound mind, a, in a sound body, 32, 33.
Spies in the enemy's camp, 50.
Standing One, the, 42.
Submission, 193.
"Sword, not peace, but a," 182, 183.
Syrophœnician woman, the story of, amplified, 40, 41.

TACTICS, the, of Peter against Simon
   Magus, 50, 51.
Teaching, the, of Christ, 78-82.
Teaching, the immoral, of the Greeks,
   illustrated, 101-105.
Temptation, the, of Christ, 147.
Traditions from our fathers, are
   they to be followed? 93.
Trick, the, of Clement upon Appion,
   101-105.
Tripolis, Peter at, 137.
Truth, cannot be found by man left
   to himself, 34; vain search of
   philosophers for, 34, 35; taught
   by the prophets, 35.
Truth and custom, 94.
Tyre, Peter at, 128; address to the
   people of, 130.

UNITY, the, of God, proved by
   Peter from the Old Testament,
   247, 250.
Universe, the, the product of mind,
   128.

Unrevealed God, the, of Simon
   Magus, 276.

VOYAGE, the, of the church, 13.

WATER, born of, 185; baptized
   with, 186, 187.
Way of salvation, the, 134.
Ways, the, of God, opposed to man's
   ways, 38, 39.
Wicked actions to be avoided, 304.
Wicked one, the, why appointed
   over the wicked by a righteous
   God? 320.
Wiles of the devil, the, 60.
Wise, the, divine things justly
   hidden from, 285.
Woman, the, of sorrowful spirit,
   198; her story, 199, etc.

ZACCHEUS, 41; appointed by Peter
   his successor, 84, 85.
Zoroaster, 150.

THE

APOSTOLICAL CONSTITUTIONS.

EDITED, WITH NOTES, BY

JAMES DONALDSON, LL.D.

EDINBURGH:
T. & T. CLARK, 38, GEORGE STREET.
MDCCCLXX.

CONTENTS.

	PAGE
INTRODUCTORY NOTICE,	3
CONTENTS OF THE APOSTOLICAL CONSTITUTIONS,	5
BOOK I. CONCERNING THE LAITY,	15
BOOK II. CONCERNING BISHOPS, PRESBYTERS, AND DEACONS,	26
BOOK III. CONCERNING WIDOWS,	93
BOOK IV. CONCERNING ORPHANS,	107
BOOK V. CONCERNING THE MARTYRS,	115
BOOK VI. CONCERNING SCHISMS,	143
BOOK VII. CONCERNING THE CHRISTIAN LIFE, AND THE EUCHARIST, AND THE INITIATION INTO CHRIST,	177
BOOK VIII. CONCERNING GIFTS, AND ORDINATIONS, AND THE ECCLESIASTICAL CANONS,	206
THE ECCLESIASTICAL CANONS OF THE SAME HOLY APOSTLES,	257

CONSTITUTIONS OF THE HOLY APOSTLES,

BY

CLEMENT, BISHOP AND CITIZEN OF ROME.

A

INTRODUCTORY NOTICE.

HERE has always existed a great diversity of opinion as to the author and date of the *Apostolical Constitutions*. Earlier writers were inclined to assign them to the apostolic age, and to Clement; but much discussion ensued, and the questions to which they give rise are still unsettled.

The most peculiar opinion in regard to them is that of Whiston, who devoted a volume (vol. iii.) of his *Primitive Christianity Revived* to prove that " they are the most sacred of the canonical books of the New Testament;" for "these sacred Christian laws or constitutions were delivered at Jerusalem, and in Mount Sion, by our Saviour to the eleven apostles there assembled after His resurrection."

Krabbe, who wrote an elaborate treatise on the origin and contents of the *Apostolical Constitutions*, tried to show that the first seven books were written "towards the end of the third century." The eighth book, he thinks, must have been written at the end of the fourth or beginning of the fifth.

Bunsen thinks that, if we expunge a few interpolations of the fourth and fifth centuries, "we find ourselves unmistakeably in the midst of the life of the church of the second and third centuries."[1] "I think," he says, "I have proved in my analysis, more clearly than has been hitherto done, the ante-Nicene origin of a book, or rather books, called by an early fiction *Apostolical Constitutions*, and consequently the still higher antiquity of the materials, both ecclesiastical and literary, which they contain. I have shown that the compilers made use of the Epistle of Barnabas, which belongs to the first half of the second century; that the eighth is an extract or transcript of Hippolytus; and that the first six books are so full of phrases found in the second interpolation of the Ignatian Epistles, that their last compiler, the author of the present text, must either have lived soon after that interpolation was made, or *vice versâ*, or the interpolator and compiler must have been one and the same person. This last circumstance renders it probable

[1] *Christianity and Mankind*, vol. ii. p. 405.

that at least the first six books of the Greek compilation, like the Ignatian forgeries, were the produce of Asia Minor. Two points are self-evident — their Oriental origin, and that they belong neither to Antioch nor to Alexandria. I suppose nobody now will trace them to Palestine."[1]

Modern critics are equally at sea in determining the date of the collections of canons given at the end of the eighth book. Most believe that some of them belong to the apostolic age, while others are of a comparatively late date. The subject is very fully discussed in Krabbe.

Bovius first gave a complete edition of the *Constitutions* (Venice, 1563), but only in a Latin form. The Greek was first edited by the Jesuit Turrianus (Venice, 1563). It was reprinted several times. Cotelerius gave it in his *Apostolical Fathers*. In the second edition of this work, as prepared by Clericus (1724), the readings of two Vienna manuscripts were given. These V. MSS. and Oxford MS. of Book viii. are supposed by Bunsen to be nearer the original than the others, alike in what they give and in what they omit. The *Constitutions* have been edited by Ültzen (1853), and by Lagarde in Bunsen's *Analecta Ante-Nicæna*, vol. ii. (1854). Lagarde has partially introduced readings from the Syriac, Arabic, Æthiopic, and Coptic forms of the *Constitutions*. Whiston devoted the second volume of his *Primitive Christianity* to the *Constitutions* and *Canons*, giving both the Greek and English. It is his translation which we have republished, with considerable alterations. We have not deemed it necessary to give a tithe of the various readings, but have confined ourselves to those that seem important. We have also given no indication of the Syriac form of the first six books. We shall give this form by itself. The translation of Whiston was reprinted by Irah Chase, D.D., very carefully revised, with a translation of Krabbe's *Essay on the Origin and Contents of the Constitutions*, and his *Dissertation on the Canons* (New York, 1848).

[1] *Christianity and Mankind*, vol. ii. p. 418.

CONTENTS OF THE APOSTOLICAL CONSTITUTIONS.

BOOK I.

1. Concerning covetousness.
2. That we ought not to return injuries, nor revenge ourselves on him that does us wrong.
3. Concerning the adornment of ourselves, and the sin which arises from thence.
4. That we ought not to be over curious about those who live wickedly, but to be intent upon our own proper employment.
5. What books of Scripture we ought to read.
6. That we ought to abstain from all the books of those that are out of the church.
7. Concerning a bad woman.
8. Concerning the subjection of a wife to her husband, and that she must be loving and modest.
9. That a woman must not bathe with men.
10. Concerning a contentious and brawling woman.

BOOK II.

1. That a bishop must be well instructed and experienced in the word.
2. What ought to be the characters of a bishop and of the rest of the clergy.
3. In what things a bishop is to be examined before he is ordained.
4. That charitable distributions are not to be made to every widow, but that sometimes a woman who has a husband is to be preferred; and that no distributions are to be made to any one who is given to gluttony, drunkenness, and idleness.
5. That a bishop must be no accepter of persons in judgment; that he must possess a gentle disposition, and be temperate in his mode of life.
6. That a bishop must not be given to filthy lucre, nor be a surety nor an advocate.
7. What ought to be the character of the initiated.
8. Concerning a person falsely accused, or a person convicted.

9. That a bishop ought not to receive bribes.

10. That a bishop who by wrong judgment spares an offender is himself guilty.

11. How a bishop ought to judge offenders.

12. Instruction as to how a bishop ought to behave himself to the penitent.

13. That we ought to beware how we make trial of any sinful course.

14. Concerning those who affirm that penitents are not to be received into the church. That a righteous person, although he converse with a sinner, will not perish with him. That no person is punished for another, but every one must give an account of himself. That we must assist those who are weak in the faith; and that a bishop must not be governed by any turbulent person among the laity.

15. That a priest must neither overlook offences, nor be rash in punishing them.

16. Of repentance, the manner of it, and rules about it.

17. That a bishop must be unblameable, and a pattern for those who are under his charge.

18. That a bishop must take care that his people do not sin, considering that he is set for a watchman among them.

19. That a shepherd who is careless of his sheep will be condemned, and that a sheep which will not be led by the shepherd is to be punished.

20. How the governed are to obey the bishops who are set over them.

21. That it is a dangerous thing to judge without hearing both sides, or to determine of punishment against a person before he is convicted.

22. That David, the Ninevites, Ezekias, and his son Manasses, are eminent examples of repentance. The prayer of Manasses king of Judah.

23. Amon may be an example to such as sin with an high hand.

24. That Christ Jesus our Lord came to save sinners by repentance.

25. Of first-fruits and tithes, and after what manner the bishop is himself to partake of them, or to distribute them to others.

26. According to what patterns and dignity every order of the clergy is appointed by God.

27. That it is a horrible thing for a man to thrust himself into any sacerdotal office, as did Corah and his company, Saul, and Uzziah.

28. Of an entertainment, and after what manner each distinct order of the clergy is to be treated by those who invite them to it.

29. What is the dignity of a bishop and of a deacon.

30. After what manner the laity are to be obedient to the deacon.

31. That the deacon must not do anything without the bishop.

32. That the deacon must not make any distributions without the consent of the bishop, because that will turn to the reproach of the bishop.

33. After what manner the bishops are to be honoured, and to be reverenced as our spiritual parents.

34. That priests are to be preferred before rulers and kings.

35. That both the law and the gospel prescribe offerings.

36. The recital of the ten commandments, and after what manner they do here prescribe to us.

37. Concerning accusers and false accusers, and how a judge is not rashly either to believe them or disbelieve them, but after an accurate examination.

38. That sinners are privately to be reproved, and the penitent to be received, according to the constitution of our Lord.

39. Examples of repentance.

40. That we are not to be implacable to him who has once or twice offended.

41. After what manner we ought to receive a penitent; how we ought to deal with offenders, and when they are to be cut off from the church.

42. That a judge must not be a respecter of persons.

43. After what manner false accusers are to be punished.

44. That the deacon is to ease the burthen of the bishops, and to order the smaller matters himself.

45. That contentions and quarrels are unbecoming Christians.

46. That believers ought not to go to law before unbelievers; nor ought any unbeliever to be called for a witness against believers.

47. That the judicatures of Christians ought to be held on the second day of the week.

48. That the same punishment is not to be inflicted for every offence, but different punishments for different offenders.

49. What are to be the characters of accusers and witnesses.

50. That former offences do sometimes render after accusations credible.

51. Against judging without hearing both sides.

52. The caution observed at heathen tribunals before the condemnation of criminals affords Christians a good example.

53. That Christians ought not to be contentious one with another.

54. That the bishops must by their deacon put the people in mind of the obligation they are under to live peaceably together.

55. An enumeration of the several instances of divine providence, and how in every age from the beginning of the world God has invited all men to repentance.

56. That it is the will of God that men should be of one mind in matters of religion, in accord with the heavenly powers.

57. An exact description of a church and the clergy, and what things in particular every one is to do in the solemn assemblies of the clergy and laity for religious worship.

58. Of commendatory letters in favour of strangers, lay persons, clergymen, and bishops; and that those who come into the church assemblies are to be received without regard to their quality.

59. That every Christian ought to frequent the church diligently both morning and evening.

60. The vain zeal which the heathens and Jews show in frequenting their temples and synagogues is a proper example and motive to excite Christians to frequent the church.

61. That we must not prefer the affairs of this life to those which concern the worship of God.

62. That Christians must abstain from all the impious practices of the heathens.

63. That no Christian that will not work must eat, as Peter and the rest of the apostles were fishermen, but Paul and Aquila tentmakers, Jude the son of James an husbandman.

BOOK III.

1. The age at which widows should be chosen.
2. That we must avoid the choice of younger widows, because of suspicion.
3. What character the widows ought to be of, and how they ought to be supported by the bishop.
4. That we ought to be charitable to all sorts of persons in want.
5. That the widows are to be very careful of their behaviour.
6. That women ought not to teach, because it is unseemly; and what women followed our Lord.
7. What are the characters of widows falsely so called.
8. That the widows ought not to accept of alms from the unworthy no more than the bishop, or any other of the faithful.
9. That women ought not to baptize, because it is impious, and contrary to the doctrine of Christ.
10. That a layman ought not to do any office of the priesthood: he ought neither to baptize, nor offer, nor lay on hands, nor give the blessing.
11. That none but a bishop and presbyter, none even of the inferior ranks of the clergy, are permitted to do the offices of the priests; that ordination belongs wholly to the bishop, and to nobody else.
12. The rejection of all uncharitable actions.
13. How the widows are to pray for those that supply their necessities.
14. That she who has been kind to the poor ought not to make a stir and tell abroad her name, according to the constitution of the Lord.
15. That it does not become us to revile our neighbours, because cursing is contrary to Christianity.
16. Concerning the sacred initiation of holy baptism.
17. What is the meaning of baptism into Christ, and on what account everything is there said or done.
18. Of what character he ought to be who is initiated.
19. What are the characters of a deacon.
20. That a bishop ought to be ordained by three or by two bishops, but not by one; for that would be invalid.

BOOK IV.

1. Those who have no children should adopt orphans, and treat them as their own children.
2. How the bishop ought to provide for the orphans.
3. Who ought to be supported according to the Lord's constitution.
4. Of the love of money.
5. With what fear men ought to partake of the Lord's oblations.
6. Whose oblations are to be received, and whose not to be received.
7. That the oblations of the unworthy, while they are such, do not only not propitiate God, but, on the contrary, provoke Him to indignation.
8. That it is better to afford, though it be inconsiderable and few, contributions to the widows from our own labours, than those which are many and large received from the ungodly; for it is better to perish by famine than to receive an oblation from the ungodly.
9. That the people ought to be exhorted by the priest to do good to the needy, as says Solomon the Wise.
10. A constitution, that if any one of the ungodly by force will cast money to the priests, they spend it in wood and coals, but not in food.
11. Of parents and children.
12. Of servants and masters.
13. In what things we ought to be subject to the rulers of this world.
14. Of virgins.

BOOK V.

1. That it is reasonable for the faithful to supply the wants of those who are afflicted for the sake of Christ by the unbelievers, according to the constitution of the Lord.
2. That we are to avoid intercourse with false brethren when they continue in their wickedness.
3. That we ought to afford an helping hand to such as are spoiled for the sake of Christ, although we should incur danger ourselves.
4. That it is an horrible and destructive thing to deny Christ.
5. That we ought to imitate Christ in suffering, and with zeal to follow His patience.
6. That a believer ought neither rashly to run into danger through security, nor to be over-timorous through pusillanimity, but to fly away for fear; yet that if he does fall into the enemy's hand, to strive earnestly, upon account of the crown that is laid up for him.
7. Several demonstrations concerning the resurrection, concerning the Sibyl, and what the Stoics say concerning the bird called the phœnix.
8. Concerning James the brother of the Lord, and Stephen the first martyr.

9. Concerning false martyrs.

10. A moral admonition, that we are to abstain from vain talking, obscene talking, jesting, drunkenness, lasciviousness, and luxury.

11. An admonition instructing men to avoid the abominable sin of idolatry.

12. That we ought not to sing an heathen or an obscene song, nor to swear by an idol; because it is an impious thing, and contrary to the knowledge of God.

13. A catalogue of the feasts of the Lord which are to be kept, and when each of them ought to be observed.

14. Concerning the passion of our Lord, and what was done on each day of His sufferings; and concerning Judas, and that Judas was not present when the Lord delivered the mysteries to His disciples.

15. Of the great week, and on what account they enjoin us to fast on Wednesday and Friday.

16. An enumeration of the prophetical predictions which declare Christ, whose completion though the Jews saw, yet out of the evil temper of their mind they did not believe He was the Christ of God, and condemned the Lord of glory to the cross.

17. How the passover ought to be celebrated.

18. A constitution concerning the great passover week.

19. Concerning the watching all the night of the great Sabbath, and concerning the day of the resurrection.

20. A prophetic prediction concerning Christ Jesus.

BOOK VI.

1. Who they were that ventured to make schisms, and did not escape punishment.

2. That it is not lawful to rise up either against the kingly or the priestly office.

3. Concerning the virtue of Moses and the incredulity of the Jewish nation, and what wonderful works God did among them.

4. That schism is made not by him who separates himself from the ungodly, but who departs from the godly.

5. Upon what account Israel, falsely so named, is rejected by God, demonstrated from the prophetic predictions.

6. That even among the Jews there arose the doctrine of several heresies hateful to God.

7. Whence the heresies sprang, and who was the ringleader of their impiety.

8. Who were the successors of Simon's impiety, and what heresies they set up.

9. How Simon, desiring to fly by some magical arts, fell down head-

long from on high at the prayers of Peter, and brake his feet, and hands, and ankle-bones.

10. How the heresies differ from each other, and from the truth.
11. An exposition of the preaching of the apostles.
12. For those that confess Christ, but are desirous to Judaize.
13. That we must separate from heretics.
14. Who were the preachers of the catholic doctrine, and which are the commandments given by them.
15. That we ought not to rebaptize, nor to receive that baptism which is given by the ungodly, which is not baptism, but a pollution.
16. Concerning books with false inscriptions.
17. Matrimonial precepts concerning clergymen.
18. An exhortation commanding to avoid the communion of the impious heretics.
19. To those that speak evil of the law.
20. Which is the law of nature, and which is that afterwards introduced, and why it was introduced.
21. That we who believe in Christ are under grace, and not under the servitude of that additional law.
22. That the law for sacrifices is additional, which Christ when He came took away.
23. How Christ became a fulfiller of the law, and what parts of it He put a period to, or changed, or transferred.
24. That it pleased the Lord that the law of righteousness should be demonstrated by the Romans.
25. How God, on account of their impiety towards Christ, made the Jews captives, and placed them under tribute.
26. That we ought to avoid the heretics as the corrupters of souls.
27. Of some Jewish and Gentile observances.
28. Of the love of boys, adultery, and fornication.
29. How wives ought to be subject to their own husbands, and husbands ought to love their own wives.
30. That it is the custom of Jews and Gentiles to observe natural purgations, and to abominate the remains of the dead; but that all this is contrary to Christianity.

BOOK VII.

1. That there are two ways—the one natural, of life, and the other introduced afterwards, of death; and that the former is from God, and the latter of error, from the snares of the adversary.
2. Moral exhortations of the Lord's constitutions agreeing with the ancient prohibitions of the divine laws. The prohibition of anger, spite, corruption, adultery, and every forbidden action.

3. The prohibition of conjuring, murder of infants, perjury, and false witness.

4. The prohibition of evil-speaking and passion, of deceitful conduct, or idle words, lies, covetousness, and hypocrisy.

5. The prohibition of malignity, acceptation of persons, wrath, malice, and envy.

6. Concerning augury and enchantments.

7. The prohibition of murmuring, insolence, pride, and arrogance.

8. Concerning long-suffering, simplicity, meekness, and patience.

9. That it is our duty to esteem our Christian teachers above our parents—the former being the means of our well-being, the other only of our being.

10. That we ought not to divide ourselves from the saints, but to make peace between those that quarrel, to judge righteously, and not to accept persons.

11. Concerning him that is double-minded and desponding.

12. Concerning doing good.

13. How masters ought to behave themselves to their servants, and how servants ought to be subject.

14. Concerning hypocrisy, and obedience to the laws, and confession of sins.

15. Concerning the observance due to parents.

16. Concerning the subjection due to the king and to rulers.

17. Concerning the pure conscience of those that pray.

18. That the way which was afterward introduced by the snares of the adversary is full of impiety and wickedness.

19. That we must not turn from the way of piety either to the right hand or to the left. An exhortation of the Lawgiver.

20. That we ought not to despise any of the sorts of food that are set before us, but gratefully and orderly to partake of them.

21. That we ought to avoid the eating of things offered to idols.

22. A constitution of our Lord, how we ought to baptize, and into whose death.

23. Which days of the week we are to fast, and which not, and for what reasons.

24. What sort of people ought to pray that prayer that was given by the Lord.

25. A mystical thanksgiving.

26. A thanksgiving at the divine participation.

27. A thanksgiving about the mystical ointment.

28. That we ought not to be indifferent about communicating.

29. A constitution concerning oblations.

30. How we ought to assemble together, and to celebrate the festival day of our Saviour's resurrection.

31. What qualifications they ought to have who are to be ordained.

CONTENTS.

32. A prediction concerning futurities.
33. A prayer declarative of God's various providence.
34. A prayer declarative of God's various creation.
35. A prayer, with thanksgiving, declarative of God's providence over the beings He has made.
36. A prayer commemorative of the incarnation of Christ, and His various providence to the saints.
37. A prayer containing the memorial of His providence, and an enumeration of the various benefits afforded the saints by the providence of God through Christ.
38. A prayer for the assistance of the righteous.
39. How the catechumens are to be instructed in the elements.
40. A constitution how the catechumens are to be blessed by the priests in their initiation, and what things are to be taught them.
41. The renunciation of the adversary, and the dedication to the Christ of God.
42. A thanksgiving concerning the anointing with the mystical oil.
43. A thanksgiving concerning the mystical water.
44. A thanksgiving concerning the mystical ointment.
45. A prayer for the new fruits.
46. Who were they that the holy apostles sent and ordained?
47. A morning prayer.
48. An evening prayer.
49. A prayer at dinner.

BOOK VIII.

1. On whose account the powers of miracles are performed.
2. Concerning unworthy bishops and presbyters.
3. That to make constitutions about the offices to be performed in the churches is of great consequence.
4. Concerning ordinations.
5. The form of prayer for the ordination of a bishop.
6. The divine liturgy, wherein is the bidding prayer for the catechumens.
7. For the energumens.
8. For the baptized.
9. The imposition of hands, and prayer for the penitents.
10. The bidding prayer for the faithful.
11. The form of prayer for the faithful.
12. The constitution of James the brother of John, the son of Zebedee.
13. The bidding prayer for the faithful after the divine oblation.
14. The bidding prayer after the participation.
15. The form of prayer after the participation.

16. Concerning the ordination of presbyters—the constitution of John, who was beloved by the Lord.
17. Concerning the ordination of deacons—the constitution of Philip.
18. The form of prayer for the ordination of a deacon.
19. Concerning the deaconess—the constitution of Bartholomew.
20. The form of prayer for the ordination of a deaconess.
21. Concerning the sub-deacons—the constitution of Thomas.
22. Concerning the readers—the constitution of Matthew.
23. Concerning the confessors—the constitution of James the son of Alpheus.
24. The same apostle's constitution concerning virgins.
25. The constitution of Lebbæus, who was surnamed Thaddæus, concerning widows.
26. The same apostle concerning the exorcist.
27. Simon the Canaanite concerning the number necessary for the ordination of a bishop.
28. The same apostle's canons concerning bishops, presbyters, deacons, and the rest of the clergy.
29. Concerning the blessing of water and oil—the constitution of Matthias.
30. The same apostle's constitution concerning first-fruits and tithes.
31. The same apostle's constitutions concerning the remaining oblations.
32. Various canons of Paul the apostle concerning those that offer themselves to be baptized—whom we are to receive, and whom to reject.
33. Upon which days servants are not to work.
34. At what hours, and why, we are to pray.
35. The constitution of James the brother of Christ concerning evening prayer.
36. The bidding prayer for the evening.
37. The thanksgiving for the evening.
38. The thanksgiving for the morning.
39. The imposition of hands for the morning.
40. The form of prayer for the first-fruits.
41. The bidding prayer for those departed.
42. How and when we ought to celebrate the memorials of the faithful departed, and that we ought then to give somewhat out of their goods to the poor.
43. That memorials or mandates do not at all profit the ungodly who are dead.
44. Concerning drunkards.
45. Concerning the receiving such as are persecuted for Christ's sake.
46. That every one ought to remain in that rank wherein he is placed, but not snatch such offices to himself which are not entrusted to him.
47. The ecclesiastical canons.

THE CONSTITUTIONS OF THE APOSTLES.

BOOK I.

CONCERNING THE LAITY.

Sec. I.—*General commandments.*

THE apostles and elders to all those who from among the Gentiles have believed in the Lord Jesus Christ; grace and peace from Almighty God, through our Lord Jesus Christ, be multiplied unto you in the acknowledgment of Him.

The catholic church is the plantation of God, and His beloved vineyard;[1] containing those who have believed in His unerring divine religion; who are the heirs by faith of His everlasting kingdom; who are partakers of His divine influence, and of the communication of the Holy Spirit; who are armed through Jesus, and have received His fear into their hearts; who enjoy the benefit of the sprinkling of the precious and innocent blood of Christ; who have free liberty to call Almighty God, Father; being fellow-heirs and joint-partakers of His beloved Son: hearken to this holy doctrine, you who enjoy His promises, as being delivered by the command of your Saviour, and agreeable to His glorious words. Take care, ye children of God, to do all things in obedience to God; and in all things please Christ our Lord.[2] For if any man follows unrighteousness, and does those things that are contrary to the will of God, such an one will be esteemed by God as the disobedient heathen.

[1] Isa. v. 7, 2.
[2] The reading of the V. MSS. The others read, "Christ our God."

I. Abstain, therefore, from all unlawful desires and injustice. For it is written in the law, " Thou shalt not covet thy neighbour's wife, nor his field, nor his man-servant, nor his maid-servant, nor his ox, nor his ass, nor anything that is thy neighbour's;"[1] for all coveting of these things is from the evil one. For he that covets his neighbour's wife, or his man-servant, or his maid-servant, is already in his mind an adulterer and a thief; and if he does not repent, is condemned by our Lord Jesus Christ: through whom[2] glory be to God for ever, Amen. For He says in the Gospel, recapitulating, and confirming, and fulfilling the ten commandments of the law: "It is written in the law, Thou shalt not commit adultery: but I say unto you, that is, I said in the law, by Moses. But now I say unto you myself, Whosoever shall look on his neighbour's wife to lust after her, hath committed adultery with her already in his heart."[3] Such an one is condemned of adultery, who covets his neighbour's wife in his mind. But does not he that covets an ox or an ass design to steal them? to apply them to his own use, and to lead them away? Or, again, does not he that covets a field, and continues in such a disposition, wickedly contrive how to remove the landmarks, and to compel the possessor to part with somewhat for nothing? For as the prophet somewhere speaks: "Woe to those who join house to house, and lay field to field, that they may deprive their neighbour of somewhat which was his."[4] Wherefore he says: "Must you alone inhabit the earth? For these things have been heard in the ears of the Lord of hosts." And elsewhere: "Cursed be he who removeth his neighbour's landmarks: and all the people shall say, Amen."[5] Wherefore Moses says: "Thou shalt not remove thy neighbour's landmarks[6] [which thy fathers have set"[7]]. Upon this account, therefore, terrors, death, tribunals, and condemnations follow such as these from

---

[1] Ex. xx. 17.
[2] "To whom" in V. MSS., and "to God" is omitted.
[3] Matt. v. 28.   [4] Isa. v. 8.
[5] Deut. xxvii. 17.   [6] Deut. xix. 14.
[7] Omitted in V. MSS.

God. But as to those who are obedient to God, there is one law of God, [simple,[1]] true, living, which is this: "Do not that to another which thou hatest another should do to thee."[2] Thou wouldst not that any one should look upon thy wife with an evil design to corrupt her; do not thou, therefore, look upon thy neighbour's wife with a wicked intention. Thou wouldst not that thy garment should be taken away; do not thou, therefore, take away another's. Thou wouldst not be beaten, reproached, affronted; do not thou, therefore, serve any other in the like manner.

II. But if any one curse thee, do thou bless him. For it is written in the book of Numbers: "He that blesseth thee is blessed, and he that curseth thee is cursed."[3] In the same manner it is written in the Gospel: "Bless them that curse you."[4] Being injured, do not avenge yourselves, but bear it with patience; for the Scripture speaks thus: "Say not thou, I will avenge myself on my enemy for what injuries he has offered me; but acquiesce under them, that the Lord may right thee, and bring vengeance upon him who injures thee."[5] For so says He again in the Gospel: "Love your enemies, do good to them that hate you, and pray for them which despitefully use you and persecute you; and ye shall be the children of your Father which is in heaven: for He maketh His sun to shine on the evil and on the good, and raineth on the just and unjust."[6] Let us therefore, beloved, attend to these commandments, that we may be found to be the children of light by doing them. Bear, therefore, with one another, ye servants and sons of God.

SEC. II.—*Commandments to men.*

Let the husband not be insolent nor arrogant towards his wife; but compassionate, bountiful, willing to please his own wife [alone[7]], and treat her honourably and obligingly, endeavouring to be agreeable to her; (III.) not adorning thyself in such a manner as may entice another woman to

[1] Omitted in V. mss.   [2] Tob. iv. 16.   [3] Num. xxiv. 9.
[4] Luke vi. 28.   [5] Prov. xx. 22.   [6] Matt. v. 44.
[7] Omitted in V. mss.

thee. For if thou art overcome by her, and sinnest with her, eternal death will overtake thee from God; and thou wilt be punished with sensible and bitter torments. Or if thou dost not perpetrate such a wicked act, but shakest her off, and refusest her, in this case thou art not wholly innocent, even though thou art not guilty of the crime itself, but only in so far as through thy adorning thou didst entice the woman to desire thee. For thou art the cause that the woman was so affected, and by her lusting after thee was guilty of adultery with thee: yet art thou not so guilty, because thou didst not send to her, who was ensnared by thee; nor didst thou desire her. Since, therefore, thou didst not deliver up thyself to her, thou shalt find mercy with the Lord thy God, who hath said, " Thou shalt not commit adultery," and, "Thou shalt not covet."[1] For if such a woman, upon sight of thee, or unseasonable meeting with thee, was smitten in her mind, and sent to thee, but thou as a religious person didst refuse her,[2] if she was wounded in her heart by thy beauty, and youth, and adorning, and fell in love with thee, thou wilt be found guilty of her transgressions, as having been the occasion of scandal to her,[3] [and shalt inherit a woe.[4]] Wherefore pray thou to the Lord God that no mischief may befall thee upon this account: for thou art not to please men, so as to commit sin; but God, so as to attain holiness of life, and be partaker of everlasting rest. That beauty which God and nature has bestowed on thee, do not further beautify; but modestly diminish it before men. Thus, do not thou permit the hair of thy head to grow too long, but rather cut it short; lest by a nice combing thy hair, and wearing it long, and anointing thyself, thou draw upon thyself such ensnared or ensnaring women. Neither do thou wear over-fine garments to seduce any; neither do thou, with an evil subtilty, affect over-fine stockings or shoes for thy feet, but only such as suit the measures of decency

---

[1] Ex. xx. 14, 17.
[2] The V. MSS. add: "didst abstain from her, and didst not sin against her."
[3] Matt. xviii. 17. [4] Not in V. MSS.

and usefulness. Neither do thou put a gold ring upon thy fingers; for all these ornaments are the signs of lasciviousness, which if thou be solicitous about in an indecent manner, thou wilt not act as becomes a good man: for it is not lawful for thee, a believer and a man of God, to permit the hair of thy head to grow long, and to bush it up together, nor to suffer it to spread abroad, nor to puff it up, nor by nice combing and platting to make it curl and shine; since that is contrary to the law, which says thus, in its additional precepts: "You shall not make to yourselves curls and round rasures."[1] Nor may men destroy the hair of their beards, and unnaturally change the form of a man. For the law says: "Ye shall not mar your beards."[1] For God the Creator has made this decent for women, but has determined that it is unsuitable for men. But if thou do these things to please men, in contradiction to the law, thou wilt be abominable with God, who created thee after His own image. If, therefore, thou wilt be acceptable to God, abstain from all those things which He hates, and do none of those things that are unpleasing to Him.

IV. Thou shalt not be as a wanderer and gadder abroad, rambling about the streets, without just cause, to spy out such as live wickedly. But by minding thy own trade and employment, endeavour to do what is acceptable to God. And keeping in mind the oracles of Christ, meditate in the same continually. For so the Scripture says to thee: "Thou shalt meditate in His law day and night; when thou walkest in the field, and when thou sittest in thine house, and when thou liest down, and when thou risest up, that thou mayest have understanding in all things."[2] Nay, although thou beest rich, and so dost not want a trade for thy maintenance, be not one that gads about, and walks abroad at random; but either go to some that are believers, and of the same religion, and confer and discourse with them about the lively oracles of God:

V. Or if thou stayest at home, read the books of the Law, of the Kings, with the Prophets; sing the hymns of David;

[1] Lev. xix. 27, xxi. 5.   [2] Josh. i. 8; Deut. vi. 7.

and peruse diligently the Gospel, which is the completion of the other.

VI. Abstain from all the heathen books. For what hast thou to do with such foreign discourses, or laws, or false prophets, which subvert the faith of the unstable? For what defect dost thou find in the law of God, that thou shouldest have recourse to those heathenish fables? For if thou hast a mind to read history, thou hast the books of the Kings; if books of wisdom or poetry, thou hast those of the Prophets, of Job, and the Proverbs, in which thou wilt find greater depth of sagacity than in all the heathen poets and sophisters, because these are the words of the Lord, the only wise God. If thou desirest something to sing, thou hast the Psalms; if the origin of things, thou hast Genesis; if laws and statutes, thou hast the glorious law of the Lord God. Do thou therefore utterly abstain from all strange and diabolical books. Nay, when thou readest the law, think not thyself bound to observe the additional precepts; though not all of them, yet some of them. Read those barely for the sake of history, in order to the knowledge of them, and to glorify God that He has delivered thee from such great and so many bonds. Propose to thyself to distinguish what rules were from the law of nature, and what were added afterwards, or were such additional rules as were introduced and given in the wilderness to the Israelites after the making of the calf; for the law contains those precepts which were spoken by the Lord God before the people fell into idolatry, and made a calf like the Egyptian Apis—that is, the ten commandments. But as to those bonds which were further laid upon them after they had sinned, do not thou draw them upon thyself: for our Saviour came for no other reason but that [He might deliver those that were obnoxious thereto from the wrath which was reserved for them, that [1]] He might fulfil the Law and the Prophets, and that He might abrogate or change those secondary bonds which were superadded to the rest of the law. For therefore did He call to us, and say, "Come un[to me [2]], all ye that labour and are heavy laden, and I

---

[1] Omitted in V. MSS.   [2] Omitted in V. MSS.

will give you rest."[1] When, therefore, thou hast read the Law, which is agreeable to the Gospel and to the Prophets, read also the books of the Kings, that thou mayest thereby learn which of the kings were righteous, and how they were prospered by God, and how the promise of eternal life continued with them from Him; but those kings which went a-whoring from God did soon perish in their apostasy by the righteous judgment of God, and were deprived of His life, inheriting, instead of rest, eternal punishment. Wherefore by reading these books thou wilt be mightily strengthened in the faith, and edified in Christ, whose body and member thou art. Moreover, when thou walkest abroad in public, and hast a mind to bathe, make use of that bath which is appropriated to men, lest, by discovering thy body in an unseemly manner to women, or by seeing a sight not seemly for men, either thou beest ensnared, or thou ensnarest and enticest to thyself [those women who easily yield to such temptations[2]]. Take care, therefore, and avoid such things, lest thou admit a snare upon thy own soul.

VII. For let us learn what the sacred word says in the book of Wisdom: "My son, keep my words, and hide my commandments with thee. Say unto Wisdom, Thou art my sister; and make understanding familiar with thee: that she may keep thee from the strange and wicked woman, in case such an one accost thee with sweet words. For from the window of her house she looks into the street, to see if she can espy some young man among the foolish children, without understanding, walking in the market-place, in the meeting of the street near her house, and talking in the dusk of the evening, or in the silence and darkness of the night. A woman meets him in the appearance of an harlot, who steals away the hearts of young persons. She rambles about, and is dissolute; her feet abide not in her house: sometimes she is without, sometimes in the streets, and lieth in wait at every corner. Then she catches him, and kisses him, and with an impudent face says unto him, I have peace-offerings with me; this day do I pay my vows: therefore came I forth to

---

[1] Matt. xi. 28. [2] Omitted in V. MSS.

meet thee; earnestly I have desired thy face, and I have found thee. I have decked my bed with coverings; with tapestry from Egypt have I adorned it. I have perfumed my bed with saffron, and my house with cinnamon. Come, let us take our fill of love until the morning; come, let us solace ourselves with love," etc. To which he adds: "With much discourse she seduced him, with snares from her lips she forced him. He goes after her like a silly bird."[1] And again: "Do not hearken to a wicked woman; for though the lips of an harlot are like drops from an honey-comb, which for a while is smooth in thy throat, yet afterwards thou wilt find her more bitter than gall, and sharper than any two-edged sword."[2] And again: "But get away quickly, and tarry not; fix not thine eyes upon her: for she hath thrown down many wounded; yea, innumerable multitudes have been slain by her."[3] "If not," says he, "yet thou wilt repent at the last, when thy flesh and thy body are consumed, and wilt say, How have I hated instruction, and my heart has avoided the reproofs of the righteous! I have not hearkened to the voice of my instructor, nor inclined mine ear to my teacher. I have almost been in all evil."[4] But we will make no more quotations; and if we have omitted any, be so prudent as to select the most valuable out of the Holy Scriptures, and confirm yourselves with them, rejecting all things that are evil, that so you may be found holy with God in eternal life.

SEC. III.—*Commandments to women.*

VIII. Let the wife be obedient to her own proper husband, because " the husband is the head of the wife."[5] But Christ is the head of that husband who walks in the way of righteousness; and " the head of Christ is God," even His Father. Therefore, O wife, next after the Almighty, our God and Father, the Lord of the present world and of the world to come, the Maker of everything that breathes, and of every power; and after His beloved Son, our Lord Jesus

[1] Prov. vii. 1, etc.   [2] Prov. v. 3.   [3] Prov. vii. 26, 27.
[4] Prov. v. 11, etc.   [5] 1 Cor. xi. 3.

Christ, through whom[1] glory be to God, do thou fear thy husband, and reverence him, pleasing him alone, rendering thyself acceptable to him in the several affairs of life, that so on thy account thy husband may be called blessed, according to the Wisdom of Solomon, which thus speaks: "Who can find a virtuous woman? for such a one is more precious than costly stones. The heart of her husband doth safely trust in her, so that she shall have no need of spoil: for she does good to her husband all the days of her life. She buyeth wool and flax, and worketh profitable things with her hands. She is like the merchants' ships, she bringeth her food from far. She riseth also while it is yet night, and giveth meat to her household, and food to her maidens. She considereth a field, and buyeth it; with the fruit of her hands she planteth a vineyard. She girdeth her loins with strength, and strengtheneth her arms. She tasteth that it is good to labour; her lamp goeth not out all the whole night. She stretcheth out her arms for useful work, and layeth her hands to the spindle. She openeth her hands to the needy; yea, she reacheth forth her hands to the poor. Her husband takes no care of the affairs of his house; for all that are with her are clothed with double garments. She maketh coats for her husband, clothings of silk and purple. Her husband is eminent in the gates, when he sitteth with the elders of the land. She maketh fine linen, and selleth it to the Phœnicians, and girdles to the Canaanites. She is clothed with glory and beauty, and she rejoices in the last days. She openeth her mouth with wisdom and discretion, and puts her words in order. The ways of her household are strict; she eateth not the bread of idleness. She will open her mouth with wisdom and caution, and upon her tongue are the laws of mercy. Her children arise up and praise her for her riches, and her husband joins in her praises. Many daughters have obtained wealth and done worthily, but thou surpassest and excellest them all. May lying flatteries and the vain beauty of a wife be far from thee. For a religious wife is blessed. Let her praise the

[1] "To whom be glory," V. MSS.

fear of the Lord: give her of the fruits of her lips, and let her husband be praised in the gates."[1] And again: "A virtuous wife is a crown to her husband."[2] And again: "Many wives have built an house."[3] You have learned what great commendations a prudent and loving wife receives from the Lord God. If thou desirest to be one of the faithful, and to please the Lord, O wife, do not superadd ornaments to thy beauty, in order to please other men; neither affect to wear fine broidering, garments, or shoes, to entice those who are allured by such things. For although thou dost not these wicked things with design of sinning thyself, but only for the sake of ornament and beauty, yet wilt thou not so escape future punishment, as having compelled another to look so hard at thee as to lust after thee, and as not having taken care both to avoid sin thyself, and the affording scandal to others. But if thou yield thyself up, and commit the crime, thou art both guilty of thy own sin, and the cause of the ruin of the other's soul also. Besides, when thou hast committed lewdness with one man, and beginnest to despair, thou wilt again turn away from thy duty, and follow others, and grow past feeling; as says the divine word: "When a wicked man comes into the depth of evil, he becomes a scorner, and then disgrace and reproach come upon him."[4] For such a woman afterward being wounded, ensnares without restraint the souls of the foolish. Let us learn, therefore, how the divine word triumphs over such women, saying: "I hated a woman who is a snare and net to the heart of men worse than death; her hands are fetters."[5] And in another passage: "As a jewel of gold in a swine's snout, so is beauty in a wicked woman."[6] And again: "As a worm in wood, so does a wicked woman destroy her husband."[7] And again: "It is better to dwell in the corner of the house-top, than with a contentious and an angry woman."[8] You, therefore, who are Christian women,

[1] Prov. xxxi. 10, etc.
[2] Prov. xii. 4.
[3] Prov. xiv. 1.
[4] Prov. xviii. 3.
[5] Eccles. vii. 26.
[6] Prov. xi. 22.
[7] Prov. xii. 4 in LXX.
[8] Prov. xxi. 9, 19.

do not imitate such as these. But thou who designest to be faithful to thine own husband, take care to please him alone. And when thou art in the streets, cover thy head; for by such a covering thou wilt avoid being viewed of idle persons. Do not paint thy face, which is God's workmanship; for there is no part of thee which wants ornament, inasmuch as all things which God has made are very good. But the lascivious additional adorning of what is already good is an affront to the bounty of the Creator. Look downward when thou walkest abroad, veiling thyself as becomes women.

IX. Avoid also that disorderly practice of bathing in the same place with men; for many are the nets of the evil one. And let not a Christian woman bathe with an hermaphrodite; for if she is to veil her face, and conceal it with modesty from strange men, how can she bear to enter naked into the bath together with men? But if the bath be appropriated to women, let her bathe orderly, modestly, and moderately. But let her not bathe without occasion, nor much, nor often, nor in the middle of the day, nor, if possible, every day; and let the tenth hour of the day be the set time for such seasonable bathing. For it is convenient that thou, who art a Christian woman, shouldst ever constantly avoid a curiosity which has many eyes.

X. But as to a spirit of contention, be sure to curb it as to all men, but principally as to thine husband; lest, if he be an unbeliever or an heathen, he may have an occasion of scandal or of blaspheming God, and thou be partaker of a woe from God. For, says He, "Woe to him by whom my name is blasphemed among the Gentiles;"[1] and lest, if thy husband be a Christian, he be forced, from his knowledge of the Scriptures, to say that which is written in the book of Wisdom: "It is better to dwell in the wilderness, than with a contentious and an angry woman."[2] You wives, therefore, demonstrate your piety by your modesty and meekness to all without the church, whether they be women or men, in order to their conversion and improvement in the faith. And since we have warned you, and instructed you briefly, whom we

[1] Isa. lii. 5.   [2] Prov. xxi. 19.

do esteem our sisters, daughters, and members, as being wise yourselves, persevere all your lives in an unblameable course of life. Seek to know such kinds of learning whereby you may arrive at the kingdom of our Lord, and please Him, and so rest for ever and ever. Amen.

BOOK II.

OF BISHOPS, PRESBYTERS, AND DEACONS.

SEC. I.—*On examining candidates for the episcopal office.*

BUT concerning bishops, we have heard from our Lord, that a pastor who is to be ordained a bishop for the churches in every parish, must be unblameable, unreprovable, free from all kinds of wickedness common among men, not under fifty years of age; for such an one is in good part past youthful disorders, and the slanders of the heathen, as well as the reproaches which are sometimes cast upon many persons by some false brethren, who do not consider the word of God in the Gospel: "Whosoever speaketh an idle word shall give an account thereof to the Lord in the day of judgment."[1] And again: "By thy words thou shalt be justified, and by thy words thou shalt be condemned."[2] Let him therefore, [if it is possible,] be well educated; [but if he be unlettered, let him at any rate be[3]] skilful in the word, and of competent age. But if in a small parish one advanced in years is not to be found,[4] let some younger person, who has a good report among his neighbours, and is esteemed by them worthy of the office of a bishop,—who has carried himself from his youth with meekness and regularity, like a much elder person,—after examination, and a general good report,

---

[1] Matt. xii. 36.   [2] Matt. xii. 37.

[3] The words within brackets occur only in the V. MSS.

[4] The V. MSS. read: "But if in a small parish one advanced in years is not to be found whom his neighbours testify to be worthy of the office of bishop, and wise enough to be appointed to it, and if there be a young man who has carried," etc.

be ordained in peace. For Solomon at twelve years of age was king of Israel,[1] and Josiah at eight years of age reigned righteously,[2] and in like manner Joash governed the people at seven years of age.[3] Wherefore, although the person be young, let him be meek, gentle, and quiet. For the Lord God says by Esaias: "Upon whom will I look, but upon him who is humble and quiet, and always trembles at my words?"[4] In like manner it is in the Gospel also: "Blessed are the meek: for they shall inherit the earth."[5] Let him also be merciful; for again it is said: "Blessed are the merciful: for they shall obtain mercy."[6] [Let him also be a peacemaker; for again it is said: "Blessed are the peacemakers: for they shall be called the sons of God."[7]] Let him also be one of a good conscience, purified from all evil, and wickedness, and unrighteousness; for it is said again: "Blessed are the pure in heart: for they shall see God."[8]

II. Let him therefore be sober, prudent, decent, firm, stable, not given to wine; no striker, but gentle; not a brawler, not covetous; "not a novice, lest, being puffed up with pride, he fall into condemnation, and the snare of the devil: for every one that exalteth himself shall be abased."[9] Such an one a bishop ought to be, who has been the "husband of one wife,"[10] who also has herself had no other husband, "ruling well his own house."[11] In this manner let examination be made when he is to receive ordination, and to be placed in his bishopric, whether he be grave, faithful, decent; whether he hath a grave and faithful wife, or has formerly had such a one; whether he hath educated his children piously, and has "brought them up in the nurture and admonition of the Lord;"[12] whether his domestics do fear and reverence him, and are all obedient to him: for if those who are immediately about him for worldly con-

---

[1] 1 Kings xii. (LXX.)
[2] 2 Kings xxii. 1.
[3] 2 Chron. xxxiv. 1; 2 Kings xi. 3, 4.
[4] Isa. lxvi. 2.
[5] Matt. v. 5.
[6] Matt. v. 7.
[7] From the V. MSS.; Matt. v. 9.
[8] Matt. v. 8.
[9] Luke xiv. 11.   [10] 1 Tim. iii. 2.
[11] 1 Tim. iii. 4.
[12] Eph. vi. 4.

cerns are seditious and disobedient, how will others not of his family, when they are under his management, become obedient to him?

III. Let examination also be made whether he be unblameable as to the concerns of this life; for it is written: "Search diligently for all the faults of him who is to be ordained for the priesthood."[1]

Sec. ii.—*On the character and teaching of the bishop.*

On which account let him also be void of anger; for Wisdom says: "Anger destroys even the prudent."[2] Let him also be merciful, of a generous and loving temper; for our Lord says: "By this shall all men know that ye are my disciples, if ye love one another."[3] Let him be also ready to give, a lover of the widow and the stranger; ready to serve, and minister, and attend; resolute in his duty; and let him know who is the most worthy of his assistance.

IV. For if there be a widow who is able to support herself, and another woman who is not a widow, but is needy by reason of sickness, or the bringing up many children, or infirmity of her hands, let him stretch out his hand in charity rather to this latter. But if any one be in want by gluttony, drunkenness, or idleness, he does not deserve any assistance, or [to be esteemed a member of] the church of God. For the Scripture, speaking of such persons, says: "The slothful hideth his hand in his bosom, and is not able to bring it to his mouth again."[4] And again: "The sluggard folds up his hands, and eats his own flesh."[5] "For every drunkard and whoremonger shall come to poverty, and every drowsy person shall be clothed with tatters [and rags[6]]."[7] And in another passage: "If thou give thine eyes to drinking and cups, thou shalt afterwards walk more naked than a pestle."[8] For certainly idleness is the mother of famine.

---

[1] Lev. xxi. 17, etc.   [2] Prov. xv. 1 (LXX.).   [3] John xiii. 35.
[4] Prov. xix. 24.   [5] Eccles. iv. 5.   [6] Not in V. mss.
[7] Prov. xxiii. 21.

[8] Prov. xxiii. 31 (LXX.). The word translated "pestle" has also been rendered "upper room," and some suppose it corrupt.

V. A bishop must be no accepter of persons; neither revering nor flattering a rich man contrary to what is right, nor overlooking nor domineering over a poor man. For, says God to Moses, "Thou shalt not accept the person of the rich, nor shalt thou pity a poor man in his cause: for the judgment is the Lord's."[1] And again: "Thou shalt with exact justice follow that which is right."[2] Let a bishop be frugal, and contented with a little in his meat and drink, that he may be ever in a sober frame, and disposed to instruct and admonish the ignorant; and let him not be costly in his diet, a pamperer of himself, given to pleasure, or fond of delicacies. Let him be patient and gentle in his admonitions, well instructed himself, meditating in and diligently studying the Lord's books, and reading them frequently, that so he may be able carefully to interpret the Scriptures, expounding the gospel in correspondence with the prophets and with the law; and let the expositions from the law and the prophets correspond to the gospel. For the Lord Jesus says: "Search the Scriptures; for they are those which testify of me."[3] And again: "For Moses wrote of me."[4] But, above all, let him carefully distinguish between the original law and the additional precepts, and show which are the laws for believers, and which the bonds for the unbelievers, lest any should fall under those bonds. Be careful, therefore, O bishop, to study the word, that thou mayest be able to explain everything exactly, and that thou mayest copiously nourish thy people with much doctrine, and enlighten them with the light of the law; for God says: "Enlighten yourselves with the light of knowledge, while we have yet opportunity."[5]

VI. Let not a bishop be given to filthy lucre, especially before the Gentiles, rather suffering than offering injuries; not covetous, nor rapacious; no purloiner; no admirer of the rich, nor hater of the poor; no evil-speaker, nor false witness; not given to anger; no brawler; not entangled with the affairs of this life; not a surety for any one, nor an

---

[1] Lev. xix. 15; Ex. xxiii. 3. [2] Deut. i. 17, xvi. 20.
[3] John v. 39. [4] John v. 46. [5] Hos. x. 12.

accuser in suits about money; not ambitious; not double-minded, nor double-tongued; not ready to hearken to calumny or evil-speaking; not a dissembler; not addicted to the heathen festivals; not given to vain deceits; not eager after worldly things, nor a lover of money. For all these things are opposite to God, and pleasing to demons. Let the bishop earnestly give all these precepts in charge to the laity also, persuading them to imitate his conduct. For, says He, "Do ye make the children of Israel pious."[1] Let him be prudent, humble, apt to admonish with the instructions of the Lord, well-disposed, one who has renounced all the wicked projects of this world, and all heathenish lusts; let him be orderly, sharp in observing the wicked, and taking heed of them, but yet a friend to all; just, discerning; and whatsoever qualities are commendable among men, let the bishop possess them in himself. For if the pastor be unblameable as to any wickedness, he will compel his own disciples, and by his very mode of life press them to become worthy imitators of his own actions. As the prophet somewhere says, "And it will be, as is the priest, so is the people;"[2] for our Lord and Teacher Jesus Christ, [the Son[3]] of God, began first to do, and then to teach, [as Luke somewhere says:[4] "which Jesus began to do and to teach"[5]]. Wherefore he says: "Whosoever shall do and teach, he shall be called great in the kingdom of God."[6] For you bishops are to be guides and watchmen to the people, as you yourselves have Christ for your guide and watchman. Do you therefore become good guides and watchmen to the people of God. For the Lord says by Ezekiel, speaking to every one of you: "Son of man, I have given thee for a watchman to the house of Israel; and thou shalt hear the word from my mouth, and shalt observe, and shalt declare it from me. When I say unto the wicked, Thou shalt surely die; if thou dost not speak to warn the wicked from his wickedness, that wicked man shall die in his iniquity, and his blood will I require at thine hand. But if thou warn the wicked from

[1] Lev. xv. 31.   [2] Hos. iv. 9.   [3] Not in V. MSS.
[4] Acts i. 1.   [5] Not in V. MSS.   [6] Matt. v. 19.

his way, that he may turn from it, and he does not turn from it, he shall die in his iniquity, and thou hast delivered thy soul."[1] "In the same manner, if the sword of war be approaching, and the people set a watchman to watch, and he see the same approach, and does not forewarn them, and the sword come and take one of them, he is taken away in his iniquity; but his blood shall be required at the watchman's hand, because he did not blow the trumpet. But if he blew the trumpet, and he who heard it would not take warning, and the sword come and take him away, his blood shall be upon him, because he heard the trumpet and took not warning. But he who took warning has delivered his soul; and the watchman, because he gave warning, shall surely live."[2] The sword here is the judgment; the trumpet is the holy gospel; the watchman is the bishop, who is set in the church, who is obliged by his preaching to testify [and vehemently to forewarn[3]] concerning that judgment. If ye do not declare and testify this to the people, the sins of those who are ignorant of it will be found upon you. Wherefore do you warn and reprove the uninstructed with boldness, teach the ignorant, confirm those that understand, bring back those that go astray. If we repeat the very same things on the same occasions, brethren, we shall not do amiss. For by frequent hearing it is to be hoped that some will be made ashamed, and at least do some good action, and avoid some wicked one. For says God by the prophet: "Testify those things to them; perhaps they will hear thy voice."[4] And again: "If perhaps they will hear, if perhaps they will submit."[5] Moses also says to the people: ["If hearing thou wilt hear the Lord God, and do that which is good and right in His eyes."[6] And again:[7]] "Hear, O Israel; the Lord our God is one Lord."[8] And our Lord is often recorded in the Gospel to have said: "He that hath ears to hear, let him hear."[9] And wise Solomon says: "My son, hear the

[1] Ezek. xxxiii. 7, etc.   [2] Ezek. xxxiii. 2, etc.   [3] Not in V. MSS.
[4] Jer. xxvi.   [5] Ezek. ii. 7, iii. 11.   [6] Ex. xv. 26.
[7] Not in V. MSS.   [8] Deut. vi. 4; Mark xii. 29.
[9] Matt. xi., xiii.

instruction of thy father, and reject not the laws of thy mother."[1] And, indeed, to this day men have not heard; for while they seem to have heard, they have not heard aright, as appears by their having left the one and only true God, and their being drawn into destructive and dangerous heresies, concerning which we shall speak again afterwards.

SEC. III.—*How the bishop is to treat the innocent, the guilty, and the penitent.*

VII. Beloved, be it known to you that those who are baptized into the death of our Lord Jesus are obliged to go on no longer in sin; for as those who are dead cannot work wickedness any longer, so those who are dead with Christ cannot practise wickedness. We do not therefore believe, brethren, that any one who has received the washing of life continues in the practice of the licentious acts of transgressors. Now he who sins after his baptism, unless he repent and forsake his sins, shall be condemned to hell-fire.

VIII. But if any one be maliciously prosecuted by the heathen, because he will not still go along with them to the same excess of riot, let him know that such an one is blessed of God, according as our Lord says in the Gospel: " Blessed are ye when men shall reproach you, or persecute you, or say all manner of evil against you falsely, for my sake. Rejoice and be exceeding glad, for your reward is great in heaven."[2] If, therefore, any one be slandered and falsely accused, such an one is blessed; for the Scripture says, "A man that is a reprobate is not tried by God."[3] But if any one be convicted as having done a wicked action, such an one not only hurts himself, but occasions the whole body of the church and its doctrine to be blasphemed; as if we Christians did not practise those things that we declare to be good and honest, and we ourselves shall be reproached by the Lord, that " they say and do not."[4] Wherefore the bishop must

---

[1] Prov. i. 8. [2] Matt. v. 11.

[3] This passage is not found in Scripture. Some compare Jas. i. 12 and Heb. xii. 8.

[4] Matt. xxiii. 3.

boldly reject such as these upon full conviction, unless they change their course of life.

IX. For the bishop must not only himself give no offence, but must be no respecter of persons; in meekness instructing those that offend. But if he himself has not a good conscience, and is a respecter of persons for the sake of filthy lucre and receiving of bribes, and spares the open offender, and permits him to continue in the church, he disregards the voice of God and of our Lord, which says, "Thou shalt exactly execute right judgment."[1] "Thou shalt not accept persons in judgment: thou shalt not justify the ungodly."[2] "Thou shalt not receive gifts against any one's life; for gifts do blind the eyes of the wise, and pervert the words of the righteous."[3] And elsewhere He says: "Take away from among yourselves that wicked person."[4] And Solomon says in his Proverbs: "Cast out a pestilent fellow from the congregation, and strife will go out along with him."[5]

X. But he who does not consider these things, will, contrary to justice, spare him who deserves punishment; as Saul spared Agag,[6] and Eli[7] his sons, "who knew not the Lord." Such an one profanes his own dignity, and that church of God which is in his parish. Such an one is esteemed unjust before God and holy men, as affording occasion of scandal to many of the newly baptized, and to the catechumens; as also to the youth of both sexes, to whom a woe belongs, and "a mill-stone about his neck,"[8] and drowning, on account of his guilt. For, observing what a person their governor is, through his wickedness and neglect of justice they will grow sceptical, and, indulging the same disease, will be compelled to perish with him; as was the case of the people joining with Jeroboam,[9] and those which were in the conspiracy with Corah.[10] But if the offender sees that the bishop and deacons are innocent and unblameable,

---

[1] Deut. xvi. 20, i. 17.   [2] Ex. xxiii. 7, LXX.   [3] Ex. xxiii. 8.
[4] Deut. xxvii. 25, xvi. 19, xvii. 7.   [5] Prov. xxii. 10.
[6] 1 Kings xv.   [7] 1 Kings ii.   [8] Matt. xviii. 6, 7.
[9] 3 Kings xii.   [10] Num. xvi.

and the flock pure, he will either not venture to despise their authority, and to enter into the church of God at all, as one smitten by his own conscience: or if he values nothing, and ventures to enter in, either he will be convicted immediately, as Uzza[1] at the ark, when he touched it to support it; and as Achan,[2] when he stole the accursed thing; and as Gehazi,[3] when he coveted the money of Naaman, and so will be immediately punished: or else he will be admonished by the pastor, and drawn to repentance. For when he looks round the whole church one by one, and can spy no blemish, neither in the bishop nor in the people who are under his care, he will be put to confusion, and pricked at the heart, and in a peaceable manner will go his way with shame and many tears, and the flock will remain pure. He will apply himself to God with tears, and will repent of his sins, and have hope. Nay, the whole flock, at the sight of his tears, will be instructed, because a sinner avoids destruction by repentance.

XI. Upon this account, therefore, O bishop, endeavour to be pure in thy actions, and to adorn thy place and dignity, which is that of one sustaining the character of God among men, as being set over all men, over priests, kings, rulers, fathers, children, teachers, and in general over all those who are subject to thee: and so sit in the church when thou speakest, as having authority to judge offenders. For to you, O bishops, it is said: " Whatsoever ye shall bind on earth shall be bound in heaven; and whatsoever ye shall loose on earth shall be loosed in heaven."[4]

XII. Do thou therefore, O bishop, judge with authority like God, yet receive the penitent; for God is a God of mercy. Rebuke those that sin, admonish those that are not converted, exhort those that stand to persevere in their goodness, receive the penitent; for the Lord God has promised with an oath to afford remission to the penitent for what things they have done amiss. For He says by Ezekiel: " Speak unto them, As I live, saith the Lord, I would not

---

[1] 2 Kings vi.
[2] Josh. vii.
[3] 4 Kings v.
[4] Matt. xviii. 18.

the death of a sinner, but that the wicked turn from his evil way, and live. Turn ye therefore from your evil ways; for why will ye die, O house of Israel?"[1] Here [the word[2]] affords hope to sinners, that if they will repent they shall have hope of salvation, lest otherwise out of despair they yield themselves up to their transgressions; but that, having hope of salvation, they may be converted, and may address to God with tears, on account of their sins, and may repent from their hearts, and so appease His displeasure towards them; so shall they receive a pardon from Him, as from a merciful Father.

XIII. Yet it is very necessary that those who are yet innocent should continue so, and not make an experiment what sin is, that they may not have occasion for trouble, sorrow, and those lamentations which are in order to forgiveness. For how dost thou know, O man, when thou sinnest, whether thou shalt live any number of days in this present state, that thou mayest have time to repent? For the time of thy departure out of this world is uncertain; and if thou diest in sin, there will remain no repentance for thee; as God says by David, "In the grave who will confess to Thee?"[3] It behoves us, therefore, to be ready in the doing of our duty, that so we may await our passage into another world without sorrow. Wherefore also the Divine Word exhorts, [speaking to thee by the wise Solomon,[4]] "Prepare thy works against thy exit, and provide all beforehand in the field,"[5] lest some of the things necessary to thy journey be wanting; as the oil of piety was deficient in the five foolish virgins[6] mentioned in the Gospel, when they, on account of their having extinguished their lamps of divine knowledge, were shut out of the bride-chamber. Wherefore he who values the security of his soul will take care to be out of danger, by keeping free from sin, that so he may preserve the advantage of his former good works to himself. Do thou, therefore, so judge as executing judgment for God. For, as the Scripture says, "the judgment is the Lord's."[7]

[1] Ezek. xxiii. 11. [2] Not in V. MSS. [3] Ps. vi. 6. [4] Not in V. MSS.
[5] Prov. xxiv. 27. [6] Matt. xxv. [7] Deut. i. 17.

In the first place, therefore, condemn the guilty person with authority; afterwards try to bring him home with mercy and compassion, and readiness to receive him, promising him salvation if he will change his course of life, and become a penitent; and when he does repent, and has submitted to his chastisement, receive him: remembering that our Lord has said, "There is joy in heaven over one sinner that repenteth."[1]

XIV. But if thou refusest to receive him that repents, thou exposest him to those who lie in wait to destroy, forgetting what David says: "Deliver not my soul, which confesses to Thee, unto destroying beasts."[2] Wherefore Jeremiah, when he is exhorting men to repentance, says thus: "Shall not he that falleth arise? or he that turneth away, cannot he return? Wherefore have my people gone back by a shameless backsliding? and they are hardened in their purpose.[3] Turn, ye backsliding children, and I will heal your backslidings."[4] Receive, therefore, without any doubting, him that repents. Be not hindered by such unmerciful men, who say that we must not be defiled with such as those, nor so much as speak to them: for such advice is from men that are unacquainted with God and His providence, and are unreasonable judges, and unmerciful brutes. These men are ignorant that we ought to avoid society with offenders, not in discourse, but in actions: for "the righteousness of the righteous shall be upon him, and the wickedness of the wicked shall be upon him."[5] And again: "If a land sinneth against me by trespassing grievously, and I stretch out my hand upon it, and break the staff of bread upon it, and send famine upon it, and destroy man and beast therein: though these three men, Noah, Job, and Daniel, were in the midst of it, they shall only save their own souls by their righteousness, saith the Lord God."[6] The Scripture most clearly shows that a righteous man that converses with a wicked man does not perish with him. For in the present world the righteous and the wicked are mingled together in

[1] Luke xv. 7.   [2] Ps. lxxiii. 19.   [3] Jer. viii. 4.
[4] Jer. iii. 22.   [5] Ezek. xviii. 20.   [6] Ezek. xiv. 13.

the common affairs of life, but not in holy communion; and
in this the friends and favourites of God are guilty of no sin.
For they do but imitate "their Father which is in heaven,
who maketh His sun to rise on the righteous and unrighteous,
and sendeth His rain on the evil and on the good;"[1] and the
righteous man undergoes no peril on this account. For those
who conquer and those who are conquered are in the same
place of running, but only those who have bravely undergone the race are where the garland is bestowed; and "no
one is crowned, unless he strive lawfully."[2] For every one
shall give account of himself, and God will not destroy the
righteous with the wicked; for with Him it is a constant rule,
that innocence is never punished. For neither did He drown
Noah, nor burn up Lot, nor destroy Rahab for company.
And if you desire to know how this matter was among us,
Judas was one of us, and took the like part of the ministry
which we had; and Simon the magician received the seal of
the Lord. Yet both the one and the other proving wicked,
the former hanged himself, and the latter, as he flew in the
air in a manner unnatural, was dashed against the earth.
Moreover, Noah and his sons with him were in the ark; but
Ham, who alone was found wicked, received punishment in
his son.[3] But if fathers are not punished for their children,
nor children for their fathers, it is thence clear that neither
will wives be punished for their husbands, nor servants for
their masters, nor one relation for another, nor one friend for
another, nor the righteous for the wicked. But every one
will be required an account of his own doing. For neither
was punishment inflicted on Noah for the world, nor was
Lot destroyed by fire for the Sodomites, nor was Rahab slain
for the inhabitants of Jericho, nor Israel for the Egyptians.
For not the dwelling together, but the agreement in their
sentiments, alone could condemn the righteous with the
wicked. We ought not therefore to hearken to such persons who call for death, and hate mankind, and love accusa-

---

[1] Matt. v. 45.   [2] 2 Tim. ii. 5.

[3] A various reading gives: "Ham, one of his sons, who alone was found wicked, received punishment."

tions, and under fair pretences bring men to death. For one man shall not die for another, but "every one is held with the chains of his own sins."[1] And, "behold, the man and his work is before his face."[2] Now we ought to assist those who are with us,[3] and are in danger, and fall, and, as far as lies in our power, to reduce them to sobriety by our exhortations, and so save them from death. For "the whole have no need of the physician, but the sick;"[4] since "it is not pleasing in the sight of your Father that one of these little ones should perish."[5] For we ought not to establish the will of hard-hearted men, but the will of the God and Father of the universe, which is revealed to us by Jesus Christ our Lord, to whom be glory for ever. Amen.

For it is not equitable that thou, O bishop, who art the head, shouldst submit to the tail, that is, to some seditious person among the laity, to the destruction of another, but to God alone. For it is thy privilege to govern those under thee, but not to be governed by them. For neither does a son, who is subject by the course of generation, govern his father; nor a slave, who is subject by law, govern his master; nor does a scholar govern his teacher, nor a soldier his king, nor any of the laity his bishop. For that there is no reason to suppose that such as converse with the wicked, in order to their instruction in the word, are defiled by or partake of their sins, Ezekiel, as it were on purpose preventing the suspicions of ill-disposed persons, says thus: "Why do you speak this proverb concerning the land of Israel? The fathers have eaten sour grapes, and the children's teeth are set on edge. As I live, saith the Lord God, ye shall not henceforth have occasion to use this proverb in Israel. For all souls are mine, in like manner as the soul of the father, so also the soul of the son is mine: the soul that sinneth, it shall die. But the man who is righteous, and does judgment and justice" (and so the prophet reckons up the rest of the virtues, and then adds for a conclusion, "Such an one is just"),

---

[1] Prov. v. 22.   [2] Isa. lxii. 11.
[3] One V. MS. reads: "those who are sick."
[4] Matt. ix. 12.   [5] Matt. xviii. 14.

"he shall surely live, saith the Lord God. And if he beget a son who is a robber, a shedder of blood, and walks not in the way of his righteous father" (and when the prophet had added what follows, he adds in the conclusion), "he shall certainly not live: he has done all this wickedness; he shall surely die; his blood shall be upon him. Yet they will ask thee, Why? Does not the son bear the iniquity of the father; or his righteousness, having exercised righteousness and mercy himself? And thou shalt say unto them, The soul that sinneth, it shall die. The son shall not bear the iniquity of the father, and the father shall not bear the iniquity of the son. The righteousness of the righteous shall be upon him, and the wickedness of the wicked shall be upon him."[1] And a little after he says: "When the righteous turneth away from his righteousness, and committeth iniquity, all his righteousness, by reason of all his wickedness which he has committed, shall not be mentioned to him: in his iniquity which he hath committed, and in his sin which he hath sinned, in them shall he die." And a little after he adds: "When the wicked turneth away from his wickedness which he hath committed, and doth judgment and justice, he hath preserved his soul, he hath turned away from all his ungodliness which he hath done; he shall surely live, he shall not die." And afterwards: "I will judge every one of you according to his ways, O house of Israel, saith the Lord God."

XV. Observe, you who are our beloved sons, how merciful yet righteous the Lord our God is; how gracious and kind to men; and yet most certainly "He will not acquit the guilty:"[2] though He welcomes the returning sinner, and revives him, leaving no room for suspicion to such as wish to judge sternly and to reject offenders entirely, and to refuse to vouchsafe to them exhortations which might bring them to repentance. In contradiction to such, God by Isaiah says to the bishops: "Comfort ye, comfort ye my people, ye priests: speak comfortably to Jerusalem." It therefore behoves you, upon hearing those words of His, to encourage those who have offended, and lead them to repent-

[1] Ezek. xviii. 2, etc. [2] Neh. i. 3.

ance, and afford them hope, and not vainly to suppose that you shall be partakers of their offences on account of such your love to them. Receive the penitent with alacrity, and rejoice over them, and with mercy and bowels of compassion judge the sinners. For if a person was walking by the side of a river, and ready to stumble, and thou shouldest push him and thrust him into the river, instead of offering him thy hand for his assistance, thou wouldst be guilty of the murder of thy brother; whereas thou oughtest rather to lend thy helping hand as he was ready to fall, lest he perish without remedy, that both the people may take warning, and the offender may not utterly perish. It is thy duty, O bishop, neither to overlook the sins of the people, nor to reject those who are penitent, that thou mayst not unskilfully destroy the Lord's flock, or dishonour His new name, which is imposed on His people, and thou thyself beest reproached as those ancient pastors were, of whom God speaks thus to Jeremiah: "Many shepherds have destroyed my vineyard; they have polluted my heritage."[1] And in another passage: "My anger is waxed hot against the shepherds, and against the lambs shall I have indignation."[2] And elsewhere: "Ye are the priests that dishonour my name."[3]

XVI. When thou seest the offender, with severity command him to be cast out; and as he is going out, let the deacons also treat him with severity, and then let them go and seek for him, and detain him out of the church; and when they come in, let them entreat thee for him. For our Saviour Himself entreated His Father for those who had sinned, as it is written in the Gospel: "Father, forgive them; for they know not what they do."[4] Then order the offender to come in; and if upon examination thou findest that he is penitent, and fit to be received at all into the church when thou hast afflicted him his days of fasting, according to the degree of his office—as two, three, five, or seven weeks—so set him at liberty, and speak such things to him as are fit to be said in way of reproof, instruction, and

[1] Jer. xii. 10.
[2] Zech. x. 3.
[3] Mal. i. 6.
[4] Luke xxiii. 34.

exhortation to a sinner for his reformation, that so he may continue privately in his humility, and pray to God to be merciful to him, saying: "If Thou, O Lord, shouldest mark iniquities, O Lord, who should stand? For with Thee there is propitiation."[1] Of this sort of declaration is that which is said in the book of Genesis to Cain: "Thou hast sinned; be quiet;"[2] that is, do not go on in sin. For that a sinner ought to be ashamed for his own sin, that oracle of God delivered to Moses concerning Miriam is a sufficient proof, when he prayed that she might be forgiven. For says God to him: "If her father had spit in her face, should she not be ashamed? Let her be shut out of the camp seven days, and afterwards let her come in again." We therefore ought to do so with offenders, when they profess their repentance,—namely, to separate them some determinate time, according to the proportion of their offence, and afterwards, like fathers to children, receive them again upon their repentance.

XVII. But if the bishop himself be an offender, how will he be able any longer to prosecute the offence of another? Or how will he be able to reprove another, either he or his deacons, if by accepting of persons, or receiving of bribes, they have not all a clear conscience? For when the ruler asks, and the judge receives, judgment is not brought to perfection; but when both are "companions of thieves, and regardless of doing justice to the widows,"[3] those who are under the bishop will not be able to support and vindicate him: for they will say to him what is written in the Gospel, "Why beholdest thou the mote that is in thy brother's eye, but considerest not the beam that is in thine own eye?"[4] Let the bishop, therefore, with his deacons, dread to hear any such thing; that is, let him give no occasion for it. For an offender, when he sees any other doing as bad as himself, will be encouraged to do the very same things; and then the wicked one, taking occasion from a single instance, works in others, which God forbid: and by that means the flock will

[1] Ps. cxxx. 3. [2] Gen. iv. 7, LXX.
[3] Isa. i. 23.   [4] Luke vi. 41.

be destroyed. For the greater number of offenders there are, the greater is the mischief that is done by them: for sin which passes without correction grows worse and worse, and spreads to others; since "a little leaven infects the whole lump,"[1] and one thief spreads the abomination over a whole nation, and "dead flies spoil the whole pot of sweet ointment;"[2] and "when a king hearkens to unrighteous counsel, all the servants under him are wicked."[3] So one scabbed sheep, if not separated from those that are whole, infects the rest with the same distemper; and a man infected with the plague is to be avoided by all men; and a mad dog is dangerous to every one that he touches. If, therefore, we neglect to separate the transgressor from the church of God, we shall make the "Lord's house a den of thieves."[4] For it is the bishop's duty not to be silent in the case of offenders, but to rebuke them, to exhort them, to beat them down, to afflict them with fastings, that so he may strike a pious dread into the rest: for, as He says, "make ye the children of Israel pious."[5] For the bishop must be one who discourages sin by his exhortations, and sets a pattern of righteousness, and proclaims those good things which are prepared by God, and declares that wrath which will come at the day of judgment, lest he contemn and neglect the plantation of God; and, on account of his carelessness, hear that which is said in Hosea: "Why have ye held your peace at impiety, and have reaped the fruit thereof?"[6]

XVIII. Let the bishop, therefore, extend his concern to all sorts of people: to those who have not offended, that they may continue innocent; to those who offend, that they may repent. For to you does the Lord speak thus: "Take heed that ye offend not one of these little ones."[7] It is your duty also to give remission to the penitent. For as soon as ever one who has offended says, in the sincerity of his soul, "I have sinned against the Lord," the Holy Spirit answers, "The Lord also hath forgiven thy sin; be of good cheer,

[1] Gal. v. 9.   [2] Eccles. x. 1.   [3] Prov. xxix. 12.
[4] Matt. xxi. 13.   [5] Lev. xv. 31.   [6] Hos. x. 13, LXX.
[7] Matt. xviii. 10.

thou shalt not die."[1] Be sensible, therefore, O bishop, of the dignity of thy place, that as thou hast received the power of binding, so hast thou also that of loosing. Having therefore the power of loosing, know thyself, and behave thyself in this world as becomes thy place, being aware that thou hast a great account to give. "For to whom," as the Scripture says, "men have entrusted much, of him they will require the more."[2] For no one man is free from sin, excepting Him that was made man for us; since it is written: "No man is pure from filthiness; no, not though he be but one day old."[3] Upon which account the lives and conduct of the ancient holy men and patriarchs are described; not that we may reproach them from our reading, but that we ourselves may repent, and have hope that we also shall obtain forgiveness. For their blemishes are to us both security and admonition, because we hence learn, when we have offended, that if we repent we shall have pardon. For it is written: "Who can boast that he has a clean heart? and who dare affirm that he is pure from sin?"[4] No man, therefore, is without sin. Do thou therefore labour to the utmost of thy power to be unblameable; and be solicitous of all the parts of thy flock, lest any one be scandalized on thy account, and thereby perish. For the layman is solicitous only for himself, but thou for all, as having a greater burden, and carrying a heavier load. For it is written: "And the Lord said unto Moses, Thou and Aaron shall bear the sins of the priesthood."[5] Since, therefore, thou art to give an account of all, take care of all. Preserve those that are sound, admonish those that sin; and when thou hast afflicted them with fasting, give them ease by remission; and when with tears the offender begs readmission, receive him, and let the whole church pray for him; and when by imposition of thy hand thou hast admitted him, give him leave to abide afterwards in the flock. But for the drowsy and the careless, do thou endeavour to convert and confirm, and warn and cure them, as sensible how great a reward thou shalt have for doing so,

[1] 2 Sam. xii. 13. [2] Luke xii. 48. [3] Job xiv. 4, LXX.
[4] Prov. xx. 9. [5] Num. xviii. 1.

and how great danger thou wilt incur if thou beest negligent therein. For Ezekiel speaks thus to those overseers who take no care of the people: " Woe unto the shepherds of Israel, for they have fed themselves; the shepherds feed not the sheep, but themselves. Ye eat the milk, and are clothed with the wool; ye slay the strong, ye do not feed the sheep. The weak have ye not strengthened, neither have ye healed that which was sick, neither have ye bound up that which was broken, neither have ye brought again that which was driven away, neither have ye sought that which was lost; but violently ye chastised them with insult: and they were scattered, because there was no shepherd; and they became meat to all the beasts of the forest." And again: "The shepherds did not search for my sheep; and the shepherds fed themselves, but they fed not my sheep." And a little after: " Behold, I am against the shepherds, and I will require my sheep at their hands, and cause them to cease from feeding my sheep, neither shall the shepherds feed themselves any more; and I will deliver my sheep out of their hands, and they shall not be meat for them." And he also adds, speaking to the people: " Behold, I will judge between sheep and sheep, and between rams and rams. Seemed it a small thing unto you to have eaten up the good pasture, and to have trodden down with your feet the residue of your pasture, and that the sheep have eaten what was trodden down with your feet?" And a little after He adds: " And ye shall know that I am the Lord, and you the sheep of my pasture; ye are my men, and I am your God, saith the Lord God."[1]

XIX. Hear, O ye bishops; and hear, O ye of the laity, how God speaks: " I will judge between ram and ram, and between sheep and sheep." And He says to the shepherds: " Ye shall be judged for your unskilfulness, and for destroying the sheep." That is, I will judge between one bishop and another, and between one lay person and another, and between one ruler and another (for these sheep and these rams are not irrational, but rational creatures): lest at any time a lay person should say, I am a sheep and not a shep-

[1] Ezek. xxxiv. 2, etc.

herd, and I am not concerned for myself; let the shepherd look to that, for he alone will be required to give an account for me. For as that sheep that will not follow its good shepherd is exposed to the wolves, to its destruction; so that which follows a bad shepherd is also exposed to unavoidable death, since his shepherd will devour him. Wherefore care must be had to avoid destructive shepherds.

XX. As to a good shepherd, let the lay person honour him, love him, reverence him as his lord, as his master, as the high priest of God, as a teacher of piety. For he that heareth him, heareth Christ; and he that rejecteth him, rejecteth Christ; and he who does not receive Christ, does not receive His God and Father: for, says He, "He that heareth you, heareth me; and he that rejecteth you, rejecteth me; and he that rejecteth me, rejecteth Him that sent me."[1] In like manner, let the bishop love the laity as his children, fostering and cherishing them with affectionate diligence; as eggs, in order to the hatching of young ones; or as young ones, taking them in his arms, to the rearing them into birds: admonishing all men; reproving all who stand in need of reproof; reproving, that is, but not striking; beating them down to make them ashamed, but not overthrowing them; warning them in order to their conversion; chiding them in order to their reformation and better course of life; watching the strong, that is, keeping him firm in the faith who is already strong; feeding the people peaceably; strengthening the weak, that is, confirming with exhortation that which is tempted; healing that which is sick, that is, curing by instruction that which is weak in the faith through doubtfulness of mind; binding up that which is broken, that is, binding up by comfortable admonitions that which is gone astray, or wounded, bruised, or broken by their sins, and put out of the way; easing it of its offences, and giving hope: by this means restore it in strength to the church, bringing it back into the flock. Bring again that which is driven away, that is, do not permit that which is in its sins, and is cast out by way of punishment, to continue excluded; but

[1] Luke x. 16.

receiving it, and bringing it back, restore it to the flock, that is, to the people of the undefiled church. Seek for that which is lost, that is, do not suffer that which desponds of its salvation, by reason of the multitude of its offences, utterly to perish. Do thou search for that which is grown sleepy, drowsy, and sluggish, and that which is unmindful of its own life, through the depth of its sleep, and which is at a great distance from its own flock, so as to be in danger of falling among the wolves, and being devoured by them. Bring it back by admonition, exhort it to be watchful; and insinuate hope, not permitting it to say that which was said by some: "Our impieties are upon us, and we pine away in them; how shall we then live?"[1] As far as possible, therefore, let the bishop make the offence his own, and say to the sinner, Do thou but return, and I will undertake to suffer death for thee, as our Lord suffered death for me, and for all men. For "the good shepherd lays down his life for the sheep; but he that is an hireling, and not the shepherd, whose own the sheep are not, seeth the wolf coming, that is, the devil, and he leaveth the sheep, and fleeth, and the wolf seizes upon them."[2] We must know, therefore, that God is very merciful to those who have offended, and hath promised repentance with an oath. But he who has offended, and is unacquainted with this promise of God concerning repentance, and does not understand His long-suffering and forbearance, and besides is ignorant of the Holy Scriptures, which proclaim repentance, inasmuch as he has never learned them from you, perishes through his folly. But do thou, like a compassionate shepherd, and a diligent feeder of the flock, search out, and keep an account of thy flock. Seek that which is wanting;[3] as the Lord God our gracious Father has sent His own Son, the good Shepherd and Saviour, our Master Jesus, and has commanded Him to "leave the ninety-nine upon the mountains, and to go in search after that which was lost, and when He had found it, to take it upon His shoulders, and to carry it into the flock, rejoicing that He had found that which was lost."[4] In like manner,

[1] Ezek. xxxiii. 10.   [2] John x. 11.   [3] Matt. xviii. 10.   [4] Luke xv. 4.

be obedient, O bishop, and do thou seek that which was lost, guide that which has wandered out of the right way, bring back that which is gone astray: for thou hast authority to bring them back, and to deliver those that are broken-hearted by remission. For by thee does our Saviour say to him who is discouraged under the sense of his sins, "Thy sins are forgiven thee: thy faith hath saved thee; go in peace."[1] But this peace and haven of tranquillity is the church of Christ, into which do thou, when thou hast loosed them from their sins, restore them, as being now sound and unblameable, of good hope, diligent, laborious in good works. As a skilful and compassionate physician, heal all such as have wandered in the ways of sin; for "they that are whole have no need of a physician, but they that are sick. For the Son of man came to save and to seek that which was lost."[2] Since thou art therefore a physician of the Lord's church, provide remedies suitable to every patient's case. Cure them, heal them by all means possible; restore them sound to the church. Feed the flock, "not with insolence and contempt, as lording it over them,"[3] but as a gentle shepherd, "gathering the lambs into thy bosom, and gently leading those which are with young."[4]

XXI. Be gentle, gracious, mild, without guile, without falsehood; not rigid, not insolent, not severe, not arrogant, not unmerciful, not puffed up, not a man-pleaser, not timorous, not double-minded, not one that insults over the people that are under thee, not one that conceals the divine laws and the promises to repentance, not hasty in thrusting out and expelling, but steady, not one that delights in severity, not heady. Do not admit less evidence to convict any one than that of three witnesses, and those of known and established reputation; inquire whether they do not accuse out of ill-will or envy: for there are many that delight in mischief, forward in discourse, slanderous, haters of the brethren, making it their business to scatter the sheep of

---

[1] Luke iv. 19; Matth. ix. 2; Mark v. 34.
[2] Matth. ix. 12; Luke xix. 10.   [3] Ezek. xxxiv. 4.
[4] Matth. xx. 25; Isa. xl. 11.

Christ; whose affirmation if thou admittest without nice scanning the same, thou wilt disperse thy flock, and betray it to be devoured by wolves, that is, by demons and wicked men, or rather not men, but wild beasts in the shape of men —by the heathen, by the Jews, and by the atheistic heretics. For those destroying wolves soon address themselves to any one that is cast out of the church, and esteem him as a lamb delivered for them to devour, reckoning his destruction their own gain. For he that is "their father, the devil, is a murderer."[1] He also who is separated unjustly by thy want of care in judging will be overwhelmed with sorrow, and be disconsolate, and so will either wander over to the heathen, or be entangled in heresies, and so will be altogether estranged from the church and from hope in God, and will be entangled in impiety, whereby thou wilt be guilty of his perdition: for it is not fair to be too hasty in casting out an offender, but slow in receiving him when he returns; to be forward in cutting off, but unmerciful when he is sorrowful, and ought to be healed. For of such as these speaks the divine Scripture: "Their feet run to mischief; they are hasty to shed blood. Destruction and misery are in their ways, and the way of peace have they not known. The fear of God is not before their eyes."[2] Now the way of peace is our Saviour Jesus Christ, who has taught us, saying: "Forgive, and ye shall be forgiven. Give, and it shall be given to you;"[3] that is, give remission of sins, and your offences shall be forgiven you. As also He instructed us by His prayer to say unto God: "Forgive us our debts, as we forgive our debtors."[4] If, therefore, you do not forgive offenders, how can you expect the remission of your own sins? Do not you rather bind yourselves faster, by pretending in your prayers to forgive, when you really do not forgive? Will you not be confronted with your own words, when you say you forgive and do not forgive? For know ye, that he who casts out one who has not behaved

[1] John viii. 44.
[2] Prov. i. 16; Isa. lix. 7; Ps. xxxv. 2; Rom. iii. 15.
[3] Mark xi. 25; Luke vi. 38.   [4] Matth. vi. 12.

himself wickedly, or who will not receive him that returns, is a murderer of his brother, and sheds his blood, as Cain did that of his brother Abel, and his "blood cries to God,"[1] and will be required. For a righteous man unjustly slain by any one will be in rest with God for ever. The same is the case of him who without cause is separated by his bishop. He who has cast him out as a pestilent fellow when he was innocent, is more furious than a murderer. Such an one has no regard to the mercy of God, nor is mindful of His goodness to those that are penitent, nor keeping in his eye the examples of those who, having been once great offenders, received forgiveness upon their repentance. Upon which account, he who casts off an innocent person is more cruel than he that murders the body. In like manner, he who does not receive the penitent, scatters the flock of Christ, being really against Him. For as God is just in judging of sinners, so is He merciful in receiving them when they return. For David, the man after God's own heart, in his hymns ascribes both mercy and judgment to Him.

XXII. It is also thy duty, O bishop, to have before thine eyes the examples of those that have gone before, and to apply them skilfully to the cases of those who want words of severity or of consolation. Besides, it is reasonable that in thy administration of justice thou shouldest follow the will of God; and as God deals with sinners, and with those who return, that thou shouldest act accordingly in thy judging. Now, did not God by Nathan reproach David for his offence? And yet as soon as he said he repented, He delivered him from death, saying, "Be of good cheer; thou shalt not die."[2] So also, when God had caused Jonah[3] to be swallowed up by the sea and the whale, upon his refusal to preach to the Ninevites, when yet he prayed to Him out of the belly of the whale, He retrieved his life from corruption. And when Hezekiah had been puffed up for a while, yet, as soon as he prayed with lamentation, He remitted his offence. But, O ye bishops, hearken to an instance useful upon this occa-

[1] Gen. iv. 10.   [2] 2 Kings xii. 13.
[3] Jonah i. 17, and iv.

sion. For it is written thus in the fourth book of Kings and the second book of Chronicles: "And Hezekiah died; and Manasseh his son reigned. He was twelve years old when he began to reign, and he reigned fifty and five years in Jerusalem; and his mother's name was Hephzibah. And he did evil in the sight of the Lord: he did not abstain from the abominations of the heathen, whom the Lord destroyed from the face of the children of Israel. And Manasses returned and built the high places which Hezekiah his father had overthrown; and he reared pillars for Baal, and set up an altar for Baal, and made groves, as did Ahab king of Israel. And he made altars in the house of the Lord, of which the Lord spake to David and to Solomon his son, saying, Therein will I put my name. And Manasseh set up altars, and by them served Baal, and said, My name shall continue for ever.[1] And he built altars to the host of heaven in the two courts of the house of the Lord; and he made his children pass through the fire in a place named Ge Benennom;[2] and he consulted enchanters, and dealt with wizards and familiar spirits, and with conjurers and observers of times, and with teraphim. And he sinned exceedingly in the eyes of the Lord, to provoke Him to anger. And he set a molten and a graven image, the image of his grove, which he made in the house of the Lord, wherein the Lord had chosen to put His name in Jerusalem, the holy city, for ever, and had said, I will no more remove my foot from the land of Israel, which I gave to their fathers; only if they will observe to do according to all that I have commanded them, and according to all the precepts that my servant Moses commanded them. And they hearkened not. And Manasseh seduced them to do more evil before the Lord than did the nations whom the Lord cast out from the face of the children of Israel. And the Lord spake concerning Manasseh and concerning His people by the hand of His servants the prophets, saying, Because Manasseh king of

[1] From "said" to "ever" is not in Scripture.
[2] Taken from 2 Chron. xxiii. 3, Sept., instead of the reading of the MSS., "Gebanai."

Judah has done all these wicked abominations in a higher degree than the Amorite did which was before him, and hath made Judah to sin with his idols, thus saith the Lord God of Israel, Behold, I bring evils upon Jerusalem and Judah, that whosoever heareth of them, both his ears shall tingle. And I will stretch over Jerusalem the line of Samaria, and the plummet of the house of Ahab; and I will blot out Jerusalem as a table-book is blotted out by wiping it. And I will turn it upside down; and I will give up the remnant of my inheritance, and will deliver them into the hands of their enemies, and they shall become a prey and a spoil to all their enemies, because of all the evils which they have done in mine eyes, and have provoked me to anger from the day that I brought their fathers out of the land of Egypt even until this day. Moreover, Manasseh shed innocent blood very much, till he had filled Jerusalem from one end to another, beside his sins wherewith he made Judah to sin in doing evil in the sight of the Lord. And the Lord brought upon him the captains of the host of the king of Assyria, and they caught Manasseh in bonds, and they bound him in fetters of brass, and brought him to Babylon; and he was bound and shackled with iron all over in the house of the prison. And bread made of bran was given unto him scantily, and by weight, and water mixed with vinegar but a little and by measure, so much as would keep him alive; and he was in straits and sore affliction. And when he was violently afflicted, he besought the face of the Lord his God, and humbled himself greatly before the face of the Lord God of his fathers. And he prayed unto the Lord, saying, O Lord, almighty God of our fathers Abraham, Isaac, and Jacob, and of their righteous seed, who hast made heaven and earth, with all the ornament thereof, who hast bound the sea by the word of Thy commandment, who hast shut up the deep, and sealed it by Thy terrible and glorious name, whom all men fear and tremble before Thy power; for the majesty of Thy glory cannot be borne, and Thine angry threatening towards sinners is insupportable. But Thy merciful promise is unmeasurable and unsearchable; for

Thou art [the most high Lord[1]], of great compassion, long-suffering, very merciful, and repentest of the evils of men. Thou, O Lord, according to Thy great goodness, hast promised repentance and forgiveness to them that have sinned against Thee, and of Thine infinite mercy hast appointed repentance unto sinners, that they may be saved. Thou therefore, O Lord, that art the God of the just, hast not appointed repentance to the just as to Abraham and Isaac and Jacob, which have not sinned against Thee; but Thou hast appointed repentance unto me that am a sinner: for I have sinned above the number of the sands of the sea. My transgressions, O Lord, are multiplied; my transgressions are multiplied, and I am not worthy to behold and see the height of heaven for the multitude of mine iniquity. I am bowed down with many iron bands; for I have provoked Thy wrath, and done evil before Thee, setting up abominations, and multiplying offences. Now, therefore, I bow the knee of mine heart, beseeching Thee of grace. I have sinned, O Lord, I have sinned, and I acknowledge mine iniquities; wherefore I humbly beseech Thee, forgive me, O Lord, forgive me, and destroy me not with mine iniquities. Be not angry with me for ever, by reserving evil for me; neither condemn me into the lower part of the earth. For Thou art the God, even the God of them that repent, and in me Thou wilt show Thy goodness; for Thou wilt save me that am unworthy, according to Thy great mercy. Therefore I will praise Thee for ever all the days of my life; for all the powers of the heavens do praise Thee, and Thine is the glory for ever and ever. Amen. And the Lord heard his voice, and had compassion upon him. And there appeared a flame of fire about him, and all the iron shackles and chains which were about him fell off; and the Lord healed Manasseh from his affliction, and brought him back to Jerusalem unto his kingdom: and Manasseh knew that the Lord He is God alone. And he worshipped the Lord God alone with all his heart, and with all his soul, all the days of his life; and he was esteemed righteous. And he took away the strange

[1] Not in MSS.

gods and the graven image out of the house of the Lord, and all the altars which he had built in the house of the Lord, and all the altars in Jerusalem, and he cast them out of the city. And he repaired the altar of the Lord, and sacrificed thereon peace-offerings and thank-offerings. And Manasseh spake to Judah to serve the Lord God of Israel. And he slept in peace with his fathers; and Amon his son reigned in his stead. And he did evil in the sight of the Lord according to all things that Manasseh his father had done in the former part of his reign. And he provoked the Lord his God to anger."[1]

Ye have heard, our beloved children, how the Lord God for a while punished him that was addicted to idols, and had slain many innocent persons; and yet that He received him when he repented, and forgave him his offences, and restored him to his kingdom. For He not only forgives the penitent, but reinstates them in their former dignity.

XXIII. There is no sin more grievous than idolatry, for it is an impiety against God: and yet even this sin has been forgiven, upon sincere repentance. But if any one sin in direct opposition, and on purpose to try whether God will punish the wicked or not, such an one shall have no remission, although he say with himself, "All is well, and I will walk according to the conversation of my evil heart." Such an one was Amon the son of Manasseh. For the Scripture says: "And Amon reasoned an evil reasoning of transgression, and said, My father from his childhood was a great transgressor, and repented in his old age; and now I will walk as my soul lusteth, and afterwards I will return unto the Lord. And he did evil in the sight of the Lord above all that were before him. And the Lord God soon destroyed him utterly from His good land. And his servants conspired against him, and slew him in his own house, and he reigned two years only."

XXIV. Take heed, therefore, ye of the laity, lest any one of you fix the reasoning of Amon in his heart, and be suddenly cut off, and perish. In the same manner, let the

[1] 2 Kings xx. xxi.; 2 Chron. xxxii. xxxiii.

bishop take all the care he can that those which are yet innocent may not fall into sin; and let him heal and receive those which turn from their sins. But if he is pitiless, and will not receive the repenting sinner, he will sin against the Lord his God, pretending to be more just than God's justice, and not receiving him whom He has received, through Christ; for whose sake He sent His Son upon earth to men, as a man; for whose sake God was pleased that He, who was the Maker of man and woman, should be born of a woman; for whose sake He did not spare Him from the cross, from death, and burial, but permitted Him to die, who by nature could not suffer, His beloved Son, God the Word, the Angel of His great council, that He might deliver those from death who were obnoxious to death. Him do those provoke to anger who do not receive the penitent. For He was not ashamed of me, Matthew, who had been formerly a publican; and admitted of Peter, when he had through fear denied Him three times, but had appeased Him by repentance, and had wept bitterly; nay, He made him a shepherd to His own lambs. Moreover, He ordained Paul, our fellow-apostle, to be of a persecutor an apostle, and declared him a chosen vessel, even when he had heaped many mischiefs upon us before, and had blasphemed His sacred name. He says also to another, a woman that was a sinner: "Thy sins, which are many, are forgiven, for thou lovest much."[1] And when the elders had set another woman which had sinned before Him, and had left the sentence to Him, and were gone out, our Lord, the Searcher of the hearts, inquiring of her whether the elders had condemned her, and being answered No, He said unto her: "Go thy way therefore, for neither do I condemn thee."[2] This Jesus, O ye bishops, our Saviour, our King, and our God, ought to be set before you as your pattern; and Him you ought to imitate, in being meek, quiet, compassionate, merciful, peaceable, without passion, apt to teach, and diligent to convert, willing to receive and to comfort; no strikers, not soon angry, not injurious, not arrogant, not supercilious, not wine-bibbers,

[1] Luke vii. 47.   [2] John viii. 11.

not drunkards, not vainly expensive, not lovers of delicacies, not extravagant, using the gifts of God not as another's, but as their own, as good stewards appointed over them, as those who will be required by God to give an account of the same.

Sec. IV.—*On the management of the resources collected for the support of the clergy, and the relief of the poor.*

Let the bishop esteem such food and raiment sufficient as suits necessity and decency. Let him not make use of the Lord's goods as another's, but moderately; "for the labourer is worthy of his reward."[1] Let him not be luxurious in diet, or fond of idle furniture, but contented with so much alone as is necessary for his sustenance.

XXV. Let him use those tenths and first-fruits, which are given according to the command of God, as a man of God; as also let him dispense in a right manner the free-will offerings which are brought in on account of the poor, to the orphans, the widows, the afflicted, and strangers in distress, as having that God for the examiner of his accounts who has committed the disposition to him. Distribute to all those in want with righteousness, and yourselves use the things which belong to the Lord, but do not abuse them; eating of them, but not eating them all up by yourselves: communicate with those that are in want, and thereby show yourselves unblameable before God. For if you shall consume them by yourselves, you will be reproached by God, who says to such unsatiable people, who alone devour all, "Ye eat up the milk, and clothe yourselves with the wool;"[2] and in another passage, "Must you alone live upon the earth?"[3] Upon which account you are commanded in the law, "Thou shalt love thy neighbour as thyself."[4] Now we say these things, not as if you might not partake of the fruits of your labours; for it is written, "Thou shalt not muzzle the mouth of the ox which treadeth out the corn;"[5] but that

[1] Luke x. 7. [2] Ezek. xxxiv. 3. [3] Isa. v. 8.
[4] Lev. xix. 18. [5] Deut. xxv. 4.

you should do it with moderation and righteousness. As, therefore, the ox that labours in the threshing-floor without a muzzle eats indeed, but does not eat all up; so do you who labour in the threshing-floor, that is, in the church of God, eat of the church: which was also the case of the Levites, who served in the tabernacle of the testimony, which was in all things a type of the church. Nay, further, its very name implied that that tabernacle was fore-appointed for a testimony of the church. Here, therefore, the Levites also, who attended upon the tabernacle, partook of those things that were offered to God by all the people,—namely, gifts, offerings, and first-fruits, and tithes, and sacrifices, and oblations, without disturbance, they and their wives, and their sons and their daughters. Since their employment was the ministration to the tabernacle, therefore they had not any lot or inheritance in the land among the children of Israel, because the oblations of the people were the lot of Levi, and the inheritance of their tribe. You, therefore, O bishops, are to your people priests and Levites, ministering to the holy tabernacle, the holy catholic church; who stand at the altar of the Lord your God, and offer to Him reasonable and unbloody sacrifices through Jesus the great High Priest. You are to the laity prophets, rulers, governors, and kings; the mediators between God and His faithful people, who receive and declare His word, well acquainted with the Scriptures. Ye are the voice of God, and witnesses of His will, who bear the sins of all, and intercede for all; whom, as you have heard, the word severely threatens if you hide the key of knowledge from men, who are liable to perdition if you do not declare His will to the people that are under you; who shall have a certain reward from God, and unspeakable honour and glory, if you duly minister to the holy tabernacle. For as yours is the burden, so you receive as your fruit the supply of food and other necessaries. For you imitate Christ the Lord; and as He "bare the sins of us all upon the tree" at His crucifixion, the innocent for those who deserved punishment, so also you ought to make the sins of the people your own. For concerning our Saviour it is said in Isaiah, " He bears our sins, and is afflicted for us."[1] And again: "He bare the sins of many, and was delivered for our offences."[2] As, therefore, you are patterns for others, so have you Christ for your pattern. As, therefore, He is concerned for all, so be you for the laity under you. For do not thou imagine that the office of a bishop is an easy or light burden. As, therefore, you bear the weight, so have you a right to partake of the fruits before others, and to impart to those that are in want, as being to give an account to Him, who without bias will examine your accounts. For those who attend upon the church ought to be maintained by the church, as being priests, Levites, presidents, and ministers of God; as it is written in the book of Numbers concerning the priests: "And the Lord said unto Aaron, Thou, and thy sons, and the house of thy family, shall bear the iniquities of the holy things of your priesthood."[3] "Behold, I have given unto you the charge of the first-fruits, from all that are sanctified to me by the children of Israel; I have given them for a reward to thee, and to thy sons after thee, by an ordinance for ever. This shall be yours out of the holy things, out of the oblations, and out of the gifts, and out of all the sacrifices, and out of every trespass-offering, and sin-offerings; and all that they render unto me out of all their holy things, they shall belong to thee, and to thy sons: in the sanctuary shall they eat them."[4] And a little after: "All the first-fruits of the oil, and of the wine, and of the wheat, all which they shall give unto the Lord, to thee have I given them; and all that is first ripe, to thee have I given it, and every devoted thing. Every first-born of man and of beast, clean and unclean, and of sacrifice, with the breast, and the right shoulder, all these appertain to the priests, and to the rest of those belonging to them, even to the Levites."[5]

Hear this, you of the laity also, the elect church of God. For the people were formerly called "the people of God,"[6] and "an holy nation."[7] You, therefore, are the holy and

[1] Isa. liii. 4. [2] Isa. liii. 12. [3] Num. xviii. 1.
[4] Num. xviii. 8, etc. [5] Num. xviii. 12, etc. [6] Ex. xix. 5, 6.
[7] Heb. xii. 23.

sacred "church of God, enrolled in heaven, a royal priesthood, an holy nation, a peculiar people,"[1] a bride adorned for the Lord God, a great church, a faithful church. Hear attentively now what was said formerly: oblations and tithes belong to Christ our High Priest, and to those who minister to Him. Tenths of salvation are the first letter of the name of Jesus. Hear, O thou holy catholic church, who hast escaped the ten plagues, and hast received the ten commandments, and hast learned the law, and hast kept the faith, and hast believed in Jesus, [and hast known the decad, and hast believed in the iota which is the first letter of the name of Jesus,[2]] and art named after His name, and art established, and shinest in the consummation of His glory. Those which were then the sacrifices now are prayers, and intercessions, and thanksgivings. Those which were then first-fruits, and tithes, and offerings, and gifts, now are oblations, which are presented by holy bishops to the Lord God, through Jesus Christ, who has died for them. For these are your high priests, as the presbyters are your priests, and your present deacons instead of your Levites; as are also your readers, your singers, your porters, your deaconesses, your widows, your virgins, and your orphans: but He who is above all these is the High Priest.

XXVI. The bishop, he is the minister of the word, the keeper of knowledge, the mediator between God and you in the several parts of your divine worship. He is the teacher of piety; and, next after God, he is your father, who has begotten you again to the adoption of sons by water and the Spirit. He is your ruler and governor; he is your king and potentate; he is, next after God, your earthly god, who has a right to be honoured by you. For concerning him, and such as he, it is that God pronounces, "I have said, Ye are gods; and ye are all children of the Most High."[3] And, "Ye shall not speak evil of the gods."[4] For let the bishop preside over you as one honoured with the authority of God, which he is to exercise over the clergy, and by

[1] 1 Pet. ii. 9.   [2] Inserted from V. MSS.
[3] Ps. lxxxii. 6.   [4] Ex. xxii. 28.

which he is to govern all the people. But let the deacon minister to him, as Christ does to His Father;[1] and let him serve him unblameably in all things, as Christ does nothing of Himself, but does always those things that please His Father. Let also the deaconess be honoured by you in the place of the Holy Ghost, and not do or say anything without the deacon; as neither does the Comforter say or do anything of Himself, but gives glory to Christ by waiting for His pleasure. And as we cannot believe on Christ without the teaching of the Spirit, so let not any woman address herself to the deacon or bishop without the deaconess. Let the presbyters be esteemed by you to represent us the apostles, and let them be the teachers of divine knowledge; since our Lord, when He sent us, said, " Go ye, and make disciples of all nations, baptizing them in the name of the Father, and of the Son, and of the Holy Ghost: teaching them to observe all things whatsoever I have commanded you."[2] Let the widows and orphans be esteemed as representing the altar of burnt-offering; and let the virgins be honoured as representing the altar of incense, and the incense itself.

XXVII. As, therefore, it was not lawful for one of another tribe, that was not a Levite, to offer anything, or to approach the altar without the priest, so also do you do nothing without the bishop;[3] for if any one does anything without the bishop, he does it to no purpose. For it will not be esteemed as of any avail to him. For as Saul, when he had offered without Samuel, was told, "It will not avail for thee;"[4] so every person among the laity, doing anything without the priest, labours in vain. And as Uzziah the king,[5] who was not a priest, and yet would exercise the functions of the priests, was smitten with leprosy for his transgression; so every lay person shall not be unpunished who despises God, and is so mad as to affront His priests, and unjustly to snatch that honour to himself: not imitating Christ, "who glorified

---

[1] The V. MSS. read, " as the powers do to God," which, Ultzen remarks, is an orthodox correction of an Arian opinion.
[2] Matth. xxviii. 19.   [3] One V. MS. reads " priest."
[4] 1 Sam. xiii. 13.   [5] 2 Chron. xxvi.

not Himself to be made an high priest;"[1] but waited till He heard from His Father, "The Lord sware, and will not repent, Thou art a priest for ever, after the order of Melchizedek."[2] If, therefore, Christ did not glorify Himself without the Father, how dare any man thrust himself into the priesthood who has not received that dignity from his superior, and do such things which it is lawful only for the priests to do? Were not the followers of Corah, even though they were of the tribe of Levi, consumed with fire, because they rose up against Moses and Aaron, and meddled with such things as did not belong to them? And Dathan and Abiram went down quick into hell; and the rod that budded put a stop to the madness of the multitude, and demonstrated who was the high priest ordained by God.[3] You ought therefore, brethren, to bring your sacrifices and your oblations to the bishop, as to your high priest, either by yourselves or by the deacons; and do you bring not those only, but also your first-fruits, and your tithes, and your free-will offerings to him. For he knows who they are that are in affliction, and gives to every one as is convenient, that so one may not receive alms twice or oftener the same day, or the same week, while another has nothing at all. For it is reasonable rather to supply the wants of those who really are in distress, than of those who only appear to be so.

XXVIII. If any determine to invite elder women to an entertainment of love, or a feast, as our Saviour calls it,[4] let them most frequently send to such an one whom the deacons know to be in distress. But let what is the pastor's due, I mean the first-fruits, be set apart in the feast for him, even though he be not at the entertainment, as being your priest, and in honour of that God who has entrusted him with the priesthood. But as much as is given to every one of the elder women, let double so much be given to the deacons, in honour of Christ. Let also a double portion be set apart for the presbyters, as for such who labour continually about the word and doctrine, upon the account of the apostles of our Lord, whose place they sustain, as the counsellors of the

[1] Heb. v. 5.   [2] Ps. cx. 4.   [3] Num. xvi.   [4] Luke xiv. 13.

bishop and the crown of the church. For they are the Sanhedrim and senate of the church. If there be a reader there, let him receive a single portion, in honour of the prophets, and let the singer and the porter have as much. Let the laity, therefore, pay proper honours in their presents, and utmost marks of respect to each distinct order. But let them not on all occasions trouble their governor, but let them signify their desires by those who minister to him, that is, by the deacons, with whom they may be more free. For neither may we address ourselves to Almighty God, but only by Christ. In the same manner, therefore, let the laity make known all their desires to the bishop by the deacon, and accordingly let them act as he shall direct them. For there was no holy thing offered or done in the temple formerly without the priest. " For the priest's lips shall keep knowledge, and they shall seek the law at his mouth," as the prophet somewhere says, " for he is the messenger of the Lord Almighty."[1] For if the worshippers of demons, in their hateful, abominable, and impure performances, imitate the sacred rules till this very day (it is a wide comparison indeed, and there is a vast distance between their abominations and God's sacred worship), in their mockeries of worship they neither offer nor do anything without their pretended priest, but esteem him as the very mouth of their idols of stone, waiting to see what commands he will lay upon them. And whatsoever he commands them, that they do, and without him they do nothing; and they honour him, their pretended priest, and esteem his name as venerable in honour of lifeless statues, and in order to the worship of wicked spirits. If these heathens, therefore, who give glory to lying vanities, and place their hope upon nothing that is firm, endeavour to imitate the sacred rules, how much more reasonable is it that you, who have a most certain faith and undoubted hope, and who expect glorious, and eternal, and never-failing promises, should honour the Lord God in those set over you, and esteem your bishop to be the mouth of God!

XXIX. For if Aaron, because he declared to Pharaoh

[1] Mal. ii. 7.

the words of God from Moses, is called a prophet; and Moses himself is called a god to Pharaoh, on account of his being at once a king and a high priest, as God says to him, " I have made thee a god to Pharaoh, and Aaron thy brother shall be thy prophet;"[1] why do not ye also esteem the mediators of the word to be prophets, and reverence them as gods?

XXX. For now the deacon is to you Aaron, and the bishop Moses. If, therefore, Moses was called a god by the Lord, let the bishop be honoured among you as a god, and the deacon as his prophet. For as Christ does nothing without His Father, so neither does the deacon do anything without his bishop; and as the Son without His Father is nothing, so is the deacon nothing without his bishop; and as the Son is subject to His Father, so is every deacon subject to his bishop; and as the Son is the messenger and prophet of the Father, so is the deacon the messenger and prophet of his bishop. Wherefore let all things that he is to do with any one be made known to the bishop, and be finally ordered by him.

XXXI. Let him not do anything at all without his bishop, nor give anything without his consent. For if he gives to any one as to a person in distress without the bishop's knowledge, he gives it so that it must tend to the reproach of the bishop, and he accuses him as careless of the distressed. But he that casts reproach on his bishop, either by word or deed, opposes God, not hearkening to what He says: " Thou shalt not speak evil of the gods."[2] For He did not make that law concerning deities of wood and of stone, which are abominable, because they are falsely called gods, but concerning the priests and the judges, to whom He also said, " Ye are gods, and children of the Most High."[3]

XXXII. If therefore, O deacon, thou knowest any one to be in distress, put the bishop in mind of him, and so give to him; but do nothing in a clandestine way, so as may tend to his reproach, lest thou raise a murmur against him; for

[1] Ex. vii. 1.   [2] Ex. xxii. 28.   [3] Ps. lxxxii. 6.

the murmur will not be against him, but against the Lord God: and the deacon, with the rest, will hear what Aaron and Miriam heard, when they spake against Moses: "How is it that ye were not afraid to speak against my servant Moses?"[1] And again, Moses says to those who rose up against him: "Your murmuring is not against us, but against the Lord our God."[2] For if he that calls one of the laity Raka,[3] or fool, shall not be unpunished, as doing injury to the name[4] of Christ, how dare any man speak against his bishop, by whom the Lord gave the Holy Spirit among you upon the laying on of his hands, by whom ye have learned the sacred doctrines, and have known God, and have believed in Christ, by whom ye were known of God, by whom ye were sealed with the oil of gladness and the ointment of understanding, by whom ye were declared to be the children of light, by whom the Lord in your illumination testified by the imposition of the bishop's hands, and sent out His sacred voice upon every one of you, saying, "Thou art my son, this day have I begotten thee?"[5] By thy bishop, O man, God adopts thee for His child. Acknowledge, O son, that right hand which was a mother to thee. Love him who, after God, is become a father to thee, and honour him.

XXXIII. For if the divine oracle says, concerning our parents according to the flesh, "Honour thy father and thy mother, that it may be well with thee;"[6] and, "He that curseth his father or his mother, let him die the death;"[7] how much more should the word exhort you to honour your spiritual parents, and to love them as your benefactors and ambassadors with God, who have regenerated you by water, and endued you with the fulness of the Holy Spirit, who have fed you with the word as with milk, who have nourished you with doctrine, who have confirmed you by their admonitions, who have imparted to you the saving body and precious blood of Christ, who have loosed you from your sins, who have made you partakers of the holy and sacred eucharist,

[1] Num. xii. 8. [2] Ex. xvi. 8. [3] Matth. v. 22.
[4] Capellius reads, "the law of Christ." [5] Ps. ii. 7.
[6] Ex. xx. 12. [7] Ex. xxi. 17.

who have admitted you to be partakers and fellow-heirs of the promise of God! Reverence these, and honour them with all kinds of honour; for they have obtained from God the power of life and death, in their judging of sinners, and condemning them to the death of eternal fire, as also of loosing returning sinners from their sins, and of restoring them to a new life.

XXXIV. Account these worthy to be esteemed your rulers and your kings, and bring them tribute as to kings; for by you they and their families ought to be maintained. As Samuel made constitutions for the people concerning a king,[1] in the first book of Kings, and Moses did so concerning priests in Leviticus, so do we also make constitutions for you concerning bishops. For if there the multitude distributed the inferior services in proportion to so great a king, ought not therefore the bishop much more now to receive of you those things which are determined by God for the sustenance of himself and of the rest of the clergy belonging to him? But if we may add somewhat further, let the bishop receive more than the other received of old: for he only managed the affairs of the soldiery, being entrusted with war and peace for the preservation of men's bodies; but the other is entrusted with the exercise of the priestly office in relation to God, in order to preserve both body and soul from dangers. By how much, therefore, the soul is more valuable than the body, so much the priestly office is beyond the kingly. For it binds and looses those that are worthy of punishment or of remission. Wherefore you ought to love the bishop as your father, and fear him as your king, and honour him as your lord, bringing to him your fruits and the works of your hands, for a blessing upon you, giving to him your first-fruits, and your tithes, and your oblations, and your gifts, as to the priest of God; the first-fruits of your wheat, and wine, and oil, and autumnal fruits, and wool,[2] and all things which the Lord God gives thee. And thy offering shall be accepted as a savour of a sweet smell to the

[1] 1 Sam. viii.
[2] One V. MS. reads "olives" instead of "wool."

Lord thy God; and the Lord will bless the works of thy hands, and will multiply the good things of the land. "For a blessing is upon the head of him that giveth."[1]

XXXV. Now you ought to know, that although the Lord has delivered you from the additional bonds, and has brought you out of them to your refreshment, and does not permit you to sacrifice irrational creatures for sin-offerings, and purifications, and scapegoats, and continual washings and sprinklings, yet has He nowhere freed you from those oblations which you owe to the priests, nor from doing good to the poor. For the Lord says to you in the Gospel: "Unless your righteousness abound more than that of the scribes and Pharisees, ye shall by no means enter into the kingdom of heaven."[2] Now herein will your righteousness exceed theirs, if you take greater care of the priests, the orphans, and the widows; as it is written: "He hath scattered abroad; he hath given to the poor; his righteousness remaineth for ever."[3] And again: "By acts of righteousness and faith iniquities are purged."[4] And again: "Every bountiful soul is blessed."[5] So therefore shalt thou do as the Lord has appointed, and shalt give to the priest what things are due to him, the first-fruits of thy floor, and of thy wine-press, and sin-offerings, as to the mediator between God and such as stand in need of purgation and forgiveness. For it is thy duty to give, and his to administer, as being the administrator and disposer of ecclesiastical affairs. Yet shalt thou not call thy bishop to account, nor watch his administration, how he does it, when, or to whom, or where, or whether he do it well or ill, or indifferently; for he has One who will call him to an account, the Lord God, who put this administration into his hands, and thought him worthy of the priesthood of so great dignity.

XXXVI. Have before thine eyes the fear of God, and always remember the ten commandments of God,—to love the one and only Lord God with all thy strength; to give no heed to idols, or any other beings, as being lifeless gods, or

---

[1] Prov. xi. 26. [2] Matth. v. 21. [3] Ps. cxii. 9.
[4] Prov. xv. 27. [5] Prov. xi. 25.

irrational beings or dæmons. Consider the manifold workmanship of God, which received its beginning through Christ. Thou shalt observe the Sabbath, on account of Him who ceased from His work of creation, but ceased not from His work of providence: it is a rest for meditation of the law, not for idleness of the hands. Reject every unlawful lust, everything destructive to men, and all anger. Honour thy parents, as the authors of thy being. Love thy neighbour as thyself. Communicate the necessaries of life to the needy. Avoid swearing falsely, and swearing often, and in vain; for thou shalt not be held guiltless. Do not appear before the priests empty, and offer thy free-will offerings continually. Moreover, do not leave the church of Christ; but go thither in the morning before all thy work, and again meet there in the evening, to return thanks to God that He has preserved thy life. Be diligent, and constant, and laborious in thy calling. Offer to the Lord thy free-will offerings; for says He, "Honour the Lord with the fruit of thy honest labours."[1] If thou art not able to cast anything considerable into the corban,[2] yet at least bestow upon the strangers one, or two, or five mites. "Lay up to thyself heavenly treasure, which neither the moth nor thieves can destroy."[3] And in doing this, do not judge thy bishop, or any of thy neighbours among the laity; for if thou judge thy brother, thou becomest a judge, without being constituted such by anybody, for the priests are only entrusted with the power of judging. For to them it is said, "Judge righteous judgment;"[4] and again, "Approve yourselves to be exact money-changers."[5] For to you this is not entrusted; for, on the contrary, it is said to those who are not of the dignity of magistrates or ministers: "Judge not, and ye shall not be judged."[6]

[1] Prov. iii. 9.
[2] The V. MSS. read: "Casting into the treasury whatever you can bestow."
[3] Matth. vi. 20.
[4] Deut. i. 16, xvi. 18.
[5] Zech. vii. 9.
[6] Luke vi. 37.

SEC. V.—*On accusations, and the treatment of accusers.*

XXXVII. But it is the duty of the bishop to judge rightly, as it is written, " Judge righteous judgment;"[1] and elsewhere, " Why do ye not even of yourselves judge what is right?"[2] Be ye therefore as skilful dealers in money: for as these reject bad money, but take to themselves what is current, in the same manner it is the bishop's duty to retain the unblameable, but either to heal, or, if they be past cure, to cast off those that are blameworthy, so as not to be hasty in cutting off, nor to believe all accusations; for it sometimes happens that some, either through passion or envy, do insist on a false accusation against a brother, as did the two elders in the case of Susanna in Babylon,[3] and the Egyptian woman in the case of Joseph.[4] Do thou therefore, as a man of God, not rashly receive such accusations, lest thou take away the innocent and slay the righteous; for he that will receive such accusations is the author of anger rather than of peace. But where there is anger, there the Lord is not; for that anger, which is the friend of Satan— I mean that which is excited unjustly by the means of false brethren—never suffers unanimity to be in the church. Wherefore, when you know such persons to be foolish, quarrelsome, passionate, and such as delight in mischief, do not give credit to them; but observe such as they are, when you hear anything from them against their brother: for murder is nothing in their eyes, and they cast a man down in such a way as one would not suspect. Do thou therefore consider diligently the accuser,[5] wisely observing his mode of life, what, and of what sort it is; and in case thou findest him a man of veracity, do according to the doctrine of our Lord,[6] and taking him who is accused, rebuke him, that he may repent, when nobody is by. But if he be not persuaded, take with thee one or two more, and so show him his fault, and admonish him with mildness and instruction; for

---

[1] John vii. 24.
[2] 1 Cor. vi. 5.
[3] Hist. Susanna.
[4] Gen. xxxix.
[5] The MSS. read, " the accused."
[6] Matth. xviii. 15.

"wisdom will rest upon an heart that is good, but is not understood in the heart of the foolish."[1]

XXXVIII. If, therefore, he be persuaded by the mouth of you three, it is well. But if any one hardens himself, "tell it to the church: but if he neglects to hear the church, let him be to thee as an heathen man and a publican;"[2] and receive him no longer into the church as a Christian, but reject him as an heathen. But if he be willing to repent, receive him. For the church does not receive an heathen or a publican to communion, before they every one repent of their former impieties; for our Lord Jesus, the Christ of God, has appointed place for the acceptance of men upon their repentance.

XXXIX. For I Matthew, one of those twelve which speak to you in this doctrine, am an apostle, having myself been formerly a publican, but now have obtained mercy through believing, and have repented of my former practices, and have been vouchsafed the honour to be an apostle and preacher of the word. And Zaccheus, whom the Lord received upon his repentance and prayers to Him, was also himself in the same manner a publican at first. And, besides, even the soldiers and multitude of publicans, who came to hear the word of the Lord about repentance, heard this from the prophet John, after he had baptized them: "Do nothing more than that which is appointed you."[3] In like manner, life is not refused to the heathen, if they repent and cast away their unbelief. Esteem, therefore, every one that is convicted of any wicked action, and has not repented as a publican or an heathen. But if he afterward repents, and turns from his error, then, as we receive the heathen, when they wish to repent, into the church indeed to hear the word, but do not receive them to communion until they have received the seal of baptism, and are made complete Christians; so do we also permit such as these to enter only to hear, until they show the fruit of repentance, that by hearing the word they may not utterly and irrecoverably perish. But let them not be admitted to communion in

[1] Prov. xiv. 33.   [2] Matth. xviii. 17.   [3] Luke iii. 13.

prayer; and let them depart after the reading of the law, and the prophets, and the gospel, that by such departure they may be made better in their course of life, by endeavouring to meet every day about the public assemblies, and to be frequent in prayer, that they also may be at length admitted, and that those who behold them may be affected, and be more secured by fearing to fall into the same condition.

XL. But yet do not thou, O bishop, presently abhor any person who has fallen into one or two offences, nor shalt thou exclude him from the word of the Lord, nor reject him from common intercourse, since neither did the Lord refuse to eat with publicans and sinners; and when He was accused by the Pharisees on this account, He said: "They that are well have no need of the physician, but they that are sick."[1] Do you, therefore, live and dwell with those who are separated from you for their sins; and take care of them, comforting them, and confirming them, and saying to them: "Be strengthened, ye weak hands and feeble knees."[2] For we ought to comfort those that mourn, and afford encouragement to the fainthearted, lest by immoderate sorrow they degenerate into distraction, since "he that is fainthearted is exceedingly distracted."[3]

XLI. But if any one returns, and shows forth the fruit of repentance, then do ye receive him to prayer, as the lost son, the prodigal, who had consumed his father's substance with harlots, who fed swine, and desired to be fed with husks, and could not obtain it.[4] This son, when he repented, and returned to his father, and said, "I have sinned against Heaven, and before thee, and am no more worthy to be called thy son;" the father, full of affection to his child, received him with music, and restored him his old robe, and ring, and shoes, and slew the fatted calf, and made merry with his friends. Do thou therefore, O bishop, act in the same manner. And as thou receivest an heathen after thou hast instructed and baptized him, so do thou let all join in

[1] Matth. ix. 12.   [2] Isa. xxxv. 3.
[3] Prov. xiv. 29, LXX.   [4] Luke xv. 21.

prayers for this man, and restore him by imposition of hands to his ancient place among the flock, as one purified by repentance; and that imposition of hands shall be to him instead of baptism: for by the laying on of our hands the Holy Ghost was given to believers. And in case some one of those brethren who had stood immoveable accuse thee, because thou art reconciled to him, say to him: "Thou art always with me, and all that I have is thine. It was meet to make merry and be glad: for this thy brother was dead, and is alive again; he was lost, and is found." For that God does not only receive the penitent, but restores them to their former dignity, holy David is a sufficient witness, who, after his sin in the matter of Uriah, prayed to God, and said: "Restore unto me the joy of Thy salvation, and uphold me with Thy free Spirit."[1] And again: "Turn Thy face from my sins, and blot out all mine offences. Create in me a clean heart, O God, and renew a right spirit in my inward parts. Cast me not away from Thy presence, and take not Thy Holy Spirit from me." Do thou therefore, as a compassionate physician, heal all that have sinned, making use of saving methods of cure; not only cutting and searing, or using corrosives, but binding up, and putting in tents, and using gentle healing medicines, and sprinkling comfortable words. If it be an hollow wound, or great gash, nourish it with a suitable plaister, that it may be filled up, and become even with the rest of the whole flesh. If it be foul, cleanse it with corrosive powder, that is, with the words of reproof. If it have proud flesh, eat it down with a sharp plaister—the threats of judgment. If it spreads further, sear it, and cut off the putrid flesh, mortifying him with fastings. But if, after all that thou hast done, thou perceivest that from the feet to the head there is no room for a fomentation, or oil, or bandage, but that the malady spreads and prevents all cure, as a gangrene which corrupts the entire member; then, with a great deal of consideration, and the advice of other skilful physicians, cut off the putrefied member, that the whole body of the church be not corrupted. Be not there-

[1] Ps. li.

fore ready and hasty to cut off, nor do thou easily have recourse to the saw, with its many teeth; but first use a lancet to lay open the wound, that the inward cause whence the pain is derived being drawn out, may keep the body free from pain. But if thou seest any one past repentance, and he is become insensible, then cut off the incurable from the church with sorrow and lamentation. For: "Take out from among yourselves that wicked person."[1] And: "Ye shall make the children of Israel to fear."[2] And again: "Thou shalt not accept the persons of the rich in judgment."[3] And: "Thou shalt not pity a poor man in his cause: for the judgment is the Lord's."[4]

XLII. But if the slanderous accusation be false, and you that are the pastors, with the deacons, admit of that falsehood for truth, either by acceptance of persons or receiving of bribes, as willing to do that which will be pleasing to the devil, and so you thrust out from the church him that is accused, but is clear of the crime, you shall give an account in the day of the Lord. For it is written: "The innocent and the righteous thou shalt not slay."[5] "Thou shalt not take gifts to smite the soul: for gifts blind the eyes of the wise, and destroy the words of the righteous."[6] And again: "They that justify the wicked for gifts, and take away the righteousness of the righteous from him."[7] Be careful, therefore, not to condemn any persons unjustly, and so to assist the wicked. For "woe to him that calls evil good, and good evil; bitter sweet, and sweet bitter; that puts light for darkness, and darkness for light."[8] [Take care, therefore, lest by any means ye become acceptors of persons, and thereby fall under this voice of the Lord.[9]] For if you condemn others unjustly, you pass sentence against yourselves. For the Lord says: "With what judgment ye judge, ye shall be judged;

---

[1] Deut. xvii. 7.
[2] Deut. i. 17; Lev. xix. 15.
[3] Ex. xxiii. 7, 8.
[4] Isa. v. 23.
[5] Lev. xv. 31.
[6] Ex. xxiii. 8.
[7] Deut. xxvii. 25, xvi. 19.
[8] Isa. v. 20.
[9] This sentence follows the passage from Isa. v. 23 in most MSS. One V. MS. has the order adopted in the text.

and as you condemn, you shall be condemned."[1] If, therefore, ye judge without respect of persons, ye will discover that accuser who bears false witness against his neighbour, and will prove him to be a sycophant, a spiteful person, and a murderer, causing perplexity by accusing the man as if he were wicked, inconstant in his words, contradicting himself in what he affirms, and entangled with the words of his own mouth; for his own lips are a dangerous snare to him: whom, when thou hast convicted him of speaking falsely, thou shalt judge severely, and shalt deliver him to the fiery sword, and thou shalt do to him as he wickedly proposed to do to his brother; for as much as in him lay he slew his brother, by forestalling the ears of the judge.[2] Now it is written, that " he that sheddeth man's blood, for that his own blood shall be shed."[3] And: "Thou shalt take away that innocent blood, which was shed without cause, from thee."[4]

XLIII. Thou shalt therefore cast him out of the congregation as a murderer of his brother. Some time afterwards, if he says that he repents, mortify him with fastings, and afterwards ye shall lay your hands upon him and receive him, but still securing him, that he does not disturb anybody a second time. But if, when he is admitted again, he be alike troublesome, and will not cease to disturb and to quarrel with his brother, spying faults out of a contentious spirit, cast him out as a pernicious person, that he may not lay waste the church of God. For such an one is the raiser of disturbances in cities; for he, though he be within, does not become the church, but is a superfluous and vain member, casting a blot, as far as in him lies, on the body of Christ. For if such men as are born with superfluous members of their body, which hang to them as fingers, or excrescences of flesh, cut them away from themselves on account of their indecency, whereby the unseemliness vanishes, and the man recovers his natural good shape by the means of the surgeon; how much more ought you, the pastors of the church (for the church is a perfect body, and sound members; of such as

[1] Matth. vii. 2; Luke vi. 37. [2] Deut. xix. 19.
[3] Gen. ix. 6. [4] Deut. xix. 13.

believe in God, in the fear of the Lord, and in love), to do the like when there is found in it a superfluous member with wicked designs, and rendering the rest of the body unseemly, and disturbing it with sedition, and war, and evil-speaking; causing fears, disturbances, blots, evil-speaking, accusations, disorders, and doing the like works of the devil, as if he were ordained by the devil to cast a reproach on the church by calumnies, and mighty disorders, and strife, and division! Such an one, therefore, when he is a second time cast out of the church, is justly cut off entirely from the congregation of the Lord. And now the church of the Lord will be more beautiful than it was before, when it had a superfluous, and to itself a disagreeable member. Wherefore henceforward it will be free from blame and reproach, and become clear of such wicked, deceitful, abusive, unmerciful, traitorous persons; of such as are "haters of those that are good, lovers of pleasure,"[1] affecters of vainglory, deceivers, and pretenders to wisdom; of such as make it their business to scatter, or rather utterly to disperse, the lambs of the Lord.

SEC. VI.—*The disputes of the faithful to be settled by the decisions of the bishop, and the faithful to be reconciled.*

Do thou therefore, O bishop, together with thy subordinate clergy, endeavour rightly to divide the word of truth. For the Lord says: "If you walk cross-grained to me, I will walk cross-grained to you."[2] And elsewhere: "With the holy Thou wilt be holy, and with the perfect man Thou wilt be perfect, and with the froward Thou wilt be froward."[3] Walk therefore holily, that you may rather appear worthy of praise from the Lord than of complaint from the adversary.

XLIV. Be ye of one mind, O ye bishops, one with another, and be at peace with one another; sympathize with one another, love the brethren, and feed the people with care; with one consent teach those that are under you to be of the same sentiments and to be of the same opinions about the same matters, "that there may be no schisms among you;

[1] 2 Tim. iii. 3, 4.   [2] Lev. xxvi. 27.   [3] Ps. xviii. 26.

that ye may be one body and one spirit, perfectly joined together in the same mind and in the same judgment,"[1] according to the appointment of the Lord. And let the deacon refer all things to the bishop, as Christ does to His Father. But let him order such things as he is able by himself, receiving power from the bishop, as the Lord did from His Father the power of creation and of providence. But the weighty matters let the bishop judge; but let the deacon be the bishop's ear, and eye, and mouth, and heart, and soul, that the bishop may not be distracted with many cares, but with such only as are more considerable, as Jethro did appoint for Moses, and his counsel was received.[2]

XLV. It is therefore a noble encomium for a Christian to have no contest with any one;[3] but if by any management or temptation a contest arises with any one, let him endeavour that it may be composed, though thereby he be obliged to lose somewhat; and let it not come before an heathen tribunal. Nay, indeed, you are not to permit that the rulers of this world should pass sentence against your people; for by them the devil contrives mischief to the servants of God, and occasions a reproach to be cast upon us, as though we had not "one wise man that is able to judge between his brethren," or to decide their controversies.

XLVI. Let not the heathen therefore know of your differences among one another, nor do you receive unbelievers as witnesses against yourselves, nor be judged by them, nor owe them anything on account of tribute or fear; but "render to Cæsar the things that are Cæsar's, and unto God the things that are God's,"[4] as tribute, taxes, or poll-money, as our Lord by giving a piece of money was freed from disturbance.[5] Choose therefore rather to suffer harm, and to endeavour after those things that make for peace, not only among the brethren, but also among the unbelievers. For by suffering loss in the affairs of this life, thou wilt be sure not to suffer in the concerns of piety, and wilt live religiously,

---

[1] 1 Cor. i. 10; Eph. iv. 4. [2] Ex. xviii.
[3] 1 Cor. vi. 1, etc. [4] Matth. xxii. 21.
[5] Matth. xvii. 24, etc.

and according to the command of Christ.[1] But if brethren have lawsuits one with another, which God forbid, you who are the rulers ought thence to learn that such as these do not do the work of brethren [in the Lord], but rather of public enemies; and one of the parties will be found to be mild, gentle, and the child of light; but the other unmerciful, insolent, and covetous. Let him, therefore, who is condemned be rebuked, let him be separated, let him undergo the punishment of his hatred to his brother. Afterwards, when he repents, let him be received; and so, when they have learned prudence, they will ease your judicatures. It is also a duty to forgive each other's trespasses—not the duty of those that judge, but of those that have quarrels; as the Lord determined when I Peter asked Him, "How oft shall my brother sin against me, and I forgive him? Till seven times?" He replied, "I say not unto thee, Until seven times, but until seventy times seven."[2] For so would our Lord have us to be truly His disciples, and never to have anything against anybody; as, for instance, anger without measure, passion without mercy, covetousness without justice, hatred without reconciliation. Draw by your instruction those who are angry to friendship, and those who are at variance to agreement. For the Lord says: "Blessed are the peacemakers, for they shall be called the children of God."[3]

XLVII. Let your judicatures be held on the second day of the week, that if any controversy arise about your sentence, having an interval till the Sabbath, you may be able to set the controversy right, and to reduce those to peace who have the contests one with another against the Lord's day. Let also the deacons and presbyters be present at your judicatures, to judge without acceptance of persons, as men of God, with righteousness. When, therefore, both the parties are come, according as the law says,[4] those that have the controversy shall stand severally in the middle of the court; and when you have heard them, give your votes holily, endea-

[1] One V. MS. reads "God" instead of "Christ."
[2] Matth. xviii. 21.   [3] Matth. v. 9.   [4] Deut. xix. 17.

vouring to make them both friends before the sentence of the bishop, that judgment against the offender may not go abroad into the world; knowing that he has in the court the Christ of God as conscious of and confirming his judgment. But if any persons are accused by any one, and their fame suffers as if they did not walk uprightly in the Lord, in like manner you shall hear both parties—the accuser and accused; but not with prejudice, nor with hearkening to one party only, but with righteousness, as passing a sentence concerning eternal life or death. For says God: "He shall prosecute that which is right justly."[1] For he that is justly punished and separated by you is rejected from eternal life and glory; he becomes dishonourable among holy men, and one condemned of God.

XLVIII. Do not pass the same sentence for every sin, but one suitable to each crime, distinguishing all the several sorts of offences with much prudence, the great from the little. Treat a wicked action after one manner, and a wicked word after another; a bare intention still otherwise. So also in the case of a contumely or suspicion. And some thou shalt curb by threatenings alone; some thou shalt punish with fines to the poor; some thou shalt mortify with fastings; and others thou shalt separate according to the greatness of their several crimes. For the law did not allot the same punishment to every offence, but had a different regard to a sin against God, against the priest, against the temple, or against the sacrifice; from a sin against the king, or ruler, or a soldier, or a fellow-subject; and so were the offences different which were against a servant, a possession, or a brute creature. And again, sins were differently rated according as they were against parents and kinsmen, and those differently which were done on purpose from those that happened involuntarily. Accordingly the punishments were different: as death either by crucifixion or by stoning, fines, scourgings, or the suffering the same mischiefs they had done to others. Wherefore do you also allot different penalties to different offences, lest any injustice should

[1] Deut. xvi. 20.

happen, and provoke God to indignation. For of what unjust judgment soever you are the instruments, of the same you shall receive the reward from God. "For with what judgment ye judge ye shall be judged."[1]

XLIX. When, therefore, you are set down at your tribunal, and the parties are both of them present (for we will not call them brethren until they receive each other in peace), examine diligently concerning those who appear before you; and first concerning the accuser, whether this be the first person he has accused, or whether he has advanced accusations against some others before, and whether this contest and accusation of theirs does not arise from some quarrel, and what sort of life the accuser leads. Yet, though he be of a good conscience, do not give credit to him alone, for that is contrary to the law; but let him have others to join in his testimony, and those of the same course of life. As the law says: "At the mouth of two or three witnesses everything shall be established."[2] But why did we say that the character of the witnesses was to be inquired after, of what sort it is? Because it frequently happens that two and more testify for mischief, and with joint consent prefer a lie; as did the two elders against Susanna in Babylon,[3] and the sons of transgressors against Naboth in Samaria,[4] and the multitude of the Jews against our Lord at Jerusalem,[5] and against Stephen His first martyr.[6] Let the witnesses therefore be meek, free from anger, full of equity, kind, prudent, continent, free from wickedness, faithful, religious; for the testimony of such persons is firm on account of their character, and true on account of their mode of life. But as to those of a different character, do not ye receive their testimony, although they seem to agree together in their evidence against the accused; for it is ordained in the law: "Thou shalt not be with a multitude for wickedness; thou shalt not receive a vain report; thou shalt not consent with a multitude to pervert judgment."[7] You ought also par-

[1] Matth. vii. 2.   [2] Deut. xix. 15.   [3] Susanna 28.
[4] 1 Kings xxi.   [5] Matth. xxvi.   [6] Acts vi. and vii.
[7] Ex. xxiii. 21.

ticularly to know him that is accused; what he is in his course
and mode of life; whether he have a good report as to his
life; whether he has been unblameable; whether he has been
zealous in holiness; whether he be a lover of the widows, a
lover of the strangers, a lover of the poor, and a lover of the
brethren; whether he be not given to filthy lucre; whether
he be not an extravagant person, or a spendthrift; whether
he be sober, and free from luxury, or a drunkard, or a
glutton; whether he be compassionate and charitable.

L. For if he has been before addicted to wicked works,
the accusations which are now brought against him will
thence in some measure appear to be true, unless justice do
plainly plead for him. For it may be, that though he had
formerly been an offender, yet that he may not be guilty of
this crime of which he is accused. Wherefore be exactly
cautious about such circumstances, and so render your sentences, when pronounced against the offender convicted, safe
and firm. And if, after his separation, he begs pardon, and
falls down before the bishop, and acknowledges his fault,
receive him. But neither do you suffer a false accuser to
go unpunished, that he may not calumniate another who lives
well, or encourage some other person to do like him. Nor,
to be sure, do ye suffer a person convicted to go off clear,
lest another be ensnared in the same crimes. For neither
shall a witness of mischiefs be unpunished, nor shall he that
offends be without censure.

LI. We said before that judgment ought not to be given
upon hearing only one of the parties; for if you hear one of
them when the other is not there, and so cannot make his defence to the accusation brought against him, and rashly give
your votes for condemnation, you will be found guilty of that
man's destruction, and partaker with the false accuser before
God, the just Judge. For "as he that holdeth the tail of
a dog, so is he that presides at unjust judgment."[1] But if ye
become imitators of the elders in Babylon, who, when they
had borne witness against Susanna, unjustly condemned her
to death, you will become obnoxious to their judgment and

[1] Prov. xxvi. 17.

condemnation. For the Lord by Daniel delivered Susanna from the hand of the ungodly, but condemned to the fire those elders who were guilty of her blood, and reproaches you by him, saying: "Are ye so foolish, ye children of Israel? Without examination, and without knowing the truth, have ye condemned a daughter of Israel? Return again to the place of judgment, for these men have borne false witness against her."[1]

LII. Consider even the judicatures of this world, by whose power we see murderers, adulterers, wizards, robbers of sepulchres, and thieves brought to trial; and those that preside, when they have received their accusations from those that brought them, ask the malefactor whether those things be so. And though he does not deny the crimes, they do not presently send him out to punishment; but for several days they make inquiry about him with a full council, and with the veil interposed. And he that is to pass the final decree and suffrage of death against him, lifts up his hands to the sun, and solemnly affirms that he is innocent of the blood of the man. Though they be heathens, and know not the Deity, nor the vengeance which will fall upon men from God on account of those that are unjustly condemned, they avoid such unjust judgments.

LIII. But you who know who our God is, and what are His judgments, how can you bear to pass an unjust judgment, since your sentence will be immediately known to God? And if you have judged righteously, you will be deemed worthy of the recompenses of righteousness, both now and hereafter; but if unrighteously, you will partake of the like. We therefore advise you, brethren, rather to deserve commendation from God than rebukes; for the commendation of God is eternal life to men, as is His rebuke everlasting death. Be ye therefore righteous judges, peacemakers, and without anger. For "he that is angry with his brother without a cause is obnoxious to the judgment."[2] But if it happens that by any one's contrivance you are angry at anybody, "let not the sun go down upon your wrath;"[3] for

---

[1] Susanna 48.   [2] Matth. v. 22.   [3] Eph. iv. 26.

says David, "Be angry and sin not;"[1] that is, be soon reconciled, lest your wrath continue so long that it turn to a settled hatred, and work sin. "For the souls of those that bear a settled hatred are to death,"[2] says Solomon. But our Lord and Saviour Jesus Christ says in the Gospels: "If thou bring thy gift to the altar, and there rememberest that thy brother hath ought against thee, leave there thy gift before the altar, and go thy way; first be reconciled to thy brother, and then come and offer thy gift to God."[3] Now the gift to God is every one's prayer and thanksgiving. If, therefore, thou hast anything against thy brother, or he has anything against thee, neither will thy prayers be heard, nor will thy thanksgivings be accepted, by reason of that hidden anger. But it is your duty, brethren, to pray continually. Yet, because God hears not those which are at enmity with their brethren by unjust quarrels, even though they should pray three times an hour, it is our duty to compose all our enmity and littleness of soul, that we may be able to pray with a pure and unpolluted heart. For the Lord commanded us to love even our enemies, and by no means to hate our friends. And the lawgiver says: "Thou shalt not hate any man; thou shalt not hate thy brother in thy mind. Thou shalt certainly reprove thy brother, and not incur sin on his account."[4] "Thou shalt not hate an Egyptian, for thou wast a sojourner with him. Thou shalt not hate an Idumæan, for he is thy brother."[5] And David says: "If I have repaid those that requited me evil."[6] Wherefore, if thou wilt be a Christian, follow the law of the Lord: "Loose every band of wickedness;"[7] for the Lord has given thee authority to remit those sins to thy brother which he has committed against thee as far as "seventy times seven,"[8] that is, four hundred and ninety times. How oft, therefore, hast thou remitted to thy brother, that thou art unwilling to do it now, when thou also hast heard Jeremiah saying, "Do not any of you impute the wickedness of his neighbour in your hearts?"[9]

[1] Ps. iv. 4.
[2] Prov. xii. 28, LXX.
[3] Matt. v. 23, 24.
[4] Lev. xix. 17.
[5] Deut. xxiii. 7.
[6] Ps. vii. 5.
[7] Isa. lviii. 6.
[8] Matt. xviii. 22.
[9] Zech. viii. 17.

But thou rememberest injuries, and keepest enmity, and comest into judgment, and art suspicious of His anger, and thy prayer is hindered. Nay, if thou hast remitted to thy brother four hundred and ninety times, do thou still multiply thy acts of gentleness more, to do good for thy own sake. Although he does not do so, yet, however, do thou endeavour to forgive thy brother for God's sake, "that thou mayest be the son of thy Father which is in heaven,"[1] and when thou prayest, mayest be heard as a friend of God.

LIV. Wherefore, O bishop, when you are to go to prayer after the lessons, and the psalmody, and the instruction out of the Scriptures, let the deacon stand nigh you, and with a loud voice say: Let none have any quarrel with another; let none come in hypocrisy; that if there be any controversy found among any of you, they may be affected in conscience, and may pray to God, and be reconciled to their brethren. For if, upon coming into any one's house, we are to say, "Peace be to this house,"[2] like sons of peace bestowing peace on those who are worthy, as it is written, "He came and preached peace to you that are nigh, and them that are far off, whom the Lord knows to be His,"[3] much more is it incumbent on those that enter into the church of God before all things to pray for the peace of God. But if he prays for it upon others, much more let himself be within the same, as a child of light; for he that has it not within himself is not fit to bestow it upon others. Wherefore, before all things, it is our duty to be at peace in our own minds; for he that does not find any disorder in himself will not quarrel with another, but will be peaceable, friendly, gathering the Lord's people, and a fellow-worker with Him, in order to the increasing the number of those that shall be saved in unanimity. For those who contrive enmities, and strifes, and contests, and lawsuits, are wicked, and aliens from God.

LV. For God, being a God of mercy from the beginning, called every generation to repentance by righteous men and prophets. He instructed those before the flood by Abel,

---

[1] Matt. v. 45. [2] Matt. x. 12.
[3] Isa. lvii. 19; Eph. ii. 7; 2 Tim. ii. 19.

and Sem, and Seth, also by Enos, and by Enoch that was translated; those at the flood by Noah; the inhabitants of Sodom by hospitable Lot; those after the flood by Melchizedek, and the patriarchs, and Job the beloved of God; the Egyptians by Moses; the Israelites by him, and Joshua, and Caleb, and Phineas, and the rest; those after the law by angels and prophets, and the same by His own incarnation [1] of the virgin; those a little before His bodily appearance by John His forerunner, and the same by the same person after Christ's birth, saying, "Repent ye, for the kingdom of heaven is at hand;"[2] those after His passion by us, the twelve apostles, and Paul the chosen vessel. We therefore, who have been vouchsafed the favour of being the witnesses of His appearance, together with James the brother of our Lord, and the other seventy-two disciples, and his seven deacons, have heard from the mouth of our Lord Jesus Christ, and by exact knowledge declare "what is the will of God, that good, and acceptable, and perfect will"[3] which is made known to us by Jesus; that none should perish, but that all men with one accord should believe in Him, and send unanimously praise to Him, and thereby live for ever.

LVI. For this is that which our Lord taught us when we pray to say to His Father, "Thy will be done, as in heaven, so upon earth;"[4] that as the heavenly natures of the incorporeal powers do all glorify God with one consent, so also upon earth all men with one mouth and one purpose may glorify the only, the one, and the true God, by Christ His only-begotten. It is therefore His will that men should praise Him with unanimity, and adore Him with one consent.[5] For this is His will in Christ, that those who are saved by Him may be many; but that you do not occasion any loss or diminution to Him, nor to the church, or lessen the number by one soul of man, as destroyed by you, which might have been saved by repentance; and which therefore perishes not only by its own sin, but also by your treachery

---

[1] One V. MS. inserts, " of the Holy Spirit and."
[2] Matt. i. 15.   [3] Rom. xii. 2.   [4] Matt. vi. 10.
[5] "And adore him with one consent" is omitted in one V. MS.

besides, whereby you fulfil that which is written, "He that gathereth not with me, scattereth."[1] Such an one is a disperser of the sheep, an adversary, an enemy of God, a destroyer of those lambs whose Shepherd was the Lord, and we were the collectors out of various nations and tongues, by much pains and danger, and perpetual labour, by watchings, by fastings, by lyings on the ground, by persecutions, by stripes, by imprisonments, that we might do the will of God, and fill the feast-chamber with guests to sit down at His table, that is, the holy and catholic church, with joyful and chosen people, singing hymns and praises to God that has called them by us to life. And you, as much as in you lies, have dispersed them. Do you also of the laity be at peace with one another, endeavouring like wise men to increase the church, and to turn back, and tame, and restore those which seem wild. For this is the greatest reward by His promise from God, "If thou fetch out the worthy and precious from the unworthy, thou shalt be as my mouth."[2]

SEC. VII.—*On assembling in the church.*

LVII. But be thou, O bishop, holy, unblameable, no striker, not soon angry, not cruel; but a builder up, a converter, apt to teach, forbearing of evil, of a gentle mind, meek, long-suffering, ready to exhort, ready to comfort, as a man of God.

When thou callest an assembly of the church as one that is the commander of a great ship, appoint the assemblies to be made with all possible skill, charging the deacons as mariners to prepare places for the brethren as for passengers, with all due care and decency. And first, let the building be long, with its head to the east, with its vestries on both sides at the east end, and so it will be like a ship. In the middle let the bishop's throne be placed, and on each side of him let the presbytery sit down; and let the deacons stand near at hand, in close and small girt garments, for they are like the mariners and managers of the ship: with regard to these, let the laity sit on the other side, with all

---

[1] Matt. xii. 30.   [2] Jer. xv. 19.

quietness and good order. And let the women sit by themselves, they also keeping silence. In the middle, let the reader stand upon some high place: let him read the books of Moses, of Joshua the son of Nun, of the Judges, and of the Kings and of the Chronicles, and those written after the return from the captivity; and besides these, the books of Job and of Solomon, and of the sixteen prophets. But when there have been two lessons severally read, let some other person sing the hymns of David, and let the people join at the conclusions of the verses. Afterwards let our Acts be read, and the Epistles of Paul our fellow-worker, which he sent to the churches under the conduct of the Holy Spirit; and afterwards let a deacon or a presbyter read the Gospels, both those which I Matthew and John have delivered to you, and those which the fellow-workers of Paul received and left to you, Luke and Mark. And while the Gospel is read, let all the presbyters and deacons, and all the people, stand up in great silence; for it is written: "Be silent, and hear, O Israel."[1] And again: "But do thou stand there, and hear."[2] In the next place, let the presbyters one by one, not all together, exhort the people, and the bishop in the last place, as being the commander. Let the porters stand at the entries of the men, and observe them. Let the deaconesses also stand at those of the women, like shipmen. For the same description and pattern was both in the tabernacle of the testimony and in the temple of God.[3] But if any one be found sitting out of his place, let him be rebuked by the deacon, as a manager of the foreship, and be removed into the place proper for him; for the church is not only like a ship, but also like a sheepfold. For as the shepherds place all the brute creatures distinctly, I mean goats and sheep, according to their kind and age, and still every one runs together, like to his like; so is it to be in the church. Let the young persons sit by themselves, if there be a place for them; if not, let them stand upright. But let those that

---

[1] Deut. xxvii. 9.   [2] Deut. v. 31.
[3] Deut. xxiii. 1. "And in the temple of God" is omitted in one V. MS.

are already stricken in years sit in order. For the children which stand, let their fathers and mothers take them to them. Let the younger women also sit by themselves, if there be a place for them; but if there be not, let them stand behind the women. Let those women which are married, and have children, be placed by themselves; but let the virgins, and the widows, and the elder women, stand or sit before all the rest; and let the deacon be the disposer of the places, that every one of those that comes in may go to his proper place, and may not sit at the entrance. In like manner, let the deacon oversee the people, that nobody may whisper, nor slumber, nor laugh, nor nod; for all ought in the church to stand wisely, and soberly, and attentively, having their attention fixed upon the word of the Lord. After this, let all rise up with one consent, and looking towards the east, after the catechumens and penitents are gone out, pray to God eastward, who ascended up to the heaven of heavens to the east; remembering also the ancient situation of paradise in the east, from whence the first man, when he had yielded to the persuasion of the serpent, and disobeyed the command of God, was expelled. As to the deacons, after the prayer is over, let some of them attend upon the oblation of the eucharist, ministering to the Lord's body with fear. Let others of them watch the multitude, and keep them silent. But let that deacon who is at the high priest's hand say to the people, Let no one have any quarrel against another; let no one come in hypocrisy. Then let the men give the men, and the women give the women, the Lord's kiss. But let no one do it with deceit, as Judas betrayed the Lord with a kiss. After this let the deacon pray for the whole church, for the whole world, and the several parts of it, and the fruits of it; for the priests and the rulers, for the high priest and the king, and the peace of the universe. After this let the high priest pray for peace upon the people, and bless them, as Moses commanded the priests to bless the people, in these words: "The Lord bless thee, and keep thee: the Lord make His face to shine upon thee,[1] and give thee peace."[2] Let the bishop pray for the people, and say: "Save Thy people, O Lord, and bless Thine inheritance, which Thou hast obtained with the precious blood of Thy Christ, and hast called a royal priesthood, and an holy nation."[3] After this let the sacrifice follow, the people standing, and praying silently; and when the oblation has been made, let every rank by itself partake of the Lord's body and precious blood in order, and approach with reverence and holy fear, as to the body of their king. Let the women approach with their heads covered, as is becoming the order of women; but let the door be watched, lest any unbeliever, or one not yet initiated, come in.

LVIII. If any brother, man or woman, come in from another parish, bringing recommendatory letters, let the deacon be the judge of that affair, inquiring whether they be of the faithful, and of the church? whether they be not defiled by heresy? and besides, whether the party be a married woman or a widow? And when he is satisfied in these questions, that they are really of the faithful, and of the same sentiments in the things of the Lord, let him conduct every one to the place proper for him. And if a presbyter comes from another parish, let him be received to communion by the presbyters; if a deacon, by the deacons; if a bishop, let him sit with the bishop, and be allowed the same honour with himself; and thou, O bishop, shalt desire him to speak to the people words of instruction: for the exhortation and admonition of strangers is very acceptable, and exceeding profitable. For, as the Scripture says, " no prophet is accepted in his own country."[4] Thou shalt also permit him to offer the eucharist; but if, out of reverence to thee, and as a wise man, to preserve the honour belonging to thee, he will not offer, at least thou shalt compel him to give the blessing to the people. But if, after the congregation is sat down, any other person comes upon you of good fashion and

---

[1] One V. MS. inserts, " and pity thee: the Lord lift His countenance upon thee."
[2] Num. vi. 24.   [3] Ps. xxviii. 8; Acts xx. 28; 1 Pet. i. 19, ii. 9.
[4] Luke iv. 24; John iv. 44.

character in the world, whether he be a stranger, or one of your own country, neither do thou, O bishop, if thou art speaking the word of God, or hearing him that sings or reads, accept persons so far as to leave the ministry of the word, that thou mayest appoint an upper place for him; but continue quiet, not interrupting thy discourse, nor thy attention. But let the brethren receive him by the deacons; and if there be not a place, let the deacon by speaking, but not in anger, raise the junior, and place the stranger there. And it is but reasonable that one that loves the brethren should do so of his own accord; but if he refuse, let him raise him up by force, and set him behind all, that the rest may be taught to give place to those that are more honourable. Nay, if a poor man, or one of a mean family, or a stranger, comes upon you, whether he be old or young, and there be no place, the deacon shall find a place for even these, and that with all his heart; that, instead of accepting persons before men, his ministration towards God may be well-pleasing. The very same thing let the deaconess do to those women, whether poor or rich, that come unto them.

LIX. When thou instructest the people, O bishop, command and exhort them to come constantly to church morning and evening every day, and by no means to forsake it on any account, but to assemble together continually; neither to diminish the church by withdrawing themselves, and causing the body of Christ to be without its member. For it is not only spoken concerning the priests, but let every one of the laity hearken to it as concerning himself, considering that it is said by the Lord: "He that is not with me is against me, and he that gathereth not with me scattereth abroad."[1] Do not you therefore scatter yourselves abroad, who are the members of Christ, by not assembling together, since you have Christ your Head, according to His promise, present, and communicating to you.[2] Be not careless of yourselves, neither deprive your Saviour of His own members, neither divide His body nor disperse His members, neither prefer the occasions of this life to the word of God;

[1] Matt. xii. 30.   [2] Matt. xxviii. 30.

but assemble yourselves together every day, morning and evening, singing psalms and praying in the Lord's house: in the morning saying the sixty-second Psalm, and in the evening the hundred and fortieth, but principally on the Sabbath-day. And on the day of our Lord's resurrection, which is the Lord's day, meet more diligently, sending praise to God that made the universe by Jesus, and sent Him to us, and condescended to let Him suffer, and raised Him from the dead. Otherwise what apology will he make to God who does not assemble on that day to hear the saving word concerning the resurrection, on which we pray thrice standing, in memory of Him who arose in three days, in which is performed the reading of the prophets, the preaching of the gospel, the oblation of the sacrifice, the gift of the holy food?

LX. And how can he be other than an adversary to God, who takes pains about temporary things night and day, but takes no care of things eternal? who takes care of washings and temporary food every day, but does not take care of those that endure for ever? How can such an one even now avoid hearing that word of the Lord, "The Gentiles are justified more than you?"[1] as He says, by way of reproach, to Jerusalem, "Sodom is justified rather than thou." For if the Gentiles every day, when they arise from sleep, run to their idols to worship them, and before all their work and all their labours do first of all pray to them, and in their feasts and in their solemnities do not keep away, but attend upon them; and not only those upon the place, but those living far distant do the same; and in their public shows all come together, as into a synagogue: in the same manner those which are vainly called Jews, when they have worked six days, on the seventh day rest, and come together into their synagogue, never leaving nor neglecting either rest from labour or assembling together, while yet they are deprived of the efficacy of the word in their unbelief, nay, and of the force of that name Judah, by which they call themselves,—for Judah is interpreted "confession,"—but these do not confess to God (having unjustly occasioned the suf-

[1] Ezek. xvi. 52.

fering on the cross), so as to be saved on their repentance;
—if, therefore, those who are not saved frequently assemble
together for such purposes as do not profit them, what apology
wilt thou make to the Lord God who forsakest His church,
not imitating so much as the heathen, but by such thy absence
growest slothful, or turnest apostate, or actest wickedness?
To whom the Lord says by Jeremiah: "Ye have not kept
my ordinances; nay, ye have not walked according to the
ordinances of the heathen, and you have in a manner exceeded them."[1] And again: "Israel has justified his soul
more than treacherous Judah."[2] And afterwards: "Will
the Gentiles change their gods which are not gods?[3] Wherefore pass over to the isles of Chittim, and behold, and send
to Kedar, and observe diligently whether such things have
been done. For those nations have not changed their ordinances; but," says He, "my people has changed its glory
for that which will not profit."[4] How, therefore, will any one
make his apology who has despised or absented himself from
the church of God?

LXI. But if any one allege the pretence of his own
work, and so is a despiser, "offering pretences for his sins,"
let such an one know that the trades of the faithful are
works by the by, but the worship of God is their great work.
Follow therefore your trades as by the by, for your maintenance, but make the worship of God your main business;
as also our Lord said: "Labour not for the meat which
perishes, but for that which endureth unto everlasting life."[5]
And again: "This is the work of God, that ye believe on
Him whom He hath sent."[6] Endeavour therefore never to
leave the church of God; but if any one overlooks it, and
goes either into a polluted temple of the heathens, or into a
synagogue of the Jews or heretics, what apology will such an
one make to God in the day of judgment, who has forsaken
the oracles of the living God, and the living and quickening

[1] Ezek. v. 7, xvi. 47.   [2] Jer. iii. 11.
[3] One V. MS. inserts here, "and elsewhere through another."
[4] Jer. ii. 11, 10.
[5] John vi. 27.   [6] John vi. 29.

oracles, such as are able to deliver from eternal punishment, and has gone into an house of demons, or into a synagogue of the murderers of Christ, or the congregation of the wicked?—not hearkening unto him that says: "I have hated the congregation of the wicked, and I will not enter with the ungodly. I have not sat with the assembly of vanity, neither will I sit with the ungodly."[1] And again: "Blessed is the man that hath not walked in the counsel of the ungodly, nor stood in the way of sinners, and hath not sat in the seat of the scornful; but his delight is in the law of the Lord, and in His law will he meditate day and night."[2] But thou, forsaking the gathering together of the faithful, the church of God, and His laws, hast respect to those "dens of thieves," calling those things holy which He has called profane, and making such things unclean which He has sanctified. And not only so, but thou already runnest after the pomps of the Gentiles, and hastenest to their theatres, being desirous to be reckoned one of those that enter into them, and to partake of unseemly, not to say abominable words; not hearkening to Jeremiah, who says, "O Lord, I have not sat in their assemblies, for they are scorners; but I was afraid because of Thy hand;"[3] nor to Job, who speaks in like manner, "If I have gone at any time with the scornful; for I shall be weighed in a just balance."[4] But why wilt thou be a partaker of the heathen oracles, which are nothing but dead men declaring by the inspiration of the devil deadly things, and such as tend to subvert the faith, and to draw those that attend to them to polytheism? Do you therefore, who attend to the laws of God, esteem those laws more honourable than the necessities of this life, and pay a greater respect to them, and run together to the church of the Lord, "which He has purchased with the blood of Christ, the beloved, the first-born of every creature."[5] For this church is the daughter of the Highest, which has been in travail of you by the word of grace, and has "formed Christ in you," of whom you are made partakers, and thereby become His holy and

[1] Ps. xxvi. 5, 4.   [2] Ps. i. 1.   [3] Jer. xv. 17.
[4] Job xxxi. 5.   [5] *Vid.* Acts xx. 28; Col. i. 15.

chosen members, "not having spot or wrinkle, or any such thing; but as being holy and unspotted in the faith, ye are complete in Him, after the image of God that created you."[1]

LXII. Take heed, therefore, not to join yourselves in your worship with those that perish, which is the assembly of the Gentiles, to your deceit and destruction. For there is no fellowship between God and the devil; for he that assembles himself with those that favour the things of the devil, will be esteemed one of them, and will inherit a woe. Avoid also indecent spectacles: I mean the theatres and the pomps of the heathens; their enchantments, observations of omens, soothsayings, purgations, divinations, observations of birds; their necromancies and invocations. For it is written: "There is no divination in Jacob, nor soothsaying in Israel."[2] And again: "Divination is iniquity."[3] And elsewhere: "Ye shall not be soothsayers, and follow observers of omens, nor diviners, nor dealers with familiar spirits. Ye shall not preserve alive wizards."[4] Wherefore Jeremiah exhorts, saying: "Walk ye not according to the ways of the heathen, and be not afraid of the signs of heaven."[5] So that it is the duty of a believer to avoid the assemblies of the ungodly, of the heathen, and of the Jews, and of the rest of the heretics, lest by uniting ourselves to them we bring snares upon our own souls; that we may not by joining in their feasts, which are celebrated in honour of demons, be partakers with them in their impiety. You are also to avoid their public meetings, and those sports which are celebrated in them. For a believer ought not to go to any of those public meetings, unless to purchase a slave, and save a soul, and at the same time to buy such other things as suit their necessities. Abstain, therefore, from all idolatrous pomp and state, all their public meetings, banquets, duels, and all shows belonging to demons.

SEC. VIII.—*On the duty of working for a livelihood.*

LXIII. Let the young persons of the church endeavour

[1] Eph. v. 27. [2] Num. xxiii. 23. [3] 1 Sam. xv. 23, LXX.
[4] Lev. xix. 26; Deut. xviii. 10. [5] Jer. x. 2.

to minister diligently in all necessaries: mind your business with all becoming seriousness, that so you may always have sufficient to support yourselves and those that are needy, and not burden the church of God. For we ourselves, besides our attention to the word of the gospel, do not neglect our inferior employments. For some of us are fishermen, some tentmakers, some husbandmen, that so we may never be idle. So says Solomon somewhere: " Go to the ant, thou sluggard; consider her ways diligently, and become wiser than she. For she, having neither field, overseer, nor ruler, prepareth her food in the summer, and layeth up a great store in the harvest. Or else go to the bee, and learn how laborious she is, and her work how valuable it is, whose labours both kings and mean men make use of for their health. She is desirable and glorious, though she be weak in strength, yet by honouring wisdom she is improved, etc. How long wilt thou lie on thy bed, O sluggard? When wilt thou awake out of thy sleep? Thou sleepest awhile, thou liest down awhile, thou slumberest awhile, thou foldest thy hands on thy breast to sleep awhile. Then poverty comes on thee like an evil traveller, and want as a swift racer. But if thou beest diligent, thy harvest shall come as a fountain, and want shall fly from thee as an evil runagate."[1] And again: " He that manageth his own land shall be filled with bread."[2] And elsewhere he says: " The slothful has folded his own hands together, and has eaten his own flesh."[3] And afterwards: " The sluggard hides his hand; he will not be able to bring it to his mouth."[4] And again: " By slothfulness of the hands a floor will be brought low."[5] Labour therefore continually; for the blot of the slothful is not to be healed. But " if any one does not work, let not such an one eat"[6] among you. For the Lord our God hates the slothful. For no one of those who are dedicated to God ought to be idle.

[1] Prov. vi. 6, etc., LXX.
[2] Prov. xii. 11.
[3] Eccles. iv. 5.
[4] Prov. xix. 24.
[5] Eccles. x. 18.
[6] 2 Thess. iii. 10.

BOOK III.

SEC. I.—*Concerning widows.*

I. Choose your "widows not under sixty years of age,"[1] that in some measure the suspicion of a second marriage may be prevented by their age. But if you admit one younger into the order of widows, and she cannot bear her widowhood in her youth, and marries, she will procure indecent reflections on the glory of the order of the widows, and shall give an account to God; not because she married a second time, but because she has "waxed wanton against Christ,"[2] and not kept her promise, [because she did not come and keep her promise with faith and the fear of God.[3]] Wherefore such a promise ought not to be rashly made, but with great caution: "for it is better for her not to vow, than to vow and not to pay."[4] But if any younger woman, who has lived but a while with her husband, and has lost him by death or some other occasion, and remains by herself, having the gift of widowhood, she will be found to be blessed, and to be like the widow of Sarepta, belonging to Sidon, with whom the holy prophet of God, Elijah,[5] lodged. Such an one may also be compared to "Anna, the daughter of Phanuel, of the tribe of Aser, which departed not from the temple, but continued in supplications and prayers night and day, who was fourscore years old, and had lived with an husband seven years from her virginity, who glorified the coming of Christ, and gave thanks to the Lord, and spake concerning Him to all those who looked for redemption in Israel."[6] Such a widow will have a good report, and will be honoured, having both glory with men upon earth, and eternal praise with God in heaven.

II. But let not the younger widows be placed in the order of widows, lest, under pretence of inability to contain in the flower of their age, they come to a second marriage, and become subject to imputation. But let them be assisted and

[1] *Vid.* 1 Tim. v. 9.   [2] 1 Tim. v. 11.   [3] Not in one V. MS.
[4] Eccles. v. 4.   [5] 1 Kings xvii. 9.   [6] Luke ii. 36.

supported, that so they may not, under pretence of being deserted, come to a second marriage, and so be ensnared in an unseemly imputation. For you ought to know this, that once marrying according to the law is righteous, as being according to the will of God; but second marriages, after the promise, are wicked, not on account of the marriage itself, but because of the falsehood. Third marriages are indications of incontinency. But such marriages as are beyond the third are manifest fornication, and unquestionable uncleanness. For God in the creation gave one woman to one man; for " they two shall be one flesh."[1] But to the younger women let a second marriage be allowed after the death of their first husband, lest they fall into the condemnation of the devil, and many snares, and foolish lusts, which are hurtful to souls, and which bring upon them punishment rather than rest.

III. But the true widows are those which have had only one husband, having a good report among the generality for good works; widows indeed, sober, chaste, faithful, pious, who have brought up their children well, and have entertained strangers unblameably, which are to be supported as devoted to God. Besides, do thou, O bishop, be mindful of the needy, both reaching out thy helping hand and making provision for them as the steward of God, distributing seasonably the oblations to every one of them, to the widows, the orphans, the friendless, and those tried with affliction.

IV. For what if some are neither widows nor widowers, but stand in need of assistance, either through poverty or some disease, or the maintenance of a great number of children? It is thy duty to oversee all people, and to take care of them all. For they that give gifts do not of their own head give them to the widows, but barely bring them in, calling them free-will offerings, that so thou that knowest those that are in affliction mayest as a good steward give them their portion of the gift. For God knows the giver, though thou distributest it to those in want when he is absent. And he has the reward of well-doing, but thou

[1] Gen. ii. 24.

the blessedness of having dispensed it with a good conscience. But do thou tell them who was the giver, that they may pray for him by name. For it is our duty to do good to all men, not fondly preferring one or another, whoever they be. For the Lord says: "Give to every one that asketh of thee."[1] It is evident that it is meant of every one that is really in want, whether he be friend or foe, whether he be a kinsman or a stranger, whether he be single or married. For in all the Scripture the Lord gives us exhortations about the needy, saying first by Isaiah: "Deal thy bread to the hungry, and bring the poor which have no covering into thine house. If thou seest the naked, do thou cover him; and thou shalt not overlook those which are of thine own family and seed."[2] And then by Daniel He says to the potentate: "Wherefore, O king, let my counsel please thee, and purge thy sins by acts of mercy, and thine iniquities by bowels of compassion to the needy."[3] And He says by Solomon: "By acts of mercy and of faith iniquities are purged."[4] And He says again by David: "Blessed is he that has regard to the poor and needy; the Lord shall deliver him in the evil day."[5] And again: "He hath dispersed abroad, he hath given to the needy, his righteousness remaineth for ever."[6] And Solomon says: "He that hath mercy on the poor lendeth to the Lord;[7] according to his gift it shall be repaid him again."[8] And afterwards: "He that stoppeth his ear, that he may not hear him that is in want, he also shall call himself, and there shall be none to hear him."[9]

V. Let every widow be meek, quiet, gentle, sincere, free from anger, not talkative, not clamorous, not hasty of speech, not given to evil-speaking, not captious, not double-tongued, not a busybody. If she see or hear anything that is not right, let her be as one that does not see, and as one that does not hear. And let the widow mind nothing but to pray for those that give, and for the whole church; and when she

---

[1] Luke vi. 30. [2] Isa. lviii. 7. [3] Dan. iv. 24.
[4] Prov. xv. 27. [5] Ps. xli. 2. [6] Ps. cxii. 9.
[7] Instead of "Lord," one V. ms. reads "God." [8] Prov. xix. 17.
[9] Prov. xxi. 13.

is asked anything by any one, let her not easily answer, excepting questions concerning the faith, and righteousness, and hope in God, remitting those that desire to be instructed in the doctrines of godliness to the governors. Let her only answer so as may tend to the subversion of the error of polytheism, and let her demonstrate the assertion concerning the monarchy of God. But of the remaining doctrines let her not answer anything rashly, lest by saying anything unlearnedly she should make the word to be blasphemed. For the Lord has taught us that the word is like "a grain of mustard seed,"[1] which is of a fiery nature, which if any one uses unskilfully, he will find it bitter. For in the mystical points we ought not to be rash, but cautious; for the Lord exhorts us, saying: "Cast not your pearls before swine, lest they trample them with their feet, and turn again and rend you."[2] For unbelievers, when they hear the doctrine concerning Christ not explained as it ought to be, but defectively, and especially that concerning His incarnation or His passion, will rather reject it with scorn, and laugh at it as false, than praise God for it. And so the aged women will be guilty of rashness, and of causing blasphemy, and will inherit a woe. For says He, "Woe to him by whom my name is blasphemed among the Gentiles."[3]

VI. We do not permit our "women to teach in the church,"[4] but only to pray and hear those that teach; for our Master and Lord, Jesus Himself, when He sent us the twelve to make disciples of the people and of the nations, did nowhere send out women to preach, although He did not want such. For there were with us the mother of our Lord and His sisters; also Mary Magdalene, and Mary the mother of James, and Martha and Mary the sisters of Lazarus; Salome, and certain others. For, had it been necessary for women to teach, He Himself had first commanded these also to instruct the people with us. For "if the head of the wife be the man,"[5] it is not reasonable that the rest of the body should govern the head. Let the

[1] Matt. xiii. 31.   [2] Matt. vii. 6.   [3] Isa. lii. 5.
[4] 1 Cor. xiv. 34.   [5] 1 Cor. xi. 3.

widow therefore own herself to be the "altar of God," and
let her sit in her house, and not enter into the houses of the
faithful, under any pretence, to receive anything; for the
altar of God never runs about, but is fixed in one place.
Let, therefore, the virgin and the widow be such as do not
run about, or gad to the houses of those who are alien from
the faith. For such as these are gadders and impudent:
they do not make their feet to rest in one place, because they
are not widows, but purses ready to receive, triflers, evil-
speakers, counsellors of strife, without shame, impudent, who
being such, are not worthy of Him that called them. For
they do not come to the common station of the congregation
on the Lord's day,[1] as those that are watchful; but either
they slumber, or trifle, or allure men, or beg, or ensnare
others, bringing them to the evil one; not suffering them to
be watchful in the Lord, but taking care that they go out as
vain as they came in, because they do not hear the word of
the Lord either taught or read. For of such as these the
prophet Isaiah says: "Hearing ye shall hear, and shall not
understand; and seeing ye shall see, and not perceive: for
the heart of this people is waxen gross,[2] [and they hear
heavily with their ears."[3]]

VII. In the same manner, therefore, the ears of the hearts
of such widows as these are stopped, that they will not sit
within in their cottages to speak to the Lord, but will run
about with the design of getting, and by their foolish prattling
fulfil the desires of the adversary. Such widows, therefore,
are not affixed to the altar of Christ: for there are some
widows which esteem gain their business; and since they
ask without shame, and receive without being satisfied, render
the generality more backward in giving. For when they
ought to be content with their subsistence from the church,
as having moderate desires, on the contrary, they run from
one of their neighbours' houses[4] to another, and disturb

[1] "On the Lord's day" not in one V. MS. [2] Isa. vi. 9.
[3] Inserted from one V. MS.
[4] Probably the reading should be, "they go round the houses of the
rich."

them, heaping up to themselves plenty of money, and lend at bitter usury, and are only solicitous about mammon, whose bag is their god; who prefer eating and drinking before all virtue, saying, "Let us eat and drink, for to-morrow we die;"[1] who esteem these things as if they were durable and not perishing things. For she that uses herself to nothing but talking of money, worships mammon instead of God,—that is, is a servant to gain, but cannot be pleasing to God, nor resigned to His worship; not being able to intercede with Him continuously on account that her mind and disposition run after money: for "where the treasure is, there will the heart be also."[2] For she is thinking in her mind whither she may go to receive, or that a certain woman her friend has forgot her, and she has somewhat to say to her. She that thinks of such things as these will no longer attend to her prayers, but to that thought which offers itself; so that though sometimes she would pray for anybody, she will not be heard, because she does not offer her petition to the Lord with her whole heart, but with a divided mind. But she that will attend to God will sit within, and mind the things of the Lord day and night, offering her sincere petition with a mouth ready to utter the same without ceasing. As therefore Judith, most famous for her wisdom, and of a good report for her modesty, "prayed to God night and day for Israel;"[3] so also the widow who is like to her will offer her intercession without ceasing for the church to God. And He will hear her, because her mind is fixed on this thing alone, and is not disposed to be either insatiable, or covetous, or expensive; when her eye is pure, and her hearing clean, and her hands undefiled, and her feet quiet, and her mouth prepared for neither gluttony nor trifling, but speaking the things that are fit, and partaking of only such things as are necessary for her maintenance. So, being grave, and giving no disturbance, she will be pleasing to God; and as soon as she asks anything, the gift will come to her: as He says, "While thou art speaking, I will say,

[1] Isa. xxii. 13; 1 Cor. xv. 32.   [2] Matt. vi. 21.
[3] Judith ix. 12.

Behold, I am here."[1] Let such an one also be free from the love of money, free from arrogance, not given to filthy lucre, not insatiable, not gluttonous, but continent, meek, giving nobody disturbance, pious, modest, sitting at home, singing, and praying, and reading, and watching, and fasting; speaking to God continually in songs and hymns. And let her take wool, and rather assist others than herself want from them; being mindful of that widow who is honoured in the Gospel with the Lord's testimony, who, coming into the temple, "cast into the treasury two mites, which make a farthing. And Christ our Lord and Master, and Searcher of hearts, saw her, and said, Verily I say unto you, that this widow hath cast into the treasury more than they all: for all they have cast in of their abundance, but this woman of her penury hath cast in all the living that she had."[2]

The widows therefore ought to be grave, obedient to their bishops, and their presbyters, and their deacons, and besides these to the deaconesses, with piety, reverence, and fear; not usurping authority, nor desiring to do anything beyond the constitution without the consent of the deacon: as, suppose, the going to any one to eat or drink with him, or to receive anything from anybody. But if without direction she does any one of these things, let her be punished with fasting, or else let her be separated on account of her rashness.

VIII. For how does such an one know of what character the person is from whom she receives? or from what sort of ministration he supplies her with food, whether it does not arise from rapine or some other ill course of life? while the widow does not remember that if she receives in a way unworthy of God, she must give an account for every one of these things. For neither will the priests at any time receive a free-will offering from such an one, as, suppose, from a rapacious person or from a harlot. For it is written, "Thou shalt not covet the goods that are thy neighbour's;"[3] and, "Thou shalt not offer the hire of an harlot to the Lord God."[4] From such as these no offerings ought to be accepted, nor

[1] Isa. lviii. 9. [2] Mark xii. 43; Luke xxi. 3.
[3] Ex. xx. 17. [4] Deut. xxiii. 18.

indeed from those that are separated from the church. Let the widows also be ready to obey the commands given them by their superiors, and let them do according to the appointment of the bishop, being obedient to him as to God; for he that receives from such an one who is worthy of blame, or from one excommunicated, and prays for him, while he purposes to go on in a wicked course, and while he is not willing at any time to repent, holds communion with him in prayer, and grieves Christ, who rejects the unrighteous, and confirms them by means of the unworthy gift, and is defiled with them, not suffering them to come to repentance, so as to fall down before God with lamentation, and pray to Him.

IX. Now, as to women's baptizing, we let you know that there is no small peril to those that undertake it. Therefore we do not advise you to it; for it is dangerous, or rather wicked and impious. For if the "man be the head of the woman,"[1] and he be originally ordained for the priesthood, it is not just to abrogate the order of the creation, and leave the principal to come to the extreme part of the body. For the woman is the body of the man, taken from his side, and subject to him, from whom she was separated for the procreation of children. For says He, "He shall rule over thee."[2] For the principal part of the woman is the man, as being her head. But if in the foregoing constitutions we have not permitted them to teach, how will any one allow them, contrary to nature, to perform the office of a priest? For this is one of the ignorant practices of the Gentile atheism, to ordain women priests to the female deities, not one of the constitutions of Christ. For if baptism were to be administered by women, certainly our Lord would have been baptized by His own mother, and not by John; or when He sent us to baptize, He would have sent along with us women also for this purpose. But now He has nowhere, either by constitution or by writing, delivered to us any such thing; as knowing the order of nature, and the decency of the action; as being the Creator of nature, and the Legislator of the constitution.

[1] 1 Cor. xi. 3.   [2] Gen. iii. 16.

X. Neither do we permit the laity to perform any of the offices belonging to the priesthood; as, for instance, neither the sacrifice, nor baptism, nor the laying on of hands, nor the blessing, whether the smaller or the greater: for "no one taketh this honour to himself, but he that is called of God."[1] For such sacred offices are conferred by the laying on of the hands of the bishop. But a person to whom such an office is not committed, but he seizes upon it for himself, he shall undergo the punishment of Uzziah.[2]

XI. Nay, further, we do not permit to the rest of the clergy to baptize,—as, for instance, neither to readers, nor singers, nor porters, nor ministers,—but to the bishops and presbyters alone, yet so that the deacons are to minister to them therein. But those who venture upon it shall undergo the punishment of the companions of Corah.[3] We do not permit presbyters to ordain deacons, or deaconesses, or readers, or ministers, or singers, or porters, but only bishops; for this is the ecclesiastical order and harmony.

XII. Now, as concerning envy, or jealousy, or evil-speaking, or strife, or the love of contention, we have said already to you, that these are alien from a Christian, and chiefly in the case of widows. But because the devil, who works in men, is in his conduct cunning, and full of various devices, he goes to those that are not truly widows, as formerly to Cain (for some say they are widows, but do not perform the injunctions agreeable to the widowhood; as neither did Cain discharge the duties due to a brother: for they do not consider how it is not the name of widowhood that will bring them to the kingdom of God, but true faith and holy[4] works). But if any one possesses the name of widowhood, but does the works of the adversary, her widowhood will not be imputed, but she will be thrust out of the kingdom, and delivered to eternal punishment. For we hear that some widows are jealous, envious calumniators, and envious at the quiet of others. Such widows as these are not the disciples of Christ, nor of His doctrine; for it becomes them, when

---

[1] Heb. v. 4.   [2] 2 Chron. xxvi.   [3] Num. xvi.
[4] Instead of "holy," one V. MS. reads "divine."

one of their fellow-widows is clothed by any one, or receives money, or meat, or drink, or shoes, at the sight of the refreshment of their sister to say:

XIII. Thou art blessed, O God, who hast refreshed my fellow-widow. Bless, O Lord, and glorify him that has bestowed these things upon her, and let his good work ascend in truth to Thee, and remember him for good in the day of his visitation. And as for my bishop, who [has so well performed his duty to Thee, and [1]] has ordered such a seasonable alms to be bestowed on my fellow-widow, who was naked, do Thou increase his [glory, and give him a [1]] crown of rejoicing in the day of the revelation of Thy visitation. In the same manner, let the widow who has received the alms join with the other in praying for him who ministered to her.

XIV. But if any woman has been good, let her, as a prudent person, conceal her own name, not sounding a trumpet before her, that her alms may be with God in secret, as the Lord says: "Thou, when thou doest thine alms, let not thy left hand know what thy right hand doth, that thine alms may be in secret."[2] And let the widow pray for him that gave her the alms, whosoever he be, as being the holy altar of Christ;[3] and "the Father, who seeth in secret, will render to him that did good openly." But those widows which will not live according to the command of God, are solicitous and inquisitive what deaconess it is that gives the charity, and what widows receive it. And when she has learned those things, she murmurs at the deaconess who distributed the charity, saying, Dost not thou see that I am in more distress, and want of thy charity? Why, therefore, hast thou preferred her before me? She says these things foolishly, not understanding that this does not depend on the will of man, but the appointment of God. For if she is herself a witness that she was nearer, and, upon inquiry, was in greater want, and more naked than the other, she ought to understand who it is that made this constitution,

---

[1] Not in one V. MS.   [2] Matt. vi. 2, 3, 4.
[3] Instead of "Christ," one V. MS. reads " of God."

and to hold her peace, and not to murmur at the deaconess who distributed the charity, but to enter into her own house, and to cast herself prostrate on her face to make supplication to God that her sin may be forgiven her. For God commanded the deaconess who brought the charity not to proclaim the same, and this widow murmured because she did not publish her name, that so she might know it, and run to receive; nay, did not only murmur, but also cursed her, forgetting Him that said: "He that blesseth thee is blessed, and he that curseth thee is cursed."[1] But the Lord says: "When ye enter into an house, say, Peace be to this house. And if the son of peace be there, your peace shall rest upon it; but if it be not worthy, your peace shall return to you."[2]

XV. If, therefore, peace returns upon those that sent it, nay, upon those that before had actually given it, because it did not find persons fit to receive it, much rather will a curse return upon the head of him that unjustly sent it, because he to whom it was sent was not worthy to receive it: for all those who abuse others without a cause curse themselves, as Solomon says: "As birds and sparrows fly away, so the curse causeless shall not come upon any one."[3] And again he says: "Those that bring reproaches are exceeding foolish."[4] But as the bee, a creature as to its strength feeble, if she stings any one, loses her sting, and becomes a drone; in the same manner you also, whatsoever injustice you do to others, will bring it upon yourselves. "He hath graven and digged a pit, and he shall fall into the same ditch that he has made."[5] And again: "He that diggeth a pit for his neighbour, shall fall into it."[6] Wherefore he that avoids a curse, let him not curse another; for "what thou hatest should be done to thee, do not thou to another."[7] Wherefore admonish the widows that are feeble-minded, strengthen those of them that are weak, and praise such of them as walk in holiness. Let them rather bless, and not calumniate. Let them make peace, and not stir up contention.

[1] Gen. xxvii. 29.
[2] Luke x. 5; Matt. x. 13.
[3] Prov. xxvi. 2.
[4] Prov. x. 18.
[5] Ps. vii. 16.
[6] Prov. xxvi. 27.
[7] Tob. iv. 16.

SEC. II.—*On deacons and deaconesses, the rest of the clergy, and on baptism.*

Let not therefore either a bishop, or a presbyter, or a deacon, or any one else of the sacerdotal catalogue, defile his tongue with calumny, lest he inherit a curse instead of a blessing; and let it also be the bishop's business and care that no lay person utter any curse: for he ought to take care of all, —of the clergy, of the virgins, of the widows, of the laity. For which reason, O bishop, do thou ordain thy fellow-workers, the labourers for life and for righteousness, such deacons as are pleasing to God, such whom thou provest to be worthy among all the people, and such as shall be ready for the necessities of their ministration. Ordain also a deaconess who is faithful and holy, for the ministrations towards women. For sometimes he cannot send a deacon, who is a man, to the women, on account of unbelievers. Thou shalt therefore send a woman, a deaconess, on account of the imaginations of the bad. For we stand in need of a woman, a deaconess, for many necessities; and first in the baptism of women, the deacon shall anoint only their forehead with the holy oil, and after him the deaconess shall anoint them: for there is no necessity that the women should be seen by the men; but only in the laying on of hands the bishop shall anoint her head, as the priests and kings were formerly anointed, not because those which are now baptized are ordained priests, but as being Christians, or anointed, from Christ the Anointed, "a royal priesthood, and an holy nation, the church of God, the pillar and ground of the marriage-chamber,"[1] who formerly were not a people, but now are beloved and chosen, upon whom is called His new name,[2] as Isaiah the prophet witnesses, saying: "And they shall call the people by His new name, which the Lord shall name for them."[3]

[1] 1 Pet. ii. 9; 1 Tim. iii. 15.
[2] The words from "upon whom" to the end of the chapter are omitted in one V. MS.
[3] Isa. lxii. 2.

XVI. Thou therefore, O bishop, according to that type, shalt anoint the head of those that are to be baptized, whether they be men or women, with the holy oil, for a type of the spiritual baptism. After that, either thou, O bishop, or a presbyter that is under thee, shall in the solemn form name over them the Father, and Son, and Holy Spirit, and shall dip them in the water; and let a deacon receive the man, and a deaconess the woman, that so the conferring of this inviolable seal may take place with a becoming decency. And after that, let the bishop anoint those that are baptized with ointment.

XVII. This baptism, therefore, is given into the death of Jesus:[1] the water is instead of the burial, and the oil instead of the Holy Ghost; the seal instead of the cross; the ointment is the confirmation of the confession; the mention of the Father as of the Author and Sender; the joint mention of the Holy Ghost as of the witness; the descent into the water the dying together with Christ; the ascent out of the water the rising again with Him. The Father is the God over all; Christ is the only-begotten God, the beloved Son, the Lord of glory; the Holy Ghost is the Comforter, who is sent by Christ, and taught by Him, and proclaims Him.

XVIII. But let him that is to be baptized be free from all iniquity; one that has left off to work sin, the friend of God, the enemy of the devil, the heir of God the Father, the fellow-heir of His Son; one that has renounced Satan, and the demons, and Satan's deceits; chaste, pure, holy, beloved of God, the son of God, praying as a son to his father, and saying, as from the common congregation of the faithful, thus: "Our Father, which art in heaven, hallowed be Thy name; Thy kingdom come; Thy will be done on earth, as it is in heaven; give us this day our daily bread; and forgive us our debts as we forgive our debtors; and lead us not into temptation, but deliver us from the evil one: for Thine is the kingdom, and the power, and the glory for ever. Amen."[2]

XIX. Let the deacons be in all things unspotted, as the

---

[1] *Vid.* Rom. vi. 3.   [2] Matt. vi. 9, etc.

bishop himself is to be, only more active; in number according to the largeness of the church, that they may minister to the infirm as workmen that are not ashamed. And let the deaconess be diligent in taking care of the women; but both of them ready to carry messages, to travel about, to minister, and to serve, as spake Isaiah concerning the Lord, saying: "To justify the righteous, who serves many faithfully."[1] Let every one therefore know his proper place, and discharge it diligently with one consent, with one mind, as knowing the reward of their ministration; but let them not be ashamed to minister to those that are in want, as even our "Lord Jesus Christ came not to be ministered unto, but to minister, and to give His life a ransom for many."[2] So therefore ought they also to do, and not to scruple it, if they should be obliged to lay down their life for a brother. For the Lord and our Saviour Jesus Christ did not scruple to "lay down His life," as Himself says, "for His friends."[3] If, therefore, the Lord of heaven and earth underwent all His sufferings for us, how then do you make a difficulty to minister to such as are in want, who ought to imitate Him who underwent servitude, and want, and stripes, and the cross for us? We ought therefore also to serve the brethren, in imitation of Christ. For says He: "He that will be great among you, let him be your minister; and he that will be first among you, let him be your servant."[4] For so did He really, and not in word only, fulfil the prediction of, "Serving many faithfully."[5] For "when He had taken a towel, He girded Himself. Afterward He puts water into a bason; and as we were sitting at meat, He came and washed the feet of us all, and wiped them with the towel."[6] By doing this He demonstrated to us His kindness and brotherly affection, that so we also might do the same to one another. If, therefore, our Lord and Master so humbled Himself, how can you, the labourers of the truth, and administrators of piety, be ashamed to do the same to such of the brethren as are weak and infirm? Minister therefore with a kind mind, not murmur-

[1] Isa. liii. 11, LXX.   [2] Matt. xx. 28.   [3] John x. 15, xv. 13.
[4] Matt. xx. 26.   [5] Isa. liii. 11.   [6] John xiii. 4.

ing nor mutinying; for ye do not do it on the account of man, but on the account of God, and shall receive from Him the reward of your ministry in the day of your visitation. It is your duty who are deacons to visit all those who stand in need of visitation. And tell your bishop of all those that are in affliction; for you ought to be like his soul and senses —active [and attentive in all things to him[1]] as to your bishop, [and father,[1]] and master.

XX. We command that a bishop be ordained by three bishops, or at least by two; but it is not lawful that he be set over you by one; for the testimony of two or three witnesses is more firm and secure. But a presbyter and a deacon are to be ordained by one bishop and the rest of the clergy. Nor must either a presbyter or a deacon ordain from the laity into the clergy; but the presbyter is only to teach, to offer, to baptize, to bless the people, and the deacon is to minister to the bishop, and to the presbyters, that is, to do the office of a ministering deacon, but not to meddle with the other offices.

BOOK IV.

Sec. I.—*On helping the poor.*

I. When any Christian becomes an orphan, whether it be a young man or a maid, it is good that some one of the brethren who is without a child should take the young man, and esteem him in the place of a son; and he that has a son about the same age, and that is marriageable, should marry the maid to him: for they which do so perform a great work, and become fathers to the orphans, and shall receive the reward of this charity from the Lord God. But if any one that walks in the way of man-pleasing is rich, and therefore is ashamed of orphans, the Father of orphans and Judge of widows will make provision for the orphans, but himself shall have such an heir as will spend what he has spared; and it

---

[1] The portions within brackets are not in one V. ms.

shall happen to him according as it is said: "What things the holy people have not eaten, those shall the Assyrians eat." As also Isaiah says: "Your land, strangers devour it in your presence."[1]

II. Do you therefore, O bishops, be solicitous about their maintenance, being in nothing wanting to them; exhibiting to the orphans the care of parents; to the widows the care of husbands; to those of suitable age, marriage; to the artificer, work; to the unable, commiseration; to the strangers, an house; to the hungry, food; to the thirsty, drink; to the naked, clothing; to the sick, visitation; to the prisoners, assistance. Besides these, have a greater care of the orphans, that nothing may be wanting to them; and that as to the maiden, till she arrives at the age of marriage, and ye give her in marriage to a brother: to the young man assistance, that he may learn a trade, and may be maintained by the advantage arising from it; that so, when he is dextrous in the management of it, he may thereby be enabled to buy himself the tools of his trade, that so he may no longer burden any of the brethren, or their sincere love to him, but may support himself: for certainly he is a happy man who is able to support himself, and does not take up the place of the orphan, the stranger, and the widow.

III. Since even the Lord said: "The giver was happier than the receiver."[2] For it is again said by Him: "Woe to those that have, and receive in hypocrisy; or who are able to support themselves, yet will receive of others: for both of them shall give an account to the Lord God in the day of judgment." But an orphan who, by reason of his youth, or he that by the feebleness of old age, or the incidence of a disease, or the bringing up of many children, receives alms, such an one shall not only not be blamed, but shall be commended: for he shall be esteemed an altar to God, and be honoured by God, because of his zealous and constant prayers for those that give to him; not receiving idly, but to the uttermost of his power recompensing what is given him by his prayer. Such an one therefore shall be blessed by God in

[1] Isa. i. 7.   [2] Acts xx. 35.

eternal life. But he that hath, and receives in hypocrisy or through idleness, instead of working and assisting others, shall be obnoxious to punishment before God, because he has snatched away the morsel of the needy.

IV. For he that has money and does not bestow it upon others, nor use it himself, is like the serpent, which they say sleeps over the treasures; and of him is that Scripture true which says, "He has gathered riches of which he shall not taste;"[1] and they will be of no use to him when he perishes justly. For it says, "Riches will not profit in the day of wrath." For such an one has not believed in God, but in his own gold; esteeming that his God, and trusting therein. Such an one is a dissembler of the truth, an accepter of persons, unfaithful, cheating, fearful, unmanly, light, of no value, a complainer, ever in pain, his own enemy, and nobody's friend. Such an one's money shall perish, and a man that is a stranger shall consume it, either by theft while he is alive, or by inheritance when he is dead. "For riches unjustly gotten shall be vomited up."[2]

V. We exhort, therefore, the widows and orphans to partake of those things that are bestowed upon them with all fear, and all pious reverence, and to return thanks to God who gives food to the needy, and to lift up their eyes to Him. For, says He, "Which of you shall eat, or who shall drink without Him? For He openeth His hand, and filleth every living thing with His kindness: giving wheat to the young men, and wine to the maidens, and oil for the joy of the living, grass for the cattle, and green herb for the service of men, flesh for the wild beasts, seeds for the birds, and suitable food for all creatures."[3] Wherefore the Lord says:[4] "Consider the fowls [of heaven[5]], that they sow not, [neither do they reap] nor gather into barns, and your Father feedeth

---

[1] Job xx. 18, LXX.; Prov. xi. 4.   [2] Job xx. 15, LXX.
[3] Eccles. ii. 25, LXX.; Ps. cxlv. 16; Zech. ix. 17, LXX.; Ps. civ. 14, 15.
[4] One V. MS. reads, "Thus also did the Lord exhort His disciples, saying."
[5] The words within brackets are not in one V. MS.

them. Are not ye much better than they? Be not therefore solicitous, saying, What shall we eat? or what shall we drink? For your Father knoweth that ye have need of all these things."[1] Since ye therefore enjoy such a providential care from Him, and are partakers of the good things that are derived from Him, you ought to return praise to Him that receives the orphan and the widow, to Almighty God, through His beloved Son Jesus Christ our Lord; through whom[2] glory be to God in spirit and truth for ever. Amen.

VI. Now the bishop ought to know whose oblations he ought to receive, and whose he ought not. For he is to avoid corrupt dealers, and not receive their gifts. "For a corrupt dealer shall not be justified from sin."[3] For of them it was that Isaiah reproached Israel, and said, "Thy corrupt dealers mingle wine with water."[4] He is also to avoid fornicators, for "thou shalt not offer the hire of an harlot to the Lord."[5] He is also to avoid extortioners, and such as covet other men's goods, and adulterers; for the sacrifices of such as these are abominable with God. Also those that oppress the widow and overbear the orphan, and fill prisons with the innocent, and abuse their own servants wickedly, I mean with stripes, and hunger, and hard service, nay, destroy whole cities; do thou, O bishop, avoid such as these, and their odious oblations. Thou shalt also refuse rogues, and such pleaders that plead on the side of injustice, and idol-makers, and thieves, and unjust publicans, and those that deceive by false balances and deceitful measures, and a soldier who is a false accuser and not content with his wages, but does violence to the needy, a murderer, a cut-throat, and an unjust judge, a subverter of causes, him that lies in wait for men, a worker of abominable wickedness, a drunkard, a blasphemer, a sodomite, an usurer, and every one that is wicked and opposes the will of God. For the Scripture says that all such as these are abominable with God. For those that receive from such persons, and thereby support the

---

[1] Matt. vi. 16.
[2] One V. MS. reads, "with whom be glory to Him, with the Spirit."
[3] Ecclus. xxvi. 29.   [4] Isa. i. 22.   [5] Deut. xxiii. 18.

widows and orphans, shall be obnoxious to the judgment-seat of God; as Adonias the prophet, in the book of Kings, when he disobeyed God, and both "eat bread and drank water in the place which the Lord had forbid him,"[1] because of the impiety of Jeroboam, was slain by a lion. For the bread which is distributed to the widows from labour is better, though it be short and little, than that from injustice and false accusation, though it be much and fine. For the Scripture says: "Better is a little to the righteous, than much riches of the sinners."[2] Now, although a widow, who eats and is filled from the impious, pray for them, she shall not be heard. For God, who knows the heart, with judgment has declared concerning the impious, saying, "If Moses and Samuel stand before my face in their behalf, I will not hear them;"[3] and, "Pray thou not for this people, and do not ask mercy for them, and do not intercede with me for them, for I will not hear thee."[4]

VII. And not these only, but those that are in sin and have not repented, will not only not be heard when they pray, but will provoke God to anger, as putting Him in mind of their own wickedness. Avoid therefore such ministrations, as you would the price of a dog and the hire of an harlot; for both of them are forbidden by the laws. For neither did Elisha receive the presents which were brought by Hazael,[5] nor Ahijah those from Jeroboam;[6] but if the prophets of God did not admit of presents from the impious, it is reasonable, O bishops, that neither should you. Nay, when Simon the magician offered money to me Peter and John,[7] and tried to obtain the invaluable grace by purchase, we did not admit it, but bound him with everlasting maledictions, because he thought to possess the gift of God, not by a pious mind towards God, but by the price of money. Avoid therefore such oblations to God's altar as are not from a good conscience. For says He: "Abstain from all injustice, and thou shalt not fear, and trembling shall not come nigh thee."[8]

[1] 1 Kings xiii.   [2] Ps. xxxvii. 16.   [3] Jer. xv. 1.   [4] Jer. vii. 16.
[5] 2 Kings viii.   [6] 1 Kings xiv.   [7] Acts viii.   [8] Isa. liv. 14.

VIII. But if ye say that those who give alms are such as these, and if we do not receive from them, whence shall we administer to the widows? And whence shall the poor among the people be maintained? Ye shall hear from us, that therefore have ye received the gift of the Levites, the oblations of your people, that ye might have enough for yourselves, and for those that are in want; and that ye might not be so straitened as to receive from the wicked. But if the churches be so straitened, it is better to perish than to receive anything from the enemies of God, to the reproach and abuse of His friends. For of such as these the prophet speaks: "Let not the oil of a sinner moisten my head."[1] Do ye therefore examine such persons, and receive from such as walk holily, and supply the afflicted. But receive not from those that are excommunicated, until they are thought worthy to become the members of the church. But if a gift be wanting, inform the brethren, and make a collection from them, and thence minister to the orphans and widows in righteousness.

IX. Say unto the people under thee what Solomon the wise says: "Honour the Lord out of thy just labours, and pay thy first-fruits to Him out of thy fruits of righteousness, that thy garners may be filled with fulness of wheat, and thy presses may burst out with wine."[2] Therefore maintain and clothe those that are in want from the righteous labour of the faithful. And such sums of money as are collected from them in the manner aforesaid, appoint to be laid out in the redemption of the saints, the deliverance of slaves, and of captives, and of prisoners, and of those that have been abused, and of those that have been condemned by tyrants to single combat and death on account of the name of Christ. For the Scripture says: "Deliver those that are led to death, and redeem those that are ready to be slain, do not spare."[3]

X. But if at any time you be forced unwillingly to receive money from any ungodly person, lay it out in wood and coals, that so neither the widow nor the orphan may receive any of it, or be forced to buy with it either meat or drink, which it

[1] Ps. cxli. 5.   [2] Prov. iii. 9, etc.   [3] Prov. xxiv. 11.

is unfit to do. For it is reasonable that such gifts of the ungodly should be fuel for the fire, and not food for the pious. And this method is plainly appointed by the law,[1] when it calls a sacrifice kept too long a thing not fit to be eaten, and commands it to be consumed with fire. For such oblations are not evil in their nature, but on account of the mind of those that bring them. And this we ordain, that we may not reject those that come to us, as knowing that the common conversation of the pious has often been very profitable to the ungodly, but religious communion with them is alone hurtful. And so much, beloved, shall suffice to have spoken to you in order to your security.

SEC. II.—*On domestic and social life.*

XI. Ye fathers, educate your children in the Lord, bringing them up in the nurture and admonition of the Lord; and teach them such trades as are agreeable and suitable to the word, lest they by such opportunity become extravagant, and continue without punishment from their parents, and so get relaxation before their time, and go astray from that which is good. Wherefore be not afraid to reprove them, and to teach them wisdom with severity. For your corrections will not kill them, but rather preserve them. As Solomon says somewhere in the book of Wisdom: "Chasten thy son, and he will refresh thee; so wilt thou have good hope of him. Thou verily shalt smite him with the rod, and shalt deliver his soul from death."[2] And again, says the same Solomon thus, "He that spareth his rod, hateth his son;"[3] and afterwards, "Beat his sides whilst he is an infant, lest he be hardened and disobey thee."[4] He, therefore, that neglects to admonish and instruct his own son, hates his own child. Do you therefore teach your children the word of the Lord. Bring them under with cutting stripes, and make them subject from their infancy, teaching them the Holy Scriptures, which are Christian and divine, and

---

[1] Lev. xix. 6. [2] Prov. xxix. 17, xix. 18, xxiii. 14.
[3] Prov. xiii. 24. [4] Ecclus. xxx. 21.

delivering to them every sacred writing, "not giving them such liberty that they get the mastery,"[1] and act against your opinion, not permitting them to club together for a treat with their equals. For so they will be turned to disorderly courses, and will fall into fornication; and if this happen by the carelessness of their parents, those that begat them will be guilty of their souls. For if the offending children get into the company of debauched persons by the negligence of those that begat them, they will not be punished alone by themselves; but their parents also will be condemned on their account. For this cause endeavour, at the time when they are of an age fit for marriage, to join them in wedlock, and settle them together, lest in the heat and fervour of their age their course of life become dissolute, and you be required to give an account by the Lord God in the day of judgment.

XII. But as to servants, what can we say more than that the slave bring a good will to his master, with the fear of God, although he be impious and wicked,[2] but yet not to yield any compliance as to his worship? And let the master love his servant, although he be his superior. Let him consider wherein they are equal, even as he is a man. And let him that has a believing master[3] love him both as his master, and as of the same faith, and as a father, but still with the preservation of his authority as his master: "not as an eye-servant, but as a lover of his master; as knowing that God will recompense to him for his subjection."[4] In like manner, let a master who has a believing servant love him as a son or as a brother, on account of their communion in the faith, but still preserving the difference of a servant.

XIII. Be ye subject to all royal power and dominion in things which are pleasing to God, as to the ministers of God, and the punishers of the ungodly.[5] Render all the fear that is due to them, all offerings, all customs, all honour, gifts, and taxes.[6] For this is God's command, that you owe

---

[1] Ecclus. xxx. 11.
[2] See Eph. vi. 5; 1 Pet. ii. 18.
[3] Col. iv. 1. See 1 Tim. vi. 2.
[4] Eph. vi. 6; Col. iii. 22.
[5] See 1 Pet. ii. 13; Tit. iii. 1.
[6] Rom. xiii. 1, 4, 7.

nothing to any one but the pledge of love, which God has commanded by Christ.[1]

XIV. Concerning virginity we have received no commandment;[2] but we leave it to the power of those that are willing, as a vow: exhorting them so far in this matter that they do not promise anything rashly; since Solomon says, "It is better not to vow, than to vow and not pay."[3] Let such a virgin, therefore, be holy in body and soul, as the temple of God,[4] as the house of Christ, as the habitation of the Holy Spirit. For she that vows ought to do such works as are suitable to her vow; and to show that her vow is real, and made on account of leisure for piety, not to cast a reproach on marriage. Let her not be a gadder abroad, nor one that rambles about unseasonably; not double-minded, but grave, continent, sober, pure, avoiding the conversation of many, and especially of those that are of ill reputation.

BOOK V.

Sec. i.—*Concerning the martyrs.*

I. If any Christian, on account of the name of Christ, and love and faith towards God, be condemned by the ungodly to the games, to the beasts, or to the mines, do not ye overlook him; but send to him from your labour and your very sweat for his sustenance, and for a reward to the soldiers, that he may be eased and be taken care of; that, as far as lies in your power, your blessed brother may not be afflicted: for he that is condemned for the name of the Lord God is an holy martyr, a brother of the Lord, the son of the Highest, a receptacle of the Holy Spirit, by whom every one of the faithful has received the illumination of the glory of the holy gospel, by being vouchsafed the incorruptible crown, and the testimony of Christ's sufferings, and the fellowship of His blood, to be made conformable to the

---

[1] Rom. xiii. 8. [2] See 1 Cor. vii. 25.
[3] Eccles. v. 4. [4] 1 Cor. vii. 34.

death of Christ for the adoption of children. For this cause do you, all ye of the faithful, by your bishop, minister to the saints of your substance and of your labour. But if any one has not, let him fast a day, and set apart that, and order it for the saints. But if any one has superfluities, let him minister more to them according to the proportion of his ability. But if he can possibly sell all his livelihood, and redeem them out of prison, he will be blessed, and a friend of Christ. For if he that gives his goods to the poor be perfect, supposing his knowledge of divine things, much more is he so that does it on account of the martyrs. For such an one is worthy of God, and will fulfil His will by supplying those who have confessed Him before nations and kings, and the children of Israel; concerning whom our Lord declared, saying: "Whosoever shall confess me before men, him will I also confess before my Father."[1] And if these be such as to be attested to by Christ before His Father, you ought not to be ashamed to go to them in the prisons. For if you do this, it will be esteemed to you for a testimony, because the real trial was to them a testimony; and your readiness will be so to you, as being partakers of their combat: for the Lord speaks somewhere to such as these, saying: "Come, ye blessed of my Father, inherit the kingdom prepared for you from the foundation of the world. For I was an hungry, and ye gave me meat; I was thirsty, and ye gave me drink; I was a stranger, and ye took me in; naked, and ye clothed me; I was sick, and ye visited me; I was in prison, and ye came unto me. Then shall the righteous answer, and say, Lord, when saw we Thee an hungered, and fed Thee? or thirsty, and gave Thee drink? When saw we Thee naked, and clothed Thee? or sick, and visited Thee? When saw we Thee a stranger, and took Thee in? or in prison, and came unto Thee? And He will answer and say unto them, Inasmuch as ye have done it unto one of the least of these my brethren, ye have done it unto me. And these shall go away into life everlasting. Then shall He say unto them on His left hand, Depart from me, ye

---

[1] Matt. x. 32.

cursed, into everlasting fire, prepared for the devil and his angels. For I was hungry, and ye gave me no meat; I was thirsty, and ye gave me no drink; I was a stranger, and ye took me not in; naked, and ye clothed me not; sick, and in prison, and ye visited me not. Then shall they also answer and say, Lord when saw we Thee hungry, or thirsty, or a stranger, or naked, or sick, or in prison, and did not minister unto Thee? Then shall He answer and say unto them, Verily I say unto you, Inasmuch as ye have not done it unto one of the least of these, neither have ye done it unto me. And these shall go away unto everlasting punishment."[1]

II. But if any one who calls himself a brother is seduced by the evil one, and acts wickedness, and is convicted and condemned to death as an adulterer, or a murderer, depart from him, that ye may be secure, and none of you may be suspected as a partner in such an abominable practice; and that no evil report may be spread abroad, as if all Christians took a pleasure in unlawful actions. Wherefore keep far from them. But do you assist with all diligence those that for the sake of Christ are abused by the ungodly and shut up in prison, or who are given over to death, or bonds, or banishment, in order to deliver your fellow-members from wicked hands. And if any one who accompanies with them is caught, and falls into misfortunes, he is blessed, because he is partaker with the martyr, and is one that imitates the sufferings of Christ; for we ourselves also, when we oftentimes received stripes from Caiaphas, and Alexander, and Annas, for Christ's sake, "went out rejoicing that we were counted worthy to suffer such things for our Saviour."[2] Do you also rejoice when ye suffer such things, for ye shall be blessed in that day.[3]

III. Receive also those that are persecuted on account of the faith, and who "fly from city to city"[4] on account of the Lord's commandment; and assist them as martyrs, rejoicing

---

[1] Matt. xxv. 34, etc. Portions of the passage from Matthew are omitted in one V. MS.; and the conclusion, beginning with "Then shall they also," is entirely omitted.

[2] Acts iv. 6, v. 40, 41.   [3] *Vid.* Luke vi. 22, 23.   [4] Matt. x. 23.

that ye are made partakers of their persecution, as knowing that they are esteemed blessed by the Lord; for Himself says: "Blessed are ye when men shall reproach you, and persecute you, and say all manner of evil against you falsely, for my sake. Rejoice, and be exceeding glad, because your reward is great in heaven: for so persecuted they the prophets which were before us."[1] And again: "If they have persecuted me, they will also persecute you."[2] And afterwards: "If they persecute you in this city, flee ye to another. For in the world ye have tribulation: for they shall deliver you into the synagogues; and ye shall be brought before rulers and kings for my sake, and for a testimony to them."[3] And, "He that endureth unto the end, the same shall be saved."[4] For he that is persecuted for the sake of the faith, and bears witness in regard to Him [Christ], and endures, is truly a man of God.

IV. But he that denies himself to be a Christian, that he may not be hated of men, and so loves his own life more than he does the Lord, in whose hand his breath is, is wretched and miserable, as being detestable and abominable, who desires to be the friend of men, but is the enemy of God, having no longer his portion with the saints, but with those that are accursed; choosing instead of the kingdom of the blessed, that eternal fire which is prepared for the devil and his angels: not being any longer hated by men, but rejected by God, and cast out from His presence. For of such an one our Lord declared, saying: "Whosoever shall deny me before men, and shall be ashamed of my name, I also will deny and be ashamed of him before my Father which is in heaven."[5] And again He speaks thus to us ourselves, His disciples: "He that loveth father or mother more than me, is not worthy of me; and he that loveth son or daughter more than me, is not worthy of me; and he that taketh not his cross, and followeth after me, is not worthy of me. He that findeth his life, shall lose it; and he that loseth his life for my sake, shall find it. For

[1] Matt. v. 11, 12. [2] John xv. 20. [3] Matt. x. 23, xvi. 33, x. 17.
[4] Matt. x. 22. [5] Matt. x. 33; Luke ix. 26.

what is a man profited, if he shall gain the whole world, and lose his own soul? or what shall a man give in exchange for his soul?"[1] And afterwards: "Fear not them that kill the body, but are not able to kill the soul; but rather fear Him who is able to destroy both soul and body in hell."[2]

V. Every one therefore who learns any art, when he sees his master by his diligence and skill perfecting his art, does himself earnestly endeavour to make what he takes in hand like to it. If he is not able, he is not perfected in his work. We therefore who have a Master, our Lord Jesus Christ, why do we not follow His doctrine?—since He renounced repose, pleasure, glory, riches, pride, the power of revenge, His mother and brethren, nay, and moreover His own life, on account of His piety towards His Father, and His love to us the race of mankind; and suffered not only persecution and stripes, reproach and mockery, but also crucifixion, that He might save the penitent, both Jews and Gentiles. If therefore He for our sakes renounced His repose, was not ashamed of the cross, and did not esteem death inglorious, why do not we imitate His sufferings, and renounce on His account even our own life, with that patience which He gives us? For He did all for our sakes, but we do it for our own sakes: for He does not stand in need of us, but we stand in need of His mercy. He only requires the sincerity and readiness of our faith, as the Scripture says: "If thou beest righteous, what doest thou give to Him? or what will He receive at thy hand? Thy wickedness is to a man like thyself, and thy righteousness to a son of man."[3]

VI. Let us therefore renounce our parents, and kinsmen, and friends, and wife, and children, and possessions, and all the enjoyments of life, when any of these things become an impediment to piety. For we ought to pray that we may not enter into temptation; but if we be called to martyrdom, with constancy to confess His precious name, and if on this account we be punished, let us rejoice, as hastening to im-

---

[1] Matt. x. 37, xvi. 26. [2] Matt. x. 28.
[3] Job xxxv. 7. One V. MS. reads "piety," instead of "wickedness," in the last sentence.

mortality. When we are persecuted, let us not think it strange; let us not love the present world, nor the praises which come from men, nor the glory and honour of rulers, according as some of the Jews wondered at the mighty works of our Lord, yet did not believe on Him, for fear of the high priests and the rest of the rulers: "For they loved the praise of men more than the praise of God."[1] But now, by confessing a good confession, we not only save ourselves, but we confirm those who are newly illuminated, and strengthen the faith of the catechumens. But if we remit any part of our confession, and deny godliness by the faintness of our persuasion, and the fear of a very short punishment, we not only deprive ourselves of everlasting glory, but we shall also become the causes of the perdition of others; and shall suffer double punishment, as affording suspicion, by our denial that that truth which we gloried in so much before is an erroneous doctrine. Wherefore neither let us be rash and hasty to thrust ourselves into dangers, for the Lord says: "Pray that ye fall not into temptation: the spirit indeed is willing, but the flesh is weak."[2] Nor let us, when we do fall into dangers, be fearful or ashamed of our profession. For if a person, by the denial of his own hope, which is Jesus the Son of God, should be delivered from a temporary death, and the next day should fall dangerously sick upon his bed, with a distemper in his bowels, his stomach, or his head, or any of the incurable diseases, as a consumption, or gangrene, or looseness, or iliac passion, or dropsy, or colic, and has a sudden catastrophe, and departs this life; is not he deprived of the things present, and loses those eternal? Or rather, he is within the verge of eternal punishment, "and goes into outer darkness, where is weeping and gnashing of teeth."[3] But let him who is vouchsafed the honour of martyrdom rejoice with joy in the Lord, as obtaining thereby so great a crown, and departing out of this life by his confession. Nay, though he be but a catechumen, let him depart without trouble; for his suffering for Christ will be to him a more genuine baptism, because he does really die with Christ, but

[1] John xii. 43. [2] Matt. xxvi. 41. [3] Matt. viii. 12.

the rest only in a figure. Let him therefore rejoice in the imitation of his Master, since is it thus ordained: "Let every one be perfect, as his Master is."[1] Now his and our Master, Jesus the Lord, was smitten for our sake: He underwent reproaches and revilings with long-suffering. He was spit upon, He was smitten on the face, He was buffeted; and when He had been scourged, He was nailed to the cross. He had vinegar and gall to drink; and when He had fulfilled all things that were written, He said to His God and Father, "Into Thy hands I commend my spirit."[2] Wherefore let him that desires to be His disciple earnestly follow His conflicts: let him imitate His patience, knowing that, although he be burned in the fire by men, he will suffer nothing, like the three children;[3] or if he does suffer anything, he shall receive a reward from the Lord, believing in the one and the only true God and Father, through Jesus Christ, the great High Priest, and Redeemer of our souls, and rewarder of our sufferings. To whom be glory for ever. Amen.

VII. For the Almighty God Himself will raise us up through our Lord Jesus Christ, according to His infallible promise, and grant us a resurrection with all those that have slept from the beginning of the world; and we shall then be such as we now are in our present form, without any defect or corruption. For we shall rise incorruptible: whether we die at sea, or are scattered on the earth, or are torn to pieces by wild beasts and birds, He will raise us by His own power; for the whole world is held together by the hand of God. Now He says: "An hair of your head shall not perish."[4] Wherefore He exhorts us, saying: "In your patience possess ye your souls."[5] But as concerning the resurrection of the dead, and the recompense of reward for the martyrs, Gabriel speaks to Daniel: "And many of them that sleep shall arise out of the dust of the earth, some to everlasting life, and some to shame and everlasting contempt. And they that understand shall shine as the sun, and as the firmament, and as the stars."[6] Therefore the most holy Gabriel foretold

[1] Luke vi. 40. [2] Luke xxiii. 46. [3] Dan. iii.
[4] Luke xxi. 18. [5] Luke xxi. 19. [6] Dan. xii. 2, 3.

that the saints should shine like the stars: for His sacred name did witness to them, that they might understand the truth. Nor is a resurrection only declared for the martyrs, but for all men, righteous and unrighteous, godly and ungodly, that every one may receive according to his desert. For God, says the Scripture, "will bring every work into judgment, with every secret thing, whether it be good or whether it be evil."[1] This resurrection was not believed by the Jews, when of old they said, "Our bones are withered, and we are gone."[2] To whom God answered, and said: "Behold, I open your graves, and will bring you out of them; and I will put my Spirit into you, and ye shall live: and ye shall know that I the Lord have spoken it, and will do it." And He says by Isaiah: "The dead shall rise, and those that are in the graves shall be raised up. And those that rest in the earth shall rejoice, for the dew which is from Thee shall be healing to them."[3] There are indeed many and various things said concerning the resurrection, and concerning the continuance of the righteous in glory, and concerning the punishment of the ungodly, their fall, rejection, condemnation, shame, "eternal fire, and endless worm."[4] Now that, if it had pleased Him that all men should be immortal, it was in His power, He showed in the examples of Enoch and Elias, while He did not suffer them to have any experience of death. Or if it had pleased Him in every generation to raise those that died, that this also He was able to do He hath made manifest both by Himself and by others; as when He raised the widow's son[5] by Elijah, and the Shunammite's son[6] by Elisha. But we are persuaded that death is not a retribution of punishment, because even the saints have undergone it; nay, even the Lord of the saints, Jesus Christ, the life of them that believe, and the resurrection of the dead. Upon this account, therefore, according to the ancient practice, for those who live in the great city, after the combats He brings a dissolution for a while, that, when He raises up every one, He may

[1] Eccles. xii. 14.   [2] Ezek. xxxvii. 11, etc.   [3] Isa. xxvi. 19.
[4] Isa. lxvi. 23.   [5] 1 Kings xvii.   [6] 2 Kings ii.

either reject him or crown him. For He that made the body of Adam out of the earth will raise up the bodies of the rest, and that of the first man, after their dissolution, [to pay what is owing to the rational nature of man; we mean the continuance in being through all ages. He, therefore, who brings on the dissolution, will Himself procure the resurrection. And He that said, "The Lord took dust from the ground, and formed man, and breathed into his face the breath of life, and man became a living soul,"[1] added after the disobedience, "Earth thou art, and unto earth shalt thou return;"[2] the same promised us a resurrection afterwards.[3]] For says He: "All that are in the graves shall hear the voice of the Son of God, and they that hear shall live."[4] Besides these arguments, we believe there is to be a resurrection also from the resurrection of our Lord. For it is He that raised Lazarus, when he had been in the grave four days,[5] and Jairus' daughter,[6] and the widow's son.[7] It is He that raised Himself by the command of the Father in the space of three days, who is the pledge of our resurrection. For says He: "I am the resurrection and the life."[8] Now He that brought Jonas[9] in the space of three days, alive and unhurt, out of the belly of the whale, and the three children out of the furnace of Babylon, and Daniel out of the mouth of the lions,[10] does not want power to raise us up also. But if the Gentiles laugh at us, and disbelieve our Scriptures, let at least their own prophetess Sibylla oblige them to believe, who says thus to them in express words:

But when all things shall be reduced to dust and ashes,
And the immortal God who kindled the fire shall have quenched it,
God shall form those bones and that ashes into a man again,
And shall place mortal men again as they were before.
And then shall be the judgment, wherein God will do justice,
And judge the world again. But as many mortals as have sinned through impiety
Shall again be covered under the earth;

---

[1] Gen. ii. 7.   [2] Gen. iii. 19.
[3] The part within brackets is not in one of the V. MSS.
[4] John v. 45.   [5] John xi.   [6] Mark v.   [7] Luke vii.
[8] John xi. 25.   [9] Jonah ii.   [10] Dan. iii. vi.

But so many as have been pious shall live again in the world.
When God puts His Spirit into them, and gives those at once that are
    godly both life and favour,
Then shall all see themselves.[1]

If, therefore, this prophetess confesses the resurrection, and does not deny the restoration of all things, and distinguishes the godly from the ungodly, it is in vain for them to deny our doctrine. Nay, indeed, they say they can show a resemblance of the resurrection, while they do not themselves believe the things they declare: for they say that there is a bird single in its kind which affords a copious demonstration of the resurrection, which they say is without a mate, and the only one in the creation. They call it a phœnix, and relate that every five hundred years it comes into Egypt, to that which is called the altar of the sun, and brings with it a great quantity of cinnamon, and cassia, and balsam-wood, and standing towards the east, as they say, and praying to the sun, of its own accord is burnt, and becomes dust; but that a worm arises again out of those ashes, and that when the same is warmed it is formed into a new-born phœnix; and when it is able to fly, it goes to Arabia, which is beyond the Egyptian countries. If, therefore, as even themselves say, a resurrection is exhibited by the means of an irrational bird, wherefore do they vainly disparage our accounts, when we profess that He who by His power brings that into being which was not in being before, is able to restore this body, and raise it up again after its dissolution? For on account of this full assurance of hope we undergo stripes, and persecutions, and deaths. Otherwise we should to no purpose undergo such things if we had not a full assurance of these promises, whereof we profess ourselves to be the preachers. As, therefore, we believe Moses when he says, "In the beginning God made the heaven and the earth;"[2] and we know that He did not want matter, but by His will alone brought those things into being which Christ was commanded to make; we mean the heaven, the earth, the sea, the light, the night, the day, the luminaries, the

[1] *Orac. Sibyl.* l. iv. *in fin.*   [2] Gen. i. 1.

stars, the fowls, the fishes, the four-footed beasts, the creeping things, the plants, and the herbs; so also will He raise all men up by His will, as not wanting any assistance. For it is the work of the same power to create the world and to raise the dead. And then He made man, who was not a man before, of different parts, giving to him a soul made out of nothing. But now He will restore the bodies, which have been dissolved, to the souls that are still in being: for the rising again belongs to things laid down, not to things which have no being. He therefore that made the original bodies out of nothing, and fashioned various [forms] of them, will also again revive and raise up those that are dead. For He that formed man in the womb out of a little seed, and created in him a soul which was not in being before,—as He Himself somewhere speaks to Jeremiah, "Before I formed thee in the womb I knew thee;"[1] and elsewhere, "I am the Lord who established the heaven, and laid the foundations of the earth, and formed the spirit of man in him,"[2] —will also raise up all men, as being His workmanship; as also the divine Scripture testifies that God said to Christ, His only-begotten, "Let us make man after our image, and after our likeness. And God made man: after the image of God made He him; male and female made He them."[3] And the most divine and patient Job, of whom the Scripture says that it is written, that "he was to rise again with those whom the Lord raises up,"[4] speaks to God thus: "Hast not Thou milked me like milk, and curdled me like cheese? Thou hast clothed me with skin and flesh, and hast fenced me with bones and sinews. Thou hast granted me life and favour, and Thy visitation hath preserved my spirit. Having these things within me, I know that Thou canst do all things, and that nothing is impossible with Thee."[5] Wherefore also[6] our Saviour and Master Jesus Christ says, that "what is impossible with men is possible

---

[1] Jer. i. 5.   [2] Zech. xii. 1.   [3] Gen. i. 26, 27.
[4] *In fin.* Job in LXX.   [5] Job x. 10.
[6] The words from "Wherefore also" to "possible with God" are omitted in one V. MS., and noticed as spurious in the other.

with God."[1] And David, the beloved of God, says: "Thine hands have made me, and fashioned me."[2] And again: "Thou knowest my frame."[3] And afterward: "Thou hast fashioned me, and laid Thine hand upon me. The knowledge of Thee is declared to be too wonderful for me; it is very great, I cannot attain unto it."[4] "Thine eyes did see my substance, being yet imperfect; and all men shall be written in Thy book."[5] Nay, and Isaiah says in his prayer to Him: "We are the clay, and Thou art the framer of us."[6] If, therefore, man be His workmanship, made by Christ, by Him most certainly will he after he is dead be raised again, with intention either of being crowned for his good actions or punished for his transgressions. But if He, being the legislator, judges with righteousness; as He punishes the ungodly, so does He do good to and saves the faithful. And those saints who for His sake have been slain by men, "some of them He will make light as the stars, and make others bright as the luminaries,"[7] as Gabriel said to Daniel. All we of the faithful, therefore, who are the disciples of Christ, believe His promises. For He that has promised it cannot lie; as says the blessed prophet David: "The Lord is faithful in all His words, and holy in all His works."[8] For He that framed for Himself a body out of a virgin, is also the former of other men. And He that raised Himself from the dead, will also raise again all that are laid down. He who raises wheat out of the ground with many stalks from one grain, He who makes the tree that is cut down send forth fresh branches, He that made Aaron's dry rod put forth buds,[9] will raise us up in glory; He that raised Him up that had the palsy whole,[10] and healed him that had the withered hand,[11] He that supplied a defective part to him that was born blind from clay and spittle,[12] will raise us up; He that satisfied five thousand men with five loaves and two fishes, and caused a remainder of

---

[1] Luke xviii. 28. [2] Ps. cxix. 73. [3] Ps. ciii. 14.
[4] Ps. cxxxix. 5. [5] Ps. cxxxix. 16. [6] Isa. lxiv. 8.
[7] Dan. xii. 3. [8] Ps. cxlv. 17. [9] Num. xvii. 8.
[10] Matt. ix. 2, etc. [11] Mark iii. 1, etc. [12] John ix. 1, etc.

twelve baskets,[1] and out of water made wine,[2] and sent a piece of money out of a fish's mouth[3] by me Peter to those that demanded tribute, will raise the dead. For we testify all these things concerning Him, and the prophets testify the other. We who have eaten and drunk with Him, and have been spectators of His wonderful works, and of His life, and of His conduct, and of His words, and of His sufferings, and of His death, and of His resurrection from the dead, and who associated with Him forty days after His resurrection,[4] and who received a command from Him to preach the gospel to all the world, and to make disciples of all nations,[5] and to baptize them into His death by the authority of the God of the universe, who is His Father, and by the testimony of the Spirit, who is His Comforter,—we teach you all these things which He appointed us by His constitutions, before " He was received up in our sight into heaven,"[6] to Him that sent Him. And if you will believe, you shall be happy; but if you will not believe, we shall be found innocent, and clear from your incredulity.

VIII. Now concerning the martyrs, we say to you that they are to be had in all honour with you, as we honour the blessed James the bishop, and the holy Stephen our fellow-servant. For these are reckoned blessed by God, and are honoured by holy men, who were pure from all transgressions, immoveable when tempted to sin, or persuaded from good works, without dispute deserving encomiums: of whom also David speaks, " Precious in the sight of the Lord is the death of His holy ones;"[7] and Solomon says, " The memory of the just is with encomiums:"[8] of whom also the prophet speaks, " Righteous men are taken away."[9]

IX. These things we have said concerning those that in truth have been martyrs for Christ, but not concerning false martyrs, concerning whom the oracle speaks, " The name of the ungodly is extinguished."[10] For " a faithful witness will

---

[1] Matt. xiv. 17.　　[2] John ii. 3.　　[3] Matt. xvii. 24.
[4] Acts i. 3.　　[5] Matt. xxviii. 19.　　[6] Acts i. 9.
[7] Ps. cxvi. 15.　　[8] Prov. x. 7.　　[9] Isa. lvii. 1, LXX.
[10] Prov. x. 7.

not lie, but an unjust witness inflames lies."[1] For he that departs this life in his testimony without lying, for the sake of the truth, is a faithful martyr, worthy to be believed in such things wherein he strove for the word of piety by his own blood.

SEC. II.—*All association with idols is to be avoided.*

X. Now we exhort you, brethren and fellow-servants, to avoid vain talk and obscene discourses, and jestings, drunkenness, lasciviousness, luxury, unbounded passions, with foolish discourses, since we do not permit you so much as on the Lord's days, which are days of joy, to speak or act anything unseemly; for the Scripture somewhere says: " Serve the Lord with fear, and rejoice unto Him with trembling."[2] Even your very rejoicings therefore ought to be done with fear and trembling: for a Christian who is faithful ought neither to repeat an heathen hymn nor an obscene song, because he will be obliged by that hymn to make mention of the idolatrous names of demons; and instead of the Holy Spirit, the wicked one will enter into him.

XI. You are also forbidden to swear by them, or to utter their abominable names through your mouth, and to worship them, or fear them as gods; for they are not gods, but either wicked demons or the ridiculous contrivances of men. For somewhere God says concerning the Israelites: " They have forsaken me, and sworn by them that are no gods."[3] And afterwards: " I will take away the names of your idols out of their mouth."[4] And elsewhere: " They have provoked me to jealousy with them that are no gods; they have provoked me to anger with their idols."[5] And in all the Scriptures these things are forbidden by the Lord God.

XII. Nor do the legislators give us only prohibitions concerning idols, but also warn us concerning the luminaries, not to swear by them, nor to serve them. For they say: " Lest, when thou seest the sun, and the moon, and the stars, thou shouldest be seduced to worship them."[6] And elsewhere:

[1] Prov. xiv. 5. [2] Ps. ii. 11. [3] Jer. v. 7.
[4] Zech. xiii. 2. [5] Deut. xxxii. 21. [6] Deut. iv. 19.

"Do not ye learn to walk after the ways of the heathen, and be not afraid of the signs of heaven."[1] For the stars and the luminaries were given to men to shine upon them, but not for worship; although the Israelites, by the perverseness of their temper, "worshipped the creature instead of the Creator," and acted insultingly to their Maker, and admired the creature more than is fit. And sometimes they made a calf, as in the wilderness;[2] sometimes they worshipped Baal-peor;[3] another time Baal, and Thamuz, and Astarte of Sidon;[4] and again Moloch and Chamos;[5] another time the sun,[6] as it is written in Ezekiel; nay, and besides, brute creatures, as among the Egyptians Apis, and the Mendesian goat, and gods of silver and gold, as in Judea.[7] On account of all which things He threatened them, and said by the prophet: "Is it a small thing to the house of Judah to do these abominations which they have done? For they have filled the land with their wickedness, to provoke me to anger: and, behold, they are as those that mock. And I will act with anger. Mine eye shall not spare, neither will I have mercy; and they shall cry in mine ears with a great voice, and I will not hearken unto them."[8] Consider, beloved, how many things the Lord declares against idolaters, and the worshippers of the sun and moon. Wherefore it is the duty of a man of God, as he is a Christian, not to swear by the sun, or by the moon, or by the stars; nor by the heaven, nor by the earth, nor by any of the elements, whether small or great. For if our Master charged us not to swear by the true God, that our word might be firmer than an oath, nor by heaven itself, for that is a piece of heathen wickedness, nor by Jerusalem, nor by the sanctuary of God, nor the altar, nor the gift, nor the gilding of the altar, nor one's own head,[9] for this custom is a piece of Judaic corruption, and on that account was forbidden; and if He exhorts the faithful that their yea be yea, and their nay, nay, and says that "what is more than these is of the

[1] Jer. x. 2.   [2] Ex. xxxii. 4.   [3] Num. xxv. 3.
[4] Judg. ii. 13.   [5] Ezek. viii. 14.   [6] 1 Kings xi. 5.
[7] Ezek. viii. 16.   [8] Ezek. viii. 17.   [9] Matt. v. 34, xxiii. 16.

evil one," how much more blameable are those who appeal to deities falsely so called as the objects of an oath, and who glorify imaginary beings instead of those that are real, whom God for their perverseness " delivered over to foolishness, to do those things that are not convenient!"[1]

SEC. III.—*On feast days and fast days.*

XIII. Brethren, observe the festival days; and first of all the birthday which you are to celebrate on the twenty-fifth of the ninth month; after which let the Epiphany be to you the most honoured, in which the Lord made to you a display of His own Godhead, and let it take place on the sixth of the tenth month; after which the fast of Lent is to be observed by you as containing a memorial of our Lord's mode of life and legislation. But let this solemnity be observed before the fast of the passover, beginning from the second day of the week, and ending at the day of the preparation. After which solemnities, breaking off your fast, begin the holy week of the passover, fasting in the same all of you with fear and trembling, praying in them for those that are about to perish.

XIV. For they began to hold a council against the Lord on the second day of the week, in the first month, which is Xanthicus; and the deliberation continued on the third day of the week; but on the fourth day they determined to take away His life by crucifixion. And Judas knowing this, who for a long time had been perverted, but was then smitten by the devil himself with the love of money, although he had been long entrusted with the purse,[2] and used to steal what was set apart for the needy, yet was he not cast off by the Lord, through much long-suffering; nay, and when we were once feasting with Him, being willing both to reduce him to his duty and instruct us in His own foreknowledge, He said: "Verily, verily, I say unto you, that one of you will betray me;" and every one of us saying, "Is it I?"[3] And the Lord being silent, I, who was one of the twelve, and more beloved by Him than the rest, arose up from lying

[1] Rom. i. 28.   [2] John xii. 6.   [3] John xiii. etc.

in His bosom, and besought Him to tell who it should be that
should betray Him. Yet neither then did our good Lord
declare His name, but gave two signs of the betrayer: one
by saying, "he that dippeth with me in the dish;" a second,
"to whom I shall give the sop when I have dipped it." Nay,
although he himself said, "Master, is it I?" the Lord did not
say Yes, but, "Thou hast said." And being willing to affright
him in the matter, He said: "Woe to that man by whom
the Son of man is betrayed! good were it for him if he had
never been born. Who, when he had heard that, went his
way, and said to the priests, What will ye give me, and I
will deliver him unto you? And they bargained with him
for thirty pieces of silver."[1] And the scripture was fulfilled,
which said, "And they took[2] the thirty pieces of silver, the
price of Him that was valued, whom they of the children of
Israel did value, and gave them for the house of the potter."[3]
And on the fifth day of the week, when we had eaten the
passover with Him, and when Judas had dipped his hand
into the dish, and received the sop, and was gone out by
night, the Lord said to us: "The hour is come that ye shall
be dispersed, and shall leave me alone;"[4] and every one
vehemently affirming that they would not forsake Him, I
Peter adding this promise, that I would even die with Him,
He said, "Verily I say unto thee, Before the cock crows,
thou shalt thrice deny that thou knowest me."[5] And when
He had delivered to us the representative mysteries of His
precious body and blood, Judas not being present with us,
He went out to the Mount of Olives, near the brook Cedron,
where there was a garden;[6] and we were with Him, and
sang an hymn according to the custom.[7] And being separated not far[8] from us, He prayed to His Father, saying:

[1] Matt. xxvi. 15.

[2] The words from "And they took" to "house of the potter" are
wanting in one V. MS. The other reads "field" of the potter, instead
of "house."

[3] Matt. xxvii. 9.   [4] John xvi. 32 ; Matt. xxvi. 31.

[5] Luke xxii. 34.   [6] John xviii. 1.   [7] Matt. xxvi. 80.

[8] "Not far," the reading of the V. MSS. The others read: "And
being separated from us, He prayed earnestly."

"Father, remove this cup away from me; yet not my will, but Thine be done."[1] And when He had done this thrice, while we out of despondency of mind were fallen asleep, He came and said: "The hour is come, and the Son of man is betrayed into the hands of sinners. And behold Judas, and with him a multitude of ungodly men,"[2] to whom he shows the signal by which he was to betray Him—a deceitful kiss. But they, when they had received the signal agreed on, took hold of the Lord; and having bound Him, they led Him to the house of Caiaphas the high priest, wherein were assembled many, not the people, but a great rout, not an holy council, but an assembly of the wicked and council of the ungodly, who did many things against Him, and left no kind of injury untried, spitting upon Him, cavilling at Him, beating Him, smiting Him on the face, reviling Him, tempting Him, seeking vain divination instead of true prophecies from Him, calling Him a deceiver, a blasphemer, a transgressor of Moses, a destroyer of the temple, a taker away of sacrifices, an enemy to the Romans, an adversary to Cæsar. And these reproaches did these bulls and dogs[3] in their madness cast upon Him, till it was very early in the morning, and then they lead Him away to Annas, who was father-in-law to Caiaphas; and when they had done the like things to Him there, it being the day of the preparation, they delivered Him to Pilate the Roman governor, accusing Him of many and great things, none of which they could prove. Whereupon the governor, as out of patience with them, said: "I find no cause against him."[4] But they bringing two lying witnesses, wished to accuse the Lord falsely; but they being found to disagree, and so their testimony not conspiring together, they altered the accusation to that of treason, saying, "This fellow says that he is a king, and forbids to give tribute to Cæsar."[5] And themselves became accusers, and witnesses, and judges, and authors of the sentence, saying, "Crucify him, crucify

---

[1] Luke xxii. 41; Matt. xxvi. 44, 43.
[2] Luke xxii. 45; Matt. xxvi. 45.　　[3] Ps. xxii. 13–17.
[4] Luke xxiii. 14; John xviii. 38.　　[5] Luke xxiii. 2.

him;"[1] that it might be fulfilled which is written by the prophets concerning Him, "Unjust witnesses were gathered together against me, and injustice lied to itself;"[2] and again, "Many dogs compassed me about, the assembly of the wicked laid siege against me;"[3] and elsewhere, "My inheritance became to me as a lion in a wood, and has sent forth her voice against me."[4] Pilate therefore, disgracing his authority by his pusillanimity, convicts himself of wickedness by regarding the multitude more than this just person, and bearing witness to Him that He was innocent, yet as guilty delivering Him up to the punishment of the cross, although the Romans had made laws that no man unconvicted should be put to death. But the executioners took the Lord of glory and nailed Him to the cross, crucifying Him indeed at the sixth hour, but having received the sentence of His condemnation at the third hour. After this they gave to Him vinegar to drink, mingled with gall. Then they divided His garments by lot. Then they crucified two malefactors with Him, on each side one, that it might be fulfilled which was written: "They gave me gall to eat, and when I was thirsty they gave me vinegar to drink."[5] And again: "They divided my garment among themselves, and upon my vesture have they cast lots."[6] And in another place: "And I was reckoned with the transgressors."[7] Then there was darkness for three hours, from the sixth to the ninth, and again light in the evening; as it is written: "It shall not be day nor night, and at the evening there shall be light."[8] All which things,[9] when those malefactors saw that were crucified with Him, the one of them reproached Him as though He was weak and unable to deliver Himself; but the other rebuked the ignorance of his fellow, and turning to the Lord, as being enlightened by Him, and acknowledg-

[1] Luke xxiii. 21.   [2] Ps. xxvii. 12.   [3] Ps. xxii. 17.   [4] Jer. xii. 8.
[5] Ps. lxix. 21.   [6] Ps. xxii. 19.   [7] Isa. lii. 12.
[8] Zech. xiv. 7. The V. MSS. read: "On that day there will not be light, but there will be cold and frost for one day."
[9] The words from "All which things" to "mystical good things" are omitted in one V. MS.

ing who He was that suffered, he prayed that He would remember him in His kingdom hereafter.[1] He then presently granted him the forgiveness of his former sins, and brought him into paradise to enjoy the mystical good things; who also cried out about the ninth hour, and said to His Father: "My God! my God! why hast Thou forsaken me?"[2] And a little afterward, when He had cried with a loud voice, "Father, forgive them, for they know not what they do,"[3] and had added, "Into Thy hands I commit my spirit," He gave up the ghost,[4] and was buried before sunset in a new sepulchre. But when the first day of the week dawned He arose from the dead, and fulfilled those things which before His passion He foretold to us, saying: "The Son of man must continue in the heart of the earth three days and three nights."[5] And when He was risen from the dead, He appeared first to Mary Magdalene, and Mary the mother of James, then to Cleopas in the way, and after that to us His disciples, who had fled away for fear of the Jews, but privately were very inquisitive about Him.[6] But these things are also written in the gospel.

XV. He therefore charged us Himself to fast these six days on account of the impiety and transgression of the Jews, commanding us withal to bewail over them, and lament for their perdition. For even He Himself "wept over them, because they knew not the time of their visitation."[7] But He commanded us to fast on the fourth and sixth days of the week; the former on account of His being betrayed, and the latter on account of His passion. But He appointed us to break our fast on the seventh day at the cock-crowing, but to fast on the Sabbath-day. Not that the Sabbath-day is a day of fasting, being the rest from the creation, but because we ought to fast on this one Sabbath only, while on this day the Creator was under the earth. For on their very

---

[1] Luke xxiii. 39, etc. [2] Matt. xxvii. 46. [3] Luke xxiii. 34.
[4] Luke xxiii. 46. [5] Matt. xii. 40.
[6] Mark xvi. 9; John xx. 11, etc.; Luke xxiv. 18; Mark xvi. 14.
[7] Luke xix. 44.

feast-day they apprehended the Lord, that that oracle might be fulfilled which says: "They placed their signs in the middle of their feast, and knew them not."[1] Ye ought therefore to bewail over them, because when the Lord came they did not believe on Him, but rejected His doctrine, judging themselves unworthy of salvation. You therefore are happy who once were not a people, but are now an holy nation, delivered from the deceit of idols, from ignorance, from impiety, who once had not obtained mercy, but now have obtained mercy through your hearty obedience: for to you, the converted Gentiles, is opened the gate of life, who formerly were not beloved, but are now beloved; a people ordained for the possession of God, to show forth His virtues, concerning whom our Saviour said, "I was found of them that sought me not; I was made manifest to them that asked not after me. I said, Behold me, to a nation which did not call upon my name."[2] For when ye did not seek after Him, then were ye sought for by Him; and you who have believed in Him have hearkened to His call, and have left the madness of polytheism, and have fled to the true monarchy, to Almighty God, through Christ Jesus, and are become the completion of the number of the saved—"ten thousand times ten thousand, and thousands of thousands;"[3] as it is written in David, "A thousand[4] shall fall beside thee, and ten thousand at thy right hand;"[5] and again, "The chariots of God are by tens of thousands, and thousands of the prosperous."[6] But unto unbelieving Israel He says: "All the day long have I stretched out mine hands to a disobedient and gainsaying people, which go in a way that is not good, but after their own sins, a people provoking me before my face."[7]

XVI. See how the people provoked the Lord by not believing in Him! Therefore He says: "They provoked the Holy Spirit, and He was turned to be their enemy."[8] For

---

[1] Ps. lxxiv. 4.   [2] Isa. lxv.   [3] Dan. vii. 10.
[4] The words from "A thousand" to "of the prosperous" are not in the V. MSS.
[5] Ps. xci. 7.   [6] Ps. lxix. 18.   [7] Ps. lxvi. 2.   [8] Isa. lxiii. 10.

blindness is cast upon them, by reason of the wickedness of their mind, because when they saw Jesus they did not believe Him to be the Christ of God, who was before all ages[1] begotten of Him, His only-begotten Son, God the Word, whom they did not own through their unbelief, neither on account of His mighty works, nor yet on account of the prophecies which were written concerning Him. For that He was to be born of a virgin, they read this prophecy: "Behold, a virgin shall be with child, and shall bring forth a Son, and they shall call His name Emanuel."[2] "For to us a Child is born, to us a Son is given, whose government is upon His shoulders; and His name is called the Angel of His great Council, the Wonderful Counsellor, the Mighty God, the Potentate, the Prince of Peace, the Father of the Future Age."[3] Now, that because of their exceeding great wickedness they would not believe in Him, the Lord shows in these words: "Who hath believed our report? and to whom hath the arm of the Lord been revealed?"[4] And afterward: "Hearing ye shall hear, and shall not understand; and seeing ye shall see, and shall not perceive: for the heart of this people is waxed gross."[5] Wherefore knowledge was taken from them, because seeing they overlooked, and hearing they heard not. But to you, the converted of the Gentiles, is the kingdom given, because you, who knew not God, have believed by preaching, and "have known Him, or rather are known of Him,"[6] through Jesus, the Saviour and Redeemer of those that hope in Him. For ye are translated from your former vain and tedious mode of life, and have contemned the lifeless idols, and despised the demons, which are in darkness, and have run to the "true light,"[7] and by it have "known the one and only true God and Father,"[8] and so are owned to be heirs of His kingdom. For since ye have "been baptized into the Lord's death,"[9] and into His resurrection,

---

[1] One V. MS. omits "ages," and the other "begotten of Him."
[2] Isa. vii. 14; Matt. i. 23.   [3] Isa. ix. 6.
[4] Isa. liii. 1.   [5] Isa. vi. 9.
[6] Gal. iv. 9.   [7] John i. 9.
[8] John xvii. 3.   [9] Rom. vi. 3.

as "new-born babes,"[1] ye ought to be wholly free from all sinful actions; "for you are not your own, but His that bought you"[2] with His own blood. For concerning the former Israel the Lord speaks thus, on account of their unbelief: "The kingdom of God shall be taken from them, and given to a nation bringing forth the fruits thereof;"[3] that is to say, that having given the kingdom to you, who were once far estranged from Him, He expects the fruits of your gratitude and probity. For ye are those that were once sent into the vineyard, and did not obey, but these they that did obey;[4] but you have repented of your denial, and you work therein now. But they, being uneasy on account of their own covenants, have not only left the vineyard uncultivated, but have also killed the stewards of the Lord of the vineyard,[5]—one with stones, another with the sword; one they sawed asunder, another they slew in the holy place, "between the temple and the altar;"[6] nay, at last they "cast the Heir Himself out of the vineyard, and slew Him."[7] And by them He was rejected as an unprofitable stone,[8] but by you was received as the corner-stone. Wherefore He says concerning you: "A people whom I knew not have served me, and at the hearing of the ear have they obeyed me."[9]

XV. It is therefore your duty, brethren, who are redeemed by the precious blood of Christ, to observe the days of the passover exactly, with all care, after the vernal equinox, lest ye be obliged to keep the memorial of the one passion twice in a year. Keep it once only in a year for Him that died but once.

[Do not you yourselves compute, but keep it when your brethren of the circumcision do so: keep it together with them; and if they err in their computation, be not you concerned. Keep your nights of watching in the middle of the days of unleavened bread. And when the Jews are feasting, do you fast and wail over them, because on the day of their

[1] 1 Pet. ii. 2. [2] 1 Cor. vi. 19. [3] Matt. xxi. 43.
[4] Matt. xxi. 28. [5] Matt. xxi. 34. [6] Heb. xi. 37.
[7] Matt. xxiii. 35. [8] Matt. xxi. 42. [9] Ps. xviii. 45.

feast they crucified Christ; and while they are lamenting and eating unleavened bread in bitterness, do you feast.[1]] But no longer be careful to keep the feast with the Jews, for we have now no communion with them; for they have been led astray in regard to the calculation itself, which they think they accomplish perfectly, that they may be led astray on every hand, and be fenced off from the truth. But do you observe carefully the vernal equinox, which occurs on the twenty-second of the twelfth month, which is Dystros (March), observing carefully until the twenty-first of the moon, lest the fourteenth of the moon shall fall on another week, and an error being committed, you should through ignorance celebrate the passover twice in the year, or celebrate the day of the resurrection of our Lord on any other day than a Sunday.

XVIII. Do you therefore fast on the days of the passover, beginning from the second day of the week until the preparation, and the Sabbath, six days, making use of only bread, and salt, and herbs, and water for your drink; but do you abstain on these days from wine and flesh, for they are days of lamentation and not of feasting. Do ye who are able fast the day of the preparation and the Sabbath-day entirely, tasting nothing till the cock-crowing of the night; but if any one is not able to join them both together, at least let him observe the Sabbath-day; for the Lord says somewhere, speaking of Himself: "When the bridegroom shall be taken away from them, in those days shall they fast."[2] In these days, therefore, He was taken from us by the Jews, falsely so named, and fastened to the cross, and "was numbered among the transgressors."[3]

XIX. Wherefore we exhort you to fast on those days, as we also fasted till the evening, when He was taken away from us; but on the rest of the days, before the day of the preparation, let every one eat at the ninth hour, or at the

---

[1] This passage does not occur in the MSS., but is taken from Epiphanius. It is believed to be genuine, in which case what follows must be regarded as the work of the interpolator.
[2] Matt. ix. 15; Mark ii. 2; Luke v. 3.   [3] Isa. liii.

evening, or as every one is able. But from the even of the fifth day till cock-crowing break your fast when it is daybreak of the first day of the week, which is the Lord's-day. From the even till cock-crowing keep awake, and assemble together in the church, watch and pray, and entreat God; reading, when you sit up all night, the Law, the Prophets, and the Psalms, until cock-crowing, and baptizing your catechumens, and reading the Gospel with fear and trembling, and speaking to the people such things as tend to their salvation: put an end to your sorrow, and beseech God that Israel may be converted, and that He will allow them place of repentance, and the remission of their impiety; for the judge, who was a stranger, " washed his hands, and said, I am innocent of the blood of this just person: see ye to it. But Israel cried out, His blood be on us, and on our children."[1] And when Pilate said, " Shall I crucify your king? they cried out, We have no king but Cæsar: crucify him, crucify him; for every one that maketh himself a king speaketh against Cæsar." And, " If thou let this man go, thou art not Cæsar's friend."[2] And Pilate the governor and Herod the king commanded Him to be crucified; and that oracle was fulfilled which says, " Why did the Gentiles rage, and the people imagine vain things? The kings of the earth set themselves, and the rulers were gathered together against the Lord, and against His Christ;"[3] and, " They cast away the Beloved, as a dead man, who is abominable."[4] And since He was crucified on the day of the preparation, and rose again at break of day on the Lord's-day, the Scripture was fulfilled which saith, " Arise, O God; judge the earth: for Thou shalt have an inheritance in all the nations;"[5] and again, " I will arise, saith the Lord; I will put Him in safety, I will wax bold through Him;"[6] and, " But Thou, Lord, have mercy upon me, and raise me up again, and I shall requite them."[7] For this reason do you also, now the Lord is risen, offer your sacrifice, concerning

[1] Matt. xxvii. 24, 25. [2] John xix. 15, 6, 12. [3] Ps. ii. 1.
[4] Isa. xiv. 19. [5] Ps. lxxxii. 8. [6] Ps. xii. 6.
[7] Ps. xli. 10.

which He made a constitution by us, saying, "Do this for a remembrance of me;"[1] and thenceforward leave off your fasting, and rejoice, and keep a festival, because Jesus Christ, the pledge of our resurrection, is risen from the dead. And let this be an everlasting ordinance till the consummation of the world, until the Lord come. For to Jews the Lord is still dead, but to Christians He is risen: to the former, by their unbelief; to the latter, by their full assurance of faith. For the hope in Him is immortal and eternal life. After eight days let there be another feast observed with honour, the eighth day itself, on which He gave me Thomas, who was hard of belief, full assurance, by showing me the print of the nails, and the wound made in His side by the spear.[2] And again, from the first Lord's-day count forty days, from the Lord's-day till the fifth day of the week, and celebrate the feast of the ascension of the Lord, whereon He finished all His dispensation and constitution, and returned to that God and Father that sent Him, and sat down at the right hand of power, and remains there until His enemies are put under His feet; who also will come at the consummation of the world with power and great glory, to judge the quick and the dead, and to recompense to every one according to his works. And then shall they see the beloved Son of God whom they pierced;[3] and when they know Him, they shall mourn for themselves, tribe by tribe, and their wives apart.[4]

XX. For even now, on the tenth day of the month Gorpiæus, when they assemble together, they read the Lamentations of Jeremiah, in which it is said, "The Spirit before our face, Christ the Lord was taken in their destructions;"[5] and Baruch, in whom it is written, "This is our God; no other shall be esteemed with Him. He found out every way of knowledge, and showed it to Jacob His son, and Israel His beloved. Afterwards He was seen upon

---

[1] Luke xxii. 19. [2] John xx. 25.
[3] Zech. xii. 10; John xix. 37.
[4] The words "and their wives apart" are not in one V. MS.
[5] Lam. iv. 20.

earth, and conversed with men."¹ And when they read them, they lament and bewail, as themselves suppose, that desolation which happened by Nebuchadnezzar; but, as the truth shows, they unwillingly make a prelude to that lamentation which will overtake them. But after ten days from the ascension, which from the first Lord's-day is the fiftieth day, do ye keep a great festival: for on that day, at the third hour, the Lord Jesus sent on us the gift of the Holy Ghost, and we were filled with His energy, and we " spake with new tongues, as that Spirit did suggest to us;"² and we preached both to Jews and Gentiles, that He is the Christ of God, who is " determined by Him to be the judge of quick and dead."³ To Him did Moses bear witness, and said: " The Lord received fire from the Lord, and rained it down."⁴ Him did Jacob see as a man, and said: " I have seen God face to face, and my soul is preserved."⁵ Him did Abraham entertain, and acknowledge to be the Judge, and his Lord.⁶ Him did Moses see in the bush;⁷ concerning Him did he speak in Deuteronomy: " A Prophet will the Lord your God raise up unto you out of your brethren, like unto me; Him shall ye hear in all things, whatsoever He shall say unto you. And it shall be, that every soul that will not hear that Prophet, shall be destroyed from among his people."⁸ Him did Joshua the son of Nun see, as the captain of the Lord's host, in armour, for their assistance against Jericho; to whom he fell down, and worshipped, as a servant does to his master.⁹ Him Samuel knew as the " anointed of God,"¹⁰ and thence named the priests and the kings the anointed. Him David knew, and sung an hymn concerning Him, " A song concerning the Beloved;"¹¹ and adds in his person, and says, " Gird Thy sword upon Thy thigh, O Thou who art mighty in Thy beauty and renown: go on, and prosper, and reign, for the sake of truth, and meekness, and righteousness; and Thy right hand shall

[1] Bar. iii. 36. [2] Acts ii. 4. [3] Acts x. 42.
[4] Gen. xix. 24. [5] Gen. xxxii. 30. [6] Gen. xviii. 25, 27.
[7] Ex. iii. 2. [8] Deut. xviii. 15. [9] Josh. v. 14.
[10] 1 Sam. xii. 3. [11] Ps. xlv.

guide Thee after a wonderful manner. Thy darts are sharpened, O Thou that art mighty; the people shall fall under Thee in the heart of the king's enemies. Wherefore God, Thy God, hath anointed Thee with the oil of gladness above Thy fellows." Concerning Him also spake Solomon, as in His person: " The Lord created me the beginning of His ways, for His works: before the world He founded me, in the beginning before He made the earth, before the fountains of waters came, before the mountains were fastened; He begat me before all the hills." [1] And again: " Wisdom built herself an house." [2] Concerning Him also Isaiah said: " A Branch shall come out of the root of Jesse, and a Flower shall spring out of his root." And, " There shall be a root of Jesse; and He that is to rise to reign over the Gentiles, in Him shall the Gentiles trust." [3] And Zechariah says: " [4]Behold, thy King cometh unto thee, just, and having salvation; meek, and riding upon an ass, and upon a colt, the foal of an ass." [5] Him Daniel describes as " the Son of man coming to the Father," [6] and receiving all judgment and honour from Him; and as " the stone cut out of the mountain without hands, and becoming a great mountain, and filling the whole earth," [7] dashing to pieces the many governments of the smaller countries, and the polytheism of gods, but preaching the one God, and ordaining the monarchy of the Romans. Concerning Him also did Jeremiah prophesy, saying: " The Spirit before His face, Christ the Lord, was taken in their snares: of whom we said, Under His shadow we shall live among the Gentiles." [8] Ezekiel also, and the following prophets, affirm everywhere that He is the Christ, the Lord, the King, the Judge, the Lawgiver, the Angel of the Father, the onlybegotten God. Him therefore do we also preach to you, and declare Him to be God the Word, who ministered to His God and Father for the creation of the universe. By

---

[1] Prov. viii. 22-25. [2] Prov. ix. 1. [3] Isa. xi. 1, 10.
[4] One V. MS. inserts: " Rejoice greatly, O daughter of Zion."
[5] Zech. ix. 9. [6] Dan. vii. 13. [7] Dan. ii. 34.
[8] Lam. iv. 20.

believing in Him you shall live, but by disbelieving you shall be punished. For "he that is disobedient to the Son shall not see life, but the wrath of God abideth on him."[1] Therefore, after you have kept the festival of Pentecost, keep one week more festival, and after that fast; for it is reasonable to rejoice for the gift of God, and to fast after that relaxation: for both Moses and Elias fasted forty days, and Daniel for "three weeks of days did not eat desirable bread, and flesh and wine did not enter into his mouth."[2] And blessed Hannah, when she asked for Samuel, said: "I have not drunk wine nor strong drink, and I pour out my soul before the Lord."[3] And the Ninevites, when they fasted three days and three nights,[4] escaped the execution of wrath. And Esther, and Mordecai, and Judith,[5] by fasting, escaped the insurrection of the ungodly Holofernes and Haman. And David says: "My knees are weak through fasting, and my flesh faileth for [want of] oil."[6] Do you therefore fast, and ask your petitions of God. We enjoin you to fast every fourth day of the week, and every day of the preparation, and the surplusage of your fast bestow upon the needy; every Sabbath-day excepting one, and every Lord's day, hold your solemn assemblies, and rejoice: for he will be guilty of sin who fasts on the Lord's-day, being the day of the resurrection, or during the time of Pentecost, or, in general, who is sad on a festival day to the Lord. For on them we ought to rejoice, and not to mourn.

BOOK VI.

Sec. I.—*On heresies.*

I. Above all things, O bishop, avoid the sad and dangerous and most atheistical heresies, eschewing them as fire that burns those that come near to it. Avoid also schisms:

[1] John iii. 36. [2] Ex. xxxiv. 28; 1 Kings xix. 8; Dan. x. 2.
[3] 1 Sam. i. 15. [4] Jonah iii. 5. [5] Esth. iv. 16; Judith viii. 6.
[6] Ps. cix. 24.

for it is neither lawful to turn one's mind towards wicked heresies, nor to separate from those of the same sentiment out of ambition. For some who ventured to set up such practices of old did not escape punishment. For Dathan and Abiram,[1] who set up in opposition to Moses, were swallowed up into the earth. But Corah, and those two hundred and fifty who with him raised a sedition against Aaron, were consumed by fire. Miriam also, who reproached Moses, was cast out of the camp for seven days; for she said that Moses had taken an Ethiopian to wife.[2] Nay, in the case of Azariah and Uzziah,[3] the latter of which was king of Judah, but venturing to usurp the priesthood, and desiring to offer incense, which it was not lawful for him to do, was hindered by Azariah the high priest, and the fourscore priests; and when he would not obey he found the leprosy to arise in his forehead, and he hastened to go out, because the Lord had reproved him.

II. Let us therefore, beloved, consider what sort of glory that of the seditious is, and what their condemnation. For if he that rises up against kings is worthy of punishment, even though he be a son or a friend, how much more he that rises up against the priests! For by how much the priesthood is more noble than the royal power, as having its concern about the soul, so much has he a greater punishment who ventures to oppose the priesthood, than he who ventures to oppose the royal power, although neither of them goes unpunished. For neither did Absalom nor Abdadan[4] escape without punishment; nor Corah and Dathan.[5] The former rose against David, and strove concerning the kingdom; the latter against Moses, concerning pre-eminence. And they both spake evil; Absalom of his father David, as of an unjust judge, saying to every one: "Thy words are good, but there is no one that will hear thee, and do thee justice. Who will make me a ruler?"[6] But Abdadan: "I have no part in David, nor any inheritance in the son of Jesse."[7] It is plain that he could not endure to be under David's

[1] Num. xvi. [2] Num. xii. 1. [3] 2 Chron. xxvi.
[4] 2 Sam. xviii.-xx. [5] Num. xvi. [6] 2 Sam. xv. 3. [7] 2 Sam. xx. 1.

government, of whom God spake: "I have found David the son of Jesse, a man after my heart, who will do all my commands."[1] But Dathan and Abiram, and the followers of Corah, said to Moses: "Is it a small thing that thou hast brought us out of the land of Egypt, out of a land flowing with milk and honey? And why hast thou put out our eyes? And wilt thou rule over us?" And they gathered together against him a great congregation; and the followers of Corah said: "Has God spoken alone to Moses? Why is it that He has given the high-priesthood to Aaron alone? Is not all the congregation of the Lord holy? And why is Aaron alone possessed of the priesthood?"[2] And before this, one said: "Who made thee a ruler and a judge over us?"[3]

III. And they raised a sedition against Moses the servant of God, the meekest of all men,[4] and faithful, and affronted[5] so great a man with the highest ingratitude; him who was their lawgiver, and guardian, and high priest, and king, the administrator of divine things; one that showed as a creator the mighty works of the Creator; the meekest man, freest from arrogance, and full of fortitude, and most benign in his temper; one who had delivered them from many dangers, and freed them from several deaths by his holiness; who had done so many signs and wonders from God before the people, and had performed glorious and wonderful works for their benefit; who had[6] brought the ten plagues upon the Egyptians; who had divided the Red Sea, and had separated the waters as a wall on this side and on that side, and had led the people through them as through a dry wilderness,[7] and had drowned Pharaoh and the Egyptians, and all that were in company with them;[8] and had made the fountain sweet for them with wood, and had brought water out of the stony rock for them when they were thirsty;[9] and had

---

[1] Acts xiii. 22. [2] Num. xvi. 13, xii. 2, xvi. 3.
[3] Ex. ii. 14.   [4] Num. xii. 3.
[5] The words from "and affronted" to "by his holiness" are not in one V. MS.
[6] The words from "who had" to "Egyptians" are not in one V. MS.
[7] Ex. vii. etc. [8] Ex. xv. 25.   [9] Ex. xvii. 6.

given them manna out of heaven, and had distributed flesh to them out of the air;[1] and had afforded them a pillar of fire in the night to enlighten and conduct them, and a pillar of a cloud to shadow them in the day, by reason of the violent heat of the sun;[2] and had exhibited to them the law of God, engraven from the mouth, and hand, and writing of God, in tables of stone, the perfect number of ten commandments;[3] "to whom God spake face to face, as if a man spake to his friend;"[4] of whom he said, "And there arose not a prophet like unto Moses."[5] Against him arose the followers of Corah, and the Reubenites,[6] and threw stones at Moses, who prayed, and said: "Accept not Thou their offering."[7] And the glory of God appeared, and sent some down into the earth, and burnt up others with fire; and so, as to those ringleaders of this schismatical deceit which said, "Let us make ourselves a leader,"[8] the earth opened its mouth, and swallowed them up, and their tents, and what appertained to them, and they went down alive into hell; but He destroyed the followers of Corah with fire.

SEC. II.—*History and doctrines of heresies.*

IV. If therefore God inflicted punishment immediately on those that made a schism on account of their ambition, how much rather will He do it upon those who are the leaders of impious heresies! Will not He inflict severer punishment on those that blaspheme His providence or His creation? But do you, brethren, who are instructed out of the Scripture, take care not to make divisions in opinion, nor divisions in unity. For those who set up unlawful opinions are marks of perdition to the people. In like manner, do not you of the laity come near to such as advance doctrines contrary to the mind of God; nor be you partakers of their impiety. For says God: "Separate yourselves from the midst of these men, lest you perish together with them."[9] And

[1] Ex. xvi.
[2] Ex. xiii. 21.
[3] Ex. xxxi. etc.
[4] Ex. xxxiii. 11.
[5] Deut. xxxiv. 10.
[6] Num. xiv. 10.
[7] Num. xvi. 15.
[8] Num. xiv. 5.
[9] Num. xvi. 21.

again: "Depart from the midst of them, and separate yourselves, says the Lord, and touch not the unclean thing, and I will receive you."[1]

V. For those are most certainly to be avoided who blaspheme God. The greatest part of the ungodly, indeed, are ignorant of God; but these men, as fighters against God, are possessed with a wilful evil disposition, as with a disease. For from the wickedness of these heretics "pollution is gone out upon all the earth,"[2] as says the prophet Jeremiah. For the wicked synagogue is now cast off by the Lord God, and His house is rejected by Him, as He somewhere speaks: "I have forsaken mine house, I have left mine inheritance."[3] And again, says Isaiah: "I will neglect my vineyard, and it shall not be pruned nor digged, and thorns shall spring up upon it, as upon a desert; and I will command the clouds that they rain no rain upon it."[4] He has therefore "left His people as a tent in a vineyard, and as a garner in a fig or olive yard, and as a besieged city."[5] He has taken away from them the Holy Spirit, and the prophetic rain, and has replenished His church with spiritual grace, as the "river of Egypt in the time of first-fruits;"[6] and has advanced the same "as an house upon an hill, or as an high mountain; as a mountain fruitful for milk and fatness, wherein it has pleased God to dwell. For the Lord will inhabit therein to the end."[7] And He says in Jeremiah: "Our sanctuary is an exalted throne of glory."[8] And He says in Isaiah: "And it shall come to pass in the last days, that the mountain of the Lord shall be glorious, and the house of the Lord shall be upon the top of the mountains, and shall be advanced above the hills."[9] Since, therefore, He has forsaken His people, He has also left His temple desolate, and rent the veil of the temple, and took from them the Holy Spirit; for says He, "Behold, your house is left unto you desolate."[10] And He has bestowed upon you, the converted of the Gentiles,

---

[1] 2 Cor. vi. 17. [2] Jer. xxiii. 15. [3] Jer. xii. 7.
[4] Isa. v. 6. [5] Isa. i. 8. [6] See Ecclus. xxiv. 25.
[7] Psa. lxviii. 16. [8] Jer. xvii. 12. [9] Isa. ii. 2.
[10] Matt. xxiii. 38.

spiritual grace, as He says by Joel: "And it shall come to pass after these things, saith God, that I will pour out of my Spirit upon all flesh; and your sons shall prophesy, and your daughters shall see visions, and your old men shall dream dreams."[1] For God has taken away all the power and efficacy of His word, and such like visitations, from that people, and has transferred it to you, the converted of the Gentiles. For on this account the devil himself is very angry at the holy church of God: he is removed to you, and has raised against you adversities, seditions, and reproaches, schisms, and heresies. For he had before subdued that people to himself, by their slaying of Christ. But you who have left his vanities he tempts in different ways, as he did the blessed Job.[2] For indeed he opposed that great high priest Joshua the son of Josedek;[3] and he oftentimes sought to sift us, that our faith might fail.[4] But our Lord and Master, having brought him to trial, said unto him: "The Lord rebuke thee, O devil; and the Lord, who hath chosen Jerusalem, rebuke thee. Is not this plucked out of the fire as a brand?"[5] And who said then to those that stood by the high priest, "Take away his ragged garments from him;" and added, "Behold, I have taken thine iniquities away from thee;" He will say now, as He said formerly of us when we were assembled together, "I have prayed that your faith may not fail."[6]

VI. For even the Jewish nation had wicked heresies: for of them were the Sadducees, who do not confess the resurrection of the dead; and the Pharisees, who ascribe the practice of sinners to fortune and fate; and the Basmotheans, who deny providence, and say that the world is made by spontaneous motion, and take away the immortality of the soul; and the Hemerobaptists, who every day, unless they wash, do not eat,—nay, and unless they cleanse their beds and tables, or platters and cups and seats, do not make use of any of them; and those who are newly risen amongst us, the Ebionites, who will have the Son of God to be a mere

---

[1] Joel ii. 28.   [2] Job i. etc.   [3] Zech. iii. 1.
[4] Luke xxii. 31.   [5] Zech. iii. 2, etc.   [6] Luke xxii. 32.

man, begotten by human pleasure, and the conjunction of Joseph and Mary. There are also those that separate themselves from all these, and observe the laws of their fathers, and these are the Essenes. These, therefore, arose among the former people. And now the evil one, who is wise to do mischief, and as for goodness, knows no such thing, has cast out some from among us, and has wrought by them heresies and schisms.

VII. Now the original of the new heresies began thus: the devil entered into one Simon, of a village called Gitthæ, a Samaritan, by profession a magician, and made him the minister of his wicked design.[1] For when Philip our fellow-apostle, by the gift of the Lord and the energy of His Spirit, performed the miracles of healing in Samaria, insomuch that the Samaritans were affected, and embraced the faith of the God of the universe, and of the Lord Jesus, and were baptized into His name; nay, and that Simon himself, when he saw the signs and wonders which were done without any magic ceremonies, fell into admiration, and believed, and was baptized, and continued in fasting and prayer,—we heard of the grace of God which was among the Samaritans by Philip, and came down to them; and enlarging much upon the word of doctrine, we laid our hands upon all that were baptized, and we conferred upon them the participation of the Spirit. But when Simon saw that the Spirit was given to believers by the imposition of our hands, he took money, and offered it to us, saying, "Give me also the power, that on whomsoever I also shall lay my hand, he may receive the Holy Ghost;"[2] being desirous that as the devil[3] deprived Adam by his tasting of the tree of that immortality which was promised him, so also that Simon might entice us by the receiving of money, and might thereby cut us off from the gift of God,[4] that so by exchange we might sell to him for money the inestimable gift of the Spirit. But as we were

---

[1] Acts viii. [2] Acts viii. 19.
[3] "The devil:" this reading is adopted from the V. MSS.
[4] The V. MSS. insert here: "Simon, therefore, being moved by the devil, brought the money."

all troubled at this offer, I Peter, with a fixed attention on that malicious serpent which was in him, said to Simon: "Let thy money go with thee to perdition, because thou hast thought to purchase the gift of God with money. Thou hast no part in this matter, nor lot in this faith; for thy heart is not right in the sight of God. Repent therefore of this thy wickedness, and pray to the Lord, if perhaps the thought of thine heart may be forgiven thee. For I perceive thou art in the gall of bitterness and the bond of iniquity."[1] But then Simon was terrified, and said: "I entreat you, pray ye to the Lord for me, that none of those things which ye have spoken come upon me."[2]

VIII. But when we went forth among the Gentiles to preach the word of life, then the devil wrought in the people to send after us false apostles to the corrupting of the word; and they sent forth one Cleobius, and joined him with Simon, and these became disciples to one Dositheus, whom they despising, put him down from the principality. Afterwards also others were the authors of absurd doctrines: Cerinthus, and Marcus, and Menander, and Basilides, and Saturnilus. Of these some own the doctrine of many gods, some only of three, but contrary to each other, without beginning, and ever with one another, and some of an infinite number of them, and those unknown ones also. And some reject marriage; and their doctrine is, that it is not the appointment of God; and others abhor some kinds of food: some are impudent in uncleanness, such as those who are falsely called Nicolaitans. And Simon meeting me Peter, first at Cæsarea Stratonis (where the faithful Cornelius, a Gentile, believed on the Lord Jesus by me), endeavoured to pervert the word of God; there being with me the holy children, Zacchæus, who was once a publican, and Barnabas; and Nicetas and Aquila, brethren of Clement the bishop and citizen of Rome, who was the disciple of Paul, our fellow-apostle and fellow-helper in the gospel. I thrice discoursed before them with him concerning the true Prophet, and concerning the monarchy of God; and when I had overcome

[1] Acts viii. 20.   [2] Acts viii. 24.

him by the power of the Lord, and had put him to silence, I drove him away into Italy.

IX. Now when he was in Rome, he mightily disturbed the church, and subverted many, and brought them over to himself, and astonished the Gentiles with his skill in magic, insomuch that once, in the middle of the day, he went into their theatre, and commanded the people that they should bring me also by force into the theatre, and promised he would fly in the air; and when all the people were in suspense at this, I prayed by myself. And indeed he was carried up into the air by demons, and did fly on high in the air, saying that he was returning into heaven, and that he would supply them with good things from thence. And the people making acclamations to him, as to a god, I stretched out my hands to heaven, with my mind, and besought God through the Lord Jesus to throw down this pestilent fellow, and to destroy the power of those demons that made use of the same for the seduction and perdition of men, to dash him against the ground, and bruise him, but not to kill him. And then, fixing my eyes on Simon, I said to him: "If I be a man of God, and a real apostle of Jesus Christ, and a teacher of piety, and not of deceit, as thou art, Simon, I command the wicked powers of the apostate from piety, by whom Simon the magician is carried, to let go their hold, that he may fall down headlong from his height, that he may be exposed to the laughter of those that have been seduced by him." When I had said these words, Simon was deprived of his powers, and fell down headlong with a great noise, and was violently dashed against the ground, and had his hip and ankle-bones broken; and the people cried out, saying, "There is one only God, whom Peter rightly preaches in truth." And many left him; but some who were worthy of perdition continued in his wicked doctrine. And after this manner the most atheistical heresy of the Simonians was first established in Rome; and the devil wrought by the rest of the false apostles also.

X. Now all these had one and the same design of atheism, to blaspheme Almighty God, to spread their doctrine that

He is an unknown being, and not the Father of Christ, nor the Creator of the world; but one who cannot be spoken of, ineffable, not to be named, and begotten by Himself; that we are not to make use of the law and the prophets; that there is no providence and no resurrection to be believed; that there is no judgment nor retribution; that the soul is not immortal; that we must only indulge our pleasures, and turn to any sort of worship without distinction. Some of them say that there are many gods, some that there are three gods without beginning, some that there are two unbegotten gods, some that there are innumerable Æons. Further, some of them teach that men are not to marry, and must abstain from flesh and wine, affirming that marriage, and the begetting of children, and the eating of certain foods, are abominable; that so, as sober persons, they may make their wicked opinions to be received as worthy of belief. And some of them absolutely prohibit the eating of flesh, as being the flesh not of brute animals, but of creatures that have a rational soul, as though those that ventured to slay them would be charged with the crime of murder. But others of them affirm that we must only abstain from swine's flesh, but may eat such as are clean by the law; and that we ought to be circumcised, according to the law, and to believe in Jesus as in an holy man and a prophet. But others teach that men ought to be impudent in uncleanness, and to abuse the flesh, and to go through all unholy practices, as if this were the only way for the soul to avoid the rulers of this world. Now all these are the instruments of the devil, and the children of wrath.

SEC. III.—*The heresies attacked by the apostles.*

XI. But we, who are the children of God and the sons of peace, do preach the holy and right word of piety, and declare one only God, the Lord of the law and of the prophets, the Maker of the world, the Father of Christ; not a being that caused Himself, or begat Himself, as they suppose, but eternal, and without original, and inhabiting light inaccessible; not two or three, or manifold, but eternally one only; not a being that cannot be known or spoken of, but who was preached by the law and the prophets; the Almighty, the Supreme Governor of all things, the All-powerful Being; the God and Father of the Only-begotten, and of the First-born of the whole creation; one God, the Father of one Son, not of many; the Maker of one Comforter by Christ, the Maker of the other orders, the one Creator of the several creatures by Christ, the same their Preserver and Legislator by Him; the cause of the resurrection, and of the judgment, and of the retribution which shall be made by Him: that this same Christ was pleased to become man, and went through life without sin, and suffered, and rose from the dead, and returned to Him that sent Him. We also say that every creature of God is good, and nothing abominable; that everything for the support of life, when it is partaken of righteously, is very good: for, according to the Scripture, "all things were very good."[1] We believe that lawful marriage, and the begetting of children, is honourable and undefiled; for difference of sexes was formed in Adam and Eve for the increase of mankind. We acknowledge with us a soul that is incorporeal and immortal,—not corruptible as bodies are, but immortal, as being rational and free. We abhor all unlawful mixtures, and that which is practised by some against nature as wicked and impious. We profess there will be a resurrection both of the just and unjust, and a retribution. We profess that Christ is not a mere man, but God the Word, and man the Mediator between God and men, the High Priest of the Father; nor are we circumcised with the Jews, as knowing that He is come "to whom the inheritance was reserved,"[2] and on whose account the families were kept distinct—"the expectation of the Gentiles,"[3] Jesus Christ, who sprang out of Judah, the Son from the branch, the flower from Jesse, whose government is upon His shoulder.[4]

XII. But because this heresy did then seem the more powerful to seduce men, and the whole church was in danger,[5]

---

[1] Gen. i. 31. [2] Gen. xlix. 10. [3] Gen. xlix. 9.
[4] Isa. xi. 1, ix. 6. [5] Acts xv.

we the twelve assembled together at Jerusalem (for Matthias was chosen to be an apostle in the room of the betrayer, and took the lot of Judas; as it is said, "His bishopric let another take"[1]). We deliberated, together with James the Lord's brother, what was to be done; and it seemed good to him and to the elders to speak to the people words of doctrine. For certain men likewise went down from Judea to Antioch, and taught the brethren who were there, saying: "Unless ye be circumcised after the manner of Moses, and walk according to the other customs which he ordained, ye cannot be saved."[2] When, therefore, there had been no small dissension and disputation, the brethren which were at Antioch, when they knew that we were all met together about this question, sent out unto us men who were faithful and understanding in the Scriptures to learn concerning this question. And they, when they were come to Jerusalem, declared to us what questions were arisen in the church of Antioch,— namely, that some said men ought to be circumcised, and to observe the other purifications. And when some said one thing, and some another, I Peter stood up, and said unto them: "Men and brethren, ye know how that from ancient days God made choice among you that the Gentiles should hear the word of the gospel by my mouth, and believe; and God, which knoweth the hearts, bare them witness.[3] For an angel of the Lord appeared on a certain time to Cornelius,[4] who was a centurion of the Roman government, and spake to him concerning me, that he should send for me, and hear the word of life from my mouth. He therefore sent for me from Joppa to Cæsarea Stratonis; and when I was ready to go to him, I would have eaten. And while they made ready I was in the upper room praying; and I saw heaven opened, and a vessel, knit at the four corners like a splendid sheet, let down to the earth, wherein were all manner of four-footed beasts, and creeping things of the earth, and fowls of the heaven. And there came a voice out of heaven to me, saying, Arise, Peter; kill, and eat. And I said, By no means, Lord: for I have never eaten anything

[1] Ps. cix. 8. [2] Acts xv. 1. [3] Acts xv. 7. [4] Acts x.

common or unclean. And there came a voice a second time, saying, What God hath cleansed, that call not thou common. And this was done thrice, and the vessel was received up again into heaven. But as I doubted what this vision should mean, the Spirit said to me, Behold, men seek thee; but rise up, and go thy way with them, nothing doubting, for I have sent them.[1] These men were those which came from the centurion, and so by reasoning I understood the word of the Lord which is written: 'Whosoever shall call on the name of the Lord shall be saved.'[2] And again: 'All the ends of the earth shall remember, and turn unto the Lord, and all the families of the heathen shall worship before Him: for the kingdom is the Lord's, and He is the governor of the nations.'[3] And observing that there were expressions everywhere concerning the calling of the Gentiles, I rose up, and went with them, and entered into the man's house. And while I was preaching the word, the Holy Spirit fell upon him, and upon those that were with him, as it did upon us at the beginning; and He put no difference between us and them, purifying their hearts by faith. And I perceived that God is no respecter of persons; but that in every nation he that feareth Him, and worketh righteousness, will be accepted with Him. But even the believers which were of the circumcision were astonished at this. Now therefore why tempt ye God, to lay an heavy yoke upon the neck of the disciples, which neither we nor our fathers were able to bear? But by the grace of the Lord, we believe we shall be saved, even as they.[4] For the Lord has loosed us from our bonds, and has made our burden light, and has loosed the heavy yoke from us by His clemency." While I spake these things, the whole multitude kept silence. But James the Lord's brother answered and said: "Men and brethren, hearken unto me; Simeon hath declared how God at first visited to take out a people from the Gentiles for His name. And to this agree the words of the prophets; as it is written: 'Afterwards I will return, and will raise again and rebuild the tabernacle

[1] Acts x. 13, etc.
[2] Joel ii. 32.
[3] Ps. xxii. 28.
[4] Acts xi. 15, 9, x. 34, 45, xv. 10.

of David, which is fallen down; and I will rebuild its ruins, and will again set it up, that the residue of men may seek after the Lord, and all the nations upon whom my name is called, saith the Lord, who doth these things.'[1] Known unto God are all His works from the beginning of the world. Wherefore my sentence is, that we do not trouble those who from among the Gentiles turn unto God: but to charge them that they abstain from the pollutions of the Gentiles, and from what is sacrificed to idols, and from blood, and from things strangled, and from fornication; which laws were given to the ancients who lived before the law, under the law of nature, Enos, Enoch, Noah, Melchizedek, Job, and if there be any other of the same sort."[2] Then it seemed good to us the apostles, and to James the bishop, and to the elders, with the whole church, to send men chosen from among our own selves, with Barnabas, and Paul of Tarsus, the apostle of the Gentiles, and Judas who was called Barsabbas, and Silas, chief men among the brethren, and wrote by their hand, as follows: "The apostles, and elders, and brethren, to the brethren of Antioch, Syria, and Cilicia of the Gentiles, send greeting: Since we have heard that some from us have troubled you with words, subverting your souls, to whom we gave no such commandment, it has seemed good to us, when we were met together with one accord, to send chosen men to you, with our beloved Barnabas and Paul, men that have hazarded their lives for our Lord Jesus Christ, by whom ye sent unto us. We have sent also with them Judas and Silas, who shall themselves declare the same things by mouth. For it seemed good to the Holy Ghost, and to us, to lay no other burden upon you than these necessary things; that ye abstain from things offered to idols, and from blood, and from things strangled, and from fornication: from which things if ye keep yourselves, ye shall do well. Fare ye well."[3] We accordingly sent this epistle; but we ourselves remained in Jerusalem many days, consulting together for the public benefit, for the well ordering of all things.

XIII. But after a long time we visited the brethren, and

[1] Amos ix. 11.   [2] Acts xv. 14.   [3] Acts xv. 23, etc.

confirmed them with the word of piety, and charged them to avoid those who, under the name of Christ and Moses, war against Christ and Moses, and in the clothing of sheep hide the wolf. For these are false Christs, and false prophets, and false apostles, deceivers and corrupters, portions of foxes, the destroyers of the herbs of the vineyards: "for whose sake the love of many will wax cold. But he that endureth stedfast to the end, the same shall be saved."[1] Concerning whom, that He might secure us, the Lord declared, saying: "There will come to you men in sheep's clothing, but inwardly they are ravening wolves. Ye shall know them by their fruits; take care of them. For false Christs and false prophets shall arise, and shall deceive many."[2]

XIV. On whose account also we, who are now assembled in one place,—Peter and Andrew; James and John, sons of Zebedee; Philip and Bartholomew; Thomas and Matthew; James the son of Alphæus, and Lebbæus who is surnamed Thaddæus; and Simon the Canaanite,[3] and Matthias, who instead of Judas was numbered with us; and James the brother of the Lord and bishop of Jerusalem, and Paul the teacher of the Gentiles, the chosen vessel, having all met together, have written to you this catholic doctrine for the confirmation of you, to whom the oversight of the universal church is committed: wherein we declare unto you, that there is only one God Almighty, besides whom there is no other, and that you must worship and adore Him alone, through Jesus Christ our Lord, in the most holy Spirit;[4] that you are to make use of the sacred Scriptures, the law, and the prophets; to honour your parents; to avoid all unlawful actions; to believe the resurrection and the judgment, and to expect the retribution; and to use all His creatures with thankfulness, as the works of God, and having no evil in them; to marry after a lawful manner, for such marriage is unblameable. For "the

---

[1] Matt. xxiv. 12.   [2] Matt. vii. 15, xxiv. 24.   [3] Matt. x. 2.
[4] One V. MS. reads as follows: "And our Lord Jesus Christ, and the most holy Spirit."

woman is suited to the man by the Lord;"[1] and the Lord says: "He that made them from the beginning, made them male and female; and said, For this cause shall a man leave his father and his mother, and shall cleave unto his wife: and they two shall be one flesh."[2] Nor let it be esteemed lawful after marriage to put her away who is without blame. For says He: "Thou shalt take care to thy spirit, and shalt not forsake the wife of thy youth; for she is the partner[3] of thy life, and the remains of thy spirit. I and no other have made her."[4] For the Lord says: "What God has joined together, let no man put asunder."[5] For the wife is the partner of life, united by God unto one body from two. But he that divides that again into two which is become one, is the enemy of the creation of God, and the adversary of His providence. In like manner, he that retains her that is corrupted is a transgressor of the law of nature; since "he that retains an adulteress is foolish and impious."[6] For says He, "Cut her off from thy flesh;"[7] for she is not an help, but a snare, bending her mind from thee to another. Nor be ye circumcised in your flesh, but let the circumcision which is of the heart by the Spirit suffice for the faithful; for He says, "Be ye circumcised to your God, and be ye circumcised in the foreskin of your heart."[8]

XV. Be ye likewise contented with one baptism alone, that which is into the death of the Lord; not that which is conferred by wicked heretics, but that which is conferred by unblameable priests, "in the name of the Father, and of the Son, and of the Holy Ghost:"[9] and let not that which comes from the ungodly be received by you, nor let that which is done by the godly be disannulled by a second. For as there is one God, one Christ, and one Comforter, and one death of the Lord in the body, so let that baptism which is unto

---

[1] Prov. xix. 14.   [2] Matt. xix. 4.
[3] The words from "for she is the partner" to "made her" are omitted in one V. MS.
[4] Mal. ii. 15, 14.   [5] Matt. xix. 6.   [6] Prov. xviii. 22.
[7] Ecclus. xxv. 26.   [8] Jer. iv. 4.   [9] Matt. xxviii. 19.

Him be but one. But those that receive polluted baptism from the ungodly will become partners in their opinions. For they are not priests. For God says to them: "Because thou hast rejected knowledge, I will also reject thee from the office of a priest to me."[1] Nor indeed are those that are baptized by them initiated, but are polluted, not receiving the remission of sins, but the bond of impiety. And, besides, they that attempt to baptize those already initiated crucify the Lord afresh, slay Him a second time, laugh at divine and ridicule holy things, affront the Spirit, dishonour the sacred blood of Christ as common blood, are impious against Him that sent, Him that suffered, and Him that witnessed. Nay, he that, out of contempt, will not be baptized, shall be condemned as an unbeliever, and shall be reproached as ungrateful and foolish. For the Lord says: "Except a man be baptized of water and of the Spirit, he shall by no means enter into the kingdom of heaven."[2] And again: "He that believeth and is baptized shall be saved; but he that believeth not shall be damned."[3] But he that says, When I am dying I will be baptized, lest I should sin and defile my baptism, is ignorant of God, and forgetful of his own nature. For "do not thou delay to turn unto the Lord, for thou knowest not what the next day will bring forth."[4] Do you also baptize your infants, and bring them up in the nurture and admonition of God. For says He: "Suffer the little children to come unto me, and forbid them not."[5]

XVI. We have sent all these things to you, that ye may know our opinion, what it is; and that ye may not receive those books which obtain in our name, but are written by the ungodly. For you are not to attend to the names of the apostles, but to the nature of the things, and their settled opinions. For we know that Simon and Cleobius, and their followers, have compiled poisonous books under the name of Christ and of His disciples, and do carry them about in order to deceive you who love Christ, and us His servants.

[1] Hos. iv. 6.   [2] John iii. 5.   [3] Mark xvi. 16.
[4] Ecclus. v. 7; Prov. xxvii. 1, iii. 28.   [5] Matt. xix. 14.

And among the ancients also some have written apocryphal books of Moses, and Enoch, and Adam, and Isaiah, and David, and Elias, and of the three patriarchs, pernicious and repugnant to the truth. The same things even now have the wicked heretics done, reproaching the creation, marriage, providence, the begetting of children, the law, and the prophets; inscribing certain barbarous names, and, as they think, of angels, but, to speak the truth, of demons, which suggest things to them: whose doctrine eschew, that ye may not be partakers of the punishment due to those that write such things for the seduction and perdition of the faithful and unblameable disciples of the Lord Jesus.

XVII. We have already said, that a bishop, a presbyter, and a deacon, when they are constituted, must be but once married, whether their wives be alive or whether they be dead; and that it is not lawful for them, if they are unmarried when they are ordained, to be married afterwards; or if they be then married, to marry a second time, but to be content with that wife which they had when they came to ordination.[1] We also appoint that the ministers, and singers, and readers, and porters, shall be only once married. But if they entered into the clergy before they were married, we permit them to marry, if they have an inclination thereto, lest they sin and incur punishment. But we do not permit any one of the clergy to take to wife either a courtezan, or a servant, or a widow, or one that is divorced, as also the law says. Let the deaconess be a pure virgin; or, at the least, a widow who has been but once married, faithful, and well esteemed.[2]

XVIII. Receive ye the penitent, for this is the will of God in Christ. Instruct the catechumens in the elements of religion, and then baptize them. Eschew the atheistical heretics, who are past repentance, and separate them from the faithful, and excommunicate them from the church of God, and charge the faithful to abstain entirely from them, and not to partake with them either in sermons or prayers: for these are those that are enemies to the church, and lay

---

[1] 1 Tim. iii. 2, 12; Tit. i. 6.   [2] Lev. xxi. 7, 14; 1 Tim. v. 9.

snares for it; who corrupt the flock, and defile the heritage of Christ, pretenders only to wisdom, and the vilest of men; concerning whom Solomon the wise said: "The wicked doers pretend to act piously." For, says he, "there is a way which seemeth right to some, but the ends thereof look to the bottom of hell."[1] These are they concerning whom the Lord declared His mind with bitterness and severity, saying that "they are false Christs and false teachers;"[2] who have blasphemed the Spirit of grace, and done despite to the gift they had from Him after the grace [of baptism], "to whom forgiveness shall not be granted, neither in this world nor in that which is to come;"[3] who are both more wicked than the Jews and more atheistical than the Gentiles; who blaspheme the God over all, and tread under foot His Son, and do despite to the doctrine of the Spirit; who deny the words of God, or pretend hypocritically to receive them, to the affronting of God, and the deceiving of those that come among them; who abuse the Holy Scriptures, and as for righteousness, they do not so much as know what it is; who spoil the church of God, as the "little foxes do the vineyard;"[4] whom we exhort you to avoid, lest you lay traps for your own souls. "For he that walketh with wise men shall be wise, but he that walketh with the foolish shall be known."[5] For we ought neither to run along with a thief, nor put in our lot with an adulterer; since holy David says: "O Lord, I have hated them that hate Thee, and I am withered away on account of Thy enemies. I hated them with a perfect hatred: they were to me as enemies."[6] And God reproaches Jehoshaphat with his friendship towards Ahab, and his league with him and with Ahaziah, by Jonah the prophet: "Art thou in friendship with a sinner? Or dost thou aid him that is hated by the Lord?"[7] "For this cause the wrath of the Lord would be upon thee suddenly, but that thy heart is found perfect with the Lord. For this cause the Lord hath spared thee; yet are thy works shattered, and

---

[1] Prov. xiv. 12. [2] Matt. xxiv. 24. [3] Matt. xii. 32.
[4] *Vid.* Cant. ii. 15. [5] Prov. xiii. 20. [6] Ps. cxxxix. 21.
[7] 2 Chron. xix. 2.

thy ships broken to pieces."[1] Eschew therefore their fellowship, and estrange yourselves from their friendship. For concerning them did the prophet declare, and say: "It is not lawful to rejoice with the ungodly,"[2] says the Lord. For these are hidden wolves, dumb dogs, that cannot bark, who at present are but few, but in process of time, when the end of the world draws nigh, will be more in number and more troublesome, of whom said the Lord, "Will the Son of man, when He comes, find faith on the earth?"[3] and, "Because iniquity shall abound, the love of many shall wax cold;" and, "There shall come false Christs and false prophets, and shall show signs in the heaven, so as, if it were possible, to deceive the elect:"[4] from whose deceit God, through Jesus Christ, who is our hope, will deliver us. For we ourselves, as we passed through the nations, and confirmed the churches, curing some with much exhortation and healing words, restored them again when they were in the certain way to death. But those that were incurable we cast out from the flock, that they might not infect the lambs, which were found with their scabby disease, but might continue before the Lord God pure and undefiled, sound and unspotted. And this we did in every city, everywhere through the whole world, and have left to you the bishops and to the rest of the priests this very catholic doctrine worthily and righteously, as a memorial or confirmation to those who have believed in God; and we have sent it by our fellow-minister Clement, our most faithful and intimate son in the Lord, together with Barnabas, and Timothy our most dearly beloved son, and the genuine Mark, together with whom we recommend to you also Titus and Luke, and Jason and Lucius, and Sosipater.[5]

Sec. IV.—*Of the law.*

By whom also we exhort you in the Lord to abstain from your old conversation, vain bonds, separations, observances,

[1] 2 Chron. xx. 37. [2] *Vid.* Isa. lvii. 21. [3] Luke xviii. 8.
[4] Matt. xxiv. 12, 24. [5] Rom. xvi. 21.

distinction of meats, and daily washings: for "old things are passed away; behold, all things are become new."¹

XIX. For since ye have known God through Jesus Christ, and all His dispensation, as it has been from the beginning, that He gave a plain law to assist the law of nature,² such an one as is pure, saving, and holy, in which His own name was inscribed, perfect, which is never to fail, being complete in ten commands,³ unspotted, converting souls;⁴ which, when the Hebrews forgot, He put them in mind of it by the prophet Malachi, saying, "Remember ye the law of Moses, the man of God, who gave you in charge commandments and ordinances."⁵ Which law is so very holy and righteous, that even our Saviour, when on a certain time He healed one leper, and afterwards nine, said to the first, "Go, show thyself to the high priest, and offer the gift which Moses commanded for a testimony unto them;"⁶ and afterwards to the nine, "Go, show yourselves to the priests."⁷ For He nowhere has dissolved the law, as Simon pretends, but fulfilled it; for He says: "One iota, or one tittle, shall not pass from the law until all be fulfilled." For says He, "I come not to dissolve the law, but to fulfil it."⁸ For Moses himself, who was at once the lawgiver, and the high priest, and the prophet, and the king, and Elijah, the zealous follower of the prophets, were present at our Lord's transfiguration in the mountain,⁹ and witnesses of His incarnation and of His sufferings, as the intimate friends of Christ, but not as enemies and strangers. Whence it is demonstrated that the law is good and holy, as also the prophets.

XX. Now the law is the decalogue, which the Lord promulgated to them with an audible voice,¹⁰ before the people made that calf which represented the Egyptian Apis. And the law is righteous, and therefore is it called the law,¹¹ because judgments are thence made according to the law of nature,

¹ 2 Cor. v. 17.   ² Isa. viii. 20, LXX.   ³ Deut. xii. 5.
⁴ Ps. xix. 8.   ⁵ Mal. iv. 4.   ⁶ Matt. viii. 4; Mark i.
⁷ Luke xvii. 14.   ⁸ Matt. v. 18, 17.   ⁹ Luke ix. 30.
¹⁰ Ex. xx.   ¹¹ Ex. xxxii.

which the followers of Simon abuse, supposing they shall
not be judged thereby, and so shall escape punishment.
This law is good, holy, and such as lays no compulsion in
things positive. For He says: "If thou wilt make me an
altar, thou shalt make it of earth."[1] It does not say, "Make
one," but, "If thou wilt make." It does not impose a necessity, but gives leave to their own free liberty. For God
does not stand in need of sacrifices, being by nature above
all want. But knowing that, as of old, Abel, beloved of God,
and Noah and Abraham, and those that succeeded, without
being required, but only moved of themselves by the law of
nature, did offer sacrifice to God out of a grateful mind; so
He did now permit the Hebrews, not commanding, but, if
they had a mind, permitting them; and if they offered from a
right intention, showing Himself pleased with their sacrifices.
Therefore He says: "If thou desirest to offer, do not offer
to me as to one that stands in need of it, for I stand in need
of nothing; for the world is mine, and the fulness thereof."[2]
But when this people became forgetful of that, and called
upon a calf as God, instead of the true God, and to him
did ascribe the cause of their coming out of Egypt, saying,
"These are thy gods, O Israel, which have brought thee out
of the land of Egypt;"[3] and when these men had committed wickedness with the "similitude of a calf that eateth
hay,"[4] and denied God who had visited them by Moses in
their afflictions, and had done signs with his hand and rod,
and had smitten the Egyptians with ten plagues; who had
divided the waters of the Red Sea into two parts; who had
led them in the midst of the water, as a horse upon the
ground; who had drowned their enemies, and those that
laid wait for them; who at Marah had made sweet the
bitter fountain; who had brought water out of the sharp
rock till they were satisfied; who had overshadowed them
with a pillar of a cloud on account of the immoderate heat,
and with a pillar of fire which enlightened and guided them
when they knew not which way they were to go; who gave

[1] Ex. xx. 24.   [2] Ps. l. 12.
[3] Ex. xxxii. 4.   [4] Ex. iv. etc.

them manna from heaven, and gave them quails for flesh from the sea;[1] who gave them the law in the mountain; whose voice He had vouchsafed to let them hear; Him did they deny, and said to Aaron, "Make us gods who shall go before us;"[2] and they made a molten calf, and sacrificed to an idol;—then was God angry, as being ungratefully treated by them, and bound them with bonds which could not be loosed, with a mortifying burden and a hard collar, and no longer said, "If thou makest," but, "Make an altar," and sacrifice perpetually; for thou art forgetful and ungrateful. Offer burnt-offerings therefore continually, that thou mayest be mindful of me. For since thou hast wickedly abused thy power, I lay a necessity upon thee for the time to come, and I command thee to abstain from certain meats; and I ordain thee the distinction of clean and unclean creatures, although every creature is good, as being made by me; and I appoint thee several separations, purgations, frequent washings and sprinklings, several purifications, and several times of rest; and if thou neglectest any of them, I determine that punishment which is proper to the disobedient, that being pressed and galled by thy collar, thou mayest depart from the error of polytheism, and laying aside that, "These are thy gods, O Israel,"[3] mayest be mindful of that, "Hear, O Israel, the Lord thy God is one Lord;"[4] and mayest run back again to that law which is inserted by me in the nature of all men, "that there is only one God in heaven and on earth, and to love Him with all thy heart, and all thy might, and all thy mind," and to fear none but Him, nor to admit the names of other gods into thy mind, nor to let thy tongue utter them out of thy mouth. He bound them for the hardness of their hearts, that by sacrificing, and resting, and purifying themselves, and by similar observances, they might come to the knowledge of God, who ordained these things for them.

XXI. "But blessed are your eyes, for they see; and your ears, for they hear."[5] Yours, I say, who have believed in

[1] Num. xi. 31.   [2] Ex. xxxii. 1.   [3] Ex. v. 4.
[4] Deut. vi. 4.   [5] Matt. xiii. 16.

the one God, not by necessity, but by a sound understanding, in obedience to Him that called you. For you are released from the bonds, and freed from the servitude. For says He:[1] "I call you no longer servants, but friends; for all things that I have heard of my Father have I made known unto you."[2] For to them that would not see nor hear, not for the want of those senses, but for the excess of their wickedness, "I gave statutes that were not good, and judgments whereby they would not live;"[3] they are looked upon as not good, as burnings and a sword, and medicines are esteemed enemies by the sick, and impossible to be observed on account of their obstinacy: whence also they brought death upon them being not obeyed.

XXII. You therefore are blessed who are delivered from the curse. For Christ, the Son of God, by His coming has confirmed and completed the law, but has taken away the additional precepts, although not all of them, yet at least the more grievous ones; having confirmed the former, and abolished the latter, and has again set the free-will of man at liberty, not subjecting him to the penalty of a temporal death, but giving laws to him according to another constitution. Wherefore He says: "If any man will come after me, let him come."[4] And again: "Will ye also go away?"[5] And besides, before His coming He refused the sacrifices of the people, while they frequently offered them, when they sinned against Him, and thought He was to be appeased by sacrifices, but not by repentance. For thus He speaks: "Why dost thou bring to me frankincense from Saba, and cinnamon from a remote land? Your burnt-offerings are not acceptable, and your sacrifices are not sweet to me."[6] And afterwards: "Gather your burnt-offerings, together with your sacrifices, and eat flesh. For I did not command you, when I brought you out of the land of Egypt, concerning burnt-offerings and sacrifices."[7] And He says by Isaiah: "To what purpose do ye bring me a multitude of sacrifices?

---

[1] One V. MS. reads: "Thus also said the Lord to us His disciples."
[2] John xv. 15.　　[3] Ezek. xx. 25.　　[4] Matt. xvi. 24.
[5] John vi. 67.　　[6] Jer. vi. 20, etc.　　[7] Jer. vii. 21.

saith the Lord. I am full of the burnt-offerings of rams, and I will not accept the fat of lambs, and the blood of bulls and of goats. Nor do you come and appear before me; for who hath required these things at your hands? Do not go on to tread my courts any more. If you bring me fine flour, it is vain: incense is an abomination unto me: your new moons, and your Sabbaths, and your great day, I cannot bear them: your fasts, and your rests, and your feasts, my soul hateth them; I am over-full of them."[1] And He says by another: "Depart from me; the sound of thine hymns, and the psalms of thy musical instruments, I will not hear."[2] And Samuel says to Saul, when he thought to sacrifice: "Obedience is better than sacrifice, and hearkening than the fat of rams. For, behold, the Lord does not so much delight in sacrifice, as in obeying Him."[3] And He says by David: "I will take no calves out of thine house, nor he-goats out of thy flock. If I should be hungry, I would not tell thee; for the whole world is mine, and the fulness thereof. Shall I eat the flesh of bulls, or drink the blood of goats? Sacrifice to God the sacrifice of praise, and pay thy vows to the Most High."[4] And in all the Scriptures in like manner He refuses their sacrifices on account of their sinning against Him. For "the sacrifices of the impious are an abomination with the Lord, since they offer them in an unlawful manner."[5] And again: "Their sacrifices are to them as bread of lamentation; all that eat of them shall be defiled."[6] If, therefore, before His coming He sought for "a clean heart and a contrite spirit"[7] more than sacrifices, much rather would He abrogate those sacrifices, I mean those by blood, when He came. Yet He so abrogated them as that He first fulfilled them. For He was both circumcised, and sprinkled, and offered sacrifices and whole burnt-offerings, and made use of the rest of their customs. And He that was the Lawgiver became Himself the fulfilling of the law; not taking away the law of nature,

---

[1] Isa. i. 11.   [2] Amos v. 23.   [3] 1 Sam. xv. 2.
[4] Ps. l. 9, 12.   [5] Prov. xxi. 27.   [6] Hos. ix. 4.
[7] Ps. li. 12, 19.

but abrogating those additional laws that were afterwards introduced, although not all of them neither.

XXIII. For He did not take away the law of nature, but confirmed it. For He that said in the law, "The Lord thy God is one Lord;"[1] the same says in the gospel, "That they might know Thee, the only true God."[2] And He that said, "Thou shalt love thy neighbour as thyself,"[3] says in the gospel, renewing the same precept, "A new commandment I give unto you, that ye love one another."[4] He who then forbade murder, does now forbid causeless anger.[5] He that forbade adultery, does now forbid all unlawful lust. He that forbade stealing, now pronounces him most happy who supplies those that are in want out of his own labours.[6] He that forbade hatred, now pronounces him blessed that loves his enemies.[7] He that forbade revenge, now commands long-suffering;[8] not as if just revenge were an unrighteous thing, but because long-suffering is more excellent. Nor did He make laws to root out our natural passions, but only to forbid the excess of them.[9] He who had commanded to honour our parents, was Himself subject to them.[10] He who had commanded to keep the Sabbath, by resting thereon for the sake of meditating on the laws, has now commanded us to consider of the law of creation, and of providence every day, and to return thanks to God. He abrogated circumcision when He had Himself fulfilled it. For He it was "to whom the inheritance was reserved, who was the expectation of the nations."[11] He who made a law for swearing rightly, and forbade perjury, has now charged us not to swear at all.[12] He has in several ways changed baptism, sacrifice, the priesthood, and the divine service, which was confined to one place; for instead of daily baptisms, He has given only one, which is that into His death. Instead of one tribe, He has appointed that out of every nation the best should be ordained for the priesthood; and that not their

[1] Deut. vi. 4.
[2] John xvii. 3.
[3] Lev. xix. 18.
[4] John xiii. 34.
[5] Matt. v. 2.
[6] Acts xx. 35.
[7] Matt. v. 7.
[8] Matt. v. 43.
[9] Matt. v. 38.
[10] Luke ii. 51.
[11] Gen. xlix. 10.
[12] Matt. v. 33.

bodies should be examined for blemishes, but their religion and their lives. Instead of a bloody sacrifice, He has appointed that reasonable and unbloody mystical one of His body and blood, which is performed to represent the death of the Lord by symbols. Instead of the divine service confined to one place, He has commanded and appointed that He should be glorified from sunrising to sunsetting in every place of His dominion.[1] He did not therefore take away the law from us, but the bonds. For concerning the law Moses says: "Thou shalt meditate on the word which I command thee, sitting in thine house, and rising up, and walking in the way."[2] And David says: "His delight is in the law of the Lord, and in His law will he meditate day and night."[3] For everywhere would He have us subject to His laws, but not transgressors of them. For says He: "Blessed are the undefiled in the way, who walk in the law of the Lord. Blessed are they that search out His testimonies; with their whole heart shall they seek Him."[4] And again: "Blessed are we, O Israel, because those things that are pleasing to God are known to us."[5] And the Lord says: "If ye know these things, happy are ye if ye do them."[6]

XXIV. Nor does He desire that the law of righteousness should only be demonstrated by us; but He is pleased that it should appear and shine by means of the Romans. For these Romans, believing in the Lord, left off their polytheism and injustice, and entertain the good, and punish the bad. But they hold the Jews under tribute, and do not suffer them to make use of their own ordinances.

XXV. Because, indeed, they drew servitude upon themselves voluntarily, when they said, "We have no king but Cæsar;"[7] and, "If we do not slay Christ, all men will believe in him, and the Romans will come and will take away both our place and nation."[8] And so they prophesied unwittingly. For accordingly the nations believed on Him, and they themselves were deprived by the Romans of their power,

---

[1] Ps. cxiii. 3; Mal. i. 11.   [2] Deut. vi. 6.   [3] Ps. i. 2.
[4] Ps. cxix. 1.   [5] Bar. iv. 4.   [6] John xiii. 17.
[7] John xix. 15.   [8] John xi. 48.

and of their legal worship; and they have been forbidden to slay whom they please, and to sacrifice when they will. Wherefore they are accursed, as not able to perform the things they are commanded to do. For says He: "Cursed be he that does not continue in all things that are written in the book of the law to do them."[1] Now it is impossible in their dispersion, while they are among the heathen, for them to perform all things in their law. For the divine Moses forbids both to rear an altar out of Jerusalem, and to read the law out of the bounds of Judea.[2] Let us therefore follow Christ, that we may inherit His blessings. Let us walk after the law and the prophets by the gospel. Let us eschew the worshippers of many gods, and the murderers of Christ, and the murderers of the prophets, and the wicked and atheistical heretics. Let us be obedient to Christ as to our King, as having authority to change several constitutions, and having, as a legislator, wisdom to make new constitutions in different circumstances; yet so that everywhere the laws of nature be immutably preserved.

SEC. V.—*The teaching of the apostles in opposition to Jewish and Gentile superstitions, especially in regard to marriage and funerals.*

XXVI. Do you therefore, O bishops, and ye of the laity, avoid all heretics who abuse the law and the prophets. For they are enemies to God Almighty, and disobey Him, and do not confess Christ to be the Son of God. For they also deny His generation according to the flesh; they are ashamed of the cross; they abuse His passion and His death; they know not His resurrection; they take away His generation before all ages. Nay, some of them are impious after another manner, imagining the Lord to be a mere man, supposing Him to consist of a soul and body. But others of them suppose that Jesus Himself is the God over all, and glorify Him as His own Father, and suppose Him to be both the Son and the Comforter; than which doctrines what can

[1] Deut. xxvii. 26; Gal. iii. 10. [2] Deut. xii.

be more detestable? Others, again, of them do refuse certain meats, and say that marriage with the procreation of children is evil, and the contrivance of the devil; and being ungodly themselves, they are not willing to rise again from the dead on account of their wickedness. Wherefore also they ridicule the resurrection, and say, We are holy people, unwilling to eat and to drink; and they fancy that they shall rise again from the dead demons without flesh, who shall be condemned for ever in eternal fire. Fly therefore from them, lest ye perish with them in their impieties.

XXVII. Now if any persons keep to the Jewish customs and observances concerning the natural gonorrhea and nocturnal pollutions, and the lawful conjugal acts,[1] let them tell us whether in those hours or days, when they undergo any such thing, they observe not to pray, or to touch a Bible, or to partake of the eucharist? And if they own it to be so, it is plain they are void of the Holy Spirit, which always continues with the faithful. For concerning holy persons Solomon says: "That every one may prepare himself, that so when he sleeps it may keep him, and when he arises it may talk with him."[2] For if thou thinkest, O woman, when thou art seven days in thy separation, that thou art void of the Holy Spirit, then if thou shouldest die suddenly thou wilt depart void of the Spirit, and without assured hope in God; or else thou must imagine that the Spirit always is inseparable from thee, as not being in a place. But thou standest in need of prayer and the eucharist, and the coming of the Holy Ghost, as having been guilty of no fault in this matter. For neither lawful mixture, nor child-bearing, nor the menstrual purgation, nor nocturnal pollution, can defile the nature of a man, or separate the Holy Spirit from him. Nothing but impiety and unlawful practice can do that. For the Holy Spirit always abides with those that are possessed of it, so long as they are worthy; and those from whom it is departed, it leaves them desolate, and exposed to the wicked spirit. Now every man is filled either with the holy or with the unclean spirit; and it is not possible to

[1] Lev. xv. [2] Prov. vi. 22.

avoid the one or the other, unless they can receive opposite spirits. For the Comforter hates every lie, and the devil hates all truth. But every one that is baptized agreeably to the truth is separated from the diabolical spirit, and is under the Holy Spirit; and the Holy Spirit remains with him so long as he is doing good, and fills him with wisdom and understanding, and suffers not the wicked spirit to approach him, but watches over his goings. Thou therefore, O woman, if, as thou sayest, in the days of thy separation thou art void of the Holy Spirit, thou art then filled with the unclean one; for by neglecting to pray and to read thou wilt invite him to thee, though he were unwilling. For this spirit, of all others, loves the ungrateful, the slothful, the careless, and the drowsy, since he himself by ingratitude was distempered with an evil mind, and was thereby deprived by God of his dignity; having rather chosen to be a devil than an archangel. Wherefore, O woman, eschew such vain words, and be ever mindful of God that created thee, and pray to Him. For He is thy Lord, and the Lord of the universe; and meditate in His laws without observing any such things, such as the natural purgation, lawful mixture, child-birth, a miscarriage, or a blemish of the body; since such observations are the vain inventions of foolish men, and such inventions as have no sense in them. Neither the burial of a man, nor a dead man's bone, nor a sepulchre, nor any particular sort of food, nor the nocturnal pollution, can defile the soul of man; but only impiety towards God, and transgression, and injustice towards one's neighbour; I mean rapine, violence, or if there be anything contrary to His righteousness, adultery or fornication. Wherefore, beloved, avoid and eschew such observations, for they are heathenish. For we do not abominate a dead man, as do they, seeing we hope that he will live again. Nor do we hate lawful mixture; for it is their practice to act impiously in such instances. For the conjunction of man and wife, if it be with righteousness, is agreeable to the mind of God. "For He that made them at the beginning made them male and female; and He blessed them, and said, Increase and multiply, and fill the earth."[1] If, therefore, the difference of sexes was made by the will of God for the generation of multitudes, then must the conjunction of male and female be also agreeable to His mind.

XXVIII. But we do not say so of that mixture that is contrary to nature, or of any unlawful practice; for such are enmity to God. For the sin of Sodom is contrary to nature, as is also that with brute beasts. But adultery and fornication are against the law; the one whereof is impiety, the other injustice, and, in a word, no other than a great sin. But neither sort of them is without its punishment in its own proper nature. For the practisers of one sort attempt the dissolution of the world, and endeavour to make the natural course of things to change for one that is unnatural; but those of the second sort—the adulterers—are unjust by corrupting others' marriages, and dividing into two what God hath made one, rendering the children suspected, and exposing the true husband to the snares of others. And fornication is the destruction of one's own flesh, not being made use of for the procreation of children, but entirely for the sake of pleasure, which is a mark of incontinency, and not a sign of virtue. All these things are forbidden by the laws; for thus say the oracles: "Thou shalt not lie with mankind as with womankind."[2] "For such an one is accursed, and ye shall stone them with stones: they have wrought abomination."[3] "Every one that lieth with a beast, slay ye him: he has wrought wickedness in his people."[4] "And if any one defile a married woman, slay ye them both: they have wrought wickedness; they are guilty; let them die."[5] And afterwards: "There shall not be a fornicator among the children of Israel, and there shall not be an whore among the daughters of Israel. Thou shalt not offer the hire of an harlot to the Lord thy God upon the altar, nor the price of a dog."[6] "For the vows arising from the hire of an harlot are not clean."[7] These things the laws have forbidden; but they have

---

[1] Matt. xix. 4; Gen. i. 28.
[2] Lev. xx. 13.
[3] Lev. xviii. 22.
[4] Ex. xxii. 19.
[5] Lev. xx. 10.
[6] Deut. xxii. 22; Deut. xxiii. 17.
[7] Prov. xix. 13, LXX.

honoured marriage, and have called it blessed, since God has blessed it, who joined male and female together.[1] And wise Solomon somewhere says: "A wife is suited to her husband by the Lord."[2] And David says: "Thy wife is like a flourishing vine in the sides of thine house; thy children like olive-branches round about thy table. Behold, thus shall the man be blessed that feareth the Lord."[3] Wherefore "marriage is honourable"[4] and comely, and the begetting of children pure, for there is no evil in that which is good. Therefore neither is the natural purgation abominable before God, who has ordered it to happen to women within the space of thirty days for their advantage and healthful state, who do less move about, and keep usually at home in the house. Nay, moreover, even in the Gospel, when the woman with the perpetual purgation of blood[5] touched the saving border of the Lord's garment in hope of being healed, He was not angry at her, nor did complain of her at all; but, on the contrary, He healed her, saying, "Thy faith hath saved thee." When the natural purgations do appear in the wives, let not their husbands approach them, out of regard to the children to be begotten; for the law has forbidden it, for it says: "Thou shalt not come near thy wife when she is in her separation."[6] Nor, indeed, let them frequent their wives' company when they are with child. For they do this not for the begetting of children, but for the sake of pleasure. Now a lover of God ought not to be a lover of pleasure.

XXIX. Ye wives, be subject to your own husbands, and have them in esteem, and serve them with fear and love, as holy Sarah honoured Abraham. For she could not endure to call him by his name, but called him lord, when she said, "My lord is old."[7] In like manner, ye husbands, love your own wives as your own members, as partners in life, and fellow-helpers for the procreation of children. For says He, "Rejoice with the wife of thy youth. Let her conversation be to thee as a loving hind, and a pleasant foal; let her alone

[1] Gen. i. 28. [2] Prov. xix. 14. [3] Ps. cxxviii. 3.
[4] Heb. xiii. 4. [5] Matt. ix. 22.
[6] Lev. xviii. 19; Ezek. xviii. 6. [7] 1 Pet. iii. 6.

guide thee, and be with thee at all times: for if thou beest every way encompassed with her friendship, thou wilt be happy in her society."[1] Love them therefore as your own members, as your very bodies; for so it is written, " The Lord has testified between thee and between the wife of thy youth; and she is thy partner, and another has not made her: and she is the remains of thy spirit;" and, "Take heed to your spirit, and do not forsake the wife of thy youth."[2] An husband, therefore, and a wife, when they company together in lawful marriage, and rise from one another, may pray without any observations, and without washing are clean. But whosoever corrupts and defiles another man's wife, or is defiled with an harlot, when he arises up from her, though he should wash himself in the entire ocean and all the rivers, cannot be clean.

Sec. vi.—*Conclusion of the work.*

XXX. Do not therefore keep any such observances about legal and natural purgations, as thinking you are defiled by them. Neither do you seek after Jewish separations, or perpetual washings, or purifications upon the touch of a dead body. But without such observations assemble in the dormitories, reading the holy books, and singing for the martyrs which are fallen asleep, and for all the saints from the beginning of the world, and for your brethren that are asleep in the Lord, and offer the acceptable eucharist, the representation of the royal body of Christ, both in your churches and in the dormitories; and in the funerals of the departed, accompany them with singing, if they were faithful in Christ. For "precious in the sight of the Lord is the death of His saints."[3] And again: "O my soul, return unto thy rest, for the Lord hath done thee good."[4] And elsewhere: "The memory of the just is with encomiums."[5] And, "The souls of the righteous are in the hands of God."[6] For those that have believed in God, although they are asleep, are not dead. For our Saviour says to the Sadducees: "But concerning

[1] Prov. v. 18, etc. [2] Mal. ii. 14, 15, 16. [3] Ps. cxvi. 15.
[4] Ps. cxv. 7. [5] Prov. x. 7. [6] Wisd. iii. 1.

the resurrection of the dead, have ye not read that which is written, I am the God of Abraham, and the God of Isaac, and the God of Jacob? God, therefore, is not the God of the dead, but of the living; for all live to Him."[1] Wherefore, of those that live with God, even their very relics are not without honour. For even Elisha the prophet, after he was fallen asleep, raised up a dead man who was slain by the pirates of Syria.[2] For his body touched the bones of Elisha, and he arose and revived. Now this would not have happened unless the body of Elisha were holy. And chaste Joseph embraced Jacob after he was dead upon his bed;[3] and Moses and Joshua the son of Nun carried away the relics of Joseph,[4] and did not esteem it a defilement. Whence you also, O bishops, and the rest, who without such observances touch the departed, ought not to think yourselves defiled. Nor abhor the relics of such persons, but avoid such observances, for they are foolish. And adorn yourselves with holiness and chastity, that ye may become partakers of immortality, and partners of the kingdom of God, and may receive the promise of God, and may rest for ever, through Jesus Christ our Saviour.

To Him, therefore, who is able to open the ears of your hearts to the receiving the oracles of God administered to you both by the gospel and by the teaching of Jesus Christ of Nazareth; who was crucified under Pontius Pilate and Herod, and died, and rose again from the dead, and will come again at the end of the world with power and great glory, and will raise the dead, and put an end to this world, and distribute to every one according to his deserts: to Him that has given us Himself for an earnest of the resurrection; who was taken up into the heavens by the power of His God and Father in our sight, who ate and drank with Him for forty days after He arose from the dead; who is sat down on the right hand of the throne of the majesty of Almighty God upon the cherubim; to whom it was said, "Sit Thou on my right hand, until I make Thine enemies Thy foot-

[1] Ex. iii. 6; Luke xx. 38.
[2] 2 Kings xiii. 21.
[3] Gen. L 1.
[4] Ex. xi. 19; Josh. xxiv. 32.

stool;"[1] whom the most blessed Stephen saw standing at the right hand of power, and cried out, and said, " Behold, I see the heavens opened, and the Son of man standing at the right hand of God,"[2] as the High Priest of all the rational orders,—through Him, worship, and majesty, and glory be given to Almighty God, both now and for evermore.[3] Amen.

BOOK VII.

CONCERNING THE CHRISTIAN LIFE, AND THE EUCHARIST, AND THE INITIATION INTO CHRIST.

SEC. I.—*On the two ways—the way of life and the way of death.*

I. The lawgiver Moses said to the Israelites, " Behold, I have set before your face the way of life and the way of death;"[4] and added, " Choose life, that thou mayest live."[5] Elijah the prophet also said to the people: " How long will you halt with both your legs? If the Lord be God, follow Him."[6] The Lord Jesus also said justly: " No one can serve two masters: for either he will hate the one, and love the other; or else he will hold to the one, and despise the other."[7] We also, following our teacher Christ, " who is the Saviour of all men, especially of those that believe,"[8] are obliged to say that there are two ways—the one of life, the other of death; which have no comparison one with another, for they are very different, or rather entirely separate; and the way of life is that of nature, but that of death was afterwards introduced,—it not being according to the mind of God, but from the snares of the adversary.[9]

---

[1] Ps. cx. 1. [2] Acts vii. 56.
[3] One V. MS. reads: " to Him be worship, and majesty, and glory, along with the Father and the co-eternal Spirit, for ever and ever. Amen."
[4] Deut. xxx. 15.   [5] Deut. xxx. 19.   [6] 1 Kings xviii. 21.
[7] Matt. vi. 24.   [8] 1 Tim. iv. 10.
[9] The Greek words properly mean: " Introduced was the way of death; not of that death which exists according to the mind of God, but that which has arisen from the plots of the adversary."

II. The first way, therefore, is that of life; and is this, which the law also does appoint: "To love the Lord God with all thy mind, and with all thy soul, who is the one and only God, besides whom there is no other;"[1] "and thy neighbour as thyself."[2] "And whatsoever thou wouldest not should be done to thee, that do not thou to another."[3] "Bless them that curse you; pray for them that despitefully use you."[4] "Love your enemies; for what thanks is it if ye love those that love you? for even the Gentiles do the same."[5] "But do ye love those that hate you, and ye shall have no enemy." For says He, "Thou shalt not hate any man; no, not an Egyptian, nor an Edomite;"[6] for they are all the workmanship of God. Avoid not the persons, but the sentiments, of the wicked. "Abstain from fleshly and worldly lusts."[7] "If any one gives thee a stroke on thy right cheek, turn to him the other also."[8] Not that revenge is evil, but that patience is more honourable. For David says, "If I have made returns to them that repaid me evil."[9] "If any one compel thee to go a mile, go with him twain."[10] And, "He that will sue thee at the law, and take away thy coat, let him have thy cloak also."[11] "And from him that taketh thy goods, require them not again."[12] "Give to him that asketh thee, and from him that would borrow of thee do not shut thy hand."[13] For "the righteous man is pitiful, and lendeth."[14] For your Father would have you give to all, who Himself "maketh His sun to rise on the evil and on the good, and sendeth His rain on the just and on the unjust."[15] It is therefore reasonable to give to all out of thine own labours; for says He, "Honour the Lord out of thy righteous labours,"[16] but so that the saints be preferred.[17] "Thou shalt not kill;" that is, thou shalt not destroy a man like thyself: for thou dissolvest what was well made. Not

---

[1] Deut. vi. 5; Mark xii. 32. [2] Lev. xix. 18.
[3] Tob. iv. 16. [4] Matt. v. 44. [5] Luke vi. 32; Matt. v. 47.
[6] Deut. xxiii. 7 [7] 1 Pet. ii. 11. [8] Matt. v. 39.
[9] Ps. viii. 5. [10] Matt. v. 41. [11] Matt. v. 40.
[12] Luke vi. 30. [13] Matt. v. 42. [14] Ps. cxii. 5.
[15] Matt. v. 45. [16] Prov. iii. 9; Ex. xx., etc. [17] Gal. vi. 10.

as if all killing were wicked, but only that of the innocent: but the killing which is just is reserved to the magistrates alone. "Thou shalt not commit adultery:" for thou dividest one flesh into two. "They two shall be one flesh:"[1] for the husband and wife are one in nature, in consent, in union, in disposition, and the conduct of life; but they are separated in sex and number. "Thou shalt not corrupt boys:"[2] for this wickedness is contrary to nature, and arose from Sodom, which was therefore entirely consumed with fire sent from God.[3] "Let such an one be accursed: and all the people shall say, So be it."[4] "Thou shalt not commit fornication:" for says He, "There shall not be a fornicator among the children of Israel."[5] "Thou shalt not steal:" for Achan, when he had stolen in Israel at Jericho, was stoned to death;[6] and Gehazi, who stole, and told a lie, inherited the leprosy of Naaman;[7] and Judas, who stole the poor's money, betrayed the Lord of glory to the Jews,[8] and repented, and hanged himself, and burst asunder in the midst, and all his bowels gushed out;[9] and Ananias, and Sapphira his wife, who stole their own goods, and "tempted the Spirit of the Lord," were immediately, at the sentence of Peter our fellow-apostle, struck dead.[10]

III. Thou shalt not use magic. Thou shalt not use witchcraft; for He says, "Ye shall not suffer a witch to live."[11] Thou shalt not slay thy child by causing abortion, nor kill that which is begotten; for "everything that is shaped, and has received a soul from God, if it be slain, shall be avenged, as being unjustly destroyed."[12] "Thou shalt not covet the things that belong to thy neighbour, as his wife, or his servant, or his ox, or his field." "Thou shalt not forswear thyself;" for it is said, "Thou shalt not swear at all."[13] But if that cannot be avoided, thou shalt swear truly; for "every one that swears by Him shall be commended."[14] "Thou

---

[1] Gen. ii. 24. [2] Lev. xviii. 20. [3] Gen. xix.
[4] Deut. xxvii. [5] Deut. xxiii. 17. [6] Josh. vii.
[7] 2 Kings v. [8] John xii. 6; Matt. xxvii. 5.
[9] Acts i. 18. [10] Acts v. [11] Ex. xxii. 18.
[12] Ex. xxi. 23, LXX. [13] Matt. v. 34. [14] Ps. lxiii. 12.

shalt not bear false witness;" for "he that falsely accuses the needy provokes to anger Him that made him."[1]

IV. Thou shalt not speak evil; for says He, "Love not to speak evil, lest thou beest taken away." Nor shalt thou be mindful of injuries; for "the ways of those that remember injuries are unto death."[2] Thou shalt not be double-minded nor double-tongued; for "a man's own lips are a strong snare to him,"[3] and "a talkative person shall not be prospered upon earth."[4] Thy words shall not be vain; for "ye shall give an account of every idle word."[5] Thou shalt not tell lies: for says He, "Thou shalt destroy all those that speak lies."[6] Thou shalt not be covetous nor rapacious: for says He, "Woe to him that is covetous towards his neighbour with an evil covetousness."[7]

V. Thou shalt not be an hypocrite, lest thy "portion be with them."[8] Thou shalt not be ill-natured nor proud: for "God resisteth the proud."[9] "Thou shalt not accept persons in judgment; for the judgment is the Lord's." "Thou shalt not hate any man; thou shalt surely reprove thy brother, and not become guilty on his account;"[10] and, "Reprove a wise man, and he will love thee."[11] Eschew all evil, and all that is like it: for says He, "Abstain from injustice, and trembling shall not come nigh thee."[12] Be not soon angry, nor spiteful, nor passionate, nor furious, nor daring, lest thou undergo the fate of Cain, and of Saul, and of Joab: for the first of these slew his brother Abel, because Abel was found to be preferred before him with God, and because Abel's sacrifice was preferred;[13] the second persecuted holy David, who had slain Goliah the Philistine, being envious of the praises of the women who danced;[14] the third slew two generals of armies—Abner of Israel, and Amasa of Judah.[15]

[1] Prov. xiv. 31.
[2] Prov. xii. 28.
[3] Prov. vi. 2.
[4] Ps. cxl. 11.
[5] Matt. xii. 36; Lev. xix. 11.
[6] Ps. v. 6.
[7] Hab. ii. 9.
[8] Matt. xv. 51.
[9] 1 Pet. v. 5.
[10] Deut. i. 17; Lev. xix. 17.
[11] Prov. ix. 8.
[12] Isa. liv. 14.
[13] Gen. iv.
[14] 1 Sam. xvii. xviii.
[15] 1 Sam. ii. 32.

VI. Be not a diviner, for that leads to idolatry; for says Samuel, "Divination is sin;"[1] and, "There shall be no divination in Jacob, nor soothsaying in Israel."[2] Thou shalt not use enchantments or purgations for thy child. Thou shall not be a soothsayer nor a diviner by great or little birds. Nor shalt thou learn wicked arts; for all these things has the law forbidden.[3] Be not one that wishes for evil, for thou wilt be led into intolerable sins.[4] Thou shalt not speak obscenely, nor use wanton glances, nor be a drunkard; for from such causes arise whoredoms and adulteries. Be not a lover of money, lest thou "serve mammon instead of God."[5] Be not vainglorious, nor haughty, nor high-minded. For from all these things arrogance does spring. Remember him who said: "Lord, my heart is not haughty, nor mine eyes lofty: I have not exercised myself in great matters, nor in things too high for me; but I was humble."[6]

VII. Be not a murmurer, remembering the punishment which those underwent who murmured against Moses. Be not self-willed, be not malicious, be not hard-hearted, be not passionate, be not mean-spirited; for all these things lead to blasphemy. But be meek, as were Moses and David,[7] since "the meek shall inherit the earth."[8]

VIII. Be slow to wrath; for such an one is very prudent, since "he that is hasty of spirit is a very fool."[9] Be merciful; for "blessed are the merciful: for they shall obtain mercy."[10] Be sincere, quiet, good, "trembling at the word of God."[11] Thou shalt not exalt thyself, as did the Pharisee; for "every one that exalteth himself shall be abased,"[12] and "that which is of high esteem with man is abomination with God."[13] Thou shalt not entertain confidence in thy soul; for "a confident man shall fall into mischief."[14] Thou shalt not go along with the foolish; but with the wise

---

[1] 1 Sam. xv. 23. [2] Num. xxiii. 23. [3] Deut. xviii. 11, 10.
[4] Lev. xix. 26, 31. [5] Matt. vi. 24. [6] Ps. cxxxi. 1.
[7] Num. xii. 3; Ps. cxxxi. 1. [8] Matt. v. 4.
[9] Prov. xiv. 29. [10] Matt. v. 7. [11] Isa. lxvi. 2.
[12] Luke xviii. 14. [13] Luke xvi. 15. [14] Prov. xiii. 17, LXX.

and righteous; for "he that walketh[1] with wise men shall be wise, but he that walketh with the foolish shall be known."[2] Receive the afflictions that fall upon thee with an even mind, and the chances of life without over-much sorrow, knowing that a reward shall be given to thee by God, as was given to Job and to Lazarus.[3]

IX. Thou shalt honour him that speaks to thee the word of God, and be mindful of him day and night; and thou shalt reverence him, not as the author of thy birth, but as one that is made the occasion of thy well-being. For where the doctrine concerning God is, there God is present. Thou shalt every day seek the face of the saints, that thou mayest acquiesce in their words.

X. Thou shalt not make schisms among the saints, but be mindful of the followers of Corah.[4] Thou shalt make peace between those that are at variance, as Moses did when he persuaded them to be friends.[5] Thou shalt judge righteously; for "the judgment is the Lord's."[6] Thou shalt not accept persons when thou reprovest for sins; but do as Elijah and Micaiah did to Ahab, and Ebedmelech the Ethiopian to Zedechiah, and Nathan to David, and John to Herod.[7]

XI. Be not of a doubtful mind in thy prayer, whether it shall be granted or no. For the Lord said to me Peter upon the sea: "O thou of little faith, wherefore didst thou doubt?"[8] "Be not thou ready to stretch out thy hand to receive, and to shut it when thou shouldst give."[9]

XII. If thou hast by the work of thy hands, give, that thou mayest labour for the redemption of thy sins; for "by alms and acts of faith sins are purged away."[10] Thou shalt not grudge to give to the poor, nor when thou hast given shalt thou murmur; for thou shalt know who will repay thee thy reward. For says he: "He that hath

---

[1] The words from "for he that walketh" to "be known" are omitted in one V. MS.
[2] Prov. xiii. 20.   [3] Job xlii.; Luke xvi.   [4] Num. xvi.
[5] Ex. ii. 13.   [6] Deut. i. 17.
[7] 1 Kings xviii. xxi. xxii.; 2 Sam. xii.; Matt. xiv.
[8] Matt. xiv. 31.   [9] Ecclus. iv. 31.   [10] Prov. xv. 27, xvi. 6.

mercy on the poor man lendeth to the Lord; according to his gift, so shall it be repaid him again."[1] Thou shalt not turn away from him that is needy; for says he: "He that stoppeth his ears, that he may not hear the cry of the needy, himself also shall call, and there shall be none to hear him."[2] Thou shalt communicate in all things to thy brother, and shalt not say [thy goods] are thine own; for the common participation of the necessaries of life is appointed to all men by God. Thou shalt not take off thine hand from thy son or from thy daughter, but shalt teach them the fear of God from their youth; for says he: "Correct thy son, so shall he afford thee good hope."[3]

XIII. Thou shalt not command thy man-servant, or thy maid-servant, who trust in the same God, with bitterness of soul, lest they groan against thee, and wrath be upon thee from God. And, ye servants, "be subject to your masters,"[4] as to the representatives of God, with attention and fear, "as to the Lord, and not to men."[5]

XIV. Thou shalt hate all hyprocrisy; and whatsoever is pleasing to the Lord, that shalt thou do. By no means forsake the commands of the Lord. But thou shalt observe what things thou hast received from Him, neither adding to them nor taking away from them. "For thou shalt not add unto His words, lest He convict thee, and thou becomest a liar."[6] Thou shalt confess thy sins unto the Lord thy God; and thou shalt not add unto them, that it may be well with thee from the Lord thy God, who willeth not the death of a sinner, but his repentance.

XV. Thou shalt be observant to thy father and mother as the causes of thy being born, that thou mayest live long on the earth which the Lord thy God giveth thee. Do not overlook thy brethren or thy kinsfolk; for "thou shalt not overlook those nearly related to thee."[7]

XVI. Thou shalt fear the king, knowing that his appointment is of the Lord. His rulers thou shalt honour as the ministers of God, for they are the revengers of all unright-

[1] Prov. xix. 17. [2] Prov. xxi. 13. [3] Prov. xix. 18. [4] Eph. vi. 5.
[5] Eph. vi. 7. [6] Prov. xxx. 6. [7] Isa. lviii. 7.

eousness; to whom pay taxes, tribute, and every oblation with a willing mind.

XVII. Thou shalt not proceed to thy prayer in the day of thy wickedness, before thou hast laid aside thy bitterness. This is the way of life, in which may ye be found, through Jesus Christ our Lord.

XVIII. But the way of death is known by its wicked practices: for therein is the ignorance of God, and the introduction of many evils, and disorders, and disturbances; whereby come murders, adulteries, fornications, perjuries, unlawful lusts, thefts, idolatries, magic arts, witchcrafts, rapines, false-witnesses, hypocrisies, double-heartedness, deceit, pride, malice, insolence, covetousness, obscene talk, jealousy, confidence, haughtiness, arrogance, impudence, persecution of the good, enmity to truth, love of lies, ignorance of righteousness. For they who do such things do not adhere to goodness, or to righteous judgment: they watch not for good, but for evil; from whom meekness and patience are far off, who love vain things, pursuing after reward, having no pity on the poor, not labouring for him that is in misery, nor knowing Him that made them; murderers of infants, destroyers of the workmanship of God, that turn away from the needy, adding affliction to the afflicted, the flatterers of the rich, the despisers of the poor, full of sin. May you, children, be delivered from all these.

XIX. See that no one seduce thee from piety; for says He: "Thou mayst not turn aside from it to the right hand, or to the left, that thou mayst have understanding in all that thou doest." [1] For if thou dost not turn out of the right way, thou wilt not be ungodly.

SEC. II.—*On the formation of the character of believers, and on giving of thanks to God.*

XX. Now concerning the several sorts of food, the Lord says to thee, "Ye shall eat the good things of the earth;" [2] and, "All sorts of flesh shall ye eat, as the green herb;" [3] but, "Thou shalt pour out the blood." [4] For "not those

[1] Deut. v. 32.   [2] Isa. i. 19.   [3] Gen. ix. 3.   [4] Deut. xv. 23.

things that go into the mouth, but those that come out of it, defile a man;"[1] I mean blasphemies, evil-speaking, and if there be any other thing of the like nature.[2] But "do thou eat the fat of the land with righteousness."[3] For "if there be anything pleasant, it is His; and if there be anything good, it is His. Wheat for the young men, and wine to cheer the maids." For "who shall eat or who shall drink without Him?"[4] Wise Ezra[5] does also admonish thee, and say: "Go your way, and eat the fat, and drink the sweet, and be not sorrowful."[6]

XXI. But do ye abstain from things offered to idols;[7] for they offer them in honour of demons, that is, to the dishonour of the one God, that ye may not become partners with demons.

XXII. Now concerning baptism, O bishop, or presbyter, we have already given direction, and we now say, that thou shalt so baptize as the Lord commanded us, saying: "Go ye, and teach all nations, baptizing them in the name of the Father, and of the Son, and of the Holy Ghost (teaching them to observe all things whatsoever I have commanded you):"[8] of the Father who sent, of Christ who came, of the Comforter who testified. But thou shalt beforehand anoint the person with the holy oil, and afterward baptize him with the water, and in the conclusion shalt seal him with the ointment; that the anointing with oil may be the participation of the Holy Spirit, and the water the symbol of the death [of Christ], and the ointment the seal of the covenants. But if there be neither oil nor ointment, water is sufficient both for the anointing, and for the seal, and for the confession of Him that is dead, or indeed is dying together [with Christ]. But before baptism, let him that is to be baptized fast; for even the Lord, when He was first baptized by John, and abode in the wilderness, did afterward fast forty days and forty nights.[9] But He was baptized,

---

[1] Matt. xv. 11. [2] Mark vii. 22. [3] Zech. ix. 17.
[4] Eccles. ii. 25, LXX.
[5] The words from "Wise Ezra" to "sorrowful" are not in one V. MS.
[6] Neh. viii. 10. [7] 1 Cor. x. 20.
[8] Matt. xxviii. 19. [9] Matt. iii. iv.

and then fasted, not having Himself any need of cleansing, or of fasting, or of purgation, who was by nature pure and holy; but that He might testify the truth to John, and afford an example to us. Wherefore our Lord was not baptized into His own passion, or death, or resurrection—for none of those things had then happened—but for another purpose. Wherefore He by His own authority fasted after His baptism, as being the Lord of John. But he who is to be initiated into His death ought first to fast, and then to be baptized. For it is not reasonable that he who has been buried [with Christ], and is risen again with Him, should appear dejected at His very resurrection. For man is not lord of our Saviour's constitution, since one is the Master and the other the servant.

XXIII. But let not your fasts be with the hypocrites; for they fast on the second and fifth days of the week. But do you either fast the entire five days, or on the fourth day of the week, and on the day of the preparation, because on the fourth day the condemnation went out against the Lord, Judas then promising to betray Him for money; and you must fast on the day of the preparation, because on that day the Lord suffered the death of the cross under Pontius Pilate. But keep the Sabbath, and the Lord's day festival; because the former is the memorial of the creation, and the latter of the resurrection. But there is one only Sabbath to be observed by you in the whole year, which is that of our Lord's burial, on which men ought to keep a fast, but not a festival. For inasmuch as the Creator was then under the earth, the sorrow for Him is more forcible than the joy for the creation; for the Creator is more honourable by nature and dignity than His own creatures.

XXIV. Now, "when ye pray, be not ye as the hypocrites;"[1] but as the Lord has appointed us in the Gospel, so pray ye: "Our Father which art in heaven, hallowed be Thy name; Thy kingdom come; Thy will be done, as in heaven, so on earth; give us this day our daily bread; and forgive us our debts, as we forgive our debtors; and lead us not into temptation, but deliver us from evil; for Thine is the king-

---

[1] Matt. vi. 5.

dom for ever. Amen."[1] Pray thus thrice in a day, preparing yourselves beforehand, that ye may be worthy of the adoption of the Father; lest, when you call Him Father unworthily, you be reproached by Him, as Israel once His firstborn son was told: "If I be a Father, where is my glory? And if I be a Lord, where is my fear?" For the glory of fathers is the holiness of their children, and the honour of masters is the fear of their servants, as the contrary is dishonour and confusion. For says He: "Through you my name is blasphemed among the Gentiles."[2]

XXV. Be ye always thankful, as faithful and honest servants; and concerning the eucharistical thanksgiving say thus: We thank Thee, our Father, for that life which Thou hast made known to us by Jesus Thy Son, by whom Thou madest all things, and takest care of the whole world; whom Thou hast sent to become man for our salvation; whom Thou hast permitted to suffer and to die; whom Thou hast raised up, and been pleased to glorify, and hast set Him down on Thy right hand; by whom Thou hast promised us the resurrection of the dead. Do thou, O Lord Almighty, everlasting God, so gather together Thy church from the ends of the earth into Thy kingdom, as this [corn] was once scattered, and is now become one loaf. We also, our Father, thank Thee for the precious blood of Jesus Christ, which was shed for us, and for His precious body, whereof we celebrate this representation, as Himself appointed us, "to show forth His death."[4] For through Him glory is to be given to Thee for ever. Amen. Let no one eat of these things that is not initiated; but those only who have been baptized into the death of the Lord. But if any one that is not initiated conceal himself, and partake of the same, "he eats eternal damnation;"[5] because, being not of the faith of Christ, he has partaken of such things as it is not lawful for him to partake of, to his own punishment. But if any one is a partaker through ignorance, instruct him quickly, and initiate him, that he may not go out and despise you.

[1] Matth. vi. 9, etc.   [2] Mal. i. 6.   [3] Isa. lii. 5.
[4] 1 Cor. xi. 26.   [5] 1 Cor. xi. 29.

XXVI. After the participation, give thanks in this manner: We thank thee, O God and Father of Jesus our Saviour, for Thy holy name, which Thou hast made to inhabit among us; and that knowledge, faith, love, and immortality which Thou hast given us through Thy Son Jesus. Thou, O Almighty Lord, the God of the universe, hast created the world, and the things that are therein, by Him; and hast planted a law in our souls, and beforehand didst prepare things for the convenience of men. O God of our holy and blameless fathers, Abraham, and Isaac, and Jacob, Thy faithful servants; Thou, O God, who art powerful, faithful, and true, and without deceit in Thy promises; who didst send upon earth Jesus Thy Christ to live with men, as a man, when He was God the Word, and man, to take away error by the roots: do Thou even now, through Him, be mindful of this Thy holy church, which Thou hast purchased with the precious blood of Thy Christ, and deliver it from all evil, and perfect it in Thy love and Thy truth, and gather us all together into Thy kingdom which Thou hast prepared. Let this Thy kingdom come. "Hosanna to the Son of David. Blessed be He that cometh in the name of the Lord"[1]—God the Lord, who was manifested to us in the flesh. If any one be holy, let him draw near; but if any one be not such, let him become such by repentance. Permit also to your presbyters to give thanks.

XXVII. Concerning the ointment give thanks in this manner: We give Thee thanks, O God, the Creator of the whole world, both for the fragrancy of the ointment, and for the immortality which Thou hast made known to us by Thy Son Jesus. For Thine is the glory and the power for ever. Amen. Whosoever comes to you, and gives thanks in this manner, receive him as a disciple of Christ. But if he preach another doctrine, different from that which Christ by us has delivered to you, such an one you must not permit to give thanks; for such an one rather affronts God than glorifies Him.

XXVIII. But whosoever comes to you, let him be first

---

[1] 1 Cor. xvi. 22; Matth. xxi. 9; Mark xi. 10.

examined, and then received; for ye have understanding, and are able to know the right hand from the left, and to distinguish false teachers from true teachers. But when a teacher comes to you, supply him with what he wants with all readiness. And even when a false teacher comes, you shall give him for his necessity, but shall not receive his error. Nor indeed may ye pray together with him, lest ye be polluted as well as he. Every true prophet or teacher that comes to you is worthy of his maintenance, as being a labourer in the word of righteousness.[1]

XXIX. All the first-fruits of the winepress, the threshing-floor, the oxen, and the sheep, shalt thou give to the priests,[2] that thy storehouses and garners and the products of thy land may be blessed, and thou mayst be strengthened with corn and wine and oil, and the herds of thy cattle and flocks of thy sheep may be increased. Thou shalt give the tenth of thy increase to the orphan, and to the widow, and to the poor, and to the stranger. All the first-fruits of thy hot bread, of thy barrels of wine, or oil, or honey, or nuts, or grapes, or the first-fruits of other things, shalt thou give to the priests; but those of silver, and of garments, and of all sort of possessions, to the orphan and to the widow.

XXX. On the day of the resurrection of the Lord, that is, the Lord's day, assemble yourselves together, without fail, giving thanks to God, and praising Him for those mercies God has bestowed upon you through Christ, and has delivered you from ignorance, error, and bondage, that your sacrifice may be unspotted, and acceptable to God, who has said concerning His universal church: "In every place shall incense and a pure sacrifice be offered unto me; for I am a great King, saith the Lord Almighty, and my name is wonderful among the heathen."[3]

XXXI. Do you first ordain bishops worthy of the Lord, and presbyters and deacons, pious men, righteous, meek, free from the love of money, lovers of truth, approved, holy, not accepters of persons, who are able to teach the word of piety, and rightly dividing the doctrines of the Lord.[4] And do ye

[1] Matth. x. 41.   [2] Num. xviii.   [3] Mal. i. 11, 14.   [4] 1 Tim. ii. 15.

honour such as your fathers, as your lords, as your benefactors, as the causes of your well-being. Reprove ye one another, not in anger, but in mildness, with kindness and peace. Observe all things that are commanded you by the Lord. Be watchful for your life. "Let your loins be girded about, and your lights burning, and ye like unto men who wait for their Lord, when He will come, at even, or in the morning, or at cock-crowing, or at midnight. For at what hour they think not, the Lord will come; and if they open to Him, blessed are those servants, because they were found watching. For He will gird Himself, and will make them to sit down to meat, and will come forth and serve them."[1] Watch therefore, and pray, that ye do not sleep unto death. For your former good deeds will not profit you, if at the last part of your life you go astray from the true faith.

XXXII. For in the last days false prophets shall be multiplied, and such as corrupt the word; and the sheep shall be changed into wolves, and love into hatred: for through the abounding of iniquity the love of many shall wax cold. For men shall hate, and persecute, and betray one another. And then shall appear the deceiver of the world, the enemy of the truth, the prince of lies,[2] whom the Lord Jesus "shall destroy with the spirit of His mouth, who takes away the wicked with His lips; and many shall be offended at Him. But they that endure to the end, the same shall be saved. And then shall appear the sign of the Son of man in heaven;"[3] and afterwards shall be the voice of a trumpet by the archangel;[4] and in that interval shall be the revival of those that were asleep. And then shall the Lord come, and all His saints with Him, with a great concussion above the clouds, with the angels of His power, in the throne of His kingdom,[5] to condemn [the devil], the deceiver of the world, and to render to every one according to his deeds. "Then shall the wicked go away into everlasting punishment, but the righteous shall go into life eternal,"[6] to inherit those things "which eye

---

[1] Luke xii. 35; Mark xiii. 35.
[2] 2 Thess. ii.
[3] Isa. xi. 4; Matth. xxiv.
[4] 1 Thess. iv. 16.
[5] Matth. xvi. 27.
[6] Matth. xxv. 46.

hath not seen, nor ear heard, nor have entered into the heart of man, such things as God hath prepared for them that love Him;"[1] and they shall rejoice in the kingdom of God, which is in Christ Jesus. Since we are vouchsafed such great blessings from Him, let us become His suppliants, and call upon Him by continual prayer, and say:

XXXIII. Our eternal Saviour, the King of gods, who alone art almighty, and the Lord, the God of all beings, and the God of our holy and blameless fathers, and of those before us; the God of Abraham, and of Isaac, and of Jacob; who art merciful and compassionate, long-suffering, and abundant in mercy; to whom every heart is naked, and by whom every heart is seen, and to whom every secret thought is revealed: to Thee do the souls of the righteous cry aloud, upon Thee do the hopes of the godly trust, Thou Father of the blameless, Thou hearer of the supplication of those that call upon Thee with uprightness, and who knowest the supplications that are not uttered: for Thy providence reaches as far as the inmost parts of mankind; and by Thy knowledge Thou searchest the thoughts of every one, and in every region of the whole earth the incense of prayer and supplication is sent up to Thee. O Thou who hast appointed this present world as a place of combat to righteousness, and hast opened to all the gate of mercy, and hast demonstrated to every man by implanted knowledge, and natural judgment, and the admonitions of the law, how the possession of riches is not everlasting, the ornament of beauty is not perpetual, our strength and force are easily dissolved; and that all is vapour and vanity; and that only the good conscience of faith unfeigned passes through the midst of the heavens, and returning with truth, takes hold of the right hand of the joy[2] which is to come. And withal, before the promise of the restoration of all things is accomplished, the soul itself exults in hope, and is joyful. For from that truth which was in our forefather Abraham, when he changed his way Thou

[1] 1 Cor. ii. 9.
[2] A conjecture of Cotelerius is adopted. The mss. read "nourishment" instead of "joy."

didst guide him by a vision, and didst teach him what kind of state this world is; and knowledge went before his faith, and faith was the consequence of his knowledge; and the covenant did follow after his faith. For Thou saidst: "I will make thy seed as the stars of heaven, and as the sand which is by the sea-shore."[1] Moreover, when Thou hadst given him Isaac, and knewest him to be like him in his mode of life, Thou wast then called his God, saying: "I will be a God to thee, and to thy seed after thee."[2] And when our father Jacob was sent into Mesopotamia, Thou showedst him Christ, and by him speakest, saying: "Behold, I am with thee, and I will increase thee, and multiply thee exceedingly."[3] And so spakest Thou to Moses, Thy faithful and holy servant, at the vision of the bush: "I am He that is; this is my name for ever, and my memorial for generations of generations."[4] O Thou great protector of the posterity of Abraham, Thou art blessed for ever.

XXXIV. Thou art blessed, O Lord, the King of ages, who by Christ hast made the whole world, and by Him in the beginning didst reduce into order the disordered parts; who dividedst the waters from the waters by a firmament, and didst put into them a spirit of life; who didst fix the earth, and stretch out the heaven, and didst dispose every creature by an accurate constitution. For by Thy power, O Lord, the world is beautified, the heaven is fixed as an arch over us, and is rendered illustrious with stars for our comfort in the darkness. The light also and the sun were begotten for days and the production of fruit, and the moon for the change of seasons, by its increase and diminutions; and one was called Night, and the other Day. And the firmament was exhibited in the midst of the abyss, and Thou commandedst the waters to be gathered together, and the dry land to appear. But as for the sea itself, who can possibly describe it, which comes with fury from the ocean, yet runs back again, being stopped by the sand at Thy command? For Thou hast said: "Thereby shall her waves be

---

[1] Gen. xiii. 16, xxii. 17.
[2] Gen. xxvi. 3.
[3] Gen. xvii. 7, xxviii. 15, xlviii. 4.
[4] Ex. iii. 14, 15.

broken."[1] Thou hast also made it capable of supporting little and great creatures, and made it navigable for ships. Then did the earth become green, and was planted with all sorts of flowers, and the variety of several trees; and the shining luminaries, the nourishers of those plants, preserve their unchangeable course, and in nothing depart from Thy command. But where Thou biddest them, there do they rise and set for signs of the seasons and of the years, making a constant return of the work of men. Afterwards the kinds of the several animals were created—those belonging to the land, to the water, to the air, and both to air and water; and the artificial wisdom of Thy providence does still impart to every one a suitable providence. For as He was not unable to produce different kinds, so neither has He disdained to exercise a different providence towards every one. And at the conclusion of the creation Thou gavest direction to Thy Wisdom, and formedst a reasonable creature as the citizen of the world, saying, "Let us make man after our image, and after our likeness;"[2] and hast exhibited him as the ornament of the world, and formed him a body out of the four elements, those primary bodies, but hadst prepared a soul out of nothing, and bestowedst upon him his five senses, and didst set over his sensations a mind as the conductor of the soul. And besides all these things, O Lord God, who can worthily declare the motion of the rainy clouds, the shining of the lightning, the noise of the thunder, in order to the supply of proper food, and the most agreeable temperature of the air? But when man was disobedient, Thou didst deprive him of the life which should have been his reward. Yet didst Thou not destroy him for ever, but laidst him to sleep for a time; and Thou didst by oath call him to a resurrection, and loosedst the bond of death, O Thou reviver of the dead, through Jesus Christ, who is our hope.

XXXV. Great art Thou, O Lord Almighty, and great is Thy power, and of Thy understanding there is no number. Our Creator and Saviour, rich in benefits, long-suffering, and the bestower of mercy, who dost not take away Thy salvation

[1] Job xxxviii. 11. [2] Gen. i. 26.

from Thy creatures: for Thou art good by nature, and sparest sinners, and invitest them to repentance; for admonition is the effect of Thy bowels of compassion. For how should we abide if we were required to come to judgment immediately, when, after so much long-suffering, we hardly get clear of our miserable condition? The heavens declare Thy dominion, and the earth shakes with earthquakes, and, hanging upon nothing, declares Thy unshaken stedfastness. The sea raging with waves, and feeding a flock of ten thousand creatures, is bounded with sand, as standing in awe at Thy command, and compels all men to cry out: "How great are Thy works, O Lord! in wisdom hast Thou made them all: the earth is full of Thy creation."[1] And the bright host of angels and the intellectual spirits say to Palmoni, "There is but one holy Being;"[2] and the holy seraphim, together with the six-winged cherubim, who sing to Thee their triumphal song, cry out with never-ceasing voices, "Holy, holy, holy, Lord God of hosts! heaven and earth are full of Thy glory;"[3] and the other multitudes of the orders, angels, archangels, thrones, dominions, principalities, authorities, and powers cry aloud, and say, "Blessed be the glory of the Lord out of His place."[4] But Israel, Thy church on earth, taken out of the Gentiles, emulating the heavenly powers night and day, with a full heart and a willing soul sings, "The chariot of God is ten thousandfold thousands of them that rejoice: the Lord is among them in Sinai, in the holy place."[5] The heaven knows Him who fixed it as a cube of stone, in the form of an arch, upon nothing, who united the land and water to one another, and scattered the vital air all abroad, and conjoined fire therewith for warmth, and the comfort against darkness. The choir of stars strikes us with admiration, declaring Him that numbers them, and showing Him that names them; the animals declare Him that puts life into them; the trees show Him that makes them grow: all which creatures, being made by Thy word, show forth the greatness of Thy power. Wherefore every man ought to send up an hymn from his

[1] Ps. civ. 24.   [2] Dan. viii. 13.   [3] Isa. vi. 3.
[4] Ezek. iii. 12.   [5] Ps. lxviii. 18.

very soul to Thee, through Christ, in the name of all the rest, since He has power over them all by Thy appointment. For Thou art kind in Thy benefits, and beneficent in Thy bowels of compassion, who alone art almighty: for when Thou willest, to be able is present with Thee; for Thy eternal power both quenches flame, and stops the mouths of lions, and tames whales, and raises up the sick, and overrules the power of all things, and overturns the host of enemies, and casts down a people numbered in their arrogance. Thou art He who art in heaven, He who art on earth, He who art in the sea, He who art in finite things, Thyself unconfined by anything. For of Thy majesty there is no boundary; for it is not ours, O Lord, but the oracle of Thy servant, who said, "And thou shalt know in thine heart that the Lord thy God He is God in heaven above, and on earth beneath, and there is none other besides Thee:"[1] for there is no God besides Thee alone, there is none holy besides Thee, the Lord, the God of knowledge, the God of the saints, holy above all holy beings; for they are sanctified by Thy hands. Thou art glorious, and highly exalted, invisible by nature, and unsearchable in Thy judgments; whose life is without want, whose duration can never alter or fail, whose operation is without toil, whose greatness is unlimited, whose excellency is perpetual, whose habitation is inaccessible, whose dwelling is unchangeable, whose knowledge is without beginning, whose truth is immutable, whose work is without assistants, whose dominion cannot be taken away, whose monarchy is without succession, whose kingdom is without end, whose strength is irresistible, whose army is very numerous: for Thou art the Father of wisdom, the Creator of the creation, by a Mediator, as the cause; the Bestower of providence, the Giver of laws, the Supplier of want, the Punisher of the ungodly, and the Rewarder of the righteous; the God and Father of Christ, and the Lord of those that are pious towards Him, whose promise is infallible, whose judgment without bribes, whose sentiments are immutable, whose piety is incessant, whose thanksgiving is everlasting, through

[1] Deut. iv. 39.

whom[1] adoration is worthily due to Thee from every rational and holy nature.

XXXVI. O Lord Almighty, Thou hast created the world by Christ, and hast appointed the Sabbath in memory thereof, because that on that day Thou hast made us rest from our works, for the meditation upon Thy laws. Thou hast also appointed festivals for the rejoicing of our souls, that we might come into the remembrance of that wisdom which was created by Thee; how He submitted to be made of a woman on our account;[2] He appeared in life, and demonstrated Himself in His baptism; how He that appeared is both God and man; He suffered for us by Thy permission, and died, and rose again by Thy power: on which account we solemnly assemble to celebrate the feast of the resurrection on the Lord's day, and rejoice on account of Him who has conquered death, and has brought life and immortality to light. For by Him Thou hast brought home the Gentiles to Thyself for a peculiar people, the true Israel, beloved of God, and seeing God. For Thou, O Lord, broughtest our fathers out of the land of Egypt, and didst deliver them out of the iron furnace, from clay and brick-making, and didst redeem them out of the hands of Pharaoh, and of those under him, and didst lead them through the sea as through dry land, and didst bear their manners in the wilderness, and bestow on them all sorts of good things. Thou didst give them the law or decalogue, which was pronounced by Thy voice and written with Thy hand. Thou didst enjoin the observation of the Sabbath, not affording them an occasion of idleness, but an opportunity of piety, for their knowledge of Thy power, and the prohibition of evils; having limited them as within an holy circuit for the sake of doctrine, for the rejoicing upon the seventh period. On this account was there appointed one week, and seven weeks, and the seventh month, and the seventh year, and the revolution of these, the jubilee, which is the fiftieth year for remission, that men might have no occasion to pretend

---

[1] One V. MS. reads, "with whom."
[2] Prov. viii. 22, LXX.

ignorance.[1] On this account He permitted men every Sabbath to rest, that so no one might be willing to send one word out of his mouth in anger on the day of the Sabbath. For the Sabbath is the ceasing of the creation, the completion of the world, the inquiry after laws, and the grateful praise to God for the blessings He has bestowed upon men. All which the Lord's day excels, and shows the Mediator Himself, the Provider, the Lawgiver, the Cause of the resurrection, the First-born of the whole creation, God the Word, and man, who was born of Mary alone, without a man, who lived holily, who was crucified under Pontius Pilate, and died, and rose again from the dead. So that the Lord's day commands us to offer unto Thee, O Lord, thanksgiving for all. For this is the grace afforded by Thee, which on account of its greatness has obscured all other blessings.

XXXVII. Thou who hast fulfilled Thy promises made by the prophets, and hast had mercy on Zion, and compassion on Jerusalem, by exalting the throne of David, Thy servant in the midst of her, by the birth of Christ, who was born of his seed according to the flesh, of a virgin alone; do Thou now, O Lord God, accept the prayers which proceed from the lips of Thy people which are of the Gentiles, which call upon Thee in truth, as Thou didst accept of the gifts of the righteous in their generations. In the first place Thou didst respect the sacrifice of Abel,[2] and accept it as Thou didst accept of the sacrifice of Noah when he went out of the ark;[3] of Abraham, when he went out of the land of the Chaldeans;[4] of Isaac at the Well of the Oath;[5] of Jacob in Bethel;[6] of Moses in the desert;[7] of Aaron between the dead and the living;[8] of Joshua the son of Nun in Gilgal;[9] of Gideon at the rock, and the fleeces, before his sin;[10] of Manoah and his wife in the field; of Samson in his thirst before the transgression;[11] of Jephtha in the war before his rash vow; of Barak and Deborah in the days of Sisera;[12] of

[1] Lev. xxiii. xxv. [2] Gen. iv. [3] Gen. viii. [4] Gen. xii.
[5] Gen. xxii. [6] Gen. xxxv. [7] Ex. xii. [8] Num. xvi.
[9] Josh. v. [10] Judg. vi. viii. [11] Judg. xiii. xv. xvi.
[12] Judg. xi. iv.

Samuel in Mizpeh;[1] of David in the threshing-floor of Ornan the Jebusite;[2] of Solomon in Gibeon and in Jerusalem;[3] of Elijah in Mount Carmel;[4] of Elisha at the barren fountain;[5] of Jehoshaphat in war;[6] of Hezekiah in his sickness, and concerning Sennacherib;[7] of Manasseh in the land of the Chaldeans, after his transgression;[8] of Josiah in Phassa;[9] of Ezra at the return;[10] of Daniel in the den of lions;[11] of Jonah in the whale's belly;[12] of the three children in the fiery furnace;[13] of Hannah in the tabernacle before the ark;[14] of Nehemiah at the rebuilding of the walls;[15] of Zerubbabel; of Mattathias and his sons in their zeal;[16] of Jael in blessings. Now also do thou receive the prayers of Thy people which are offered to Thee with knowledge, through Christ in the Spirit.

XXXVIII. We give Thee thanks for all things, O Lord Almighty, that Thou hast not taken away Thy mercies and Thy compassions from us; but in every succeeding generation Thou dost save, and deliver, and assist, and protect: for Thou didst assist in the days of Enos and Enoch, in the days of Moses and Joshua, in the days of the judges, in the days of Samuel and of Elijah and of the prophets, in the days of David and of the kings, in the days of Esther and Mordecai, in the days of Judith, in the days of Judas Maccabeus and his brethren, and in our days hast Thou assisted us by Thy great High Priest, Jesus Christ Thy Son. For He has delivered us from the sword, and hath freed us from famine, and sustained us; has delivered us from sickness, has preserved us from an evil tongue. For all which things do we give Thee thanks through Christ, who has given us an articulate voice to confess withal, and added to it a suitable tongue as an instrument to modulate withal, and a proper taste, and

[1] 1 Sam. vii.   [2] 1 Chron. xxi.   [3] 1 Kings iii. viii.
[4] 1 Kings xviii.   [5] 2 Kings ii.   [6] 2 Chron. xviii.
[7] 2 Kings xx. xix.   [8] 2 Chron. xxxiii.
[9] 2 Chron. xxxv. Cotelerius conjectures "in his passover," instead of "in Phassa."
[10] Ezra viii.   [11] Dan. vi. 14.   [12] Jonah ii.
[13] Dan. iii.   [14] 1 Sam. i.   [15] Ezra iii.
[16] 1 Macc. i. etc.

a suitable touch, and a sight for contemplation, and the hearing of sounds, and the smelling of vapours, and hands for work, and feet for walking. And all these members dost Thou form from a little drop in the womb; and after the formation dost Thou bestow on it an immortal soul, and producest it into the light as a rational creature, even man. Thou hast instructed him by Thy laws, improved him by Thy statutes; and when Thou bringest on a dissolution for a while, Thou hast promised a resurrection. Wherefore what life is sufficient, what length of ages will be long enough, for men to be thankful? To do it worthily it is impossible, but to do it according to our ability is just and right. For Thou hast delivered us from the impiety of polytheism, and from the heresy of the murderers of Christ; Thou hast delivered us from error and ignorance; Thou hast sent Christ among men as a man, being the only begotten God; Thou hast made the Comforter to inhabit among us; Thou hast set angels over us; Thou hast put the devil to shame; Thou hast brought us into being when we were not; Thou takest care of us when made; Thou measurest out life to us; Thou affordest us food; Thou hast promised repentance. Glory and worship be to Thee for all these things, through Jesus Christ,[1] now and ever, and through all ages. Amen. Meditate on these things, brethren; and the Lord be with you upon earth, and in the kingdom of His Father, who both sent Him, and has "delivered us by Him from the bondage of corruption into His glorious liberty;"[2] and has promised life to those who through Him have believed in the God of the whole world.

SEC. III.—*On the instruction of catechumens, and their initiation into baptism.*

Now, after what manner those ought to live that are initiated into Christ, and what thanksgivings they ought to send up to God through Christ, has been said in the foregoing directions. But it is reasonable not to leave even those who are not yet initiated without assistance.

[1] One V. MS. reads, "with Christ and the Holy Spirit." [2] Rom. viii. 12.

XXXIX. Let him, therefore, who is to be taught the truth in regard to piety be instructed before his baptism in the knowledge of the unbegotten God, in the understanding of His only begotten Son, in the assured acknowledgment of the Holy Ghost. Let him learn the order of the several parts of the creation, the series of providence, the different dispensations of Thy laws. Let him be instructed why the world was made, and why man was appointed to be a citizen therein; let him also know his own nature, of what sort it is; let him be taught how God punished the wicked with water and fire, and did glorify the saints in every generation —I mean Seth, and Enos, and Enoch, and Noah, and Abraham and his posterity, and Melchizedek, and Job, and Moses, and Joshua, and Caleb, and Phineas the priest, and those that were holy in every generation; and how God still took care of and did not reject mankind, but called them from their error and vanity to the acknowledgment of the truth at various seasons, reducing them from bondage and impiety unto liberty and piety, from injustice to righteousness, from death eternal to everlasting life. Let him that offers himself to baptism learn these and the like things during the time that he is a catechumen; and let him who lays his hands upon him adore God, the Lord of the whole world, and thank Him for His creation, for His sending Christ His only begotten Son, that He might save man by blotting out his transgressions, and that He might remit ungodliness and sins, and might "purify him from all filthiness of flesh and spirit,"[1] and sanctify man according to the good pleasure of His kindness, that He might inspire him with the knowledge of His will, and enlighten the eyes of his heart to consider of His wonderful works, and make known to him the judgments of righteousness, that so he might hate every way of iniquity, and walk in the way of truth, that he might be thought worthy of the laver of regeneration, to the adoption of sons, which is in Christ, that "being planted together in the likeness of the death of Christ,"[2] in hopes of a glorious communication, he may be

[1] 2 Cor. vii. 1.   [2] Rom. vi. 5.

mortified to sin, and may live to God, as to his mind, and word, and deed, and may be numbered together in the book of the living. And after this thanksgiving, let him instruct him in the doctrines concerning our Lord's incarnation, and in those concerning His passion, and resurrection from the dead, and assumption.

XL. And when it remains that the catechumen is to be baptized, let him learn what concerns the renunciation of the devil, and the joining himself with Christ; for it is fit that he should first abstain from things contrary, and then be admitted to the mysteries. He must beforehand purify his heart from all wickedness of disposition, from all spot and wrinkle, and then partake of the holy things; for as the skilfullest husbandman does first purge his ground of the thorns which are grown up therein, and does then sow his wheat, so ought you also to take away all impiety from them, and then to sow the seeds of piety in them, and vouchsafe them baptism. For even our Lord did in this manner exhort us, saying first, "Make disciples of all nations;"[1] and then He adds this, "and baptize them into the name of the Father, and of the Son, and of the Holy Ghost." Let, therefore, the candidate for baptism declare thus in his renunciation:

XLI. I renounce Satan, and his works, and his pomps, and his worships, and his angels, and his inventions, and all things that are under him. And after his renunciation let him in his consociation say: And I associate myself to Christ, and believe, and am baptized into one unbegotten Being, the only true God Almighty, the Father of Christ, the Creator and Maker of all things, from whom are all things; and into the Lord Jesus Christ, His only begotten Son, the First-born of the whole creation, who before the ages was begotten by the good pleasure of the Father, by whom all things were made, both those in heaven and those on earth, visible and invisible; who in the last days descended from heaven, and took flesh, and was born of the holy Virgin Mary, and did converse holily according to the laws of His God and Father, and was crucified under Pontius Pilate, and died for us, and

[1] Matt. xxviii. 19.

rose again from the dead after His passion the third day, and ascended into the heavens, and sitteth at the right hand of the Father, and again is to come at the end of the world with glory to judge the quick and the dead, of whose kingdom there shall be no end. And I am baptized into the Holy Ghost, that is, the Comforter, who wrought in all the saints from the beginning of the world, but was afterwards sent to the apostles by the Father, according to the promise of our Saviour and Lord, Jesus Christ; and after the apostles, to all those that believe in the holy catholic church; into the resurrection of the flesh, and into the remission of sins, and into the kingdom of heaven, and into the life of the world to come. And after this vow, he comes in order to the anointing with oil.

XLII. Now this is blessed by the high priest for the remission of sins, and the first preparation for baptism. For he calls thus upon the unbegotten God, the Father of Christ, the King of all sensible and intelligible natures, that He would sanctify the oil in the name of the Lord Jesus, and impart to it spiritual grace and efficacious strength, the remission of sins, and the first preparation for the confession of baptism, that so the candidate for baptism, when he is anointed, may be freed from all ungodliness, and may become worthy of initiation, according to the command of the Only-begotten.

XLIII. After this he comes to the water, and blesses and glorifies the Lord God Almighty, the Father of the only begotten God;[1] and the priest returns thanks that He has sent His Son to become man on our account, that He might save us; that He has permitted that He should in all things become obedient to the laws of that incarnation, to preach the kingdom of heaven, the remission of sins, and the resurrection of the dead. Moreover, he adores the only begotten God Himself, after His Father, and for Him, giving Him thanks that He undertook to die for all men by

[1] One V. MS. has "Son" instead of "God." Cotelerius remarks that this change was made in the interests of orthodoxy; for the expression "only begotten God" had become common with the Arians.

the cross, the type of which He has appointed to be the baptism of regeneration. He glorifies Him also, for that God who is the Lord of the whole world, in the name of Christ, and by His Holy Spirit, has not cast off mankind, but has suited His providence to the difference of seasons: at first giving to Adam himself paradise for an habitation of pleasure, and afterwards giving a command on account of providence, and casting out the offender justly, but through His goodness not utterly casting him off, but instructing his posterity in succeeding ages after various manners; on whose account, in the conclusion of the world, He has sent His Son to become man for man's sake, and to undergo all human passions without sin. Him, therefore, let the priest even now call upon in baptism, and let him say: Look down from heaven, and sanctify this water, and give it grace and power, that so he that is to be baptized, according to the command of Thy Christ, may be crucified with Him, and may die with Him, and may be buried with Him, and may rise with Him to the adoption which is in Him, that he may be dead to sin and live to righteousness. And after this, when he has baptized him in the name of the Father, and of the Son, and of the Holy Ghost, he shall anoint him with ointment, and shall add as follows:—

XLIV. O Lord God, who art without generation, and without a superior, the Lord of the whole world, who hast scattered the sweet odour of the knowledge of the gospel among all nations, do Thou grant at this time that this ointment may be efficacious upon him that is baptized, that so the sweet odour of Thy Christ may continue upon him firm and fixed; and that now he has died with Him, he may arise and live with Him. Let him say these and the like things, for this is the efficacy of the laying on of hands on every one; for unless there be such a recital made by a pious priest over every one of these, the candidate for baptism does only descend into the water as do the Jews, and he only puts off the filth of the body, not the filth of the soul. After this let him stand up, and pray that prayer which the Lord taught us. But, of necessity, he who is risen again ought to stand up and pray, because he that is raised up stands upright. Let him, therefore, who has been dead with Christ, and is raised up with Him, stand up. But let him pray towards the east. For this also is written in the second book of the Chronicles, that after the temple of the Lord was finished by King Solomon, in the very feast of dedication the priests and the Levites and the singers stood up towards the east, praising and thanking God with cymbals and psalteries, and saying, " Praise the Lord, for He is good; for His mercy endureth for ever." [1]

XLV. But let him pray thus after the foregoing prayer, and say: O God Almighty, the Father of Thy Christ, Thy only begotten Son, give me a body undefiled, a heart pure, a mind watchful, an unerring knowledge, the influence of the Holy Ghost for the obtaining and assured enjoying of the truth, through Thy Christ, by whom [2] glory be to Thee, in the Holy Spirit, for ever. Amen. We have thought it reasonable to make these constitutions concerning the catechumens.

SEC. IV.—*Enumeration ordained by apostles.*

XLVI. Now concerning those bishops which have been ordained in our lifetime, we let you know that they are these:—James the bishop of Jerusalem, the brother of our Lord; upon whose death the second was Simeon the son of Cleopas; after whom the third was Judas the son of James. Of Cæsarea of Palestine, the first was Zaccheus, who was once a publican; after whom was Cornelius, and the third Theophilus. Of Antioch, Euodius, ordained by me Peter; and Ignatius by Paul. Of Alexandria, Annianus was the first, ordained by Mark the evangelist; the second Avilius by Luke, who was also an evangelist. Of the church of Rome, Linus the son of Claudia was the first, ordained by Paul; [3] and Clemens, after Linus' death, the second, ordained by me Peter. Of Ephesus, Timotheus, ordained by Paul; and

---

[1] 2 Chron. v. 13.

[2] One V. MS. reads, "with whom glory be to Thee, along with the Holy Spirit."

[3] 2 Tim. iv. 21.

John, by me John. Of Smyrna, Aristo the first; after whom Strataeas the son of Lois;[1] and the third Aristo. Of Pergamus, Gaius. Of Philadelphia, Demetrius, by me. Of Cenchrea, Lucius, by Paul. Of Crete, Titus. Of Athens, Dionysius. Of Tripoli in Phœnicia, Marathones. Of Laodicea in Phrygia, Archippus. Of Colossæ, Philemon.[2] Of Borea in Macedonia, Onesimus, once the servant of Philemon. Of the churches of Galatia, Crescens. Of the parishes of Asia, Aquila and Nicetas. Of the church of Æginæ, Crispus. These are the bishops who are entrusted by us with the parishes in the Lord; whose doctrine keep ye always in mind, and observe our words. And may the Lord be with you now, and to endless ages, as Himself said to us when He was about to be taken up to His own God and Father. For says He, "Lo, I am with you all the days, until the end of the world. Amen."[3]

Sec. v.—*Daily prayers.*

XLVII. "Glory be to God in the highest, and upon earth peace, good-will among men."[4] We praise Thee, we sing hymns to Thee, we bless Thee, we glorify Thee, we worship Thee by Thy great High Priest; Thee who art the true God, who art the One Unbegotten, the only inaccessible Being. For Thy great glory, O Lord and heavenly King, O God the Father Almighty, O Lord God,[5] the Father of Christ the immaculate Lamb, who taketh away the sin of the world, receive our prayer, Thou that sittest upon the cherubim. For Thou only art holy, Thou only art the Lord Jesus, the Christ of the God of all created nature, and our King, by whom glory, honour, and worship be to Thee.

---

[1] 2 Tim. i. 5.   [2] Philem. 10.
[3] Matt. xxviii. 20.   [4] Luke ii. 14.
[5] One V. MS. gives a more orthodox form to this prayer: "O Lord, only begotten Son, and Holy Spirit, Lord God, the Lamb of God, the Son of the Father, who takest away the sins of the world, receive our prayer. Thou who sittest at the right hand of the Father, have mercy upon us, for Thou only art holy; Thou only art Christ, Jesus Christ, to the glory of God the Father. Amen."

XLVIII. "Ye children, praise the Lord: praise the name of the Lord."[1] We praise Thee, we sing hymns to Thee, we bless Thee for Thy great glory, O Lord our King, the Father of Christ the immaculate Lamb, who taketh away the sin of the world. Praise becomes Thee, hymns become Thee, glory becomes Thee, the God and Father,[2] through the Son, in the most holy Spirit, for ever and ever. Amen. "Now, O Lord, lettest Thou Thy servant depart in peace, according to Thy word; for mine eyes have seen Thy salvation, which Thou hast prepared before the face of all people, a light for the revelation to the Gentiles, and the glory of Thy people Israel."[3]

XLIX. Thou art blessed, O Lord, who nourishest me from my youth, who givest food to all flesh. Fill our hearts with joy and gladness, that having always what is sufficient for us, we may abound to every good work, in Christ Jesus our Lord, through whom[4] glory, honour, and power be to Thee for ever. Amen.

BOOK VIII.

CONCERNING GIFTS, AND ORDINATIONS, AND THE ECCLESIASTICAL CANONS.

SEC. I.—*On the diversity of spiritual gifts.*

Jesus Christ, our God and Saviour, delivered to us the great mystery of godliness, and called both Jews and Gentiles to the acknowledgment of the one and only[5] true God His Father,[6] as Himself somewhere says, when He was giving

---

[1] Ps. cxiii. 1.

[2] One V. MS. omits "the God and;" then reads, "to Father, Son, and Holy Ghost."

[3] Luke ii. 29.   [4] One V. MS. reads, "with whom."

[5] The words "one and only" are omitted in the Syriac and Coptic.

[6] One V. MS. omits "His Father." The Syriac and Coptic have "the only Father."

thanks for the salvation of those that had believed, "I have manifested Thy name to men, I have finished the work Thou gavest me;"[1] and said concerning us to His Father, "Holy Father, although the world has not known Thee, yet have I known Thee; and these have known Thee."[2] With good reason did He say to all of us together, when we were perfected concerning those gifts which were given from Him by the Spirit: "Now these signs shall follow them that have believed in my name: they shall cast out devils; they shall speak with new tongues; they shall take up serpents; and if they drink any deadly thing, it shall by no means hurt them: they shall lay their hands on the sick, and they shall recover."[3] These gifts were first bestowed on us the apostles when we were about to preach the gospel to every creature, and afterwards were of necessity afforded to those who had by our means believed; not for the advantage of those who perform them, but for the conviction of the unbelievers, that those whom the word did not persuade, the power of signs might put to shame: for signs are not for us who believe, but for the unbelievers, both for the Jews and Gentiles. For neither is it any profit to us to cast out demons, but to those who are so cleansed by the power of the Lord; as the Lord[4] Himself somewhere instructs us, and shows, saying: "Rejoice ye, not because the spirits are subject unto you; but rejoice, because your names are written in heaven."[5] Since the former is done by His power, but this by our good disposition and diligence, yet (it is manifest) by His assistance. It is not therefore necessary that every one of the faithful should cast out demons, or raise the dead, or speak with tongues; but such an one only who is vouchsafed this gift, for some cause which may be advantage to the salvation of the unbelievers, who are often put to shame, not with the demonstration of the word, but by the power of the signs; that is, such as are worthy of salvation: for all the ungodly are not affected by wonders; and hereof God Himself is a

[1] John xvii. 6, 4.
[2] John xvii. 11, 25.
[3] Mark xvi. 17.
[4] The Coptic reads "our God."
[5] Luke x. 20.

witness, as when He says in the law: "With other tongues will I speak to this people, and with other lips, and yet will they by no means believe."[1] For neither did the Egyptians believe in God, when Moses had done so many signs and wonders;[2] nor did the multitude of the Jews believe in Christ, as they believed Moses, who yet had healed every sickness and every disease among them.[3] Nor were the former shamed by the rod which was turned into a living serpent, nor by the hand which was made white with leprosy, nor by the river Nile turned into blood; nor the latter by the blind who recovered their sight, nor by the lame who walked, nor by the dead who were raised.[4] The one was resisted by Jannes and Jambres, the other by Annas and Caiaphas.[5] Thus signs do not shame all into belief, but only those of a good disposition; for whose sake also it is that God is pleased, as a wise steward of a family, to appoint miracles to be wrought, not by the power of men, but by His own will. Now we say these things, that those who have received such gifts may not exalt themselves against those who have not received them; such gifts, we mean, as are for the working of miracles. For otherwise there is no man who has believed in God through Christ,[6] that has not received some spiritual gift: for this very thing, having been delivered from the impiety of polytheism, and having believed in God the Father through Christ,[7] this is a gift of God. And the having cast off the veil of Judaism, and having believed that, by the good pleasure of God, His only begotten Son, who was before all ages,[8] was in the last time born of a virgin,[9] without the company of a man, and that He lived as a man, yet without sin, and fulfilled all that righteousness which is of the law; and that, by the permission of God, He who was God

---

[1] Isa. xxviii. 11; 1 Cor. xiv. 21.   [3] Deut. xviii.
[2] Ex. vii. and iv.   [4] Matt. xi. 5.   [5] 1 Tim. iii. 8.
[6] Instead of "Christ," the Coptic reads, "through His holy Son."
[7] The Coptic reads, "and in Christ and the Holy Spirit."
[8] The Coptic reads, "and His only begotten Son, who was with the Father and the life-giving Holy Spirit before all the ages."
[9] The Coptic reads, "spotless virgin."

the Word endured the cross, and despised the shame; and that He died, and was buried, and rose within three days; and that after His resurrection, having continued forty days with His apostles, and completed His whole constitutions, He was taken up in their sight to His God and Father, who sent Him: he who has believed these things, not at random and irrationally, but with judgment and full assurance, has received the gift of God. So also has He who is delivered from every heresy. Let not, therefore, any one that works signs and wonders judge any one of the faithful who is not vouchsafed the same: for the gifts of God which are bestowed by Him through Christ are various; and one man receives one gift, and another another. For perhaps one has the word of wisdom, and another the word of knowledge;[1] another, discerning of spirits; another, foreknowledge of things to come; another, the word of teaching; another, long-suffering; another, continence according to the law: for even Moses, the man of God, when he wrought signs in Egypt, did not exalt himself against his equals; and when he was called a god, he did not arrogantly despise his own prophet Aaron.[2] Nor did Joshua the son of Nun, who was the leader of the people after him, though in the war with the Jebusites he had made the sun stand still over against Gibeon, and the moon over against the valley of Ajalon,[3] because the day was not long enough for their victory, insult over Phineas or Caleb. Nor did Samuel, who had done so many surprising things, disregard David the beloved of God: yet they were both prophets, and the one was high priest, and the other was king. And when there were only seven thousand holy men in Israel who had not bowed the knee to Baal,[4] Elijah alone among them, and his disciple Elisha, were workers of miracles. Yet neither did Elijah despise Obadiah the steward, who feared God, but wrought no signs; nor did Elisha despise his own disciple when he trembled at the enemies.[5] Moreover, neither did the wise Daniel who was twice delivered from the mouths of the lions, nor the

[1] 1 Cor. xii. 8.   [2] Ex. vii. 1.   [3] Josh. x.
[4] 1 Kings xix. 18; Rom. xi. 4.   [5] 2 Kings vi.

three children who were delivered from the furnace of fire,[1] despise the rest of their fellow-Israelites: for they knew that they had not escaped these terrible miseries by their own might; but by the power of God did they both work miracles, and were delivered from miseries. Wherefore let none of you exalt himself against his brother, though he be a prophet, or though he be a worker of miracles: for if it happens that there be no longer an unbeliever, all the power of signs will thenceforwards be superfluous. For to be pious is from any one's good disposition; but to work wonders is from the power of Him that works them by us: the first of which respects ourselves; but the second respects God that works them, for the reasons which we have already mentioned. Wherefore neither let a king despise his officers that are under him, nor the rulers those who are subject. For where there are none to be ruled over, rulers are superfluous; and where there are no officers, the kingdom will not stand. Moreover, let not a bishop be exalted against his deacons and presbyters, nor the presbyters against the people: for the subsistence of the congregation depends on each other. For the bishops and the presbyters are the priests with relation to the people; and the laity are the laity with relation to the clergy. And to be a Christian is in our own power; but to be an apostle, or a bishop, or in any other such office, is not in our own power, but at the disposal of God, who bestows the gifts. And thus much concerning those who are vouchsafed gifts and dignities.

II. We add, in the next place, that neither is every one that prophesies holy, nor every one that casts out devils religious: for even Balaam the son of Beor the prophet did prophesy,[2] though he was himself ungodly; as also did Caiaphas, the falsely-named high priest.[3] Nay, the devil foretells many things, and the demons, about Him; and yet for all that, there is not a spark of piety in them: for they are oppressed with ignorance, by reason of their voluntary wickedness. It is manifest, therefore, that the ungodly, although they prophesy, do not by their prophesying cover their own impiety; nor will

[1] Dan. vi. 14, iii.   [2] Num. xx. and xxiv.   [3] John xi. 51.

those who cast out demons be sanctified by the demons being made subject to them: for they only mock one another, as they do who play childish tricks for mirth, and destroy those who give heed to them. For neither is a wicked king any longer a king, but a tyrant; nor is a bishop oppressed with ignorance or an evil disposition a bishop, but falsely so called, being not one sent out by God, but by men, as Ananiah and Samœah in Jerusalem, and Zedechiah and Achiah the false prophets in Babylon.[1] And indeed Balaam the prophet, when he had corrupted Israel by Baal-peor, suffered punishment;[2] and Caiaphas at last was his own murderer;[3] and the sons of Sceva, endeavouring to cast out demons, were wounded by them, and fled away in an unseemly manner; and the kings of Israel and of Judah, when they became impious, suffered all sorts of punishments. It is therefore evident how bishops and presbyters, also falsely so called, will not escape the judgment of God. For it will be said to them even now: "O ye priests that despise my name, I will deliver you up to the slaughter, as I did Zedekiah and Achiah, whom the king of Babylon fried in a frying-pan,"[4] as says Jeremiah the prophet.[5] We say these things, not in contempt of true prophecies, for we know that they are wrought in holy men by the inspiration of God, but to put a stop to the boldness of vainglorious men; and add this withal, that from such as these God takes away His grace: for "God resisteth the proud, but giveth grace to the humble."[6] Now Silas and Agabus prophesied in our times;[7] yet did they not equal themselves to the apostles, nor did they exceed their own measures though they were beloved of God. Now women prophesied also. Of old, Miriam the sister of Moses and Aaron,[8] and after her Deborah,[9] and after these Huldah[10] and Judith[11]—the former under Josiah, the latter under Darius. The mother of the Lord did also prophesy, and her kinswoman Elisabeth, and Anna;[12] and in our time the daughters

[1] Jer. xxviii. and xxix.
[2] Num. xxv. and xxxi.
[3] Acts xix. 14.
[4] Mal. i. 6.
[5] Jer. xxix. 22.
[6] 1 Pet. v. 5.
[7] Acts xv. 32, xxi. 10.
[8] Ex. xv. 20.
[9] Judg. iv. 4.
[10] 2 Kings xxii. 14.
[11] Judith viii.
[12] Luke i. and ii.

of Philip:[1] yet were not these elated against their husbands, but preserved their own measures. Wherefore if among you also there be a man or a woman, and such an one obtains any gift, let him be humble, that God may be pleased with him. For says He: "Upon whom will I look, but upon him that is humble and quiet, and trembles at my words?"[2]

SEC. II.—*Election and ordination of bishops: form of service on Sundays.*

III. We have now finished the first part of this discourse concerning gifts, whatever they be, which God has bestowed upon men according to His own will; and how He rebuked the ways of those who either attempted to speak lies, or were moved by the spirit of the adversary; and that God often employed the wicked[3] for prophecy and the performance of wonders. But now our discourse hastens as to the principal part, that is, the constitution of ecclesiastical affairs, that so, when ye have learned this constitution from us, ye who are ordained bishops by us at the command of Christ, may perform all things according to the commands delivered you, knowing that he that heareth us heareth Christ, and he that heareth Christ heareth His God and Father,[4] to whom be glory for ever. Amen.

IV. Wherefore we, the twelve apostles of the Lord, who are now together, give you in charge those divine constitutions concerning every ecclesiastical form, there being present with us Paul the chosen vessel, our fellow-apostle, and James the bishop, and the rest of the presbyters, and the seven deacons.[5]

---

[1] Acts xxi. 9.   [2] Isa. lxvi. 2.

[3] We have adopted the reading of one V. MS., ἀπεχρήσατο. It means more than is in the text—that God used the wicked in a way in which they would not be naturally used; lit., "abused," or "misused." The other MSS. and the Coptic read ἐπεχαρίσατο, "gave His gifts to the wicked for prophecy." Whiston has tried to make sense by giving a new meaning to ἀπεχαρίσατο, "taking away His grace from the wicked."

[4] Luke x. 16.

[5] The Coptic and one V. MS. omit from the commencement of the chapter to "deacons." The V. MS. has: "Peter, the chief of the apostles,

In the first place, therefore, I Peter say,[1] *that a bishop to be ordained is to be,* as we have already, all of us, appointed, unblameable in all things, a select person,[2] *chosen by the whole people, who, when he is named and approved, let the people assemble, with the presbytery and bishops* that are present, *on the Lord's day,* and let them give their consent. *And let the principal of the bishops ask the presbytery and people whether this be the person whom they desire for their ruler. And if they give their consent, let him ask further whether he has a good testimony from all men as to his worthiness for so great and glorious an authority; whether all things relating to his piety towards God be right; whether justice towards men has been observed by him; whether the affairs of his family have been well ordered by him; whether he has been unblameable in the course of his life. And if all the assembly together do according to truth, and not according to prejudice, witness that he is such an one, let them the third time, as before God the Judge, and Christ,* the Holy Ghost being also present, as well as all the holy and ministering spirits, *ask again whether he be truly worthy of this ministry, that so "in the mouth of two or three witnesses every word may be established."* [3] *And if they agree the third time that he is worthy, let them all be demanded their vote; and when they all give it willingly, let them be heard. And silence being made, let one of the principal bishops, together with two others, stand near to the altar, the rest of the bishops and presbyters praying silently, and the deacons holding the divine Gospels open upon the head of him that is to be ordained,* and say to God thus:[4]

proclaimed the gospel to Pontus, Galatia, Cappadocia, Asia, Bithynia, and finally in Rome, where he was crucified by the prefect in the reign of Nero, and where also he is buried."

[1] From this to the end of ch. xxvi., only small portions of what is now in the received text occur in the Coptic version. The Oxford MS. is also deficient. It has only a portion of the fifth, nothing of ch. vi. to xvi., and only a single sentence in ch. xxii. The portions in Coptic are printed in italics.

[2] Omitted in one V. MS.

[3] Matt. xviii. 19.

[4] The Coptic has, "let the bishop pray for him."

V. O Thou the great Being, O Lord God Almighty, who alone art unbegotten, and ruled over by none; who always art, and wast before the world; who standest in need of nothing, and art above all cause and beginning; who only art true, who only art wise; who alone art the most high; who art by nature invisible; whose knowledge is without beginning; who only art good, and beyond compare; who knowest all things before they are; who art acquainted with the most secret things; who art inaccessible, and without a superior; the God and Father of Thy only begotten Son, of our God and Saviour; the Creator of the whole world by Him; whose providence provides for and takes the care of all; the Father of mercies, and God of all consolation;[2] who dwellest in the highest heavens,[3] and yet lookest down on things below: Thou who didst appoint the rules of the church, by the coming of Thy Christ in the flesh; of which the Holy Ghost is the witness, by Thy apostles, and by us the bishops, who by Thy grace are here present; who hast fore-ordained priests from the beginning for

OXFORD MS.[1]

V. God and Father of our Lord, Jesus Christ, the Father of mercies and the God of all consolation, who knowest all things before they take place; Thou who didst appoint the rules of the church through the word of Thy grace; who didst appoint beforehand the race righteous from the beginning that came from Abraham to be rulers, and didst constitute them priests, not leaving Thy sanctuary without ministers; who from the foundation of the world didst delight in those whom Thou chosest to be glorified in; and now pour down the influence of Thy free Spirit, which through Thy beloved Son Jesus Christ Thou hast bestowed on Thy holy apostles, who set up the church in the place of the sanctuary, to unending glory and praise of Thy name: O Thou, who knowest the hearts of all, grant that this Thy servant whom Thou

---

[1] The Oxford MS. has this chapter in an abbreviated form as in the parallel columns.

[2] 2 Cor. i. 3.   [3] Ps. cxiii. 5.

the government of Thy people— Abel in the first place, Seth and Enos, and Enoch and Noah, and Melchisedeck and Job; who didst appoint Abraham, and the rest of the patriarchs, with Thy faithful servants Moses and Aaron, and Eleazar and Phineas; who didst choose from among them rulers and priests in the tabernacle of Thy testimony; who didst choose Samuel for a priest and a prophet; who didst not leave Thy sanctuary without ministers; who didst delight in those whom Thou chosest to be glorified in. Do Thou, by us, pour down the influence of Thy free Spirit, through the mediation of Thy Christ, which is committed to Thy beloved Son Jesus Christ; which He bestowed according to Thy will on the holy apostles of Thee the eternal God. Grant by Thy name, O God, who searchest the hearts, that this Thy servant, whom Thou hast chosen to be a bishop, may feed Thy holy flock, and discharge the office of an high priest to Thee, and minister to Thee unblameably hast chosen to the holy office of Thy bishop, may discharge the duty of a high priest to Thee, and minister to Thee unblameably night and day; that he may appease Thee unceasingly, and present to Thee the gifts of Thy holy church, and in the spirit of the high-priesthood have power to remit sins according to Thy commandment, to give lots according to Thy injunction, to loose every bond according to the power which Thou hast given to the apostles, and be well-pleasing to Thee, in meekness and a pure heart offering a smell of sweet savour through Thy Son Jesus Christ our Lord, with whom to Thee be glory, power, and honour, along with the Holy Spirit, now and for ever. Amen.

night and day; that he may appease Thee, and gather together the number of those that shall be saved, and may offer to Thee the gifts of Thy holy church. Grant to him, O Lord Almighty, through Thy Christ, the fellowship of the Holy Spirit, that so he may have power to remit sins according to Thy command; to give forth lots according to Thy command; to loose every bond, according to the power which Thou gavest the apostles; that he may please Thee in meekness and a pure heart, with a stedfast, unblameable, and unreprovable mind; to offer to Thee a pure and unbloody sacrifice, which by Thy Christ Thou hast appointed as the mystery of the new covenant, for a sweet savour, through Thy holy child Jesus Christ, our God and Saviour, through whom[1] glory, honour, and worship be to Thee in the Holy Spirit, now and always, and for all ages. And when he has prayed for these things, let the rest of the priests add, Amen; and together with them all the people. *And after the prayer let one of the bishops elevate the sacrifice upon the hands of him that is ordained, and* early in the morning *let him be placed in his throne, in a place set apart for him among the rest of the bishops, they* all *giving him the kiss in the Lord.*[2] *And after the reading of the* Law[3] *and the Prophets, and our Epistles, and Acts, and the Gospels, let him that is ordained salute the church, saying, The grace of our Lord Jesus Christ, the love of God and the Father, and the fellowship of the Holy Ghost, be with you all; and let them all answer, And with Thy Spirit. And after these words let him speak to the people the words of exhortation; and when he has ended his word of doctrine* (I Andrew[4] the brother of Peter speak), all standing up, *let the deacon ascend upon some high seat, and proclaim,* Let none of the hearers, *let none of the unbelievers stay;* and silence being made, let him say:

VI. Ye catechumens, pray, and let all the faithful pray for them in their mind, saying: Lord, have mercy upon them. And let the deacon bid prayers for them, saying: Let us all pray unto God for the catechumens, that He that is good, He that is the lover of mankind, will mercifully hear their prayers and their supplications, and so accept their petitions as to assist them and give them those desires of their hearts

---

[1] One V. MS. reads, "with whom."

[2] The Coptic inserts, "let the holy Gospels be read."

[3] The Coptic reads "Gospel" instead of "Law."

[4] One V. MS. has the following note: "Andrew the brother of Peter preaches the gospel to the Scythians, Sogdiani, and Thracians, who on account of preaching Christ is crowned with the martyrdom of the cross by Ægæa the proconsul, and was buried in Patræ. Afterwards he was removed to Constantinople by the Emperor Constantine."

which are for their advantage, and reveal to them the gospel of His Christ; give them illumination and understanding, instruct them in the knowledge of God, teach them His commands and His ordinances, implant in them His pure and saving fear, open the ears of their hearts, that they may exercise themselves in His law day and night; strengthen them in piety, unite them to and number them with His holy flock; vouchsafe them the laver of regeneration, and the garment of incorruption, which is the true life; and deliver them from all ungodliness, and give no place to the adversary against them; "and cleanse them from all filthiness of flesh and spirit, and dwell in them, and walk in them, by His Christ; bless their goings out and their comings in, and order their affairs for their good."[1] Let us still earnestly put up our supplications for them, that they may obtain the forgiveness of their transgressions by their admission, and so may be thought worthy of the holy mysteries, and of constant communion with the saints. Rise up, ye catechumens, beg for yourselves the peace of God through His Christ, a peaceable day, and free from sin, and the like for the whole time of your life, and your Christian ends of it; a compassionate and merciful God; and the forgiveness of your transgressions. Dedicate yourselves to the only unbegotten God, through His Christ. Bow down your heads, and receive the blessing. But at the naming of every one by the deacon, as we said before, let the people say, Lord, have mercy upon him; and let the children say it first. And as they have bowed down their heads, let the bishop who is newly ordained bless them with this blessing: O God Almighty, unbegotten and inaccessible, who only art the true God, the God and Father of Thy Christ, Thy only begotten Son; the God[2] of the Comforter, and Lord of the whole world; who by Christ didst appoint Thy disciples to be teachers for the teaching of piety; do Thou now also look down upon Thy servants, who are receiving instruction in the gospel of Thy Christ, and

---

[1] 2 Cor. vii. 1, vi. 16; Ps. cxxi. 8.

[2] One V. MS. has προβολεύς, "the sender forth," or "producer," instead of "God."

"give them a new heart, and renew a right spirit in their inward parts,"[1] that they may both know and do Thy will with full purpose of heart, and with a willing soul. Vouchsafe them an holy admission, and unite them to Thy holy church, and make them partakers of Thy divine mysteries, through Christ, who is our hope, and who died for them; by whom glory and worship be given to Thee in the Holy Spirit for ever. Amen. And after this, let the deacon say: Go out, ye catechumens, in peace. And after they are gone out, let him say: Ye energumens, afflicted with unclean spirits, pray, and let us all earnestly pray for them, that God, the lover of mankind, will by Christ rebuke the unclean and wicked spirits, and deliver His supplicants from the dominion of the adversary. May He that rebuked the legion of demons,[2] and the devil, the prince of wickedness, even now rebuke these apostates from piety, and deliver His own workmanship from his power, and cleanse those creatures which He has made with great wisdom. Let us still pray earnestly for them. Save them, O God, and raise them up by Thy power. Bow down your heads, ye energumens, and receive the blessings. And let the bishop add this prayer, and say:

VII. Thou, who hast bound the strong man, and spoiled all that was in his house, who hast given us power over serpents and scorpions to tread upon them, and upon all the power of the enemy;[3] who hast delivered the serpent, that murderer of men, bound to us, as a sparrow to children, whom all things dread, and tremble before the face of Thy power;[4] who hast cast him down as lightning from heaven to earth,[5] not with a fall from a place, but from honour to dishonour, on account of his voluntary evil disposition; whose look dries the abysses, and threatening melts the mountains, and whose truth remains for ever; whom the infants praise, and sucking babes bless; whom angels sing hymns to, and adore; who lookest upon the earth, and makest it tremble; who touchest the mountains, and they smoke; who threatenest the sea, and driest it up, and makest all its

[1] Ps. li. 12. [2] Mark v. 9; Zech. iii. 2.
[3] Matt. xii. 29; Luke x. 19. [4] Job xl. 24, LXX. [5] Luke x. 18.

rivers as desert, and the clouds are the dust of His feet; who walkest upon the sea as upon the firm ground;[1] Thou only begotten God, the Son of the great Father, rebuke these wicked spirits, and deliver the works of Thy hands from the power of the adverse spirit. For to Thee is due glory, honour, and worship, and by Thee to Thy Father, in the Holy Spirit, for ever. Amen. And let the deacon say: Go out, ye energumens. And after them, let him cry aloud: Ye that are to be illuminated, pray. Let all us, the faithful, earnestly pray for them, that the Lord will vouchsafe that, being initiated into the death of Christ, they may rise with Him, and become partakers of His kingdom, and may be admitted to the communion of His mysteries; unite them to, number them among, those that are saved in His holy church. Save them, and raise them up by Thy grace. And being sealed to God through His Christ, let them bow down their heads, and receive this blessing from the bishop:

VIII. Thou who hast formerly said by Thy holy prophets to those that be initiated, "Wash ye, become clean,"[2] and hast appointed spiritual regeneration by Christ, do Thou now also look down upon these that are baptized, and bless them, and sanctify them, and prepare them that they may become worthy of Thy spiritual gift, and of the true adoption of Thy spiritual mysteries, of being gathered together with those that are saved through Christ our Saviour; by whom glory, honour, and worship be to Thee, in the Holy Ghost, for ever. Amen. And let the deacon say: Go out, ye that are preparing for illumination. And after that let him proclaim: Ye penitents, pray; let us all earnestly pray for our brethren in the state of penitence, that God, the lover of compassion, will show them the way of repentance, and accept their return and their confession, and bruise Satan under their feet suddenly,[3] and redeem them from the snare of the devil, and the ill-usage of the demons, and free them from every unlawful word, and every absurd practice and

---

[1] Ps. cvi. 9; Isa. li. 10; Ps. xcvii. 5; Isa. lxiv. 1; Ps. cxvii. 2, ix. 3, xcvii. 3, civ. 32; Nah. i. 4, 3; Job ix. 8, LXX.
[2] Isa. i. 16.   [3] Rom. xvi. 20.

wicked thought; forgive them all their offences, both voluntary and involuntary, and blot out that handwriting which is against them,[1] and write them in the book of life;[2] cleanse them from all filthiness of flesh and spirit,[3] and restore and unite them to His holy flock. For He knoweth our frame. For who can glory that he has a clean heart? And who can boldly say, that he is pure from sin?[4] For we are all among the blameworthy. Let us still pray for them more earnestly, for there is joy in heaven over one sinner that repenteth,[5] that, being converted from every evil work, they may be joined to all good practice; that God, the lover of mankind, will suddenly accept their petitions, will restore[6] to them the joy of His salvation, and strengthen them with His free Spirit;[7] that they may not be any more shaken,[8] but be admitted to the communion of His most holy things, and become partakers of His divine mysteries, that appearing worthy of His adoption, they may obtain eternal life. Let us all still earnestly say on their account: Lord, have mercy upon them. Save them, O God, and raise them up by Thy mercy. Rise up, and bow your heads to God through His Christ, and receive the blessings. Let the bishop then add this prayer:

IX. Almighty, eternal God, Lord of the whole world, the Creator and Governor of all things, who hast exhibited man as the ornament of the world through Christ, and didst give him a law both naturally implanted and written, that he might live according to law, as a rational creature; and when he had sinned, Thou gavest him Thy goodness as a pledge in order to his repentance: Look down upon these persons who have bended the neck of their soul and body to Thee; for Thou desirest not the death of a sinner, but his repentance, that he turn from his wicked way, and live.[9] Thou

[1] Col. ii. 13, 14.   [2] Phil. iv. 3.   [3] 2 Cor. vii. 1.
[4] Prov. xx. 9.   [5] Luke xv. 7.
[6] The V. mss. read, "restore them to their former position, and give them the joy," etc.
[7] Ps. li. 14.
[8] The V. mss. add, "in their footsteps, but may be deemed worthy to be admitted," etc.
[9] Ezek. xviii. and xxxiii.

who didst accept the repentance of the Ninevites, who willest that all men be saved, and come to the acknowledgment of the truth;[1] who didst accept of that son who had consumed his substance in riotous living,[2] with the bowels of a father, on account of his repentance; do Thou now accept of the repentance of Thy supplicants: for there is no man that will not sin; for "if Thou, O Lord, markest iniquities, O Lord, who shall stand? For with Thee there is propitiation."[3] And do Thou restore them to Thy holy church, into their former dignity and honour, through Christ our God and Saviour, by whom glory and adoration be to Thee, in the Holy Ghost, for ever. Amen. Then let the deacon say, Depart, ye penitents; and let him add, Let none of those who ought not to come draw near. All we of the faithful, let us bend our knee; let us all entreat God through His Christ; let us earnestly beseech God through His Christ.

X. Let us pray for the peace and happy settlement of the world, and of the holy churches; that the God of the whole world may afford us His everlasting peace, and such as may not be taken away from us; that He may preserve us in a full prosecution of such virtue as is according to godliness. Let us pray for the holy catholic and apostolic church which is spread from one end of the earth to the other; that God would preserve and keep it unshaken, and free from the waves of this life, until the end of the world, as founded upon a rock; and for the holy parish in this place, that the Lord of the whole world may vouchsafe us without failure to follow after His heavenly hope, and without ceasing to pay Him the debt of our prayer. Let us pray for every episcopacy which is under the whole heaven, of those that rightly divide the word of Thy truth. And let us pray for our bishop James, and his parishes; let us pray for our bishop Clement, and his parishes; let us pray for our bishop Euodius, and his parishes; let us pray for our bishop Annianus, and his parishes: that the compassionate God may grant them to continue in His holy churches in health, honour, and long life, and afford them an honourable

---
[1] Jonah iii.; 1 Tim. ii. 4.   [2] Luke xv.   [3] 1 Kings viii. 46.

old age in godliness and righteousness. And let us pray for our presbyters, that the Lord may deliver them from every unreasonable and wicked action, and afford them a presbyterate in health and honour. Let us pray for all the deacons and ministers in Christ, that the Lord may grant them an unblameable ministration. Let us pray for the readers, singers, virgins, widows, and orphans. Let us pray for those that are in marriage and in child-bearing, that the Lord may have mercy upon them all. Let us pray for the eunuchs who walk holily. Let us pray for those in a state of continence and piety. Let us pray for those that bear fruit in the holy church, and give alms to the needy. And let us pray for those who offer sacrifices and oblations to the Lord our God, that God, the fountain of all goodness, may recompense them with His heavenly gifts, and " give them in this world an hundredfold, and in the world to come life everlasting;"[1] and bestow upon them for their temporal things, those that are eternal; for earthly things, those that are heavenly. Let us pray for our brethren newly enlightened, that the Lord may strengthen and confirm them. Let us pray for our brethren exercised with sickness, that the Lord may deliver them from every sickness and every disease, and restore them sound into His holy church. Let us pray for those that travel by water or by land. Let us pray for those that are in the mines, in banishments, in prisons, and in bonds, for the name of the Lord. Let us pray for those that are afflicted with bitter servitude. Let us pray for our enemies, and those that hate us. Let us pray for those that persecute us for the name of the Lord, that the Lord may pacify their anger, and scatter their wrath against us. Let us pray for those that are without, and are wandered out of the way, that the Lord may convert them. Let us be mindful of the infants of the church, that the Lord may perfect them in His fear, and bring them to a complete age. Let us pray one for another, that the Lord may keep us and preserve us by His grace to the end, and deliver us from the evil one, and from all the scandals of those that work ini-

[1] Matth. xix. 19.

quity, and preserve us unto His heavenly kingdom. Let us pray for every Christian soul. Save us, and raise us up, O God, by Thy mercy. Let us rise up, and let us pray earnestly, and dedicate ourselves and one another to the living God, through His Christ. And let the high priest add this prayer, and say:

XI. O Lord Almighty, the Most High, who dwellest on high, the Holy One, that restest among the saints, without beginning, the Only Potentate, who hast given to us by Christ the preaching of knowledge, to the acknowledgment of Thy glory and of Thy name, which He has made known to us, for our comprehension, do Thou now also look down through Him upon this Thy flock, and deliver it from all ignorance and wicked practice, and grant that we may fear Thee in earnest, and love Thee with affection, and have a due reverence of Thy glory. Be gracious and merciful to them, and hearken to them when they pray unto Thee; and keep them, that they may be unmoveable, unblameable, and unreprovable, that they may be holy in body and spirit, not having spot or wrinkle, or any such thing; but that they may be complete, and none of them may be defective or imperfect. O our support, our powerful God, who dost not accept persons, be Thou the assister of this Thy people,[1] which Thou hast redeemed with the precious blood of Thy Christ; be Thou their protector, aider, provider, and guardian, their strong wall of defence, their bulwark and security. For "none can snatch out of Thy hand:"[2] for there is no other God like Thee; for on Thee is our reliance. "Sanctify them by Thy truth: for Thy word is truth."[3] Thou who dost nothing for favour, Thou whom none can deceive, deliver them from every sickness, and every disease, and every offence, every injury and deceit, "from fear of the enemy, from the dart that flieth in the day, from the mischief that walketh about in darkness;"[4] and vouchsafe them that everlasting life which is in Christ Thy only begotten Son, our God and Saviour, through whom glory and

---

[1] The V. mss. insert, " whom Thou hast selected out of myriads."
[2] John x. 29. [3] John xvi. 17. [4] Ps. lxiv. 2, xci. 6.

worship be to Thee, in the Holy Spirit, now and always, and for ever and ever. Amen. And after this let the deacon say, Let us attend. And let the bishop salute the church, and say, The peace of God be with you all. And let the people answer, And with thy spirit; and *let the deacon say to all, Salute ye one another with the holy kiss. And let the clergy salute the bishop, the men of the laity salute the men, the women the women. And let the children stand at the reading-desk; and let another deacon stand by them, that they may not be* disorderly.[1] *And let other deacons walk about and watch the men and women, that no tumult may be made, and that no one nod, or whisper, or slumber; and let* the deacons[2] *stand at the doors of the men, and the* sub-deacons *at those of the women, that no one go out, nor a door be opened, although it be for one of the faithful, at the time of the oblation. But let one of the sub-deacons bring water to wash the hands of the priests, which is a symbol of the purity of those souls that are devoted to God.*

XII. And I James,[3] the brother of John, the son of Zebedee, say, that *the deacon shall* immediately *say, Let none of the catechumens, let none of the hearers, let none of the unbelievers, let none of the heterodox, stay here. You who have prayed the foregoing prayer, depart. Let the mothers receive their children; let no one have anything against any one; let no one come in hypocrisy; let us stand upright before the Lord with fear and trembling, to offer. When this is done, let the deacons bring the gifts to the bishop at the altar; and let the presbyters stand on his right hand, and on his left, as disciples stand before their Master. But let two of the deacons, on each side of the altar, hold a fan, made up of thin membranes, or of the feathers of the peacock, or of fine cloth, and let them silently drive away the small animals that fly about, that they may not come near to the cups. Let the high priest, therefore,* together

---

[1] The meaning in Coptic seems to be uncertain.
[2] The Coptic reads, "sub-deacons."
[3] One V. MS. gives the following note: "James the son of Zebedee, brother of John, preached the gospel in Judea, was slain with the sword by Herod the tetrarch, and lies in Cæsarea.

with the priests, *pray*[1] by himself; and let him put on his shining garment, and stand at the altar, and make the sign of the cross upon his forehead with his hand,[2] and say: The grace of Almighty God, and the love of our Lord Jesus Christ, and the fellowship of the Holy Ghost, be with you all. And let all with one voice say: And with thy spirit. The high priest: Lift up your mind. All the people: We lift it up unto the Lord. The high priest: Let us give thanks to the Lord. All the people: It is meet and right so to do. Then let the high priest say: It is very meet and right before all things to sing an hymn to Thee, who art the true God, who art before all beings, "from whom the whole family in heaven and earth is named;"[3] who only art unbegotten, and without beginning, and without a ruler, and without a master; who standest in need of nothing; who art the bestower of everything that is good; who art beyond all cause and generation; who art alway and immutably the same; from whom all things came into being, as from their proper original. For Thou art eternal knowledge, everlasting sight, unbegotten hearing, untaught wisdom, the first by nature, and the measure of being, and beyond all number; who didst bring all things out of nothing into being by Thy only begotten Son, but didst beget Him before all ages by Thy will, Thy power, and Thy goodness, without any instrument, the only begotten Son, God the Word, the living Wisdom, "the first-born of every creature, the angel of Thy great counsel,"[4] and Thy High Priest, but the King and Lord of every intellectual and sensible nature, who was before all things, by whom were all things. For Thou, O eternal God, didst make all things by Him, and through Him it is that Thou vouchsafest Thy suitable providence over the whole

---

[1] The Coptic adds, "over the oblation, that the Holy Spirit may descend upon it, making the bread the body of Christ, and the cup the blood of Christ; and prayers being ended." It then goes on with the words in italics in ch. xiii.

[2] The common text has, "before all the people," omitted by one V. ms.

[3] Eph. iii. 15.   [4] Col. i. 15; Isa. ix. 6, LXX.

world; for by the very same that Thou bestowedst being, didst Thou also bestow well-being: the God and Father of Thy only begotten Son, who by Him didst make before all things the cherubim and the seraphim, the æons and hosts, the powers and authorities, the principalities and thrones, the archangels and angels; and after all these, didst by Him make this visible world, and all things that are therein. For Thou art He who didst frame the heaven as an arch, and "stretch it out like the covering of a tent,"[1] and didst found the earth upon nothing by Thy mere will; who didst fix the firmament, and prepare the night and the day; who didst bring the light out of Thy treasures, and on its departure didst bring on darkness, for the rest of the living creatures that move up and down in the world; who didst appoint the sun in heaven to rule over the day, and the moon to rule over the night, and didst inscribe in heaven the choir of stars to praise Thy glorious majesty; who didst make the water for drink and for cleansing, the air in which we live for respiration and the affording of sounds, by the means of the tongue, which strikes the air, and the hearing, which co-operates therewith, so as to perceive speech when it is received by it, and falls upon it; who madest fire for our consolation in darkness, for the supply of our want, and that we might be warmed and enlightened by it; who didst separate the great sea from the land, and didst render the former navigable and the latter fit for walking, and didst replenish the former with small and great living creatures, and filledst the latter with the same, both tame and wild; didst furnish it with various plants, and crown it with herbs, and beautify it with flowers, and enrich it with seeds; who didst ordain the great deep, and on every side madest a mighty cavity for it, which contains seas of salt waters heaped together,[2] yet didst Thou every way bound them with barriers of the smallest sand; who sometimes dost raise it to the height of mountains by the winds, and sometimes dost smooth it into a plain; sometimes dost enrage it with a tem-

---

[1] Gen. i.; 4 Esd. xvi. 59; Ps. civ. 2.
[2] Job xxxviii.; Jer. v.

pest, and sometimes dost still it with a calm, that it may be easy to seafaring men in their voyages; who didst encompass this world, which was made by Thee through Christ, with rivers, and water it with currents, and moisten it with springs that never fail, and didst bind it round with mountains for the immoveable and secure consistence of the earth: for Thou hast replenished Thy world, and adorned it with sweet-smelling and with healing herbs, with many and various living creatures, strong and weak, for food and for labour, tame and wild; with the noises of creeping things, the sounds of various sorts of flying creatures; with the circuits of the years, the numbers of months and days, the order of the seasons, the courses of the rainy clouds, for the production of the fruits and the support of living creatures. Thou hast also appointed the station of the winds, which blow when commanded by Thee, and the multitude of the plants and herbs. And Thou hast not only created the world itself, but hast also made man for a citizen of the world, exhibiting him as the ornament of the world; for Thou didst say to Thy Wisdom: "Let us make man according to our image, and according to our likeness; and let them have dominion over the fish of the sea, and over the fowls of the heaven."[1] Wherefore also Thou hast made him of an immortal soul, and of a body liable to dissolution—the former out of nothing, the latter out of the four elements—and hast given him as to his soul rational knowledge, the discerning of piety and impiety, and the observation of right and wrong; and as to his body, Thou hast granted him five senses and progressive motion: for Thou, O God Almighty, didst by Thy Christ plant a paradise in Eden,[2] in the east, adorned with all plants fit for food, and didst introduce him into it, as into a rich banquet. And when Thou madest him, Thou gavest him a law implanted within him, that so he might have at home and within himself the seeds of divine knowledge; and when Thou hadst brought him into the paradise of pleasure, Thou allowedst him the privilege of enjoying all things, only forbidding the tasting of one tree, in hopes of greater blessings;

[1] Gen. i. 26.   [2] Gen. iii.

that in case he would keep that command, he might receive the reward of it, which was immortality. But when he neglected that command, and tasted of the forbidden fruit, by the seduction of the serpent and the counsel of his wife, Thou didst justly cast him out of paradise. Yet of Thy goodness Thou didst not overlook him, nor suffer him to perish utterly, for he was Thy creature; but Thou didst subject the whole creation to him, and didst grant him liberty to procure himself food by his own sweat and labours, whilst Thou didst cause all the fruits of the earth to spring up, to grow, and to ripen. But when Thou hadst laid him asleep for a while, Thou didst with an oath call him to a restoration again, didst loose the bond of death, and promise him life after the resurrection. And not this only; but when Thou hadst increased his posterity to an innumerable multitude, those that continued with Thee Thou didst glorify, and those who did apostatize from Thee Thou didst punish. And while Thou didst accept of the sacrifice of Abel[1] as of an holy person, Thou didst reject the gift of Cain, the murderer of his brother, as of an abhorred wretch. And besides these, Thou didst accept of Seth and Enos,[2] and didst translate Enoch:[3] for Thou art the Creator of men, and the giver of life, and the supplier of want, and the giver of laws, and the rewarder of those that observe them, and the avenger of those that transgress them; who didst bring the great flood upon the world by reason of the multitude of the ungodly,[4] and didst deliver righteous Noah from that flood by an ark,[5] with eight souls, the end of the foregoing generations, and the beginning of those that were to come; who didst kindle a fearful fire against the five cities of Sodom, and "didst turn a fruitful land into a salt lake for the wickedness of them that dwelt therein,"[6] but didst snatch holy Lot out of the conflagration. Thou art He who didst deliver Abraham from the impiety of his forefathers, and didst appoint him to be the heir of the world, and didst discover to him Thy

[1] Gen. iv.
[2] Gen. iv. and v.
[3] Ecclus. xlix. 19.
[4] Gen. vi. and vii.
[5] 1 Pet. iii. 20.
[6] Gen. xix.; Wisd. x. 6; Ps. cvii. 34.

Christ; who didst aforehand ordain Melchisedec an high priest for Thy worship;[1] who didst render Thy patient servant Job the conqueror of that serpent who is the patron of wickedness; who madest Isaac the son of the promise, and Jacob the father of twelve sons, and didst increase his posterity to a multitude, and bring him into Egypt with seventy-five souls.[2] Thou, O Lord, didst not overlook Joseph, but grantedst him, as a reward of his chastity for Thy sake, the government over the Egyptians.[3] Thou, O Lord, didst not overlook the Hebrews when they were afflicted by the Egyptians, on account of the promises made unto their fathers; but Thou didst deliver them, and punish the Egyptians. And when men had corrupted the law of nature, and had sometimes esteemed the creation the effect of chance, and sometimes honoured it more than they ought, and equalled it to the God of the universe, Thou didst not, however, suffer them to go astray, but didst raise up Thy holy servant Moses, and by him didst give the written law for the assistance of the law of nature,[4] and didst show that the creation was Thy work, and didst banish away the error of polytheism. Thou didst adorn Aaron and his posterity with the priesthood, and didst punish the Hebrews when they sinned, and receive them again when they returned to Thee. Thou didst punish the Egyptians with a judgment of ten plagues, and didst divide the sea, and bring the Israelites through it, and drown and destroy the Egyptians who pursued after them. Thou didst sweeten the bitter water with wood; Thou didst bring water out of the rock of stone; Thou didst rain manna from heaven, and quails, as meat out of the air; Thou didst afford them a pillar of fire by night to give them light, and a pillar of a cloud by day to overshadow them from the heat; Thou didst declare Joshua to be the general of the army, and didst overthrow the seven nations of Canaan by him;[5] Thou didst divide Jordan, and dry up the rivers of Etham;[6] Thou didst overthrow walls without instruments or the hand of man.[7]

[1] Gen. xii. etc. [2] Gen. xlvi. 27, LXX. [3] Ex. i. etc.
[4] See Isa. viii. 20, LXX. [5] Josh. iii. 10, etc.
[6] Ps. lxxiv. 15. [7] Josh. vi.

For all these things, glory be to Thee, O Lord Almighty. Thee do the innumerable hosts of angels, archangels, thrones, dominions, principalities, authorities, and powers, Thine everlasting armies, adore. The cherubim and the six-winged seraphim, with twain covering their feet, with twain their heads, and with twain flying,[1] say, together with thousand thousands of archangels, and ten thousand times ten thousand of angels,[2] incessantly, and with constant and loud voices, and let all the people say it with them: "Holy, holy, holy, Lord of hosts, heaven and earth are full of His glory: be Thou blessed for ever. Amen."[3] And afterwards let the high priest say: For Thou art truly holy, and most holy, the highest and most highly exalted for ever. Holy also is Thy only begotten Son our Lord and God, Jesus Christ, who in all things ministered to His God and Father, both in Thy various creation and Thy suitable providence, and has not overlooked lost mankind. But after the law of nature, after the exhortations in the positive law, after the prophetical reproofs and the government of the angels, when men had perverted both the positive law and that of nature, and had cast out of their mind the memory of the flood, the burning of Sodom, the plagues of the Egyptians, and the slaughters of the inhabitants of Palestine, and being just ready to perish universally after an unparalleled manner, He was pleased by Thy good will to become man, who was man's Creator; to be under the laws, who was the Legislator; to be a sacrifice, who was an High Priest; to be a sheep, who was the Shepherd. And He appeased Thee, His God and Father, and reconciled Thee to the world, and freed all men from the wrath to come, and was made of a virgin, and was in flesh, being God the Word, the beloved Son, the first-born of the whole creation, and was, according to the prophecies which were foretold concerning Him by Himself, of the seed of David and Abraham, of the tribe of Judah. And He was made in the womb of a virgin, who formed all mankind that are born into the world; He took flesh, who was without flesh; He who was begotten before time, was born in time; He lived holily, and taught

[1] Isa. vi. 2.   [2] Dan. vii. 10.   [3] Isa. vi. 3; Rom. i. 25.

according to the law; He drove away every sickness and every disease from men, and wrought signs and wonders among the people; and He was partaker of meat, and drink, and sleep, who nourishes all that stand in need of food, and "fills every living creature with His goodness;"[1] "He manifested His name to those that knew it not;"[2] He drave away ignorance; He revived piety, and fulfilled Thy will; He finished the work which Thou gavest Him to do; and when He had set all these things right, He was seized by the hands of the ungodly, of the high priests and priests, falsely so called, and of the disobedient people, by the betraying of him who was possessed of wickedness as with a confirmed disease; He suffered many things from them, and endured all sorts of ignominy by Thy permission; He was delivered to Pilate the governor, and He that was the Judge was judged, and He that was the Saviour was condemned; He that was impassible was nailed to the cross, and He who was by nature immortal died, and He that is the giver of life was buried, that He might loose those for whose sake He came from suffering and death, and might break the bonds of the devil, and deliver mankind from his deceit. He arose from the dead the third day; and when He had continued with His disciples forty days, He was taken up into the heavens, and is sat down on the right hand of Thee, who art His God and Father. Being mindful, therefore, of those things that He endured for our sakes, we give Thee thanks, O God Almighty, not in such a manner as we ought, but as we are able, and fulfil His constitution: "For in the same night that He was betrayed, He took bread"[3] in His holy and undefiled hands, and, looking up to Thee His God and Father, "He brake it, and gave it to His disciples, saying, This is the mystery of the new covenant: take of it, and eat. This is my body, which is broken for many, for the remission of sins."[4] In like manner also "He took the cup," and mixed it of wine and water, and sanctified it, and delivered it to them, saying: "Drink ye all of this; for this is

[1] Ps. cv. 16.
[2] John xvii. 6, 4.
[3] 1 Cor. xi.
[4] Matth. xxvi.; Mark xiv.; Luke xxii.

my blood which is shed for many, for the remission of sins: do this in remembrance of me. For as often as ye eat this bread and drink this cup, ye do show forth my death until I come." Being mindful, therefore, of His passion, and death, and resurrection from the dead, and return into the heavens, and His future second appearing, wherein He is to come with glory and power to judge the quick and the dead, and to recompense to every one according to his works, we offer to Thee, our King and our God, according to His constitution, this bread and this cup, giving Thee thanks, through Him, that Thou hast thought us worthy to stand before Thee, and to sacrifice to Thee; and we beseech Thee that Thou wilt mercifully look down upon these gifts which are here set before Thee, O Thou God, who standest in need of none of our offerings. And do Thou accept them, to the honour of Thy Christ, and send down upon this sacrifice Thine Holy Spirit, the Witness of the Lord Jesus' sufferings, that He may show this bread to be the body of Thy Christ, and the cup to be the blood of Thy Christ, that those who are partakers thereof may be strengthened for piety, may obtain the remission of their sins, may be delivered from the devil and his deceit, may be filled with the Holy Ghost, may be made worthy of Thy Christ, and may obtain eternal life upon Thy reconciliation to them, O Lord Almighty. We further pray unto Thee, O Lord, for Thy holy church spread from one end of the world to another, which Thou hast purchased with the precious blood of Thy Christ, that Thou wilt preserve it unshaken and free from disturbance until the end of the world; for every episcopate who rightly divides the word of truth. We further pray to Thee for me, who am nothing, who offer to Thee, for the whole presbytery, for the deacons and all the clergy, that Thou wilt make them wise, and replenish them with the Holy Spirit. We further pray to Thee, O Lord, "for the king and all in authority,"[1] for the whole army, that they may be peaceable towards us, that so, leading the whole time of our life in quietness and unanimity, we may glorify Thee through Jesus Christ,

---

[1] 1 Tim. ii. 2.

who is our hope. We further offer to Thee also for all those holy persons who have pleased Thee from the beginning of the world—patriarchs, prophets, righteous men, apostles, martyrs, confessors, bishops, presbyters, deacons, sub-deacons, readers, singers, virgins, widows, and lay persons, with all whose names Thou knowest. We further offer to Thee for this people, that Thou wilt render them, to the praise of Thy Christ, " a royal priesthood and an holy nation;"[1] for those that are in virginity and purity; for the widows of the church; for those in honourable marriage and child-bearing; for the infants of Thy people; that Thou wilt not permit any of us to " become castaways." We further beseech Thee also for this city and its inhabitants; for those that are sick; for those in bitter servitude; for those in banishments; for those in prison; for those that travel by water or by land; that Thou, the helper and assister of all men, wilt be their supporter. We further also beseech Thee for those that hate us and persecute us for Thy name's sake; for those that are without, and wander out of the way; that Thou wilt convert them to goodness, and pacify their anger. We further also beseech Thee for the catechumens of the church, and for those that are vexed by the adversary, and for our brethren the penitents, that Thou wilt perfect the first in the faith, that Thou wilt deliver the second from the energy of the evil one, and that Thou wilt accept the repentance of the last, and forgive both them and us our offences. We further offer to Thee also for the good temperature of the air, and the fertility of the fruits, that so, partaking perpetually of the good things derived from Thee, we may praise Thee without ceasing, " who gavest food to all flesh."[2] We further beseech Thee also for those who are absent on a just cause, that Thou wilt keep us all in piety, and gather us together in the kingdom of Thy Christ, the God of all sensible and intelligent nature, our King; that Thou wouldst keep us immoveable, unblameable, and unreprovable: for to Thee belongs all glory, and worship, and thanksgiving, honour and adoration, the Father, with the Son, and to the Holy Ghost,

[1] 1 Pet. ii. 9.   [2] Ps. cxxxvi. 25.

both now and always, and for everlasting, and endless ages for ever. And let all the people say, Amen. And let the bishop say, "The peace of God be with you all." And let all the people say, "And with thy spirit." And let the deacon proclaim again:

XIII. Let us still further beseech God through His Christ, and let us beseech Him on account of the gift which is offered to the Lord God, that the good God will accept it, through the mediation of His Christ, upon His heavenly altar, for a sweet-smelling savour. Let us pray for this church and people. Let us pray for every episcopate, every presbytery, all the deacons and ministers in Christ, for the whole congregation, that the Lord will keep and preserve them all. Let us pray "for kings and those in authority," that they may be peaceable toward us, "that so we may have and lead a quiet and peaceable life in all godliness and honesty."[1] Let us be mindful of the holy martyrs, that we may be thought worthy to be partakers of their trial. Let us pray for those that are departed in the faith. Let us pray for the good temperature of the air, and the perfect maturity of the fruits. Let us pray for those that are newly enlightened, that they may be strengthened in the faith, and all may be mutually comforted by one another.[2] Raise us up, O God, by Thy grace. Let us stand up, and dedicate ourselves to God, through His Christ. And let the bishop say: O God, who art great, and whose name is great, who art great in counsel and mighty in works, the God and Father of Thy holy child Jesus, our Saviour; look down upon us, and upon this Thy flock, which Thou hast chosen by Him to the glory of Thy name; and sanctify our body and soul, and grant us the favour to be "made pure from all filthiness of flesh and spirit,"[3] and may obtain the good things laid up for us, and do not account any of us unworthy;

---

[1] 1 Tim. ii. 2.
[2] This is not a fair translation of the Greek, which, as the text stands, does not make sense. One V. MS. reads, "Let us beseech in behalf of one another."
[3] 2 Cor. vii. 1.

but be Thou our comforter, helper, and protector, through Thy Christ, with whom glory, honour, praise, doxology, and thanksgiving be to Thee and to the Holy Ghost for ever. Amen. And after that all have said Amen, let the deacon say: Let us attend. And let the bishop speak thus to the people: Holy things for holy persons. And let the people answer: There is One that is holy; there is one Lord, one Jesus Christ, blessed for ever, to the glory of God the Father. Amen. "Glory to God in the highest, and on earth peace, good-will among men. Hosanna to the son of David! Blessed be He that cometh in the name of the Lord," being the Lord God who appeared to us, "Hosanna in the highest."[1] *And after that, let the bishop partake, then the presbyters, and deacons, and*[2] sub-deacons, and the readers, and the singers, and the ascetics; and then of the women, the deaconesses, and the virgins, and the widows; then the children; *and then all the people in order, with reverence and godly fear, without tumult. And let the bishop give the oblation, saying, The body of Christ; and let him that receiveth say, Amen. And let the deacon take the cup; and when he gives it, say, The blood of Christ, the cup of life; and let him that drinketh say, Amen.*[3] And let the thirty-third psalm be said, while all the rest are partaking; *and when all*, both men and women, *have partaken*, let the deacons carry what remains into the vestry. *And when the singer has done, let the deacon say:*

XIV. *Now we have received the precious body and* the precious *blood of Christ, let us give thanks to Him who has thought us worthy to partake of these His holy*[5] *mysteries;* and let us beseech Him that it may not be to us for condemnation, but for salvation, to the advantage of soul and body, to the preservation of piety, to the remission of sins, and to the life of

---

[1] Luke ii. 14; Matth. xxi. 9.
[2] The Coptic adds, "the rest of the clergy in their order."
[3] The Coptic has, "and let them sing psalms during the distribution, until the whole congregation has received it."
[4] The Coptic has, "let all the women receive it also."
[5] The Coptic, "these His holy and immortal mysteries, which are numbered in heaven."

the world to come. Let us arise, and by the grace of Christ let us dedicate ourselves to God, to the only unbegotten God, and to His Christ. And let the bishop give thanks:

XV. O Lord God Almighty, the Father of Thy Christ, Thy blessed Son, who hearest those who call upon Thee with uprightness, who also knowest the supplications of those who are silent; we thank Thee that Thou hast thought us worthy to partake of Thy holy mysteries, which Thou hast bestowed upon us, for the entire confirmation of those things we have rightly known, for the preservation of piety, for the remission of our offences; for the name of Thy Christ is called upon us, and we are joined to Thee. O Thou that hast separated us from the communion of the ungodly, unite us with those that are consecrated to Thee in holiness; confirm us in the truth, by the assistance of Thy Holy Spirit; reveal to us what things we are ignorant of, supply what things we are defective in, confirm us in what things we already know, preserve the priests blameless in Thy worship; keep the kings in peace, and the rulers in righteousness, the air in a good temperature, the fruits in fertility, the world in an all-powerful providence; pacify the warring nations, convert those that are gone astray, sanctify Thy people, keep those that are in virginity, preserve those in the faith that are in marriage, strengthen those that are in purity, bring the infants to complete age, confirm the newly admitted; instruct the catechumens, and render them worthy of admission; and gather us all together into Thy kingdom of heaven, by Jesus Christ our Lord, with whom glory, honour, and worship be to Thee, in the Holy Ghost, for ever. Amen. And *let the deacon say: Bow down to*[1] *God through His Christ, and receive the blessing.* And let the bishop add this prayer, and say: O God Almighty, the true God, to whom nothing can be compared, who art everywhere, and present in all things, and art in nothing as one of the things themselves; who art not bounded by place, nor grown old by time; who art not terminated by ages, nor deceived by words; who art not subject to generation, and wantest no guardian; who art above all

---

[1] The Coptic has, "the Lord."

corruption, free from all change, and invariable by nature; "who inhabitest light inaccessible;"[1] who art by nature invisible, and yet art known to all reasonable natures who seek Thee with a good mind, and art comprehended by those that seek after Thee with a good mind; the God of Israel, Thy people which truly see, and which have believed in Christ: Be gracious to me, and hear me, for Thy name's sake, and bless those that bow down their necks unto Thee, and grant them the petitions of their hearts, which are for their good, and do not reject any one of them from Thy kingdom; but sanctify, guard, cover, and assist them; deliver them from the adversary and every enemy; keep their houses, and guard "their comings in and their goings out."[2] For to Thee belongs the glory, praise, majesty, worship, and adoration, and to Thy Son Jesus, Thy Christ, our Lord and God and King, and to the Holy Ghost, now and always, for ever and ever. Amen. And[3] *the deacon shall say, Depart in peace.*[4] *These constitutions concerning this mystical worship, we,* the apostles, *do ordain for you, the bishops, presbyters, and deacons.*

SEC. III.—*Ordination and duties of the clergy.*

XVI. Concerning the ordination of presbyters, I[5] who am loved by the Lord make this constitution for you the bishops: *When thou ordainest a presbyter, O bishop, lay thy hand upon his head, in the presence of the presbyters and*

---

[1] 1 Tim. vi. 16.   [2] Ps. cxxi. 8.

[3] The Coptic adds: "And let the presbyters and deacons watch the few fragments that are left, that they may perceive that there is nothing superfluous; lest they fall into the great judgment, like the sons of Aaron and Eli, whom the Holy Spirit destroyed, because they did not refrain from despising the sacrifice of the Lord: how much more those who despise the body and blood of the Lord, thinking that to be merely material food which they receive, and not spiritual!"

[4] The Coptic inserts, "when they have been blessed."

[5] One V. MS. has this note: "John the evangelist, the brother of James, was banished by Domitian to the island of Patmos, and there composed the Gospel according to him. He died a natural death, in the third year of Trajan's reign, in Ephesus. His remains were sought, but have not been found."

deacons,[1] and pray, saying: O Lord Almighty, our God, who hast created all things by Christ, and dost in like manner take care of the whole world by Him; for He who had power to make different creatures, has also power to take care of them, according to their different natures; on which account, O God, Thou takest care of immortal beings by bare preservation, but of those that are mortal by succession —of the soul by the provision of laws, of the body by the supply of its wants. Do Thou therefore now also look down upon Thy holy church, and increase the same, and multiply those that preside in it, and grant them power, that they may labour both in word and work for the edification of Thy people. Do Thou now also look down upon this Thy servant, who is put into the presbytery by the vote and determination of the whole clergy; and do Thou replenish him with the Spirit of grace and counsel, to assist and govern Thy people with a pure heart, in the same manner as Thou didst look down upon Thy chosen people, and didst command Moses to choose elders, whom Thou didst fill with Thy Spirit.[2] Do Thou also now, O Lord, grant this, and preserve in us the Spirit of Thy grace, that this person, being filled with the gifts of healing and the word of teaching, may in meekness instruct Thy people, and sincerely serve Thee with a pure mind and a willing soul, and may fully discharge the holy ministrations for Thy people, through Thy Christ, with whom glory, honour, and worship be to Thee, and to the Holy Ghost, for ever. Amen.

XVII. Concerning the ordination of deacons, I Philip[3] make this constitution: Thou shalt ordain a deacon, O bishop, by laying thy hands upon him in the presence of the whole presbytery, and of the deacons, and shalt pray, and say:

[1] The Coptic adds: "While you pray, he is ordained; and thou shalt ordain the deacon also according to this constitution alone."

[2] Ex. xviii. xxiv. xxviii.

[3] One V. MS. has the following note: "Philip having proclaimed the life-giving word to the Asiatic diocese, has been buried in Hierapolis of Phrygia along with his daughters, having been crowned with martyrdom in the reign of the Emperor Domitian. Philip, who has the daughters, is one of the seven; it was he also who baptized the eunuch."

XVIII. O God Almighty, the true and faithful God, who art rich unto all that call upon Thee in truth, who art fearful in counsels, and wise in understanding, who art powerful and great, hear our prayer, O Lord, and let Thine ears receive our supplication, and "cause the light of Thy countenance to shine upon this Thy servant," who is to be ordained for Thee to the office of a deacon; and replenish him with Thy Holy Spirit, and with power, as Thou didst replenish Stephen, who was Thy martyr, and follower of the sufferings of Thy Christ.[1] Do Thou render him worthy to discharge acceptably the ministration of a deacon, steadily, unblameably, and without reproof, that thereby he may attain an higher degree, through the mediation of Thy only begotten Son, with whom glory, honour, and worship be to Thee and the Holy Spirit for ever. Amen.

XIX. Concerning a deaconess, I Bartholomew[2] make this constitution: O bishop, thou shalt lay thy hands upon her in the presence of the presbytery, and of the deacons and deaconesses, and shalt say:

XX. O Eternal God, the Father of our Lord Jesus Christ, the Creator of man and of woman, who didst replenish with the Spirit Miriam, and Deborah, and Anna, and Huldah;[3] who didst not disdain that Thy only begotten Son should be born of a woman; who also in the tabernacle of the testimony, and in the temple, didst ordain women to be keepers of Thy holy gates,—do Thou now also look down upon this Thy servant, who is to be ordained to the office of a deaconess, and grant her Thy Holy Spirit, and "cleanse her from all filthiness of flesh and spirit,"[4] that she may worthily discharge the work which is committed to her to Thy glory, and the praise of Thy Christ, with whom glory and adoration be to Thee and the Holy Spirit for ever. Amen.

---

[1] Acts vi. and vii.

[2] One V. MS. has the following note: "Bartholomew preached the Gospel according to Matthew to the Indians, who also has been buried in India."

[3] Ex. xv. 20; Judg. iv. 4; Luke ii. 36; 2 Kings xxii. 14.

[4] 2 Cor. vii. 1.

XXI. Concerning the sub-deacons, I Thomas[1] make this constitution for you the bishops:[2] When thou dost ordain a sub-deacon, O bishop, thou shalt lay thy hands upon him, and say: O Lord God, the Creator of heaven and earth, and of all things that are therein; who also in the tabernacle of the testimony didst appoint overseers and keepers of Thy holy vessels;[3] do Thou now look down upon this Thy servant, appointed a sub-deacon; and grant him the Holy Spirit, that he may worthily handle the vessels of Thy ministry, and do Thy will always, through Thy Christ, with whom glory, honour, and worship be to Thee and to the Holy Spirit for ever. Amen.

XXII. Concerning readers,[4] I Matthew, also called Levi, who was once a tax-gatherer, make a constitution: Ordain a reader by laying thy hands upon him, and pray unto God, and say: O Eternal God, who art plenteous in mercy and compassions, who hast made manifest the constitution of the world by Thy operations therein, and keepest the number of Thine elect, do Thou also now look down upon Thy servant, who is to be entrusted to read Thy holy Scriptures to Thy people, and give him Thy Holy Spirit, the prophetic Spirit. Thou who didst instruct Esdras Thy servant to read Thy laws to the people,[5] do Thou now also at our prayers instruct Thy servant, and grant that he may without blame perfect the work committed to him, and thereby be declared worthy of an higher degree, through Christ, with whom glory and worship be to Thee and to the Holy Ghost for ever. Amen.

XXIII. And I James, the son of Alphæus, make a constitution in regard to confessors: *A confessor is not ordained; for he is so by choice and patience, and is worthy of great*

[1] One V. MS. has the following note: "Thomas preached to the Parthians, Medes, Persians, Germans, Hyrcanians, Bactrians, Bardians, who also, having been a martyr, lies in Edessa of Osdroene."

[2] The words "for you the bishops" are omitted in the Oxford MS.

[3] Num. iii.; 1 Chron. i.

[4] The Oxford MS. has no part of this chapter. It reads: "A reader is appointed when the bishop gives him a book; for there is no imposition of hands."

[5] Neh. viii.

honour, as having confessed the name of God, and of His Christ, before nations and kings. But if there be occasion, he is to be ordained[1] *either a bishop, priest, or deacon. But if any one of the confessors who is not ordained snatches to himself any such dignity upon account of his confession, let the same person be deprived and rejected; for he is not in such an office, since he has denied the constitution of Christ, and is "worse than an infidel."* [2]

XXIV. I, the same, make a constitution in regard to virgins: *A virgin is not ordained, for we have no such command from the Lord;*[3] *for this is a state of voluntary trial, not for the reproach of marriage, but on account of leisure for piety.*

XXV. And I Lebbæus,[4] surnamed Thaddæus, make this constitution in regard to widows: *A widow is not ordained; yet if she has lost her husband a great while, and has lived soberly and unblameably, and has taken extraordinary care of her family, as Judith*[5] *and Anna*[6]—*those women of great reputation—let her be chosen into the order of widows. But if she has lately lost her yokefellow, let her not be believed, but let her youth be judged of by the time; for the affections do sometimes grow aged with men, if they be not restrained by a better bridle.*

XXVI. I the same make a constitution in regard to an exorcist. *An exorcist is not ordained. For it is a trial of voluntary goodness, and of the grace of God through Christ by the inspiration of the Holy Spirit. For he who has received the gift of healing is declared by revelation from God, the grace which is in him being manifest to all.* But if there be occasion for him, he must be ordained[7] *a bishop, or a presbyter, or a deacon.*

[1] The Coptic reads, "let him be ordained."
[2] 1 Tim. v. 8.   [3] 1 Cor. vii. 25.
[4] The two V. MSS. have the following note: "Thaddæus, also called Lebbæus, and who was surnamed Judas the Zealot, preached the truth to the Edessenes and the people of Mesopotamia when Abgarus ruled over Edessa, and has been buried in Berytus of Phœnicia."
[5] Judith xvi. 21, 23.   [6] Luke ii. 36, etc.
[7] The Coptic has, "let him be ordained."

XXVII.[1] And I Simon the Canaanite[2] make a constitution to determine by how many a bishop ought to be elected. Let a bishop be ordained by three or two bishops; but if any one be ordained by one bishop, let him be deprived, both himself and he that ordained him. But if there be a necessity that he have only one to ordain him, because more bishops cannot come together, as in time of persecution, or for such like causes, let him bring the suffrage of permission from more bishops.

XXVIII. Concerning[3] the canons I the same make a constitution. A bishop blesses, but does not receive the blessing. He lays on hands, ordains, offers, receives the blessing from bishops, but by no means from presbyters. A bishop deprives any clergyman who deserves deprivation, excepting a bishop; for of himself he has not power to do that. A presbyter blesses, but does not receive the blessing; yet does he receive the blessing from the bishop or a fellow-presbyter. In like manner does he give it to a fellow-presbyter. He lays on hands, but does not ordain; he does not deprive, yet does he separate those that are under him, if they be liable to such a punishment. A deacon does not bless, does not give the blessing, but receives it from the bishop and presbyter: he does not baptize, he does not offer; but when a bishop or presbyter has offered, he distributes to the people, not as a priest, but as one that ministers to the priests. But it is not lawful for any one of the other clergy to do the work of a deacon. A deaconess does not bless, nor perform anything belonging to the office of presbyters or deacons, but only is to keep the doors, and to minister to the presbyters in the baptizing of women, on account of decency. A deacon separates a sub-deacon, a

---

[1] Ch. xxvii., xxviii., xxx.-xxxiv., and ch. xlii.-xlvii., occur in Syriac and Coptic, as well as in the Greek MSS.

[2] One V. MS. has the following note: "Simon the Canaanite, preacher of the truth, is crowned with martyrdom in Judea in the reign of Domitian."

[3] The words from "concerning" to "constitution" are omitted in the Oxford MS., in Syriac, and Coptic.

reader, a singer, and a deaconess, if there be any occasion, in the absence of a presbyter. It is not lawful for a sub-deacon to separate either one of the clergy or laity; nor for a reader, nor for a singer, nor for a deaconess, for they are the ministers to the deacons.

SEC. IV.—*Certain prayers and laws.*

XXIX.[1] Concerning the water and the oil, I Matthias make a constitution. Let the bishop bless the water, or the oil. But if he be not there, let the presbyter bless it, the deacon standing by. But if the bishop be present, let the presbyter and deacon stand by, and let him say thus: O Lord of hosts, the God of powers, the creator of the waters, and the supplier of oil, who art compassionate, and a lover of mankind, who hast given water for drink and for cleansing, and oil to give man a cheerful and joyful countenance;[2] do Thou now also sanctify this water and this oil through Thy Christ, in the name of him or her that has offered them, and grant them a power to restore health, to drive away diseases, to banish demons, and to disperse all snares through Christ our hope, with whom glory, honour, and worship be to Thee, and to the Holy Ghost, for ever. Amen.

XXX. I[3] the same make a constitution in regard to first-fruits and tithes. Let all first-fruits be brought to the bishop, and to the presbyters, and to the deacons,[4] for their maintenance; but let all the tithe be for the maintenance of the rest of the clergy, and of the virgins and widows, and of those under the trial of poverty. For the first-fruits belong to the priests, and to those deacons that minister to them.

XXXI. I the same make a constitution in regard to re-

[1] This chapter is not found in the Coptic and Syriac. One V. MS. has the following note: "Matthew [probably a mistake for Matthias] taught the doctrines of Christ in Judea, and was one of the seventy disciples. After the ascension of Christ he was numbered with the twelve apostles, instead of Judas, who was the betrayer. He lies in Jerusalem."

[2] Ps. civ. 15.

[3] The Oxford MS. reads: "I the same, Simon the Canaanite, make a constitution."

[4] "Deacons" omitted in Oxford MS. and in Coptic.

mainders. Those eulogies which remain at the mysteries, let the deacons distribute them among the clergy, according to the mind of the bishop or the presbyters: to a bishop, four parts; to a presbyter, three[1] parts; to a deacon, two[2] parts; and to the rest of the sub-deacons, or readers, or singers, or deaconesses, one part. For this is good and acceptable in the sight of God, that every one be honoured according to his dignity; for the church is the school, not of confusion, but of good order.

XXXII. [I also, Paul,[3] the least of the apostles, do make the following constitutions for you, the bishops, and presbyters, and deacons, concerning canons.] Those that first come to the mystery of godliness, let them be brought to the bishop or to the presbyters by the deacons, and let them be examined as to the causes wherefore they come to the word of the Lord; and let those that bring them exactly inquire about their character, and give them their testimony. Let their manners and their life be inquired into, and whether they be slaves or freemen. And if any one be a slave, let him be asked who is his master. If he be slave to one of the faithful, let his master be asked if he can give him a good character. If he cannot, let him be rejected, until he show himself to be worthy to his master. But if he does give him a good character, let him be admitted. But if he be household slave to an heathen, let him be taught to please his master, that the word be not blasphemed. If, then, he have a wife, or a woman hath an husband, let them be taught to be content with each other; but if they be unmarried, let them learn not to commit fornication, but to enter into lawful marriage. But if his master be one of the faithful, and knows that he is guilty of fornication, and yet does not give him a wife, or to the woman an husband, let him

---

[1] "Two," Oxford MS.   [2] "One," Oxford MS.
[3] One V. MS. has the following instead of the title: "Paul, the teacher of the Gentiles, having proclaimed the gospel of Christ to the Gentiles from Jerusalem even to Illyricum, was cut off in Rome while teaching the truth, by Nero and King Agrippa, being beheaded, and has been buried in Rome itself."

be separated; but if any one hath a demon, let him indeed be taught piety, but not received into communion before he be cleansed; yet if death be near, let him be received. If any one be a maintainer of harlots, let him either leave off to prostitute women, or else let him be rejected. If a harlot come, let her leave off whoredom, or else let her be rejected. If a maker of idols come, let him either leave off his employment, or let him be rejected. If one belonging to the theatre come, whether it be man or woman, or charioteer, or dueller, or racer, or player of prizes, or Olympic gamester, or one that plays on the pipe, on the lute, or on the harp at those games, or a dancing-master, or an huckster, either let them leave off their employments, or let them be rejected. If a soldier come, let him be taught to "do no injustice, to accuse no man falsely, and to be content with his allotted wages:"[1] if he submit to those rules, let him be received; but if he refuse them, let him be rejected. He that is guilty of sins not to be named, a sodomite, an effeminate person, a magician, an enchanter, an astrologer, a diviner, an user of magic verses, a juggler, a mountebank, one that makes amulets, a charmer, a soothsayer, a fortune-teller, an observer of palmistry; he that, when he meets you, observes defects in the eyes or feet of the birds or cats, or noises, or symbolical sounds: let these be proved for some time, for this sort of wickedness is hard to be washed away; and if they leave off those practices, let them be received; but if they will not agree to that, let them be rejected. Let a concubine, who is slave to an unbeliever, and confines herself to her master alone, be received; but if she be incontinent with others, let her be rejected. If one of the faithful hath a concubine, if she be a bond-servant, let him leave off that way, and marry in a legal manner: if she be a free woman, let him marry her in a lawful manner; if he does not, let him be rejected. Let him that follows the Gentile customs, or Jewish fables, either reform, or let him be rejected. If any one follows the sports of the theatre, their huntings, or horse-races, or combats, either let him leave them off, or let him

[1] Luke iii. 14.

be rejected. Let him who is to be a catechumen be a catechumen for three years; but if any one be diligent, and has a good-will to his business, let him be admitted: for it is not the length of time, but the course of life, that is judged. Let him that teaches, although he be one of the laity, yet, if he be skilful in the word and grave in his manners, teach; for "they shall be all taught of God."[1] Let all the faithful, whether men or women, when they rise from sleep, before they go to work, when they have washed themselves, pray; but if any catechetic instruction be held, let the faithful person prefer the word of piety before his work. Let the faithful person, whether man or woman, treat servants kindly, as we have ordained in the foregoing books, and have taught in our epistles.[2]

XXXIII. I Peter and Paul do make the following constitutions. Let the slaves work five days; but on the Sabbath-day and the Lord's day let them have leisure to go to church for instruction in piety. We have said that the Sabbath is on account of the creation, and the Lord's day of the resurrection. Let slaves rest from their work all the great week, and that which follows it—for the one in memory of the passion, and the other of the resurrection; and there is need they should be instructed who it is that suffered and rose again, and who it is permitted Him to suffer, and raised Him again. Let them have rest from their work on the ascension, because it was the conclusion of the dispensation by Christ. Let them rest at Pentecost, because of the coming of the Holy Spirit, which was given to those that believed in Christ. Let them rest on the festival of His birth, because on it the unexpected favour was granted to men, that Jesus Christ, the Logos of God, should be born of the Virgin Mary,[3] for the salvation of the world. Let them rest on the festival of Epiphany, because on it a manifestation took place of the divinity of Christ, for the Father bore testimony to Him at the baptism; and the Paraclete, in the form of a dove, pointed out to the bystanders Him to

[1] John vi. 45. [2] Eph. vi.; Col. iv.; Philem.
[3] The Coptic adds, "the holy mother of God."

whom testimony was borne. Let them rest on the days of the apostles: for they were appointed your teachers [to bring you] to Christ, and made you worthy of the Spirit. Let them rest on the day of the first[1] martyr Stephen, and of the other holy martyrs who preferred Christ to their own life.

XXXIV. Offer up your prayers in the morning, at the third hour, the sixth, the ninth, the evening, and at cock-crowing: in the morning, returning thanks that the Lord has sent you light, that He has brought you past the night, and brought on the day; at the third hour, because at that hour the Lord received the sentence of condemnation from Pilate; at the sixth, because at that hour He was crucified;[2] at the ninth, because all things were in commotion at the crucifixion of the Lord, as trembling at the bold attempt of the impious Jews, and not bearing the injury offered to their Lord; in the evening, giving thanks that He has given you the night to rest from the daily labours; at cock-crowing, because that hour brings the good news of the coming on of the day for the operations proper for the light. But if it be not possible to go to the church on account of the unbelievers, thou, O bishop, shalt assemble them in a house, that a godly man may not enter into an assembly of the ungodly. For it is not the place that sanctifies the man, but the man the place. And if the ungodly possess the place, do thou avoid it, because it is profaned by them. For as holy priests sanctify a place, so do the profane ones defile it. If it be not possible to assemble either in the church or in a house, let every one by himself sing, and read, and pray, or two or three together. For "where two or three are gathered together in my name, there am I in the midst of them."[3] Let not one of the faithful pray with a catechumen, no, not in the house: for it is not reasonable that he who is admitted should be polluted with one not admitted. Let not one of the godly pray with an heretic, no, not in the house.

[1] One V. MS., Coptic, and Syriac, omit "first."
[2] The Syriac and Coptic add: "and His side being wounded, blood and water came forth."
[3] Matth. xviii. 20.

For "what fellowship hath light with darkness?"[1] Let Christians, whether men or women, who have connections with slaves, either leave them off, or let them be rejected.

XXXV. I James,[2] the brother of Christ according to the flesh, but His servant as the only begotten God, and one appointed bishop of Jerusalem by the Lord Himself, and the apostles, do ordain thus: When it is evening, thou, O bishop, shalt assemble the church; and after the repetition of the psalm at the lighting up the lights, the deacon shall bid prayers for the catechumens, the energumens, the illuminated, and the penitents, as we have formerly said. But after the dismission of these, the deacon shall say: So many as are of the faithful, let us pray to the Lord. And after the bidding prayer, which is formerly set down, he shall say:

XXXVI. Save us, O God, and raise us up by Thy Christ. Let us stand up, and beg for the mercies of the Lord, and His compassions, for the angel of peace, for what things are good and profitable, for a Christian departure out of this life, an evening and a night of peace, and free from sin; and let us beg that the whole course of our life may be unblameable. Let us dedicate ourselves and one another to the living God through His Christ. And let the bishop add this prayer, and say:

XXXVII. O God, who art without beginning and without end, the Maker of the whole world by Christ, and the Provider for it, but before all[3] His God and Father, the Lord[4] of the Spirit, and the King of intelligible and sensible beings; who hast made the day for the works of light, and the night for the refreshment of our infirmity,—for "the day is Thine, the night also is Thine: Thou hast prepared

[1] 2 Cor. vi. 14.
[2] The words from "I James" to "ordain thus" are omitted in the V. MSS., and the following words are given instead in the two V. MSS.: "James, the brother of the Lord, has been killed with stones (the other MS. reads, 'with sticks') by the Jews in Jerusalem on account of the doctrines of Christ." Ch. xxxv.-xli. are omitted in the Oxford MS., and in Syriac and Coptic.
[3] "Before all" is omitted in one V. MS.
[4] One V. MS. reads "sender forth" instead of "Lord."

the light and the sun," [1]—do Thou now, O Lord, Thou lover of mankind, and Fountain of all good, mercifully accept of this our evening thanksgiving. Thou who hast brought us through the length of the day, and hast brought us to the beginnings of the night, preserve us by Thy Christ, afford us a peaceable evening, and a night free from sin, and vouchsafe us everlasting life by Thy Christ, through whom glory, honour, and worship be to Thee in [2] the Holy Spirit for ever. Amen. And let the deacon say: Bow down for the laying on of hands. And let the bishop say: O God of our fathers, and Lord of mercy, who didst form man of Thy wisdom a rational creature, and beloved of God more than the other beings upon this earth, and didst give him authority to rule over the creatures upon the earth, and didst ordain by Thy will rulers and priests—the former for the security of life, the latter for a regular worship,—do Thou now also look down, O Lord Almighty, and cause Thy face to shine upon Thy people, who bow down the neck of their heart, and bless them by Christ; through whom Thou hast enlightened us with the light of knowledge, and hast revealed Thyself to us; with whom worthy adoration is due from every rational and holy nature to Thee, and to the Spirit, who is the Comforter, for ever. Amen. And let the deacon say: "Depart in peace." In like manner, in the morning, after the repetition of the morning psalm, and his dismission of the catechumens, the energumens, the candidates for baptism, and the penitents, and after the usual bidding of prayers, that we may not again repeat the same things, let the deacon add after the words, Save us, O God, and raise us up by Thy grace: Let us beg of the Lord His mercies and His compassions, that this morning and this day may be with peace and without sin, as also all the time of our sojourning; that He will grant us His angel of peace, a Christian departure out of this life, and that God will be merciful and gracious. Let us dedicate ourselves and one another to the living God through His Only-begotten. And let the bishop add this prayer, and say:

[1] Ps. lxxiv. 16.   [2] One V. ms. reads "with" instead of "in."

XXXVIII. O God, the God of spirits and of all flesh, who art beyond compare, and standest in need of nothing, who hast given the sun to have rule over the day, and the moon and the stars to have rule over the night, do Thou now also look down upon us with gracious eyes, and receive our morning thanksgivings, and have mercy upon us; for we have not "spread out our hands unto a strange God;"[1] for there is not among us any new God, but Thou, the eternal God, who art without end, who hast given us our being through Christ, and given us our well-being through Him. Do Thou vouchsafe us also, through Him, eternal life; with whom glory, and honour, and worship be to Thee and to the Holy Spirit for ever. Amen. And let the deacon say: Bow down for the laying on of hands. And let the bishop add this prayer, saying:

XXXIX. O God, who art faithful and true, who "hast mercy on thousands and ten thousands of them that love Thee,"[2] the lover of the humble, and the protector of the needy, of whom all things stand in need, for all things are subject to Thee; look down upon this Thy people, who bow down their heads to Thee, and bless them with spiritual blessing. "Keep them as the apple of an eye,"[3] preserve them in piety and righteousness, and vouchsafe them eternal life in Christ Jesus Thy beloved Son, with whom glory, honour, and worship be to Thee and to the Holy Spirit, now and always, and for ever and ever. Amen. And let the deacon say: "Depart in peace." And when the first-fruits are offered, the bishop gives thanks in this manner:

XL. We give thanks to Thee, O Lord Almighty, the Creator of the whole world, and its Preserver, through Thy only begotten Son Jesus Christ our Lord, for the first-fruits which are offered to Thee, not in such a manner as we ought, but as we are able. For what man is there that can worthily give Thee thanks for those things Thou hast given them to partake of? The God of Abraham, and of Isaac, and of Jacob, and of all the saints, who madest all things fruitful by Thy word, and didst command the earth to bring forth

---

[1] Ps. xliv. 20. [2] Ex. xxxiv. and xx. [3] Ps. xvii. 8.

various fruits for our rejoicing and our food; who hast given to the duller and more sheepish sort of creatures juices—herbs to them that feed on herbs, and to some flesh, to others seeds, but to us corn, as advantageous and proper food, and many other things—some for our necessities, some for our health, and some for our pleasure. On all these accounts, therefore, art Thou worthy of exalted hymns of praise for Thy beneficence by Christ, through whom[1] glory, honour, and worship be to Thee, in the Holy Spirit, for ever. Amen. Concerning those that are at rest in Christ: After the bidding prayer, that we may not repeat it again, the deacon shall add as follows:

XLI. Let us pray for our brethren that are at rest in Christ, that God, the lover of mankind, who has received his soul, may forgive him every sin, voluntary and involuntary, and may be merciful and gracious to him, and give him his lot in the land of the pious that are sent into the bosom of Abraham, and Isaac, and Jacob, with all those that have pleased Him and done His will from the beginning of the world, whence all sorrow, grief, and lamentation are banished. Let us arise, let us dedicate ourselves and one another to the eternal God, through that Word which was in the beginning. And let the bishop say: O Thou who art by nature immortal, and hast no end of Thy being, from whom every creature, whether immortal or mortal, is derived; who didst make man a rational creature, the citizen of this world, in his constitution mortal, and didst add the promise of a resurrection; who didst not suffer Enoch and Elias to taste of death; "the God of Abraham, the God of Isaac, and the God of Jacob, who art the God of them, not as of dead, but as of living persons: for the souls of all men live with Thee, and the spirits of the righteous are in Thy hand, which no torment can touch;"[2] for they are all sanctified under Thy hand: do Thou now also look upon this Thy servant, whom Thou hast selected and received into another state, and forgive him if voluntarily or involuntarily he has sinned, and afford him

---

[1] One V. ms. reads, "with whom," and "with the Holy Spirit."
[2] Matth. xxii. 32; Wisd. iii. 1.

merciful angels, and place him in the bosom of the patriarchs, and prophets, and apostles, and of all those that have pleased Thee from the beginning of the world, where there is no grief, sorrow, nor lamentation; but the peaceable region of the godly, and the undisturbed land of the upright, and of those that therein see the glory of Thy Christ; by whom[1] glory, honour, and worship, thanksgiving, and adoration be to Thee, in the Holy Spirit, for ever. Amen. And let the deacon say: Bow down, and receive the blessing. And let the bishop give thanks for them, saying as follows: "O Lord, save Thy people, and bless Thine inheritance,"[2] which Thou hast purchased with the precious blood of Thy Christ. Feed them under Thy right hand, and cover them under Thy wings, and grant that they may "fight the good fight, and finish their course, and keep the faith"[3] immutably, unblameably, and unreproveably, through our Lord Jesus Christ, Thy beloved Son, with whom glory, honour, and worship be to Thee and to the Holy Spirit for ever. Amen.

XLII. Let the third day of the departed be celebrated with psalms, and lessons, and prayers, on account of Him who arose within the space of three days; and let the ninth day be celebrated in remembrance of the living, and of the departed; and the fortieth[4] day according to the ancient pattern: for so did the people lament Moses, and the anniversary day in memory of him.[5] And let alms be given to the poor out of his goods for a memorial of him.

XLIII. These things we say concerning the pious; for as to the ungodly, if thou givest all the world to the poor, thou wilt not benefit him at all. For to whom the Deity was an enemy while he was alive, it is certain it will be so also when he is departed; for there is no unrighteousness with Him. For "the Lord[6] is righteous, and has loved righteousness."[7] And, "Behold the man and his work."[8]

---

[1] "With whom," one V. MS.   [2] Ps. xxviii. 9.   [3] 2 Tim. iv. 7.
[4] The Syriac and a Greek marginal reading give "the thirtieth."
[5] Deut. xxxiv. 8.
[6] The Syriac and the Oxford MS. read "God" instead of "Lord."
[7] Ps. xi. 8.   [8] Isa. lxii. 11.

XLIV. Now, when you are invited to their memorials, do you feast with good order, and the fear of God, as disposed to intercede for those that are departed. For since you are the presbyters and deacons of Christ, you ought always to be sober, both among yourselves and among others, that so you may be able to warn the unruly. Now the Scripture says, "The men in power are passionate. But let them not drink wine, lest by drinking they forget wisdom, and are not able to judge aright."[1] Wherefore[2] both the presbyters and the deacons are those of authority in the church next to God Almighty and His beloved Son.[3] We say this, not they are not to drink at all, otherwise it would be to the reproach of what God has made for cheerfulness, but that they be not disordered with wine. For the Scripture does not say, Do not drink wine; but what says it? "Drink not wine to drunkenness;" and again, "Thorns spring up in the hand of the drunkard."[4] Nor do we say this only to those of the clergy, but also to every lay Christian, upon whom the name of our Lord Jesus Christ is called. For to them also it is said, "Who hath woe? who hath sorrow? who hath uneasiness? who hath babbling? who hath red eyes? who hath wounds without cause? Do not these things belong to those that tarry long at the wine, and that go to seek where drinking meetings are?"[5]

XLV. Receive ye those that are persecuted on account of the faith, and who fly from city to city,[6] as mindful of the words of the Lord. For, knowing that though "the spirit be willing, the flesh is weak,"[7] they fly away, and prefer the spoiling of their goods, that they may preserve the name of Christ in themselves without denying it. Supply them therefore with what they want, and thereby fulfil the commandment of the Lord.

[1] Prov. xxxi. 4, LXX.
[2] The Syriac, the Coptic, and the Oxford MS. add, "the bishops." The Coptic omits "the deacons."
[3] The Coptic adds, "Jesus Christ and the Holy Spirit."
[4] Prov. xxiii.; Ecclus. xxxi.; Eph. v.; Prov. xxvi. 9.
[5] Prov. xxiii. 29. [6] Matth. x. 23. [7] Matth. xxvi. 4.

SEC. V.—*All the apostles urge the observance of the order of the church.*

XLVI. Now this we all in common do charge you, that every one remain in that rank which is appointed him, and do not transgress his proper bounds; for they are not ours, but God's. For says the Lord: "He that heareth you, heareth me; and he that heareth me, heareth Him that sent me." And, "He that despiseth you, despiseth me; and he that despiseth me, despiseth Him that sent me."[1] For if those things that are without life do observe good order, as the night, the day, the sun, the moon, the stars, the elements, the seasons, the months, the weeks, the days, and the hours, and are subservient to the uses appointed them, according to that which is said, "Thou hast set them a bound which they shall not pass;"[2] and again, concerning the sea, "I have set bounds thereto, and have encompassed it with bars and gates; and I said to it, Hitherto shalt thou come, and thou shalt go no farther;"[3] how much more ought ye not to venture to remove those things which we, according to God's will, have determined for you! But because many think this a small matter, and venture to confound the orders, and to remove the ordination which belongs to them severally, snatching to themselves dignities which were never given them, and allowing themselves to bestow that authority in a tyrannical manner which they have not themselves, and thereby provoke God to anger (as did the followers of Corah and King Uzziah,[4] who, having no authority, usurped the high-priesthood without commission from God; and the former were burnt with fire, and the latter was struck with a leprosy in his forehead); and provoke Christ Jesus to anger, who has made this constitution; and also grieve the Holy Spirit, and make void His testimony: therefore, foreknowing the danger that hangs over those who do such things, and the neglect about the sacrifices and eucharistical offices which will arise from their being impiously offered by those who

[1] Luke; Matth. x. 40; John xiii. 20. [2] Ps. civ. 9.
[3] Job xxxvii. 10. [4] Num. xvi.; 2 Chron. xxvi.

ought not to offer them; who think the honour of the high-priesthood, which is an imitation of the great High Priest Jesus Christ our King, to be a matter of sport; we have found it necessary to give you warning in this matter also. For some are already turned aside after their own vanity. We say that Moses the servant of God ("to whom God spake face to face, as if a man spake to his friend;"[1] to whom He said, "I know thee above all men;" to whom He spake directly, and not by obscure methods, or dreams, or angels, or riddles),—this person, when he made constitutions and divine laws, distinguished what things were to be performed by the high priests, what by the priests, and what by the Levites; distributing to every one his proper and suitable office in the divine service. And those things which are allotted for the high priests to do, those might not be meddled with by the priests; and what things were allotted to the priests, the Levites might not meddle with; but every one observed those ministrations which were written down and appointed for them. And if any would meddle beyond the tradition, death was his punishment. And Saul's example does show this most plainly, who, thinking he might offer sacrifice without the prophet and high priest Samuel,[2] drew upon himself a sin and a curse without remedy. Nor did even his having anointed him king discourage the prophet. But God showed the same by a more visible effect in the case of Uzziah,[3] when He without delay exacted the punishment due to this transgression, and he that madly coveted after the high-priesthood was rejected from his kingdom also. As to those things that have happened amongst us, you yourselves are not ignorant of them. For ye know undoubtedly that those that are by us named bishops, and presbyters, and deacons, were made by prayer, and by the laying on of hands; and that by the difference of their names is showed the difference of their employments. For not every one that will is ordained, as the case was in that spurious and counterfeit priesthood of the calves under Jeroboam;[4] but he only who is called of

[1] Num. xii. 7, 8; Ex. xxxiii. 11, 17.
[2] 1 Sam. xiii.
[3] 2 Chron. xxvi.
[4] 1 Kings xiii. 33.

God. For if there were no rule or distinction of orders, it would suffice to perform all the offices under one name. But being taught by the Lord the series of things, we distributed the functions of the high-priesthood to the bishops, those of the priesthood to the presbyters, and the ministration under them both to the deacons; that the divine worship might be performed in purity. For it is not lawful for a deacon to offer the sacrifice, or to baptize, or to give either the greater or the lesser blessing. Nor may a presbyter perform ordination; for it is not agreeable to holiness to have this order perverted. For "God is not the God of confusion,"[1] that the subordinate persons should tyrannically assume to themselves the functions belonging to their superiors, forming a new scheme of laws to their own mischief, not knowing that "it is hard for them to kick against the pricks;"[2] for such as these do not fight against us, or against the bishops, but against the universal bishop, and the high priest of the Father, Jesus Christ our Lord.[3] High priests, priests, and Levites were ordained by Moses,[4] the most beloved of God. By our Saviour[5] were we apostles, thirteen in number, ordained; and by the apostles I James, and I Clement, and others with us, were ordained, that we may not make the catalogue of all those bishops over again. And in common, presbyters, and deacons, and sub-deacons, and readers, were ordained by all of us. The great High Priest therefore, who is so by nature, is Christ the only begotten; not having snatched that honour to Himself, but having been appointed such by the Father; who being made man for our sake, and offering the spiritual sacrifice to His God and Father, before His suffering gave it us alone in charge to do this, although there were others with us who had believed in Him. But he that believes is not presently appointed a priest, or obtains the dignity of the high-priesthood. But after His ascension we offered, according to His constitution, the pure and unbloody sacrifice; and ordained bishops, and presbyters, and deacons, seven in

---

[1] 1 Cor. xiv. 33.   [2] Acts ix. 5.
[3] The Coptic adds, "the Son of God, and true God."
[4] Ex. xxviii. and xxix.   [5] The Coptic adds "God."

number: one of which was Stephen,[1] that blessed martyr, who was not inferior to us as to his pious disposition of mind towards God; who showed so great piety towards God, by his faith and love towards our Lord Jesus Christ, as to give his life for Him, and was stoned to death by the Jews, the murderers of the Lord. Yet still this so great and good a man, who was fervent in spirit, who saw Christ on the right hand of God, and the gates of heaven opened, does nowhere appear to have exercised functions which did not appertain to his office of a deacon, nor to have offered the sacrifices, nor to have laid hands upon any, but kept his order of a deacon unto the end. For so it became him, who was a martyr for Christ, to preserve good order. But if some do blame Philip[2] our deacon, and Ananias[3] our faithful brother, that the one did baptize the eunuch, and the other me Paul, these men do not understand what we say. For we have affirmed only that no one snatches the sacerdotal dignity to himself, but either receives it from God, as Melchisedec and Job, or from the high priest, as Aaron from Moses. Wherefore Philip and Ananias did not constitute themselves, but were appointed by Christ, the High Priest of that God to whom no being is to be compared.

THE ECCLESIASTICAL CANONS OF THE SAME HOLY APOSTLES.

XLVII. Let a bishop be ordained by two or three bishops.

2. A presbyter by one bishop, as also a deacon, and the rest of the clergy.

---

[1] Acts vi. and vii.

[2] One V. MS. has the following note: "That he who baptized the Ethiopian eunuch was not the Apostle Philip, but one of those who were chosen along with St. Stephen to be deacons, and who also had four daughters, as says Luke in the Acts."

[3] Acts viii. and ix.

3. If any bishop or presbyter, otherwise than our Lord has ordained concerning the sacrifice, offer other things at the altar [of God], as honey, milk, or strong beer instead of wine, any necessaries, or birds, or animals, or pulse, otherwise than is ordained, let him be deprived; excepting grains of new corn, or ears of wheat, or bunches of grapes in their season.

4. For it is not lawful to offer anything besides these at the altar, and oil for the holy lamp, and incense in the time of the divine oblation.

5. But let all other fruits be sent to the house of the bishop, as first-fruits to him and to the presbyters, but not to the altar. Now it is plain that the bishop and presbyters are to divide them to the deacons and to the rest of the clergy.

6. Let not a bishop, a priest, or a deacon cast off his own wife under pretence of piety; but if he does cast her off, let him be suspended. If he go on in it, let him be deprived.

7. Let not a bishop, a priest, or deacon undertake the cares of this world; but if he do, let him be deprived.

8. If any bishop, or presbyter, or deacon shall celebrate the holiday of the passover before the vernal equinox with the Jews, let him be deprived.

9. If any bishop, or presbyter, or deacon, or any one of the catalogue of the priesthood, when the oblation is over, does not communicate, let him give his reason; and if it be just, let him be forgiven; but if he does not do it, let him be suspended, as becoming the cause of damage to the people, and occasioning a suspicion against him that offered, as of one that did not rightly offer.

10. All those of the faithful that enter [into the holy church of God], and hear the sacred Scriptures, but do not stay during prayer and the holy communion, must be suspended, as causing disorder in the church.

11. If any one, even in the house, prays with a person excommunicate, let him also be suspended.

12. If any clergyman prays with one deprived as with a clergyman, let himself also be deprived.

13. If any clergyman or layman who is suspended, or

ought not to be received,[1] goes away, and is received in another city without commendatory letters, let both those who received him and he that was received be suspended. But if he be already suspended, let his suspension be lengthened, as lying to and deceiving the church of God.

14. A bishop ought not to leave his own parish and leap to another, although the multitude should compel him, unless there be some good reason forcing him to do this, as that he can contribute much greater profit to the people of the new parish by the word of piety; but this is not to be settled by himself, but by the judgment of many bishops, and very great supplication.

15. If any presbyter or deacon, or any one of the catalogue of the clergy, leaves his own parish and goes to another, and, entirely removing himself, continues in that other parish without the consent of his own bishop, him we command no longer to go on in his ministry, especially in case his bishop calls upon him to return, and he does not obey, but continues in his disorder. However, let him communicate there as a layman.

16. But if the bishop with whom they are undervalues the deprivation decreed against them, and receives them as clergymen, let him be suspended as a teacher of disorder.

17. He who has been twice married after his baptism, or has had a concubine, cannot be made a bishop, or presbyter, or deacon, or indeed any one of the sacerdotal catalogue.

18. He who has taken a widow, or a divorced woman, or an harlot, or a servant, or one belonging to the theatre, cannot be either a bishop, priest, or deacon, or indeed any one of the sacerdotal catalogue.

19. He who has married two sisters, or his brother's or sister's daughter, cannot be a clergyman.

20. Let a clergyman who becomes a surety be deprived.

21. Let an eunuch, if he be such by the injury of men, or his testicles were taken away in the persecution, or he was born such, and yet is worthy of episcopacy, be made a bishop.

---

[1] Dionysius Exiguus translates "communicans," in which case the Greek reading must be δεκτός, or, "who can be received."

22. Let not him who has disabled himself be made a clergyman; for he is a self-murderer, and an enemy to the creation of God.

23. If any one who is of the clergy disables himself, let him be deprived, for he is a murderer of himself.

24. Let a layman who disables himself be separated for three years, for he lays a snare for his own life.

25. Let a bishop, or presbyter, or deacon who is taken in fornication, or perjury, or stealing, be deprived, [but not suspended; for the Scripture says: "Thou shalt not avenge twice for the same crime by affliction."[1]]

26. In like manner also as to the rest of the clergy.

27. Of those who come into the clergy unmarried, we permit only the readers and singers, if they have a mind, to marry afterward.

28. We command that a bishop, or presbyter, or deacon who strikes the faithful that offend, or the unbelievers who do wickedly, and thinks to terrify them by such means, be deprived, for our Lord has nowhere taught us such things. On the contrary, "when Himself was stricken, He did not strike again; when He was reviled, He reviled not again; when He suffered, He threatened not."[2]

29. If any bishop, or presbyter, or deacon who is deprived justly for manifest crimes, does venture to meddle with that ministration which was once entrusted to him, let the same person be entirely cut off from the church.

30. If any bishop obtains that dignity by money, or even a presbyter or deacon, let him and the person that ordained him be deprived; and let him be entirely cut off from communion, as Simon Magus was by [me] Peter.

31. If any bishop makes use of the rulers of this world, and by their means obtains to be a bishop of a church, let him be deprived and suspended, and all that communicate with him.

32. If any presbyter despises his own bishop, and assembles separately, and fixes another altar, when he has nothing to condemn in his bishop either as to piety or righteousness, let

---

[1] Nah. i. 9.   [2] 1 Pet. ii. 23.

him be deprived as an ambitious person; for he is a tyrant, and the rest of the clergy, whoever join themselves to him. And let the laity be suspended. But let these things be done after one, and a second, or even a third admonition from the bishop.

33. If any presbyter or deacon be put under suspension by his bishop, it is not lawful for any other to receive him, but for him only who put him under suspension, unless it happens that he who put him under suspension die.

34. Do not ye receive any stranger, whether bishop, or presbyter, or deacon, without commendatory letters; and when such are offered, let them be examined. And if they be preachers of piety, let them be received; but if not, supply their wants, but do not receive them to communion: for many things are done by surprise.

35. The bishops of every country ought to know who is the chief among them, and to esteem him as their head, and not to do any great thing without his consent; but every one to manage only the affairs that belong to his own parish, and the places subject to it. But let him not do anything without the consent of all; for it is by this means there will be unanimity, and God will be glorified by Christ, in the Holy Spirit.

36. A bishop must not venture to ordain out of his own bounds for cities or countries that are not subject to him. But if he be convicted of having done so without the consent of such as governed those cities or countries, let him be deprived, both the bishop himself and those whom he has ordained.

37. If any bishop that is ordained does not undertake his office, nor take care of the people committed to him, let him be suspended until he do undertake it; and in the like manner a presbyter and a deacon. But if he goes, and is not received, not because of the want of his own consent, but because of the ill temper of the people, let him continue bishop; but let the clergy of that city be suspended, because they have not taught that disobedient people better.

38. Let a synod of bishops be held twice in the year, and

let them ask one another the doctrines of piety; and let them determine the ecclesiastical disputes that happen—once in the fourth week of Pentecost, and again on the twelfth of the month Hyperberetæus.

39. Let the bishop have the care of ecclesiastical revenues, and administer them as in the presence of God. But it is not lawful for him to appropriate any part of them to himself, or to give the things of God to his own kindred. But if they be poor, let him support them as poor; but let him not, under such pretences, alienate the revenues of the church.

40. Let not the presbyters and deacons do anything without the consent of the bishop, for it is he who is entrusted with the people of the Lord, and will be required to give an account of their souls. Let the proper goods of the bishop, if he has any, and those belonging to the Lord, be openly distinguished, that he may have power when he dies to leave his own goods as he pleases, and to whom he pleases; that, under pretence of the ecclesiastical revenues, the bishop's own may not come short, who sometimes has a wife and children, or kinsfolk, or servants. For this is just before God and men, that neither the church suffer any loss by the not knowing which revenues are the bishop's own, nor his kindred, under pretence of the church, be undone, or his relations fall into lawsuits, and so his death be liable to reproach.

41. We command that the bishop have power over the goods of the church; for if he be entrusted with the precious souls of men, much more ought he to give directions about goods, that they all be distributed to those in want, according to his authority, by the presbyters and deacons, and be used for their support with the fear of God, and with all reverence. He is also to partake of those things he wants, if he does want them, for his necessary occasions, and those of the brethren who live with him, that they may not by any means be in straits: for the law of God appointed that those who waited at the altar should be maintained by the altar; since not so much as a soldier does at any time bear arms against the enemies at his own charges.

42. Let a bishop, or presbyter, or deacon who indulges

himself in dice or drinking, either leave off those practices, or let him be deprived.

43. If a sub-deacon, a reader, or a singer does the like, either let him leave off, or let him be suspended; and so for one of the laity.

44. Let a bishop, or presbyter, or deacon who requires usury of those he lends to, either leave off to do so, or let him be deprived.

45. Let a bishop, or presbyter, or deacon who only prays with heretics, be suspended; but if he also permit them to perform any part of the office of a clergyman, let him be deprived.

46. We command that a bishop, or presbyter, or deacon who receives the baptism, or the sacrifice of heretics, be deprived: "For what agreement is there between Christ and Belial? or what part hath a believer with an infidel?"[1]

47. If a bishop or presbyter rebaptizes him who has had true baptism, or does not baptize him who is polluted by the ungodly, let him be deprived, as ridiculing the cross and the death of the Lord, and not distinguishing between real priests and counterfeit ones.

48. If a layman divorces his own wife, and takes another, or one divorced by another, let him be suspended.

49. If any bishop or presbyter does not baptize according to the Lord's constitution, into the Father, the Son, and the Holy Ghost, but into three beings without beginning, or into three Sons, or three Comforters, let him be deprived.

50. If any bishop or presbyter does not perform the three immersions of the one admission, but one immersion, which is given into the death of Christ, let him be deprived; for the Lord did not say, "Baptize into my death," but, "Go ye and make disciples of all nations, baptizing them into the name of the Father, and of the Son, and of the Holy Ghost." Do ye, therefore, O bishops, baptize thrice into one Father, and Son, and Holy Ghost, according to the will of Christ, and our constitution by the Spirit.[2]

[1] 2 Cor. vi. 15.
[2] At the end of this canon, in the collection of John of Antioch, the

51. If any bishop, or presbyter, or deacon, or indeed any one of the sacerdotal catalogue, abstains from marriage, flesh, and wine, not for his own exercise, but because he abominates these things, forgetting that "all things were very good,"[1] and that "God made man male and female,"[2] and blasphemously abuses the creation, either let him reform, or let him be deprived, and be cast out of the church; and the same for one of the laity.

52. If any bishop or presbyter does not receive him that returns from his sin, but rejects him, let him be deprived; because he grieves Christ, who says, "There is joy in heaven over one sinner that repenteth."[3]

53. If any bishop, or presbyter, or deacon does not on festival days partake of flesh or wine, let him be deprived, as "having a seared conscience,"[4] and becoming a cause of scandal to many.

following words are added: "Let him that is baptized be taught that the Father was not crucified, nor endured to be born of man, nor indeed that the Holy Spirit became man, or even endured suffering, for He was not made flesh; but the only begotten Son ransomed the world from the wrath which lay upon it: for He became man through His love of man, having fashioned a body for Himself from a virgin. For Wisdom built a house for herself as a Creator; but He willingly endured the cross, and rescued the world from the wrath that lies on it, namely, those who are baptized into the name of the Father, and the Son, and the Holy Spirit. But let those who do not thus baptize be suspended, as being ignorant of the mystery of piety." The same collection gives the following as Canon 51: "He who says that the Father suffered is more impious than the Jews, nailing along with Christ the Father also. He who denies that the only begotten Son was made flesh for us, and endured the cross, fights with God, and is an enemy of the saints. He that names the Holy Spirit Father or Son, is ignorant and foolish; for the Son is Creator along with the Father, and has the same throne, and is Lawgiver along with Him, and Judge, and the cause of the resurrection; and the Holy Spirit is the same in substance: for the Godhead has three Persons, the same in substance. For in our day Simon the magician gave forth [his doctrines], drawing the speechless, delusive, unstable, and wicked spirit to himself, and babbling that there is one God with three names, and sometimes erasing the passion and birth of Christ. Do you, then, most beloved ones, baptize into one Father, and Son, and the Holy Spirit as third, according to the will of the Lord, and our constitution made in the spirit."

[1] Gen. i. 31.   [2] Gen. i. 26.   [3] Luke xv. 7.   [4] 1 Tim. iv. 2.

54. If any one of the clergy be taken eating in a tavern, let him be suspended, excepting when he is forced to bait at an inn upon the road.

55. If any one of the clergy abuses his bishop unjustly, let him be deprived; for says the Scripture, "Thou shalt not speak evil of the ruler of thy people."[1]

56. If any one of the clergy abuses a presbyter or a deacon, let him be separated.

57. If any one of the clergy mocks at a lame, a deaf, or a blind man, or at one maimed in his feet, let him be suspended; and the like for the laity.

58. Let a bishop or presbyter, who takes no care of the clergy or people, and does not instruct them in piety, be separated; and if he continues in his negligence, let him be deprived.

59. If any bishop or presbyter, when any one of the clergy is in want, does not supply his necessity, let him be suspended; and if he continues in it, let him be deprived, as having killed his brother.

60. If any one publicly reads in the church the spurious books of the ungodly, as if they were holy, to the destruction of the people and of the clergy, let him be deprived.

61. If there be an accusation against a Christian for fornication, or adultery, or any other forbidden action, and he be convicted, let him not be promoted into the clergy.

62. If any one of the clergy for fear of men, as of a Jew, or a Gentile, or an heretic, shall deny the name of Christ, let him be suspended; but if he deny the name of a clergyman, let him be deprived; but when he repents, let him be received as one of the laity.

63. If any bishop, or presbyter, or deacon, or indeed any one of the sacerdotal catalogue, eats flesh with the blood of its life, or that which is torn by beasts, or which died of itself, let him be deprived; for this the law itself has forbidden.[2] But if he be one of the laity, let him be suspended.

64. If any one of the clergy be found to fast on the Lord's

[1] Ex. xxii. 28.   [2] Gen. ix.; Lev. xvii.

day, or on the Sabbath-day, excepting one only, let him be deprived; but if he be one of the laity, let him be suspended.

65. If any one, either of the clergy or laity, enters into a synagogue of the Jews or heretics to pray, let him be deprived and suspended.

66. If any one of the clergy strikes one in a quarrel, and kills him by that one stroke, let him be deprived, on account of his rashness; but if he be one of the laity, let him be suspended.

67. If any one has offered violence to a virgin not betrothed, and keeps her, let him be suspended. But it is not lawful for him to take another to wife; but he must retain her whom he has chosen, although she be poor.

68. If any bishop, or presbyter, or deacon, receives a second ordination from any one, let him be deprived, and the person who ordained him, unless he can show that his former ordination was from the heretics; for those that are either baptized or ordained by such as these, can be neither Christians nor clergymen.

69. If any bishop, or presbyter, or deacon, or reader, or singer, does not fast the fast of forty days, or the fourth day of the week, and the day of the preparation, let him be deprived, except he be hindered by weakness of body. But if he be one of the laity, let him be suspended.

70. If any bishop, or any other of the clergy, fasts with the Jews, or keeps the festivals with them, or accepts of the presents from their festivals, as unleavened bread or some such thing, let him be deprived; but if he be one of the laity, let him be suspended.

71. If any Christian carries oil into an heathen temple, or into a synagogue of the Jews, or lights up lamps in their festivals, let him be suspended.

72. If any one, either of the clergy or laity, takes away from the holy church an honeycomb, or oil, let him be suspended, and let him add the fifth part to that which he took away.[1]

73. A vessel of silver, or gold, or linen, which is sancti-

[1] Lev. v. 16.

fied, let no one appropriate to his own use, for it is unjust; but if any one be caught, let him be punished with suspension.

74. If a bishop be accused of any crime by credible and faithful persons, it is necessary that he be cited by the bishops; and if he comes and makes his apology, and yet is convicted, let his punishment be determined. But if, when he is cited, he does not obey, let him be cited a second time, by two bishops sent to him. But if even then he despises them, and will not come, let the synod pass what sentence they please against him, that he may not appear to gain advantage by avoiding their judgment.

75. Do not ye receive an heretic in a testimony against a bishop; nor a Christian if he be single. For the law says, "In the mouth of two or three witnesses every word shall be established."[1]

76. A bishop must not gratify his brother, or his son, or any other kinsman, with the episcopal dignity, or ordain whom he pleases; for it is not just to make heirs to episcopacy, and to gratify human affections in divine matters. For we must not put the church of God under the laws of inheritance; but if any one shall do so, let his ordination be invalid, and let him be punished with suspension.

77. If any one be maimed in an eye, or lame of his leg, but is worthy of the episcopal dignity, let him be made a bishop; for it is not a blemish of the body that can defile him, but the pollution of the soul.

78. But if he be deaf and blind, let him not be made a bishop; not as being a defiled person, but that the ecclesiastical affairs may not be hindered.

79. If any one hath a demon, let him not be made one of the clergy. Nay, let him not pray with the faithful; but when he is cleansed, let him be received; and if he be worthy, let him be ordained.

80. It is not right to ordain him bishop presently who is just come in from the Gentiles, and baptized; or from a wicked mode of life: for it is unjust that he who has not

[1] Deut. xix. 15.

yet afforded any trial of himself should be a teacher of others, unless it anywhere happens by divine grace.

81. We have said that a bishop ought not to let himself into public administrations, but to attend on all opportunities upon the necessary affairs of the church.[1] Either therefore let him agree not to do so, or let him be deprived. For "no one can serve two masters,"[2] according to the Lord's admonition.

82. We do not permit servants to be ordained into the clergy without their masters' consent; for this would grieve those that owned them. For such a practice would occasion the subversion of families. But if at any time a servant appears worthy to be ordained into an high office, such as our Onesimus appeared to be, and if his master allows of it, and gives him his freedom, and dismisses him from his house, let him be ordained.

83. Let a bishop, or presbyter, or deacon, who goes to the army, and desires to retain both the Roman government and the sacerdotal administration, be deprived. For "the things of Cæsar belong to Cæsar, and the things of God to God."[3]

84. Whosoever shall abuse the king or the governor unjustly, let him suffer punishment; and if he be a clergyman, let him be deprived; but if he be a layman, let him be suspended.

85. Let the following books be esteemed venerable and holy by you, both of the clergy and laity. Of the Old Covenant: the five books of Moses—Genesis, Exodus, Leviticus, Numbers, and Deuteronomy; one of Joshua the son of Nun, one of the Judges, one of Ruth, four of the Kings, two of the Chronicles, two of Ezra, one of Esther, [one of Judith,] three of the Maccabees, one of Job, one hundred and fifty psalms; three books of Solomon—Proverbs, Ecclesiastes, and the Song of Songs; sixteen prophets. And besides these, take care that your young persons learn the Wisdom of the very learned Sirach. But our sacred books, that is, those of the New Covenant, are these: the four Gospels of Matthew, Mark, Luke, and John; the fourteen Epistles of Paul; two

[1] Can. iv. *prius.* [2] Matt. vi. 24. [3] Matt. xxii. 21.

Epistles of Peter, three of John, one of James, one of Jude; two Epistles of Clement; and the Constitutions dedicated to you the bishops by me Clement, in eight books; which it is not fit to publish before all, because of the mysteries contained in them; and the Acts of us the Apostles.

Let these canonical rules be established by us for you, O ye bishops; and if you continue to observe them, ye shall be saved, and shall have peace; but if you be disobedient, you shall be punished, and have everlasting war one with another, and undergo a penalty suitable to your disobedience.

Now, God who alone is unbegotten, and the Maker of the whole world, unite you all through His peace, in the Holy Spirit; perfect you unto every good work, immoveable, unblameable, and unreprovable; and vouchsafe to you eternal life with us, through the mediation of His beloved Son Jesus Christ our God and Saviour; with whom glory be to Thee, the God over all, and the Father, in the Holy Spirit the Comforter, now and always, and for ever and ever.   Amen.

The end of the Constitutions of the Holy Apostles by Clement, which are the catholic doctrine.

INDEXES.

I.—INDEX OF TEXTS OF SCRIPTURE.

GENESIS.

i. 1,	124, 176, **226**
i. 26,	193, 227, 264
i. 26, 27,	125
i. 28,	173, 174
i. 31,	153, 264
ii. 7,	123
ii. 24,	94, 179
iii. 16,	110
iii. 19,	123
iv.,	180, 195
iv., v.,'.	228
iv. 7,	41
iv. 10,	49
vi., viii.,	228
viii.,	197
ix.,	265
ix. 3,	184
ix. 6,	72
xii.,	197, 229
xiii. 16,	192
xv. 20,	211
xvii. 7,	192
xviii. 25, 27,	141
xix.,	179, 228
xix. 24,	141
xxii.,	197
xxii. 17,	192
xxvi. 3,	192
xxvii. 29,	103
xxviii. 15,	192
xxix.,	67
xxxii. 30,	141
xxxv.,	197
xlvi. 27,	229
xlviii. 4,	192
xlix. 9,	143
xlix. 10,	153, 168

EXODUS.

i.,	229
ii. 13,	182
ii. 14,	145
iii. 2,	141
iii. 6,	176
iii. 14, 15,	192
iv. etc.,	164
v. 4,	165
vii., iv.,	208
vii. etc.,	145
vii. 1,	62, 209
xi. 19,	176
xii.,	197
xiii. 21,	146
xv. 20,	211, 239
xv. 25,	145
xv. 26,	31
xvi.,	146
xvi. 8,	63
xvii. 6,	145
xviii.,	74
xviii., xxiv., xxviii.,	238
xix. 5, 6,	57
xx.,	163, 178
xx., xxxiv.,	250
xx. 10,	173
xx. 12,	63
xx. 14-17,	18
xx. 17,	16, 99
xx. 24,	164
xxi. 17,	63
xxi. 21,	77
xxi. 23,	179
xxii. 18,	179
xxii. 19,	173
xxii. 28,	58, 62, 265
xxiii. 3,	29, 71
xxiii. 7,	33
xxiii. 7, 8,	71
xxiii. 8,	33
xxviii., xxix.,	256
xxxi. etc.,	146
xxxii.,	163
xxxii. 4,	129, 164
xxxiii. 11,	146
xxxiii. 11, 17,	255
xxxiv. 28,	143

LEVITICUS.

v. 16,	266
xv.,	171
xv. 31,	30, 42, 71
xvii.,	265
xviii. 19,	174
xviii. 20,	179
xviii. 22,	173
xix. 6,	113
xix. 11,	180
xix. 15,	29
xix. 17,	80, 180
xix. 18,	55, 168, 178
xix. 26,	91
xix. 26, 31,	181
xix. 27,	19
xx. 10,	173
xx. 13,	173
xxi. 7, 14,	160
xxi. 17,	28
xxiii., xxv.,	197
xxvi. 27,	73

NUMBERS.

iii.,	240
vi. 24,	86
xi. 31,	165
xii. 1,	144
xii. 2,	145
xii. 3,	145
xii. 7, 8,	255
xii. 8,	63
xiv. 5,	146
xiv. 10,	146
xvi.,	33, 60, 44, 182, 197, 254
xvi. 3,	145
xvi. 21,	146
xvii. 8,	126
xviii.,	189

xviii. 1,		43, 57	vi.,		. 229	xvii. 9,		. 93
xviii. 8,		. 57	vii.,		34, 179	xx., xix.,		. 198
xviii. 12,		. 57	x.,		. 209	xx., xxi.,		. 53
xx., xxiv.,		. 210	xxiv. 32,		. 176	xxii. 1,		. 27
xxiii. 23,		91, 181				xxii. 14,		211, 239
xxiv. 9,		. 17	JUDGES.					
xxv. 3,		. 129	ii. 13,		. 129	1 CHRONICLES.		
xxv., xxxi.,		. 211	iv. 4,		211, 239	i.,		. 240
			iv., xi.,		. 197	xxi.,		. 198
DEUTERONOMY.			vi., viii.,		. 197			
i. 16,		. 66	xiii., xv., xvi.,		. 197	2 CHRONICLES.		
i. 17,		29, 33, 35, 71,				v. 13,		. 204
		180, 182	1 SAMUEL.			xviii.,		. 198
iv. 19,		. 128	i.,		. 198	xix. 2,		. 161
iv. 39,		. 195	i. 15,		. 143	xx. 37,		. 162
v. 31,		. 84	ii. 32,		. 180	xxiii. 3,		. 50
v. 32,		. 184	vii.,		. 198	xxiv. 1,		. 27
vi. 4,		31, 165, 168	viii.,		. 64	xxvi.,		59, 104, 144,
vi. 5,		. 178	xii. 3,		. 141			254, 256
vi. 6,		. 169	xiii.,		. 255	xxxii., xxxiii.,		. 53
vi. 7,		. 19	xiii. 13,		. 59	xxxiii.,		. 198
xii.,		. 170	xv. 2,		. 167	xxxv.,		. 198
xii. 5,		. 163	xv. 23,		. 181			
xv. 23,		. 184	xvii., xviii.,		. 180	EZRA.		
xvi. 18,		. 66	xviii., xxi., xxii.,		182	iii.,		. 198
xvi. 19,		33, 71				viii.,		. 198
xvi. 20,		29, 33, 76	2 SAMUEL.					
xvii. 7,		33, 71	xii.,		. 182	NEHEMIAH.		
xviii.,		. 208	xii. 13,		. 43	i. 3,		. 39
xviii. 10,		. 91	xv. 3,		. 144	viii.,		. 2
xviii. 11, 10,		. 181	xviii.-xx.,		. 144	viii. 10,		. 185
xviii. 15,		. 141	xx. 1,		. 144			
xix. 13,		. 72				ESTHER.		
xix. 14,		. 16	1 KINGS.			iv. 16,		. 143
xix. 15,		77, 267	ii.,		. 33			
xix. 17,		. 75	iii., viii.,		. 198	JOB.		
xix. 19,		. 72	viii. 46,		. 221	i. etc.,		. 148
xxii. 22,		. 173	i. 5,		. 129	ix. 8,		. 219
xxiii. 1,		. 84	xii.,		27, 33	x. 10,		. 125
xxiii. 7,		80, 178	xiii.,		. 111	xiv. 4,		. 43
xxiii. 17,		173, 179	xiii. 33,		. 255	xx. 15,		. 109
xxiii. 18,		99, 110	xiv.,		. 111	xx. 18,		. 109
xxiv. 10,		. 146	xv.,		. 33	xxviii. 1,		. 193
xxv. 4,		. 55	xv. 23,		. 91	xxxi. 5,		. 90
xxvii.,		. 179	xvii.,		. 122	xxxv. 7,		. 119
xxvii. 9,		. 84	xviii.,		. 198	xxxvii. 10,		. 254
xxvii. 17,		. 16	xviii. 21,		. 177	xxxviii.,		. 226
xxvii. 25,		33, 71	xix. 8,		. 143	xl. 24,		. 218
xxvii. 26,		. 170	xix. 18,		. 209	xlii.,		. 182
xxx. 15,		. 177	xxi.,		. 77			
xxx. 19,		. 177				PSALMS.		
xxxii. 21,		. 128	2 KINGS.			i. 1,		. 90
xxxiv. 8,		. 252	ii.,		122, 198	i. 2,		. 169
			v.,		34, 179	ii. 1,		. 139
JOSHUA.			vi.,		34, 209	ii. 7,		. 63
i. 8,		. 19	viii.,		. 111	ii. 11,		. 128
iii. 10,		. 229	xi. 3, 4,		. 27	iv. 4,		. 80
v. 14,		. 197	xii. 13,		. 49	v. 6,		. 180
v. 14,		. 141	xiii. 21,		. 176	vi. 6,		. 35

vii. 5,	.	. 80	cix. 8,	. . 154	xiv. 12,	.	. 161
vii. 16,	.	. 103	cx. 1,	. . 177	xiv. 29,	.	69, 181
viii. 5,	.	. 178	cx. 4,	. . 60	xiv. 31,	.	. 180
ix. 3,	.	. 219	cxi. 9,	. . 95	xiv. 33,	.	. 68
xi. 8,	.	. 252	cxii. 5,	. . 178	xv. 1,	.	. 28
xii. 6,	.	. 139	cxii. 9,	. . 65	xv. 27,	.	65, 95, 182
xvii. 8,	.	. 250	cxiii. 1,	. . 206	xviii. 3,	.	. 24
xvii. 26,	.	. 73	cxiii. 3,	. . 169	xviii. 22,	.	. 158
xviii. 35,	.	. 137	cxiii. 5,	. . 214	xix. 14,	.	158, 175
xix. 8,	.	. 163	cxv. 7,	. . 175	xix. 17,	.	95, 183
xxii. 13, 14,	.	. 132	cxvi. 15,	127, 175	xix. 18,	.	113, 183
xxii. 17,	.	. 133	cxvii. 2,	. . 219	xix. 24,	.	28, 92
xxii. 19,	.	. 133	cxix. 1,	. . 169	xx. 9,	.	. 43
xxii. 28,	.	. 155	cxix. 22,	. . 143	xx. 22,	.	. 17
xxv. 4, 5,	.	. 90	cxix. 73,	. . 126	xxi. 9, 19,	.	. 24
xxvii. 8,	.	. 86	cxxi. 8,	217, 237	xxi. 13,	.	. 95
xxvii. 12,	.	. 133	cxxxi. 1,	181 bis	xxi. 19,	.	. 25
xxviii. 9,	.	. 252	cxxxvi. 25,	. . 233	xxi. 27,	.	. 167
xxxv. 2,	.	. 48	cxxxviii. 3,	. . 174	xxii. 10,	.	. 33
xxxvii. 16,	.	. 111	cxxxix. 5,	. . 126	xxiii.,	.	. 253
xl. 2,	.	. 95	cxxxix. 16,	. . 126	xxiii. 14,	.	. 113
xli. 10,	.	. 139	cxxxix. 21,	. . 161	xxiii. 21,	.	. 28
xliv. 20,	.	. 250	cxli. 12,	. . 12	xxiii. 29,	.	. 253
xlv.,	.	. 141	cxliv. 16,	. . 109	xxiii. 31,	.	. 28
xlix. 21,	.	. 133	cxlv. 17,	. . 126	xxiv. 11,	.	. 112
l,	.	. 70			xxiv. 27,	.	. 35
l. 9, 12,	.	. 167	PROVERBS.		xxvi. 2,	.	. 103
l. 12,	.	. 164	i. 8,	. . 32	xxvi. 9,	.	. 253
li. 12,	.	. 218	i. 16,	. . 48	xxvi. 17,	.	. 78
li. 12, 19,	.	. 167	iii. 9,	66, 112, 178	xxvi. 27,	.	. 103
li. 14,	.	. 220	iii. 28,	. . 159	xxvii. 1,	.	. 159
lvi. 3, 4,	.	. 85	v. 3,	. . 22	xxix. 12,	.	. 42
lxiii. 12,	.	. 179	v. 11,	. . 22	xxix. 17,	.	. 113
lxiv. 2,	.	. 223	v. 18,	. . 175	xxx. 6,	.	. 183
lxvi. 2,	.	. 135	v. 22,	. . 38	xxxi. 4,	.	. 253
lxviii. 16,	.	. 147	vi. 2,	. . 180	xxxi. 10, etc.,		. 24
lxix. 18,	.	. 135	vi. 6,	. . 92	xxxi. 13,	.	. 183
lxxii. 6,	.	. 62	vi. 22,	. . 171			
lxxii. 8,	.	. 139	vii. 1, etc.,	. . 22	ECCLESIASTES.		
lxxiii. 19,	.	. 36	vii. 26, 27,	. . 22	ii. 25,	.	109, 185
lxxiv. 4,	.	. 135	viii. 22,	. . 196	iv. 5,	.	28, 92
lxxiv. 15,	.	. 229	viii. 22-25,	. . 142	v. 4,	.	. 93
lxxiv. 16,	.	. 249	ix. 1,	. . 142	v. 10,	.	. 115
lxxxii. 6,	.	. 58	ix. 8,	. . 180	vii. 26,	.	. 24
lxxxviii. 18,	.	. 194	x. 7,	127, 175	x. 1,	.	. 42
xci. 6,	.	. 223	x. 9,	. . 220	x. 18,	.	. 92
xci. 7,	.	. 135	x. 18,	. . 103	xii. 14,	.	. 122
xcvii. 3,	.	. 219	xi. 4,	. . 109			
xcvii. 5,	.	. 219	xi. 22,	. . 24	CANTICLES.		
ciii. 14,	.	. 126	xi. 25,	. . 65	ii. 15,	.	. 161
ciii. 14, 15,	.	. 109	xi. 26,	. . 65			
civ. 2,	.	89, 226	xii. 4,	. . 24	ISAIAH.		
civ. 9,	.	. 254	xii. 28,	80, 180	i. 7,	.	. 108
civ. 15,	.	. 243	xiii. 17,	. . 181	i. 8,	.	. 147
civ. 24,	.	. 194	xiii. 19,	. . 173	i. 11,	.	. 167
civ. 32,	.	. 219	xiii. 20,	161, 182	i. 16,	.	. 219
cv. 16,	.	. 231	xiii. 24,	. . 113	i. 19,	.	. 183
cvi. 9,	.	. 219	xiv. 1,	. . 24	i. 22,	.	. 110
cvii. 34,	.	. 228	xiv. 5,	. . 128	i. 23,	.	. 4

ii. 2,	. . .	147	xii. 7,	. . .	147	JOEL.		
v. 6,	. . .	147	xii. 8,	. . .	133	ii. 28,	. . .	148
v. 7, 2,	. . .	15	xii. 10,	. . .	40	ii. 32,	. . .	155
v. 8,	. . 16,	55	xv. 1,	. . .	111			
v. 20,	. . .	71	xv. 17,	. . .	90	AMOS.		
v. 23,	. . .	71	xv. 19,	. . .	83	v. 23,	. . .	148
vi. 2,	. . .	230	xvii. 12,	. . .	147			
vi. 3,	. . 194,	230	xxvi.,	. . .	31	JONAH.		
vi. 9,	. . 97,	136	xxviii., xxix.,	. . .	211	i. 17,	. . .	49
vii. 14,	. . .	136	xxix. 22,	. . .	211	ii.,	. . 123,	198
viii. 20,	. . 163,	229	xxxiii. 15,	. . .	147	iii.,	. . .	221
ix. 6,	. 136, 153,	225				iii. 5,	. . .	143
xi. 1,	. . .	153	LAMENTATIONS.			iv.,	. . .	49
xi. 1, 10,	. . .	142	iv. 20,	. . 140,	142			
xi. 4,	. . .	190				NAHUM.		
xiv. 19,	. . .	139	EZEKIEL.			i. 9,	. . .	260
xxii. 13,	. . .	98	ii. 7,	. . .	31			
xxvi. 19,	. . .	121	iii. 11,	. . .	31	HABAKKUK.		
xxviii. 11,	. . .	208	iii. 12,	. . .	194	ii. 9,	. . .	180
xxxv. 3,	. . .	69	v. 7,	. . .	89			
xl. 11,	. . .	47	viii. 14,	. . .	129	ZECHARIAH.		
li. 10,	. . .	219	viii. 16,	. . .	129	iii. 1,	. . .	148
lii. 5,	. . 25,	96	viii. 17,	. . .	129	iii. 2,	. . 148,	218
lii. 6,	. . .	187	xvi. 47,	. . .	89	vii. 9,	. . .	66
lii. 12,	. . .	133	xvi. 52,	. . .	88	viii. 17,	. . .	80
liii.,	. . .	138	xviii. 2, etc.,	. . .	39	ix. 12,	. . .	142
liii. 1,	. . .	136	xviii. 6,	. . .	174	ix. 17,	. . 109,	185
liii. 4,	. . .	57	xviii. 20,	. . .	36	x. 3,	. . .	40
liii. 11,	. . 106	bis	xviii., xxxiii.,	. . .	220	xii. 1,	. . .	125
liii. 12,	. . .	57	xx. 25,	. . .	166	xii. 10,	. . .	140
liv. 14,	. . 111,	180	xxiii. 11,	. . .	35	xiii. 2,	. . .	128
lvii. 1,	. . .	127	xxxiii. 2,	. . .	31	xiv. 7,	. . .	133
lvii. 19,	. . .	81	xxxiii. 7,	. . .	31			
lvii. 21,	. . .	162	xxxiii. 10,	. . .	45	MALACHI.		
lviii. 6,	. . .	80	xxxiv. 2,	. . .	44	i. 6,	40, 187,	211
lviii. 7,	. . 95,	183	xxxiv. 3,	. . .	55	i. 11,	. . .	169
lviii. 9,	. . .	99	xxxiv. 4,	. . .	47	i. 11, 14,	. . .	189
lix. 7,	. . .	48	xxxvii. 11,	. . .	122	ii. 7,	. . .	61
lxii. 2,	. . .	104				ii. 14, 15, 16,	. . .	175
lxii. 11,	. . 38,	252	DANIEL.			ii. 15, 14,	. . .	158
lxiii. 10,	. . .	135	ii. 34,	. . .	142	iv. 4,	. . .	163
lxiv. 1,	. . .	219	iii.,	. . 121,	210			
lxiv. 8,	. . .	126	iii., vi.,	. . .	123	1 MACCABEES.		
lxv.,	. . .	135	iv. 24,	. . .	95	i. etc.,	. . .	198
lxvi. 2,	27, 181,	212	vi. 14,	. . 198,	210			
			vii. 10,	. . 135,	230	4 ESDRAS.		
JEREMIAH.			vii. 13,	. . .	142	xvi. 59,	. . .	226
i. 3,	. . .	125	viii. 13,	. . .	194			
ii. 11, 10,	. . .	89	x. 2,	. . .	143	TOBIT.		
iii. 11,	. . .	89	xii. 2, 3,	. . .	121	iv. 16,	. . 17, 103,	178
iii. 22,	. . .	36	xii. 3,	. . .	126			
iv. 4,	. . .	158				JUDITH.		
v.,	. . .	226	HOSEA.			viii.,	. . .	211
v. 7,	. . .	128	iv. 6,	. . .	159	viii. 6,	. . .	143
vi. 20,	. . .	166	iv. 9,	. . .	30	ix. 12,	. . .	98
vii. 16,	. . .	111	ix. 4,	. . .	167	xvi. 21, 23,	. . .	241
vii. 21,	. . .	166	x. 12,	. . .	29			
viii. 4,	. . .	36	x. 13,	. . .	42	WISDOM.		
x. 2,	. . 91,	129				iii. 1,	. . 175,	251
						x. 6,	. . .	228

ECCLESIASTICUS.		ix. 12, . . 38, 49, 69	xxii. 32, . . 251
iv. 31, .	. 182	ix. 15, . . . 138	xxiii. 3, . . 32
v. 7, .	. 159	ix. 22, . . . 174	xxiii. 16, . . 129
xxiv. 25,	. 147	x. 2, . . . 157	xxiii. 35, . . 137
xxv. 26,	. 158	x. 12, . . . 81	xxiii. 38, . . 147
xxvi. 29,	. 110	x. 13, . . . 103	xxiv., . . . 190
xxx. 11,	. 114	x. 17, . . . 118	xxiv, 12, . . 157
xxxi.,	. 253	x. 22, . . . 118	xxiv. 12, 24, . 162
xxxi. 21,	. 113	x. 23, . . 118, 253	xxiv. 24, . 157, 161
xlix. 19,	. 228	x. 25, . . . 208	xxiv. 51, . . 180
		x. 26, . . . 119	xxv. 46, . . 190
BARUCH.		x. 28, . . . 119	xxvi., . . 77, 231
iii. 36, .	. 141	x. 32, . . . 116	xxvi. 4, . . 253
iv. 4, .	. 169	x. 33, . . . 118	xxvi. 15, . . 131
		x. 37, . . . 119	xxvi. 24, . . 74
HIST. OF SUSANNA, 67,		x. 40, . . . 254	xxvi. 30, . . 131
	77, 79	x. 41, . . . 189	xxvi. 31, . . 131
MATTHEW.		xi. 5, . . . 208	xxvi. 44, 43, . 132
i. 15, .	. 82	xi. 28, . . . 21	xxvi. 45, . . 132
i. 23, .	. 136	xii. 9, . . . 218	xxvii. 5, . . 179
iii., iv.,	. 185	xii. 30, . 83, 87	xxvii. 9, . . 131
v. 2, .	. 168	xii. 32, . . 161	xxvii. 24, 25, . 139
v. 4, .	. 181	xii. 36, . 26, 179	xxvii. 46, . . 134
v. 5, .	. 27	xii. 37, . . 26	xxviii. 19, . 127, 158,
v. 7, .	27, 168, 181	xii. 40, . . 134	185, 201, 213
v. 8, .	. 27	xiii. 9, . . . 31	xxviii. 20, . 87, 205
v. 9, .	. 27, 75	xiii. 16, . . 165	
v. 11, .	. 32	xiii. 31, . . 96	MARK.
v. 11, 12,	. 118	xiv., . . . 182	i., ... 163
v. 18, 17,	. 163	xiv. 17, . . 127	ii. 2, . . . 138
v. 21, .	. 65	xiv. 31, . . 182	iii. 1, etc., . . 126
v. 22, .	. 79	xv. 11, . . 185	v., ... 123
v. 23, .	. 63	xvi. 24, . . 166	v. 9, . . . 218
v. 23, 24,	. 80	xvi. 27, . . 190	v. 34, . . . 47
v. 28, .	. 16	xvi. 26, . . 119	vii. 22, . . 185
v. 34, .	129, 179	xvi. 33, . . 118	xi. 10, . . 188
v. 38, .	. 168	xvii. 24, . . 127	xi. 25, . . . 48
v. 39, .	. 178	xviii. 6, 7, . 33	xii. 29, . . 31
v. 40, .	. 178	xviii. 14, . . 38	xii. 32, . . 178
v. 42, .	. 178	xviii. 18, . 38, 42, 46	xii. 43, . . 99
v. 44, .	. 178	xviii. 15, . . 67	xiii. 35, . . 190
v. 45, .	37, 178	xviii. 17, . 18, 68	xiv., . . . 231
v. 46, .	. 81	xviii. 20, . . 247	xvi. 9, . . . 134
v. 47, .	. 178	xviii. 21, . . 75	xvi. 14, . . 134
vi. 2, 34,	. 102	xviii. 22, . . 80	xvi. 16, . . 159
vi. 5, .	. 186	xix. 4, . . 158, 173	xvi. 17, . . 207
vi. 9, etc.,	. 103, 187	xix. 6, . . . 158	
vi. 10, .	. 82	xix. 14, . . 159	LUKE.
vi. 12, .	. 48	xix. 18, . . 222	i., ii., . . . 211
vi. 16, .	. 110	xx. 25, . . . 47	ii. 14, . . 205, 235
vi. 20, .	. 66	xx. 26, . . . 106	ii. 29, . . . 206
vi. 21, .	. 98	xx. 28, . . . 106	ii. 36, . . 92, 239
vi. 24, .	177, 181, 268	xxi. 9, . . 188, 235	ii. 51, . . . 168
vii. 2, .	. 72, 77	xxi. 13, . . . 42	iii. 13, . . . 68
vii. 6, .	. 96	xxi. 28, . . . 137	iii. 14, . . . 245
vii. 15, .	. 157	xxi. 34, . . . 137	iv. 19, . . . 47
viii. 4, .	. 163	xxi. 42, . . . 137	iv. 24, . . . 86
viii. 12,	. 120	xxi. 43, . . . 137	v. 3, . . . 138
ix. 2, .	. 126	xxii. 21, . 74, 268	vi. 22, 23, . . 117

vi. 28,	.	.	17	v. 45,	.	.	.	123
vi. 30,	.	.	95, 178	v. 46,	.	.	.	29
vi. 32,	.	.	178, 241	vi. 27,	.	.	.	89
vi. 37,	.	.	66, 72	vi. 29,	.	.	.	89
vi. 38,	.	.	. 48	vi. 45,	.	.	.	246
vi. 40,	.	.	. 121	vi. 67,	.	.	.	166
vi. 41,	.	.	. 41	vii. 24,	.	.	.	67
vii. 4,	.	.	. 123	viii. 11,	.	.	.	54
vii. 47,	.	.	. 54	viii. 44,	.	.	.	48
viii. 14,	.	.	. 181	ix. 1,	.	.	.	126
ix. 26,	.	.	. 118	x. 11,	.	.	.	46
ix. 30,	.	.	. 163	x. 15,	.	.	.	106
x. 5,	.	.	. 103	x. 29,	.	.	.	223
x. 7,	.	.	. 55	xi.,	.	.	.	123
x. 16,	.	.	45, 212	xi. 25,	.	.	.	123
x. 18,	.	.	. 218	xi. 48,	.	.	.	169
x. 19,	.	.	. 218	xi. 51,	.	.	.	210
x. 20,	.	.	. 207	xii. 6,	.	.	130, 179
xii. 35,	.	.	. 190	xii. 43,	.	.	.	119
xii. 48,	.	.	. 43	xiii.,	.	.	.	130
xiv. 11,	.	.	. 27	xiii. 4,	.	.	.	106
xiv. 13,	.	.	. 60	xiii. 17,	.	.	.	169
xv.,	.	.	. 221	xiii. 20,	.	.	.	254
xv. 4,	.	.	. 46	xiii. 34,	.	.	.	168
xv. 7,	.	36, 220, 264	xiii. 35,	.	.	.	28
xv. 21,	.	.	. 69	xv. 13,	.	.	.	106
xvi.,	.	.	. 182	xv. 16,	.	.	.	166
xvi. 15,	.	.	. 181	xv. 20,	.	.	.	118
xvii. 14,	.	.	. 163	xvi. 17,	.	.	.	223
xviii. 8,	.	.	. 162	xvi. 32,	.	.	.	131
xviii. 28,	.	.	. 126	xvii. 3,	.	.	136, 168
xix. 10,	.	.	. 47	xvii. 6, 4,	.	207, 231
xix. 44,	.	.	. 134	xvii. 11, 25,	.	.	207
xx. 38,	.	.	. 176	xviii. 1,	.	.	.	131
xxi. 3,	.	.	. 99	xviii. 38,	.	.	.	132
xxi. 18,	.	.	. 121	xix. 15,	.	.	.	169
xxi. 19,	.	.	. 121	xix. 6, 12,	.	.	139
xxii.,	.	.	. 231	xix. 37,	.	.	.	140
xxii. 19,	.	.	. 140	xx. 11,	.	.	.	134
xxii. 31,	.	.	. 148	xx. 25,	.	.	.	140
xxii. 32,	.	.	. 148					
xxii. 34,	.	.	. 131					
xxii. 41,	.	.	. 132					
xxii. 45,	.	.	. 132					
xxiii. 2,	.	.	. 132					
xxiii. 14,	.	.	. 132					
xxiii. 21,	.	.	. 133					
xxiii. 34,	.	40, 134					
xxiii. 39, etc.,	.	. 134					
xxiii. 46,	.	121, 134					
xxiv. 18,	.	.	. 134					

x.,	.	.	.	154
x. 13,	.	.	.	155
x. 34, 45,	.	.	155
x. 42,	.	.	.	141
xi. 15, 9,	.	.	155
xv.,	.	.	.	153
xv. 1,	.	.	.	153
xv. 7,	.	.	.	154
xv. 10,	.	.	.	155
xv. 14,	.	.	.	156
xv. 23, etc.,	.	.	156
xv. 32,	.	.	.	211
xix. 14,	.	.	.	211
xx. 28,	.	.	86, 90
xx. 35,	.	.	.	108
xxi. 9,	.	.	.	212
xxi. 10,	.	.	.	211
xxiii. 32,	.	.	.	145

ROMANS.

i. 25,	.	.	.	230
i. 28,	.	.	.	130
iii. 15,	.	.	.	48
vi. 3,	.	.	105, 136
vi. 5,	.	.	.	200
vii. 25,	.	.	.	241
viii. 12,	.	.	.	199
xi. 4,	.	.	.	209
xii. 2,	.	.	.	82
xiii. 1, 4, 7,	.	.	114
xiii. 8,	.	.	.	115
xvi. 20,	.	.	.	219
xvi. 21,	.	.	.	162

1 CORINTHIANS.

i. 10,	.	.	.	74
ii. 9,	.	.	.	191
vi. 1,	.	.	.	74
vi. 5,	.	.	.	67
vi. 19,	.	.	.	137
vii. 25,	.	.	.	115
vii. 34,	.	.	.	115
x. 20,	.	.	.	185
xi.,	.	.	.	231
xi. 3,	.	.	96, 100
xi. 26,	.	.	.	187
xi. 29,	.	.	.	187
xii. 8,	.	.	.	209
xiv. 21,	.	.	.	208
xiv. 33,	.	.	.	256
xiv. 34,	.	.	.	96
xv. 32,	.	.	.	98
xvi. 22,	.	.	.	188

2 CORINTHIANS.

i. 3,	.	.	.	214
v. 17,	.	.	.	163
vi. 14,	.	.	.	248
vi. 15,	.	.	.	263

ACTS.

i. 1,	.	.	.	30
i. 3,	.	.	.	127
i. 9,	.	.	.	127
i. 18,	.	.	.	179
ii. 4,	.	.	.	141
iv. 6,	.	.	.	117
v.,	.	.	.	179
v. 40, 41,	.	.	117
vi., vii.,	77, 239, 257
vii. 56,	.	.	.	177
viii.,	.	111, 149
viii. 19,	.	.	.	149
viii. 20,	.	.	.	150
viii. 24,	.	.	.	150
viii., ix.,	.	.	257
ix. 5,	.	.	.	256
ix. 11,	.	.	.	156

JOHN.

i. 9,	.	.	.	136
ii. 3,	.	.	.	127
iii. 5,	.	.	.	159
iii. 36,	.	.	.	143
iv. 44,	.	.	.	86
v. 39,	.	.	.	29

276   THE APOSTOLICAL CONSTITUTIONS.

vi. 16,	.	. 217	iv.,	.	. 246	iv. 7,	.	. 252
vii. 1,	.	217, 220, 234, 239	iv. 1,	.	. 114	iv. 21,	.	. 204
xi. 3,	.	. 22	1 THESSALONIANS.			TITUS.		
xvi. 17,	.	. 147	iv. 16,	.	. 190	i. 6,	.	. 160
						iii. 1,	.	. 114
GALATIANS.			2 THESSALONIANS.					
iii. 10,	.	. 170	ii.,	.	. 189	PHILEMON.		
iv. 9,	.	. 136	iii. 10,	.	. 92	ver. 10,	.	. 205
v. 9,	.	. 42						
vi. 10,	.	. 178	1 TIMOTHY.			HEBREWS.		
			ii. 2,	.	232, 234	v. 4,	.	. 101
EPHESIANS.			ii. 4,	.	. 221	v. 5,	.	. 60
ii. 7,	.	. 81	ii. 15,	.	. 189	xi. 37,	.	. 137
iii. 15,	.	. 225	iii. 2,	.	. 27	xii. 8,	.	. 32
iv. 4,	.	. 74	iii. 2, 12,	.	. 160	xii. 23,	.	. 57
iv. 26,	.	. 79	iii. 4,	.	. 27	xiii. 4,	.	. 174
v.,	.	. 253	iii. 8,	.	. 208			
v. 27,	.	. 91	iii. 15,	.	. 104	JAMES.		
vi.,	.	. 246	iv. 2,	.	. 264	i. 12,	.	. 32
vi. 4,	.	. 27	iv. 10,	.	. 177			
vi. 5,	.	114, 183	v. 8,	.	. 241	1 PETER.		
vi. 6,	.	. 114	v. 9,	.	93, 160	i. 19,	.	. 86
vi. 7,	.	. 183	v. 11,	.	. 93	ii. 2,	.	. 137
			vi. 2,	.	. 114	ii. 9,	58, 86, 104, 233	
PHILIPPIANS.			vi. 16,	.	. 237	ii. 11,	.	. 178
iv. 3,	.	. 220				ii. 13,	.	. 114
			2 TIMOTHY.			ii. 18,	.	. 114
COLOSSIANS.			i. 5,	.	. 205	ii. 23,	.	. 260
i. 15,	.	90, 225	ii. 5,	.	. 37	iii. 6,	.	. 174
ii. 13, 14,	.	. 220	ii. 19,	.	. 81	iii. 20,	.	. 228
iii. 22,	.	. 114	iii. 3, 4,	.	. 73	v. 5,	.	180, 211

II.—INDEX OF PRINCIPAL SUBJECTS.

ACCUSERS and accused, the treatment of, 67, 77, 78 ; false, how to be punished, 72.
Adonias, 111.
Adultery and kindred vices condemned, 173.
Alms avail not the ungodly, 252.
Amon, a presumptuous sinner, 53.
Anointing the baptized, 185, 202 ; form of thanksgiving at, 188 ; forms of thanksgiving connected with, 188, 203.
Apocryphal books to be avoided, 159, 160.
Apostles, an exposition of the preaching of, 152, etc.
Assembling in the church, 83.

Augury and divination forbidden, 181.

BAPTISM, the various characters of those who may offer themselves for, 24-26.
Baptism, the one, 158 ; the guilt of rejecting, 159 ; customs connected with, 159, 201, 202, etc. ; instruction before, 191, etc. ; three immersions in, 264.
Baptism into the death of Jesus, 105.
Baptism, infant, 159.
Baptism of women, 105.
Baptism, a polluted, 159.
Baptism by women and the lower clergy, forbidden, 100, 101.

THE APOSTOLICAL CONSTITUTIONS. 277

Baptized, the, the character required in, 32, 105; the renunciation made by, 201; prayer for, 219.
Bartholomew, the constitution of, respecting deaconesses, 239.
Baths, indiscriminate and frequent, to be avoided by women, 25.
Bishops, the qualifications, moral and literary, required in, 26, 32; character required in, 27-32; duties of, 28; how they are to treat the innocent, the guilty, and the penitent, 32-55; as the head, not to be governed by the tail, 38; not to be themselves offenders, 41; to extend their concern to all sorts of people, 43; to be honoured and revered, 45; their management of the funds collected for the clergy and the poor, 55; to the laity, priests, Levites, and prophets, 56; the teachers, rulers, king, and, next to God, the earthly gods of the laity, 58, 62; nothing to be done without, 59, 62; a portion to be set apart for, at feasts, although not present, 60; the deacons to be subject to, 62; to be honoured as spiritual parents, 63; to be honoured before kings, 64; offerings for, 65; exhorted to unity—the deacons to aid, 74; to compose contentions, 74; the duty of, in judgments, 75, etc., 78, etc.; to exhort the people to peace and harmony, 81; to be ordained by two or three bishops, 107, 237; not to receive alms from the impious, 111, 112; but from the righteous only, 112; the election and ordination of, 212, 213; form of prayer for the ordination of, 214; nothing to be done by presbyters or deacons without the consent of, 262; to have power over the goods of the church, 262; what physical defects unfit for the office of, 267; various canons regulating the conduct of, 257-268.
Bishops, the number and names of those ordained by apostles, 204, etc.
Blesses, who it is that, 242.
Blessing, to be returned for cursing, 17.
Blessing the oil and water used in baptism, 243.
Books, those esteemed venerable and holy, 268.

Books of the heathen to be abstained from, 20.
Books, spurious, taking the names of apostles, to be avoided, 159, 160, 265.
Bribes, a bishop must not take, 111.

CANDIDATES for baptism, who to be received, and who to be refused, 244-246.
Canons, ecclesiastical, various, 257-269.
Catechumens, the instruction of, 199, etc.; bidding prayers for, 216.
Catholic church, the, 15.
Children, the instruction of, 113, etc.
Christ, confessing and denying, 116, 118; His example of self-abasement, 119-121; betrayal of, by Judas, 130, 131; agony of, 132; before Caiaphas and Pilate, 132, 133; the crucifixion of, 133; predictions respecting, in the Old Testament, 136, etc., 141, etc.
Church, the true, who compose, 15.
Church, a, a description of its order, etc., 83-86; diligent attendance in, enjoined, 87; excuses for non-attendance in, 89; the order of, to be observed, 254.
Clergy, the precepts respecting the marriage of, 159, 160; ordination and duties of, 237, etc.; respective duties of the various orders of, 242; canons for the regulation of the procedure of, 257, etc.
Coming, the second, of the Lord, 180.
Commandments, the Ten, 65, 66.
Communion with heretics, to be avoided, 160-162.
Confessing Christ, 116, 118, 120; the reward of, 121.
Confessors, constitutions respecting, 240, 241.
Contention, the spirit of, to be curbed by women, 25, 26.
Contentions, unbecoming Christians, 74.
Corah, 144, 145.
Cursing, forbidden, 103.
Customs of the heathen, to be shunned, 91.

DEACONS and deaconesses, to be honoured, 59; a double portion to be set apart for, at feasts, 60; to do nothing without the bishop,

but to be subject to him, 62; to aid the bishop, 74; the character of, 105, 106; ordination of, 238, etc.; and, of sub-deacons, 240.
Deaconesses, needed—ordination of, 104; Bartholomew's constitution respecting, 239.
Dead, the, and the relics of, not unclean, 175, 176.
Dead in Christ, prayers for the, 251.
Death, the way of, 184.
Decalogue, the, 63.
Denying Christ, 118.
Domestic and social life, counsels respecting, 113.
Drunkards, 253.

Election of bishops, 213.
Energumens, bidding prayer for, 218, 219.
Eucharist, the, mode of procedure in celebrating, and prayers connected with, 224-237.
Eucharistic thanksgiving, 187, 188.
Evening, prayers for, 249, 250.
Evil-speaking forbidden, 180.
Excommunication, 68; reception into the church of such as have undergone the sentence of, 68, 69; treatment of those under sentence of, 69, 70.
Exorcists, constitution of Lebbæus respecting, 241.

Faithful, the, bidding prayer for, 221; form of prayer for, 223.
False accusers to be punished, 72.
Fast and feast days, 130, 134, 138.
Fasts, when to be kept, 186.
Fasting in connection with baptism, 185, 186.
Feast and fast days, 130, 134, 138.
First-fruits and tithes, 55, 243; forms of prayer for, 251, 252.
Gifts, spiritual, diversities of, 206-210; the possessors of the higher forms of, not to despise those of others, 210.
Giving, the duty and happiness of, 109.

Heathen books, to be abstained from, 20.
Heathenish customs, to be avoided, 91.
Heresies, 143.
Heretics, history and doctrines of, 146; attacked by the apostles, 152; communion with, to be avoided, 160, 161; to be excommunicated, 162; impious opinions of, 170, 171.
Holy days, and days of rest and worship, 246.
Husbands, the duty of, 17, etc.; to love their wives, 174, 175.

Idols, all association with, to be avoided, 128.
Illuminated, prayer for the, 219.
Impious, the, 111; when they pray, provoke God's anger, 111, 112; alms not to be received from, 111, 112.
Infant baptism, 159.
Initiated, the, the instruction of, 199, etc.
Instruction of children, 113.
Israelites, the idolatrous propensities of the, 129.

James the son of Alphæus, the constitutions of, 240.
James the brother of Christ, the constitutions of, 248.
James the brother of John, the constitutions of, 224, etc.
Jewish customs, absurd, respecting purgations, marriage, and the dead, to be avoided, 117, etc., 175, 176.
Jews, the, brought dispersion and misery upon themselves by their rejection of Christ, 169, 170.
John, the constitutions of, 237, etc.
Judas, 130, 131.
Judging, the office of, reserved for priests, 66; mode of procedure to be observed in, 73, etc.
Judicatures, when to be held, 75.

Kings, the bishop to be honoured before, 64.

Laity, the, general considerations respecting, 15, etc.; men, 15-22; women, 22, etc.; addressed on the subject of tithes and first-fruits, 57, 58; to recognise the superiority of the bishop, and to honour him, 58, 59; to do nothing in connection with religious service without the bishop, 59.
Law, the, not abolished, but fulfilled, 163; the decalogue and the superadded, 163-165; Christians not in servitude to the superadded, 165, 166; of sacri-

fice, how to be regarded,—taken away by Christ, 166-168; the moral, confirmed and extended by Christ, 168, 169.
Laws regulating the Christian life, 178, etc.
Laymen, not to perform the work of priests, 101.
Lebbæus, his constitution respecting widows, 241.
Letters, recommendatory, 86.
Life, the way of, 178.
Life, the Christian, laws regulating, 178, etc.
Liturgy, the divine, 216, etc.
Lord's second coming, the, 180.
Lord's day, the, assembling on, 189.
Lord's Supper, the, form of thanksgiving for, 187; the uninitiated not to partake of, 187; form of thanksgiving after, 188.
Luminaries, the, Christians not to swear by, 128, etc.

MALEFACTORS, the two, crucified with Jesus, 133.
Manasses, his sin, punishment, and pardon, 51-53.
Marriage, 153.
Marriage, second, of the clergy, forbidden, 160.
Martyrs, to be cared for, 115, 116, 117; to be honoured, 127.
Martyrs, false, 127, 128.
Masters and servants, 114.
Matthew, his constitution respecting readers, 240.
Matthias, his constitution respecting water and oil, 143.
Men, Christian, to avoid ornamentation and over-refinement of dress, 18; not to wander about to spy out evil, 19; to be keepers at home, attending to their own business and reading the Scriptures, 19, 20; to abstain from heathen books, and study the Scriptures, 20, 21; to shun the wicked woman, 21, 22.
Miracles, the evidence of, may be resisted, 208.
Moral laws for the regulation of Christian life, 178-184.
Money, the love of, 109.
Money, given by the ungodly to the priest, how to be expended, 112.
Morning, prayers for, 249, 250.

NEPOTISM condemned, 267.

OBLATIONS, whose to be received, and whose rejected, 110.
Offerings for the clergy and the poor, 65, 189.
Oil used in baptism, 185, 202.
Oil and water, the blessing of, 243.
Order, the, of the church, to be observed, 254.
Ordination, 30, 189; mode of procedure to be observed in, 212, etc.; of bishops, 107, 257; of presbyters, 237; of deacons, 238; second, forbidden, 266.

PARENTS, how they should train their children, 113.
Passover, the holy, 130; the time of the observance of, 137, 138.
Paul, the constitutions of, 244; and of Peter, 246.
Penitent, the, how to be received into communion, 68, 69.
Penitent, the, prayer for, 219-221.
Pentecost, 142, 143.
Persecuted, the, to be aided, 117, 118; and received, 253.
Peter and Paul, the constitutions of, 246.
Peter, and Simon Magus, 150, 151; vision seen by, and visit of, to Cornelius, 154, 155.
Philip, the constitution of, 238.
Phœnix, the story of, an emblem of the resurrection, 124.
Poor, on helping the, 107, etc.
Prayer, what sort required, and when to be used, 186, 187.
Prayer, various forms of, and of thanksgiving, 191-199, 204, 214, etc., 223.
Prayer, forms of, for evening use, 248, 249; for morning, 249, 250.
Prayer, hours of, 247.
Prayer, the, of the impious will not be heard, 111.
Prayers, daily, 205, 206.
Prayers for the dead, 251.
Presbyters, the ordination and duties of, 237, etc.
Priests, to be honoured before kings, 64; offerings for, 65; the proper work of, not to be performed by laymen, 101.
Prophets, not all holy, 210.
Prophets, false, 190.
Punishments, to be graduated according to crimes, 76.

READERS, the ordination of, 240.

Re-baptism, to be avoided, 158.
Remainders of oblations, how to be distributed, 244.
Renunciation, the, of the devil, etc., to be made by the baptized, 201.
Respect of persons, to be avoided by the judge, 71.
Resurrection, the day of the, 189.
Resurrection of the dead, the, 121; the Sibylla quoted as to, 123, 124.
Romans, the, the law of righteousness demonstrated by, 169.
Rulers, the duty of submission to, 114, 115.

Schisms, 143, 144.
Scriptures, an exhortation to read and study, 19, 20.
Sects, Jewish, 143.
Sedition, 144; the, of Korah, 145.
Servants and masters, the relative duties of, 114.
Servants, on what days they are not to work, 246.
Sibylla, the, quoted respecting the resurrection, 123, 124.
Simon the Canaanite, the constitutions of, 242.
Simon Magus, the sin of, to be avoided, 111; the heresy of, 149, 150; meets Peter, 150; at Rome, attempts to fly, but is foiled by Peter's prayers, and falls down headlong, 151.
Subjection to rulers, the duty of, 114, 115.
Superstitious observances, certain Jewish, in regard to marriage and funerals, etc., condemned, 171-175, 176.

Teachers, true and false, how to be treated, 188, 189.
Temperance in the use of wine, 253.
Ten commandments, the, 65, 66.
Tenths, or tithes, and first-fruits, 55, 56, 243.

Thanksgiving, forms of, at the eucharist and anointing, 187, 188, 203.
Thomas, the constitution of, 240.

Unction at baptism, 185, 202.
Ungodly, the, alms avail not, 252.
Unity and unanimity, the cultivation of, among Christians, urged, 82.
Unnatural lusts, condemned, 173.

Virginity, optional, 115.

Water, the blessing of, 243.
Way of death, the, 184, etc.
Way of life, the, 178, etc.
Ways, the two, 177.
Widows, rules and advice respecting, 93, etc.; character and duties of, 96, 98, 99; some, falsely so called, 97; ought not to accept alms from the unworthy, 99; to avoid envy, jealousy, and all evil-speaking, 101; how they should pray for benefactors, 102; the constitution of Lebbæus respecting, 241.
Wife, a bishop or presbyter should not cast off his, under pretence of piety, 268.
Wine, to be used moderately, 253.
Witnesses and accusers, 77.
Wives, the duties of, 22; to be subject to their husbands, 174, 175.
Woman, the wicked, to be shunned, 21, 22.
Women, commandments to, 22; not to bathe with men, 25; the spirit of contention to be restrained by, 25, 26.
Women, ought not to teach in the church, 96, etc.; ought not to baptize, 100.
Working for a livelihood, the duty of, 91, etc.

The Works of St. Augustine.

MESSRS. CLARK beg to announce that they have in preparation Translations of a Selection from the WRITINGS of ST. AUGUSTINE, on the plan of their ANTE-NICENE LIBRARY, and under the editorship of the Rev. MARCUS DODS, A.M. They append a list of the works which they intend to include in the Series, each work being given entire, unless otherwise specified.

> All the TREATISES in the PELAGIAN, and the four leading TREATISES in the DONATIST CONTROVERSY.
>
> The TREATISES against FAUSTUS the Manichæan; on CHRISTIAN DOCTRINE; the TRINITY; the HARMONY OF THE EVANGELISTS; the SERMON ON THE MOUNT.
>
> Also the LECTURES on the GOSPEL OF ST. JOHN, the CONFESSIONS, the CITY OF GOD, and a SELECTION from the LETTERS.

All these works are of first-rate importance, and only a small proportion of them have yet appeared in an English dress. The SERMONS and the COMMENTARIES ON THE PSALMS having been already given by the Oxford Translators, it is not intended, at least in the first instance, to publish them.

The Series will include a LIFE OF ST. AUGUSTINE, by ROBERT RAINY, D.D., Professor of Church History, New College, Edinburgh.

The Series will probably extend to Twelve or Fourteen Volumes. It will not be commenced for some time, so as to allow the ANTE-NICENE SERIES to approach nearer to completion; but the Publishers will be glad to receive the *Names* of Subscribers.

The form and mode of printing have not yet been finally settled; but in any case the quantity of matter will be equal to the subscription of Four Volumes for a Guinea, as in the case of the ANTE-NICENE SERIES.

T. and T. Clark's Publications.

LANGE'S
COMMENTARIES ON THE OLD AND NEW TESTAMENTS,
IN IMPERIAL 8VO.

MESSRS. CLARK have now pleasure in intimating their arrangements, in conjunction with the well-known firm of SCRIBNER AND CO., of New York, and under the Editorship of Dr. PHILIP SCHAFF, for the Publication of Translations of the Commentaries of Dr. LANGE and his *Collaborateurs*, on the Old and New Testaments.

Of the OLD TESTAMENT they have published the Commentary on
THE BOOK OF GENESIS, One Volume;
to which is prefixed a Theological and Homiletical Introduction to the Old Testament, and a Special Introduction to Genesis, etc.; and
PROVERBS, ECCLESIASTES, and SONG OF SOLOMON, in One Volume.

They have already published in the Foreign Theological Library the Commentaries on St. Matthew, St. Mark, St. Luke, and the Acts of the Apostles. They propose to issue in the same form the Commentary on St. John's Gospel, which will not, however, be ready for some time.

There are now ready, of the NEW TESTAMENT—

ROMANS. One Volume.
1st and 2d CORINTHIANS. One Volume.
THESSALONIANS, TIMOTHY, TITUS, PHILEMON, and HEBREWS. One Volume.
PETER, JOHN JAMES, and JUDE. One Volume.

And during the year they hope to publish—

GALATIANS, EPHESIANS, PHILIPPIANS, and COLOSSIANS. One Volume.
REVELATION. One Volume.

Messrs. CLARK will, as early as possible, announce further arrangements for the translation of the Commentaries on the Old Testament Books.

The Commentaries on Matthew, in one volume; Mark and Luke, in one volume; and on Acts, in one volume, may be had uniform with the above if desired.

Each of the above volumes will be supplied to Subscribers to the FOREIGN THEOLOGICAL LIBRARY and ANTE-NICENE LIBRARY at 15s. The price to others will be 21s.

www.ingramcontent.com/pod-product-compliance
Lightning Source LLC
Chambersburg PA
CBHW021224300426
44111CB00007B/420